Frommer's®

Cuba

4th Edition

by Claire Boobbyer

Here's what the critics say about Frommer's:

"Amazingly easy to use. Very portable, very complete."
—BOOKLIST

"Detailed, accurate, and easy-to-read information
for all price ranges."
—GLAMOUR MAGAZINE

"Hotel information is close to encyclopedic."
—DES MOINES SUNDAY REGISTER

"Frommer's Guides have a way of giving you a real feel
for a place."
—KNIGHT RIDDER NEWSPAPERS

WILEY

Wiley Publishing, Inc.

ABOUT THE AUTHOR

Claire Boobbyer is a travel writer, photographer, and editor who fell in love with Latin America more than 10 years ago, after several backpacking trips around the region. She first went to Cuba in 1998 to spend a newly reinstated Christmas Day holiday in Havana and has been returning ever since. She is the author of several other guidebooks on the region and her photographic work has appeared in various guidebooks. She is the author and photographer of the forthcoming *Frommer's Cuba Day by Day*.

Published by:

WILEY PUBLISHING, INC.

111 River St.
Hoboken, NJ 07030-5774

ISBN: 978-0-470-34542-9

Editor: Shelley W. Bance with Maureen Clarke
Production Editor: Erin Amick
Cartographer: Guy Ruggiero
Photo Editor: Richard Fox
Production by Wiley Indianapolis Composition Services

Front cover photo: A bass player in Trinidad
Back cover photo: A family holiday at Varadero

For information on our other products and services or to obtain technical support, please contact our Customer Care Department within the U.S. at 800/762-2974, outside the U.S. at 317/572-3993 or fax 317/572-4002.

Wiley also publishes its books in a variety of electronic formats. Some content that appears in print may not be available in electronic formats.

Manufactured in the United States of America

5 4 3 2

CONTENTS

WHAT'S NEW IN CUBA 1

1 THE BEST OF CUBA 4

1 The Best Cuban Travel Experiences 4

2 The Best Historical Sights 5

3 The Best of Natural Cuba 6

4 The Best Outdoor Adventures 7

5 The Best Beaches 8

6 The Best Resort Hotels 9

7 The Best Hotels 10

8 The Best Casas Particulares 11

9 The Best Restaurants & Paladares 12

10 The Best of Cuban Music & Nightlife 13

11 The Best of Cuba Online 14

2 CUBA IN DEPTH 15

1 Cuba Today 15

2 Looking Back at Cuba 19

3 Cuba in Popular Culture 23

4 Eating & Drinking in Cuba 25

3 PLANNING YOUR TRIP TO CUBA 28

1 Visitor Information 28

2 Entry Requirements 29

Gifts & Other Assistance 32

3 When to Go 33

Calendar of Events 34

4 Getting There & Getting Around 37

5 Money & Costs 41

What Things Cost in Cuba 42

6 Health 44

7 Safety 47

8 Specialized Travel Resources 47

Race Relations in Cuba 49

9 Escorted General-Interest Tours 51

Frommers.com: The Complete Travel Resource 51

10 Special-Interest Trips 52

11 Staying Connected 56

Online Traveler's Toolbox 57

12 Tips on Accommodations 58

4 SUGGESTED CUBA ITINERARIES — 61

1 The Regions in Brief............61
2 Cuba in 1 Week..................64
3 Cuba in 2 Weeks 66
4 Cuba for Families.................69
5 Colonial Treasures
Highlights Tour 70
6 Havana in 3 Days.................71

5 HAVANA — 75

1 Orientation 75
2 Getting Around 83
Fast Facts: Havana..................85
3 Where to Stay....................87
4 Where to Dine 101
5 What to See & Do..............109
*A Quick Key to Havana's Parks
& Plazas*............................110
Luis Posada Carriles...............113
*Frommer's Favorite
Havana Experiences* 115
6 Outdoor Pursuits...............119
7 Shopping 121
8 Havana After Dark..............125

6 VIÑALES & WESTERN CUBA — 130

1 Pinar del Río 130
Smoke 'Em If You Got 'Em..........132
2 Viñales 135
3 Sierra del Rosario Biosphere
Reserve & San Diego
de los Baños 141
4 Cayo Levisa 145
5 María la Gorda 147
6 Isla de la Juventud 149
7 Cayo Largo del Sur 153

7 VARADERO & MATANZAS PROVINCE — 156

1 Matanzas 156
2 Varadero 159
3 The Zapata Peninsula &
Playa Girón 172
The Bay of Pigs.....................174

8 TRINIDAD & CENTRAL CUBA — 177

1 Santa Clara 177
Che Guevara........................180
2 Cienfuegos 186
Beny Moré...........................191
3 Trinidad 194
4 Sancti Spíritus...................207

9 CAMAGÜEY & THE NORTHEASTERN COAST — 213

1 Cayo Coco & Cayo Guillermo ... 213
Papa & the Cayos 216

A Stopover in Morón 218
2 Camagüey 223

10 EL ORIENTE — 233

1 Guardalavaca 233
2 Bayamo & the Sierra Maestra ... 245
Dear Granma 250

Goin' (or Not) to Gitmo 254
3 Baracoa 255

11 SANTIAGO DE CUBA — 263

1 Orientation 263
Santiago, City of Struggle & Rebellion 267
2 Getting Around 268
Fast Facts: Santiago de Cuba 269
3 What to See & Do 270
4 Where to Stay 274

5 Where to Dine 278
6 Shopping 280
7 Santiago de Cuba After Dark 281
Carnival & Other Santiago Festivals 282
8 Side Trips from Santiago de Cuba 285

APPENDIX A: FAST FACTS, TOLL-FREE NUMBERS & WEBSITES — 288

1 Fast Facts: Cuba 288

2 Toll-Free Numbers & Websites 294

APPENDIX B: CUBAN SPANISH TERMS & PHRASES — 297

1 Basic Words & Phrases 297
2 More Useful Phrases 299

3 Typical Cuban Words & Phrases 300

INDEX — 382

LIST OF MAPS

The Regions in Brief 62

Cuba in 1 Week/Cuba
  in 2 Weeks 66

Colonial Treasures 72

Havana at a Glance 77

La Habana Vieja & Centro
  Habana 79

Vedado 80

Playa 81

The Viñales Valley 137

Varadero 160

Santa Clara 179

Cienfuegos 187

Trinidad 195

Sancti Spíritus 209

Cayo Coco & Cayo Guillermo 215

Camagüey 225

El Oriente 235

Bayamo 249

Baracoa 257

Santiago de Cuba 264

ACKNOWLEDGEMENTS

Claire Boobbyer would like to thank the many Cubans who assisted her on the ground throughout the country. Thanks also to Maureen Clarke and Shelley Bance for their in-house help.

AN INVITATION TO THE READER

In researching this book, we discovered many wonderful places—hotels, restaurants, shops, and more. We're sure you'll find others. Please tell us about them, so we can share the information with your fellow travelers in upcoming editions. If you were disappointed with a recommendation, we'd love to know that, too. Please write to:

Frommer's Cuba, 4th Edition
Wiley Publishing, Inc. • 111 River St. • Hoboken, NJ 07030-5774

AN ADDITIONAL NOTE

Please be advised that travel information is subject to change at any time—and this is especially true of prices. We therefore suggest that you write or call ahead for confirmation when making your travel plans. The authors, editors, and publisher cannot be held responsible for the experiences of readers while traveling. Your safety is important to us, however, so we encourage you to stay alert and be aware of your surroundings. Keep a close eye on cameras, purses, and wallets, all favorite targets of thieves and pickpockets.

Other Great Guides for Your Trip:

Frommer's Spanish PhraseFinder & Dictionary

Frommer's Cuba Day by Day

Frommer's Belize

Frommer's Caribbean

Frommer's Costa Rica

Frommer's Mexico

Frommer's Portable Dominican Republic

Frommer's South America

FROMMER'S STAR RATINGS, ICONS & ABBREVIATIONS

Every hotel, restaurant, and attraction listing in this guide has been ranked for quality, value, service, amenities, and special features using a star-rating system. In country, state, and regional guides, we also rate towns and regions to help you narrow down your choices and budget your time accordingly. Hotels and restaurants are rated on a scale of zero (recommended) to three stars (exceptional). Attractions, shopping, nightlife, towns, and regions are rated according to the following scale: zero stars (recommended), one star (highly recommended), two stars (very highly recommended), and three stars (must-see).

In addition to the star-rating system, we also use **seven feature icons** that point you to the great deals, in-the-know advice, and unique experiences that separate travelers from tourists. Throughout the book, look for:

Finds	Special finds—those places only insiders know about
Fun Facts	Fun facts—details that make travelers more informed and their trips more fun
Kids	Best bets for kids and advice for the whole family
Moments	Special moments—those experiences that memories are made of
Overrated	Places or experiences not worth your time or money
Tips	Insider tips—great ways to save time and money
Value	Great values—where to get the best deals

The following **abbreviations** are used for credit cards:

AE	American Express	**DISC**	Discover	**V**	Visa
DC	Diners Club	**MC**	MasterCard		

FROMMERS.COM

Now that you have the guidebook to a great trip, visit our website at **www.frommers.com** for additional travel information on more than 4,000 destinations. We update features regularly to give you instant access to the most current trip-planning information available. At Frommers.com, you'll find scoops on the best airfares, lodging rates, and car rental bargains. You can even book your travel online through our travel booking partners. Other popular features include:

- Online updates to our most popular guidebooks
- Vacation sweepstakes and contest giveaways
- Newsletter highlighting the hottest travel trends
- Online travel message boards with featured travel discussions

What's New in Cuba

The most exciting news is that travel restrictions between the U.S. and Cuba will likely ease soon with the incoming administration of Barack Obama, whose presidency signals changes in U.S.-Cuba policy. Family travel between Miami and Cuba will probably be first affected by the relaxation of the travel embargo. Inside Cuban borders, however, some things never change including the government, the architecture, and the fleet of old American cars. But those things over which the government has no control—including the drop in tourist numbers—have prompted officials to open the way for further capital ventures in association with foreign companies. According to the Ministry of Tourism, Cuba aims to open 10,000 more hotel rooms in the next few years. Where leisure is concerned, there are folks moving into town. The most important changes and new developments in the tourism field are noted throughout this guide.

Note: For details on damage incurred by Hurricanes Gustav and Ike in late August and early September 2008, see "Hurricane Update," below.

HAVANA

The most exciting development in Havana will be the opening of Cuba's first designer hotel in spring 2009. The **Hotel Victoria** in Vedado will be transformed by Esencia Hotels & Resorts (www.esenciahotelsand resorts.com) into a Conran & Partners–designed hotel.

The **NH Parque Central Torre** (© 7/ 860-6627; www.nh-hoteles.es) is a smart, modern annex of 149 new rooms due to open in autumn 2008 behind the NH Parque Central.

Habaguanex opened the **Marqués del Prado Ameno** hotel in spring 2008. The Old Havana hotel company is currently restoring a building on the corner of Calle Morro and Genios in La Habana Vieja, which will become the **Hotel Packard.** The company also plans to open the hotels **San Felipe, Santiago,** and **Palacio Cueto,** although scheduled opening dates are not yet known. Habaguanex has plans to restore hotels along the Malecón. It now manages 527 rooms and hopes to eventually open and run a total of 2,000 rooms.

The **Hotel Habana Libre** in Vedado is open while undergoing a refurbishment program and a redesign of its swimming pool area.

The **Hotel Plaza** on Parque Central is undergoing refurbishment without closure to mark its 100th anniversary in 2009.

The Spanish hotel chain Barceló will open the **Barceló Habana Ciudad** in April 2009 with 186 rooms.

The Spanish CRaytur Caribe hotel chain will take over the running of the three-star **Atlántico** in Playas del Este and the **Villa los Pinos** complex of 26 modern chalets, which will become a four-star facility.

The **Melia Las Antillas** in Varadero became an adults-only (ages 16 and above) resort in November 2008.

VIÑALES & WESTERN CUBA

Esencia Hotels & Resorts will open the **Casa Viñales,** a 70-room eco-spa resort in the valley, scheduled to open at the end of 2009.

Avalon (www.avalons.net), which operates fishing and diving tours in Cuba, has opened **Villa Marinera** on Cayo Largo for its clients.

VARADERO & MATANZAS PROVINCE

The **Carbonera Country Club Resort** will be built by Esencia Hotels & Resorts just north of the international airport in Varadero by the end of 2010. It will house a PGA 18-hole golf course, boutique hotel, spa, and maritime center.

Oasis recently took over the running of the 444-room **Brisas del Caribe** in Varadero. The Spanish CRaytur Caribe hotel chain will take over operation of the four-star **Barlovento Hotel,** also in Varadero.

The **Barceló Arenas Blancas** will open in early 2009 with 358 rooms.

The **Hotel Sirenis La Salina** opened in 2008 in a zone of recent construction near the Tryp Peninsula Varadero at the end of the Varadero peninsula. Next to La Salina, the **Iberostar Laguna Azul,** with 814 rooms, is due to open in March 2009.

TRINIDAD & CENTRAL CUBA

In Trinidad, the **Hotel La Ronda** is due to open as a boutique Hoteles E in 2009. The **El Mesón del Regidor,** also in Trinidad, was closed during 2008 for refurbishment by Cubanacán and is due to reopen in 2009. The **Hotel Plaza** in Sancti Spíritus is being converted into a Hoteles E–branded hotel by Cubanacán in 2008 and 2009, as is the **Hotel Mascotte** in Remedios. The Hotel Plaza has some rooms open during the Hoteles E makeover, but the Hotel Mascotte is closed. They will be joined by a new Hoteles E, the **Hotel Barcelona,** scheduled to open in 2009.

Cubanacán will also be opening the **Casa Verde** and **San Carlos** in Cienfuegos, as Hoteles E establishments in the next few years. Just outside Cienfuegos, across the bay, the restoration of the **Jagua Fortress** was announced in mid-2008.

The group of islands called Cayo Santa María will be focused on a rebranding as **Cayos de Villa Clara** (www.villaclarakeys. com), with the aim of increasing the room capacity from 2,000 to 11,000 rooms. Spanish hotel chain Barceló alone will open 6,849 rooms by 2011. The **Barceló Cayo Santa Maria** will be an enormous complex made up of four hotels. The first 2,780 rooms are due to open at the end of 2008. The complex will boast a whopping 21 restaurants, 28 bars, two theaters, and a 2,200m (7,218-ft.) spa, among other facilities.

The Cayo Santa María island group is also slated to get an aquarium, three shopping complexes, a fitness center, a nightclub, and an amphitheater. The current Cayo Las Brujas marina will be expanded and a new marina built farther out on the key. Caibarien, the rather forlorn town that sits at the entrance of the *pedraplén* (concrete causeway), will get a **golf course** in its vicinity.

Over the next few years, Esencia Hotels & Resorts will open the **Casa Cienfuegos** along the Malecón in the coastal city.

CAMAGÜEY & THE NORTHEASTERN COAST

A joint Cuban-Venezuelan venture will result in a hotel built on **Cayo Paredón Grande.**

EL ORIENTE

Hotel Royalton in Bayamo will become a Hoteles E boutique hotel run by Cubanacán. The **Hostal La Habanera,** currently a Hoteles E establishment, will come under the management of Gaviota in Baracoa.

The nearby **Hotel Rusa,** also to be managed by Gaviota, will be transformed into a Hoteles E hotel.

Holguin and Gibara will get new hotels: The **Hotel Ordóñez** will be built in Gibara and the **Libertad** and **La Caballeriza** will open in Holguin. The latter will open under the Hoteles E brand.

Gibara is also the proud owner of a new marina that opened in May 2008, with sailboats, aquatic bikes, and catamarans.

SANTIAGO DE CUBA

The **Moncada Barracks** in Santiago closed its doors in mid-2008 for an overhaul of the exhibits. It should reopen in time for the 50th anniversary of the Revolution in 2009.

Esencia Hotels & Resorts will remodel the well-known **Casa Granda,** currently run by Gran Caribe, as part of its Cuba hotels and resorts program in the next few years.

HURRICANE UPDATE

Hurricanes Gustav and Ike hit Cuba at the end of August and early September 2008, causing about US$9.4 billion worth of losses. Some 200,000 homes were damaged and 30,000 were destroyed. Agriculture was affected, including the banana, coffee, guava, avocado, manioc, and tobacco industries. Nearly a third of the island's crops and half the annual sugar crop have been destroyed.

Pinar del Río province and the special municipality of Isla de la Juventud were particularly hard struck, as was Baracoa and other eastern areas of the island.

Many areas of Cuba were generally unaffected in any serious way, such as Havana, Trinidad, Santa Clara, and the tourist enclave of Varadero. However, in affected areas, hurricane recovery has been slowed in the wake of Hurricane Paloma, which swept over the eastern part of the island in early November 2008.

As tourism is the biggest source of income in Cuba, one of the first priorities has been to ensure that hotels and tourist infrastructure are up and running. Indeed, Sol Melía, the largest international hotel chain operating on the island, has confirmed to *Frommer's* that all its hotels are fully operational, except those with scheduled closures for renovation projects.

While Cuba has one of the most effective hurricane evacuation programs in the world, ensuring the absolute minimum loss of life, it still has struggled to deal with the logistical aftermath. Reports from inside Cuba suggest that there is not enough food to go around and that prices have soared for food, soap, detergent, and petrol. Some areas were still without power a month after the hurricane, but the Cuban government has made it a priority to repair the national grid.

It is difficult, at all times, to gain accurate information from inside Cuba. Readers planning on visiting Cuba independently should make direct contact with hotels and *casas particulares* to ensure that they are still operational after the hurricane season.

One should be aware that not only in hurricane conditions, but also after heavy rain, buildings do collapse in Cuba. Visitors should take care in streets in the poorer barrios of Havana, for example, where old Spanish colonial buildings have been known to crumble without prior warning.

The Best of Cuba

Cuba is unlike any other place on earth. What draws people to this fascinating Caribbean island is much more than beaches, sun, and cheap drinks, though there is plenty of all three for those who want them. One of the last Communist-bloc nations left, it doesn't suffer from the drab and desultory demeanor of its disappeared peers. Cuba's rich culture, unique political history, and continued survival through ongoing economic hardship make it one of the most eye-opening countries that experienced travelers can still discover. Seeing the best of Cuba means grooving to its intoxicating music, marveling at how Cubans improvise on a daily basis to make ends meet, and visiting a land in which the past 50 years seem to have passed by in some odd state of frozen animation.

1 THE BEST CUBAN TRAVEL EXPERIENCES

- **Patronizing *Paladares* and *Casas Particulares:*** The best way to appreciate Cubans, as well as to have the opportunity to exchange ideas about Cuba and the outside world, is by stepping inside a *paladar* restaurant or a *casa particular,* the Cuban version of a simple bed-and-breakfast. These private initiatives, heavily taxed by the state, are one of the only ways Cubans can earn badly needed hard currency, and they allow travelers a rewarding chance to see the country beyond the state-run hotels and restaurants.

- **Exploring la Habana Vieja (Old Havana):** No trip to Cuba is complete without at least a day (or more) spent in Habana Vieja. The streets and alleys of this colonial-era city center have been immaculately restored. You'll feel sucked back in time as you visit the plazas, churches, and forts here. Be sure to take a break from sightseeing and museum-hopping to stock up on souvenirs at the Calle Tacón market, your best one-stop shop in the country for this sort of stuff. See "What to See & Do" in chapter 5.

- **Spending an Afternoon at the Callejón de Hammel:** This short alley is lined with Salvador González's colorful murals and punctuated with scrap sculptures and shrines to Afro-Cuban deities. If you can make it on a Sunday afternoon in Havana, you'll be treated to a popular Afro-Cuban dance and music celebration. See "What to See & Do" in chapter 5.

- **Walking along Havana's Malecón:** Your best bet is to start in Habana Vieja and work your way toward the Hotel Nacional in Vedado. Take your time to stop and sit on the sea wall for a spell, and be sure to talk to some of the locals on your way. If you time it right, you will reach the Hotel Nacional in the late afternoon—a good time to grab a cool drink and enjoy the setting sun from the "Compass Card" outdoor terrace. See "What to See & Do" in chapter 5.

- **Celebrating Las Parrandas:** As the end of the year rolls around, the little colonial town of Remedios gears up to host Las Parrandas, one of Cuba's grandest street parties and religious carnivals. Everything culminates on Christmas Eve in an orgy of drums, floats, and fireworks. See "Santa Clara" in chapter 8.

- **Hopping a Steam Train to the Valley of the Sugar Mills:** The colonial mansions in Trinidad were built with the riches of a booming Cuban sugar trade of the 18th and 19th centuries. The best way to see the Valle de los Ingenios, an extraordinarily lush valley once home to 60 sugar mills, is aboard a vintage 1907 American steam train to one of the sugar estates, Manaca-Iznaga, where you can survey the valley's many shades of green from a fantastic tower. See "Trinidad" in chapter 8.

- **Following in Fidel's Footsteps:** Waging a guerrilla war against the Batista dictatorship, Fidel Castro and his young comrades hid out in the Sierra Maestra mountains in the late 1950s. Their small-scale rebel base camp was never discovered, but visitors today can hike a trail through remote cloud forest up to Comandancia de la Plata, the command post where Fidel turned a country on its

head. It's a fascinating glimpse of history from up close. See "Bayamo & the Sierra Maestra" in chapter 10.

- **Joining a Carnival Conga Line:** In the intense heat of summer, Santiago de Cuba explodes with the island's best carnival, an evocative celebration of the city's Afro-Caribbean roots. Ripe with rumba music, conga processions, booming percussion, fanciful floats, and wild costumes, it's a participatory party that has nothing to do with those cheesy conga lines people do on cruise ships. See "Carnival & Other Santiago Festivals" in chapter 11.
- **Beach time:** Lying on one of Cuba's white-sand beaches sipping a *mojito* (Cuban rum cocktail) before dipping into the sparkling waters of the warm Caribbean sea is one of the best things you can do.

2 THE BEST HISTORICAL SIGHTS

- **Catedral de San Cristóbal** and **Plaza de la Catedral,** Havana (© 7/861-7771): Havana's cathedral and the plaza it sits on are perhaps Old Havana's most distinctive historical sites. The twin towers and worn baroque facade of this ancient church are beautiful both by day and night. The small plaza it fronts is an atmospheric cobblestone square surrounded by perfectly restored colonial-era buildings with shops, museums, galleries, and restaurants. See p. 110.
- **Museo de la Ciudad,** Havana (© 7/861-6130): Old Havana's preeminent museum displays colonial-era art and artifacts. It's worth the price of admission alone to stroll the rooms, outdoor courtyards, and interior veranda of the former Palacio de los Capitanes Generales (Palace of the Captains General), which houses the museum. See p. 112.
- **Parque Histórico Morro y Cabaña,** Havana (© 7/863-7063 for El Morro, and © 7/862-0617 for La Cabaña):

Across the harbor from Old Havana, the Morro & Cabaña Historic Park complex is comprised of two major forts charged with protecting Havana's narrow and strategic harbor entrance. There's a lighthouse, several museums, restored barracks, batteries of cannons, and a handful of restaurants to explore, and a nightly *cañonazo* (cannon blast) ceremony is held here. See p. 118.

- **Cementerio de Colón,** Havana (© 7/832-1050): Columbus Cemetery is an impressive collection of mausoleums, crypts, family chapels and vaults, soaring sculptures, and ornate gravestones. All of the dead are laid to rest aboveground, and you'll be awed by the surfeit of marble and sun-bleached alabaster. The whole thing is laid out in an orderly grid of streets. See p. 116.
- **Monumento Ernesto Che Guevara,** Santa Clara (© 42/20-5878): Featuring a huge sculpture of the revolutionary hero overlooking a vast plaza, this

place is deeply revered by Cubans. Underneath the statue is a museum with exhibits detailing the life and exploits of "El Che," as well as a mausoleum holding Guevara's remains and the tombstones of 37 other revolutionary fighters killed with Guevara in Bolivia. See "Santa Clara" in chapter 8.

- **Trinidad:** The entire town of Trinidad qualifies as a historical site. The impeccably preserved relic—several blocks square of perfect pastel-colored mansions, churches, and cobblestone streets—is one of the greatest collections of colonial architecture to be found anywhere in the Americas. The star among Trinidad's colonial set pieces is the **Museo Romántico** (© **41/99-4363**), in an 18th-century mansion right on the main square. See "Trinidad" in chapter 8.

- **Plaza San Juan de Dios,** Camagüey (© **32/29-1318**): This dignified square is the highlight of Camagüey's colonial quarter, one of the largest in Cuba with more than a dozen 16th-, 17th-, and 18th-century colonial churches. Marked by cobblestones and colonial houses with red-tile roofs and iron window grilles, the understated plaza is home to a 17th-century baroque church and hospital of the order of San Juan de Dios. See p. 228.

- **Museo El Chorro de Maíta,** Guardalavaca (© **24/43-0421**): Guardalavaca is in the midst of the most important archaeological zone of Native American groups in Cuba. This small museum site is a Taíno burial ground from the late–15th and early–16th centuries, the biggest and finest American Indian cemetery discovered in Cuba. The well-preserved remains of more than 100 members of the community reveal important clues about native groups after the arrival of the Spanish conquistadors. The museum displays ceramics and objects found at the site. See "Guardalavaca" in chapter 10.

- **Casa Velázquez (Museo de Ambiente Colonial Cubano),** Santiago de Cuba (© **22/65-2652**): Diego Velázquez founded the original seven *villas* (towns/ settlements) in Cuba, and his 1515 mansion in Santiago de Cuba, the oldest house in the country and one of the oldest in the Americas, is still standing. Today it's a museum of colonial furnishings from the 16th to the 19th century. Individual pieces are splendid, but none manages to upstage the historical impact of the restored house itself. See p. 270.

- **Castillo El Morro,** Santiago de Cuba (© **22/69-1569**): Although nowhere near as expansive as its sister fort in Havana, this massive fortress is nonetheless quite impressive. You can almost feel like you're part of the history here while walking the mazelike alleyways, and the views are wonderful as well. See p. 271.

---

3 THE BEST OF NATURAL CUBA

- **The Viñales Valley:** This broad, flat valley is punctuated by a series of limestone karst hill formations, or *mogotes*. The views from the small mountains surrounding the valley are spectacular. The area provides great opportunities for hiking, mountain biking, bird-watching, and rock climbing, and there are plenty of caves to explore. See "Viñales" in chapter 6.

- **Las Terrazas:** This planned ecotourism project is set amid the Sierra del Rosario Biosphere Reserve. There are a host of trails and attractions here, including lakes, swimming holes, and a zip-line canopy tour. The bird-watching is excellent. See "Sierra del Rosario Bio-sphere Reserve & San Diego de los Baños" in chapter 6.

- **Parque Nacional Ciénaga de Zapata:** The Zapata Swamp National Park is a massive expanse of mangroves, swamp, and wetlands housing an abundant variety of flora and fauna. The area is a mecca for bird-watchers, naturalists, and anglers. Your best bet for exploring the park is Playa Larga, a simple beach-resort area catering to scuba divers. See "The Zapata Peninsula & Playa Girón" in chapter 7.

- **Parque Nacional Topes de Collantes:** The dense pine-covered mountains of the Sierra del Escambray lurk on the outskirts of Trinidad, and the Topes de Collantes National Park is a lovely, cool refuge from the town's stone streets. It's great for hiking, with several well-established trails, the best of which culminate in refreshing waterfalls. See "Trinidad" in chapter 8.

- **Baracoa:** Cuba's first settlement, over-looking a beautiful oyster-shaped bay, remains a natural paradise, with thick tropical vegetation, 10 rivers, and a distinctive flat-topped mountain called El Yunque, a UNESCO Biosphere Reserve that beckons hikers. Travelers into rafting, beaches, and boating will also find ample opportunities to explore this isolated area. See "Baracoa" in chapter 10.

- **Sierra Maestra:** The highest and longest mountain range in Cuba, the Sierra Maestra is full of lore for Cubans—it's where Fidel Castro and his band of rebels hid out and waged guerilla warfare against the Batista government in the 1950s. Stretching across three provinces, its peaks are almost on top of the rocky southern coastline. The Gran Parque Nacional Sierra Maestra and Parque Nacional de Turquino are perfect for hikers and nature lovers. See "Bayamo & the Sierra Maestra" in chapter 10.

4 THE BEST OUTDOOR ADVENTURES

- **Landing a Marlin or Sailfish:** If you really want to emulate Ernest Heming-way, you'll head out to sea to fish. The waters off Cuba's coast are excellent for sportfishing year-round. Big game fish are best sought off the northern coast, while bonefish and tarpon are better stalked off the southern coast. Nautica Marlin (www.nauticamarlin.com) and Gaviota (www.gaviota-grupo.com) run a string of marinas with modern, well-equipped sport-fishing fleets all around Cuba's coastline.

- **Rock Climbing the *Mogotes* of the Viñales Valley:** Although in its infancy, rock climbing is a rapidly developing sport in Cuba, and Viñales Valley is the place to come and climb. More than 60 routes and 100 pitches have been marked and climbed, and more climbs

are constantly being uncovered. See "Viñales" in chapter 6.

- **Scuba Diving at María la Gorda:** Cuba has many excellent dive destina-tions, but María la Gorda probably edges out the rest by having consistently excellent conditions, a variety of sites, an amazing setting, and an excellent dive operation. However, there's excel-lent diving off much of Cuba's coast, and if you want to combine diving with other attractions, you can do so from just about any destination on the island. See "María la Gorda" in chapter 6.

- **Bird-Watching in the Zapata Penin-sula:** A dedicated (and lucky) bird-watcher might be able to spot 18 of Cuba's 24 endemic species in the swamps, mangroves, and wetlands of the Zapata Peninsula. In addition to the endemic species, ornithologists and lay bird-watchers can spot more than 100 other varieties of shore birds, transients, and waterfowl in this rich, wild region. See "The Zapata Peninsula & Playa Girón" in chapter 7. Other top bird-watching destinations include **La Güira National Park** (see chapter 6), as well as the areas around **Cayo Coco** and **Cayo Guillermo** (see chapter 9) and **Baracoa** (see chapter 10).

- **Hiking and Rafting in Baracoa:** Baracoa, long isolated by impenetrable tropical vegetation, steep mountains, and rushing rivers, is an adventurer's dream. El Yunque, a curiously flat-topped limestone mountain, is home to dozens of bird species, orchids, and unique tropical plants and forest; it's also great for climbing. The Río Toa, the widest river in Cuba, is one of the few spots in Cuba for rafting. See "Baracoa" in chapter 10.

- **Hiking Pico Turquino:** Pico Turquino, tucked within the celebrated Sierra Maestra National Park, is the highest peak in Cuba at just under 2,000m (6,562 ft.). The trail to the summit is swathed in cloud forest and tropical flora. Mountaineers in good physical condition can do the 15km (9-mile) round-trip journey in a day, but most camp overnight below the summit. The panoramic views of the coast and Caribbean Sea are breathtaking. See "Bayamo & the Sierra Maestra" in chapter 10.

5 THE BEST BEACHES

- **Playa Paraíso** and **Playa Sirena:** These two connected beaches are the most outstanding of the uniformly spectacular stretches of sand along the length of Cayo Largo del Sur. Located on the more protected western end of the island, these are broad expanses of glistening, fine white sand, bordering the clear Caribbean Sea. There's a simple beachside restaurant on Playa Paraíso, and not much else here—and that's a large part of their charm. See "Cayo Largo del Sur" in chapter 6.

- **Varadero:** This is Cuba's premier beach-resort destination, and it ranks right up there with the best in the Caribbean. We personally prefer some of the island's less-developed stretches of sand. But if you're looking for a well-run all-inclusive resort loaded with amenities and activities, Varadero is a good choice. The 21km (13 miles) of nearly uninterrupted beach here is fabulous. See "Varadero" in chapter 7.

- **Playa Ensenachos** and **Playa Mégano:** Located on the tiny islet of Cayo Ensenachos, which is part of la Cayería del Norte, these protected crescents of sand drop off very gently, allowing bathers to wade 90m (295 ft.) or more out into the calm, crystal-clear waters. You'll have to shell out big bucks to visit these beaches, either staying at the Occidental Royal Hideaway Ensenachos or paying its hefty day-use fee. Both of these beaches are astoundingly beautiful, but we slightly prefer Playa Mégano. See "Santa Clara" in chapter 8.

- **Playa Ancón:** A wonderful white-sand beach and close runner-up to the more spectacular beaches of Cuba, attractive Ancón has one huge advantage: It's just minutes from one of the country's true treasures, Trinidad, and perfectly positioned for those who'd like a bit of colonial culture with their sun and sand (or vice versa). With good diving and one very nice resort hotel, it's sure to be built up soon. See "Trinidad" in chapter 8.

- **Cayos Coco** and **Guillermo:** These tiny cays off the north coast, separated from the Cuban mainland by a long man-made causeway, are tucked into shallow waters that flow into the Atlantic. There's barely a sign of the "real Cuba," but what you do get is stunning, unspoiled beaches, excellent diving, and a full contingent of watersports. See "Cayo Coco & Cayo Guillermo" in chapter 9.

- **Cayo Sabinal:** If it's seclusion and pristine nature you're after, find your way to this small cay on the northeastern coast. It has brilliant beaches protected by stunning coral reefs and almost no facilities to speak of. With its rich flora and fauna, Cayo Sabinal is an ecotourist's dreamland. See "Camagüey" in chapter 9.

- **Guardalavaca:** Probably Cuba's prettiest resort area, Guardalavaca is a hot spot, but not overheated like Varadero. The area, a prime archaeological zone of pre-Columbian Cuba, is one of lush tropical vegetation, brilliant white sands, and clear turquoise waters. Long stretches of coastline are interrupted by charming little cove beaches, and some of Cuba's finest resort hotels are here. See "Guardalavaca" in chapter 10.

6 THE BEST RESORT HOTELS

- **Paradisus Varadero,** Varadero (© 45/66-8700): This is the Sol Meliá's fanciest resort hotel in Varadero, with expansive grounds, a huge free-form pool, and all the activities and amenities you could hope for. There's a variety of dining options and they create the feel of an intimate, romantic getaway better than any of the other large resort hotels in Varadero. See p. 167.

- **Tryp Península Varadero,** Varadero (© 45/66-8800): This is my top choice for a family resort in Varadero and an excellent all-around resort in its own right. The setting, facilities, and service are all tops, and the rooms are quite spacious and well equipped. The children's pools and play area are the best in Cuba. See p. 169.

- **Meliá Sol Cayo Santa María,** Cayo Santa María (© 42/35-0200): This resort is yet another of the Sol Meliá's excellent all-inclusive properties. This one is located on a very beautiful and very isolated patch of beach in la Cayería del Norte. The facilities are certainly top-notch, and the setting is just spectacular. See p. 184.

- **Brisas Trinidad del Mar,** Península Ancón, Trinidad (© 41/99-6500): This resort hotel on Playa Ancón has excellent sea and mountain views and is

only minutes from the most beautiful colonial city in Cuba. The well-conceived design echoes the handsome architecture of Trinidad. See p. 202.

- **Meliá Cayo Coco,** Cayo Coco (© 33/30-1180): Of the several fine hotels on Cayo Coco, Sol Meliá's top property on the cays is the most sophisticated and stylish, with cool bungalows overlooking a natural lagoon, elegant decor throughout, good restaurants, a beautiful pool area, and a great stretch of beach on a natural cove. See p. 218.

- **Sol Cayo Guillermo,** Cayo Guillermo (© 33/30-1760): Relaxed and unpretentious, this lively resort hotel is less staid and prepackaged than many of the big hotels on the cays. The cheery bungalow-style rooms are perfect for a younger crowd. See p. 221.

- **Paradisus Río de Oro,** Playa Esmeralda (© 24/43-0090): Perhaps Cuba's most sybaritic all-inclusive resort hotel, this sprawling Sol Meliá property hugs a rocky cliff and is distinguished by some of the most luxuriously designed grounds you'll find anywhere. Rooms are large, refined, and private. Sunbathers will have a hard time deciding between the terrific main beach, the nearly private small cove beaches, and the extraordinary pool area—not to mention the massage hut that hangs out from the cliff over the sea. See p. 239.

- **Hotel Cayo Levisa,** Cayo Levisa (© 48/75-6506): Land one of the oceanfront bungalows here and you may never want to leave this idyllic little island resort. For those on a budget, these standard beachfront bungalows are a passport to paradise. See p. 146.

- **Villa Las Brujas,** Cayo Santa Maria (© 42/35-0199): Perched on a rocky outcrop over the turquoise Caribbean, the very reasonably priced, stylish, comfortable, individual and duplex villas here are connected by a raised, rugged wooden walkway through scrub and mangrove and face a long stretch of beautiful white-sand beach. Staff members are very friendly here, too. See p. 186.

7 THE BEST HOTELS

- **Hotel Florida,** Havana (© 7/862-4127): This is probably my favorite of the Habaguanex properties in Old Havana. The building features a wonderful open-air central courtyard, checkerboard marble floors, and oodles of colonial-era charm. The whole operation is elegant and refined, and located right on the pulse of things on busy Calle Obispo. See p. 88.

- **Hotel Saratoga,** Havana (© 7/868-1000): Set right on the Paseo del Prado, with stunning views of El Capitolio from many of its rooms, this new hotel has the most comfortable and luxurious rooms of any hotel in or near Habana Vieja. Add to that a wonderful rooftop pool and bar, and this hotel is clearly one of the top choices in the city. See p. 89.

- **NH Parque Central,** Havana (© 7/860-2667): This modern, upscale hotel dominates the northern end of Havana's small Central Park. It boasts luxury spacious rooms and marble bathrooms and a lovely rooftop pool. Its ultramodern annex, the NH Parque Central Torre hotel, is due to open by the end of 2008. See p. 89.

- **Hotel Los Jazmines,** Viñales (© 48/79-6205): With a spectacular setting on a hillside overlooking the Viñales Valley, this is hands down the best option in town. If you land one of the third-floor rooms with a balcony, you'll

forgive the somewhat smallish rooms and minimal amenities. Los Jazmines makes a great base for exploring this region. See p. 139.

- **Grand Hotel Iberostar Trinidad,** Trinidad (© 41/99-6073): This new hotel has seriously upped the bar in terms of comfort and luxury in Trinidad. Set fronting a quiet little park in the heart of downtown, this is clearly the top high-end choice in Trinidad. See p. 200.

- **Hotel La Unión,** Cienfuegos (© 43/55-1020): Housed in a marvelously restored colonial mansion right in the heart of downtown Cienfuegos, this is one of the nicest boutique hotels in the country. With a couple of interior courtyards, neoclassical furnishings, and architectural touches, La Unión captures the elegance and charm of Cuba's bygone era. It's worth the small splurge for one of the spacious junior suites. See p. 191.

- **Hostal del Rijo,** Sancti Spíritus (© 41/32-8588): The concept of small boutique hotels with historic character is catching on in Cuba, and this boutique hotel in unassuming Sancti Spíritus is among the best of its kind in the country. In a beautifully restored colonial mansion, it has massive rooms with restrained decor, and it just might rank as the best hotel bargain in Cuba. See p. 211.

- **Gran Hotel,** Camagüey (© 32/29-2093): In the heart of Camagüey's colonial quarter, this 1930s hotel has real old-world character, a selection of atmospheric bars, and a small terrace pool. The Gran Hotel offers tons of style at a bargain price—especially if you get one of the spacious corner rooms. See p. 229.
- **Hotel El Castillo,** Baracoa (© 21/64-5194): This hotel has history, charm, and a location to die for. Inside the walls of one of the town's oldest fortresses, up on a hill where the pool comes with splendid panoramic views of Baracoa and the bay, this is the kind of place you won't want to leave. Relaxed and unpretentious, it suits Baracoa perfectly. See p. 259.
- **Hotel Casa Granda,** Santiago de Cuba (© 22/65-3021): It's not Santiago's

biggest or most expensive hotel, but the Casa Granda, in an elegant landmark building on Parque Céspedes in the heart of the city, is the place to stay if you want to be in the heady mix that is the Oriente region's capital. Renovation has dramatically improved the rooms, and the terrific terrace bars are among the best people-watching places in the city. See p. 275.

- **Hostal Basilio,** Santiago de Cuba (© 22/65-1702): This little hotel is in a beautifully restored old home in the heart of downtown Santiago de Cuba and now operates under the boutique Hoteles E brand. The good-size rooms have very high ceilings with ornate crown molding. Throughout the hotel, you'll find attractive tile work on the floors, wainscoting, and smart bathrooms. See p. 275.

8 THE BEST CASAS PARTICULARES

- **Casa de Evora Rodríguez,** Havana (© 7/861-7932): This top-floor "penthouse" belonging to the welcoming Evora has stunning panoramic views and the top-floor flat is full of potted plants. See p. 93.
- **Casa Sandra,** Havana (© 7/832-402): On the 13th floor of a 1950s block of flats, this enormous flat has spectacular views of Vedado and the Malecón. The rooms are spacious and attractively decorated and guests share a nice living room. Run by Lilly and her family, this is a gorgeous place to stay. See p. 97.
- **Casa Amistad,** Cienfuegos (© 432/51-6143): Run by the superfriendly and knowledgeable Armando and Leonor, this colonial house with a wonderful front living room has two rooms and some hearty home-cooked food; the house is a stone's throw from Parque José Martí. See p. 192.

- **Hostal Casa Múñoz,** Trinidad (© 41/99-3673): Historic Trinidad is well stocked with beautiful colonial houses and rental rooms, but this one is distinguished by its impressive living room and ever-expanding facilities; its informative host is a photographer who knows Trinidad like the back of his hand. See p. 201.
- **Casa Font,** Trinidad (© 41/99-3683): A gorgeous late-18th-century colonial house in the heart of the old center, this family home has a great collection of antiques and a light, airy feel. For a *casa particular,* this is about as grand as it gets: chandeliers of Baccarat crystal, thick wood doors, colonial- and republican-era oil paintings, and mediopunto (stained-glass, fan-shaped) windows above the doors. See p. 201.
- **Hostal Florida Center,** Santa Clara (© 42/20-8161): This is a gorgeous

1876 colonial house filled with interesting historic furniture and blessed with a flourishing garden and welcoming host, Angel. The food served here is some of the best in Cuba. See p. 181.

- **Casa La Colina,** Baracoa (© 21/64-2729): One of the things that makes Baracoa so extraordinary is its spectacular natural setting, and this handsome house has a fantastic terrace with panoramic views of the entire town and the bay leading out to the sea. The rooms are large and comfortable, and your host is a charm. See p. 260.

- **Casa Daniel Salomón Paján,** Baracoa (© 21/64-2122): This is one of the friendliest *casas* in Cuba. Daniel works at the museum and knows a lot about Baracoa's history. He has one comfortable room with a large bathroom and a central covered patio. See p. 260

- **Casa Maruchi,** Santiago de Cuba (© 22/62-0767): A lovely colonial house with a wonderful patio stuffed with orchids and other plants is run by the friendly Maruchi. Two chic, comfortable rooms with exposed brickwork, Spanish colonial furniture, lace bedspreads, and candlesticks are off the patio. See p. 276.

- **Casa Hugo & Adela,** Santiago de Cuba (© 22/62-6359): Most of Santiago's best *casas* are in the leafy outer neighborhoods, but if you want to be in the thick of Santiago, with a comfortable room and a huge private rooftop terrace overlooking the old city and harbor, grab this room. See p. 276.

- **Casa Asensio,** Santiago de Cuba (© 22/62-4600): Facility-wise, this house may be unrivaled in Cuba. It's a very large apartment with its own kitchen and a massive, private rooftop terrace. It's perfect for anyone planning to stay awhile to explore Santiago de Cuba and the surrounding area in depth. See p. 277.

9 THE BEST RESTAURANTS & PALADARES

- **Café del Oriente,** Havana (© 7/860-6686): Arguably the most elegant restaurant and cafe in Habana Vieja, this place serves well-prepared and creative international fare in a beautiful room just off the Plaza San Francisco. When the weather is nice, you can even sit at an outdoor table right on the plaza. See p. 102.

- **El Templete,** Havana (© 7/866-8807): This is truly fine dining portside in Old Havana, with outside seating with roadside and harbor views and sophisticated interior dining. See p. 110.

- **La Guarida,** Havana (© 7/862-9047): Atmosphere, fame, good food, and good times all combine in equal measure at perhaps the most famous *paladar* in Cuba. To walk up the rickety steps to this third-floor private restaurant is an experience in itself. See p. 105.

- **Roof Garden Restaurant,** Havana (© 7/860-8560): The creative French-inspired menu and stunning setting make this probably the best high-end dining option in Havana. Try for a window table on the elevated area ringing the restaurant. See p. 103.

- **La Cocina de Lilliam,** Havana (© 7/209-6514): Lilliam Domínguez has raised the bar for *paladares* around Havana. Her delicious *criolla* cooking always makes the most of whatever ingredients are locally available, and her softly lit garden setting is stunning. See p. 107.

- **La Fonda de Mercedes,** Las Terrazas (© 8/577-8647): Working out of her apartment's simple kitchen, Doña Mercedes Dache serves up wonderfully prepared *criolla* cuisine. Meals are served on large tables in an open-air terrace overlooking a mountain lake. If you come to Las Terrazas, don't leave without eating here. See p. 143.

- **Paladar Estela,** Trinidad (© 41/99-4329): A colonial house with a pretty garden patio dining area, this private home restaurant in the heart of the historic quarter of Trinidad serves epic proportions of well-prepared Cuban specialties. The friendly owners also rent a room. See p. 203.
- **La Campana de Toledo,** Camagüey (© 32/28-6812): Located on one of the most authentic and elegant colonial squares in Cuba, this handsome, rustic restaurant with a pretty patio is a great spot for a midday break from the heat or a relaxed dinner. Dishes are more imaginative than the basic Cuban fare at most state-run establishments. See p. 231.
- **Hostal Florida Center,** Santa Clara (© 42/20-8161): This is a popular *casa particular* serving dinners with enormous platters of delicious seafood and chicken, plus salads and fruit dishes. The garden is candelit at night. See p. 182.
- **La Colonial,** Baracoa (© 21/64-5391): The government seems to support the competition of private restaurants only nominally, and this is the last surviving *paladar* in Baracoa. The nicely decorated colonial house easily outclasses the state-run options in town, and it has good service and a changing menu with several fresh fish dishes. See p. 261.

- **Restaurant El Morro,** Santiago de Cuba (© 22/69-1576): Perched along the cliff next to the El Morro fortress, with spectacular views of the Caribbean, this popular open-air restaurant is a good-value lunch spot. There are plenty of fish dishes and a fixed-price midday meal, all served under a canopy of hanging plants that help patrons beat the heat. See p. 280.
- **ZunZún,** Santiago de Cuba (© 22/64-1528): One of the few upscale dining experiences in eastern Cuba, this elegant restaurant has several small, private dining rooms scattered throughout a large 1940s house in one of Santiago de Cuba's most pleasant suburbs. Attention to detail and presentation—dining elements seldom given much thought in Cuba—are a welcome surprise. It's best known for its top-quality seafood. See p. 279.
- **Paladar Salón Tropical,** Santiago de Cuba (© 22/64-1161): One of the most elegant *paladares* in Cuba, this attractively decorated place offers a smorgasbord of tasty choices. It's just such a shame that the service is glacially slow. See p. 279.

10 THE BEST OF CUBAN MUSIC & NIGHTLIFE

- **Tropicana,** Havana (© 7/267-1010): This is the original and still reigning cabaret show in Cuba. The Tropicana has been at it for over 60 years and it shows no signs of slowing down. The sea of lithe dancers, the exuberance of their costumes, and the sheer excess of it is worth the trip. It all occurs under the stars in the shadow of tall overhanging trees. There's a second Tropicana in Matanzas for visitors to Varadero, and another in Santiago. See p. 127.

- **El Gato Tuerto,** Havana (© 7/838-2696): The mood is dark and bohemian, although the decor mixes Art Deco and kitsch in equal measure. The nightly show usually features three or four distinct acts, which can range from sultry boleros to up-tempo jazz. A storyteller, poet, or comedian might perform between sets. See p. 128.
- **La Zorra y El Cuervo,** Havana (© 7/833-2402): This is Havana's best jazz club, and that's saying a lot. The vibe is

mellow and unpretentious in this compact basement club, but the music and acts are usually culled from the best Cuba has to offer. See p. 128.

- **Callejón de Hammel,** Havana. At noon each Sunday, this is the site of a weekly Afro-Cuban music and dance show and celebration headed up by the renowned folkloric group Clavé y Guaguanco. The vibe is fantastic. See p. 114.

- **Trinidad:** Trinidad's popularity has ensured a steady menu of live-music offerings. Cuban bands play under the stars on the steps of the **Casa de la Música** until more energetic dancing and music get underway inside. The **Palenque de los Congos Reales** regularly hosts an outstanding folkloric Afro-Cuban music and dance performance. Small, relaxed spots like the patio bars **La Canchánchara** and **Ruinas de Segarte** feature live *son.* If that's too traditional, then check out **La Cueva,** a funky dance club in a cave. See "Trinidad" in chapter 8.

- **Casas de la Trova,** Camagüey and Santiago de Cuba: Perhaps the country's two best *Casas de la Trova,* the traditional Cuban live-music spots, are in Camagüey and Santiago de Cuba. Camagüey's casa is agreeably low-key, while Santiago's is legendary, having given birth to dozens of Cuba's most respected musicians and bands. Both are great places to mix with locals, try out some dance moves, and sip a *mojito.* See "Camagüey" in chapter 9 and p. 284 in chapter 11.

- **Casa de las Tradiciones,** Santiago: This neighborhood music venue oozes charm and authenticity. It's not touristy and makes for a great night out regardless of the changing musical genre. See p. 283.

- **Calle Antonio Maceo,** Baracoa: Tiny Baracoa rocks at night with its own little version of Bourbon Street. People spill out of a half-dozen cafes, bars, and live-music venues, shifting gears from traditional *trova* to *son* and dance music to full-throttle dance club. Amiable emcees entertain audiences with romantic poetry and humor. See "Baracoa" in chapter 10.

11 THE BEST OF CUBA ONLINE

- **http://lanic.utexas.edu/la/cb/cuba**: Hosted by the University of Texas Latin American Studies Department, this site houses a vast collection of information about Cuba. This is hands down the best one-stop shop for Web browsing.

- **www.cubanacan.cu:** Cubanacán is probably the largest state-run tourism company, with hotels, transportation, and receptive tourism arms. They also have the best-developed website of the handful of state-run agencies, though that's not necessarily saying much.

- **www.cubasi.cu:** CubaSí is the best of the state-sponsored, all-purpose information sites on Cuba. It has an English-language mirror of the principal site, as well as a good search engine and easy

links to an online version of the Cuban telephone book.

- **www.casaparticular.info:** We find this the best of the clearinghouse sites for *casas particulares.* It has lots of links to *casas* in the main tourist destinations around Cuba.

- **www.cubamania.com:** This site is a lively, sometimes conflictive and controversial, forum site for all things Cuban, but there's plenty of good information to be had here.

- **http://havanajournal.com**: This site run out of Cape Cod collates an interesting and diverse amount of news, tourism, and culture stories. The forums are also lively and useful; it's an excellent resource.

Cuba in Depth

Cuba is an ongoing and enduring enigma. By any conventional measure, this Caribbean island should be a speck in the global geopolitical ocean. Yet for half a century, this complicated nation of 11.4 million people has commanded the world stage in a manner wholly incommensurate with its small size and economic insignificance. A former colony of Spain and playground of American high rollers, Cuba struck out on its own in the late 1950s, and the nation remains a hot topic in the corridors of the world's power brokers. Fiercely independent but rarely free, and the unlikeliest of major players, Cuba arouses passions like perhaps no other nation.

For decades, those inflamed feelings have focused on the Communist regime that one man, Fidel Castro, brazenly engineered. Hated and worshiped in almost equal measure, Fidel Castro defied critics, confounded pundits, and frustrated his own followers. His brother, Raúl Castro, became president in February 2008, and walks the same walk with Cuba's unique brand of home-grown communism. Slowly, though, the world is learning that Cuba is more than a coveted property in a high-stakes game of Risk. Wider exposure to Cuban culture (especially its music), the island's colonial treasures, and the Cuban people has given rise to a love affair that transcends international politics.

---

1 CUBA TODAY

Cuba was one of the major stories of the 20th century, from the stunning overthrow of the dictator Fulgencio Batista in 1959 by a ragtag revolutionary army to Fidel Castro's tenacious hold on power. And although virtually everything about Cuba is filtered through an ideological lens, Cuba is a fascinating living laboratory of social and political experimentation, and a test case for a people's perseverance. A defiant Fidel Castro weathered the fierce opposition of the U.S. government and the hostility of Cuban exiles in Miami, just 145km (90 miles) to the north. While some of his radical reform goals have been achieved, Cubans have also been greatly disheartened by the regime's abject failures. The Cuban people have been forced to make unfathomable sacrifices in the face of a poorly planned (and worse performing) economy and the ongoing American trade embargo.

Cuba was once the dazzling iconoclast, held in awe by much of Latin America for its willingness to stand up to the United States. In recent years, though, Fidel Castro found himself increasingly isolated, and few are those who don't believe that Cuba is a Communist dinosaur. Although Castro promoted foreign investment and joint ventures in oil, mining, and tourism, Cuba remains willfully individualistic.

The country's uniqueness is also the source of its phenomenal appeal. Cuba is a puzzling anachronism, a creaky and sputtering country caught in a tortuous time warp. Many of Havana's crumbling colonial buildings are little more than facades, propped up like a movie set. While most of the planet plunges ahead at a dizzying digital pace, Cuba crawls along in slow motion. Homes, which Cubans do not actually own but are instead given title to by the state, have only the most rudimentary appliances—if they have any at all. Vintage Chevy and Cadillac jalopies from the '40s and '50s, their chrome fenders pock-marked and their engines patched together with a hodgepodge of parts, lumber down the streets of dimly lit cities. In rural areas, even antique cars are a luxury; transportation is more commonly by oxen-led cart and rickety iron bicycle.

To many visitors, Cuba offers a mystifying, but welcome retreat from the whiz-bang of technology and convenience to which most of us have become accustomed. Groups of underemployed men while away the hours playing dominoes on card tables set up in the street. Septets of octogenarian musicians play traditional Cuban *son,* music with roots in the 1920s and whose rhythms are largely unaffected by outside influence and changing global tastes. Neighbors gather on doorsteps in the wilting heat of the late afternoon to chat and fan themselves, and they form friendly networks working together to solve problems of accommodations, transportation, plumbing, and electricity.

Many travelers, convinced that Cuba cannot forever remain a land of time travel, hasten to experience the country before it gets reeled in by a ravenous Western world. Cuba's tourist potential is almost unlimited, and the government has embraced tourism as its best and perhaps only hope to bring in hard currency and employ large numbers of people. The largest island in the Caribbean, Cuba is abundantly blessed with palm trees, sultry temperatures, hip-swiveling rhythms, stunning beaches, warm people, a surfeit of rum, and the world's finest hand-rolled cigars. In the mid-1980s, only about 250,000 visitors traveled to Cuba annually; in 2007, there were more than two million visitors. Tourism has now surpassed the source of Cuba's original wealth, the sugar industry, to become the country's top revenue earner. If all Americans were allowed to travel legally, politicians and hoteliers reason, Cuba might receive as many as 10 million visitors annually. Yet massive tourism is still a dream in Cuba.

Most travelers still cling to package tours and tourist resorts clustered on beaches.

Modern Cuba is a tangled mass of contradictions. The centralized economy is dependent upon capitalistic joint ventures with foreign investors from Canada, Great Britain, Germany, Italy, and Spain. Plenty of Cubans survive only with the assistance of political and religious opponents of the regime who've fled the country and send hundreds of millions of dollars in hard currency each year to relatives. Until the change of head of state in February 2008, the socialist regime, ostensibly founded upon an egalitarian revolution, didn't allow its own citizens to step foot into certain tourist enclaves, including many resorts, hotels, and restaurants, and a long list of goods and services readily available to foreigners could not be enjoyed by nationals. Many of these goods still cannot be enjoyed by Cubans. Although now allowed to own mobile phones and computers, for example, these consumer goods are beyond the reach of the vast majority of Cubans. Start-up mobile-phone contracts cost CUC$110 (US$119/£59) but with average salaries of around CUC$10 (US$11/£5.40) a month, owning a mobile phone is a pipe dream.

Cubans often fall back on an all-purpose national refrain to describe what their lives are like: *No es fácil.* It isn't easy. Cubans are specialists in what might be called the *arte de inventar,* the art of inventing solutions where there are none. That means fighting to make ends meet through odd jobs and hustling. Setting up neighborhood networks that distribute contraband goods, such as cigars nicked from the tobacco factory. Running illicit *paladares* in living rooms and backyards, serving black-market lobster or beef. Cuba is an entire nation jimmy-rigged and bandaged with duct tape.

Unless you're ensconced in a gleaming, all-inclusive beach resort, where the realities of Cuban life are whitewashed for the benefit of tourists, the grinding deficiencies of the Cuban economy and bottomless needs of the Cuban people are hard to ignore. Talk to almost any Cuban and he'll tell you about appallingly overcrowded housing and transport conditions, state rations that don't cover basic needs, the scarcity of basic commodities, and the CUC$10-to-CUC$20 monthly salaries paid in Cuban currency, the peso. Workers trained by the state as engineers and doctors instead scramble for more lucrative positions as bellboys, while others cobble together a few dollars worth of hard currency from occasional, often extralegal, odd jobs. Ration booklets allow Cuban citizens to buy a certain amount of basic goods at highly subsidized prices in Cuban pesos. However, the rations allotted do not suffice: just 6 pounds of rice and sugar, 20 ounces of beans, 1 pound of chicken, two bottles of cooking oil, some bread, plus some cigarettes, coffee, and a few other goods on an irregular basis such as fish, ham, and toothpaste. Anything beyond those miserly provisions—the odd piece of beef, a pair of decent shoes—must be purchased on the black market or in hard currency–only stores.

Yet Cuba is remarkably free of the crushing poverty sadly common in Africa, India, and even other parts of Latin America. Housing is provided by the state—homeless people sleeping on the streets are nowhere to be seen in Cuba—and all citizens receive regular food rations. Many appear surprisingly well dressed, no doubt a privilege of possessing a job that earns a few dollars or having family members outside of Cuba who send money that helps ease the pain.

Fidel Castro took power in 1959 with a commitment to remake the nation by overhauling its economy, land ownership, education system, and healthcare. On a social agenda, Cuba has been remarkably successful. All Cubans receive free healthcare. However, most hospitals and pharmacies lack the most basic supplies, like aspirin and X-ray plates. The fabric and interior of some hospitals are appallingly outdated and back-up electricity generators for *apagónes* (power cuts) have been known to fail while operating theaters are in use. Compulsory state education through high school is free, and the national university system has produced some extremely accomplished professionals in medicine and the sciences. Average life expectancy rose from 57 years in 1958 to 77 in 2006—the highest in Latin America. Infant mortality, just 6.22 per 1,000 births, is the lowest in the region and equal to or better than many developed countries. Literacy rates are above 95% (the government claims to have erased illiteracy entirely), violent crime is almost nonexistent, and the pervasive sexism and racism of pre-revolutionary Cuba have given way to a more equitable landscape.

Those achievements receive less attention, though, than Cuba's strangled economy and continued political repression. Opponents of the socialist regime, both outside of Cuba and increasingly within the country, make the case that Cuba is a nation with no semblance of democracy. A single political party dominates all Cuban life. Cubans cannot speak freely, the media are state-owned and closely orchestrated by the Communist Party, and ordinary citizens have no rights to travel freely beyond Cuba. This latter point has been raised as a possible issue for reform. Raúl Castro's daughter stated in May 2008 that Cubans should be free to travel abroad without restrictions and without requiring permits. As yet, this idea has not come to fruition.

Hundreds of thousands of Fidel Castro's early opponents fled Cuba in the early days of the Revolution, when the state was busy expropriating private property, land, and businesses. Since then, thousands more have tried, only a few successfully, to make it to U.S. shores, often in rickety *balseros* (rafts). The less daring, but equally hopeful form daily queues at the U.S. Interests Office in Havana and other foreign embassies, desperately hoping for exit visas. On three major occasions, including the Mariel Boatlift in 1980, Fidel Castro sought to relieve pressure by allowing large groups, many of them deemed "undesirables," to emigrate.

The U.S. trade embargo and travel restrictions are still firmly in place, and President George W. Bush has made them even more stringent. But the embargo has done nothing to bring down the Castros' regime and little to force them to adopt more inclusive, democratic policies. In fact, the U.S. stance emboldened Fidel Castro, giving him a tangible enemy to rally his troops against, and may have even stifled change in Cuba. As one Cuban told me, "Fidel eats well every day. Don't worry about him. As for the rest of us, well, that's another question."

Despite years of difficulty and isolation, *La Revolución,* now 50 years old, continues to be the nation's rallying cry and raison d'être. Schoolchildren don't become Boy or Girl Scouts, but Young Communist Pioneers. Secretive local chapters of the Committee for the Defense of the Revolution (CDR) keep tabs on dissenters and those not upholding the party line. Throughout the country, giant billboards function like government pep talks to convince a population more worried about shoes and food than ideology to stay on the path. Billboards proclaim quaint notions like VICTORIA DE IDEAS (A Victory of Ideas), VIVIMOS EN UN PAIS LIBRE (We Live in a Free Country), LA REVOLUCION SOMOS NOSOTROS (We Are the Revolution), and even the melancholy rationalization SOMOS FELICES AQUI (We're Happy Here). Larger-than-life portraits of heroes and martyrs like Che Guevara (the roguish icon of revolution the world over), José Martí, Camilo Cienfuegos, and "Los Cinco" (five suspected spies convicted and imprisoned in the United States) guard the entrances to towns and are plastered on the walls of shops, offices, and homes. Perhaps fittingly, most of these billboards and portraits are now worn and faded.

Amid the extraordinary dilapidation of Havana and other decaying towns, it's near impossible for travelers not to wonder: What must this place once have looked like? Formerly grand, and now just badly faded and deteriorated buildings stand—if barely so—as harsh evidence of 4 decades of frustration, empty state coffers, and bankrupt promises of an idealistic, battle-hardened regime. Cubans are exhorted to fight on to bring the Revolution to fruition, but many Cubans, especially the young who've known nothing but Fidel, are weary of waiting. *Un año más*—one more year, they say.

When Raúl Castro replaced his ailing brother in early 2008, there was much talk of hope and great reforms. Many Cubans thought a corner had been turned. Between February and July 2008, Castro instituted certain reforms (see "Cuba Under Raúl Castro," later in this chapter).

Cuba, though, is as exhilarating as it is perplexing. One of the most exciting, mind-bending, and sensation-tingling countries you can visit, Cuba is a flood of indelible images. Many are inspiring, others heartbreaking. An open-air cafe with a smiling band of preternaturally cool musicians locked in a perfect groove. Huge crowds of hitchhiking Cubans gathered on the side of the road, desperate for a lift. Noisy Carnival rumbas and conga groups piercing the heat with Afro-Caribbean rhythms. Sexy couples with well-oiled hips gliding across dance floors. Those combative billboards forlornly pitched along the side of empty highways. Crowded *camellos,* crazy people-hauler flatbed trucks that look like urban transportation in a post-apocalyptic world. Mile-long lines for ice cream at Coppelia shops. Kids playing *pelota,* the national pastime of baseball, with a stick in the hollows of a ruined building.

But perhaps the truest picture of Cuba comes from the people themselves. Resilient and eternally patient Cubans somehow find the will to rise above devastating poverty, shortages, dense bureaucracy, and political authoritarianism. With wonderful senses of humor and hospitable like few others, they invite visitors into their cramped homes even if they've nothing to offer them. Schoolchildren, like an ad for the UN in identical maroon and mustard-colored uniforms, smile sweetly for photographs.

Cuba remains a quandary and a country full of potential. Hope can be seen in the painstaking restoration of landmark colonial buildings in Habana Vieja, whose decrepitude only a few years ago was the perfect metaphor for Cuba. Now that the ailing Fidel Castro is in the background, all eyes are firmly on Raúl Castro and any additional reforms that might be forthcoming. Hope grows on both sides of the political spectrum for greater engagement, but as always, intransigence lingers. And— as the Castros prepare to celebrate the 50th anniversary of what the country calls "El Triunfo de la Revolución"—Cuba soldiers on.

2 LOOKING BACK AT CUBA

In the first half of the 20th century, the United States, the primary purchaser of Cuba's sugar, dominated the island's economy and to a considerable extent controlled its political processes. Until the 1950s, Cuba was besieged by political corruption and violence. Fulgencio Batista, though only a sergeant in the army, managed to dictate Cuba's internal affairs through a series of puppet presidents for nearly a decade before winning the presidency outright in 1940. Though Batista retired in 1944, he staged a military coup and returned to power in 1952. Batista's corrupt dictatorship, supported by the United States, overlooked growing poverty across the country while Batista fattened his overseas bank accounts.

Havana was effectively ruled by a group of millionaires more powerful than anywhere else in Latin America, a distortion that allowed Cuban officials to claim that Cuba had the second-highest per capita income in the region. The capital was overrun by brothels, casinos, and gangsters, with high rollers in zoot suits transforming the city into their personal playground. Meanwhile, most of the country was mired in poverty, and more than half of all Cubans were undernourished in 1950. The nascent republic's unequivocal dependence on the United States, corruption, and absence of social equality reinforced the seeds of discontent that had been planted as far back as the 1920s.

GUERRILLA WARFARE & REVOLUTION

By the 1950s, the climate was ripe for revolution, though it would come in fits and starts. A band of young rebels attacked the Moncada Barracks, the country's second-most-important military base, in Santiago de Cuba on July 26, 1953 (the rebels would later take the date of the attack as the name for their movement, calling it the *Movimiento 26 de Julio*). The effort failed miserably, and many of the rebels were killed or later captured and tortured by the military. But the attack gave its young leader, a lawyer named Fidel Castro Ruz, the bully pulpit he needed. Jailed and tried for offenses against the nation, Castro's legendary 2-hour defense—presaging an uncanny ability to speak for hours at length about Cuba and the Revolution— included the now-famous words, "History will absolve me" (the title of Castro's revolutionary manifesto). Castro was imprisoned offshore on the Isla de la Juventud until May 1955, when Batista granted an amnesty to political prisoners.

Castro fled to Mexico, where he spent a year in exile planning his return to Cuba and the resumption of his plans to overthrow the government. The following year, Castro sneaked back to the southeastern coast of Cuba, along with a force of 81 guerrillas, including Ernesto "Che" Guevara and Castro's brother Raúl, aboard a small yacht, the *Granma.* The journey was beset by myriad problems and delays, including unfortunate weather, and Batista's forces were tipped off to the rebels' imminent arrival. Only 15 rebels reached their planned destination, the Sierra Maestra mountains. From such unlikely beginnings, the rebel forces evolved into a formidable guerrilla army, largely through the assistance of peasants who were promised land reforms in exchange for their support.

Following 2 years of dramatic fighting in the mountains and strategic points, Castro's insurrection gained strength and legitimacy among a broad swath of the Cuban population. Batista saw the end in sight and on January 1, 1959, he fled the country for the Dominican Republic. The combat-weary but triumphant rebels, known as the *barbudos* (the bearded ones), declared victory in Santiago de Cuba and then entered Havana a week later.

CUBA UNDER FIDEL CASTRO

The new government immediately set about restructuring Cuban society: It reduced rents, instituted agrarian reform, and limited estates to 400 hectares (1,000 acres). As part of a comprehensive nationalization program, the government expropriated utilities, factories, and private lands. The fledgling government also embarked upon wide-ranging programs designed to eradicate illiteracy and provide universal healthcare and free schooling.

The Revolution's lofty aims were mitigated by cruder attempts to consolidate state power. The transition to a centralized, all-powerful state antagonized many Cubans, mostly elites. Castro placed the media under state control, as it remains today, and he promised elections that were never held. Local Committees for the Defense of the Revolution (CDRs) kept tabs on dissenters. In the early years of Castro's reign, many thousands of people suspected of opposing the Revolution were interrogated, imprisoned, or sent to labor camps, along with other social "undesirables," such as homosexuals and priests.

In just 3 years after the triumph of the Revolution, nearly a quarter of a million Cubans—mostly professionals and wealthy landowners—fled the country. They settled in nearby Florida and established a colony of conservative Cuban Americans, which, in the coming decades, achieved not only economic success, but also a level of political clout that was disproportionate to its size.

Washington, opposed to Cuba's political evolution and spurred on by politically active Cubans living in Miami, continued to try to isolate Castro in Latin America. Just 1 year after Castro took power, in 1960, the U.S. government launched a trade embargo against Cuba in retaliation for Cuba's state appropriations and seizures of the assets of U.S. businesses. The trade embargo, which Cuba terms a blockade, and travel restrictions later imposed on most U.S. citizens, continue to this day. In 1961, the United States broke diplomatic relations with Cuba, and CIA-trained Cuban exiles launched an attempt to overthrow the Castro government. The Bay of Pigs mission was an utter fiasco and a severe black mark against the Kennedy administration. Cuba's resistance strengthened Castro's resolve to stand up to the United States.

Castro had not revealed any Communist leanings in the decade since coming to power, but soon after the Bay of Pigs, Castro declared himself a Marxist-Leninist. Some historians have argued that the aggressive ploys of the U.S. government were fundamental in pushing the Cuban government into the arms of the American enemy in the Cold War, the Soviet Union and its Eastern bloc of potential trading partners. The USSR was only too eager to develop a strategic relationship with an ideological opponent of Washington in the backyard of the United States. By the end of the 1980s, the USSR dominated Cuban trade and provided Cuba with subsidies worth an estimated $5 billion annually.

In the fall of 1962, the Soviet Union under Nikita Khrushchev installed 42 medium-range nuclear missiles in Cuba. A tense standoff ensued when President Kennedy ordered a naval blockade on the island and demanded that the existing missiles be dismantled. The world waited anxiously for 6 days until Khrushchev finally caved to U.S. demands to turn back his ships. The possibility of a nuclear war was averted in return for a U.S. promise never to invade Cuba.

Another 200,000 people abandoned Cuba as part of the Freedom Flights Program between 1965 and 1971. In 1980, Castro lifted travel restrictions and opened the port of Mariel (west of Havana); during the Mariel Boatlift, at least 125,000 Cubans—many of whom Washington charged were criminals and drug addicts—made it to U.S. shores before President Carter forced Castro to close the floodgates.

THE SPECIAL PERIOD

Soviet trade and subsidies propped up Cuba's heavily centralized and poorly performing economy until the end of the 1980s. But the fall of the Berlin Wall and dismantling of the Soviet Union suddenly left Cuba in an untenable position, as supplies of food, oil, and hard currency were cut off while the U.S. trade embargo continued.

The Cuban government initiated a "Special Period" in 1990—a euphemism for harsh new austerity measures and hardship to be borne by the large majority of Cubans. Rationing of basic goods had existed for most of Castro's years in power, but limited government distribution now included many more necessities. During the Special Period and years since, most Cubans found it virtually impossible to subsist on rations alone.

Complicating the delicate situation was the 1992 Cuba Democracy Act, which broadened the U.S. embargo to cover a ban on trade with Cuba for foreign subsidiaries of U.S. companies. Though the U.S. government denies that its trade embargo can be blamed for the shortcomings in the Cuban economy and resulting shortages of food and medicine, many analysts believe that the embargo has greatly exacerbated the difficulties experienced by ordinary Cubans. Meanwhile, Castro held onto power and made few concessions, even using the U.S. trade restrictions to his advantage: They gave him something and someone to blame for Cuba's grinding poverty and lack of goods.

With the economy in shambles, the Cuban government has been forced to introduce a limited number of capitalist measures. Foreign investment, which has taken the form of joint ventures primarily in the fields of tourism and mineral and oil exploration, has been openly encouraged. Castro, with inescapable irony, legalized the U.S. dollar in 1993—even establishing state-owned, dollar-only stores, small-scale private enterprises like *casas particulares* and *paladares* (private homestays and restaurants), and the introduction of private farmers' markets. While these capitalist initiatives have benefited some Cubans, giving them access to dollars (through jobs in tourism or relatives sending remittances from abroad), the dual economy has ultimately turned many other Cubans into have-nots, unequal in a socialist society.

In August 1994, in a frantic safety-valve measure designed to alleviate some of the economic pressure on the state, Castro lifted restrictions on those wishing to leave. More than 30,000 Cubans accepted the invitation and set out across dangerous waters to Florida on *balseros* (homemade rafts). Faced with the political embarrassment of an influx of poor Cubans, President Clinton abolished the standing U.S. policy granting automatic asylum to Cuban refugees. Instead, they were returned to the Guantánamo Bay Naval Base to await repatriation.

After Castro visited the Vatican in 1996, Pope John Paul II returned the favor. His visit to Cuba in 1998 prompted a relaxation of the government's harsh views of the Catholic Church in Cuba. In late 1999, 6-year-old Elián González became the latest face of political animosity between the United States and Cuba. González survived for 2 days alone on a raft after his mother and other escapees had perished, only to become the object of an international tug-of-war. Castro and most Cubans, in huge demonstrations, demanded the boy's return to be with his father in northern Cuba. Castro's opponents in the United States sought to allow the boy to stay with distant relatives in Miami. After weeks of wrangling, the Immigration and Naturalization Service returned Elián to his father and Cuba, where he received a hero's welcome.

The normally quiet U.S. naval base at Guantánamo Bay has been in the news in recent years after Al Qaeda prisoners from the wars in Afghanistan and Iraq were taken to the base for interrogation and detention. Former President Jimmy Carter made a historic visit to Cuba in the spring of 2002, voicing support for Castro's call for an end to the trade embargo and travel restrictions while also criticizing the Cuban government's lack of democracy. Carter met with dissidents and gave an uncensored and at times harshly critical speech in front of Castro that was broadcast on Cuban television.

However, Carter's visit had little lasting effect. In 2003, Castro jailed some 75 prominent dissidents and government critics, imposing stiff sentences following abbreviated trials. In early 2004 and again in 2006, the Bush administration tightened the screws on U.S. citizens' right to travel to Cuba, virtually eliminating all educational and humanitarian licenses and severely reducing the amount of time and money that Cuban Americans can spend in Cuba.

In July 2006, Fidel Castro fell ill and withdrew from public life. His younger brother Raúl became acting president. Fidel Castro relinquished power in February 2008 and Raúl was unanimously elected as Cuba's new president by the country's National Assembly.

CUBA UNDER RAUL CASTRO

One of the first reforms that Raúl instituted following his election as Cuba's new president was the lifting of restrictions on Cubans owning TVs, DVD players, computers, and other electrical appliances. This was followed by a move to decentralize the state-run agricultural economy, including allowing farmers to till fallow land and to buy their own equipment. In June 2008, Raúl abolished the egalitarian wage system, allowing hard-working employees to earn a better salary, and raised the state pension. In July 2008, Raúl authorized land grants for private farming. This move was aimed at boosting agricultural production and reducing the amount of food that Cuba imports. Then came the lifting of the restriction on cellphone ownership and the prohibition preventing Cubans from staying in tourist hotels.

However, during a speech he made on July 26, 2008, he dashed hopes for further reforms by alluding to the global economic downturn and saying Cuba would have to tighten its belt, reduce expectations for material goods, and not always expect good news.

Freedom to travel abroad is still restricted and access to the Internet is also restricted. Talk of reforming the dual monetary system is on everyone's lips, but no confirmation of a plan of action has been forthcoming.

3 CUBA IN POPULAR CULTURE

CUBAN MUSIC

Perhaps no other nation—certainly no other nation of its size—is as spectacularly endowed musically as is Cuba. The seductive sounds of richly percussive Cuban music are, in many people's minds, Cuba's greatest export. In the late 1990s, a series of records and a documentary film brought a group of aging Cuban musicians to the world's attention. The unexpected popularity abroad of the Buena Vista Social Club and its individual artists—Ibrahim Ferrer, Compay Segundo, Rubén González, Eliades Ochoa, and Omara Portuondo—made traditional Cuban sounds very much in demand throughout Cuba and internationally. Buena Vista and company, though, is only the latest round of Cuban music to circle the globe, echoing the earlier mambo and cha-cha-chá crazes that took the United States and Europe by storm in the 1950s.

Within Cuba, music is a daily presence across the island, from rural areas and dusty provincial towns to the capital. It seeps out of cafes and *casas de la trova* (music clubs) in the midafternoon and thunders out of dance halls as the sun rises over the Malecón (promenade). The musical diet is a dizzying menu of styles with uncommon appeal, so emphatically tropical that you can almost hear the humidity in the vocals, chords, and percussion.

Cuba's musical heritage, an onomatopoeic stew of salsa, rumba, mambo, *son, danzón,* and cha-cha-chá, stems from the country's rich mix of African, Spanish, French, and Haitian cultures. The roots of contemporary Cuban popular music lie in the 19th century's combination of African drums and rhythms along with Spanish guitar and melody. Most forms of Cuban music feature Latin stringed instruments, African bongos, congas, and claves (wooden percussion sticks), and auxiliary instruments such as maracas and guiros.

The heartbeat of Cuban music is the clave, which refers to a distinctive rhythm and the instrument used to play it. While the actual instrument is not necessarily played in every song, all Cuban rhythms are built up from the simple concept of the clave. The perennial form of Cuban traditional music is *son* (literally, "sound"; pronounced *sohn*), a style of popular dance music that originated in the eastern, poorer half of the country known as El Oriente in the early 1900s.

You can and will hear live music anywhere you go in Cuba, but the best places for authentic traditional *son* and more modern styles are Havana, Trinidad, Camagüey, Santiago de Cuba, and Baracoa. The last three possess the best *casas de la trova* (music clubs) in the country, spots thick with sultry air, slowly rotating ceiling fans, and grinning octogenarians plunking away on weathered guitars and stand-up basses. Cubans seem only too happy to share the dance floor with tentative foreigners.

BOOKS ON CUBA

There's a wealth of books on Cuba's history and politics. For a good historical overview, try Jaime Suchlicki's latest edition of **Cuba: From Columbus to Castro and Beyond** (Brasseys, 2002), or Richard Gott's **Cuba: A New History** (Yale University Press, 2004). More than 1,800 pages,

Hugh Thomas's *Cuba, or The Pursuit of Freedom* (Da Capo Press, 1998) is far more comprehensive and fascinating, but it takes a while to read.

A unique account of post-revolutionary Cuba comes from a well-known Latin American journalist, Alma Guillermoprieto, who writes of the 6 months she spent in Cuba in the early '70s teaching dance. *Dancing with Cuba: A Memoir of the Revolution* (Vintage, 2005) is a portrait of the artistic world of Cuba in the '70s and a self-reflective memoir of the author's political awakening.

No reading list for Cuba would be complete without a biography or two of Fidel Castro and Che Guevara. The best are Leycester Coltman's *The Real Fidel Castro* (Yale University Press, 2005), Tad Szulc's *Fidel: A Critical Portrait* (Avon Books, 2000), and Jon Lee Anderson's *Che Guevara: A Revolutionary Life* (Grove, 1997). The latest addition to the biography shelves is *My Life: Fidel Castro* (Penguin, 2007) by journalist Ignacio Ramonet. Also worth a read are *Guerilla Prince: The Untold Story of Fidel Castro* (Little, Brown, 2002) by Georgie Anne Geyer, and *The Life and Death of Che Guevara* (Vintage, 1998) by Jorge Castañeda. There are also several volumes of writings worth looking into by both Fidel and Che. Che's own *The Motorcycle Diaries: Notes on a Latin American Journey* (Ocean Press, 2003) provides an interesting glimpse into the social and psychological genesis of this great revolutionary figure, although it deals with the period in Che's life prior to meeting Fidel and going to Cuba. The book was made into a very successful film (*The Motorcycle Diaries*) by director Walter Salles.

Another compelling perspective on the Revolution is offered by Enrique Oltuski, a former Shell Oil engineer and a leader in the 26th of July movement, in *Vida Clandestina: My Life in the Cuban Revolution* (Jossey-Bass, 2002).

Any exploration into Cuban literature should include the works of poets José Martí and Nicolás Guillén, as well as the novels and prose writings of Alejo Carpentier and José Lezama Lima. Prominent works that exist in English include Guillermo Cabrera Infante's *Three Trapped Tigers* (Marlow, 1997), and several of Reinaldo Arenas's novels and his best-selling autobiography *Before Night Falls* (Penguin, 1994), made into a stunning film by Julian Schnabel.

Also worth reading is Cristina García's novel, *Dreaming in Cuban* (Ballantine, 1993), which chronicles the lives of three Cuban women after the Revolution. If you like García's book, you might also enjoy Ana Menéndez's *Loving Che* (Atlantic Monthly Press, 2003), the story of one woman's quest to uncover the mysteries and romance of her mother's past.

Of course, it goes without saying that you've already read Hemingway's *The Old Man and the Sea* (Scribner, 1952) and Graham Greene's *Our Man in Havana* (Heinemann, 1958).

CUBAN FILMS

In addition to the poignant *Before Night Falls* and the excellent *The Motorcycle Diaries,* mentioned above, there are a host of wonderful films that can be rented prior to any trip to Cuba or bought while you are there from ARTex stores (www.cubacine.cu). One true classic film available on DVD is *Soy Cuba (I Am Cuba)* by the great Russian director Mikhail Kalatozov, who shot this Communist-era piece of social-realist propaganda in Cuba shortly after the Revolution. The film features a screenplay by Russian poet Yevgeny Yevtushenko and the Cuban writer and filmmaker Enrique Piñeda Barnet.

Cuba's own film industry has produced several fine films, including the celebrated *Fresa y Chocolate* (Strawberry and Chocolate), *Memorias del Subdesarrollo* (Memories of Underdevelopment), and *Muerte de un Burócrata* (Death of a Bureaucrat), all by Tomás Gutiérrez Alea. The animated comedy *Vampiros de la Habana* (Vampires of Havana) by Juan Padrón proved popular. Three of my favorite Cuban films are *Guantanamera* by Tomás Gutiérrez Alea and Juan Carlos Tabío, *Lista de Espera* by Juan Carlos Tabío, and *El Benny* by Jorge Luis Sánchez. Also look out for *Suite Habana* by Fernando Pérez.

For a good look into the conflict between Cubans in Cuba and their relatives and friends in the United States, check out *Azucar Amarga* (Bitter Sugar) by Leon Ichaso, or *Quién Diablos es Julieta* (Who the Hell Is Juliette?) by Carlos Marcovich. The movie *Buena Vista Social Club* documents the rediscovery and newfound fame of some of Cuba's great traditional musicians. The accompanying Grammy Award–winning CD *Buena Vista Social Club* is as good a place as any to start listening to Cuban music.

SANTERIA & AFRO-CUBAN CULTURE

Cuba's prominent African-influenced culture is one of the nation's defining characteristics. African culture brought by slaves and developed within the context of the Spanish colony has had a profound impact on religion, music, and indeed, virtually all of Cuban society.

One of the most salient aspects of Afro-Cuban culture is Santeria (also called *Regla de Ocha*). Frequently misunderstood and misinterpreted as a religious cult or form of voodoo, Santeria is in fact a major syncretic and animistic religion that, by most estimates, has a greater following in Cuba than does Catholicism. Its practice is not restricted to Afro-Cubans or a certain socioeconomic class.

Havana's **Casa de Africa Museum,** Obrapía 157, between San Ignacio and Mercaderes in La Habana Vieja (② **7/861-5798**), has exhibits on Santeria for those interested in learning more. The museum is open Tuesday through Saturday from 9am to 5pm and Sunday from 9am to 1pm. Through local contacts, Spanish-speaking visitors can sometimes arrange for a *santero* or *babalao* (high priest) to perform ritualistic divinations.

4 EATING & DRINKING IN CUBA

Do not come to Cuba for fine dining. While it's possible to minimize the pain, finding good food, service, and value is a challenge in Cuba. About 98% of restaurants that cater to tourists are run by large state-owned corporations, and as a whole, they are often overpriced and mediocre. Even the popular and highly touted restaurants here often suffer from inconsistency and indifferent service. *Note:* Be especially on the lookout for overcharging, either in the form of phantom charges or inflated prices.

In addition to hotel restaurants and official state-run tourist restaurants, the principal dining option in Cuba is the *paladar.* Like *casas particulares, paladares* are private homes that have been granted permission to serve foreign tourists. *Paladares* are small, with a seating limit of just 12, and subject to various limitations (although you will find in Havana that a few of the popular choices clearly do not adhere to the rules and are still operational). They cannot serve shrimp or lobster for instance, and cannot accept credit cards. They are also heavily taxed by the state. However, Cubans are a creative lot and you will find *paladares* that have figured ways around many of these limitations. *Paladares* tend to open and close, move, or change their name or menu with great frequency. They also often run out of menu items, or simply can't find the raw materials to begin the day with. However, there are some dependable and long-standing *paladares.* In fact, several of these are among the best restaurants in the country. At these, you'll almost certainly need a reservation, or be prepared to wait.

In general, you should tip between 10% and 15%, keeping in mind that this represents a huge amount of hard currency for most Cubans. Some restaurants add a 10% service charge to bills; this will not go to the waitstaff. Also, if you show up at a *paladar* on the recommendation of a taxi driver or *jinetero,* you can expect to pay a commission of between CUC\$3 and CUC\$5 (US\$3.25–US\$5.40/£1.60–£2.70), which is often added to your bill after being paid to the driver or *jinetero* by the paladar.

Given the unique economic and social conditions of Cuba, there is little street food to speak of, aside from a few odd pizza and ice-cream vendors. Cuban street pizza has heavy dough, with a molten mess of sauce and gooey cheese topping, served as small individual discs on wax paper. Peanuts sold in newspaper cones and a peanut- and- toffee bar are also popular.

With a recent influx of foreign capital and a move toward modernization, fast-food chains have begun popping up around Cuba. The most prominent of these is El Rápido, which has numerous outlets serving fried chicken, burgers, hot dogs, microwave pizzas, and other fast-food staples. Another chain worth mentioning is Pizza Nova, which has several outlets in Havana and in various provincial cities. This chain specializes in thin-crust pizza and good pastas.

LOCAL CUISINE

Cuban, or *criolla,* cuisine is a mix of European (predominantly Spanish) and Afro-Caribbean influences. The staples of the cuisine include roasted and fried pork, beef, and chicken, usually accompanied by rice, beans, plantains, and yucca. Oddly, Cubans do not eat large amounts of seafood, although fish and lobster dishes are on the menu at most tourist restaurants. In general, Cubans do not use aggressive amounts of spice or hot peppers, although onions, garlic, and, to a much lesser extent, cumin are used fairly liberally.

With the exception of breakfast, most meals are accompanied by some combination of white rice and beans. *Arroz moro,* or *moros y cristianos* (Moors and Christians), is the common name for black beans mixed with white rice. *Congrí* is a similar dish of red beans and white rice already mixed. Sometimes the rice and beans are served separately.

The national dish—which, unfortunately, you won't often find on restaurant menus, but it's worth sampling if you do—is *ajiaco,* a chunky meat and vegetable stew. *Ajiaco* comes from the Taíno word *aji* for chile pepper, although the dish is seldom prepared very spicy. You're much more likely to find *ropa vieja* (literally, "old clothes"), a sauté of shredded beef, onions, and peppers; or *picadillo,* a similar concoction made with ground beef and sometimes featuring olives and raisins in the mix.

If you're looking for a light snack, try a *bocadito,* literally a "little bite," which is what they call a simple sandwich, usually made of ham and/or cheese.

Aside from the excellent Coppelia ice creams, you'll generally find rather slim pickings for dessert. Flan is popular, but

---

Fun Facts   La Bomba

If you want to order papaya, remember to call it *fruta bomba*. In Cuba, the word *papaya* is almost always used as pejorative slang referring to a woman's most private part.

seldom outstanding. I feel similarly about *natilla,* a simple sweet pudding that usually comes in either chocolate or coconut flavors. Many dessert menus will feature some sort of sweet marmalade, usually *guayaba,* papaya, or coconut, accompanied by cheese. Unfortunately, the cheeses are generally bland and nondescript.

WETTING YOUR WHISTLE

Most Cubans simply drink water or any number of popular soft drinks, including Sprite and Coca-Cola, whose locally produced equivalents are called Cachito and Tu Cola, respectively. While many hotels and restaurants serve freshly squeezed orange juice for breakfast, you'll have a harder time finding other fresh fruit juices than you'd expect in the Caribbean tropics unless you are staying in a *casa particular.*

One of the more interesting nonalcoholic drinks is *guarapo,* the sweet juice of freshly pressed sugar cane.

Cubans also drink plenty of coffee, and they like to brew it strong. Order *café espresso* for a straight shot, or *café con leche* if you'd like it mixed with warm milk. Ask for *café americano* if you want a milder brew.

Cuba produces a small handful of pretty good lager beers. Cristal, Bucanero, and Mayabe are the most popular. If you want something slightly darker and stronger, try a Bucanero dark. Cuba does produce excellent rums. Most visitors soon have their fill of *mojitos* (light rum with lime juice, fresh mint, sugar, and club soda) and daiquiris. Another popular cocktail is the *cuba libre* ("Free Cuba"), which is simply a rum and Coke with lime.

Planning Your Trip to Cuba

U.S. citizens are not allowed to travel directly to Cuba without a U.S. Treasury Department license. Travel is sometimes arranged through a third country instead (see "Entry Requirements," below). Once in Cuba, U.S. citizens will encounter no restrictions. All travelers must be aware that hurricanes may strike from June until November. Cuba has a very effective hurricane response operation. If planning to visit during an important carnival, make arrangements for your accommodations and rental car in advance; the supply of rental cars sometimes runs out.

For additional help in planning your trip and for more on-the-ground resources in Cuba, please see "Fast Facts, Toll-Free Numbers & Websites" in Appendix A on p. 288.

1 VISITOR INFORMATION

Tourism is Cuba's number-one source of hard currency, and the government is actively involved in promoting tourism internationally. As a result, there's a network of tourism boards and agencies in major cities around the world; some are better than others. Some offices are run by the Ministry of Tourism, others by one of the major state-run agencies like **Cubanacán, Havanatur,** or **Cubatur.** No matter the bureau, the focus is almost entirely on organized tours, but they can also give you some basic information. Agencies to contact include **Cuba Tourist Board Canada,** 1200 Bay St., Suite 305, Toronto M5R 2A5 (© **416/362-0700;** www.gocuba.ca), or 2075, rue University, Bureau 460, Montreal H3A 2L1 (© **514/ 848-0668**); **Cuba Tourist Board Great Britain,** 154 Shaftesbury Ave., 1st Floor, London WC2H 8HL (© **0207/240- 6655;** tourism@cubasi.info); and, in the United States, the **Cuban Interests Section** (© **202/797-8518;** http://embacu. cubaminrex.cu).

A host of other information is available online. The **Latin America Network Information Center** (http://lanic.utexas. edu/la/cb/cuba) is hands down the best one-stop shop for helpful links to a wide range of travel and general information sites.

The Cuban government sponsors a number of websites, including **Cuba Travel** (www.cubatravel.cu), **CubaSi** (www. cubasi.cu), and **Directorio Turístico de Cuba** (www.dtcuba.com). All provide a fair amount of travel-related information and links. State-run tourism agency websites—including **Cubanacán** (www. cubanacan.cu) and **Cubatur** (www.cubatur. cu)—are also good places to check for hotels, transportation, and package deals.

Infotur (www.infotur.cu), based in Cuba, also provides fairly detailed information on the country's provinces through a series of portable document files (PDFs).

To read travelogues about Cuba, try the forum section at **www.cubamania.com**. You can search for other blogs about Cuba at **Travelblog.com** or post your own travelogue at **Travelblog.org.** For blogs that cover general travel news and highlight various destinations, try **Writtenroad.com** or Gawker Media's snarky **Gridskipper.com.** For more literary travel essays, try **Worldhum.com,** which has an extensive list of other travel-related journals, blogs, online communities, newspaper coverage, and bookstores.

The best road map to Cuba is the Guía de Carreteras published by Limusa; it can be bought at El Navegante, Calle Mercaderes 115 between Obispo and Obrapía, La Habana Vieja.

2 ENTRY REQUIREMENTS

PASSPORTS
All travelers to Cuba must possess a valid passport, a return ticket, and a visa or tourist visa. Unlicensed U.S. citizens may be allowed a stay of up to 90 days upon entry. British citizens are granted 30 days upon entry. This can be extended for another 30 days only within Cuba. Canadian citizens are granted a visa for 90 days. This can be extended for 90 days only.

VISAS
Tourist visas are generally issued by the ticketing airline or travel agent. (If you book a flight with Air Canada, the visa is included in the price.) In a worst-case scenario, the visa can usually be bought on the spot upon clearing Customs. Tourist visas cost between CUC$22 (US$24/£12) and CUC$35 (US$38/£19), depending upon the issuing agent, and are good for up to 90 days for U.S. and Canadian citizens, although Customs agents will sometimes issue them for just 30 days, or until the date of your return flight, unless you request otherwise. They can be extended for another 30 days (90 days for Canadians) once you arrive in Cuba for an additional minimum CUC$25 (US$27/£14) fee. In order to extend your tourist visa, you must personally go to any immigration office in the country. An additional 90-day extension for Canadians can be granted once at any immigration office for a cost of approximately CUC$22 (US$24/£12). For further information in Canada, contact the Cuban Embassy at www.embacubacanada.net; or the Cuban consulate in

Toronto at cubacon1@on.aibn.com; or the Cuba tourist board in Canada at www.gocuba.ca.

In the U.K., if you buy a ticket for an independent flight, you will need to purchase a separate tourist visa. Some travel companies are charging exorbitant costs for this (up to £50). While the visa is also available from the **Cuban Embassy** in London for £15 plus postage (www.cubaldn.com), the cheapest, most efficient and reliable place is directly from **www.visacuba.co.uk**. U.K. citizens are granted entry for 30 days. This can be extended once at any immigration office for an additional 30 days for CUC$25 (£14).

Note that when seeking a tourist visa extension, you need to purchase bank stamps for the value of the extension you need. To avoid making unnecessary journeys, ask your hotel or *casa particular* (the Cuban version of a simple bed-and-breakfast) to call the local immigration office and ask the price of the extension *for your nationality* before heading to a bank authorized to sell the stamps.

In the event you need a specific work visa, or if your travel agent or airline will not provide you with the tourist visa, you should contact the Cuban consulate or embassy in your home country.

For Residents of the United States
While it is not illegal for U.S. citizens to travel to Cuba, most are prohibited from spending any money in Cuba. This, in effect, is the "travel ban." The complicated

prohibition, which allows for various exceptions, is governed by the U.S. Treasury Department and the Office of Foreign Assets Control (OFAC). Further information can be found at www.treas. gov/offices/enforcement/ofac.

The Treasury Department grants certain licenses. Some of these licenses are implicit, such as those for full-time journalists and government workers on official business. Other licenses must be applied for on a case-by-case basis with the U.S. Treasury Department, including Cuban-American citizens making humanitarian visits to close family. Licenses granted for educational travel and certain humanitarian trips, particularly those organized by religious groups, used to be a major route for legal travel to Cuba, but these were severely curtailed by the Bush administration in 2004, with even tighter restrictions placed on licensed travel in 2005 and 2006.

Travel arrangements for licensed travelers can be made by an authorized Travel Service Provider (TSP), and travel can be made directly from U.S. gateway cities on regular charter flights. There are hundreds of authorized TSPs. A couple of the most dependable are **ABC Charters** (© **305/263-6829**; www.abc-charters.com) and **Tico Travel** (© **800/493-8426** in the U.S. or Canada, or 954/493-8426; www.destination cuba.com).

Be careful about signing on for a "fully hosted" trip. According to the regulations, a U.S. citizen can travel to Cuba without violating the Treasury ban provided he or she does not pay for any goods or services, including food and lodging, or provide any services to Cuba or a Cuban national while in the country. This provision had been widely used by U.S. citizens to buy packages from Canadian, Mexican, or Bahamian tour agencies. However, the Treasury Department has caught on to this tactic and has declared any "fully hosted" trip that is clearly for pleasure or tourism is in violation of the regulations.

Failure to comply with Department of Treasury regulations may result in civil penalties and criminal prosecution upon return to the United States. For more information, contact the **Office of Foreign Assets Control,** U.S. Department of the Treasury, 1500 Pennsylvania Ave. NW, Treasury Annex, Washington, DC 20220 (© **800/540-6322** or 202/622-2490; www. treas.gov/ofac).

As far as Cuba is concerned, U.S. travelers are welcomed with open arms. In fact, as an aid to those seeking to circumvent the Treasury ban, in most cases, Cuban immigration does not actually stamp U.S. passports, or any for that matter (but you should ask the officer to be sure). For current information on Cuban entry and Customs requirements, you can contact the **Cuban Interests Section** (© **202/797-8518**).

UNLICENSED TRAVEL It is estimated that as many as 200,000 U.S. citizens travel to Cuba each year without a Treasury Department license. The vast majority of travelers use third-country gateway cities like Toronto, Montreal, Cancún, Mexico City, Nassau, George Town on Grand Cayman, or Kingston in Jamaica, and are never questioned or bothered by U.S. authorities upon return. However, the Bush administration has cracked down on unlicensed travelers, and reports of tourists being caught have increased dramatically.

WHAT TO DO IF YOU GET BUSTED Officially, U.S. citizens who violate the ban face up to 10 years in prison, $250,000 in criminal fines, and $55,000 in civil fines, but according to the Treasury, penalties range from $3,000 to $7,500. Just 21 people were penalized in 2006. If you are stopped upon returning from an unlicensed trip to Cuba and directly asked by the Customs and Immigration agents, you should give as little information as possible. United States citizens cannot be compelled to provide self-incriminating information. Furthermore,

Tips Pick Your Poison

Some operators and guidebooks recommend lying if asked whether or not you were in Cuba. If you lie, you then place yourself at risk for perjury charges, which in the end are easier for the United States government to prosecute and are potentially more serious. I recommend you say little or nothing about your travel to Cuba, but I don't recommend that you lie. Remember, under U.S. law you have the right to refuse to incriminate yourself.

you cannot be denied reentry into the U.S. for traveling to Cuba. You will likely face a long and uncomfortable search and questioning session, and be sent on your way. This will probably be followed by the receipt of a pre-penalty notice from the OFAC. The letter will request specific information to prove or disprove your alleged travel to Cuba, and to threaten the various fines and penalties. At this point, you should contact the **Center for Constitutional Rights** (© 212/614-6470; www.ccr-ny.org), which runs the Cuba Travel Project and works in conjunction with the **National Lawyers Guild** (www.nlg.org/cuba) to provide legal assistance to U.S. citizens facing prosecution for traveling to Cuba. Typically, after the initial pre-penalty letter, the OFAC offers to settle the case for a reduced fine in the neighborhood of $1,500 to $2,500. Many travelers have opted to go this route. A very, very small number of cases have ever fully gone to trial.

For Cuban Nationals

The Cuban government doesn't recognize dual nationality of travelers from other countries who are Cuban-born or are the children of Cuban parents, particularly those who chose exile in the United States. The Cuban government requires some individuals whom it considers to be Cuban to enter and depart Cuba using a Cuban passport. Using a Cuban passport for this purpose does not jeopardize one's foreign citizenship; however, you will probably have to use your home country's passport to exit and enter that country. Other

Cuban nationals and exiles just need a visa, but acquiring this visa is more complicated than acquiring the simple tourist visa used by most other travelers.

If you are Cuban-born or the child of Cuban-born parents, you should check with the Cuban embassy or consulate in your country of residence, as well as your local immigration authorities. In Canada, contact the **Cuban Embassy,** 388 Main St., Ottawa, Ontario, K1S 1E3 (© 613/563-0141; www.embacubacanada.net); there are also consulates in Montreal and Toronto. In the U.K., contact the **Cuban Embassy,** 167 High Holborn, London, WC1 6PA (© 0207/240-2488; www.cubaldn.com). In the U.S., contact the **Cuban Interests Section,** 2630 16th St. NW, Washington, DC 20009 (© 202/797-8518).

MEDICAL REQUIREMENTS

It is suggested that you have all the vaccines recommended for international travel. These are tetanus, polio, diptheria, hepatitis A, and cholera. Vaccinations for yellow fever and cholera are not required unless you are arriving from a country where they are prevalent.

CUSTOMS
What You Can Bring Into Cuba

You may bring in all manner of personal effects, including video and still cameras, personal electronic devices, jewelry, and sports equipment. In addition, visitors

Gifts & Other Assistance

Cuba is greatly lacking in many consumer and health-related products, and many visitors make a point of bringing items that are hard to find or prohibitively expensive to give as gifts. However, some visitors may be concerned about paternalism or setting an example that influences Cubans to look upon all travelers as bearers of material goods (in many areas popular with tourists, begging has become an issue). One possible solution is to take along gifts to offer to those who welcome you into their homes or with whom you have some sort of meaningful interaction. Another is to seek out schools and local officials to ensure that gifts are properly distributed. Items greatly appreciated by all Cubans include toothpaste; aspirin and other medicines; sporting goods and equipment, especially baseballs, bats, and gloves; pens and colored pencils; makeup; soap; clothing; and disposable diapers.

—Neil E. Schlecht

may bring in up to two bottles of liquor, a carton of cigarettes, and up to 10 kilograms of medications, provided they are in the original packaging. Anything that might be deemed an import destined to be sold or given as a gift to a Cuban citizen will raise eyebrows and may be subject to stiff import duties and/or confiscation. This includes TVs, VCR or large DVD players, telephones, fax machines, desktop computers, and most types of appliances. In fact, by law you may only import up to CUC$1,000 (US$1,080/£540) worth of any merchandise, and there is a 100% duty on all but the first CUC$50 (US$54/£27) worth. In practice, most visitors can freely bring in reasonable quantities of basic goods, like dried foods, vitamins, pharmaceuticals, and household supplies, without them being taxed or confiscated.

Note: You may bring unlimited amounts of cash, but you must declare quantities in excess of US$5,000 (£2,500), as you may have trouble exporting large quantities of cash, if discovered upon departure. For current and more detailed information, check out **www.aduana.co.cu**.

What You Can Take Home from Cuba

Travelers may export up to 50 cigars with no questions asked. Larger quantities can be exported, provided you show proof that they were bought in official Habanos S.A. outlets. There are restrictions on certain works of art, books, publications, and coins. Consult **www.aduana.co.cu** for further information. Travelers are officially limited to bringing home two bottles of rum or other spirits, although this limit is rarely enforced. Still, if the Customs officials deem your purchases to be of a commercial nature, you could face fines or confiscation.

To export works of art, you will need a permit from the **Registro Nacional de Bienes Culturales (National Register of Cultural Heritage)**, Calle 17 no. 1009 between Calles 10 and 12, Vedado (© 7/831-3362; www.cnpc.cult.cu; both in Spanish only). Theoretically, any reputable gallery or shop will provide you with this permit along with your purchase. Handicrafts and artwork bought at street fairs are exempt from this requirement, although I have heard of cases of people being hassled upon departure for not having a permit for artwork that should be exempt.

Note: There's a CUC$25 (US$27/£14) departure tax. You must pay this in cash, so be sure to have it on hand.

U.S. Citizens: Travelers bringing back Cuban-made goods will be considered in violation of the Treasury embargo and their goods will be confiscated. It is also illegal for U.S. citizens to import Cuban products even if they never stepped foot on the island. It does no good to try to convince the Customs agent confiscating your stogies that you bought them in a cigar shop in Canada or Mexico or Costa Rica.

Canadian Citizens: For a clear summary of Canadian rules, write for the booklet *I Declare,* issued by the **Canada Border Services Agency** (*C* **800/461-9999** in Canada, or 204/983-3500; **www.cbsa-asfc.gc.ca**). Canada allows its citizens a C$750 exemption, and you're allowed to bring back duty-free 200 cigarettes, 1 can of tobacco, 40 imperial ounces of liquor, and 50 cigars. In addition, you're allowed to mail gifts to Canada valued at less than C$60 a day, provided they're unsolicited and don't contain alcohol or tobacco (write on the package "Unsolicited gift, under $60 value"). All valuables should be declared on the Y-38 form before departure from Canada, including serial numbers of valuables you already own, such as expensive foreign cameras. *Note:* The C$750 exemption can only be used once a year and only after an absence of 7 days.

U.K. Citizens: Those returning from **a non-E.U. country** have a customs allowance of 200 cigarettes **or** 50 cigars **or** 250 grams of smoking tobacco; 2 liters of still table wine; 1 liter of spirits or strong liqueurs (over 22% volume); **or** 2 liters of fortified wine, sparkling wine, or other liqueurs; 60cc (ml) perfume; 250cc (ml) of toilet water; and £145 worth of all other goods, including gifts and souvenirs. People under 17 years cannot have the tobacco or alcohol allowance. For more information, contact **HM Customs & Excise** at *C* **0845/010-9000** (from outside the U.K., *C* 44 2920/501-261), or consult their website at **www.hmrc.gov.uk**.

Australian Citizens: The duty-free allowance in Australia is A$900 or, for those under 18, A$450. Citizens can bring in 250 cigarettes **or** 250 grams of either loose tobacco or cigars, and 2.25 liters of alcohol. If you're returning with valuables you already own, such as foreign-made cameras, you should file form B263. A helpful brochure available from Australian consulates or Customs offices is *Know Before You Go.* For more information, call the **Australian Customs Service** at *C* **1300/363-263,** or log on to **www.customs.gov.au**.

New Zealand Citizens: The duty-free allowance is NZ$700. Citizens over 17 can bring in 200 cigarettes **or** 50 cigars **or** 250 grams of tobacco (or a mixture of all three if their combined weight doesn't exceed 250g); plus 4.5 liters of wine or beer or 1.125 liters of liquor. New Zealand currency does not carry import or export restrictions. Fill out a certificate of export, listing the valuables you are taking out of the country; that way, you can bring them back without paying duty. Most questions are answered in a free pamphlet available at New Zealand consulates and Customs offices: *New Zealand Customs Guide for Travellers, Notice no. 4.* For more information, contact **New Zealand Customs,** The Customhouse, 17–21 Whitmore St., Box 2218, Wellington (*C* **04/473-6099** or 0800/428-786; **www.customs.govt.nz**).

---

3 WHEN TO GO

The tourist high season runs from December through March, coinciding with the winter months in most northern countries. It also coincides with Cuba's dry season. Throughout this season, and especially around the Christmas and Easter holidays, the beaches and resorts are relatively full, prices are somewhat higher, and it may be harder to find an available rental car or room. In addition, overbooking—a widespread problem in the Cuban tourism industry—is certainly much more of a problem during the high season. During the low season, you should be able to find discounts on rooms, car rentals, and tour options. Moreover, resorts and attractions are much less crowded. However, temperatures are somewhat higher throughout the low season, and periods of extended rainfall are not uncommon.

CLIMATE

Cuba has two distinct seasons, rainy (May–Oct) and dry (Nov–Apr). The dry season is characterized by consistently sunny and temperate weather, with daytime temperatures averaging between 75° and 80°F (24°–27°C). However, temperature swings are greater during this period, and it can actually get somewhat chilly when cold fronts—or "northers"—creep down the eastern seaboard of the United States, particularly in the months of January and February. In contrast, the rainy season is overall a slightly warmer period in Cuba, with less dramatic same-day temperature swings. There's a small dry spell most years during August, which is also the hottest month to visit Cuba. The entire Caribbean basin is affected by an annual hurricane season (June–Nov), with September and October having the highest number of hurricanes.

HOLIDAYS

Cuba has a very limited number of official holidays, and aside from Christmas Day, no religious holidays are recognized by the state. The official holidays are **January 1** (Liberation Day), **May 1** (May Day, or Labor Day), **July 26** (Revolution Day), **October 10** (anniversary of the beginning of the 1868 War of Independence), and **December 25** (Christmas Day). However, the state has such total control that it's not uncommon for mass rallies or entire national mobilizations to be called as it sees fit. Other important dates that sometimes bring Cuba to a de facto state of national holiday include: **January 28** (Birth of José Martí), **February 24** (anniversary of the beginning of the 1895 War of Independence), **March 8** (International Women's Day), **April 19** (anniversary of Bay of Pigs victory), **July 30** (Day of the Martyrs of the Revolution), **October 8** (anniversary of the death of Che Guevara), **October 28** (anniversary of the death of Camilo Cienfuegos), and **December 7** (anniversary of the death of Antonio Maceo).

CALENDAR OF EVENTS

Cuba has a packed schedule of festivals, congresses, and carnivals, and it seems like more are being held each year. If no specific contact information for a particular event is offered below, you can contact **Paradiso** (✆ 7/836-4931; www.paradiso.cu/eventos. asp), the tour agency arm of the national arts and cultural organization ARTex. Paradiso organizes theme tours and escorted trips based around most of the major festivals and cultural events occurring throughout the year. You can also find pretty good information at **www.cubatravel.cu** and **www.cult.cu** (the latter is in Spanish only).

For an exhaustive list of events beyond those listed here, check http://events.frommers.com, where you'll find a searchable, up-to-the-minute roster of what's happening in cities all over the world.

FEBRUARY

International Book Fair, Havana. This large gathering of authors, publishers, and distributors is really only of interest to those who can read in Spanish. But if you can, this is an excellent Latin American book fair. For more information, visit www.cubaliteraria.cu. Second week of February.

International Jazz Festival, Havana. This festival, which used to be held in December, is organized by none other than Chucho Valdés. The festival usually draws a handful of top international bands and soloists to share the stage and billing with a strong stable of Cuba's best jazz talents. For more information, visit www.festivaljazzplaza.icm.cu. Mid-February.

Habanos Festival, Havana. Cigar smokers won't want to miss this annual celebration of the Cuban stogie. Run by the official state cigar company, Habanos, S.A., events include lectures, factory visits, tastings, and a gala dinner with an auction of rare cigars. For more information, visit www.habanos.com. Late February.

MARCH

International Festival of "La Trova" Pepe Sánchez, Santiago de Cuba. If you like the sounds of traditional Cuban folk music, you'll want to hit this festival. Buena Vista Social Club member Eliades Ochoa organized a recent festival. Local Santiagueros are the heart of the festival, but singers and groups come from the entire island and throughout Latin America. Mid-March.

Celebration of Classic Cars, Havana. Recognizing the appeal of its huge fleet of classic American cars, Cuba has organized a weeklong celebration of these Detroit dinosaurs. Events include lectures, mechanical workshops, and parades. Owners from other countries are encouraged to bring their wheels to Cuba, and a caravan from Havana to another colonial city is usually orchestrated. Mid-March.

APRIL

International Percussion Festival PERCUBA, Havana. This large meeting of percussionists draws national and international scholars and players working in genres ranging from classical to fusion. Lectures, workshops, concerts, and colloquiums are all part of a dense bill. Call © 7/838-2270 or visit www.cult.cu for more information. Mid-April.

MAY

May Day parades, nationwide. If you're in Cuba on May Day, the traditional socialist celebration of Labor Day, you'll want to join (or at least watch) one of the many parades and public gatherings. The big daddy of them all takes place at the Plaza de la Revolución in Havana, where more than 100,000 people usually gather to listen to the president's annual May Day speech. May 1.

JUNE

International Festival "Boleros de Oro," Havana. You'll be crying in your *mojito* (Cuban highball cocktail) . . . and loving it. Theaters, clubs, and concert halls across Havana will be filled with the sweet and melancholy sounds of bolero. Concerts are also staged in Santiago and other major cities. Late June.

JULY

Fiesta del Fuego, Santiago de Cuba. This event features lectures, concerts, parades, and street fairs celebrating Afro-Caribbean culture. Speakers, guests, and musical groups from around the Caribbean are usually invited. For more information, visit www.casadelcaribe.cult.cu. July 3–9.

International "Old Man and the Sea" Billfish Tournament, Playas del Este, Havana. Marina Tarará is the host to this annual big-game fishing tournament. Call © 7/897-1462 for more information. Mid- to late July.

Carnival, Santiago de Cuba. The most "African" city in Cuba throws an excellent annual carnival. Street parties and concerts are everywhere, and the colonial city is flooded with masked revelers and long conga lines. Second half of July.

August

Carnival, Havana. Although not nearly as colorful or charismatic as Santiago's Carnival, there's still a good dose of public merriment, street parties, open-air music concerts, and the occasional parade. For more information, visit www.sancristobal.cult.cu. August 3–15.

Carnival, Matanzas. If you're looking for a good time, try to get to Matanzas during the third week of August. Although not as massive or elaborate as Carnival celebrations in Havana or Santiago, Matanzas still puts on a good party. The town has strong Afro-Cuban roots, and you'll experience this in body, flesh, food, and song throughout the week. Third week of August.

Beny Moré International Festival of Popular Music, Cienfuegos. Although he was actually born a few kilometers away in the little hamlet of Santa Isabel de las Lajas, Moré is celebrated here with a heavy schedule of concerts throughout most of the latter part of August, and sometimes into September. Late August to early September.

September

Fiesta de la Virgen del Cobre, El Cobre, Santiago de Cuba. Cuba's national saint, the Virgin of Cobre, is revered by Roman Catholics and Santeras alike. There are pilgrimages to her altar in the small town of El Cobre, and celebrations in her honor nationwide. September 8.

International Blue Marlin Tournament, Havana. The Marina Hemingway is the fitting site for this annual big-game fishing tournament. For more information, call © 7/204-6848 or visit www.cubanacan.cu. Late September.

October

Days of Cuban Culture, nationwide. In yet another show of Cuba's omnipresent anticolonial spirit, the period traditionally marking Christopher Columbus's stumbling upon the New World are given over to celebrations of Cuban and Afro-Cuban culture. October 10–20.

International Festival "Matamoros Son," Santiago de Cuba. The silky sounds of Cuban *son* fill the streets and theaters of Santiago. Organized by the reigning champion of the genre, Adalberto Alvarez, this is a great chance to hear a solid week of some wonderful music. Mid-October.

Havana International Ballet Festival, Havana. Alicia Alonso, amazingly, is still going strong as the director of the Cuban National Ballet, still one of the most highly regarded troupes on the planet. Alicia uses this cachet to stage a wonderful annual international festival in the Gran Teatro de La Habana. For more information, call © 7/855-3084 or visit www.balletcuba.cult.cu. Late October.

November

Havana Biennale, Havana. This is one of the premier Latin American art shows, bringing together and exhibiting a wide range of contemporary Latin American artists who work in a broad range of mediums and styles. For more information, visit www. bienalhabana.cult.cu. Occurring in even-numbered years from mid-November to mid-December.

December

International Festival of New Latin American Film, Havana. This is one of the premier film festivals in Latin America. A packed schedule of films is shown in theaters over a period of 10 days throughout Havana, but predominantly in Vedado. For more information, check out www.habanafilmfestival.com. Early December.

Las Parrandas, Remedios. This extravagant public carnival features late-night parades with ornate floats, costumed revelers, and a serious amount of fireworks. The big event occurs on December 24, but between the preparations, practice runs, and smaller imitations in neighboring towns, you'll be able to catch some of the excitement throughout most of late December. Late December.

4 GETTING THERE & GETTING AROUND

GETTING TO CUBA
By Plane

Cuba has 10 international airports. Havana is by far the principal gateway, although there are numerous regularly scheduled and charter flights to Varadero (VRA) and Santiago de Cuba (SCU) as well. To a lesser extent, international charter flights from Canada and Europe service Cayo Largo del Sur (CYO), Cienfuegos (CFG), Santa Clara (SNU), Camagüey (CMW), Ciego de Avila (AVI), Holguín (HOG), and Cayo Coco (CCC).

It's roughly a 70-minute flight from Miami to Havana; 3 hours and 30 minutes from New York to Havana; 4 hours and 30 minutes from Toronto or Montreal to Havana; and 10 hours from London to Havana. Most of the principal Caribbean basin gateway cities—Cancún, George Town (Grand Cayman), Kingston, Nassau, and Santo Domingo—are between 30 and 90 minutes to Havana by air.

Airfares vary widely, depending on the season, demand, and certain ticketing restrictions. But given the high number of charter flights and package tours to Cuba, combined with the stiff competition for vacation travel throughout the Caribbean, airfares are relatively cheap, and bargains abound. It really pays to shop around.

Cubana (© 7/834-4446; www.cubana.cu) is Cuba's national airline and the principal carrier to the island, with regularly scheduled flights to a score of cities throughout the Americas, Europe, and Canada. Other carriers with regularly scheduled or charter service to Cuba include **Air Jamaica, Air Canada, Air Europa, Air Transat, Blue Panorama, Condor Airways, Grupo Taca, Iberia, Martinair, Mexicana, and Virgin Atlantic.** For toll-free phone numbers and websites for these and other airlines, see Appendix A, p. 294.

There is no regularly scheduled service between the United States and Cuba, although there are numerous charter flights from Miami, and to a lesser extent from New York and Los Angeles. Licensed U.S. travelers are eligible to use these flights. For more information, see "Escorted General-Interest Tours" and "Special-Interest Trips," later in this chapter.

Arriving at the Airport

IMMIGRATION & CUSTOMS CLEARANCE Queues can be extremely long when you pass through the Havana airport immigration booths, where you are studied by officials and a camera. Once through, you must have your hand luggage scanned again, collect your bags from one of the two carousels (they're not connected, despite appearances), and clear customs. The last process is now remarkably speedy.

Getting into Town from the Airport

Taxis line up outside the arrivals hall and you will be shepherded to the first in the queue. Despite it being illegal to carry passengers without using the meter, airport taxi drivers will refuse to use them and charge a flat fee of around CUC$20 (US$22/ £11) to Vedado and CUC$25 (US$27/£14) to the airport. The metered fee is around CUC$15 (US$16/£8). However, you have no other options if you have no prebooked pickup. *Note:* All taxis have been brought under the Ministry of Transport umbrella and are known as **Cubataxi** throughout the country; however, the different companies, such as Panataxi and Taxi OK, continue to operate with their own cars and different prices.

By Boat

When arriving by sea, contact the port authorities before entering Cuban waters 19km (12 miles) offshore on VHF channels 16, 19, or 72, or HF channels 2790, 7462, 2420, or 2460. Skippers do not need to give advance notice or have a prior visa. A visa can be granted on arrival. All crew members must have current passports, and U.S. Treasury Department restrictions (see "Entry Requirements" and "Customs," earlier in this chapter) apply to all U.S. citizens. Skippers will also need to register their vessel upon arrival. A special permit, or *permiso especial de navegación,* is issued. This permit costs around CUC$50 (US$54/£27) depending on the length of the vessel.

Cuba has a network of state-run, full-service marinas, many run by Nautica Marlin (www.nauticamarlin.com) and Gaviota (www.gaviota-grupo.com). Marinas that function as official points of entry and exit include those in Jardines del Rey, María la Gorda, Cayo Largo del Sur, Cienfuegos, and Santiago de Cuba, as well as the Marina Hemingway in Havana and Marina Dársena in Varadero. For more information on the specific marinas, see the respective destination chapters in this book.

Good resources for any sailor planning to visit Cuba are Simon Charles's *The Cruising Guide to Cuba* (Cruising Guide Publications, 1997) and Nigel Calder's *Cuba: A Cruising Guide* (Imray, Laurie, Norie & Wilson, 1999). While a little dated, both books are full of invaluable information, tips, and firsthand experiences aimed at cruising sailors.

GETTING AROUND
By Bus

For all intents and purposes, the only buses tourists will ride in Cuba are those run by **Víazul** (© 7/881-1413; www. viazul.com). (*Note:* This website is not updated. Although the timetable and prices are incorrect, they are not hugely off the mark. If you plan a trip using the displayed timetable, your trip won't be completely thrown off kilter.) Víazul buses are modern and comfortable with lavatories on board. Since the tickets must be paid in hard currency, which precludes many Cubans from using them, there is less demand and greater availability. While it is possible for tourists to travel on standard Cuban buses, it is often complex, impractical, and problematic—and you will almost certainly be charged in CUC, at rates just slightly cheaper than Víazul.

Víazul travels to most major tourist destinations in Cuba. The main Víazul station is located in Nuevo Vedado, Havana, across from the metropolitan zoo. However, some of its routes, including the popular Viñales and Pinar del Río route, can be booked and boarded at the main bus terminal near the Plaza de la Revolución. For schedules and prices, see the regional chapters that follow.

You can also book Víazul tickets in the international airport and at Infotur in La Habana Vieja. Many tour agencies across the country are now selling Víazul tickets at no extra cost to the purchaser. This is a great service, especially when many bus stations are a big sprint out of town. This also means travelers do not have to turn up early in order to purchase tickets before the bus departure. Note that in high season in some places, such as Baracoa, tickets are booked up well in advance and travelers are known to have been stuck for a few days; if you have a tight schedule, buy your return ticket for this route in Santiago de Cuba.

By Car

Driving a rental car is an excellent way to travel around Cuba. (The legal age requirement is 18.) It gives you great flexibility and allows you to access beautiful off-the-beaten-track places. Many roads are in acceptable condition, while many are severely substandard. And, while there's very little traffic, you'll have to keep a sharp eye out for horse-drawn carriages, slow-moving tractors, scores of bicyclists, and pedestrians taking over major roadways.

It is completely inadvisable to drive at night. It is very unsafe because there is no lighting on highways. Animal-drawn transport, some lorries, bicycles, and pedestrians are also not illuminated, giving rise to highly dangerous driving situations.

The speed limit for cars is 50kmph (31 mph) in the cities, 90kmph (56 mph) on the *carretera,* and 100kmph (62 mph) on the Autopista.

In all cities, there are *parqueos* where you can leave your vehicle attended for 24 hours. This costs from CUC$1 to CUC$2 (US$1.10–US$2.15/55p–£1.10) a night. It may be unwise to leave the vehicle unattended in cities, as theft of wheels and wipers is not unknown.

There is a handful of state-run car-rental companies, with a large, modern fleet of rental cars to choose from. Prices and selection are rather standard, with an abundance of small, economy Japanese and Korean cars. A rental car should cost you between CUC$45 (US$49/£24) and CUC$80 (US$86/£43) per day, including insurance and unlimited mileage, depending on the model and the season. Low-season prices are, obviously, cheaper. Some agencies start you off with a full tank of gas for which they charge you—in addition to the rental fee—then give no credit for any gas left in the tank upon the return

of the car. Discounts are available for multiday rentals. It's always a good idea to have a reservation in advance, especially during peak periods, when cars can get a little scarce. However, there's a Catch-22 here, in that many of the state-run agencies don't have a trustworthy international reservations system. As is the case with rampant overbooking of hotel rooms, when demand outstrips supply, the car-rental agencies will often not honor your supposedly confirmed reservation.

Cubans may now drive rental cars and can be included on your insurance for an additional cost, as can a second foreign driver. Insurance is voided if an accident is shown to be caused by a driver under the influence of alcohol.

For listings of the major car rental agencies in Cuba, see "Toll-Free Numbers & Websites" in Appendix A, p. 294. All have desks at the airport and at a host of major hotels around Havana and the rest of the country. If you book your car online, the best deals are usually found at the rental-car company websites, although all the major online travel agencies also offer rental-car reservation services.

All car-rental agencies in Cuba, except Transtur, offer insurance coverage for between CUC$10 (US$11/£5.40) and CUC$20 (US$22/£11) per day. Transtur, which runs Cubacar and Rex, charges a minimum CUC$15 (US$16/£8.10) for coverage for rentals that start in Havana. Most agencies carry a deductible of CUC$200 (US$216/£108) to CUC$1,000 (US$1,080/£540). Transtur's deductible is a minimum of CUC$350 (US$378/£189) on rentals that start in Havana. Some do not cover theft, but this is a very minor problem in Cuba. If you hold a private auto insurance policy, you may be covered abroad for loss or damage to the car, and liability in case a passenger is injured. The credit card you use to rent the car also may provide some coverage. However, be sure to check whether or not your insurance company or credit card coverage excludes rental cars in Cuba. Moreover, this type of coverage probably does not cover liability if you caused the accident. Check your own auto insurance policy, the rental company policy, and your credit card coverage for the extent of coverage.

Be very thorough when checking out your car, and make sure that all accouterments (like a spare tire, jack, and radio) are present and accounted for. Moreover, be sure to have the agent note every little nick and scratch, or you run a great risk of being charged for them upon your car's return. You will also be charged for small nicks caused by flying stones on some of Cuba's poorer roads.

Gasoline costs CUC\$.95 (US\$1/50p) especial per liter (*por litro*), or CUC\$.85 (US90¢/45p) regular per liter. Diesel is CUC\$.75 (US80¢/40p) per liter. Gone are the gas shortages of several years ago. Service stations are plentiful and conveniently located on the major highways and on the outskirts of all major centers, as well as in major towns and cities.

Every car-rental agency will provide you with a decent road map. Alternately, you can try to get a copy of the **International Travel Map: Cuba** (ITMB Publishing; www.itmb.com) before arriving. However, the best road map is the Guia de Carreteras (p. 86).

While driving is generally easy and stress-free, there are a couple of concerns for most foreign drivers here. First (and most annoying) is the fact that there are **very, very few road signs** and directional aids. The Ministry of Tourism is aware that this is a major problem, and I have been expecting it to be addressed for the past 5 years or so. As of yet, very little progress has been made. Secondly, there's the issue of **hitchhikers.** Cuba's public transportation network is grossly overburdened and hitchhiking is a way of life. The highways sometimes seem like one long line, with periodic swellings, of people asking for a lift, or *botella*. While cases of

kidnappings and muggings of drivers who give lifts are rare, you should still be careful about whom you pick up. It is not advisable to pick up hitchhikers after dark. However, the biggest hassle of offering rides is twofold: When you stop, you are likely to be swarmed by supplicants, who will want to stuff your car to the brink of its carrying capacity; and most hitchhikers are looking for relatively short hops, so once you pick up a load, you might find yourself suddenly making constant stops to let your passengers off—at which point there will almost certainly be a new rider immediately vying to snag the just-emptied seat. (You can, however, stop at an official *botella* point, identified by the mustard-yellow uniformed official with a clipboard.) However, that said, you will be providing the public-transport-starved Cubans with a much-needed ride.

One final note: **Stop at all railroad crossings!** It's the law, and it's also an important safety measure. Cuba's railroad network crisscrosses its highway system at numerous points. Trains rarely slow down and even rarer still are protective crossbars or warning lights. Police often hang out at railroad crossings, both to warn drivers when a train is coming and to dole out tickets to those who don't come to a stop.

By Plane

Cubana (© 7/834-4446; www.cubana. cu) is the principal national and international carrier for Cuba. The other principal commuter and charter carrier is **AeroCaribbean** (© 7/879-7524). There's a full schedule of commuter flights connecting Havana and Varadero with the destination cities of Baracoa, Bayamo, Camagüey, Ciego de Avila, Manzanillo, Nueva Gerona (Isla de la Juventud), Guantánamo, Holguín, Santiago de Cuba, Las Tunas, Cayo Largo, and Cayo Coco. Fares average from CUC\$84 (US\$91/£45) to CUC\$131 (US\$141/£71) one-way. The exception is Isla de la Juventud, which costs just CUC\$43 (US\$46/£23) each way from Havana. If you know you'll need an internal flight, try to have your travel agent or tour operator book it in advance. If not, you can easily book flights from the tour desks at almost any hotel in Cuba.

By Train

The state-run train agency, **Ferrocuba** (© 7/861-8540 or 7/862-8081, ext. 252), has offices in each train station. Havana is connected to Pinar del Río in the west, and Santiago de Cuba in the east by regular rail traffic. There are usually one or two trains a day heading west, and a half dozen or so heading east. Intermediate cities with regular service include Matanzas, Santa Clara, Ciego de Avila, Camagüey, Las Tunas, and Holguín. The principal train station, or **Estación Central,** is located in Havana at Calle Egido and Calle Arsenal, Habana Vieja (© **7/861-4259**).

Unlike the state-run bus service, there are usually seats available on most trains. However, most trains are in rather bad shape, with uncomfortable seats and limited amenities. Be sure to bring along some food and something to drink. Even if there's a cafeteria car onboard, which isn't always the case, you might not find any of the offerings particularly appealing, and they might just run out of food somewhere along the line. Moreover, train travel in Cuba is notoriously erratic, with frequent schedule changes and delays. It is always best to check current schedules and conditions before buying a ticket and undertaking a train journey.

The most attractive rail option for travelers is the 12-hour express train to Santiago de Cuba, leaving Havana each evening at 6:05pm; the fare is CUC$50 (US$54/£27) to CUC$62 (US$67/£33). This train only makes stops in Santa Clara and Camagüey, and is the most modern and comfortable train in the whole national system. For more information on traveling by train, see the regional chapters that follow.

5 MONEY & COSTS

Cuba is not a particularly cheap island to travel around for tourists and is not cheap at all compared to its neighboring Central American countries. You can reduce costs by traveling on the Víazul bus system and staying in *casas particulares* (private homes with rooms for rent), but note that single travelers rarely get a discount on a double room in a private house. You can easily pay out CUC$25 (US$27/£14) in a 2-week trip just on tipping the ubiquitous music bands that play in restaurants.

Cuba's state banking system is trying to keep up with the rise in international tourism and joint business ventures. Both the **Banco de Crédito y Comercio** and **Banco Financiero Internacional** have opened up branches in most major business and tourist areas; most are open Monday through Friday from 8am to 4pm and a handful are open on Saturday mornings. These banks are the place to go for cash withdrawals off of your non-U.S.-issued credit cards. They'll also work for cashing traveler's checks or changing currency, but your best bet for money-exchange transactions is the national chain of *casas de cambio* (money-exchange houses), **CADECA, S.A.** You'll find CADECA branches in most major cities and tourist destinations, as well as at all the international airports. Don't be scared off by the long lines in front of most CADECA offices. These are invariably Cubans looking to buy Cuban Convertible Pesos, or CUC *(chavitos).* Foreigners wanting to sell dollars *(dólares)* and sterling *(Libra Esterlina)* for Cuban Convertible Pesos can almost always jump to the head of the line and walk right in. This is also the place to change your CUCs into national pesos *(moneda nacional)* for the odd purchase of *maní* (peanuts

What Things Cost in Cuba

	CUC$	US$	UK£
Casa particular (per night)	25.00	27.00	14.00
Beer	1.25	1.35	0.67
Mojito	3.00–5.00	3.25–5.40	1.60–2.70
Taxi ride from Havana airport to downtown	20.00–25.00	22.00–27.00	11.00–14.00
Tip for ubiquitous music band	1.00	1.10	0.55
Coffee	0.25–1	0.25–1.10	0.14–0.54
Internet card	6.00	6.50	3.25
Moderate-to-good, three-course meal without alcohol	10.00–15.00	11.00–16.00	5.40–8.00
Moderately priced hotel room in a provincial city	50.00–100.00	54.00–108.00	27.00–54.00
Moderately priced, all-inclusive hotel room in a beach resort	100.00–150.00	108.00–162.00	54.00–81.00
Museum admission	1.00–5.00	1.10–5.40	0.55–1.70

in a paper cone), Granma, or a peso pizza and peso beer.

CURRENCY

Although Castro has replaced the U.S. dollar with the Cuban convertible peso, or CUC, Cuba has always operated under a de facto dollarized economy. The CUC is an internationally unsupported currency, and it is, for all intents and purposes, pegged to the U.S. dollar. All of the CADECA branches and major banks will change U.S. dollars, euros, British pounds, and Canadian dollars.

There are, in fact, two distinct kinds of currency circulating in Cuba: the *moneda libremente convertible* ("convertible peso" or CUC), and the *moneda nacional* (Cuban peso or MN). Both are distinguished by the dollar $ symbol, leading to some confusion occasionally. Both the CUC and *moneda nacional* are divided up into units of 100 centavos. To complicate matters, the euro is

also legal tender in many of the hotels, restaurants, and shops in several of the larger, isolated beach resort destinations.

The convertible peso functions on a near one-to-one parity with the dollar—at press time, the official exchange rate was US$1=CUC$.93 and £1=CUC$1.85. However, U.S. dollars are penalized by a 10% surcharge on all money exchange operations into convertible pesos. For this reason, it is best to carry any hard currency you plan on spending in Cuba as euros, British pounds, or Canadian dollars. All of these are freely exchanged at all CADECA branches and most banks around Cuba. Be sure to bring relatively fresh and new bills. Cuban banks will sometimes refuse to accept bills with even slight tears or markings. Also, it is wise to bring a calculator with you and carefully monitor the exchange process, as tellers have been known to deliberately shortchange unsuspecting and overly trusting tourists.

Convertible pesos come in 1, 3, 5, 10, 20, 50, and 100 peso bills. Convertible peso coins come in denominations of 5, 10, 25, and 50 centavos, and 1 peso. Although the government has long abandoned its official posture of a one-to-one parity between the Cuban peso (MN) and the U.S. dollar, the habit of converting *moneda nacional* prices directly into dollars is still common in many situations. Currently, Cuban pesos can be exchanged legally for U.S. dollars or CUC (and vice versa) at any CADECA money exchange office, most banks, and many hotels. The official exchange rate as of press time was around 24 Cuban pesos to the CUC. While opportunities for travelers to pay in Cuban pesos are few and far between, it is not a bad idea to exchange around CUC$1 to CUC$2 (US$1.10–US$2.15/55p–£1.10) for pesos soon after arrival. It may be possible to pay for some meals, movie tickets, and other goods or services in Cuban pesos, and the savings are substantial. If "MN" is displayed on the prices, you should theoretically be paying Cuban pesos. However, in most cases, vendors will try to insist that any non-Cuban pay in convertible pesos, often at a one-to-one rate of exchange. For up-to-date currency conversions, consult www.oanda.com.

You can exchange any remaining convertible pesos for U.S. dollars, sterling, or euros at the airport before leaving. Do so, as the convertible pesos will be useless outside of Cuba.

Note: Cubans still often use the terms *peso* and *dollar* interchangeably. If you are quoted a price in pesos, it may not be the bargain you think it to be. To be clear, "*moneda nacional*" or "MN" always refers to Cuban pesos. Other terms for a CUC include *divisa, chavito, verde, guano,* and *fula.* Cash is known as *efectivo.*

CREDIT CARDS

MasterCard and **Visa** are widely accepted at hotels, car-rental agencies, and official restaurants and shops, with the caveat that they cannot be issued by a United States bank or financial institution. **Diners Club** is also accepted, although to a much lesser extent. **American Express** cards are not accepted anywhere on the island. It is always best to check with your home bank before traveling to see if your card will work in Cuba. If you have ignored all advice, contact **Asistur** (p. 289), which can advise you on a company in Santo Domingo that can arrange a transaction between your U.S. bank and Asistur.

You are also fabulously ripped off when taking money out on your debit or credit card in Cuba. No matter what the country of origin of your card, your transaction will first be converted into dollars, thereby incurring a charge of up to a staggering 12.5%, before you are given the CUC. On a CUC$800 (US$864/£432) withdrawal, you'll pay a whopping CUC$100 (US$108/£54) fee. This also happens at ATMs where your request for CUC is converted to U.S. dollars at that day's exchange rate. You are then charged 3% of the transaction in dollars at the point of withdrawal. Thus, a CUC$100 withdrawal in 2008 resulted in a conversion to US$108 plus a commission of US$3.25 with a total debit of US$111.25.

Most *paladares* (private-home restaurants), *casas particulares* (private-home accommodations), and small businesses do not accept credit cards. In the more remote destinations, you should count on using cash for all transactions. Moreover, shaky phone connections and other logistical problems often get in the way of credit card usage. I actually saw some British travelers unable to use a card at a major hotel because the hotel was out of receipt tape, and the staff weren't sure when they would get more. Do not count on paying a hotel bill with a credit card unless it is a very expensive hotel and/or linked to an international chain such as Sol Melia.

If your credit card is lost or stolen while you're in Cuba, you can contact **Fincimex-Western Union in the Focsa building,**

Tips **Small Change**

When you change money, ask for some small bills or loose change. Petty cash will come in handy for tipping and public transportation. Consider keeping the change separate from your larger bills, so that it's readily accessible.

corner of Calle 17 and Calle N, Vedado, Havana (© **7/833-0128/9**). However, you're best off having written down in advance your issuing bank's telephone number and calling the bank directly. Banks will usually accept collect calls from anywhere in the world. You can also contact Asistur (p. 289).

ATMS

Cuba has a modestly expanding network of ATMs (automated teller machines) associated with a string of new banks, like the **Banco de Crédito y Comercio** and **Banco Financiero Internacional.** No credit or debit cards issued by U.S.-based companies will work at any of these machines. However, travelers from other countries can easily extract convertible pesos from ATMs at the international airport and most major tourist destinations. As with credit cards, it is always best to check with your home bank before traveling to see if your ATM card will work in Cuba.

Note: Remember that many banks impose a fee every time you use a card at another bank's ATM, and that fee can be higher for international transactions (up to $5 or more) than for domestic ones

(where they're rarely more than $2 in the U.S.).

You can use your credit card to receive cash advances at ATMs. Keep in mind that credit card companies protect themselves from theft by limiting maximum withdrawals outside their home country, so call your credit card company before you leave home. And keep in mind that you'll pay interest from the moment of your withdrawal, even if you pay your monthly bills on time.

TRAVELER'S CHECKS

In Cuba, traveler's checks are accepted at most major hotels, government-run or chain restaurants, and major attractions, but far less readily than credit cards. The same prohibition against U.S. bank-issued tender applies to traveler's checks. If you are a die-hard fan of traveler's checks, **Thomas Cook** (visit www.thomascook. com to find your nearest branch) and **Visa** (© **0800/89-5078** in the U.K.) traveler's checks issued outside of the United States are still your best bet. Most banks, CADECA offices, hotels, and businesses charge commissions of around 3.5% and 4% on weekends for cashing traveler's checks.

6 HEALTH

STAYING HEALTHY

Despite ongoing economic troubles and shortages, Cuba's healthcare system remains one of the best in Latin America. The country takes extremely proactive steps toward preventive public health, and

common tropical diseases like cholera, malaria, and dengue fever are either uncommon or have been totally eradicated. You don't need any vaccinations to travel to Cuba, unless you are coming from a region with cholera or yellow fever, in which case the Cuban authorities will require proof of immunization.

Staying healthy on a trip to Cuba is predominantly a matter of common sense: **Know your physical limits** and don't overexert yourself in the ocean, on hikes, or in athletic activities. Cuba is a tropical country, so limit your **exposure to the sun,** especially during the first few days of your trip and, thereafter, from 11am to 3pm. (It is often much hotter in Cuba btw. 2–3pm than at midday.) Use a sunscreen with a high protection factor and apply it liberally. Remember that children need more protection than adults do.

There are no poisonous snakes in Cuba, which will put many minds at ease. In terms of **biting bugs,** your standard array of bees, wasps, mosquitoes, and sand fleas are present. Sand fleas are a slight nuisance at most beaches if there's no offshore breeze to clear them, particularly around sunrise and sunset. While there are also ticks and chiggers, so far Lyme disease is not considered a problem. Bring repellent and wear light, long-sleeved clothing.

Overall, while **water** is potable throughout most of Cuba, I recommend you stick primarily to bottled water, just to err on the side of safety. Every hotel and restaurant catering to travelers will carry bottled water. Ask for *agua mineral natural* (still) or *agua mineral con gas* (sparkling water).

Contact the **International Association for Medical Assistance to Travelers (IAMAT)** (② 716/754-4883 or 416/652-0137 in Canada; www.iamat.org) for tips on travel and health concerns and for lists of local, English-speaking doctors. The United States **Centers for Disease Control and Prevention** (② 800/311-3435; www.cdc.gov) provides up-to-date information on health hazards by region or country and offers tips on food safety. The website **www.tripprep.com**, sponsored by a consortium of travel medicine practitioners, also offers helpful advice on traveling abroad. You can find listings of reliable clinics overseas at the **International Society of Travel Medicine** website, www.istm.org.

General Availability of Health Care

Due to the U.S. embargo and other problems, common medicines are restricted or routinely unavailable in Cuba. It is wise to bring a full medical pack containing basic medicines. Travelers may also want to consider carrying ciprofloxacin if they are susceptible to stomach bugs that need treating with an antibiotic. Having said that, there are international health clinics in Cuba for emergencies, but it would still be better to bring what you can with you. All prescription medicines should be brought with you as well.

COMMON AILMENTS AND DANGERS

Visitors to Cuba should keep in mind its tropical setting and the common ailments and dangers that result.

TROPICAL ILLNESSES Cuba does experience dengue outbreaks from time to time and you would be wise to keep your ear to the ground about this.

EXTREME WEATHER Hurricanes can occur between June and November in Cuba, but they do not arrive every year. The National Hurricane Center's website (www.nhc.noaa.gov) offers details on any storms in the Caribbean basin. It also has a hurricane preparedness section. In the event of a hurricane, Cuba has a very well-organized preparedness program. In the event of extreme danger, thousands can be evacuated, minimizing or avoiding deaths completely. Listen to all authorities in the event of an emergency.

During the rainy season, tropical storms with plenty of lightning are common. According to the Cuban Meteorological Institute, around 65 Cubans die each year from lightning strikes. During a storm, stay inside or in your vehicle. Move out of the sea and away from the beach and move away from high ground.

The tropical sun in Cuba is extremely fierce. The highest sun protection factor, hats, and protective clothing should be worn. Stay out of the sun between 11am and 3pm and drink plenty of water to avoid dehydration.

WHAT TO DO IF YOU GET SICK AWAY FROM HOME

Cuba has an excellent nationwide system of hospitals and clinics, as well as international clinics, and you should have no trouble finding prompt and competent medical care in the case of an emergency. See the "Orientation" section of the individual destination chapters, or "Fast Facts" in Appendix A for specific recommendations. The system is entirely free for Cubans, but foreigners are charged for services. This is actually a significant means of income for the country; however, fees for private medical care are relatively inexpensive by most Western standards.

The country has a network of pharmacies, though due to the U.S. embargo, certain medicines are restricted or often unavailable. That said, it is always a good idea to carry a sufficient supply of any necessary prescription medicines you may need (packed in their original containers in your carry-on luggage), and a small first-aid kit with basic analgesic, antihistamine, and anti-diarrhea medications. You might also bring a copy of your prescriptions, with the generic name of the medication in case the pharmacist doesn't recognize the brand name. Don't forget an extra pair of contact lenses or prescription glasses.

If you suffer from a chronic illness, consult your doctor before your departure.

For conditions like epilepsy, diabetes, or heart problems, wear a **MedicAlert identification tag** ((℃ **888/633-4298**; www.medicalert.org), which will immediately alert doctors to your condition and give them access to your records through MedicAlert's 24-hour hotline.

A full list of international clinics, international drugstores, and opticians is available on the Servimed website (**www.servimed cuba.com//en/directory.php**). The Clincia Central Cira Garcia, Calle 20 no. 4101, on the corner of Avenida 41, Playa, Havana ((℃ **7/204-2811**; www.cirag.cu) is the largest center in the country catering to foreigners. It is also possible to have medical treatments, cosmetic surgery, and undergo drug-addiction programs in Cuba for a fraction of the cost elsewhere. All the details are listed under the Servimed website. Servimed is part of the agency Cubanacán.

Asistur, Prado 208 between Calles Trocadero and Colón ((℃ **7/866-4499**; 7/866-8521 emergency number; www.asistur.cu) will help you with medical reports and the management of medical expenses if you end up in the hospital. Its addresses outside Havana are available on www.asistur.cu/mapa.html.

Called *farmacias* in Spanish, drugstores are relatively common throughout the country, although not necessarily well stocked. Those at hospitals and major clinics are often open 24 hours. Many hotels, particularly the larger ones, have either a small pharmacy or a basic medical clinic on-site. There's a 24-hour pharmacy at the international terminal of the José Martí International Airport ((℃ 7/266-4105) in Havana.

We list **additional emergency numbers** in "Fast Facts" Appendix A, p. 289.

Cuba is an extremely safe country. Street crime is relatively rare. With the recent upsurge in tourism, there have been some reports of pickpocketing and muggings in Old Havana and Centro Havana, but these are by far the exceptions to the rule. There's a strong security and police presence in most popular tourist destinations, and even outside the well-worn tourist routes, theft and assaults are quite uncommon.

That said, you should still be careful and use common sense. Given the nature of Cuba's socialist system, a huge disparity in wealth exists between the average Cuban and any foreign visitor, even budget travelers. Don't flash ostentatious signs of wealth, and avoid getting too far off the beaten path, especially at night. Don't leave valuables unattended, and always use the safe in your hotel room or at the front desk.

Should you find yourself robbed, you will need a police report for insurance purposes. If you don't speak Spanish, go accompanied by a Spanish speaker; otherwise, you will make little headway.

The U.S. State Department (**http://travel.state.gov**) and the U.K. Foreign and Commonwealth Office (**www.fco.gov.uk**) issue updated advice for travelers.

Meddling in drugs and firearms brings stiff penalties. There are also prohibitions relating to blood products, obscene or pornographic literature, or any anti-state literature. Getting on the wrong side of the law is not advisable in any way.

Also, see "Women Travelers," below, and "Etiquette & Customs" in Fast Facts, Appendix A, p. 289.

8 SPECIALIZED TRAVEL RESOURCES

TRAVELERS WITH DISABILITIES

Most disabilities shouldn't stop anyone from traveling. There are more options and resources out there than ever before, and Cuba has been very forward thinking in the recognition of the rights of people with disabilities. Still, overall, Cuba is not an easy country for them. While a few hotels are equipped for travelers with disabilities, these are far from the norm. Moreover, there's almost no private or public transportation service geared toward such travelers. The streets of Havana are rugged and crowded, and sidewalks, in particular, are often either totally absent or badly torn up. The Cuban people, however, are quite conscientious and embracing in their treatment of people with disabilities.

Asociación Cubana de Limitados Físicos-Motores (The Cuban Disabled Association), Calle 6 no. 106, between Avenidas 1 and 3, Miramar, Havana (© 7/209-3049; aclifim@infomed.sld.cu), is a Cuban organization charged with ensuring accessibility and lobbying for rights. The association is a member of the Disabled Peoples' International (DPI), and probably the best contact for travelers with disabilities in Cuba.

The Society for Accessible Travel & Hospitality (© 212/447-7284; www.sath.org) offers a wealth of travel resources for those with all types of disabilities and informed recommendations on destinations, access guides, travel agents, tour operators, vehicle rentals, and companion services. Annual membership costs $49 for adults, $29 for seniors and students.

For more on organizations that offer resources to disabled travelers, go to www.frommers.com/planning.

GAY & LESBIAN TRAVELERS Homosexuality is not illegal in Cuba, but in general, Cuba has a poor record on gay and lesbian rights, and while the situation has improved somewhat, there are still high levels of homophobia and broad societal rejection of gays and lesbians. For decades following the Revolution, gays and lesbians were closeted and persecuted. (Read Reinaldo Arenas' horrifying account in *Before Night Falls*.) The harsh measures they faced included forced labor and prison. The blockbuster movie *Fresa y Chocolate* (Strawberry and Chocolate) certainly brought the issue to the forefront, yet little has changed in the prevailing views of this macho society. There are no openly accepted gay or lesbian establishments in Cuba, and none of the established gay and lesbian tour operators run trips to the island.

Santa Clara is perhaps the most openly gay city in Cuba and there is an annual gay and transvestite carnival in the middle of May. In June 2008, Cuba authorized sex-change operations. Raúl Castro's daughter, Mariela Castro, heads the National Center for Sex Education and champions homosexual, bisexual, and transgender rights. In mid-May 2008, the state-television network transmitted *Brokeback Mountain* on TV, the first time a gay film has been broadcast in Cuba. Cuba also held an anti-homophobia day for the second time in May 2008, promoted by Mariela Castro. The legalization of same-sex marriage has also been talked about.

While travelers are generally not hassled in Cuba and given some leeway in terms of social mores, same-sex signs of physical affection are rare and frowned upon across the country. Gay and lesbian couples and singles should take the prevailing social climate into account when traveling in Cuba.

The documentary film, *Gay Cuba,* by Sonja de Vries (Frameline Films; www.frameline.org), is an honest look at the treatment of gays and lesbians in modern Cuba.

The International Gay and Lesbian Travel Association (IGLTA) (© 954/630-1637; www.iglta.org) is the trade association for the gay and lesbian travel industry, and offers an online directory of gay- and lesbian-friendly travel businesses; go to its website and click on "Members."

For more gay and lesbian travel resources visit www.frommers.com/planning.

SENIOR TRAVELERS

Cuba is a comfortable destination for senior travelers. Seniors are treated with deference and respect in Cuba. Moreover, it's a particularly safe country, with low levels of street crime, and the food and water are generally safe as well.

Mention the fact that you're a senior when you make your travel reservations—some of the hotel chains and package tour operators still offer discounts for seniors. However, don't expect to find specific senior discounts once you arrive in Cuba, where you will be lumped into the category of rich foreigner and gouged as much as possible, like all the rest.

ElderTreks (© 800/741-7956 in North America and 0808-234-1717 in the U.K.; www.eldertreks.com) is a Canadian-based company that arranges small-group (up to 16 people) adventure trips for those 50 and older to Cuba.

In the U.K., trips to Cuba are offered by **Saga,** The Saga Building, Enbrook Park, Folkestone, Kent, CT20 3SE (© 0800/096-0078; www.saga.co.uk).

For more information and resources on travel for seniors, see www.frommers.com/planning.

TRAVELING WITH FAMILY

Cuba is an excellent destination for families, particularly if you want an all-inclusive beach vacation with a broad range of

Race Relations in Cuba

The Cuban population is—very conservatively—estimated to be about one-third black or mixed-race (in reality, the percentage is probably closer to two-thirds or more). Cuba officially declares itself to be colorblind and, at least on the surface, the obvious mixed-race heritage and the strong presence of Afro-Cuban culture seem to support that notion. Though as a society, Cuba is much less racist and male dominated than it was before the Revolution, racism still exists, even if much of it is under the radar. Economic racism is widespread; relatively few black Cubans occupy positions of authority in the government, state enterprise, or tourism. Racist comments are as regrettably common as they are in other countries. Many Cubans assume blacks to be the majority of *jineteros* (male hustlers) and *jineteras* (female escorts), even though the reality is that hustling in Cuba is universal. Most Cubans also believe that the police harass blacks to a disproportionate degree, and travelers of African and Hispanic descent may experience the same. Spanish-speaking travelers accompanying Anglo-looking tourists are sometimes followed and questioned by police who ignorantly assume them to be Cuban hustlers working a beat. In fact, one other disturbing aspect of this situation is that black tourists are sometimes mistaken for Cuban *jineteros* and may be given a hard time by security personnel upon entering hotels, although now that it is legal for Cubans to enter and stay in hotels with foreigners, this should no longer happen.

—Neil E. Schlecht

tours, activities, and entertainment options. Toward this end, Varadero would probably be your top choice, with a wealth of watersports activities and land-based adventures, including nearby caves to explore. The beach destinations of Cayo Coco, Cayo Guillermo, and Guardalavaca are also worth considering. If you do go the all-inclusive route, be sure the resort you choose has a well-run children's program, with a full plate of activities.

If your children are old enough, they should enjoy the colonial wonders of Habana Vieja (Old Havana), including its forts and castles. Hotels and attractions throughout Cuba often give discounts for children under 12 years old.

However, hotels with regular, dependable babysitting service are few and far between. If you'll need babysitting service, make sure your hotel provides it before you leave home. To locate those accommodations, restaurants, and attractions that are particularly kid-friendly, refer to the "Kids" icon throughout this guide.

For a list of more family-friendly travel resources, visit www.frommers.com/planning.

WOMEN TRAVELERS

Women should be careful when walking alone at night, both in Havana and in other more remote destinations. Cuba is a somewhat typical "macho" Latin American nation, with an open and extroverted sense of sexuality. Single women can expect their fair share of catcalls, whistles, and propositions known as *piropo*, especially in Havana. The best advice is to ignore the unwanted attention, rather than try to come up with a witty or antagonistic rejoinder. Cuban men are pretty persistent, but they should soon get the message if you ignore them. If they don't, say *"Déjeme en paz"* (Leave me in peace). If it gets out of control, a swear word will usually work.

Women travelers should check out the award-winning website **Journeywoman** (www.journeywoman.com), a "real life" women's travel-information network where you can sign up for a free e-mail newsletter and get advice on everything from etiquette and dress to safety; or the travel guide *Safety and Security for Women Who Travel* by Sheila Swan and Peter Laufer (Travelers' Tales, 2nd ed., 2004), which gives common-sense tips on safe travel.

Also, see the sections on "Safety," above, and "Single Travelers," below.

For general travel resources for women, go to www.frommers.com/planning.

STUDENT TRAVELERS

Check out the **International Student Travel Confederation (ISTC;** www.istc. org) website for comprehensive travel services information and details on how to get an **International Student Identity Card (ISIC),** which qualifies students for substantial savings on rail passes, plane tickets, entrance fees, and more. It also provides students with basic health and life insurance and a 24-hour helpline. The card is valid for a maximum of 18 months. You can apply for the card online or in person at **STA Travel** (© **800/781-4040** in North America, 132-782 in Australia, or 087/1-2-300-040 in the U.K.; www. statravel.com), the biggest student travel agency in the world; check out the website to locate STA Travel offices worldwide. If you're no longer a student, but are still under 26, you can get an **International Youth Travel Card (IYTC)** from the same people, which entitles you to some discounts. **Travel CUTS** (© **800/592-2887;** www.travelcuts.com) offers similar services

for both Canadians and U.S. residents. Irish students may prefer to turn to **USIT** (© **01/602-1906;** www.usit.ie), an Ireland-based specialist in student, youth, and independent travel.

SINGLE TRAVELERS

Cuba is generally extremely safe for travelers. Single travelers face no real specific threats or dangers. That said, don't throw common sense out the window. Single travelers—and women in particular—should still be careful when walking alone at night, both in Havana and in other more remote destinations.

I have never felt unsafe traveling on my own and there are few other countries in the world, like Cuba, where I would consider taking an illegal taxi with a strange man for hundreds of kilometers down back roads. Remember also that there are severe repercussions for Cubans who commit crimes against tourists.

Perhaps the biggest issue facing single travelers is that of *jineterismo,* which is a way of life in Cuba. In its most disturbing form, it has become synonymous with prostitution. Sex tourism and prostitution flourish in Cuba, and single travelers of both genders and any sexual persuasion will encounter constant offers for companionship, and usually more. In some cases, the terms are quite clear and a cash value is set. In others, the *jinetera* or *jinetero* is just looking for some restaurant meals, store-bought clothing, food, daily necessities, and sometimes even a good time. Many are looking to cement relationships with foreign tourists that could lead to marriage and a means of improving their standard of living on a long-term basis, either on the island or abroad.

For more information on traveling single, go to www.frommers.com/planning.

VEGETARIAN TRAVELERS

Cuba is not a society geared up for vegetarianism. Vegetables are not plentiful, although fruits are widely available. Eggs

Frommers.com: The Complete Travel Resource

Planning a trip or just returned from one? Head to **Frommers.com,** voted Best Travel Site by *PC Magazine*. We think you'll find our site indispensable before, during, and after your travels—with expert advice and tips; independent reviews of hotels, restaurants, attractions, and preferred shopping and nightlife venues; vacation giveaways; and an online booking tool. We publish the complete contents of over 135 travel guides in our **Destinations** section, covering over 4,000 places worldwide. Each weekday, we publish original articles that report on **Deals and News** via our free **Frommers.com Newsletters.** What's more, **Arthur Frommer** himself blogs 5 days a week, with cutting opinions about the state of travel in the modern world. We're betting you'll find our **Events** listings an invaluable resource; it's an up-to-the-minute roster of what's happening in cities everywhere—including concerts, festivals, lectures, and more. We've also added weekly **podcasts, interactive maps,** and hundreds of new images across the site. Finally, don't forget to visit our **Message Boards,** where you can join in conversations with thousands of fellow Frommer's travelers and post your trip report once you return.

are widely available and peanuts *(mani)* are sold on the street. Fish can be found in abundance. Travelers should locate the small vegetable markets *(agromercados)* where private trading of products is allowed. Rice and beans *(moros y cristianos)* are plentiful. Dairy products are not always available. Cartons of fruit juices and biscuits and tins of olives are always available in town supermarkets. In short, a vegetarian won't starve, but this is no place to come for any innovative cuisine.

For more vegetarian-friendly travel resources, go to www.frommers.com/planning.

9 ESCORTED GENERAL-INTEREST TOURS

There are more than 100 licensed travel service providers in the United States; almost all offer charter flights and packages. Some of these operators arrange well-organized escorted general-interest tours. A couple of the best and most reputable are:

- **ABC Charters** ★ (© **305/263-6829;** www.abc-charters.com) is an excellent travel service provider and charter company based in Miami.
- **Tico Travel** ★ (© **800/493-8426** in the U.S. or Canada, or 954/493-8426;

www.destinationcuba.com) is a dependable company with operations throughout much of Latin America.

From Canada
In addition to the agencies listed below, Canadian travelers and others using Canada as a gateway can check directly with **Air Transat Holidays** (© **866/322-6649** in the U.S. and Canada; www.airtransat holidays.com), the tour agency arm of one of the principal charter flight companies to Cuba.

- **Sol Meliá Cuba** (www.solmeliacuba.ca) is the Canadian-based tour agency arm of the Sol Meliá company.
- **Signature Travel** ★ (© 866/324-2883; www.signaturevacations.com) is the largest tour and package operator in Canada, with offices in Burnaby, Mississauga, Montreal, and Winnipeg.

From the U.K.

- **Cuba Welcome** ★ (© 020/7731-6871; www.cubawelcome.com) is a good U.K.-based operator with a knowledgeable and dependable operation on the ground in Cuba.
- **Regent Holidays** ★ (© 0845/277-33661; www.regent-cuba.com) is the specialized Cuba unit of this U.K. tour operator.
- **Journey Latin America** (© 020/8747-3108; www.journeylatinamerica.co.uk) is a large U.K.-based operator for trips throughout the hemisphere, with often very good deals on airfare.
- **Cuba Direct** (© 0844/415-5510; www.cubadirect.co.uk) is a good Cuban-owned operator running a variety of tours.
- **Thomas Cook** ★ (© 0870/750-5711; www.thomascook.com) is a major U.K.-based operator for trips around the world, with excellent operations in Cuba.

From Australia & New Zealand

- **Caribbean Bound** (© 02/9267-2555; www.caribbean.com.au) is a specialist in travel throughout the Caribbean.
- **Caribbean Destinations** (© 03/9571-3744; www.caribbeanislands.com.au) is another Australian-based specialist in travel throughout the Caribbean.

Cuba-Based Agencies

- **Cubalinda** (© 7/836-4062; www.cubalinda.com) is an excellent agency that provides hands-on service and is especially adept at helping nonlicensed U.S. travelers understand and work with the various options open to them.
- **Cuba Welcome** ★ (© 020/7731-6871 in the U.K.; or Office 608, Bacardi Building, Calle Monserrate, La Habana Vieja, © 7/863-3885 in Cuba; www.cubawelcome.com) is a U.K.-based operator that has an excellent operation on the ground in Cuba.

For more information on escorted general-interest tours, including questions to ask before booking your trip, see www.frommers.com/planning.

---

10 SPECIAL-INTEREST TRIPS

There are plenty of options for a special-interest or theme vacation to Cuba. Popular themes include cigars, Ernest Hemingway, classic cars, bird-watching, diving, fishing, and Latin dance. In addition to the agencies and operators listed below, most of the package- and escorted-tour operators listed above offer a selection of themed specialty tours.

- **GAP Adventures** ★ (© 800/708-7761 in the U.S. and Canada, or 0870/999-0144 in the U.K.; www.gapadventures.com) is a major international adventure

and educational tour operator with a full plate of theme tours to Cuba.
- **Global Exchange** ★ (© 800/497-1994, ext 242; www.globalexchange.org) is a nonprofit organization working to increase international understanding by conducting small-scale tours that emphasize educational or social aid themes.
- **Paradiso** ★ (© 7/836-4931; www.paradiso.cu) is the tour agency arm of the Cuban arts and cultural organization ARTex. Paradiso organizes theme

tours and escorted trips, including tours based around most of the major festivals and cultural events, as well as participatory learning trips with instruction in a variety of arts.

Active tourism is still in its infancy in Cuba, but opportunities have opened up in the last few years. The island offers myriad opportunities to add a bit of adrenaline and adventure to your vacation. Watersports are the main draw here, and Cuba abounds with outstanding opportunities to fish, sail, snorkel, and scuba dive. For those looking for some dry-land adventure activities, there are great options for biking and rock climbing, and you might even be able to get on a diamond to play some baseball.

BASEBALL Baseball is the national sport and, after dancing and sex, Cuba's greatest national passion. Cuba's amateur players are considered some of the best in the world, and the premier players are aggressively scouted and courted by Major League Baseball. The regular season runs November through March, and playoffs and the final championship usually carry the season on into May. Most major towns and cities have a local team. Some of the consistently better teams include Pinar del Río, Sancti Spíritus, Santiago de Cuba, Santa Clara, and of course Havana's Industriales. It's usually easy to buy tickets at the box office for less than 5 Cuban pesos, or ask at your hotel and perhaps they can get you tickets in advance.

If you want to actually get out and play, you should be able to find a pickup game to join. Although they have temporarily suspended their organized trips, check out the website of **Baseball Adventures** (© 707/937-4478; www.baseballadventures. com), which used to offer fully hosted trips geared toward serious players looking to play and train with local Cuban pros.

Tip: If you're planning on playing, bring some extra equipment—balls, bats,

and gloves—to leave behind. It'll be greatly appreciated and is a great means of getting into a game.

BIKING With a local reliance on bicycles for everyday transportation and a relatively well-maintained road network serving a small motor vehicular fleet, Cuba is a great country to tour by bicycle. There are very few operations renting decent bikes in Cuba, so it's best to bring your own. I also recommend organized trips, as the logistics of traveling through Cuba still make it a bit difficult for independent bike touring. One dependable operation with regular bike tours and quality bike rentals in Cuba is **Wow Cuba** (© **800/969-2822** or 902/368-2453; www.wowcuba.com). Anyone thinking of bicycling in Cuba should pick up a copy of Wally and Barbara Smith's *Bicycling Cuba: Fifty Days of Detailed Rides from Havana to Pinar Del Río and the Oriente* (Backcountry Guides, 2002).

BIRD-WATCHING Over 350 resident and migratory species of birds can be spotted in Cuba, including some 24 endemic species. Cuba is also home to the smallest hummingbird in the world, the endemic bee hummingbird. A couple of organized tour options are offered by the British company **Cuba Welcome** (© **020/7731-6871** in the U.K.; www.cubawelcome. com) and the Canadian operation **Quest Nature Tours** (© **416/633-5666**; www. questnaturetours.com). Some of the best places to go bird-watching in Cuba include **La Güira National Park,** the **Zapata Peninsula, Cayo Coco** and **Cayo Guillermo, La Belen** reserve near Camagüey, the **Sierra Maestra** region, and **Baracoa.** Birdwatchers will want to bring a copy of *Field Guide to the Birds of Cuba* (Comstock, 2000), by Orlando Garrido et al.

CIGARS CubaWelcome (© **020/7731-6871** in the U.K.; www.cubawelcome. com) offers a 5-day cigar tour including factory visits, a visit to the famous Vuelta Abajo tobacco-growing region in western

Cuba, and the chance to meet with Alejandro Robaina, the famous tobacco grower. Tobacco plants mature by February, and February and March are good months to visit Vuelta Abajo.

FISHING There's fabulous deep-sea sportfishing for marlin, sailfish, tuna, dorado, and more off most of Cuba's extensive coastline, while the Zapata Peninsula and Cayo Largo del Sur may just be some of the best and least exploited bonefishing spots left in the hemisphere. The mountain lake and resort of Hanabanilla is getting good grades as a freshwater ground for widemouth and black bass. There's a broad network of state-run marinas all around Cuba; the greatest number are run by **Grupo Empresarial de Náutica y Marinas Marlin** (www.nauticamarlin.com) and **Gaviota** (© 7/66-9668; www.gaviotagrupo.com). All offer sportfishing charters. For more information, see individual destination chapters. **Cuba Welcome** (www.cubawelcome.com) and **Avalon** (www.avalonfishingcenter.com) run reputable operations. Cuba Welcome runs tours to Las Salinas in **Zapata National Park** and Avalon operates out of **Jardines de la Reina, Isla de la Juventud,** and **Cayo Largo.**

GOLF The country's only regulation 18-hole golf course is the **Varadero Golf Club** (© 45/66-8442; www.varaderogolfclub.com). The course is a relatively flat resort course, with lots of water, plenty of sand, great views, and almost no rough. Golfers will probably want to stay at the adjacent **Meliá Las Américas** (© 45/66-7600; www.solmeliacuba.com), although you can make reservations and play here from any hotel in the area.

In Havana, there's the **Club de Golf Habana,** Carretera Vento Km 8, Capdevila, Rancho Boyeros (© 7/649-8918, ext. 111), which has a decent little 9-hole course.

KITE SURFING Great kite surfing can be found on Cayo Guillermo. You will need to bring all your own equipment

though. Canadian hobbyists have been coming here for years.

MOUNTAIN & ROCK CLIMBING These sports are in their infancy in Cuba, but excellent opportunities abound, especially around the Viñales Valley. **Cuba Climbing** (www.cubaclimbing.com) can point you to the right rocks and answer any questions you might have.

SAILING Whether you take a day sail, or decide to go cruising the coastline for a week or so, opportunities to sail the clear waters off Cuba abound. The state-run marinas in Varadero, Jardines del Rey, Camagüey, Santiago, Cienfuegos, and Cayo Largo del Sur all offer charter sailboats, as well as a variety of day sailing options. See the individual destination chapters for more information.

SCUBA DIVING & SNORKELING There are fabulous scuba-diving and snorkeling opportunities on the coral reefs, ocean walls, and ancient wrecks that lie just off Cuba's coasts. **María la Gorda, Isla de la Juventud, Playa Larga, Playa Girón,** and **Los Jardines de la Reina** are widely considered the absolute top scuba-diving destinations, but in each case, the majority of the accommodations options are either rustic or decidedly geared toward hard-core dive enthusiasts and almost no one else. You will also find perfectly acceptable dive opportunities and operations in **Varadero, Cayo Coco, Cayo Guillermo, Guardalavaca,** and **Cayo Largo del Sur,** as well as far more comfortable and varied accommodations. For more information, see specific destination chapters.

SURFING Cuba is not considered a world-class surfing destination, and there are very few Cuban surfers or surf tourists. Still, this is part of the charm of surfing in Cuba, and there are waves and breaks all along the island's long coastline, including right off the Malecón in Havana. For good information and a primer, check out **www.havanasurf-cuba.com**. You will definitely have to bring your own board, and I would recommend bringing a board (or two) that you wouldn't mind leaving behind for some very appreciative Cuban surfer.

TENNIS Many of the large-scale beach resorts have tennis courts. Almost all are outdoor courts, and very few are lit. If you're set on playing tennis on your trip, be sure to check in advance whether your hotel or resort has courts. Your options are much more limited in Havana, unless you're staying at one of the few city hotels with a court. Your best bet in Havana is to try to book a court at the **Occidental Miramar,** Avenida 5, between Calles 78 and 80, Miramar, Playa (© 7/204-3584), which has six courts; or head to the **Club Habana,** Avenida 5, between Calles 188 and 192, Reparto Flores, Playa (© 7/204-5700); or **Club de Golf Habana,** Carretera Vento Km 8, Capdevila, Rancho Boyeros (© 7/55-8746). Each have a few courts open to the general public. All charge around CUC$10 (US$11/£5.40) per hour.

ACADEMIC TRIPS & LANGUAGE CLASSES The **University of Havana** offers language classes from CUC$100 (US$108/£54) a month starting on the first Monday of every month. A 60-hour Cuban culture class is offered every second month. The **University of the Oriente** in Santiago de Cuba also offers Spanish classes from CUC$231 (US$250/£125). On their website (www.uo.edu.cu), click on "Estudios"; the information is in Spanish only. **Caledonia** (© 0131/621-7721; www.caledonialanguages.com) offers Spanish courses in Havana and Santiago from CUC$1,005 (US$1,085/£543) for 2 weeks.

MUSIC & DANCE TRIPS **Caledonia** (© 0131/621-7721; www.caledonia languages.com) offers music and dance trips to Cuba with prices starting at

CUC$802 (US$866/£433). It is also possible to combine these activities with language classes. The site has links to the annual Cuban Music School (www.jazz summerschool.com/cuban_music_school). Caledonia is listed as a responsible travel operator by www.responsibletravel.com.

PHOTOGRAPHY & WRITING TRIPS **Cuba Welcome** (© 020/7731-6871 in the U.K.; www.cubawelcome.com) arranges photography workshop tours with British photographer Keith Cardwell. Tours are run in conjunction with Cuban photographer Julio Muñoz based in Trinidad (www. trinidadphoto.com). An 11-day tour is £1,370 (US$2,726) per person, excluding food and flights.

British travel writing and photography agency **Travellers' Tales** (www.travellerstales. org) has added Cuba to its program. A week-long trip starts at £1,440 (US$2,866), excluding flights.

ADVENTURE & WELLNESS TRIPS Most tour operators listed can arrange trekking tours. **Caledonia** (© 0131/621-7721; www.caledonialanguages.com) organizes trekking trips in the Sierra Maestra. There is only one fully oriented spa center independent of hotels in Cuba, the Acuavida Centro Spa-Talaso on Cayo Coco. **Cuba Direct** (© 0844/415-5510; www.cubadi rect.co.uk) can organize week-long trips for £999 (US$1,988) including flights, domestic flight transfers, and 4 days of treatments. The spa situation will change with the building of the Esencia properties (p. 59) in Cuba over the next few years.

VOLUNTEER & WORKING TRIPS The **Cuban Solidarity Campaign** (© 020/ 8800-0155; www.cuba-solidarity.org/ brigades.asp) runs international work brigades twice a year for up to 22 days for £900 (US$1,791) per person, including all flights, accommodations, and food. See also **Global Exchange,** p. 52.

PLANNING YOUR TRIP TO CUBA

3

STAYING CONNECTED

TELEPHONES

The phone numbering system inside Cuba is being modernized, but it remains quite confusing. Havana's city code is one digit. Other area codes are two digits; individual phone numbers can range from five to seven digits. You do not need to use the city or area code for local calls, but you must dial 01 followed by the city or area code for any long-distance call within Cuba or to a cellphone, except when calling to or from Havana. From Havana to any other province or from a province to Havana, you would dial only the zero before the area code. Thus, a call from Trinidad to Pinar del Rio would start 01-48. A call from Havana to Pinar del Rio would begin 0-48. The same rules apply for a cellphone call. All Cuba cellphones begin with a 5. To dial a cellphone from a fixed line in Havana, dial 0-5, then the rest of the cellphone number. If you call a cellphone from any other province, dial 01-5, then the rest of cellphone number. If you dial cellphone to cellphone, just dial 5, then the rest of cellphone number.

To call Cuba: If you're calling Cuba from the United States:

- First dial 011, the international access code.
- Then dial 53, the country code.
- And last, dial the area code and then the number.
- The whole number you'd dial for a number in Havana (area code 7) would be 011-53-7-XXX-XXXX.

To make international calls: To make international calls from Cuba, first dial 119 and then the country code (U.S. or Canada 1, U.K. 44, Ireland 353, Australia 61, New Zealand 64). Next dial the area code and number. For example, if you want to call the British Embassy in Washington, D.C., you would dial

119/1-202-588-7800. You can make collect calls to Canada, Spain, the U.S., France, Italy, and the U.K.

For directory and operator assistance: Dial ✆ 113 if you're looking for a number inside Cuba and for domestic help, and dial ✆ 180 for numbers to all other countries and for help with collect calls.

Nearly all hotels and some *casas particulares* have phones in their rooms. Dialing instructions should be available in rooms; if not, contact the reception desk. Cuba has a wide range of **public telephone booths** where Cuban pesos *(moneda nacional)* and a variety of cards can be used. Any older sky-blue phone or newer royal-blue phone with a coin slot will take *moneda nacional*. This is the cheapest option where you can talk for a very long time for 1 peso. New royal-blue phones will take cards expressed in CUC (from CUC\$5/US\$5.40/£2.70) and *moneda nacional*. Only buy the CUC cards to make international calls, as making a local call means you are paying more than several times the peso amount. You can also buy cards of certain values with codes that allow you to make calls from a private phone or a public phone by dialing an access code first and then your card number and then the phone number you wish to dial. These cards are available in CUC and in *moneda nacional* and may be worth purchasing if you plan to make a lot of local calls on your trip.

Note that many public phone booths, especially in Havana, frequently break down. Those that are working suffer from long queues in Havana and, if you are in a rush, this may not be your best option.

Note that if you stay in a *casa particular* and wish to confirm your subsequent *casa* in another town, your *casa* owner will make this courtesy call for you.

Online Traveler's Toolbox

Veteran travelers usually carry some essential items to make their trips easier. Following is a selection of handy websites to bookmark and use.

- **Airplane Food** (www.airlinemeals.net)
- **Airplane Seating** (www.seatguru.com; www.airlinequality.com)
- **Events** (www.cubaescena.cult.cu; www.paradiso.cu; www.thehmagazine. com/agenda/havana_listings.php; www.cubaabsolutely.com/events/ whats_on.htm)
- **Foreign Languages for Travelers** (www.travlang.com)
- **Maps** (www.mapquest.com)
- **Time and Date** (www.timeanddate.com)
- **Travel Warnings** (http://travel.state.gov; www.fco.gov.uk/travel; www.voyage. gc.ca; www.smartraveller.gov.au)
- **Universal Currency Converter** (www.oanda.com)
- **Weather** (www.intellicast.com; www.weather.com)

CELLPHONES

In Cuba, cellular service is controlled by **Cubacel,** Avenida 5 and Calle 76, Edificio Barcelona, Centro de Negocios, Miramar (© **5/264-2266;** www.cubacel.cu). Cubacel has offices at the José Martí International Airport and in Havana and most major cities and tourist destinations. Cubacel offers cellphone rentals for CUC$6 (US$6.50/£3.25) per day, with a CUC$3 (US$3.25/£1.60) daily activation fee. You'll have to leave a deposit and purchase a prepaid calling card. If you have your own phone, you will just have to pay the CUC$3 (US$3.25/£1.60) daily activation fee. Cubacel works with both TDMA phones and GSM systems. Prepaid calling cards are sold in denominations of CUC$10 (US$11/£5.40), CUC$20 (US$22/£11), and CUC$40 (US$43/£22). Rates inside Cuba run between CUC40¢ (US45¢/20p) and CUC60 (US65¢/30p) per minute for outgoing calls, depending on the hour and destination called. Incoming calls are charged between CUC$.35 (US40¢/20p) and CUC$.45 (US45¢/20p) per minute. Rates to the rest of the world run between CUC$2 (US$2.15/£1.10) and CUC$4 (US$4.30/£2.15) per minute. Text (SMS) messages are free to receive, but cost CUC16 ¢ (US20¢/10p) to send within Cuba and CUC$1 (US$1.10/55p) to send abroad. If you intend to only make a few calls or send a few text messages, it will be cheaper to bring your own phone than pay the cumulative daily Cubacel charges. (Remember to dial Cuba's country code of 53 before any area code and the number you wish to dial in the country before using your own phone.)

Note: Any phone with an SIM from a U.S. provider will not work in Cuba.

INTERNET & E-MAIL
With Your Own Computer

A handful of hotels have Wi-Fi (wireless fidelity) "hot spots," from which you can get a high-speed connection without cable wires, networking hardware, or a phone line (see below). These include the Meliá Cohiba, the NH Parque Central, Hotel Saratoga, and Hotel Chateau Miramar.

Wherever you go, bring a **connection kit** of the right power and phone adapters, a spare phone cord, and a spare Ethernet network cable—or find out whether your hotel supplies them to guests. Throughout Cuba, electricity is 110-volt AC, and most outlets are U.S.-style two- or three-prong. However, many of the large hotels and resorts that cater primarily to Canadian and European clientele are wired for 220 volts.

Without Your Own Computer

Internet access has greatly improved in Cuba and so has the speed, but it is by no means high speed. In all the major cities, you will now find Etecsa offices with Internet connections for which you must buy a CUC$6 (US$6.50/£3.25) per hour card. Control has also increased and you could be asked to sign your name, passport number, and Internet card code on a list of Internet users in these telephone/telepunto/minipunto offices. All upscale hotels and resorts also provide for guest connectivity in one form or another. Many of these operate with Etecsa cards, but you must buy your card at the hotel, because an Etecsa card bought elsewhere will not operate on the hotel's computer.

Some high-end hotels in Havana charge more than CUC$6 (US$6.50/£3.25) an hour.

The **José Martí International Airport** in Havana also has Internet access.

12   TIPS ON ACCOMMODATIONS

Cuba's accommodations for tourists range from top-class historic hotels to budget, basic uniform blocks in the cities. These are complemented by *casas particulares,* a system of excellent value Cuban guesthouses where Cubans can rent out a maximum of two of their rooms to guests. At **beach resorts,** hotels range from top-class luxury to above-basic facilities at slightly inflated prices, with a few very good exceptions at the more reasonable/lower end of the market. In most areas, *casas particulares* right on the beach are rare due to government restrictions. In rural areas, there is a mix of high-end to moderately priced, attractive accommodations as well as some unattractive government hotels.

Hotels are either owned or run by the Cuban state or are run as joint ventures with foreign companies. There are no 100% foreign-owned hotels in Cuba.

Most hotel options in Cuba have been divvied up among a few large state-run chains: **Islazul** (www.islazul.cu), **Gaviota** (www.gaviota-grupo.com), **Cubanacán** (www.hotelescubanacan.com), **Gran Caribe** (www.gran-caribe.com), and **Habaguanex** (www.habaguanexhotels.com). These chains generally stake out distinct territories. Habaguanex has near monopoly control over the hotel scene in Habana Vieja in Havana. Their properties tend to be midrange to upper end, and most are in beautifully restored colonial buildings. Gaviota, Cubanacán, and Gran Caribe divvy up the remainder of the midrange to upper-end hotels around the country. Islazul runs the most economical hotels, although it has begun refurbishing some real gems in the colonial heart of some of Cuba's more interesting cities. Cubanacán is also upgrading properties with its Hoteles E brand.

These large state-run companies have signed management contracts with international hotel chains, usually resulting in improved service and hospitality. While the international **Barceló** (www.barcelo.com), **NH Hoteles** (www.nh-hotels.com), **Iberostar** (www.iberostar.com), **Accor** (www.accor.com), and **Occidental** (www.occidental-hoteles.com) chains run a few hotels each, predominantly in Havana and Varadero, the major player is the Spanish **Sol Meliá** chain, which manages 24 midrange to high-end properties in Cuba. In general, the Sol Meliá hotels are some of the best run and most comfortable in the country.

Watch out for the British company Havana Holdings, which has set up **Esencia Hotels & Resorts** (www.esenciahotels andresorts.com) to upgrade and build new hotels in Cuba in association with Gran Caribe.

Be prepared for some pitfalls when booking directly through hotel websites in Cuba. Many of the state-run chains—**Gaviota, Habaguanex,** and **Cubanacán**—have primitive or poorly maintained websites, and their online booking mechanisms can be cumbersome and inconsistent. You'll definitely do better with the larger international chains like **Sol Meliá** (www.solmeliacuba. com), **Occidental** (www.occidental-hoteles. com), and **Barceló** (www.barcelo.com).

Aside from official hotels and resorts, the other principal lodging option in Cuba is a **casa particular,** or private house. To meet demand and inject just a bit of economic relief (and nascent capitalism) into the system, the government has authorized certain households to rent out rooms. An official *casa particular* should display a small plaque or sticker declaring it to be a government sanctioned *casa*. The newest symbol appears to be a blue capital "H" set on its side, with slightly bent horizontal lines, and the top horizontal line longer than the bottom one. (It also looks like an anchor.) It should also say *Arrendador Divisa*. This means the owner of the house is allowed to rent rooms for *divisa* (hard currency). Houses with red symbols can only rent to Cubans for *moneda nacional.*

Casas charge from CUC$15 to CUC$25 (US$14–US$23/£8–£14) in the low season and CUC$25 to CUC$35 (US$23–US$38/£14–£19) in the high season. In addition to the season, price variations depend on the number of guests, the length of stay, your status (students often receive discounts), the location of the house in the country (for example, the more remote or less touristy the area, the cheaper it could be), and the amount of tax that owners pay on the room. Those with impressive colonial homes often charge more.

During low season, do negotiate for a lower nightly rate and always try to negotiate a lower rate for a long stay. Note that it is very difficult to get a discount for single travelers. Pairs/couples and families with children under 18 who share the same room enjoy the most value.

On arrival, *casa* owners must ask for your passport and enter the information into a registration book that must be taken to the immigration office within 24 hours of your arrival. You will be asked to sign next to your information in this book. If you are not asked to sign or are not asked for your passport, your *casa* may not be legal. *Casas particulares* can have no more than two rooms for rent. Each room can only hold two adults and children under 18. The owners must pay a tax of between CUC$100 and CUC$250 (US$108–US$270/£54–£135) per room per month (the price depends on the house location), plus the now obligatory monthly gastronomic tax, plus a tax on areas used by tourists such as a garage and lounge. At the end of the year, depending on what has been earned, a further tax of between 10% and 30% is paid on the total annual earnings. Most are quite modest—you are basically living with a Cuban family. Rooms for rent will either have their own private bathroom or a bathroom shared with other tourists, not with the family. Your room will most likely have air-conditioning. There are few *casas* now that only have fans. If there is no air-conditioning, you should pay less. The minimum facilities you will receive are clean sheets and towels, probably a bedside lamp, a wardrobe closet, and a sideboard. Some *casas* now have security boxes. Most houses will provide locked rooms with a key. You may or may not be given the keys to the house depending on the rules of the owners. Some *casas* have independent entrances, which appeal to some travelers. Most colonial houses that often make the most attractive *casas* do not have en suite bathrooms due to the configuration of the houses. Either way, en suite or not, the bathroom will be clean and will have a working lavatory, toilet paper, and a shower or bath with hot water.

Most *casas particulares* serve huge, varied, and tasty meals (breakfasts and dinners) at very reasonable prices, especially since the optional gastronomic tax of CUC$30 (US$32/£16) a month has become obligatory. The biggest and most wonderful advantage of staying in a *casa* is that it is a great way to meet and interact with Cubans, something you cannot really do at "official" hotels and resorts. Most owners will also bend over backwards to assist you with your plans—whether that means answering your questions, arranging transport, or making phone calls for you. Most will also do laundry.

If you have a reservation for your *casa,* your hosts should honor it. If you just turn up without a reservation and the house is full, the owner will farm you out to a friend or relative at a nearby house. You are not under any obligation to take these places, but they could save you a lot of hassle. Make sure they are legal houses, though. Even with a reservation, it is wise to make a follow-up confirmation by e-mail or by phone. *Casa* owners are happy to phone ahead to your next *casa* to tell the future host you are on your way.

Be aware that if you show up at a *casa particular* on the recommendation of a taxi driver or *jinetero,* either of them will expect a commission of between CUC$1 and CUC$5 (US$1.10–US$5.40/55p–£2.70), which invariably is indirectly added onto the bill at your *casa particular.*

Frommer's has received reports of the occasional theft from *casas particulares.* This is an extremely rare occurrence, since renting rooms to tourists is the main source of hard currency for Cubans. Putting this at risk is, quite frankly, idiotic in Cuba's economic climate.

For tips on surfing for hotel deals online, visit www.frommers.com/planning.

Suggested Cuba Itineraries

Cuba is a big island—the largest in the Caribbean—and its attractions and charms run the gamut from the hustle and bustle of Havana, to the colonial grandeur of Trinidad and a host of other small and well-preserved old cities and towns, to the steamy, vibrant streets of Santiago, and the sparkling waters and white sands of a half-dozen or more top-notch beach destinations. So, you will need to plan well to make the most out of any trip here. The following itineraries should be used as rough outlines. Other options include specialized itineraries focused on a particular interest or activity. Bird-watchers could design an itinerary that visits a series of prime bird-watching sites. Latin dance or art enthusiasts could arrange a specialized trip to focus on these interests. And revolutionary history buffs could build a trip around visits to the Moncada barracks (Cuartel de Moncada) in Santiago, the Che Guevara Memorial (Monumento Ernesto Che Guevara) in Santa Clara, and the Bay of Pigs (Playa Girón). Feel free to pick and choose—you can combine a bit of one, with a smidgen of another, or come up with something entirely on your own.

1 THE REGIONS IN BRIEF

Cuba is probably the most intensely diverse island destination in the Caribbean, with everything from standard fun-in-the-sun beach resort getaways to colonial city circuits, myriad land and sea adventure opportunities, tobacco and classic-car theme tours, and a wide array of cultural and artistic offerings. There's a lot to see and do in Cuba, and most travelers will have to carefully pick and choose. This chapter will provide you with descriptions of the country's regions, along with itineraries that will help you get the most from your visit.

Cuba is the westernmost and largest of the entire chain of Caribbean islands, located at the convergence of the Caribbean Sea, the Gulf of Mexico, and the Atlantic Ocean just 145km (90 miles) south of Florida. They say that Cuba—if you use your imagination—looks something like a crocodile: The head is in the east, a line of small islands form the ridges along its back, the Sierra Maestra national park forms the front legs, the Zapata Peninsula forms the rear legs, and Pinar del Río province is the tail. Cuba is in fact a closely linked string of archipelagos, made up of more than 4,000 separate little islands and cays.

Cuba's two major cities, Havana and Santiago de Cuba, are port cities with large protected harbors. Most of the island's other principal cities lie along its centerline, either right on or just off the Autopista Nacional (National Hwy.), the country's principal trade and transportation route.

HAVANA & PLAYAS DEL ESTE **Havana** is Cuba's capital and the country's most important cultural, political, and economic hub. With a wealth of museums, antique buildings, old forts, the Malecón seaside promenade, and modern restaurants, clubs, and cabarets, Havana is one of the liveliest and most engaging cities in Latin America. Just

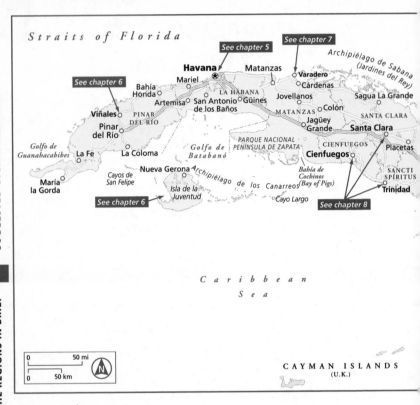

east of the city center are some 15km (9 miles) of very respectable white-sand beach, the **Playas del Este.** While nowhere near as stunning as some of Cuba's more celebrated beach destinations, the Playas del Este are certainly a suitable alternative, either as a base for exploring Havana or as an easily accessible place for sun, sand, and sea.

VIÑALES & WESTERN CUBA   Comprising the province of Pinar del Río, western Cuba is a wonderfully rustic region of farms and forests, flanked by some beautiful and relatively underpopulated beaches. The only real city in the province, **Pinar del Río,** is of limited interest on its own, but it serves as a gateway to **Viñales** and the **Vuelta Abajo,** Cuba's premiere tobacco-growing and cigar-manufacturing region. Just north of Pinar del Río, Viñales is a pretty little hamlet in an even prettier valley, surrounded by stunning karst hill formations. Viñales is Cuba's prime ecotourist destination, with great opportunities for hiking, bird-watching, mountain biking, and cave exploration. On the far western tip of the island sits the tiny resort of **María la Gorda,** arguably home to the best of Cuba's overall excellent scuba diving. Lying off the southern coast of this region in the Caribbean Sea are the island destinations of **Isla de la Juventud,** yet another of Cuba's premiere scuba-diving destinations, and **Cayo Largo del Sur,** another long stretch of dazzling and isolated white sand.

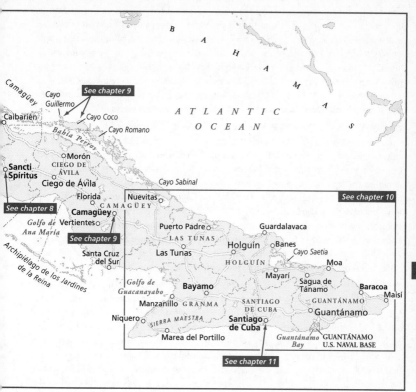

VARADERO & MATANZAS PROVINCE   Matanzas is Cuba's second-largest province and home to its most important beach destination, **Varadero.** Boasting some 21km (13 miles) of nearly uninterrupted white-sand beach, Varadero is Cuba's quintessential sun-and-fun destination, with a host of luxurious all-inclusive resorts strung along the length of this narrow peninsula. In addition to Varadero, Matanzas province is home to the colonial-era cities of **Matanzas** and **Cárdenas.**

In the southern section of the province is the **Ciénaga de Zapata,** a vast wetlands area of mangrove and swamp, renowned for its wildlife-viewing, bird-watching, and fishing opportunities. This is also where you'll find the **Bahía de Cochinos (Bay of Pigs),** where the nascent Cuban revolutionary state defeated an invasion force trained, supplied, and abetted by the United States. The beaches of **Playa Girón** and **Playa Larga** serve as a base for access to some of Cuba's best scuba diving.

TRINIDAD & CENTRAL CUBA   Beginning with the provinces of Villa Clara and Cienfuegos, and including the neighboring province of Sancti Spíritus, central Cuba is the start of the country's rural heartland. Vast regions of sugar cane, tobacco, and cattle ranges spread out on either side of the Autopista Nacional, which more or less bisects this region as it heads east.

Trinidad is perhaps Cuba's quintessential colonial-era city, with beautifully maintained and restored buildings set on winding cobblestone streets. The cities of **Santa Clara, Cienfuegos,** and **Sancti Spíritus** are considered lesser lights on the tourism circuit, but all have ample charms of their own. Santa Clara is a lively university town, and is considered the "City of Che Guevara," with its massive memorial to the fallen revolutionary leader. To the north of Santa Clara lie the tiny colonial city of **Remedios** and the up-and-coming beach resorts of **la Cayería del Norte.** Cienfuegos is a charming port town with the country's second-longest seaside promenade. Sancti Spíritus is one of the original seven *villas* of Cuba, with some wonderful old historic churches and buildings, and a more natural feel than you'll find in other more touristy towns.

CAMAGÜEY & NORTHEASTERN CUBA   This section of mainland Cuba is little more than a string of rural towns and small cities, anchored by two colonial-era cities. This is Cuba at its quietest, stuck in time and in no rush to break free. However, off the northern coast here lie a series of modern beach resorts built on long stretches of soft and silvery white sand, connected to the mainland by a long narrow causeway that seems to barely skirt the surface of the sea. The sister resort islands of **Cayo Coco** and **Cayo Guillermo** are two of the finest and most popular resort destinations in Cuba. Several less-developed beach resorts stretch east along the coast on the string of islands making up the Archipiélago de Camagüey, better known as the Jardines del Rey (King's Gardens). The cities of **Ciego de Avila** and **Camagüey** are seldom explored colonial-era cities. The latter, in particular, has loads of charms and attractions, and is being restored to highlight much of its former glory.

EL ORIENTE   For most of the country's history, the whole eastern end of Cuba was known as El Oriente. Today, it is comprised of four separate provinces: Holguín, Granma, Santiago de Cuba, and Guantánamo. This is a large region with a host of gorgeous natural attractions, highlighted by the mountains of the **Sierra Maestra**—a mecca for naturalists and adventure travelers as well as those looking to follow in the revolutionary footsteps of Fidel and Che—and the beautiful beaches of **Guardalavaca,** yet another of Cuba's premier beach resort destinations, with unimaginably fine white sand and calm turquoise waters. Of the cities here, only Santiago de Cuba is a tourist draw in its own right, although visitors to **Holguín, Bayamo,** or **Baracoa** will experience Cuba at its most authentic.

SANTIAGO DE CUBA   This is Cuba's second largest city. Set between the Sierra Maestra mountains and the sea, Santiago is a vibrant city with a rich artistic and cultural heritage. Santiago is considered the heart of Cuba's Afro-Cuban and Afro-Caribbean heritage, which is expressed in the music, dance, and religion you'll find here. Santiago's Carnival celebrations are by far the best in Cuba, and some of the best in the entire Caribbean.

The city itself has a charming colonial-era center and a host of interesting museums and attractions, including José Martí's tomb and mausoleum, the original Bacardí rum factory, and the impressive Castillo del Morro protecting the city's harbor. Nearby sites worth visiting include the El Cobre shrine to the island's patron saint, La Virgin de Caridad, and the Gran Piedra, a massive rock outcropping allowing for great hiking and views.

2 CUBA IN 1 WEEK

This is a tough one. Many visitors are content to spend an entire week soaking up the rays and lying in the sand at an all-inclusive beach resort. I sometimes devote an entire week to Havana. However, the following itinerary seeks to pack a handful of Cuba's top

Day ❶: Arrive & Settle into Havana

Arrive and check in to your hotel. Take an afternoon walk along the **Malecón** and have a sunset cocktail at the **Hotel Nacional de Cuba** ★★ (p. 94). For dinner, head to either **La Guarida** ★★ (p. 105) or **La Cocina de Lilliam** ★★ (p. 107), two of the city's best *paladares*. Be sure to make a reservation as soon as you get to your hotel, because these places book up fast. After dinner, catch some jazz at **La Zorra y el Cuervo** ★★ (p. 107) if you're not jet-lagged.

Day ❷: Step Back in Time

Start the morning off in **Habana Vieja** (p. 109). Visit the **Plaza de la Catedral,** the **Plaza de Armas, Plaza Vieja,** and **Plaza de San Francisco.** Be sure to tour the **Museo de la Ciudad** ★★ (p. 112), the **Castillo de la Real Fuerza** ★ (p. 109), and any other attractions that catch your attention. Have lunch at **La Bodeguita del Medio** ★ (p. 102). After lunch, head toward Parque Central and visit **El Capitolio** ★ (p. 114), and then later, either the **Museo Nacional de las Bellas Artes** ★★ (p. 112), or the **Museo de la Revolución** ★ (p. 112). Finish up your afternoon strolling along the outdoor art exhibit that is **Callejón de Hammel** ★★★ (p. 114), but if your second day is a Sunday, arrive here earlier for the Sunday rumba sessions. If you have a spare half-hour, drive by the Plaza de la Revolución ★ to see the José Martí memorial and the iconic iron sculpture of the face of Che Guevara on the Ministry of the Interior building. In the evening, go to the **Tropicana** ★★★ (p. 127) for dinner and a show.

Day ❸: Time for Trinidad

Head for Trinidad. Stay either in the new **Grand Hotel Iberostar Trinidad** ★★ (p. 200), the **Hotel Las Cuevas** ★, or one of the many *casas particulares* right in the colonial center of this classic little city. Spend the afternoon touring Trinidad's colonial-era landmarks, including the **Plaza Mayor,** the **Plazuela El Jigüe,** the **Iglesia de la Santísima Trinidad,** and the **Museo Romántico** ★★ (p. 198). For dinner, make a reservation at **Paladar Estela** ★★ (p. 203) or **Sol y Son** ★★. After dinner, stroll around the Plaza Mayor and listen for where the action is. It might be a salsa or *son* band playing on the steps below the **Casa de la Música** ★ (p. 203), or it might be in any one of several clubs nearby, including the excellent **Palenque de los Congos Reales** ★★.

Day ❹: Checking in with Che

Spend the morning walking around Trinidad, and shopping at the various little street markets around town. From Trinidad, head north to **Santa Clara** ★, Che Guevara's city. Your first and most important stop here is the massive and impressive **Monumento Ernesto Che Guevara** ★ (p. 179), set on the Plaza de la Revolución Che Guevara. In the early evening, head to **Parque Vidal,** the downtown heart and soul of Santa Clara. Stop in to tour the **Teatro La Caridad,** and then head to **Hostal Florida Center** ★★ (p. 182) for dinner. After dinner, see if there's anything happening at **Club Mejunje** ★★ (p. 183).

Days ❺ & ❻: Hit the Beach

From Santa Clara, head to **La Cayería del Norte** ★★★ (p. 184), where you will find a handful of large, luxurious resorts on some of the finest beaches in Cuba. Be sure to stop for a bit in the tiny, colonial-era town of **Remedios** ★★★ (p. 183) on your way. And then settle in for some serious relaxation. There's excellent snorkeling and scuba diving, as well as numerous opportunities to indulge in other watersports. Or you can just chill.

START: Cuba in 1 Week   START: Cuba in 2 Weeks

Straits of Florida

START: Cuba in 1 Week
Havana **1–2**
Trinidad **3–4**
Santa Clara **4**
La Cayería del Norte **5**
Remedios **6**
Havana **7**

START: Cuba in 2 Weeks
Havana **1–2**
Viñales Valley **3**
Cienfuegos **4**
Trinidad **5–6**
Santa Clara **6**
Remedios **7**
Havana **7**&**14**
Baracoa **8–9**
Santiago de Cuba **10–11**
Cayo Largo del Sur **12–14**

Day ❼: Going Home
Return to **Havana** in time for your international connection. If you have extra time, head to the **Calle Tacón** street market ★★ (p. 124) to do some last-minute shopping before you go.

---

3 CUBA IN 2 WEEKS

If you've got 2 weeks, you'll be able to hit all the highlights mentioned above, as well as some others, including Cuba's second city Santiago, a side trip to the gorgeous *mogotes* (limestone formations) and tobacco farms of the Viñales valley, and visits to Cienfuegos and Baracoa, two underappreciated Cuban cities. And, you get to do all this at a slightly more relaxed pace to boot. This itinerary starts off very similar to the 1-week version above, but soon diverges.

Day ❶: Arrive & Settle into Havana
Arrive and settle in to your hotel. Spend the afternoon walking along the **Malecón** ★★★ and have a sunset cocktail at the **Hotel Nacional** ★★ (p. 94). After sunset, head over for dinner at **Los Doce**

Apóstoles ★ (p. 108) in the **Parque Histórico Morro y Cabaña** ★★ (p. 118). Stick around for the *cañonazo* (cannon-firing) ceremony.

Day ❷: Step Back in Time

Start the morning off in **Habana Vieja** ★★★. Visit the **Plaza de la Catedral**, the **Plaza de Armas, Plaza Vieja**, and **Plaza de San Francisco.** Be sure to tour the **Museo de la Ciudad** ★★ (p. 112), the **Castillo de la Real Fuerza** ★ (p. 109), and any other attractions that catch your attention. Have lunch at **La Bodeguita del Medio** ★ (p. 102). After lunch, head toward Parque Central and visit **El Capitolio** ★ (p. 114), then either the **Museo Nacional de las Bellas**

Artes ★★ (p. 112), or the **Museo de la Revolución** ★ (p. 112). Finish up your afternoon strolling along the outdoor art exhibit that is **Callejón de Hammel** ★★★ (p. 112), but if your second day is a Sunday, arrive here earlier for the Sunday rumba sessions. If you have a spare half-hour, drive by the Plaza de la Revolución ★ to see the José Martí memorial and the iconic iron sculpture of the face of Che Guevara on the Ministry of the Interior building. In the evening, head to the **Tropicana** ★★ ★ (p. 127) for dinner and a show.

Day ❸: The Viñales Valley by Day, Jazz at Night

Sign on for an organized day tour of the **Viñales valley** ★★★. You'll get to take in some of Cuba's best natural scenery, and also visit a tobacco farm and cigar-rolling facility. You'll probably also visit the Guayabitas liquor factory in **Pinar del Río** (p. 130), and take a quick tour through **La Cueva del Indio** (p. 136). This jam-packed day tour should still get you back to Havana in time for a dinner at one of the city's standout *paladares* (private home restaurants), followed by some hot jazz at **La Zorra y el Cuervo** ★★ (p. 128) or the **Jazz Café** ★ (p. 128).

Day ④: Cienfuegos, la Perla del Sur

Pick up a rental car and head for **Cienfuegos** ★, a bustling port city on the southern coast, with a compact, yet very attractive colonial-era core. Get to know the old center around **Parque José Martí,** visiting the **Catedral de la Purísima Concepción** and the **Teatro Tomás Terry** ★ (p. 189). In the afternoon, head out to the Punta Gorda district and have a sunset drink at the **Cienfuegos Yacht Club** (p. 190). For dinner, try the historic old **Palacio del Valle** ★★ (p. 193).

Day ⑤: Time for Trinidad

From Cienfuegos, it's a short hop to **Trinidad** ★★★, with some beautiful scenery along the coast. Stay either in the new **Grand Hotel Iberostar Trinidad** ★★ (p. 200), the **Hotel Las Cuevas** ★, or one of the many *casas particulares* right in the colonial center of this classic little city. Spend the afternoon touring Trinidad's colonial-era landmarks, including the **Plaza Mayor,** the **Plazuela El Jigüe,** the **Iglesia de la Santísima Trinidad,** and the **Museo Romántico** ★★ (p. 198). For dinner, make a reservation at **Paladar Estela** ★★ (p. 203) or **Sol y Son** ★★. After dinner, stroll the area around the Plaza Mayor and listen for where the action is. It might be a salsa or *son* band playing on the steps below the **Casa de la Música** ★ (p. 202), or it might be in any one of several clubs nearby, including the excellent **Palenque de los Congos Reales** ★★.

Day ⑥: Checking in with Che

Spend the morning walking around Trinidad and shopping at the various little street markets around town. From Trinidad, head north to **Santa Clara** ★, Che Guevara's city. Your first and most important stop here is the massive and impressive **Monumento Ernesto Che Guevara** ★ (p. 179), set on the Plaza de la Revolución Che Guevara. In the early evening, head to **Parque Vidal,** the downtown heart and soul of Santa Clara. Stop in to tour the **Teatro La Caridad,** and then head to **Hostal Florida Center** ★★ (p. 182) for dinner. After dinner, see if there's anything happening at **Club Mejunje** ★★ (p. 183).

Day ⑦: Remedios and Back to Havana

In the morning, drive to the nearby town of **Remedios** ★★★ (p. 183). This is one of Cuba's smallest and best-preserved old colonial-era towns. Tour the **Iglesia de San Juan Bautista** ★★ (p. 183), with its intricately carved and ornate baroque altar, and stop for a cool drink or light lunch at the open-air **Café El Louvre** ★ (p. 183) right on the town's central plaza. Allow yourself a little over 4 hours to drive from Remedios back to Havana, where you'll turn in your rental car before taking a flight for the rest of your trip.

Days ⑧ & ⑨: Head East to Baracoa

From Havana, take a flight (booked well in advance) to **Baracoa** ★★★ (p. 255), the oldest, and arguably most beautiful city in Cuba. You'll definitely want to stay in the **Hotel El Castillo** ★★ (p. 259), with its commanding setting on a hillside over the city. Spend 1 day exploring the architecture and old-world charms of the city, and another hiking the lush forests around **El Yunque** ★★ (p. 258). Despite its diminutive size, Baracoa is a bustling little burg with excellent nightlife.

Days ⑩ & ⑪: Sweltering Santiago

In Baracoa, you can arrange for a transfer or private taxi to **Santiago de Cuba** ★★★, the island's second-largest city. If you want to be in the heart of downtown, choose the **Hotel Casa Granda** ★★ (p. 275), while if you're looking for more comfort, amenities, and facilities, you should book a room in the **Meliá Santiago de Cuba** ★★ (p. 277) or stay in some of the city's lovely *casas particulares*. You'll need 2 days to fully explore this colonial-era port city, with its host of historical and architectural attractions. Be sure to schedule at least 1 night at Santiago's fabulous **Casa de la Trova** ★★ (p. 284) or its even better **Casa de las Tradiciones** ★★★.

Days ⑫, ⑬ & ⑭: Hot Sun, Cool Sands, Clear Water

Finish your trip off with some downtime at an all-inclusive resort on **Cayo Largo del Sur** ★★★ (p. 153). You'll have to fly here from Havana, and you're best off just buying a 3-day/2-night package from any of the tour desks in Havana or Santiago. You should easily be able to arrange a flight from Santiago to Havana that connects with a flight to Cayo Largo; be sure that your flight back from Cayo Largo gets you into Havana in time for your international connection and flight home. If you have time pressures, opt for one of the top-end all-inclusives at Varadero ★★.

69

SUGGESTED CUBA ITINERARIES

---

4 CUBA FOR FAMILIES

Most of Cuba's principal attractions—its art, architecture, history, music, cigars, and so on—are geared toward adults. There are, in fact, few attractions or activities geared for the very young. This is why I recommend families base themselves out of a town that has a large all-inclusive resort with a well-developed children's program. For my money, Varadero is the best bet, although a case can be made for Guardalavaca, as well. Both have a host of excellent all-inclusive resorts. If your children are worldly and inquisitive, feel free to swap out some resort days for the more cultural side trips to cities, destinations, and attractions described in some of the other itineraries in this chapter.

Day ❶: Arrive in Varadero

Fly directly into **Varadero.** I recommend the **Tryp Península Varadero** ★★★ (p. 169), which has an excellent children's program and tons of activity and tour options. After settling into your room, check out the **children's program** and any **activities** or **tours** scheduled for the coming days. Feel free to adapt the following days' suggestions accordingly. Spend some time on the beach or at the pool. After dinner, attend the hotel's nightly cabaret show.

Day ❷: Take in an Attraction or Two

Varadero is chock-full of attractions geared toward the whole family. You can head to the lovely **Josone** (p. 162), or see the

dolphin show at the local **Delfinario** (p. 162). If your family is adventurous, try the **Boat Adventure** ★, which is a fast and furious trip through the mangroves aboard sit-on-top motorized watercraft.

Day ❸: A Trip to Trinidad

All of the hotel tour desks offer day trips to **Trinidad** ★★★. While some travel via bus, you should splurge and take a plane. Trinidad is an immaculately preserved colonial city, with a very compact central core that shouldn't tire or bore your children. In fact, they should get a kick out of the rough cobblestone streets, ancient architecture, vibrant street markets, and a real glimpse into everyday Cuban life.

4

CUBA FOR FAMILIES

Day ❹: Parents' Day Off

Drop the kids off with the **children's program** for at least 1 full day and treat yourselves to some time alone. If you play golf, schedule a round at the **Varadero Golf Club** ★ (p. 163). Or, if you want to pamper yourself, take advantage of the excellent **spa services** right at the Tryp Peninsula Varadero. Pick up the kids and treat them to dinner off of the resort grounds. I recommend the **Mesón del Quijote** (p. 170), which is housed in a building with a medieval-style turret beside it.

Day ❺: Head for the High Seas

Sign up for a day cruise on one of the many sailboats operating out of Varadero. These cruises head out to nearby cays, and include some snorkeling time, as well as lunch either on the boat or on some private little island beach.

Day ❻: Parents' Night Off

This is your last day, so take advantage of the resort's in-house facilities and activities, but be sure to reserve a babysitter for the evening and make reservations for dinner and a show at the **Tropicana Matanzas** ★★ (p. 171).

Day ❼: Heading Home

Use any spare time you have before your flight out of **Varadero** to buy last-minute souvenirs and gifts, or just laze on the beach or by the pool.

5 COLONIAL TREASURES HIGHLIGHTS TOUR

Cuba's colonial cities are some of the best-preserved and architecturally intact examples to be found anywhere in the hemisphere. From the remarkable restored grandeur of Old Havana to the rugged realism of Trinidad to tiny Baracoa—the oldest colonial city in the Americas—there's a wealth of history, culture, and overall beauty to be found in the country's colonial treasures.

Days ❶ & ❷: Havana

Follow the itinerary as described above in "Cuba in 2 Weeks."

Day ❸: Cienfuegos

Pick up a rental car and head for **Cienfuegos** ★, a bustling port city on the southern coast, with a compact, yet very attractive, colonial-era core. Get to know the old center around **Parque José Martí**, visiting the **Catedral de la Purísima Concepción** and the **Teatro Tomás Terry** ★ (p. 189). In the afternoon, head out to the Punta Gorda district and have a sunset drink at the **Cienfuegos Yacht Club** (p. 190). For dinner, head to the historic old **Palacio del Valle** ★★ (p. 193).

Day ❹: Trinidad

From Cienfuegos, it's a short hop to **Trinidad** ★★★, with some beautiful scenery along the coast. Stay either in the new **Gran Hotel Iberostar Trinidad** ★★ (p. 200), the **Hotel Las Cuevas** ★, or one of the many *casas particulares* right in the colonial center of this classic little city. Spend the afternoon touring Trinidad's colonial-era landmarks, including the **Plaza Mayor,** the **Plazuela El Jigüe,** the **Iglesia de la Santísima Trinidad,** and the **Museo Romántico** ★★ (p. 198). For dinner, make a reservation at **Paladar Estela** ★★ (p. 203) or **Sol y Son** ★★. After dinner, stroll around the Plaza Mayor and listen for where the action is. It might be a salsa or *son* band playing on the steps below the **Casa de la Música** ★ (p. 202), or it might be in any one of several clubs nearby including the excellent **Palenque de los Congos Reales** ★★.

Day ⑤: Sancti Spíritus

While its colonial center is modest in size and level of restoration, **Sancti Spíritus** nonetheless retains a wonderful sense of its former glory and receives far less tourist traffic than any other city on this tour. You'll definitely want to walk along **Calle Llano** ★, a narrow cobblestone alleyway of pastel-colored and tile-roof houses. You'll also want to have lunch or dinner at one of the outdoor patio tables overlooking the old stone **Puente Yayabo (Yayabo bridge),** which was built in 1825. Be sure to book a room at the **Hostal del Rijo** ★★, a very comfortable hotel in a restored old mansion set right on a quiet little plaza.

Days ⑥ & ⑦: Camagüey

Although far less celebrated—or visited—than Trinidad, **Camagüey** ★★ just may be Cuba's richest colonial-era city, outside of Old Havana, in terms of art, architecture, and general ambience. The city's colonial core retains its highly irregular layout and an unequaled collection of impressive 16th-, 17th-, and 18th-century churches. The city's **Plaza del Carmen** ★★ (p. 228) and **Plaza San Juan de Dios** ★★★ (p. 228) are two impeccable and evocative city squares. Sitting right near the center of all the ancient action, the old **Gran Hotel** ★ (p. 229) should be your first choice.

Day ⑧: Bayamo

Even though most of this city was deliberately torched in 1869 as an act of civil disobedience, it still makes a wonderful stop on a route taking in Cuba's principal colonial cities. You'll definitely want to stay at the new refurbished boutique **Hotel Royalton** ★★ (p. 248), which sits right on the central **Parque Céspedes** ★★.

You'll also want to visit the **Casa Natal de Céspedes** ★ (p. 247), the birthplace of the "father of the Cuban nation," and the only house on the square that escaped destruction from the fire.

Days ⑨ & ⑩: Santiago de Cuba

This is a colonial highlights tour, so you'll want to stay in the heart of downtown; choose either the **Hotel Casa Granda** ★★ (p. 275), the **Hostal Basilio** ★ (p. 275), or the private **Casa Leonardo y Rosa** ★ (p. 276) or **Casa Maruchi** ★. You'll need 2 days to fully explore this beautiful colonial-era port city, with its host of historical and architectural attractions. Be sure to schedule at least 1 night at Santiago's fabulous **Casa de la Trova** ★★★ (p. 284) or its even better **Casa de los Tradiciones** ★★★. Turn in your rental car here in Santiago.

Day ⑪: Baracoa

From Santiago, take a Víazul bus or private taxi to **Baracoa** ★★★ (p. 255), the oldest and arguably most beautiful city in Cuba. It's fitting to finish off this tour in the oldest city on the island. You'll definitely want to stay in the **Hotel El Castillo** ★★ (p. 259), with its commanding setting on a hillside over the city. Spend your time here exploring the architecture and old-world charms of the city. Despite its diminutive size, Baracoa is also a bustling little city with excellent nightlife.

Day ⑫: Heading Home

From Baracoa, take a flight back to **Havana** in time for your international connection. If you have extra time, head to the **Calle Tacón** street market ★★ (p. 124) to do some last-minute shopping before you go.

6 HAVANA IN 3 DAYS

Havana is an amazing—at times, overwhelming—city, overflowing with history, art, architecture, culture, nightlife, and more. Three days will allow you to visit its most important attractions, and maybe even discover some of its lesser-known charms.

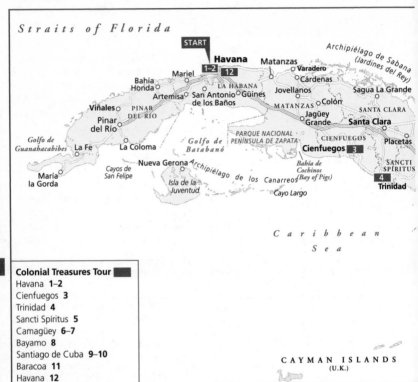

Straits of Florida

START

Havana Matanzas

Archipiélago de Sabana
(Jardines del Rey)

1–2 12

Varadero
Mariel ○Cárdenas
Bahía ○ LA HABANA Jovellanos
Honda ○ San Antonio ○Güines Sagua La Grande
Artemisa○ de los Baños MATANZAS ○Colón
Viñales○ PINAR SANTA CLARA
DEL RÍO Jagüey
Pinar ○ Grande **Santa Clara**
del Río
Golfo de *Golfo de* PARQUE NACIONAL CIENFUEGOS ○Placetas
Guanahacabibes La Fe○ La Coloma *Batabanó* PENÍNSULA DE ZAPATA **Cienfuegos** 3
○ Nueva Gerona *Archipiélago* *Bahía de* SANCTI
Cayos de *Cochinos* SPÍRITUS
María San Felipe *de los Canarreos* (Bay of Pigs) 4
la Gorda Isla de la **Trinidad**
Juventud Cayo Largo

C a r i b b e a n

S e a

Colonial Treasures Tour

Havana **1–2**
Cienfuegos **3**
Trinidad **4**
Sancti Spíritus **5**
Camagüey **6–7**
Bayamo **8**
Santiago de Cuba **9–10**
Baracoa **11**
Havana **12**

C A Y M A N I S L A N D S
(U.K.)

Day ❶: Start in the Old City

Start your day in Habana Vieja. Visit the **Plaza de la Catedral**, the **Plaza de Armas**, **Plaza Vieja**, and **Plaza de San Francisco**. Be sure to tour the **Museo de la Ciudad** ★★ (p. 112), the **Castillo de la Real Fuerza** ★ (p. 109), and any other attractions that catch your attention. Have lunch at **La Bodeguita del Medio** ★ (p. 102). Spend the afternoon exploring the area around Parque Central, which includes **El Capitolio** ★ (p. 114), the **Museo Nacional de las Bellas Artes** ★★ (p. 112), and the **Museo de la Revolución** ★ (p. 112). Make a reservation in advance and take the 2pm tour of the Partagas cigar factory (p. 115). You will not have

time to visit four attractions in one afternoon, so prioritize them beforehand.

As the day cools down, take a stroll on the **Malecón** ★★★ (p. 114). If you've got the energy, you should be able to make the 20-minute walk to the **Hotel Nacional** ★★ (p. 94) in time for a sunset *mojito* at their outdoor bar.

LA GUARIDA ★★★
For dinner, you'll want to climb the rickety, dimly lit steps to La Guarida (p. 105), the city's most celebrated *paladar*. Reservations here are essential.

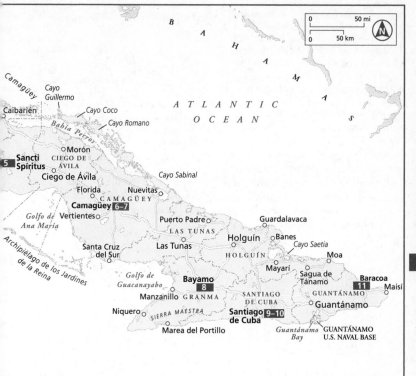

Day ❷: Vedado & Miramar

Start the morning strolling along the beautiful tombs and mausoleums of **Cementerio de Colón** ★★ (p. 116). From here, head over to the outdoor art exhibit that is the **Callejón de Hammel** ★★★ (p. 114). By now, you should have worked up enough of a sweat for a refreshing bowl of ice cream at **Coppelia** ★ (p. 116).

From Vedado, take a Coco Taxi to Miramar and the Playa district. Be sure to visit the **Maqueta de la Habana** ★ (p. 117), a rather impressive mock-up model of the entire city. Since you're out in this neck of the woods, have a late lunch at **La Cocina de Lilliam** ★★★ (p. 107), on the one hand because it's an excellent restaurant, and on the other, because your dinner tonight will be pedestrian at best (though the cabaret show will be unforgettable). After lunch, head to the **José Martí Memorial** (p. 116), and enjoy the panoramic view from the highest spot in Havana. Then, imagine the Plaza de la Revolución fit to bursting during a political rally and admire the iconic **image of Che Guevara cast in iron** ★ on the Ministry of the Interior building opposite the memorial.

TROPICANA ★★★
It's time to pull out all the stops and head to the **Tropicana** (p. 127) for dinner and a show. This place is the original and still the best cabaret show in Cuba. Stick around after the show for some serious salsa dancing in the adjacent Salón Arcos de Cristal club.

Day ❸: More Habana Vieja

Give yourself another day in **Habana Vieja**—there's just no way you've seen it all in 1 day. Be sure to visit some of the art galleries and to spend some time shopping at the **Calle Tacón** outdoor market ★★ (p. 124). Have lunch on one of the ancient plazas here. I recommend either the restaurant **Santo Angel** ★ (p. 103) or the **Cafetería El Portal** (p. 104). In the late afternoon, head over to the **Parque Histórico Morro y Cabaña** ★★ (p. 118) and explore the forts and museums at this complex.

LOS DOCE APÓSTOLES ★
After touring the complex, grab an outdoor table near sunset at **Los Doce Apóstoles** (p. 108), and enjoy the view of Havana across the harbor from this restaurant. Be sure to finish your dinner in time for the *cañonazo* ceremony.

After dinner and the *cañonazo*, head to **Zorra y el Cuervo** ★★ (p. 128) for a late-night jazz concert.

Havana

It's hard to convey the wonder, sensuality, and alluring fallen beauty of Havana. It's hard to imagine a city with such rhythm and verve, a city at once so tremendously vibrant and at the same time laid-back—that is, until you've taken a lazy stroll along the Malecón, gotten lost in the time warp of La Habana Vieja's colonial cobblestone streets, taken a ride in a 1940 Dodge taxi through crumbling Centro Habana, danced salsa until dawn after catching the Tropicana floor show, or witnessed Afro-Cuban religious rituals on the street.

Originally established in 1514 on Cuba's southern coast, San Cristóbal de la Habana had been moved by 1519 to its present-day location on the island's north coast, at the mouth of a deep and spacious harbor with a narrow, protected harbor channel. Before long, Havana had become the most important port in the Spanish colonial empire, a natural final gathering place for the resupply and embarkation of the Spanish fleet before returning to the Old Country laden with bounty. By 1607, Havana had been declared the capital of colonial Cuba, and by the early 1700s, it was the third-largest city in the Spanish empire, behind Mexico City and Lima.

Subsequent centuries saw Havana grow steadily in wealth, size, and prominence. Havana was luckily spared the bulk of the violence and fighting that occurred in Cuba's Wars of Independence, and later revolutionary war. Following the sinking of the USS *Maine* in Havana harbor in 1898, a long period of direct U.S. control and indirect U.S. influence followed. This period saw the first indications of suburban sprawl and the growing importance of the western neighborhoods of Vedado and Miramar. This era was also marked by a strong presence of mob activity, with the likes of Al Capone, Meyer Lansky, and Lucky Luciano setting up shop in Havana.

Havana has been largely frozen in time in the wake of the 1959 Revolution. Decades of economic crisis and shortages have left much of Havana in severe decay and decomposition. The great exception to this rule is La Habana Vieja, where parts have been meticulously restored to much of its colonial glory. Although the situation in Havana is beginning to change, with the recent boom in tourism and tourism-related growth, what new construction has occurred over the past 40 years has largely borne the drab architectural stamp of the former Soviet Union and its central state planning. Luckily, most of this has taken place outside the boundaries of the traditional city center. Today, Havana, with some 2.5 million inhabitants, is the largest city in the Caribbean and Cuba's undisputed political, business, and cultural center.

---

1 ORIENTATION

ARRIVING
By Plane

Arriving international passengers clear Customs on the ground level of Terminal 3 at the **José Martí International Airport** (© 7/266-4133; airport code HAV). All of the major car-rental agencies have kiosks or booths just outside of Customs. There's also an **Infotur** kiosk ((© 7/266-4094; www.infotur.cu), where you can buy a map and pick up some brochures, and you should even be able to get help with reservations.

There's an ATM among all the booths and kiosks on the ground floor, and another on the second floor, where departing passengers check in. Etecsa, the national phone company, has booths with card-operated pay phones on this level, as well as on the second floor. You can either buy a card from them, if their booth is manned, or from one of the souvenir vendors on the second floor.

Taxis wait in a long line just outside the ground-floor exit. Cars are marked with different names, such as **Taxi OK** or **Panataxi.** However, in summer 2008, all taxis changed their name to Cubataxi and all are run by the Ministry of Transport. The rate to any hotel in downtown Havana is CUC$20 to CUC$25 (US$22–US$27/£11–£14); airport taxis refuse to use their meters on this run.

Some charter flights and all national flights arrive at either Terminal 1 or 2. Both terminals also have Infotur offices or kiosks, an ATM or two, telephones, and taxis.

If you're driving from the airport, the main artery into Havana is Avenida de Rancho Boyeros. This will bring you to the Plaza de la Revolución and the towering José Martí Memorial. In general terms, if you continue straight, or roughly north toward the sea, you will hit the University of Havana and Vedado. Miramar and Playa will be to the left (west) and are best reached via the Malecón, while Centro Habana and La Habana Vieja will be to the right (east).

By Car

Entering Havana by car is a confusing mess. Almost none of the major arteries into downtown are marked. This is especially true of the Autopista Nacional coming in from the east, which dumps you unceremoniously into the midst of an urban mess of some of the city's outer neighborhoods. Similarly, while there is ostensibly a beltway, or *Circunvalación,* around the downtown area, it and its various exits are virtually entirely unmarked.

One good tactic for navigating Havana is to somehow find your way to the Malecón; from there, the entire city is relatively easily accessible. The main thoroughfare through Miramar and Playa is Avenida 5.

By Train

The principal train station, or **Estación Central,** is located in La Habana Vieja at Calle Egido and Calle Arsenal ((© 7/861-4259). There are always plenty of taxis waiting at the station.

By Bus

The main **Víazul** bus station ((© 7/881-1413 or 7/881-5652; www.viazul.com) is located at Avenida 26 and Zoológico in Nuevo Vedado, on the outskirts of downtown. From here, it is a CUC$3 (US$3.25/£1.60) taxi ride to Vedado and CUC$4 to CUC$5 (US$4.30–US$5.40/£2.15–£2.70) to La Habana Vieja. **Astro** buses ((© 7/870-9401) arrive at their main terminal at Avenida de la Independencia and Calle 19 de Mayo, near the Plaza de la Revolución. There are always taxis available at both stations.

By Boat

Marlin's Marina Hemingway, Avenida 5 and Calle 248, Santa Fe, Playa ((© 7/204-1150 or 7/204-6848; www.nauticamarlin.com), is the principal port of call and official point of entry for clearing Customs and Immigration. When arriving by sea, contact the

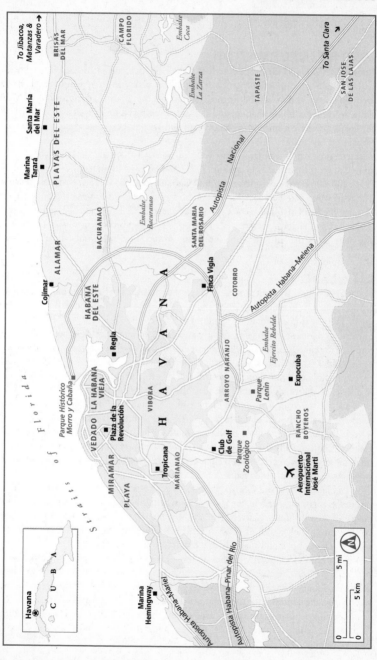

HAVANA

5

ORIENTATION

To Jibacoa, Matanzas & Varadero →

To Santa Clara ↗

BRISAS DEL MAR

CAMPO FLORIDO

Embalse Coca

TAPASTE

SAN JOSE DE LAS LAJAS

Santa Maria del Mar

PLAYAS DEL ESTE

Embalse La Zarza

Marina Tarará

Nacional

Autopista

Embalse Bacuranao

SANTA MARIA DEL ROSARIO

BACURANAO

ALAMAR

Cojimar

HABANA DEL ESTE

Finca Vigia

COTORRO

Autopista Habana–Melena

Regla

Embalse Ejercito Rebelde

ARROYO NARANJO

Parque Histórico Morro y Cabaña

LA HABANA VIEJA

VIBORA

Expocuba

H A V A N A

VEDADO

Plaza de la Revolución

Club de Golf

Parque Lenin

RANCHO BOYEROS

MIRAMAR

Tropicana

MARIANAO

Parque Zoológico

PLAYA

Aeropuerto Internacional José Marti

✈

S t r a i t s   o f   F l o r i d a

Havana ✴

C U B A

Marina Hemingway

Autopista Habana–Mariel

Autopista Habana–Pinar del Rio

N

5 mi

5 km

0

0

marina before entering Cuban waters (19km/12 miles offshore) on VHF channels 16 or 72, or HF channel 7462.

Commercial cruise ships dock at the Sierra Maestra Terminal in La Habana Vieja, just off the Plaza de San Francisco.

VISITOR INFORMATION

Infotur (© 7/866-3333; www.infotur.cu), Calle Obispo, corner of Bernaza, is the official state-run tourist information agency. It has offices or kiosks in several strategic spots around Havana, and in each of the three terminals at the airport. It can provide you with some brochures and information, and can usually help you make reservations. Most of the kiosks also have a small selection of maps and various local tourist guides and books for sale.

There are a handful of large, state-run tour agencies that have desks at most hotels around town; these include **Havanatur** (© 7/204-8409; www.havanatur.cu), **Cubanacán** (© 7/208-6044; www.cubanacan.cu), and **Cubatur** (© 7/835-4155; www.cubatur.cu). These are your best bets for information and tour bookings around the country. In Havana, the **San Cristóbal** agency, part of Habaguanex, Calle Oficios 110 bajos between Calles Lamparilla and Amarguar (© 7/861-9171; www.viajessancristobal.cu) also provides city tours that include some interesting sociocultural tours not offered by other agencies.

CITY LAYOUT

Havana is a major city built around its ample and protected harbor. The oldest colonial-era buildings are closest to the harbor, and the bulk of the expansion heads out west from there. The city is bordered along its northern edge by the Caribbean Sea. The majority of Havana's denizens live in large, densely populated working-class neighborhoods to the south of the principal downtown business and tourist neighborhoods. While there are communities on the eastern side of the harbor, the most important neighborhoods and developments are all found on the western side. These communities are generally laid out in a series of abutting grids, although they often abut at odd angles.

While the streets in Vedado and Playa tend to be numbered or carry a letter designation, the neighborhoods of La Habana Vieja and Centro Habana have only named streets. To make matters more confusing, most of the streets in La Habana Vieja and Centro Habana have two or more names—those that appear on maps and street signs are often different from their common names. Wherever possible, I've tried to give the most common and popularly used name.

In La Habana Vieja and Centro Habana, street names are generally displayed on little plaques or signs attached to the sides of corner buildings at street intersections. The plaques tend to be hung relatively high, at about 3m (10 ft.) or so. In Vedado and Playa, you'll want to look lower, as most intersections feature a .5m-high (1½-ft.) concrete block in a sort of pyramid shape, with the street name engraved on it.

Street addresses are usually given as follows: Prado no. 22, e/Tejadillo y Empedrado; or 23 e/L y M. In the case of the first example, the address is for building 22 on Paseo del Prado, located between the cross streets Calle Tejadillo and Calle Empedrado. In the second case, the address is for an unnumbered building on Calle 23 between Calles L and M. Note that Cuban addresses frequently omit the word "Calle" or "Avenida." Also, Cubans usually refer to Avenida 5 as "Quinta Avenida," "5ta Avenida," or—most commonly—simply "5ta."

HAVANA

5

ORIENTATION

ACCOMMODATIONS ■
Hotel Ambos Mundos **13**
Hotel Conde de Villanueva **7**
Hotel Deauville **42**
Hotel del Tejadillo **21**
Hotel Florida **16**
Hotel Inglaterra **35**
Hotel Lido **28**
Hotel Los Frailes **4**
Hotel Plaza **32**
Hotel Raquel **2**
Hotel Santa Isabel **9**
Hotel Saratoga **39**
Hotel Sevilla **30**
Hotel Telégrafo **34**
NH Parque Central **31**
Park View Hotel **27**

DINING ◆
Café del Oriente **6**
Café La Mina **14**
Café Taberna **3**
Cafetería El Portal **18**
El Bodegón Criollo **23**
El Floridita **33**
El Templete **10**
La Bodeguita del Medio **17**
La Divina Pastora **24**
La Dominica **12**
La Guarida **41**
La Paella **8**
La Taberna de la Muralla **1**
Los Doce Apóstoles **25**
Los Nardos **38**
Restaurant-Pizzeria El
Asturianito **38**

Roof Garden Restaurant **30**
Santo Angel **5**

ATTRACTIONS ●
Castillo de la Real Fuerza **11**
Catedral de San Cristóbal **19**
Centro Wifredo Lam **20**
Chinatown **40**
El Capitolio **36**
El Templete **10**
Fábrica de Tabaco Partagas **37**
Museo de la Ciudad **15**
Museo de la Revolucíon y
Memorial *Granma* **26**
Museo Nacional de Bellas Artes **29**
Parque la Maestranza **22**

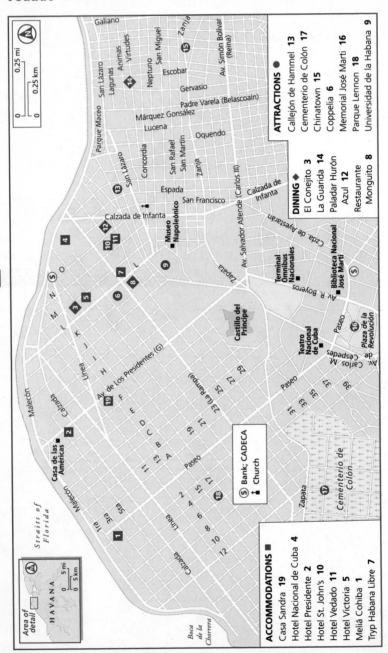

0   0.25 mi
0   0.25 km

Straits of
Florida

Boca
de la
Chorrera

Galiano
San Miguel
Zanja
Av. Simón Bolívar
(Reina)
San Lázaro
Animas
Virtudes
Lagunas
Neptuno
Escobar
Gervasio
Padre Varela (Belascoaín)
Márquez González
Lucena
Oquendo
Zanja
San Rafael
San Martín
Concordia
Espada
San Francisco
Calzada de
Infanta
Calzada de Infanta
Parque Maceo
San Lázaro

**Museo
Napoleónico**

Av. Salvador Allende (Carlos III)
Cda. de Ayestarán
Zapata
Av. Boyeros

**Terminal
Omnibus
Nacionales**

**Biblioteca Nacional
José Martí**

**Castillo del
Príncipe**

**Teatro
Nacional
de Cuba**

Carlos M.
Av. de
Céspedes

**Plaza de la
Revolución**

Paseo
Paseo
Zapata

**Cementerio de
Colón**

Malecón
Calzada
Línea
Av. de Los Presidentes (G)
Casa de las
Américas
23 (la Rampa)
Paseo

1ra
5ta
Línea
Calzada
Paseo

Bank; CADECA
Church

DINING ◆
El Conejito **3**
La Guarida **14**
Paladar Hurón
Azul **12**
Restaurante
Monguito **8**

ATTRACTIONS ●
Callejón de Hammel **13**
Cementerio de Colón **17**
Chinatown **15**
Coppelia **6**
Memorial José Martí **16**
Parque Lennon **18**
Universidad de la Habana **9**

ACCOMMODATIONS ■
Casa Sandra **19**
Hotel Nacional de Cuba **4**
Hotel Presidente **2**
Hotel St. John's **10**
Hotel Vedado **11**
Hotel Victoria **5**
Meliá Cohiba **1**
Tryp Habana Libre **7**

ACCOMMODATIONS ■
Aparthotel
  Montehabana **5**
Hotel Chateau Miramar **6**
Hotel Comodoro **2**
Meliá Habana **3**
Occidental Miramar **4**
Residencias Miramar **8**

DINING ◆
Don Cangrejo **13**
El Aljibe **10**
El Tocororo **14**
La Cocina de Lilliam **9**

ATTRACTIONS ●
Acuario Nacional **7**
Casa Compay Segundo **12**
Maqueta de la Habana **11**
Marina Hemingway **1**

$ Bank; CADECA
✝ Church

Area of detail

HAVANA

0   5 mi
0   5 km

0   0.25 mi
0   0.25 km

Straits of Florida

Almendares

Boca de la Chorrera

Teatro Karl Marx

MIRAMAR

Parque Miramar

Santa Rita de Cassia

KOHLY

LA SIERRA

ALMENDARES

AMPLIACIÓN DE ALMENDARES

QUEREJETA

NEIGHBORHOODS IN BRIEF

La Habana Vieja La Habana Vieja (Old Havana) is the historic colonial heart of Havana. Situated at the eastern edge of the city, in the area beginning around the Paseo del Prado, or Paseo de Martí, and the Parque Central, and extending to the Harbor Channel, it is a dense collection of colonial-era and neocolonial houses, mansions, churches, seminaries, and apartment buildings punctuated by a few picturesque plazas and parks. UNESCO declared La Habana Vieja a World Heritage Site in 1982, and today it is one of the most beautiful restored colonial cities in the world. You will find the city's greatest collection of museums and attractions here, as well as a broad selection of restaurants and beautifully restored boutique hotels. This is an area best explored on foot.

Centro Habana In many ways, Central Havana is little more than the necessary and neglected area connecting La Habana Vieja with Vedado. It is defined on its northern edge by the Malecón, the seaside pedestrian walkway that stretches from La Habana Vieja to the end of Vedado. The stretch of the Malecón (and everything inland from it) between the Hotel Nacional and La Habana Vieja is a study in decay and decomposition. Still, it is quite picturesque and charming in its own way. Centro Habana is primarily a residential area, although it does have a high concentration of *casas particulares* (private rooms for rent).

Beware: I cannot stress enough the level of decay and decomposition here. Balconies, crown molding, and other large chunks of brick, mortar, and stone regularly drop off buildings here, sometimes injuring passersby below.

Vedado & the Plaza de la Revolución Beginning more or less at the Hotel Nacional and extending west to the Almendares River, and south to the Plaza de la Revolución, Vedado is a busy mix of middle- to upper-class houses and businesses. As the older sections of La Habana Vieja and Centro Habana began to overflow, residential and business growth centered on Vedado. Calle 23, or La Rampa, is the principal avenue defining Vedado, and it's where you'll find Coppelia, the Tryp Habana Libre (former Havana Hilton), and the Hotel Nacional. The broad Plaza de la Revolución sits on high ground on the southern edge of Vedado and houses several government agencies, in addition to the towering José Martí Memorial, the National Theater, and the National Library.

Playa This upscale residential district is located just west of Vedado, past the Almendares River. The most important neighborhood here is **Miramar,** home to many prominent businesses and most of the resident foreign community in Cuba. Almost all of the various embassies and diplomatic missions have set up shop in the various Batista-era mansions that make up this neighborhood. There are several large and luxurious, business-class hotels here, as well as many private rooms for rent in wonderfully maintained, neocolonial mansions.

Habana del Este & Playas del Este On the eastern banks of the harbor is Habana del Este, and about 11km (6³/₄ miles) farther east along the coast are the Playas del Este, or eastern beaches, which stretch on for about 15km (9 miles) of their own. Habana del Este and Playas del Este are connected to the rest of Havana by a tunnel running between La Habana Vieja and the area around the Morro Castle. There are also frequent little passenger ferries running between La Habana Vieja and the neighborhoods of Regla and Casablanca. The towns that comprise Habana del Este, Alamar, Cojímar, and Ciudad Panamericana are working class and industrial. The beaches of Playas del Este, on the other hand, are beautiful stretches of white sand fronting the Caribbean Sea. These beaches are popular with both Cubans and travelers alike.

Near the Airport The area near and around the airport is an industrial wasteland. There are no hotels or facilities for tourists in the area directly around the airport. Playa and Miramar, about a 15- to 20-minute drive away, are the closest neighborhoods for travelers looking for quick access to the airport; however, the extra time and distance to hotels in Vedado or La Habana Vieja are rather negligible.

2 GETTING AROUND

BY TAXI

There is a host of different taxi cars with modern fleets geared toward the tourist trade. They have all just been reunited under Ministry of Transport management and, although they continue to carry the names of the previous companies such as Panataxi, Taxi OK, and Transgaviota, they are now all called **Cubataxi** and can be called on a central number (© 7/855-5555-59). All tourist taxis have meters. (Taxi drivers claiming their meters are broken are gearing up to rip off tourists.) Rates vary somewhat, but most of the meters start at CUC$1 (US$1.10/55p) for the first kilometer and then charge between CUC$.50 and CUC$.85 (US55¢–US90¢/25p–45p) for each additional kilometer. The most economical cabs are the yellow old-style Panataxis without air-conditioning, followed by the new yellow models with air-conditioning. Fénix (© 7/866-6666) is the most expensive cab service in Havana and is the only one (in addition to the Gran Car service, see below) that continues to operate under its own name.

Other options include horse-drawn carriages; the so-called **Coco Taxis** (© 7/873-1411), round open-air two seaters powered by a motorcycle; and antique cars that range from a Ford Model T to a 1957 Chevy. Both the horse-drawn carriages and Coco Taxis cost from CUC$5 to CUC$10 (US$5.40–US$11/£2.70–£5.40) per hour, with a minimum of around CUC$3 (US$3.25/£1.60). **Gran Car** (© 7/881-0992) is the most reputable agent for antique-car rentals. Gran Car rates, with a driver, run CUC$25 (US$27/£14) per hour or CUC$125 (US$135/£68) per day, or CUC$30 (US$32/£16) per hour and CUC$150 (US$162/£81) per day for convertibles.

Peso taxis, *bicitaxis* (bicycle taxis), and freelance taxis are lesser options for most tourists. All are illegal for tourists, although it's the driver, not the rider, who is at risk. If you choose one of these options, be sure to fix your price beforehand, and don't be surprised if the driver is somewhat paranoid about the money transfer, and/or refuses to drop you off right at your hotel, or changes the route when he spots the police.

BY FOOT

Havana is a great town to walk around. It's almost entirely flat and very safe. Early morning, late afternoon, and early evening are the prime times to walk. High heat and heavy humidity can make long walks, particularly around midday, a little uncomfortable. La Habana Vieja is best explored on foot, and a walk along the Malecón is obligatory.

Attractions in Vedado and Miramar are a little spread out, making them less desirable to explore on foot, although a walk along La Rampa in Vedado, or Quinta Avenida (Av. 5) in Miramar, are both rewarding.

BY CAR

There's really no reason for tourists to rent a car to explore Havana. Taxis are plentiful and relatively inexpensive. Moreover, streets are poorly marked and it's a confusing city to navigate.

One exception would be to rent an antique car from **Gran Car** (© 7/881-0992). Gran Car's fleet runs from restored 1930s open-air Ford cruisers to classic 1950s Chevys, Buicks, De Sotos, and Studebakers. Rates, with a driver, run around CUC$25 (US$27/£14) per hour up to CUC$150 (US$162/£81) per day, depending on whether the car is a convertible or not.

If you do want to rent a modern car while in Havana, there is a host of options, including **Cubacar** (© 7/273-2277; cubacar@transtur.cu); **Havanautos** (© 7/835-3142; havanautos@transtur.cu); and **Rex** (© 7/835-6830 or 7/683-0303). All three are run by **Transtur** (© 7/862-2686 or 7/861-5885; www.transtur.cu). **Micar** (© 7/204-7777) and **Vía Rent a Car** (© 7/861-4465; www.gaviota-grupo.com) are also options. All of the above companies have desks at the airport and at a host of major hotels around Havana. See "Getting Around" in chapter 3 for more information.

In general, traffic is much lighter than you'd find in most major urban areas. However, you do have to pay more attention to a wide range of obstacles, from pedestrians and bicyclists to horse-drawn carriages. While most roads in Havana are in pretty decent shape, it's not uncommon to come across huge potholes or torn-up sections of road with no markings or warnings. Moreover, street markings and signs are minimal, making navigation challenging.

BY BUS

For all intents and purposes, Havana's woefully overburdened urban bus system is not a viable option for tourists. Routes and service are inconsistent, the buses are overcrowded, and there are no readily available route maps and schedules.

Truly hearty travelers and independent souls can give the local buses a try. Your best bet is to query locals about routes and hours and where to find the appropriate stop. A large number of metro buses either originate or have a stop at the Parque de la Fraternidad, a block south of the Capitolio. A new bus service, known as *taxi rutero,* has begun, costing five Cuban pesos. Most buses are entered from the front, although some are still entered from the rear and use an honor system of passing your coins forward. Some have separate lines for those wanting a seat *(sentado)* and those willing to stand *(parado).* Fares run around 40 centavos to one peso in Cuban pesos *(moneda nacional).*

Transtur has started operating red **HabanaBusTour** coaches (© 7/831-7333; www.transtur.cu) on three routes with a hop-on/hop-off service for CUC$5 (US$5.40/£2.70) a day. The routes cover La Habana Vieja to the Plaza de la Revolución, Plaza de la Revolución to Marina Hemingway through Miramar, and Parque Central to Playas del Este. They run from 9am to 9:20pm daily. All schedules are marked at the bright red bus stops.

Fast Facts **Havana**

Airport See "Arriving," earlier in this chapter.

Babysitters Your hotel front desk is your best bet for finding a babysitter.

Bookstores In La Habana Vieja, check out **La Moderna Poesía,** Calle Obispo 527 (© **7/861-6640**), or **La Librería Internacional,** Calle Obispo 526 (© **7/861-3283**), which are directly across the street from each other. In Vedado, head to **Ateneo,** Calle Linea, between Calles 12 and 14 (© **7/833-9609**).

Car Rentals See "Getting Around," above.

Currency Exchange Currency exchange offices are ubiquitous around Havana. There are branches of the state-run *casa de cambio* **CADECA** (© **7/855-5701**) throughout Havana, as well as at the airport and in the lobbies of most major hotels. Most banks will also exchange money.

Dentists **Hospital Cira García,** Calle 20 no. 4101, Playa (© **7/204-4300** or 204-2811; www.cirag.cu), and other major medical centers also provide dental care. If you want a specific recommendation, contact your embassy, or ask at your hotel's front desk. Alternately, you can contact **Asistur** (© **7/866-4499;** www.asistur.cu), which can help you with dental emergencies.

Doctors Cuba has a surfeit of doctors and many hotels catering to tourists have one or two on staff. If not, your hotel is still probably your best bet for a recommendation. You can also try contacting your embassy or **Asistur** (© **7/866-4499;** www.asistur. cu), which specializes in emergency medical care and insurance for travelers.

Drugstores Well-stocked drugstores are few and far between in Havana. There's a 24-hour pharmacy at the international terminal of the José Martí airport (© **7/266-4105**). The pharmacies at the **Hotel Plaza** (© **7/861-5703**) in La Habana Vieja, and **Tryp Havana Libre** (© **7/838-4593**) in Vedado, are usually decently stocked. In Miramar, you can try the **Farmacia Internacional,** Avenida 41 and Calle 20 (© **7/204-2051**), also at Avenida 3 and Calle 82 (© **7/204-4515**) and Avenida 7 and Calle 26 (© **7/204-7980**).

Embassies & Consulates See "Fast Facts: Cuba," in Appendix A.

Emergencies Dial © **106** for **police;** © **838-1185** or 838-2185 for an **ambulance;** and © **105** for the **fire department.** At none of these numbers can you assume you will find an English-speaking person on the other end. Also, you can try contacting **Asistur** (© **7/866-4499**), which specializes in emergency medical care for travelers.

Express Mail Services The main office of **DHL,** Calle 26 and Avenida 1, Miramar (© **7/204-1578;** www.dhl.com), will pick up and deliver anywhere in Havana. **EMS Cubapost,** Calle 21 no. 1009, between Calles 10 and 12, Vedado (© **7/831-3328**), is a Cuban-run express mail service with a desk at most post offices.

Eyeglasses Look for the word *óptica.* **Optica Miramar,** Avenida 7 and Calle 24, Miramar (© **7/204-2269**), is one of the better *ópticas* catering to foreign residents and visitors. It has a branch in downtown Havana at Calle Neptuno 411, between San Nicolás and Manrique (© **7/862-1292**).

Hospitals Your best bet is **Hospital Cira García,** Calle 20 no. 4101, Playa (© **7/204-4300** or 7/204-2811; www.cirag.cu), which provides emergency services and long-term care. Another possibility is the **Hospital Hermanos Almeijeiras,** Calles San Lázaro and Belascoaín, Centro Habana (© 7/876-1000).

Internet Access Internet access is becoming more common and available in Havana. The most popular Internet cafe in town is located at **El Capitolio** (p. 114). The rate here is CUC$5 (US$5.40/£2.70) per hour, and the 10 machines here are often booked solid. Aside from this, your best options are the various hotels with business centers and/or Internet cafes; most of these charge between CUC$6 and CUC$8 (US$6.50–US$8.65/£3.25–£4.30) per hour, with even higher rates occasionally charged at the fancier hotels. Alternately, you can go to any **Etecsa** office. These offices sell disposable access cards at CUC$6 (US$6.50/£3.25) per hour, which are good at any Internet-equipped Etecsa office in the country. There's one at Calles Obispo, corner of Calle Habana, in La Habana Vieja.

Maps The various Infotur booths and kiosks around town sell a pretty decent map of Havana for CUC$1 (US$1.10/55p); sometimes they'll even give you a copy for free. Most rental-car agencies and hotels can also give you a copy of the same, or a similar, map. The Cuban Geographic and Cartographic Institute publishes a couple of much more detailed maps of Havana, including the *Ciudad de la Habana Mapa Turistica,* which you can get at most tourist gift shops and Infotur kiosks. You'll also find good maps online at **www.cubaroutes.com** and **www.cubamapa.com**. The best road map to Cuba is the Guía de Carreteras published by Limusa; it can be bought at El Navegante, Calle Mercaderes 115 between Obispo and Obrapía.

Photographic Needs Most of your photographic needs will be met by the rival chains of **Photoservice** and **Photoclub**. Their shops offer 1-hour or overnight developing services and usually carry an assortment of film and some replacement batteries. Between the two chains, there are numerous outlets across Havana. For any repairs or more complicated needs, try **Fotografía Luz Habana,** Calle Tacón 22, between Calles O'Reilly and Empedrado, La Habana Vieja (© 7/863-4263).

Police Dial © **106.** Although it's possible for someone who speaks English to be rounded up, do not expect to find an English-speaking person on the other end. In the event of serious danger, you are probably better off contacting your embassy (nonlicensed U.S. citizens should contact the U.S. Interests Section only as a last resort).

Post Office Most major hotels either have small post office branches, or will sell you stamps and post letters. This is generally your best bet, as the *correos* (public post office branches) are often crowded and inefficient. In La Habana Vieja, there's a *correo* on the west end of the Plaza de San Francisco. There's another on the side of the Gran Teatro toward the Capitolio. Both are open Monday through Saturday from 8am to 5pm.

Safety Havana is a very safe city. There's a strong police presence and street crime is uncommon, especially in tourist areas. But because streetlights are virtually nonexistent, it's wise to avoid the dark alleys and side streets of Havana after dark. Popular tourist spots are relatively safe at night. Still, given the vast economic gap between Cubans and tourists, you should be careful about where you walk and whom you engage. It is best not to wear much jewelry or make other showy signs of wealth.

Taxis See "Getting Around," earlier in this chapter.

3 WHERE TO STAY

There's a wide range of hotel options and *casas particulares* (private rooms) for rent in Havana. Hotel options are divvied up among the large state-run chains. **Habaguanex** has monopoly control over the hotel scene in La Habana Vieja, and **Gaviota, Cubanacán,** and **Gran Caribe** own the remainder of the midrange to upper-end hotels around Havana. Of the international hotel chains, the major player in town is the Spanish-owned **Sol Meliá,** which manages three large, high-end properties in Havana. Havana will get its first designer hotel when British company Esencia Hotels & Resorts reopens the Hotel Victoria in Vedado in spring 2009. Given the fact that hotel chains control so much of the market, one major problem is a generalized lax attitude toward overbooking. Habaguanex and Gran Caribe are particularly notorious for this. Confirmed reservations at Gran Caribe's Hotel Nacional or Habaguanex's Santa Isabel have been shuttled off to one of their sister properties, usually with no compensation and little sympathy.

There are hundreds of *casas particulares* in Havana. The neighborhoods of Centro Habana, Vedado, and Playa have the greatest concentration of *casas particulares,* although La Habana Vieja is starting to catch up. In general, the rooms and homes are kept very clean, while the furnishings and amenities are quite simple. The rates average between CUC$20 and CUC$35 (US$22–US$38/£11–£19) per room, and meals are often available at very reasonable prices. With the broad range of *casa particulares* and rapid turnover in the market, it's impossible to list a representative selection. I've tried to include the most dependable and long-standing options in each neighborhood below. In addition, you can check out www.casaparticular.info and www.casaparticular.org.

Given the compact nature of Havana, the proximity of its major attractions, and the wide availability of relatively inexpensive taxis, the neighborhood you choose is not a limiting factor. In general, most visitors will want to spend most of their time exploring La Habana Vieja, so the hotels there or nearby in Centro Habana are best for direct walking access. Large group and package tourists, as well as business travelers, are usually funneled toward hotels in Miramar and Playa, about a 10- to 15-minute ride away from most of the action, although the area is home to some of the better dining and nightlife spots. Vedado is a sort of middle ground, with plenty of accommodations and dining choices, easy access to the rest of the city's attractions, and quite a few natural charms of its own.

Note: While 110-volt electricity with standard U.S.-style plugs are the national norm, the high percentage of European travelers has led many hotels to add on 220-volt outlets or to fully convert. The Meliá chain, for example, has mostly 220-volt outlets, although it usually provides at least one 110-volt outlet in each bathroom.

LA HABANA VIEJA

With few exceptions, all of the hotels in Old Havana are run by the Cuban chain **Habaguanex.** All of these are intimate boutique hotels in beautifully refurbished old buildings. I've listed my favorite Habaguanex hotels below, but there are others that are nearly as nice; check www.habaguanexhotels.com for the complete listing. One nice perk of staying at a Habaguanex hotel is that you get free admission to most of the museums in Old Havana.

Very Expensive

Hotel Conde de Villanueva ★ This place is geared toward cigar freaks, and only true aficionados should stay here. The hotel features one of the better and most respected cigar shops in town, La Casa del Habano, which rents out private humidors so that regular clients can always have their own personal reserve. The rooms are large and soaked in old-world charm, not to mention the scent of tobacco—all are smoking rooms, of course. The better and more expensive rooms come with views over the street. The building dates back to the end of the 18th century, and features a large portrait of its namesake count in the entryway. Sebastian, the pet peacock, roams the large central courtyard. The semiformal Vuelta Abajo restaurant serves good Cuban cuisine, and there's a wonderful, shady little park just across the street.

Calle Mercaderes 202 (btw. Calles Lamparilla and Amargura), La Habana Vieja. ℂ 7/862-9293. Fax 7/862-9682. www.habaguanexhotels.com. 9 units. CUC$130–CUC$160 (US$140–US$173/£70–£86) double; CUC$200–CUC$242 (US$216–US$261/£108–£131) suite. Rates include breakfast. MC, V. Free parking. **Amenities:** Restaurant; bar; concierge; 24-hr room service; laundry service; dry cleaning. *In room:* A/C, TV, minibar, safe.

Hotel Florida ★★ (Finds)   This is my favorite of the converted old colonial mansions in La Habana Vieja. Built in 1836 and turned into a hotel in 1885, the Florida is stately and elegant and I'd give it an unqualified nod over the Hotel Santa Isabel (see below), except for the fact that a couple of the rooms don't have any windows. However, if you do get one of the window rooms or one of the suites, you may find it hard to head out and explore the city. The rooms are decorated with a mix of imitation and real antique furnishings, wrought-iron beds, checkerboard marble floors, and tasteful framed prints. The entrance is right on the busy Calle Obispo, and it's possible to miss it amid all the hustle and bustle. The tranquil central courtyard provides immediate relief, surrounded by soaring stone columns connected by high arches. If the Florida is full, the newly opened Hotel Marqués de Prado Ameno (253 O'Reilly btw. Cuba and Aguiar), with its cloistered courtyard, is accessed through the Florida and shares the same management. Its 16 spacious rooms with marble floors still retain parts of the original friezes.

Calle Obispo (corner of Calle Cuba), La Habana Vieja. ℂ 7/862-4127. Fax 7/862-4117. www.habaguanexhotels.com. 25 units. CUC$130–CUC$160 (US$140–US$173/£70–£86) double; CUC$180–CUC$200 (US$194–US$216/£97–£108) suite. Rates include breakfast. Rates slightly lower during off season, higher during peak weeks. MC, V. Free valet parking. **Amenities:** 2 restaurants; 2 bars; concierge; tour desk; car-rental desk; 24-hr. room service; laundry service; dry cleaning. *In room:* A/C, TV, minibar, hair dryer, safe.

Hotel Raquel ★   This is one of the newer additions to the Habaguanex chain, and yet another stunningly restored old building. The facade is a visual orgy of bas-relief work, while the centerpiece of the marble-tiled lobby here is a soaring stained-glass atrium ceiling. The third-floor rooms share a large rooftop terrace, with wonderful views over Old Havana. The rooms themselves are spacious and attractively decorated with lamp fixtures and headboards of artistically crafted iron. However, at these prices I'd expect more than a 13-inch television and two twin beds (only two of the standard rooms here have a queen-size bed, although the suites do come with a king-size bed). This is often called "the Jewish hotel." The restaurant features borscht and latkes, while various lobby displays pay homage to Cuba's small, but active Jewish tradition. In fact, many of the staff members are drawn from the local Jewish community.

Calle Amargura, at the corner of San Ignacio, La Habana Vieja. ℂ 7/860-8280. Fax 7/860-8275. www.habaguanexhotels.com. 25 units. CUC$160–CUC$200 (US$173–US$216/£86–£108) double; CUC$230–CUC$250 (US$248–US$270/£124–£135) suite. Rates include breakfast. Rates slightly lower during off season, higher during peak weeks. MC, V. Free valet parking. **Amenities:** Restaurant; bar; gym; concierge; tour desk; 24-hr. room service; laundry service. *In room:* A/C, TV, minibar, hair dryer, safe.

Hotel Santa Isabel ★★   This is one of the most highly touted hotels of the Habaguanex chain, and it *is* a lovely little hotel, wonderfully located on the eastern end of the

Plaza de Armas. Still, they're stretching things when they tout it as a top-tier luxury hotel. Sure, it's elegant and charming, and definitely a top choice in Old Havana, but the rooms and bathrooms are rather compact, and you won't find many of the amenities you'd expect at most luxury hotels. The rooms themselves are dark and understated, with high ceilings and iron bed frames. The junior suites have a small sitting room and extra television, as well as Jacuzzi jets in their standard-size tubs. However, the best rooms in the house, aside from the sumptuous Santovenia suite, are nos. 304 through 314, which come with large rooftop terraces overlooking the plaza. The central open-air patio courtyard with a bubbling fountain is a great spot for breakfast or a quiet break from midday heat.

Calle Baratillo 9 (btw. Calles Obispo and Narciso López), Plaza de Armas, La Habana Vieja. ℂ 7/860-8201. Fax 7/860-8391. www.habaguanexhotels.com. 27 units. CUC$240–CUC$282 (US$259–US$302/£130–£151) double; CUC$340–CUC$382 (US$367–US$413/£184–£206) junior suite; CUC$400–CUC$442 (US$432–US$477/£216–£239) Santovenia suite. Rates include breakfast. MC, V. Free valet parking. **Amenities:** Restaurant; 2 bars; secretarial services; 24-hr. room service; babysitting; laundry service; dry cleaning; nonsmoking rooms. *In room:* A/C, TV, minibar, hair dryer, safe.

Hotel Saratoga ★★★ (Finds) This hotel has the most luxurious rooms and appointments of any La Habana Vieja property. Even the standard rooms are very spacious, with marble or tile floors, elegant furnishings, and all the modern amenities. Each comes with a tub and separate shower. Many have a private balcony and view over Havana's bustling streets. Several of the suites here are truly special. I like the Suite Capitolio, which is a corner unit with a fabulous view of the Capitol dome from the king-size bed. The Prado and Habana suites are also top-notch rooms. Despite having nearly 100 rooms, this place still feels like a boutique hotel. Two of the best features here are the delightful rooftop pool with stunning views and probably the best breakfast in Cuba. Perhaps my only criticism of this hotel is the fact that its mezzanine bar area is a bit on the small side.

Paseo del Prado 603, La Habana Vieja. ℂ 7/868-1000. Fax 7/868-1001. www.hotel-saratoga.com. 96 units. CUC$235–CUC$305 (US$254–US$329/£127–£165) double; CUC$385–CUC$670 (US$416–US$724/£208–£362) suite. Rates include breakfast. MC, V. Free parking. **Amenities:** Restaurant; 2 bars; rooftop pool; small gym; concierge; tour desk; Wi-Fi; 24-hr. room service; laundry service; dry cleaning; nonsmoking rooms. *In room:* A/C, TV, dataport; minibar, hair dryer, safe.

Hotel Sevilla ★★ This is the best of the three grand old hotels (Sevilla, Inglaterra, and Plaza) near the Parque Central. Plus, it's got a lovely street-level pool and well-equipped little health club, which the other old dames lack. Still, all three are easily eclipsed by the new Hotel Saratoga (see above). Some of the standard rooms are a bit small and lackluster, and it's definitely worth the splurge for a superior or junior suite—you'll get a lot more space. The hotel was actually built in two stages, and all of the current rooms are in the newer Biltmore addition, which dates from the 1920s. The original (ca. 1908) Grand Sevilla operates as a hotel training school, although the original ornate, Moorish-influenced lobby area is still working and quite impressive. The ninth-floor **Roof Garden Restaurant** (p. 103) is one of the top dining options in town.

Calle Trocadero 55 (corner of Calle Prado), La Habana Vieja. ℂ 7/860-8560. Fax 7/860-8875. www.grancaribe.com. 178 units. CUC$197–CUC$206 (US$213–US$222/£106–£111) standard; CUC$206–CUC$256 (US$222–US$276/£111–£138) superior or junior suite. Rates include breakfast. MC, V. Free valet parking. **Amenities:** 2 restaurants; 2 bars; outdoor pool; health club; concierge; tour desk; car-rental desk; 24-hr. room service; massage; babysitting; laundry service; dry cleaning. *In room:* A/C, TV, minibar, hair dryer, safe.

NH Parque Central ★★ This modern, upscale hotel dominates the northern end of Havana's small Central Park. Behind a wall of glass doors fronting the park sits the large atrium lobby area. The rooms are new and spacious, with dark colors, thick fabrics, and fresh carpeting. The marble bathrooms even have a separate bathtub and shower. These are probably the most comfortable luxury rooms in La Habana Vieja, and the hotel has a broad array of amenities and services—although it lacks the old-world charm and sense of time travel provided by other hotels in this part of town. The suites are huge, and some have private balconies with nice views over the park and toward El Capitolio. Service is relatively efficient and attentive, something that cannot always be said about most other hotels in La Habana Vieja. The new, modern NH Parque Central Torre hotel is due to open in late 2008.

Calle Neptuno (btw. Calles Prado and Zulueta), La Habana Vieja. © **7/860-6627.** Fax 7/860-6630. www. nh-hotels.com. 227 units. CUC$270 (US$292/£146) standard double; CUC$325 (US$351/£176) superior double; CUC$330–CUC$550 (US$356–US$594/£178–£297) suite. MC, V. Free valet parking. **Amenities:** 2 restaurants; 2 bars; 2 lounges; small rooftop pool; health club; Jacuzzi; concierge; tour desk; car-rental desk; well-equipped business center; Wi-Fi; 24-hr. room service; massage; babysitting; laundry service; dry cleaning; nonsmoking rooms. *In room:* A/C, TV, dataport, minibar, hair dryer, safe.

Expensive

Hotel Ambos Mundos ★

Hemingway claimed this was "a good place to write," and the room (no. 511) where he wrote parts of *For Whom the Bell Tolls* is a shrine to the late author, featuring his typewriter and photocopies of some handwritten drafts and notes. The hotel is a popular stop on the tourist trail and a good base for exploring La Habana Vieja. The rooms are simple and somewhat spartan, but they are clean and comfortable, and most have high French doors opening to some views of the bustling streets. A few even have small balconies. Most folks love the compact old, iron-grated elevator running up the inside of the central staircase; however, it's woefully inadequate to meet demand, so if you're staying on an upper floor, you might find waiting for it frustrating. Breakfast is served on the rooftop patio under shady arbors with a wonderful view of the harbor and La Habana Vieja; this is also a great spot for a refreshing drink any time of day or night. The lobby bar is also popular, and features live piano music most of the day and much of the night.

Calle Obispo 153 (corner of Calle Mercaderes), La Habana Vieja. © **7/860-9530.** Fax 7/860-9532. www. habaguanexhotels.com. 52 units. CUC$130 (US$140/£70) double; CUC$160 (US$173/£86) minisuite. Rates include breakfast. Rates slightly lower during off season, higher during peak weeks. MC, V. Street parking nearby. **Amenities:** Restaurant; 2 bars; tour desk; car-rental desk; in-room massage; babysitting; laundry service. *In room:* A/C, TV, fridge, safe.

Hotel del Tejadillo ★

It's hard to find a better located hotel in La Habana Vieja. Just a half-block from the Plaza de la Catedral and La Bodeguita del Medio, and about 2 blocks from the Malecón, this recently renovated old mansion provides decent value and ample colonial charm. The spacious rooms have high ceilings, comfortable new beds, and Oriental throw rugs. About half of them come with fully equipped kitchenettes. Most are set around a typical central courtyard, with a central fountain surrounded by lush tropical plants and large sculptures. The biggest drawback here is the fact that quite a few rooms have no windows. Breakfast is served in a little dining room, or in a separate open-air courtyard. There's a lively little bar here and it's far enough removed from the rooms so as not to keep you up.

Calle Tejadillo 12 (corner of Calle San Ignacio), La Habana Vieja. © **7/863-7283.** Fax 7/863-8830. www. habaguanexhotels.com. 32 units. CUC$110–CUC$130 (US$119–US$140/£59–£70) double; CUC$130–CUC$150 (US$140–US$162/£70–£81) suite. Rates include breakfast. MC, V. Street parking nearby. **Amenities:** Restaurant; bar; concierge; tour desk; laundry service; dry cleaning. *In room:* A/C, TV, kitchenette (in some), fridge, safe.

Hotel Los Frailes ★ (Finds)   While I find the staff dressed in mock monk garb a little bit cheesy (not to mention how hot and uncomfortable it must be for them), this is still a lovely little hotel located in the heart of La Habana Vieja. The rooms have high ceilings, smooth stucco walls, and heavy wooden beds. Unfortunately, most of the rooms here lack windows, and only two of the four minisuites come with queen-size beds (the rest come with two twins). The narrow central courtyard is engulfed in lush tropical foliage cascading down from the second-floor hallways, and features a murmuring fountain, traveling art expositions, and a Plexiglas viewing port into the building's 19th-century water-collection system.

Calle Teniente Rey 8 (btw. Calles Mercaderes and Oficios), La Habana Vieja. ✆ **7/862-9383.** Fax 7/862-9718. www.habaguanexhotels.com. 22 units. CUC$110–CUC$130 (US$119–US$140/£59–£70) double; CUC$150–CUC$170 (US$162–US$184/£81–£92) minisuite. Rates include breakfast. MC, V. Street parking nearby. **Amenities:** Bar; concierge; tour desk; 24-hr. room service; laundry service; dry cleaning. *In room:* A/C, TV, minibar, safe.

Hotel Plaza ★   Built in 1909, this is one of the more historic hotels in La Habana Vieja. Suite no. 216 is still rented out, replete with bat and ball and other memorabilia from one of its more famous guests, the Sultan of Swat, Babe Ruth. Albert Einstein and Isadora Duncan were also guests here. The building also served as the headquarters of *El Diario de la Marina* newspaper. However, historic charm is in greater supply than actual comfort or luxury; although rooms have attractive dark-wood furniture and the bathrooms have tubs, they are a little spartan. You'll find just as many famous ghosts haunting the nearby Hotel Sevilla (see above), while enjoying more comfortable accommodations in some, but not all rooms. Still, the rooms are spacious and clean, and quite a few have narrow, private balconies. The hotel is undergoing major renovations throughout 2009, its 100th anniversary year. The lobby is worth checking out, whether you're staying here or not, for its intricate mosaic tile floor, bas-relief trim, and stained-glass atrium skylights. And, by all means, come by for an afternoon drink at the rooftop **Solarium Bar** ★★, with great views of Havana and the neighboring Bacardí building.

Calle Ignacio Agramonte 267, La Habana Vieja. ✆ **7/860-8583** or 7/867-1075. Fax 7/860-8591. www.hotelplazacuba.com. 188 units. CUC$120–CUC$160 (US$130–US$173/£65–£86) double; CUC$145–CUC$185 (US$157–US$200/£78–£100) suite. Rates include breakfast. MC, V. Free valet parking. **Amenities:** 3 restaurants; 3 bars; concierge; tour desk; car-rental desk; 24-hr. room service; laundry service; dry cleaning. *In room:* A/C, TV, minibar, hair dryer, safe.

Moderate

Park View Hotel (Value)   This is one of the newer additions to the Habaguanex stable and one of its better values. This old hotel, originally opened in 1928, has been entirely restored and remodeled. Rooms, while by no means large, are comfortable and inviting. Their biggest drawbacks are the tiny, 13-inch television sets and the smallish bathrooms, which have slightly cramped corner shower units. Three interior units on each floor have no window, while the end rooms are slightly larger and come with a small balcony overlooking the shady little park that gives this hotel its name. The seventh-floor restaurant serves up standard Cuban and international fare, but with a wonderful view over the Morro Castle.

Calle Colón (corner of Calle Morro), La Habana Vieja. ✆ **7/861-3293.** Fax 7/863-6036. www.habaguanexhotels.com. 55 units. CUC$76–CUC$95 (US$82–US$103/£41–£51) double. Rates include breakfast. MC, V. Free valet parking. **Amenities:** Restaurant; 2 bars; tour desk; laundry service. *In room:* A/C, TV, minibar, safe.

Due to Habaguanex's almost complete control of the area, there are no budget hotel options in La Habana Vieja. This is one of the best locations in Havana, and the following *casas particulares* are recommended. **Chez Nous,** Calle Teniente Rey 115, between Calles Cuba and San Ignacio (℃ 7/862-6287; cheznous@ceniai.inf.cu), is a friendly house and a stone's throw from Plaza Vieja. The two rooms share a bathroom and there's a great terrace and interesting living room. **Casa Lisette y Orlando,** Calle Aguacate 509, Aptos 301 y 102 between Calles Sol and Muralla (℃ 7/867-5768; lisettesobrino@yahoo.es), is a clean, modern, quiet apartment run by a lovely, friendly couple. **Casa Eduardo Canciano,** Calle Refugio 103 between Calles Prado and Morro (℃ 7/863-0523; www.winpict.com/cuba/index.htm; eduardo.canciano@infomed.sld.cu), is a first-floor flat run by a friendly family. It has a wonderful Sevillana patio and Spanish wooden colonial windows. The large bedroom equipped with air-conditioning and a fan has an adjoining, original jet-black-and-yellow bathroom. The dining room is next to the sweet balcony overlooking the street. **La Casona de Obrapía,** Calle Obrapia 405 between Calles Aguacate and Compostela (℃ 7/862-8285; reymond_15@yahoo.es), is a restored, spacious colonial home run by Reymond and Raydel with two interior rooms. There's wonderful original tiling throughout and a large living room with a balcony overlooking the street. **Casa Mary,** Calle Cárcel-Capdevila No. 59, 2nd floor, between Calles Morro and Zulueta (℃ 7/861-5911; http://xoomer.alice.it/gianni_franci; mariange2850@yahoo.com), is a flat with an enormous terrace overlooking El Morro. It is next to the Spanish Embassy in a quiet location. The two small rooms both have doors out onto the terrace, where you may lounge on painted iron chairs.

CENTRO HABANA

With the exception of Hotel Deauville, all of the hotels listed here are either right on, or very close to, the dividing line between La Habana Vieja and Centro Habana, and so are convenient for exploring Old Havana.

Expensive

Hotel Telégrafo ★   This restored hotel is actually over a century old, yet it has the boldest and most contemporary architecture and interior design in town. Instead of trying to recapture a sense of the past, this place offers a brash mix of Art Deco furnishings, playful light fixtures, and modern Cuban art and sculpture throughout the hotel. The rooms have soaring high ceilings, and proportionately high painted headboards. A majority have views over the Parque Central, although a few let out onto the interior courtyard. Unfortunately, the hyperhip interior design ends up leaving the rooms feeling a bit spartan and uninviting. The hotel's snack bar is located in a first-floor courtyard under ancient brick-and-stone arches in ruin, which set off a massive and intricate mosaic wall, small pool, and modern track lighting. It's open 24 hours. The hotel has a few computers with Internet connections, and this is one of the hotel's finest features. This is definitely a great spot for a coffee, drink, or light snack.

Calle Prado 408 (corner of Neptuno), Centro Havana. ℃ 7/861-1010. Fax 7/861-4844. www.habaguanex hotels.com. 63 units. CUC$130–CUC$160 (US$140–US$173/£70–£86) double; CUC$180–CUC$200 (US$194–US$216/£97–£108) suite. Rates include breakfast. MC, V. Free valet parking. **Amenities:** Restaurant; bar; tour desk; car-rental desk; 24-hr. room service; laundry service. *In room:* A/C, TV, minibar, hair dryer, safe.

Moderate

Hotel Deauville This place doesn't look like much from the outside and things don't get significantly better inside. The entire structure suffers from significant wear and tear, but throughout 2008, rooms were getting a complete makeover. However, it is located right on the Malecón and most rooms have a private balcony overlooking the sea. The views from the rooms on the higher floors are wonderful, and the corner rooms—with windows on two sides—are particularly nice. The Deauville does a brisk business in package tours, and is often full with French and German groups. The rooftop pool here is a popular spot. The hotel's advertised rates are a bit high for what you get, but if you're booked here as part of a package, or if you can get a lower rate, this is a pretty good option for a few days in Havana. The restaurants and inclusive buffet breakfast are embarrassments.

Calle Galiano 1 (btw. the Malecón and San Lázaro), Centro Habana. © **7/866-8813.** Fax 7/866-8148. 144 units. CUC$53–CUC$85 (US$57–US$92/£29–£46) double. Rates include breakfast buffet. MC, V. Street parking nearby. **Amenities:** 2 restaurants; 2 bars; dance club; outdoor pool; tour desk; car-rental desk; laundry service; dry cleaning. *In room:* A/C, TV, safe.

Hotel Inglaterra ★ This is yet another of the more historic and better located hotels in Havana, although it's definitely showing its age—it's been in business since 1875. The ornate lobby, with its colorful Moorish mosaics, and the lively streetside cafe, are the best features here. Rooms are perennially desultory and dated, and most have small bathrooms. However, quite a few of the rooms do come with a small balcony overlooking the Parque Central, a nice perk. The rooftop bar is one of the few such perches to stay open relatively late (closed Sat), although the concrete balustrade obstructs the views when seated at your table.

Paseo del Prado 416 (in front of Parque Central), Centro Havana. © **7/860-8595.** Fax 7/860-8254. www.gran-caribe.com. 83 units. CUC$120 (US$130/£65) double; CUC$175 (US$189/£95) suite. Rates include breakfast. MC, V. Free valet parking. **Amenities:** 3 restaurants; 2 bars; concierge; tour desk; car-rental desk; 24-hr. room service; laundry service; dry cleaning. *In room:* A/C, TV, minibar, hair dryer, safe.

Inexpensive

There are literally hundreds of official and unofficial rooms for rent in private homes throughout Centro Habana. Many are quite dilapidated and run-down, but a few are well maintained and charming. Stunning views are enjoyed from the top-floor "penthouse" of **Casa de Evora Rodríguez** ★, Paseo del Prado 20, 9th floor, between San Lázaro and Cárcel (© **7/861-7932;** evorahabana@yahoo.com). Nearby is the super-friendly, modern apartment of a young couple, **Federico and Yamelis Llanes,** with a balcony overlooking Prado, Calle Cárcel 156 between Calles San Lázaro and Prado (© **7/861-7817;** fllanes@gmail.com). Another great option with en suite rooms, incredible balcony views, and an independent kitchen and living room is the apartment of **Melba and Alberto,** ★ Calle Galiano 115, Apto 81, between Calles Animas and Trocadero (©) **7/863-5178;** barracuda1752@yahoo.es). Other popular options include the lovely **Casa Esther Cardosa,** Calle Aguila 367, between Calles San Miguel and Neptuno (© **7/862-0401;** esthercv2551@cubarte.cult.cu), with a great terrace, and interesting furniture and prints on the walls. **Casa Viky,** Calle Barcelona 60, between Calles Aguila and Amistad (© **7/863-8923;** mvictoriau@infomed.sid.cu), is a flat on the renovated Calle Barcelona, laid with gorgeous pink, blue, and cream Art Deco tiles. The elegant first room with two beds is equipped with handsome furniture and a chandelier and comes with an original 1950s bathroom that is shared with the other room. **Casa del**

Científico, Paseo de Martí 212, at the corner of Calle Trocadero (📞 **7/862-4511**), is a small, historic hotel right on the Prado, with a wonderful marble staircase, exquisite stained glass, and basic, but comfortable rooms.

Hotel Lido (**Value**)   Although a block removed from the Prado, this is a much better bet than its nearby sister, the Hotel Caribbean. In general, the rooms are larger and more comfortable. Interior rooms lack windows and are a tad stuffy, but the end rooms have wonderful private balconies overlooking Calle Consulado. The fifth-floor rooftop restaurant serves uninspired budget fare, but has good views over Havana.

Calle Consulado 216 (btw. Calles Animas and Trocadero), Centro Habana. 📞/fax **7/866-8814**. www. islazul.cu. 64 units. CUC$36–CUC$41 (US$39–US$44/£19–£22) double. Rates include breakfast. Street parking nearby. **Amenities:** Restaurant; bar; tour desk. *In room:* A/C, TV, safe.

VEDADO & THE PLAZA DE LA REVOLUCION AREA
Very Expensive
Hotel Nacional de Cuba ★★   Sitting on a high bluff overlooking the Malecón, this is Havana's signature hotel, and it's loaded with atmosphere. Two massive turrets loom overhead as you approach the entrance along its palm-lined driveway. The long, tiled lobby, with its high ceilings and heavy painted beams, is the heart and hub of this joint, and it's almost always bustling. The rooms themselves are large and well-appointed, although somewhat drab and showing their age. Some of the standard rooms have quite small bathrooms and no dressers with drawers. The suites and deluxe rooms are generally quite nice, however. Over half the rooms have ocean views, although only a rare few have private balconies. The hotel has a vast lawn area on its high bluff that opens out toward the sea. My favorite spot here is the "Compass Card," an outdoor terrace made of marble inlaid in the pattern of a nautical compass. This is a great place to grab a table for a sunset drink overlooking the Malecón, with giant cannons protecting you on either side.

Calle O (corner of Calle 21), Vedado. 📞 **7/873-3564-3567**. Fax 7/836-5171. www.gran-caribe.com. 457 units. CUC$170 (US$184/£92) double; CUC$390 (US$421/£211) suite; CUC$1,000 (US$1,080/£540) presidential suite. Rates include breakfast buffet. MC, V. Free valet parking. **Amenities:** 3 restaurants; 6 bars; 2 lounges; cabaret; 2 outdoor pools; lit outdoor tennis court; concierge; tour desk; car-rental desk; business center; salon; 24-hr. room service; in-room massage; babysitting; laundry service; dry cleaning. *In room:* A/C, TV, minibar, hair dryer, safe.

Hotel Victoria ★★★   This little business-class hotel (ca. 1928) is open, but will probably be closed for a lengthy period while being transformed into Cuba's first designer hotel. British company Esencia Hotels & Resorts will reopen the new hotel in late spring 2009. Conran & Partners will design the interiors of the rooms, restaurant, bar, and swimming pool terrace. The refurbished hotel will feature a larger restaurant, cocktail bar, and a guests-only bar. Rooms will feature Wi-Fi, a built-in plasma screen, sound system, and desk-drawer humidor, among other facilities. The hotel will also have a gym as well as health and beauty treatments.

The current hotel in 2008 is a small, attractive business hotel close to the action in Vedado. Be careful here: The neighboring FOCSA building funnels the sea breezes right at the Victoria's entrance. When the winds are up, they can almost knock you off your feet.

Calles 19 and M, Vedado. 📞 **7/833-3510**. Fax 7/833-3109. www.esenciahotelsandresorts.com. 31 units. CUC$80–CUC$100 (US$86–US$108/£43–£54) double. CUC$130 (US$140/£70) suite. Rates include breakfast. New rates to start at CUC$111 (US$120/£60). MC, V. Free parking. **Amenities:** Restaurant; snack bar; bar; lounge; small outdoor pool; concierge; tour desk; car-rental desk; small business center; 24-hr. room service; babysitting; laundry service. *In room:* A/C, TV, minibar, hair dryer, safe.

Meliá Cohiba ★★ Sitting just off the Malecón, this high-rise hotel, with its sharp angles and alternating walls of stone and glass, is probably the most modern building in Havana. Moreover, the Meliá Cohiba, along with its sister hotel, the Meliá Habana (p. 97), provide all the services and amenities luxury travelers are looking for in a top-rated hotel. Rooms are large and comfortable, and most have excellent views, particularly those on the higher floors. The executive floors and services here make this by far the best choice for business travelers, and it's got a wonderful outdoor pool and the best-equipped health club I've found at any hotel in Havana. The Cohiba has a wide range of restaurants and shops, and even its buffet restaurant is a treat, with live cook stations and enough space and flow so as not to feel like a cattle car. The **Habana Café** ★ is one of the better club/restaurants in town, with a nightly floor show and live music. The executive floors and *Servicio Real* upgrade, which includes Internet and business-center privileges, as well as a constantly refreshed and extensive buffet in the executive lounge, make this by far the best choice for business travelers.

Av. Paseo (btw. Avs. 1 and 3), Vedado. © **7/833-3636.** Fax 7/834-4555. www.solmeliacuba.com. 462 units. CUC$225 (US$243/£122) double; CUC$275 (US$297/£160) junior suite; CUC$370 (US$400/£200) suite; CUC$100–CUC$185 (US$108–US$200/£54–£100) supplement for *Servicio Real* upgrade. MC, V. Valet parking CUC$8 (US$8.65/£4.30) per day. **Amenities:** 4 restaurants; 4 bars; 2 lounges; large outdoor pool; indoor squash court; well-equipped health club; Jacuzzi; sauna; concierge; tour desk; car-rental desk; business center; Wi-Fi; shopping arcade; salon; 24-hr. room service; in-room massage; babysitting; laundry service; dry cleaning; nonsmoking rooms. *In room:* A/C, TV, dataport, minibar, hair dryer, safe.

Tryp Habana Libre ★★ Formerly the Havana Hilton, this historic landmark is the place Fidel Castro first called home following the fall of Batista. Rising high above Havana from a spot on La Rampa, this hotel provides some of my favorite views of the city and sea from most of its rooms. The two-story open lobby area is striking, with its amoeba-shaped pool and massive modern sculpture surrounded by plants and palms. The rooms themselves are large and comfortable, although they feel dated, despite the fact that most of the carpets and furniture are new. Of the dining and entertainment options, I find the famous Trader Vic's–style Polinesio an overpriced disappointment, although you might appreciate the 24-hour diner-style La Rampa Cafetería—I did. The 25th-floor Turquino Cabaret might not have the best floor show in town, but it does have the best view and regularly stages A-list concerts and performances. In mid-2008, the hotel began a refurbishment program that includes the swimming pool area.

Calles L and 23, Vedado. © **7/838-4011.** Fax 7/834-6365. www.solmeliacuba.com. 572 units. CUC$200 (US$216/£58) double; CUC$300 (US$324/£162) junior suite; CUC$300 (US$324/£162) suite. Rates include buffet breakfast. Children 11 and under stay free in parent's room. MC, V. Valet parking CUC$6 (US$6.50/£3.25) per day. **Amenities:** 5 restaurants; 3 bars; 2 lounges; dance club; outdoor pool; concierge; tour desk; car-rental desk; business center; shopping arcade; salon; 24-hr. room service; babysitting; laundry service; dry cleaning; nonsmoking rooms. *In room:* A/C, TV, dataport, minibar, hair dryer, safe.

Expensive

Hotel Presidente ★★ (Finds) This is an elegant Vedado hotel. The impeccable Victorian-style lobby features black-and-white marble floors, pink marble wainscoting, and real antiques. Some of the standard rooms are a bit compact, while others are quite spacious. About half (generally the even-numbered rooms) have good ocean views. On the 10th floor, you'll find two large suites with wonderfully inviting oceanview terraces. There's a refreshing outdoor pool on the ground level, and a poolside bar and grill. While the hotel is just 2 blocks from the Malecón, it's not very close to much else.

Calle Calzada 110 (corner of Av. de los Presidentes), Vedado. ⓒ **7/838-1001.** Fax 7/838-2956. www. hotelesc.com. 158 units. CUC$140 (US$151/£76) double; CUC$200 (US$216/£108) suite. Rates include buffet breakfast. MC, V. Free valet parking. **Amenities:** Restaurant; bar; outdoor pool; tour desk; car-rental desk; laundry service; dry cleaning. *In room:* A/C, TV, minibar, hair dryer, safe.

Moderate

Hotel St. John's ⟮**Value**⟯   This is a perennially popular choice for budget and midrange travelers. It definitely gets the nod over its nearby neighbor, the Hotel Vedado (see below). Rooms are clean and simple. Most are pretty spacious and the furnishings are relatively modern. Rooms on the 9th floor and above have wonderful views. If you don't have a room on a higher floor, you can always spend time in the tiny rooftop pool or the new adjoining bar and events space. The hotel is right in the heart of Vedado, just a block off La Rampa.

Calle O No. 206 (btw. Calles 23 and 25), Vedado. ⓒ **7/833-3740.** Fax 7/833-3561. www.gran-caribe.com. 87 units. CUC$67–CUC$80 (US$72–US$86/£36–£43) double. Rates include breakfast buffet. MC, V. Street parking nearby. **Amenities:** 2 restaurants; 2 bars; dance club; outdoor pool; tour desk; car-rental desk; laundry service; dry cleaning. *In room:* A/C, TV, safe.

Hotel Vedado   This popular Vedado hotel is somewhat nondescript. Sure, it'll do in a pinch, but it's rather uninspired and uninspiring. Rooms are distributed in two neighboring towers, and there's a kidney-shaped pool on the ground floor between them. Opened in 1952, the lobby retains the original Art Deco feel. The hotel has a tiny exercise room, where the best feature is a little sauna. The surly reception staff needs replacing.

Calle O (btw. Calles 23 and 25), Vedado. ⓒ **7/836-4072.** www.gran-caribe.com. 203 units. CUC$69 (US$75/£37) double. Rates include breakfast buffet. MC, V. **Amenities:** 2 restaurants; 3 bars; outdoor pool; exercise room; sauna; tour desk; car-rental desk. *In room:* A/C, TV, safe.

Inexpensive

Given that this is one of Havana's prime middle-class neighborhoods, there's a glut of *casas particulares,* many in wonderful old neoclassical and Art Deco homes and apartment buildings. The following are all recommended. **Casa María Elena Matos Fernández,** Calle 13 no. 106, between Calles L and M, Apartment 5 (ⓒ **7/832-4346;** ernesto. mato@infomed.sld.cu): This is a huge, smart flat with elegant proportions in an Art Deco building close to the Malecón. The one room has two beds and pretty floor tiles and an adjoining large 1950s bubble-gum pink bathroom. **Casa Aidée and Jorge,** Calle 15, no. 278 between Calles J and I, Apto 2 (bajos) (ⓒ **7/832-7655;** jorcanci@yahoo.es): offers two ground-floor apartments, one much larger than the other, with independent entrances. They are clean and comfortable and an extraordinarily good value. There's an extra daily charge if you wish to use the kitchen. **Casa Luis Alberto Gómez Garcés,** Calle 15, no. 305 (bajos), between Calles H and I (ⓒ **7/836-3954;** mroche@infomed. sld.cu), is a quirky house with its Spanish turret. It has one large room with a small kitchenette and an independent entrance. The room is next to a small patio. The main house interior decor is shabby chic with a chandelier, some choice pieces of furniture, and lovely hallway tiling. **Casa María D'García (Lola),** Calle I, no. 355, between Calles 17 and 19, Apartamento 1, 2nd floor (ⓒ **7/832-1525;** lazaro.goenaga@infomed.sld.cu). This house has an attractive, nicely furnished room in a grand house on an atmospheric street. The terrace overlooking the street is perfect for rocking in chairs and gossiping. **Casa Jorge Coalla Potts,** Calle I between Calles 21 and 23, no. 456, Apto 11 (ⓒ **7/832-9032;** www.havanaroomrental.com; jorgepotts@correodecuba.cu), is managed by Jorge and Marisel, helpful and very hospitable hosts. Their ground-floor apartment is in an excellent location in a handsome, modern white apartment building.

Casa Sandra ★ On the 13th floor of this 1950s block, this enormous flat affords spectacular views of Vedado and the Malecón. The rooms are spacious and attractively decorated and guests share a spacious, minimally decorated living room enhanced by Asian influences. Breakfasts are served up on the elegant long dining table or on the wraparound terrace. Run by Lilly and her family, who work in film, this is a gorgeous place to stay.

Calle G, no. 301 (at the corner of Calle 13), 13th floor. ✆ **7/832-4021.** www.casalilly.com. 2 units. CUC$30–CUC$40 (US$32–US$43/£16–£22) double. No credit cards. Guarded parking available beneath the flats. *In room:* A/C, no phone.

PLAYA

Very Expensive

Meliá Habana ★★ This modern luxury hotel is set on a coral ledge on the edge of the Caribbean. Its rows of balconies are draped with flowing ferns, and the building gets wider as it gets higher, giving it an inverted pyramid effect. Most of the rooms here have excellent ocean views from their good-size private balconies. The rooms are large and comfortable, with high ceilings and big bathrooms. The most striking feature here is the ground-level lagoon surrounded by lush tropical gardens and filled by man-made waterfalls set under soaring columns. The lagoon almost seems to blend into the free-form pool, which is billed as the largest in Cuba. As at the Meliá Cohiba, the executive floors and services are top-notch here, making it a good choice for business travelers. The hotel is the unofficial default hub of the business scene in Miramar.

Av. 3 (btw. Calles 76 and 80), Miramar, Playa. ✆ **7/204-8500.** Fax 7/204-8505. www.solmeliacuba.com. 397 units. CUC$220 (US$238/£119) double; CUC$370 (US$400/£200) junior suite; CUC$520 (US$562/£281) suite. MC, V. Valet parking CUC$4 (US$4.30/£2.15) per day. **Amenities:** 6 restaurants; 3 bars; 2 lounges; coffee shop; large outdoor pool; 2 outdoor tennis courts; small, well-equipped exercise room; sauna; concierge; tour desk; car-rental desk; business center; shopping arcade; salon; 24-hr. room service; babysitting; laundry service; dry cleaning; nonsmoking rooms. *In room:* A/C, TV, dataport, minibar, hair dryer, safe.

Occidental Miramar ★★ This modern and massive luxury hotel is an impressive and imposing presence in the heart of Miramar's business district. It has nicer rooms than the Meliá Habana (see above), but it's 2 blocks from the sea and has fewer dining and entertainment options. The rooms are all at least junior suites, with one queen-size bed and a comfortable sitting area. The beds are some of the firmest I've found in Havana. The bathrooms are just a tad on the small size in proportion to everything else here. Only the eight end-unit suites here have balconies, although these balconies are large. This place does a brisk business in group and conference travel.

Av. 5 (btw. Calles 72 and 76), Miramar, Playa. ✆ **7/204-3584.** Fax 7/204-9227. www.occidental-hoteles. com/miramar. 427 units. CUC$130 (US$140/£70) double; CUC$190 (US$205/£103) suite; CUC$300 (US$324/£162) senior suite. Rates include breakfast. MC, V. Free valet parking. **Amenities:** 3 restaurants; 2 bars; lounge; large outdoor pool; 6 outdoor tennis courts (2 lit); indoor squash court; well-equipped exercise room; sauna; children's center; concierge; tour desk; car-rental desk; business center; shopping arcade; salon; 24-hr. room service; babysitting; laundry service; dry cleaning; nonsmoking rooms. *In room:* A/C, TV, dataport, minibar, hair dryer, safe.

Expensive

Aparthotel Montehabana (**Value**) While this place won't win any architectural or interior design awards, the spacious serviced apartments are convenient for long stays and are an extraordinarily good value for the location. The apartments have small, fully equipped kitchens, living rooms, and spacious bedrooms. Balconies, with not much of a view, come with sun loungers. The building also has large, standard hotel rooms. There's a bar, small supermarket, and Internet access on site. Guests can make use of the pool and tennis courts of the Occidental Miramar, a short walk away through the property.

Calle 70 (btw. Av. 5 and Av. 7), Miramar, Playa. ⓒ **7/204-1952.** www.gaviota-grupo.com. 177 units. CUC$80 (US$86/£43) double; CUC$90 (US$97/£49) double studio apartment; CUC$100 (US$108/£54) double apartment; CUC$160 (US$173/£86) double apartment and double room. MC, V. Free valet parking. **Amenities:** Snack bar; 1 bar; car-rental desk; shuttle bus to city center; laundry service. *In room:* A/C, TV, dataport, minibar, hair dryer, safe.

Hotel Chateau Miramar   This place is attempting to stake out the boutique business-class market. For lack of any competition, it is doing just that, although it doesn't have the warmth, charm, or personality I'd expect in a high-end boutique hotel; for anyone here on business, I'd recommend any of the large business-class hotels in town over this option. The standard rooms here are on the small side, while the junior suites and suites are more than ample. The decor is rather nondescript and impersonal, although the marble bathrooms are spacious. Most rooms come with a private balcony, and some of these are quite roomy. Suite no. 416 is the best room and view in the house, while any room with a number ending in 09 through 16 will have an ocean view. One of the more unique and appealing features here is the fact that each room comes with a 21-inch flatscreen television, equipped with Wi-Fi. The hotel is right on the waterfront, just behind the National Aquarium.

Av. 1 (btw. Calles 60 and 62), Miramar, Playa. ⓒ **7/204-1952.** Fax 7/204-0224. www.hotelescubanacan. com. 50 units. CUC$120 (US$130/£65) double; CUC$170 (US$184/£92) suite. Rates include breakfast. MC, V. Free valet parking. **Amenities:** Restaurant; snack bar; bar; lounge; outdoor pool; car-rental desk; business center; 24-hr. room service; laundry service. *In room:* A/C, TV, Wi-Fi, minibar, hair dryer, safe.

Hotel Comodoro   Located next to the Meliá Habana (see above), this complex has the feel of a South Florida condo community. The hotel rooms in the main building are acceptable, although I'd definitely opt for one of the one- or two-bedroom bungalows, which are housed in a series of two-story blocks spread around a maze of free-form pools. The bungalows all come with kitchenettes or full kitchens, making them a good option for longer stays. All of the rooms here have a balcony or patio. The Comodoro has a tiny patch of beach sand, which has been hauled in and set next to a natural pool created by a break wall just off the coast here.

Av. 3 and Calle 84, Miramar, Playa. ⓒ **7/204-5551.** Fax 7/204-2089. www.hotelescubanacan.com. 300 units. CUC$90–CUC$110 (US$97–US$119/£49–£59) double; CUC$135–CUC$155 (US$146–US$167/£73–£84) suite; CUC$118–CUC$137 (US$127–US$148/£64–£75) bungalow. MC, V. Free parking. **Amenities:** 3 restaurants; snack bar; 3 bars; dance club; natural saltwater pool; a series of free-form freshwater pools; watersports equipment/rentals; concierge; tour desk; car-rental desk; business center; shopping arcade; salon; 24-hr. room service; massage; laundry service; dry cleaning. *In room:* A/C, TV, safe.

Inexpensive

As in Vedado and Centro Habana, there are scores of *casas particulares* and private rooms for rent in Playa. Given the fact that this was a popular upper-class residential neighborhood prior to the Revolution, most are housed in large, comfortable homes and apartments. In addition to the *casa* described below, you could try **Casa Gina,** Calle 86 no. 526, between Avenidas 5 and 7 (ⓒ **7/203-4034**). Alternately, you could see if there's space at the Ministry of Education's **Hostal Icemar,** Calle 16 no. 104, between Avenidas

1 and 3 (©/fax **7/203-7735**), a dependable budget option popular with students and backpackers, with additional three-bed apartments for rent. Doubles are CUC$44 (US$48/£24).

Residencias Miramar ★   This is an excellent *casa particular* with wonderful hosts. The rooms are clean and modern, and each comes with its own phone and a small fridge. Common areas include a comfortable living room, and a shady patio area amid well-tended gardens. Meals are served throughout the day for very reasonable prices, and Eva can help arrange tours and activities, as well as arrange homestays with friends in La Habana Vieja and Vedado.

Av. 7 no. 4403 (btw. Calles 44 and 46), Miramar, Playa. © **7/202-1075.** evahabanasol@yahoo.com. 2 units. CUC$30 (US$32/£16) double. No credit cards. Free parking. **Amenities:** Restaurant; laundry service. *In room:* A/C, TV, minifridge, hair dryer.

NEAR THE AIRPORT

There are no hotels at or truly near the airport. Luckily, the bulk of Havana hotels are just a 15- to 30-minute car ride away. The closest hotels to the airport are those in Playa.

HABANA DEL ESTE & PLAYAS DEL ESTE

The beaches of Playas del Este are quite beautiful. Moreover, the four long, consecutive beaches here are just a 15- to 25-minute taxi or car ride from La Habana Vieja, making it a good choice for combining your fun in the sun with some city pleasures. However, the hotel choices here are limited and rather desultory. While there are several all-inclusive resorts, offering a whole range of entertainment and activities options, they are far less polished and attractive than similar options in Varadero or other prime all-inclusive destinations. In fact, if you want a beautiful beach resort just a little bit farther east of Playas del Este, head to **Breezes Jibacoa** (see below).

Expensive

Blau Club Arenal ★   Sandwiched between the Itabo lagoon and Playa Santa María, this is the best of the former Horizontes all-inclusives in this area, and it has become even better after being taken over by the Spanish Blau chain. The rooms are of good size and have plenty of windows or big, sliding glass doors opening onto private balconies or terraces. I think it's worth the slight splurge for one of the superior rooms or junior suites. The hotel does a brisk business in European group travel.

Laguna Itabo, btw. Santa María del Mar and Boca Ciega. © **7/797-1272.** Fax 7/797-1280. www.blau-hotels.com. 169 units. CUC$110–CUC$142 (US$119–US$153/£59–£77) double; CUC$110–CUC$142 (US$119–US$153/£59–£77) suite. Rates are all-inclusive. MC, V. Free parking. **Amenities:** 2 restaurants; 3 bars; dance club; large outdoor pool; small gym; 2 tennis courts; free watersports equipment; tour desk; car-rental desk; babysitting; laundry service. *In room:* A/C, TV, fridge, safe.

Club Atlántico   Not to be confused with the Apartotel Atlántico, this is a comfortable and relatively modern, all-inclusive option. The rooms are standard-issue affairs, mostly with two twin beds and a little balcony or terrace. The buffet meals here are nothing to write home about or look forward to, but on the upside, the all-inclusive rates include all your drinks and the use of nonmotorized watersports equipment. There's an inviting and refreshing, kidney-shaped pool that overlooks and lets out onto the beautiful beach here. Try for an oceanview third-floor room.

Av. Las Terrazas, Santa María del Mar, Playas del Este. © **7/797-1085.** www.gran-caribe.com. 92 units. CUC$130–CUC$150 (US$140–US$162/£70–£81) double. Rates are all-inclusive. MC, V. Free parking.

Amenities: Restaurant; snack bar; 2 bars; outdoor pool; outdoor tennis court; free watersports equipment; tour desk; car-rental desk; in-room massage; babysitting; laundry service. *In room:* A/C, TV, minibar, safe.

Villas Los Pinos ★ These independent villas are probably the plushest accommodations in Playas del Este and well suited to longer stays. The villas are a mix of two-, three-, and four-bedroom units in a series of two- and three-story buildings. Most villas come with their own swimming pool. The entire complex, moreover, borders a beautiful section of beach. The rooms vary considerably, but most are quite spacious, with rattan furnishings and well-equipped kitchenettes. Some have wonderful raised decks with ocean views. I like unit nos. 44 and 45 for their views, while no. 34 has its own squash court. For CUC$25 (US$27/£14) per day, you can hire your own cook and personal housekeeper.

Av. Las Terrazas 21 (btw. Calles 4 and 5), Santa María del Mar, Playas del Este. ✆ 7/797-1361. www.grancaribe.com. 70 units. CUC$114–CUC$152 (US$123–US$164/£62–£82) 2-bedroom villa; CUC$162–CUC$200 (US$175–US$216/£87–£108) 3-bedroom villa; CUC$200–CUC$238 (US$216–US$257/£108–£129) 4-bedroom villa. MC, V. Free parking. **Amenities:** 3 restaurants; 2 bars; 20 outdoor pools; 2 outdoor tennis courts; small exercise room; sauna; watersports equipment rentals; tour desk; car-rental desk; in-room massage; babysitting; laundry service. *In room:* A/C, TV, kitchenette, fridge, safe.

Inexpensive

In addition to the hotel listed below, the Playas del Este beach town of Guanabo has a high concentration of *casas particulares.* Try **Casa Trullijo,** Av. Quebec 55, between Calles 478 and 482, Guanabo (✆ 7/796-3325; www.cubanasol.com). At Santa María del Mar, set a kilometer back from the beach due to restrictions on beachfront *casas,* is the house of **Orlando Odio López,** Av. de las Banderas 909 between Calles 9 and 11 (✆ 7/797-1219).

Hotel Tropicoco ⟨Value⟩ This imposing, five-story hotel stretches on for a hundred yards or so in each direction from its blocky concrete lobby. This place hosts many group and package tours, and it's usually pretty lively. Still, it's hard not to find the Soviet-style architecture of this resort a little depressing, particularly the rectangular pool, wedged into a shady area in an alcove of the building. The whole complex has been remodeled and the rooms and facilities are in decent shape. Most of the rooms face the sea, although only a few have balconies, and overall they are unspectacular and on the small side. The best feature here is a beautiful and extremely popular section of beach just across the street.

Avs. Sur and Las Terrazas, Santa María del Mar. ✆ 7/797-1371. Fax 7/797-1389. www.hotelescubanacan.com. 188 units. CUC$99 (US$107/£53) double. Rates are all-inclusive. MC, V. Free parking. **Amenities:** 2 restaurants; 3 bars; large outdoor pool; small exercise room; sauna; watersports equipment rentals; tour desk; car-rental desk; salon; in-room massage; babysitting; laundry service. *In room:* A/C, TV, kitchenette, fridge, safe.

A LITTLE FARTHER EAST

Breezes Jibacoa ★★ This plush, all-inclusive resort is set on a beautiful patch of beach, about halfway between Havana and Varadero. The hotel is less than an hour's drive from downtown Havana, making day trips, and even evening outings to the capital, convenient. The standard rooms are large, comfortable, and modern and many come with just one king-size bed. This resort is geared toward single adults and couples, and no children under 14 are allowed. The tropical oceanview rooms have a separate sitting area, fridge, CD player, and the best beach views in the house. All rooms come with a private balcony. A huge swimming pool is set in the center of the resort, and a wide range of activities is offered.

(US$106/£53) per person standard room; CUC$113 (US$122/£61) per person oceanview room. Rates are all-inclusive. MC, V. No children under 14 allowed. **Amenities:** 4 restaurants; 6 bars; cabaret; large outdoor pool; small, well-equipped gym; 2 tennis courts; free watersports equipment; free bicycles; tour desk; car-rental desk; in-room massage; laundry service. *In room:* A/C, TV, fridge (in suite), coffeemaker, hair dryer, safe, CD player (in suite).

4 WHERE TO DINE

It has been said before, and it's worth repeating: Do not come to Cuba for fine dining. In addition to mediocre food and service, overcharging is attempted with disheartening frequency.

Paladares (private restaurants) are common in Havana. They are officially limited to no more than 12 seats, and cannot serve lobster or shrimp. Quite a few have established themselves as some of the better, long-standing restaurant options in Havana. In fact, the best of these outshine most of the official government-run options.

Aside from the restaurants listed below, fast-food chains have started to pop up around Havana. The most prominent of these is **El Rápido,** which has numerous outlets serving fried chicken, burgers, hot dogs, microwave pizzas, and other fast-food staples. Another chain worth mentioning is **Pizza Nova,** Calle 248 and Avenida 5, Miramar (© **7/204-6969**), which also has outlets in Marina Hemingway and several provincial cities. This place has good thin-crust pizza and respectable pastas. Finally, for breakfast or a quick bite, look out for **Pain de Paris** storefronts, featuring a wide range of fresh-baked breads, croissants, and pastries, as well as simple sandwiches. For a coffee-and-cake pit stop, the attractive, newly renovated **Cafe Santo Domingo,** Calle Obispo between Calles San Ignacio and Mercaderes (© **7/860-9326**) above the Panadería San José, serves a smorgasbord of creamy cakes, tarts, meat pies, and fruit and ice-cream smoothies.

LA HABANA VIEJA

In addition to the places mentioned below, budget travelers swear by the **Restaurante Hanoi,** Calles Teniente Rey and Oficios (© **7/867-1029**), although I was rather disappointed to find virtually no Vietnamese influence on the decidedly mediocre *criolla* and Chinese cuisine here. There's also the new **Restaurante Europa,** Calle Obispo 112, corner of Aguiar (© **7/866-4484**), a former candy shop, serving up a host of adventurous sauces in well-presented food. The set menu for CUC$15 (US$16/£8.10) is a good value.

Very Expensive

El Floridita ★ CRIOLLA/INTERNATIONAL   This is by far the classiest of the many Hemingway hangouts in Havana. In fact, El Floridita is so upscale, I have a hard time imagining the rugged writer really enjoying this place. It'll cost you CUC$6 (US$6.50/£3.25) for a daiquiri in "The Cradle of the Daiquiri"—be sure to get it shaken, not blended. The bartenders' deep-red jackets blend perfectly with the plush decor. The long bar takes up a good portion of the front room. There's quieter and more formal seating in the back, although even if you land a table just off the bar, this place is never rowdy. The food here is acceptable, but can't justify the hefty price tags. If you do stick around for a meal, stick to the seafood. The sautéed shrimp, which is prepared tableside, is a good bet. I recommend El Floridita mostly as a cool and refreshing place to stop for a drink after walking around Havana in the middle of a hot afternoon.

Calle Obispo 557 (corner of Calle Monserrate). ✆ **7/866-8856.** Reservations recommended. Main courses CUC$16–CUC$30 (US$17–US$32/£8.65–£16). MC, V. Bar daily 11:30am–11pm. Restaurant daily noon–11pm.

El Templete ★★ (Finds) INTERNATIONAL/SEAFOOD   This is truly fine dining portside with tables on the roadside overlooking the harbor and sophisticated interior dining inside. The eclectic menu notes dishes such as beef carpaccio with foie gras and red wine reduction, baby eels, and a delicious tuna crusted with sesame seeds and Marmitako sauce. This place has gained currency for those in the know and is a hot dining spot for government officials and other bigwigs; the service is excellent. The only drawback is that some of the outside tables are too close to the road.

Avenida del Puerto (corner of Narciso López). ✆ **7/866-8807.** Main courses CUC$8–CUC$30 (US$8.65–US$32/£4.30–£16). MC, V. Daily noon–midnight.

Expensive

Café del Oriente ★ INTERNATIONAL   This elegant little restaurant sits just off the Plaza San Francisco and, when the weather permits, has a few outdoor tables. Inside you'll find a cool, large room, with a beautiful patterned marble floor, high ceilings, and dark wainscoting on the walls. In the center of the restaurant is a large, U-shaped bar. The menu here is one of the more extravagant in Havana, but it isn't adventurous as it used to be. For the main course, I like the wild rabbit with oregano or the fish filet in lime coulis. Even if you don't take a full meal here, this is a great place to stop for a drink or cup of coffee while touring Old Havana. In fact, it's open 24 hours daily for a very late night or early morning pick-me-up.

Calle Oficios 112 (corner of Calle Armargura). ✆ **7/860-6686.** Reservations recommended. Main courses CUC$9–CUC$21 (US$9.70–US$23/£4.85–£11). MC, V. Daily noon–midnight.

La Bodeguita del Medio ★ CRIOLLA   The "B del M," as it's also known, oozes history and suffers from overcrowding. Still, it's still a must for any first-time trip to Havana. The collage of famous photos and signatures that crowd the walls here are legend. You'll definitely want a reservation (in high season), although even with a reservation, you'll probably end up waiting for a table—this place is just that popular. Tradition would have you start things off with a *mojito,* although the *mojitos* here are notoriously weak and unjustifiably expensive. Definitely order one with 3- or 5-year-old *añejo* rum if you plan on enjoying it. The food—simple and well-prepared Cuban dishes—is pretty good. The slow-roasted pork is my favorite, although the *ropa vieja* (shredded beef) gives it a run for its money. No matter what you order, make sure you have it served with plenty of yuca with *mojo* (gravy) and the *moros y cristianos,* black beans with rice. This place is crowded and rowdy, so don't come expecting anything less. There's live music in the squashed bar.

Calle Empedrado 207 (btw. Calles San Ignacio and Cuba). ✆ **7/867-1374.** Reservations recommended. Main courses CUC$12–CUC$16 (US$13–US$17/£6.50–£8.65). MC, V. Daily noon–midnight.

La Domínica ★★ ITALIAN   This is the best Italian restaurant in town. Skip the formal and stuffy seating inside and grab one of the outdoor tables under a canvas umbrella on the old brick streets. If the band were playing "'O Sole Mio" instead of "Guantanamera," you might almost forget you're in Havana and think you were dining at a sidewalk trattoria in Rome. There's a wood-burning oven turning out excellent thin-crust pizzas. The pastas are cooked al dente and served in big portions. My favorite is the *penne alla putanesca,* which comes in a tomato cream sauce seasoned with anchovies and capers. For main dishes, I'd recommend the *saltimbocca alla Romana* (veal scallops wrapped in sage and prosciutto ham). Finish everything off with some *cassata sicilliana* (a cake dessert) and an espresso.

Calles O'Reilly and Mercaderes. © **7/860-2918.** Reservations recommended. Main courses CUC$10–CUC$26 (US$11–US$28/£5.40–£14); pizzas and pastas CUC$6–CUC$12 (US$6.50–US$13/£3.25–£6.50). MC, V. Daily noon–11pm.

Roof Garden Restaurant ★★ (Finds) FRENCH/INTERNATIONAL   Located on the top floor of the Hotel Sevilla, this is one of the finer restaurants in Havana, with arguably the finest setting. The large dining room has a massively high ceiling with intricate bas-relief work and moldings. The room is ringed by floor-to-almost-ceiling windows that are left open in all but the most inclement weather. Marble floors and huge chandeliers complete the ambience. The menu is one of the more adventurous in town, with main dishes such as king prawns in aged rum, squid ragout in its own ink, and a delicious lamb ragout *(cordero estofado).* For starters, I recommend the salad of pickled duck with artichokes and poached egg in red wine. To finish off the night decadently, go for the profiteroles with ice cream and chocolate sauce. The set three-course meal at CUC$17 (US$18/£9.20) is a good value, as are the Cuban colonial cuisine dishes. This place is also known as the "Torre del Oro."

Calle Trocadero 55 (corner of Calle Prado). © **7/860-8560.** Reservations recommended. Main courses CUC$9–CUC$32 (US$9.70–US$35/£4.85–£17). MC, V. Daily 7–10:30pm.

Santo Angel ★ (Finds) INTERNATIONAL   With a handful of outdoor tables right on the Plaza Vieja, as well as others on the broad covered veranda facing the plaza, this is arguably one of the most atmospheric restaurants in Old Havana. You'll definitely want to choose one of the aforementioned tables over those in the indoor dining rooms. The adventurous menu attempts to match the grandeur of the ambience, with mixed results. You can start things off with *malanga* (vegetable) soup and blue cheese or some seafood bisque. For a main dish, I like the lamb in red wine and honey. The chefs here are inconsistent, and at times I've left very pleased, while on other occasions I've been sorely disappointed.

Calle Teniente Rey 60, at the corner of Calle San Ignacio. © **7/861-1626.** Reservations recommended. Main courses CUC$8–CUC$28 (US$8.65–US$30/£4.30–£15). MC, V. Daily 11:30am–11pm.

Moderate

Café La Mina CRIOLLA   This popular place has a privileged location right on the Plaza de Armas. There's covered seating in three separate patios, with ferns and arbors and caged parakeets providing additional atmosphere, as well as several dining rooms spread through the interior of a couple of connected buildings. The food is standard and acceptable tourist fare. The combo *Caribeña La Mina* is a sauté of chunks of chicken, pork, and shrimp in a tasty sauce with a hint of rum. The Traditional Cuban Combo comes with a *mojito,* black beans and rice, some grilled pork in *mojo* (gravy), and dessert. There's an attached ice-cream parlor and informal cafe. This is a good place to while away a few hours midday, or to take a break while walking around La Habana Vieja.

Calles Obispo and Oficios, Plaza de Armas. © **7/862-0216.** Reservations not required. Main courses CUC$7–CUC$28 (US$7.55–US$30/£3.80–£15). MC, V. Daily 24 hr.

La Paella ★ SPANISH   This is the premier paella place in Havana. The paellas are well prepared—in fact, they have won a few international prizes. Stick to a paella with chicken and sausage, or splurge on a lobster and seafood special. This place used to be a real bargain, but prices have doubled. They also have a host of meat, poultry, and seafood items, but go with the house specialty. The atmosphere is warm and lively, with heavy wooden tables and colorful ceramic accents everywhere.

In the Hostal Valencia at Calle Oficios 53 (btw. Calles Lamparilla and Obrapía). (C) **7/867-1037.** Reservations recommended. Main courses CUC$8–CUC$24 (US$8.65–US$26/£4.30–£13). MC, V. Daily noon–10pm.

Inexpensive

Café Taberna (Value) CRIOLLA/INTERNATIONAL   This lively joint is housed in a beautifully restored, 18th-century building with high ceilings, just off the Plaza Vieja. Photos of Beny Moré and other popular mambo acts adorn the walls, and there's a long bar with an impressive wall of booze stacked behind it. The food is standard and uninspired fare, but this is one of the few places in La Habana Vieja that won't break your bank for a simple meal. The outdoor seating seems like an afterthought, and feels a little too far removed from the action and ambience.

Calles Mercaderes and Teniente Rey, Plaza Vieja. (C) **7/861-1637.** Reservations not required. Main courses CUC$4–CUC$25 (US$4.30–US$27/£2.15–£14). MC, V. Daily noon–midnight.

Cafetería El Portal CRIOLLA   The El Patio restaurant complex has a handful of dining options, and this is the only one really worth a visit. With seating on the large covered patio, and a couple of dozen small tables set right on the Plaza de la Catedral, it's hard to find a spot with more character in La Habana Vieja. The menu is small, but this place is big on atmosphere. The only real splurge here is the lobster supreme in a light vinaigrette, which, although small, is a decent deal at CUC$10 (US$11/£5.40). If you're hungrier, you can have a Cuban sandwich or a small steak, both of which will come with French fries and fill you up. The *mojitos* here are acceptable and will run you CUC$3 (US$3.25/£1.60). The outdoor tables start getting some shade around 2pm, and all night long they provide wonderful views of the cathedral's lit bell towers. This is a great spot for a drink and light meal, day or night. If you do opt for one of the pricier tables inside, be sure to snag one of the few tables on the second-floor balconies overlooking the plaza.

Calle San Ignacio 54 (corner of Calle Empedrado), Plaza de la Catedral. (C) **7/867-1034.** Reservations not accepted. Main courses CUC$4–CUC$17 (US$4.30–US$18/£2.15–£9.20). MC, V. Daily noon–midnight.

La Taberna de la Muralla ★ (Finds) GRILL   Havana's only brewpub is blessed with a beautiful setting on a corner overlooking Plaza Vieja. Grab a seat at one of the wrought-iron tables under a broad canvas umbrella on the edge of the plaza when the weather's right, or one of the heavy wooden tables on the covered patio or indoor dining room when it's not. The small and simple menu is made up almost entirely of grilled-to-order pork chops, chicken breasts, or fish filets, or kabobs of chicken, shrimp, lobster, or a mix of the three. Order a pint of the home-brewed amber or dark beer and admire the large copper brewing tanks just behind the bar. Large groups or heavy drinkers can order a *dispensa,* a tall, clear glass tube filled with beer, featuring a spout at the bottom and a thinner tube filled with ice running up its center. Service can be annoyingly slack when it's busy.

Calle San Ignacio (corner of Calle Muralla), Plaza Vieja. (C) **7/866-4453.** Reservations not accepted. Main courses CUC$4–CUC$8 (US$4.30–US$8.65/£2.15–£4.30). MC, V. Daily noon–midnight.

Los Nardos ★ (Value) INTERNATIONAL/SPANISH   A small neon sign and a doorman mark the entrance to this hidden restaurant that serves up some of the largest and tastiest platters in Havana. Los Nardos, run by a cooperative, can be found on the top floor in the arches next to the Sala Kid Chocolate, conveniently located in the center of town opposite the Capitolio. Dine by candlelight—at lunch time and in the evening—on large wooden tables accompanied by a live band. The walls are impressively lined with wine vaults and trophies; colored-glass windows with candlelight cast an attractive light across the room. The servings of food are enormous: huge lobster platters or chicken with plenty of vegetables at very reasonable prices. Those who can't manage to finish the meal may take the leftovers home with them. It's extremely popular and you will almost always have to wait a short while to get served.

Paseo del Prado 565 (btw. Teniente Rey and Dragones, across from El Capitolio). ℂ **7/863-2985.** Reservations not accepted. Main courses CUC$5–CUC$14 (US$5.40–US$15/£2.70–£7.55). No credit cards. Daily 11:30am–11:30pm.

Restaurante-Pizzeria El Asturianito ★ (**Value**) ITALIAN   Climb right to the very top of the Los Nardos building for this Italian-style eatery. It's run by the same crew as Los Nardos and it serves plenty of similar dishes, but without the waiting line, candlelight, ambience, and live music. However, the service and standards are the same and the seating is more spacious. Although there are Cuban platters served, you'll probably come for the Italian fare. There are 11 spaghetti dishes, plus lasagna. I recommend the great-value three-meals-in-one Juventud Asturiana pizza on a thin crust, which comes piled with ham, chorizo, salami, *camarones* (shrimp), tuna, and Bolognese sauce in separate quarters; the Bolognese sauce is a bit heavy for pizza, though.

Paseo del Prado 560 btw. Teniente Rey and Dragones ℂ **7/863-2985.** Reservations not accepted. Main courses CUC$2.50–CUC$12 (US$2.70–US$13/£1.35–£6.50). No credit cards. Daily noon–midnight.

CENTRO HABANA

I am decidedly unimpressed with the Asian food available in Cuba. This goes for the handful of Chinese restaurants in Havana's little Chinatown, too. However, if you do venture to the block-long Cuchillo de Zanja, or just crave a change from *criolla* cooking, your best bets are **Los Tres Chinitos,** Dragoes 355 (ℂ **7/860-4318**) and **Viejo Amigo,** Dragones 356 (ℂ **7/861-8095**).

Moderate

La Guarida ★★ CRIOLLA   The most famous *paladar* in Cuba owes its renown in equal parts to the wonderful ambience, excellent cuisine, and the starring role it played in several scenes in the Cuban blockbuster film *Fresa y Chocolate.* The three small rooms of this converted apartment are reached by climbing three flights of steep, run-down, and poorly lit stairs. The signed celebrity headshots allow a glimpse at the stars in whose steps you have just followed. Start things off with some seviche, gazpacho, or their signature appetizer of eggplant caviar, a tasty vegetable paste with the texture the name implies. *Caimanero* (fresh red snapper) might come in a white-wine, orange, or sweet-and-sour sauce—all are good, as is the honey-mustard chicken and pork medallions in mango sauce. There's an extensive selection of Spanish, French, Italian, and Chilean wines. Just make sure you're not seated at the table between the kitchen and the restrooms. The ornate facade and balcony balustrades make this place worth a peek during the daytime. (To locate this *paladar,* see the "Vedado" map on p. 80, or better yet, just tell its name to any taxi driver.)

Calle Concordia 418 (btw. Calles Gervasio and Escobar). ℂ **7/866-9047.** www.laguarida.com. Reservations required. Main courses CUC$11–CUC$17 (US$12–US$18/£5.95–£9.20). No credit cards. Daily noon–4:30pm and 7pm–midnight.

In addition to the places listed below, you might try **Sierra Maestra** (℗ 7/838-4011), which serves nouvelle Cuban cuisine in an elegant setting on the 25th floor of the Tryp Habana Libre hotel.

Moderate

El Conejito INTERNATIONAL   The name means "little rabbit," but there's more than just a little bit of rabbit on the menu here: grilled, baked, *a la criolla,* or *ali oli* (in garlic *mojo,* or gravy) are just some of the treatments our furry friend gets—not to mention rabbit sausage, rabbit terrine, and rabbit ham for starters. Almost all the rabbit dishes are reasonably priced at from CUC$4 to CUC$6.20 (US$4.30–US$6.70/ £2.15–£3.35). Avoid the house specialty, *conejo a la financiera,* which comes in a busy yet bland sauce, and stick to simpler preparations. There are also more traditional meat and seafood options, but I'd go with the bunny. The place is modeled on an English Tudor pub, with brick walls and heavy, dark interior beams. There's a small attached bar that is usually pretty quiet.

Calles M and 17. ℗ **7/832-4671.** Reservations not required. Main courses CUC$4–CUC$20 (US$4.30–US$22/£2.15–£11). No credit cards. Daily noon–11pm.

Paladar Hurón Azul ★★ CRIOLLA/INTERNATIONAL   Tucked away on a lightly trafficked street, yet still close to the hustle and bustle of Vedado, this small restaurant is a calm and elegant joint that's very popular with tourists and the Cuban elite. The indoor dining rooms display beautiful paintings by prominent local artists. While not as festive or popular as La Guarida (see above), the food and service here are excellent. Several house combo plates are offered, based around either a chicken or pork main dish. This place is not to be confused with the open-air patio bar of the same name run by the Union de Escritores y Artistas Cubanos (UNEAC).

Calle Humboldt 153 (corner of Calle P). ℗ **7/836-3636.** www.huronazul.com. Reservations recommended. Main courses CUC$8–CUC$14 (US$8.65–US$15/£4.30–£7.55). No credit cards. Daily noon–midnight.

Inexpensive

Restaurante Monguito Finds CRIOLLA   This little joint has just five plastic tables with plastic lawn chairs in a narrow room. Plastic flowers in cheap vases, a couple of squawking parrots in the back, and kitschy, semiholographic nature scenes on the main wall complete the ambience. The *bistec uruguayo,* a kind of deep-fried pork *cordon bleu,* is huge, and the *pollo a la cacerola,* baked chicken in a tomato sauce, is excellent. Try to get a seat near one of the fans, because—despite the massive air-conditioning unit—this place can get a little stuffy, especially midday.

Calle L (btw. Calles 23 and 25, directly across from Tryp Habana Libre). ℗ **7/831-2615.** Reservations not accepted. Main courses CUC$4–CUC$7.50 (US$4.30–US$8.10/£2.15–£4.05). No credit cards. Fri–Wed noon–11pm.

PLAYA

Very Expensive

El Tocororo ★ CRIOLLA/INTERNATIONAL   Like its progeny, La Finca, this is a place whose reputation precedes it, and whose actual performance can't quite justify the prices and renown. The food and service are fine, but they don't live up to the fanfare. There's no fixed menu, but if the waiter's suggestions don't hit the mark, ask and they may be able to accommodate your request. Most main dishes run between CUC$24 and CUC$35 (US$26–US$38/£13–£19), with lobster—which you choose from a tank— topping things off at around CUC$40 ($43/£22) a pop. They sometimes have exotic game here, ranging from ostrich to crocodile. Almost anything can be prepared with whatever sauce or preparation you might desire. The restaurant is housed in an attractive old Miramar mansion; the decor is cluttered and eclectic, with Tiffany lamps, stained glass, assorted hanging plants, and carved parrots dominating the scene. There's also an attached little sushi bar and restaurant, **Sakura,** serving traditional and respectable Japanese cuisine, although sometimes certain ingredients are lacking.

Av. 3 and Calle 18. © **7/204-2209.** Reservations recommended. Main courses CUC$10–CUC$40 (US$11–US$43/£5.40–£22); sushi CUC$6–CUC$12 (US$6.50–US$13/£3.25–£6.50). MC, V. Mon–Sat noon–midnight.

Expensive
Don Cangrejo ★ SEAFOOD   This oceanfront restaurant is one of the better and most dependable options for seafood in Havana. The menu is extensive, but your best bet is to stick to a piece of simply prepared fresh snapper or grouper. If you want something heavier, they prepare a lot of cheese and gratin sauces, often with shrimp, crab, or lobster thrown in. Weather permitting, the best seats are outdoors on the open-air patio right beside the water, and around the little courtyard swimming pool. The indoor seating is semiformal and heavily air-conditioned. If you're going to dine indoors, try to snag one of the second-floor window tables just off the little bar. The place has a decent and reasonably priced wine list and a knowledgeable sommelier.

Av. 1 (btw. Calles 16 and 18). © **7/204-4169.** Reservations recommended. Main courses CUC$8–CUC$30 (US$8.65–US$32/£4.30–£16). MC, V. Daily noon–midnight.

Moderate
If you can't get a table at La Cocina de Lilliam (see below), **La Esperanza,** Calle 16 no. 105 between Avenidas 1 and 3 (© **7/202-4361**), is another excellent *paladar* set up in an old sprawling home in Miramar (Mon–Sat 7–11pm; CUC$13/US$14/£7).

El Aljibe ★ CRIOLLA   This popular tourist restaurant is a pleasant surprise. The fixed-price *pollo asado El Aljibe* (CUC$12/US$13/£6.50) is the way to go here. Served all-you-can-eat family style with white rice, black beans, fried plantain, French fries, and salad, the slow-roasted chicken comes in a wonderful, slightly sweet-and-sour garlic *mojo* (gravy) that goes well over the rice. This place serves busloads of people on a regular basis, and despite the assembly-line efficiency of the operation, you can still enjoy the pleasant open-air restaurant, with its tall, steeply pitched thatched roof and rustic red-tile floors. Sure there is a handful of meat and seafood options, but trust me, stick to the house specialty.

Av. 7 (btw. Calles 24 and 26). © **7/204-1583** or 7/204-4233. Reservations recommended. Main courses CUC$10–CUC$24 (US$11–US$26/£5.40–£13). MC, V. Daily noon–midnight.

La Cocina de Lilliam ★★ (Finds) CRIOLLA   The elegant, softly lit outdoor garden seating here would be enough to recommend this family-run *paladar,* but the food is excellent as well. Lilliam Domínguez has a deft touch. Try the garbanzo, ham, and onion appetizer, and then opt for a piece of fresh fish, usually grouper or snapper, simply grilled. The menu varies, but if it's available, order the *ropa vieja,* made with shredded lamb here instead of the traditional beef. This place is getting quite popular, so reservations are essential, especially if you want one of the outdoor tables.

Calle 48 no. 1311 (btw. Calles 13 and 15). © **7/209-6514.** Reservations highly recommended. Main courses CUC$10–CUC$15 (US$11–US$16/£5.40–£8.10). No credit cards. Sun–Fri noon–3pm and 7–10pm.

HABANA DEL ESTE & PLAYAS DEL ESTE
Expensive

La Divina Pastora SEAFOOD/CRIOLLA This place has a wonderful setting, just behind a battery of big cannons below the Fortaleza de la Cabaña, near the water and overlooking La Habana Vieja. However, you'll be paying extra for the setting, and most of the seating is indoors, with no views of the city. The food here, while acceptable, does nothing to justify the prices. You might as well order the lobster, as it's the only thing that costs more or less what you'd pay for it anywhere else—and you know they're fresh, since you get to pick your dinner from a large tank of live ones. If you're not especially hungry, check out the **El Mirador** bar next-door, which has better views from its outdoor tables, and a small, simple menu of sandwiches and light meals.

Parque Histórico Morro y Cabaña, Carretera de La Cabaña. © **7/860-8341.** Reservations recommended. Main courses CUC$14–CUC$30 (US$15–US$32/£7.55–£16). MC, V. Daily noon–midnight.

Moderate

El Bodegón Criollo CRIOLLA A couple of huge wine casks hanging over the door mark the entrance to this, the principal restaurant at the Fortaleza de la Cabaña complex (see "Parque Histórico Morro y Cabaña," p. 118). The dining room occupies a long, wide, former storage room in the old fortress, with arched ceilings and brick floors. A small bar dominates a much smaller, adjacent room. The food is simple and filling. I recommend the *grillada criolla,* which is a mixed plate of grilled beef, chicken, and pork served with *moros y cristianos* (black beans and rice). The grilled lobster is a good choice as well. Make a reservation for around 7pm if you want to eat and be out in time to snag a good spot for the nightly *cañonazo* (cannon-firing) ceremony. The Fortaleza de la Cabaña complex is popular with Cubans and actually has several restaurants—you might want to try the nearby **La Fortaleza,** a pesos-only *(moneda nacional)* restaurant that serves similar and slightly less-expensive food in a much less formal setting.

Fortaleza de la Cabaña. © **7/861-9504.** Reservations recommended. Main courses CUC$5–CUC$20 (US$5.40–US$22/£2.70–£11). MC, V. Daily noon–11pm.

La Terraza ★ SEAFOOD/CRIOLLA This place is de rigueur for any Hemingway tour of the island. The ghosts of Papa and his pal Gregorio Fuentes are omnipresent here—just saunter through the swinging saloon-style doors and look around. The small restaurant is actually somewhat unable to cope with its fame, but if you get here early or have a firm reservation, you won't have to wait to enjoy the well-prepared seafood, cool sea breezes, and a great view across the small plaza in Cojímar to the sea. The seafood paella is pretty good, and the lobster is usually fresh.

Calle 152 no. 161, Cojímar. © **7/766-5151.** Reservations recommended. Main courses CUC$6–CUC$25 (US$6.50–US$27/£3.25–£14). MC, V. Daily 11am–11pm.

Los Doce Apóstoles ★ CRIOLLA I prefer this place to the far more pretentious and nearby La Divina Pastora (see above). Set at the base of the Morro Castle, just behind a battery of 12 cannons—hence the name "The Twelve Apostles"—the setting is actually nicer than that at La Divina Pastora, with great views day or night at a collection of open-air patio tables. When it's raining or the sun's too strong, you can take a seat at one of the less picturesque, indoor tables. Stick to the reasonably priced *criolla* fare and, if you've

Parque Histórico Morro y Cabaña, Carretera de La Cabaña. © **7/863-8295.** Reservations recommended.
Main courses CUC$8–CUC$28 (US$8.65–US$30/£4.30–£15). MC, V. Daily noon–11pm.

---

5 WHAT TO SEE & DO

Havana is a city with a rich historical and architectural legacy. There are scores of sights
and attractions, ranging from museums and churches to city squares and colonial forts—
and more. There's easily a week's worth of worthy attractions. I've tried to select and
describe the most important sights below.

At many attractions, a CUC$2 to CUC$5 (US$2.15–US$5.40/£1.10–£2.70) fee is
added on for the taking of photos, and as much as CUC$50 (US$54/£27) for shooting
video. This policy seems to be applied somewhat erratically.

All of the major tour agencies offer **city tours.** These affairs generally take in as many
attractions as can be fitted into the allotted time period. The most common tours include
stops at the José Martí Memorial, a ride along the Malecón, and a walk around La
Habana Vieja (including stops at a handful of churches and attractions, and, of course,
La Bodeguita del Medio). Some include tours of any number of the attractions listed
below, with perhaps a visit to El Morro or the Hemingway Museum thrown in, while
others are theme based—castles and forts, churches, tobacco, art, or Hemingway, for
example. Different tour agencies mix and match the various attractions at their discretion. If you want to see something specific, be sure it's on the tour you sign up for. The
tours can range from 4 to 8 hours in length and cost between CUC$15 and CUC$50
(US$16–US$54/£8.10–£27) per person.

THE TOP ATTRACTIONS
La Habana Vieja
In addition to the places mentioned below, there are scores of other interesting little
museums and attractions. Moreover, many of the hotels and restaurants mentioned above
(including El Floridita, Hotel Santa Isabel, and Hotel Ambos Mundos, to name just a
few) are practically attractions in their own right, and worth a quick visit on any walking
tour.

One of the prime attractions in La Habana Vieja is the expansive daily street market
of arts and crafts ★★, open from 9am until around 6pm, from Wednesday to Sunday,
on Calle Tacón, facing the Harbor Channel. See "Shopping," later in this chapter, for
more information.

Castillo de la Real Fuerza ★   This well-preserved, 16th-century fort sits within a
broad cloverleaf moat. This is the oldest fort in Havana, and the oldest surviving fort in
the hemisphere. It was actually pretty much a failure, built too small and too far from the
harbor entrance to be of much use. Still, crossing over the old drawbridge and walking
around the ancient stone battlements gives you a great sense of history. The most distinctive feature of this compact fort is the weathervane, **La Giraldilla,** which has come to be
the city's defining symbol. The original 1634 bronze sculpture is actually on display
at the Museo de la Ciudad, but a copy still adorns the top of the fort's bell tower. Today,
the fort also contains the **Artistic Ceramic Museum,** with ceramic works by Wifredo

A Quick Key to Havana's Parks & Plazas

Any tour of La Habana Vieja will be oriented around the several colonial plazas or squares, and the Parque Central (Central Park). Although relatively close together, each is almost a world of its own. The principal attractions of each are described in greater detail below, but here's a general overview.

The smallest, **Plaza de la Catedral,** is probably the most visited. Named for the cathedral that defines its northern boundary, this compact cobblestone square is surrounded by a series of stunning, colonial-era buildings and former palaces. With the cathedral's bell towers lit up each night, this is a great plaza to visit after dark. Within a 1-block radius in any direction, you will find La Bodeguita del Medio, the Centro Wifredo Lam, the Museo de Arte Colonial, and the lively Calle Tacón street market.

The **Plaza de Armas** probably has the most dense concentration of historic buildings and attractions. Surrounding the shady urban park that now takes up the plaza, you'll find the Palacio de los Capitanes Generales and Museo de la Ciudad, the Castillo de la Real Fuerza, El Templete, and the Hotel Santa Isabel, housed in the former palace of the Count of Santovenia. Most days, the square is lined with stands set up by scores of used-book sellers.

The oldest plaza, **Plaza Vieja,** was first laid out in 1599 and was dubbed "Plaza Nueva" (New Square). It soon lost prominence to the better located Plaza de Armas and Plaza de la Catedral. In fact, for most of the last half of the 20th century, it served simply as a parking lot. However, it has recently been meticulously restored. At the center of the broad open square is a replica of an 18th-century fountain. Surrounding it are historic buildings representing 4 centuries of construction.

Lam, Amelia Peláez, and Mirta García Bus, among others, and brand-new exhibits with items salvaged from shipwrecks and with replicas of Spanish colonial boats.

Calle O'Reilly 2 (at Av. del Puerto). *C* **7/861-5010.** Admission CUC$2 (US$2.15/£1.10) adults, free for children under 12. Daily 8am–7pm.

Catedral de San Cristóbal ★★★ This is Old Havana's classic cathedral. The plaza fronting the cathedral and the church's baroque facade, with its asymmetrical towers, are the most visited attractions in La Habana Vieja. Inside, the cathedral is simple, almost to the point of austerity, thanks to a radical, 19th-century neoclassical makeover. Still, the vaulted ceilings, massive stone pillars, and modest collection of art and antiquities certainly make it worth a visit. Of these, the 17th-century wooden sculpture of Saint Christopher is quite interesting—note the shortened legs, which were cut in order to get the piece into place. Despite the official visiting hours listed below, the church is frequently closed tight. If you're lucky, you might be able to attend Mass here at 9:30am on Sunday.

Calle Empedrado 156, Plaza de la Catedral. *C* **7/861-7771.** Free admission. Mon–Fri 11am–3pm; Sat 11am–2pm; Sun (Mass) 9:30am–12:30pm.

Near the waterfront, you'll find the **Plaza de San Francisco.** Asymmetrical in shape, this is the most open and uncluttered plaza in La Habana Vieja. Facing the Sierra Maestra ship terminal, it is anchored by the Fuente de los Leones (Lion's Fountain), which was carved in 1836 by Italian sculptor Giuseppe Gaggini, modeled after a sister fountain in the Alhambra in Granada, Spain. The area's former importance as a business center is quickly noted in the imposing facades of the Lonja de Comercio (Stock Exchange) and a couple of large banks and money exchange houses that dominate the northern side of the plaza. The southern edge is defined by the lovely, 16th-century Basílica Menor de San Francisco de Asís. Be sure to climb the bell tower here, the tallest church tower in Havana, for a wonderful view of La Habana Vieja and its harbor.

Parque Central marks the western boundary of La Habana Vieja. This is a popular local gathering spot, particularly known for its heated conversations about baseball. It is bordered on the west by the Paseo de Martí, or Prado, featuring El Capitolio and the Gran Teatro de la Habana. On the eastern edge, you'll find the Palacio del Centro Asturiano, which now holds the international collection of the Museo Nacional de Bellas Artes. Classic hotels that ring the park include the Hotel Inglaterra, Hotel Plaza, and the Hotel Telégrafo, as well as the modern Hotel Parque Central. A short stroll down the Prado will soon bring you to the Museo Nacional de Bellas Artes, Museo de la Revolución, and the Memorial *Granma;* while just 1 block in the other direction, heading toward La Habana Vieja on Calle Obispo, you'll hit El Floridita.

Centro Wifredo Lam ★   This little museum and gallery is dedicated to the memory of Cuba's most treasured modern artist. The museum houses a sizable collection of Lam's lithographs and acrylic works, as well as works of art and sculpture from the artist's personal collection. There's usually an interesting traveling exhibit in a separate gallery space. If you want to take a break, there's a simple cafe in a cool central courtyard. The museum has been closed for some time and is due to reopen in June 2009.

Calle San Ignacio (corner of Calle Empedrado). ℂ **7/861-3419.** Admission CUC$2 (US$2.15/£1.10) adults, free for children under 12. Mon–Sat 10am–5pm.

El Templete   A tall (and still growing) ceiba tree stands in front of this neoclassical Doric temple. The tree is the younger cousin of a fallen giant that stood here, on the site where local citizens celebrated the town's first Mass and town meetings in the early 1500s. Behind the tree stands the "little temple," which was built between 1754 and 1828. Inside, you'll find three large canvases by Jean-Baptiste Vermay depicting the inauguration of the temple, as well as depictions of those town meetings and masses. You'll also find a bust of the artist beside an urn containing his ashes.

Calles Baratillo and O'Reilly, Plaza de Armas. ℂ **7/861-2876.** Admission CUC$3 (US$3.25/£1.60) adults, free for children under 12. Daily 9am–6pm.

(Moments) **Strolling Calle Obispo**

Calle Obispo is one of the most charming and distinctive streets in La Habana Vieja. This bustling pedestrian-only boulevard conveniently connects Parque Central and the nearby Capitolio with the Plaza de Armas and its many surrounding attractions, making it a classic route for any walking tour of La Habana Vieja.

HAVANA

5

WHAT TO SEE & DO

Museo de la Ciudad ★★ The Museum of the City is housed in the Palacio de los Capitanes Generales (Palace of the Captain Generals), a beautiful example of 18th-century Cuban baroque architecture, and one of the most important and well-preserved buildings in La Habana Vieja. The seat of Cuba's government for more than 100 years, the building now features a dozen or so rooms with polished marble floors and ornate architectural details, which have displays of colonial-era relics and artifacts. It's worth the price of admission just to stroll along the broad second-floor interior veranda overlooking the lush central courtyard, with its white marble statue of Christopher Columbus. And don't miss the Throne Room, with its thick red-velvet draperies, an array of treasures, and plush throne built for use by Spain's visiting monarchs. Allow yourself at least an hour to tour the museum.

Calle Tacón (btw. Calles O'Reilly and Obispo), Plaza de Armas. ✆ 7/861-6130 or 7/861-2876. Admission CUC$3 (US$3.25/£1.60) adults, free for children under 12. Daily 9am–6pm.

Museo de la Revolución y Memorial Granma ★ Housed in the former Presidential Palace, the Museum of the Revolution and *Granma* Memorial outline Cuba's history in copious detail, with an emphasis on its independence and revolutionary struggles. In addition to the history lessons, exhibits, and memorabilia, there are wonderful works of art and some stunning architectural details, including a replica of Versaille's Hall of Mirrors, ornate bas-relief work, and interior decorations by Tiffany. Outside, you'll find several trucks, tanks, planes, and even a bit of a shot-down U2 spy plane, all surrounding the glass-enclosed *Granma,* the 59-foot motor launch that carried Fidel Castro, Che Guevara, and 80 other fighters to the island in 1956. Give yourself at least 1¹/₂ hour to see it all.

Calle Refugio 1 (btw. Calles Monserrate and Zulueta). ✆ 7/862-4091. Admission CUC$5 (US$5.40/£2.70) adults, free for children under 12. Guided tours are given throughout the day and cost an additional CUC$2 (US$2.15/£1.10). Daily 10am–5pm.

Museo Nacional de Bellas Artes ★★ The National Fine Arts Museum fills three floors of this square-city-block building, and the design—with a central courtyard and zigzagging ramped stairwell—can make navigating the upper floors confusing, so allow yourself plenty of time, and be prepared to get mildly lost inside. An extensive collection of Cuban art and sculpture is on display at the newly renovated main building here. Modern masters like Wifredo Lam, Raúl Martínez, Amelia Peláez, and Rene Portocarrero are well represented. The international collection is now housed in a recently restored, early-20th-century gem of a building. This collection leans heavily on classical and neoclassical European works, with some fine portraits and still lifes from the Dutch Golden Age, although there are some American, Latin American, and Oriental works on display. Brits will be interested in Canaletto's 1751 painting of Chelsea College and the River Thames; the other half hangs in a National Trust property in Norfolk. Give yourself at

Luis Posada Carriles

On October 6, 1976, Cubana de Aviación flight 455 was blown up by plastic explosives, killing all 73 people aboard. The victims included Cuba's entire Olympic fencing team. The man implicated in the bombing, Luis Posada Carriles, is emblematic of the confusing and contradictory nature of U.S.-Cuba relations, and relevant in terms of the current War on Terror.

A former CIA operative and U.S. Army officer, the 80-year-old Posada Carriles took part in the failed Bay of Pigs invasion and later worked with the Nicaraguan contras to destabilize the Sandinista government. He has bragged, and later denied, being responsible for the Cubana airplane bombing, as well as a string of bombings at hotels and tourism facilities in Cuba in which several civilians and tourists were killed. Along with Orlando Bosch, he is implicated in the 1976 car bombing in Washington, D.C., that killed Chilean ambassador Orlando Letelier.

Posada Carriles has been jailed in both Venezuela and Panama. He broke out of jail in Venezuela in the mid-1980s, but was later arrested on charges of attempting to assassinate Fidel Castro at a 2000 regional summit in Panama. In July 2005, Posada Carriles was pardoned by outgoing President Mireya Moscoso. Between 2005 and May 2007, he was held in an immigration detention center as the result of his illegally entering the United States, after his requests for political asylum were denied. Charges were then dropped and he remains a free man. However, in June 2008, the Panamanian Supreme Court overturned the presidential pardon. This has opened up the possibility of extradition to Panama.

Posada Carilles represents an embarrassment to the United States. A self-proclaimed and proud "terrorist," he is seen as being coddled by the Bush administration, which has so far refused to prosecute him under any terrorist statutes or grant extradition officially requested by both Cuba and Venezuela. In Havana, you can see him vilified along with George W. Bush and Adolf Hitler on propaganda billboards.

HAVANA

5

WHAT TO SEE & DO

least 2 hours to tour the collection in either building, or more if you want to get a good feel for the extensive Cuban art collection.

Calle Trocadero (btw. Calles Zulueta and Monserrate) and Calle San Rafael (btw. Calles Zulueta and Monserrate). ✆ **7/861-0241.** www.museonacional.cult.cu. Admission CUC$5 (US$5.40/£2.70) adults, free for children under 14. Tues–Sat 10am–6pm; Sun 10am–2pm.

Parque La Maestranza (Kids)   Located on the edge of La Habana Vieja, this 2-block stretch of city park is dedicated to the little ones. There are pony rides and a little train ride, as well as jungle gyms and inflatable rooms for romping around in. There are usually some clowns or mimes on hand, and balloons, popcorn, and soft drinks are for sale. This place is decidedly low-key and low-tech by Western standards, but the mix of mostly Cuban and some foreign kids never seem to mind.

Calle Cuarteles (btw. Calle Tacón and Av. del Puerto). Admission CUC$2 (US$2.15/£1.10). Daily 9am–5pm.

Callejón de Hammel ★★★ (**Finds**)   Nearly every inch of this narrow, 2-block-long alleyway is painted in bright colors, the work of painter Salvador González. Most are mural-size depictions of Afro-Cuban deities. There are also sculptures made from scrap and old bike parts, as well as a *Nganga,* a sacred place for the celebration of Palo Monte rituals centered on a giant cauldron. There are crafts and food for sale in this open-air bazaar, and González also has a small gallery here. At noon each Sunday, this is the site of a weekly Afro-Cuban music and dance show and celebration headed up by the renowned folkloric group Clavé y Guaguanco. (To locate this alleyway, see the "Vedado" map on p. 80.)

Callejón de Hammel, btw. Calles Espada and Aramburu. Free admission. Daily 24 hr.

Chinatown (**Overrated**)   You'll see Havana's Chinatown touted in local literature, tour offerings, and other guidebooks. Overall, it's quite a disappointment. Occupying a small section of Centro Habana, it has few distinguishing features, a very small population of residents of Chinese descent, and none of the vibrancy of Chinatowns in cities like New York, San Francisco, or Toronto. A block-long pedestrian-only street, **El Cuchillo de Zanja,** is packed with nondescript and unimpressive Chinese restaurants and shops. The biggest attraction here is the large, pagoda-style **Dragon's Gate** at the corner of Calle Dragones and Calle Amistad. Perhaps the most interesting attraction is the **Iglesia de la Caridad,** which features a statue of a Virgin that some say has Asian features. (To locate this area, see the "Vedado" map on p. 80.)

In the area bordered by Calles Dragones, Zanja, Rayo, and San Nicolás. Free admission. Daily 24 hr.

El Capitolio ★   Modeled after its U.S. cousin, the Cuban Capitol is a stunning architectural work of grand scale—it's actually a tiny bit taller and longer than the Washington, D.C. version. There's not a whole lot to see here, but it's worth climbing the steep steps and taking a quick tour. I was impressed by its scale and the intricately inlaid marble floors. The entrance hall has a replica of a 25-carat diamond imbedded in the floor from which all highway distances radiating out from Havana are measured. There's also the *Statue of the Republic,* a 17m-tall (56-ft.), 49-ton Roman goddess covered in gold leaf, which some claim is Jupiter. You can walk around the old parliamentary hall and, if you're lucky, visit the library. Regular guided tours are offered for CUC$1 (US$1.10/55p) per person. There are some Arts-and-Crafts galleries inside the Capitolio, as well as a simple restaurant and a popular Internet cafe.

Calle Prado (btw. Calles San José and Dragones). (*C*) **7/861-5519.** Admission CUC$3 (US$3.25/£1.60) adults, free for children under 12. Daily 8am–5pm.

El Malecón ★★★   This oceanside pedestrian walkway stretches all the way from the Castillo de San Salvador de la Punta in La Habana Vieja to the Almendares River that separates Vedado from Miramar (about 7km/4¼ miles in total). No trip to Havana is complete without at least some time spent strolling and lingering along the Malecón, which is the social center for a wide range of Cubans. Throughout the day, you'll see children swimming and men fishing off the coral outcroppings that border the walkway, and at night, you're sure to see lovers entwined on cozy perches and groups of revelers all along the seawall.

   The section fronting Centro Habana is perhaps the most picturesque, with the crumbling facades and faded paint of neoclassical and neo-Moorish buildings and apartments

Frommer's Favorite Havana Experiences

- Take a walk along the **Malecón,** and then, for a slight change of pace, grab a Coco Taxi or horse-drawn carriage for a different take on Havana's most popular promenade.
- Wander the streets of **La Habana Vieja.** Allow yourself to get lost in time and in the beautiful architecture of its colonial streets, buildings, and plazas.
- Have dinner at the delicious and atmospheric *paladar* **La Guarida,** housed in a crumbling old building used in the famous Cuban film *Fresa y Chocolate.*
- Visit the **Plaza de la Catedral** ★★★ at night, stopping to grab an outdoor table at **Cafetería El Portal** to sip a drink and soak in the sight of the **Catedral de San Cristóbal's** illuminated bell towers.
- Visit a **cigar factory** and enjoy the aromas of Cuba's top export being manufactured in timeless fashion before your very eyes.
- Head to the **Callejón de Hammel** to admire the street art and murals of this Centro Habana neighborhood. Try to come on a Sunday afternoon and you'll be able to enjoy the spectacle of an Afro-Cuban religious show and celebration.
- Pull out all the stops and treat yourself to dinner and a show at the **Tropicana.**

HAVANA

5

WHAT TO SEE & DO

lining the avenue that separates the Malecón from the city. If you've got the legs and time, a walk from the Hotel Nacional to La Habana Vieja (or vice versa) is in order, and should only take you about 20 to 25 minutes. On rough days, you may have to time your steps—or cross the street—as waves break furiously over the seawall. Alternatively, you can hire a horse-drawn carriage or Coco Taxi for the trip.

Free admission. Daily 24 hr.

Fábrica de Tabaco Partagas ★ Founded in 1845, this is Cuba's largest and perhaps most renowned cigar factory, producing around 5 million cigars a year. The off-yellow-and-rust trimmed, neoclassical facade is resplendent in the Havana morning sunlight. (You can take your best photos of it from the west-side windows of El Capitolio.) Official tours are held only at 10am and 2pm daily, although you can sometimes work your way into one of the many tour groups that come through all day long. Throughout the day, you can stop in and buy cigars from the well-stocked shop, La Casa del Habano.

Alternately, or in conjunction, you can visit the nearby **Fábrica de Tabaco H. Upmann,** Calle Amistad 407, between Calles Barcelona and Dragones (© 7/862-0081), or the **Fábrica de Tabaco La Corona,** Calle Zulueta 106, between Calles Colón and Refugio (© 7/862-6173), which are similarly charged with producing some of the country's finest cigars.

Calle Industria 524 (behind the Capitolio). © **7/862-4604.** 45-min. guided tour CUC$10 (US$11/£5.40); reservations recommended. Mon–Sat 9:30–11am and 12:30–2:30pm.

(Finds Imagine

Beatles fans will want to stop by the little **Parque Lennon (Lennon Park)** at Calles 17 and 6 in Vedado, where you'll find a life-size statue of John Lennon seated on a park bench. The "smart Beatle" is quite revered here, and there is an annual open-air concert in this park every December 8, featuring a wide range of prominent Cuban musicians, singing his songs and commemorating his assassination on that day.

Vedado

Cementerio de Colón ★★   A miniature city of mausoleums, crypts, family chapels and vaults, soaring sculptures, and ornate gravestones, Columbus Cemetery covers 55 hectares (136 acres). Designed by Spanish architect Calixto de Loira in the mid-1800s, it is laid out in grids around a central chapel. The main entrance features a large sculpture of Faith, Hope, and Charity in Carrara marble. There's also a large monument to fallen soldiers of the Revolutionary Armed Forces, and an impressive stainless steel sculpture capping a memorial to the martyrs of the 1957 attack on Batista's Presidential Palace. One of the most popular graves is that of La Milagrosa (The Miraculous One). The story goes that when Amelia Goyri de la Hoz died in childbirth in 1901, she was buried with her stillborn daughter placed at her feet. When the tomb was opened a few years later, the baby was found in her arms. Amelia is now considered the protector of pregnant women and newborn children. Pilgrims paying homage must not turn their backs to the tomb upon leaving. Brief guided tours are available (for free, but a tip is generally expected), or you can buy a little guidebook with a detailed map (CUC$5/US$5.40/£2.70) at the entrance.

Calles Zapata and 12. Ⓒ **7/832-1050.** Admission CUC$1 (US$1.10/£55) adults, free for children under 12. Daily 8am–5pm.

Coppelia ★ (Moments   Made famous in Tomás Gutiérez Alea's hit film *Fresa y Chocolate* (Strawberry and Chocolate), this is the main branch of the Cuban national ice-cream company. At the center of the block-long complex is a postmodern building of curving concrete and glass, surrounded by a series of open courtyards with wrought-iron tables, where customers are served bowls of the frozen nectar. There are actually a dozen or so small booths selling cones and bowls spread around the park. Still, Coppelia is yet another glaring case of tourist apartheid: Cubans form long lines to wait their turn at a table or stand while tourists, who are paying in hard currency and not Cuban pesos, are always taken to the head of the line, or shown to a separate convertible peso stand. There are usually only two or three flavors available on any given day; if you're there on a rum raisin day, you're in for a treat. Ice cream in wrappers for tourists starts at about CUC$1.30 (US$1.40/70p); it costs a couple of pesos in *moneda nacional.*

Calles 23 and L. Ⓒ **7/832-6184.** Tues–Sun 11am–10pm.

Memorial José Martí   The 109m (358-ft.) marble tower here is the highest point in Havana. At the base of the tower is a massive statue of the poet and national independence hero José Martí. Inside the base is a small museum dedicated to Martí featuring manuscripts, memorabilia, portraits, and other informative displays. An elevator takes visitors up to a series of lookout rooms atop the tower, providing far-reaching panoramic views of Havana. The lookout is by far the most interesting and popular attraction here, although there's also a little theater where concerts and poetry readings are sometimes held. The memorial sits in the Plaza de la Revolución, host to all political rallies, and faces the Ministry of Interior building with the iconic image of Che Guevara's face cast in iron ★.

Plaza de la Revolución, Nuevo Vedado. ⓒ **7/859-2347** or 7/859-2347. Admission museum CUC$3 (US$3.25/£1.60) adults, CUC$1.50 (US$1.60/80p) children under 12; mirador CUC$2 (US$2.15/£1.10) adults, CUC$1.50(US$1.60/80p) children under 12. Mon–Sat 9am–5pm.

Universidad de la Habana   The compact campus of Havana's main university sits on some high ground in Vedado close to the former Havana Hilton. The broad staircase leading up to the school, with its signature *Alma Mater* statue of a seated woman with outstretched arms, is a popular gathering spot for students, and you can sometimes catch impromptu concerts here. There are a couple of unimpressive museums on campus— those of Natural Sciences and Montane Anthropology—as well as the nearby and slightly more interesting Museo Napoleónico, Calle San Miguel 1159, at the corner of La Ronda (ⓒ 7/873-6564), with its large collection of Napoleonic-era memorabilia.

Calles L and 27, La Ronda. ⓒ **7/879-3488.** Free admission to the university; CUC$3 (US$3.25/£1.60) for museum. Mon–Sat 8am–6pm.

Playa

Acuario Nacional (Kids)   A few years ago, the National Aquarium got a major face-lift and improvements are ongoing. It's not Sea World or the Baltimore Aquarium, but this is a pretty spiffy attempt for Cuba. A variety of tanks and pools re-create all the major water habitats of Cuba, and sea lion and dolphin shows are presented throughout the day. There are a couple of simple cafeteria-style restaurants, and one pseudo-fancy option, the Gran Azul Restaurant, with a huge Plexiglas wall opening onto a large tank where two sad and claustrophobic dolphins swim. This place is very popular with Cuban families and school groups, so it's a great place to mingle.

Av. 3 and Calle 62, Miramar. ⓒ **7/202-5872** or 7/203-6401. www.acuarionacional.cu. Admission CUC$7 (US$7.55/£3.80) adults, CUC$3 (US$3.25/£1.60) students and children under 12. Winter Tues–Sun 10am– 6pm. Summer Tues—Sun 10am–10pm.

Casa Compay Segundo   The megafamous Buena Vista Social Club star who died in 2003 lived in this house for the last six years of his life. It is filled with memorabilia, his awards, newspaper articles, and dozens of photographs that his fans will love. His pre-served bedroom provides a rare glimpse of photos taken in his youth.

Calle 22 no. 103 (btw. Avs. 1 and 3), Miramar, ⓒ **7/202-5922.** www.compaysegundo.es. Mon–Fri 9am–4pm.

Maqueta de la Habana ★   I was prepared to dislike this miniature display of Havana, but left oddly impressed. The realistic scale model of the city takes up almost 144sq. m (1,550 sq. ft.). You can walk around it on the ground level, or climb a narrow interior balcony that rings three walls here. There's usually some traveling art exhibition on the walls surrounding the model. A guide can be hired for CUC$5 to CUC$10 (US$5.40–US$11/£2.70–£5.40). This is not to be confused with a similar (and much smaller) scale model of Old Havana, found in Old Havana, of course.

Calle 28 (btw. Avs. 1 and 3), Miramar. ⓒ **7/202-7322.** Admission CUC$3 (US$3.25/£1.60); CUC$2 (US$2.15/ £1.10) to take photos; CUC$5 (US$5.40/£2.70) to take video. Mon–Sat 9:30am–5:30pm.

(Moments) The Cañonazo

The **cañonazo (cannon blast)** ★ is a picturesque ritual that takes place at La Fortaleza de San Carlos de la Cabaña every night. An honor guard in 18th-century military garb emerges from the barracks at about 8:40pm and conducts a small parade to a bank of cannons overlooking Havana's harbor channel. With pomp and circumstance, the cannon is loaded and fired precisely at 9pm. About 1,000 people show up each night, the vast majority of them Cubans. Arrive early if you want a good vantage point. The blast itself is quite loud—you can hear it in most parts of Havana—so protect your ears. You can combine the ceremony with a meal at one of the nearby restaurants.

Outside Downtown

Museo Ernest Hemingway   I have mixed feelings about the experience of visiting this place, since visitors are not allowed into the former home of the famous writer. Sure, you get a bit of the feel for Hemingway, but you also end up feeling like a Peeping Tom. Circling the ground floor, you can see the house more or less as it was when Hemingway was living and writing here. There's a copious collection of books, paintings, and stuffed animal heads. In addition to an old typewriter, the works of art by Picasso, Miró, and Klee are some of the more prized possessions. There's a small tower separate from the main house, which has a gift shop and some rooms with rudimentary exhibits, and you can even climb it for a better view all around. In the surrounding gardens, you can see Papa's pet cemetery and the author's dry-docked fishing boat, *Pilar.*

Finca la Vigía, San Francisco de Paula, Carretera Central Km 12.5. ✆ **7/891-0809.** Admission CUC$3 (US$3.25/£1.60) adults, free for children under 12; CUC$1 (US$1.10/55p) for a guide; CUC$5 (US$5.40/£2.70) to take photos; CUC$50 (US$54/£27) to take video. Mon–Sat 10am–5pm; Sun 10am–1pm.

Parque Histórico Morro y Cabaña ★★   Located across the harbor channel from La Habana Vieja, this historic park of forts, battlements, and barracks was responsible for the protection of Havana for centuries. The complex is actually made up of two separate forts, or attractions: the **Castillo del Morro** and **La Fortaleza de San Carlos de la Cabaña.**

The Morro Castle, or "El Morro" as it is most commonly known, is the first fort you'll come to after crossing under the harbor channel tunnel. Sitting on the point overlooking Havana's narrow harbor channel, it was built between 1589 and 1630 and served as an important line of defense against pirate attacks and naval invasions. In addition to its ramparts, barracks, and banks of cannons, El Morro has a series of exhibition rooms and minimuseums. You can walk the fort's ancient streets and even climb the still-functioning, 19th-century lighthouse here. El Morro affords excellent views of Havana and the curve of the Malecón, and there are several restaurants and bars here.

About a kilometer (¹/₂-mile) away, and separated by a deep ravine, is the larger La Fortaleza de San Carlos de la Cabaña, more popularly referred to as simply "la Cabaña." Built between 1764 and 1774, in response to the British invasion, the long fort is a miniature city, with a high perch overlooking the harbor channel and La Habana Vieja. As at El Morro, there are several exhibition halls and a handful of restaurants, bars, and gift shops here. One of the more popular exhibition halls is the **Comandancia de Che Guevara,** a room where the revolutionary leader briefly set up a command post after storming the fort in January 1959. Be sure to stop in at the cigar shop, which features the longest cigar in the world, an 11m (36-ft.) stogie that hangs above your head and is duly registered in the Guinness Book of World Records.

There are separate entrance fees for each attraction. A taxi to the complex from Havana costs between CUC$5 and CUC$7 (US$5.40—US$7.55/£2.70–£3.80). You can walk between the two forts—it's about a 15-minute walk that's only moderately strenuous if you stick to the high ground—or you can take a taxi between the two for under CUC$2 (US$2.15/£1.10).

Carretera de La Cabaña, Habana del Este. (✆ **7/863-7063** for El Morro; (✆ **7/862-0617** for La Cabaña. Admission El Morro CUC$3 (US$3.25/£1.60) adults, free for children under 12; La Cabaña CUC$3 (US$3.25/£1.60) adults before 6pm, CUC$5 (US$5.40/£2.70) adults after 6pm, free for children under 12. El Morro daily 8am–8pm; La Cabaña daily 10am–midnight.

---

6 OUTDOOR PURSUITS

BASEBALL Baseball is the national sport and, after salsa dancing and sex, the greatest national passion. Cuba's amateur players are considered some of the best in the world, and the premier players are aggressively scouted and courted by the Major Leagues. Quite a few have defected and signed with major-league clubs, while other outstanding players are content to stay, turning down lucrative offers. The regular season runs November through March, and playoffs and the final championship usually carry the season on into May. **Industriales,** the main Havana team, plays at the **Estadio Latinoamericano,** Calle Zequeira 312, Cerro (✆ 7/870-6526). It's usually easy to buy tickets at the box office for less than 5 Cuban pesos, or ask at your hotel and perhaps they can get tickets for you in advance—although for these, you'll probably end up paying CUC$1 to CUC$3 (US$1.10–US$3.25/55p–£1.60).

BIKING Despite the fact that so much of Havana's transportation is conducted on bicycles, there are no rental agencies or outlets for tourists wishing to get around town by bike. Your best bet for bicycling in Cuba is to bring your own set of wheels and head outside Havana.

GOLF While the only regulation 18-hole course in the country is located in Varadero (see chapter 7), the **Club de Golf Habana,** Carretera Vento Km 8, Capdevila, **Rancho Boyeros** (✆ **7/649-8918, ext. 111**), has a decent little 9-hole course for true golf junkies. A round of 9 holes will run you CUC$20 (US$22/£11). Each hole actually has two sets of tees, so you can really play 18 holes, and fake the impression that it's a regulation course. A round of 18 holes costs CUC$30 (US$32/£16). Club rental is an extra CUC$10 (US$11/£5.40) and a caddy will cost you CUC$5 (US$5.40/£2.70).

GYMS There are no chains of modern gyms in Havana. Visitors looking for a regular workout on modern gym equipment or an aerobics class should stick to the larger hotels with well-equipped facilities (see "Where to Stay," earlier in this chapter). If you're not staying at one of these hotels, you can use the facilities at the **Meliá Habana** or **Meliá Cohiba** for CUC$10 (US$11/£5.40).

Club Habana, Avenida 5, between Calles 188 and 192, Reparto Flores, Playa (✆ **7/204-5700** or 7/204-3300), has a decent gym and will let guests use the facilities for CUC$20 to CUC$30 (US$22–US$32/£11–£16) per day.

JOGGING The **Malecón** is a fabulous place to jog. Early mornings and early evenings, when the heat has somewhat abated, are best. You'll have to watch your step in certain sections where the sidewalk is torn up or deteriorated, but overall this is the choice route for jogging. Farther afield, joggers could try **Parque Lenin,** Calle 100 and Carretera de la Presa (© 7/644-3026), which is open Tuesday through Sunday from 9am to 5:30pm. This massive park is a major recreational area for locals and has several trails and internal roadways good for jogging.

SCUBA DIVING   While the diving is nowhere near as good as you'll find in more dedicated dive destinations in Cuba, it's certainly possible to do some underwater exploring out of Havana. Your best bet is to head over to Cubanacán's **Club Acuario,** Avenida 5 and Calle 248, Santa Fe, Playa (© 7/204-1150), or **Marina Tarará,** Vía Blanca Km 18, Playa Tarará, Habana del Este (© 7/797-1500), located 18km (11 miles) east of the city. It costs between CUC$50 and CUC$85 (US$54–US$92/£27–£46) for two tank dives, including equipment and lunch. You might also consider a day trip to Varadero or Playa Girón for generally better conditions, and not much more cost.

SPORTFISHING   It's easy to follow in Hemingway's wake and try your luck at landing a big one. As with diving, your best bet is to head over to Cubanacán's **Club Acuario,** Avenida 5 and Calle 248, Santa Fe, Playa (© 7/204-1150), or **Marina Tarará,** Vía Blanca Km 18, Playa Tarará, Habana del Este (© 7/797-1500). Depending on the size of the boat and number of fishermen, a half-day of sportfishing costs between CUC$150 and CUC$500 (US$162–US$540/£81–£270), while a full day will run you between CUC$400 and CUC$1,400 (US$432–US$1,512/£216–£756), including gear and lunch.

SWIMMING   If your hotel does not have a swimming pool, most of the larger hotels allow nonguests use of their pool facilities for a price. Rates generally range between CUC$5 and CUC$18 (US$5.40–US$19/£2.70–£9.70) per person. The nicer options include the **Meliá Habana** and **Club Habana** in Playa; the **Hotel Nacional** and **Meliá Cohiba** in Vedado; and the **NH Parque Central, Hotel Saratoga,** and **Hotel Sevilla** in La Habana Vieja.

Although it's possible to use the small beach at the Club Habana, the nearby Playas del Este is your best bet for some beach time. Most tour agencies and hotel tour desks offer a day trip to Playa Santa María del Mar for CUC$25 to CUC$40 (US$27–US$43/£14–£22), including round-trip transportation, lunch, and often free run of the facilities at one of the all-inclusive hotels out there.

Note: Do not be tempted to join the locals you see swimming off the coral outcroppings just below the Malecón. The coral is jagged and sharp, and the seas can get suddenly rough. Moreover, in recent years there have been complaints that the water is very polluted.

TENNIS   Unless you're staying at one of the few Havana hotels with a court, your options are limited. Your best bet is to try to book a court at the **Occidental Miramar,** Avenida 5, between Calles 78 and 80, Miramar, Playa (© 7/204-8158), which has six courts; or head to the **Club Habana,** Avenida 5, between Calles 188 and 192, Reparto Flores, Playa (© 7/204-3300); or **Club de Golf Habana,** Carretera Vento Km 8, Capdevila, Rancho Boyeros (© 7/649-8820), each of which has a few courts open to the general public. All charge around CUC$10 (US$11/£5.40) per hour.

7 SHOPPING

THE SHOPPING SCENE

Havana is by no means a great shopping city (although it is the best in Cuba). Given the reality of the Cuban economy, all shops selling any goods above and beyond the basic necessities are by default geared entirely toward tourists, a small community of foreign diplomats and workers, and an even smaller community of Cubans earning enough hard currency to afford such luxuries. Hence, it's a challenge to find interesting shops with unique local items at good prices. In general, stores throughout Havana are open from 9am to 5pm, 7 days a week. Some may open earlier and close later, particularly in heavily trafficked tourist areas. Virtually none close for lunch.

All shops selling to tourists operate exclusively with Cuban convertible pesos. Most are run by big, state-owned enterprises. The most common stores belong to the **Caracol** chain, which is geared primarily to tourists, while the **Tiendas Panamericanas** chain specializes in household and domestic items aimed at foreign residents. In recent years, modern malls have begun popping up. Everything stated above holds true for the merchandise you'll find here.

ARTex ★ (© 7/204-0813; www.soycubano.com) is the state-run company in charge of managing Cuba's artistic export products (hence the name "ARTex"). Its job runs the gamut from promoting Cuban musicians and artists abroad to marketing their goods and negotiating contracts. ARTex operates a series of storefronts around the country, either stand-alone affairs or shops placed in prominent hotels or tourist attractions. Depending on the size and location, these usually carry a good selection of Cuban music, Cuban films, tourist T-shirts, and kitschy arts and crafts. The better ones have decent quality drums and percussion instruments, as well as art prints and posters. In Miramar, head to ARTex's **Bazar Volveré,** Calle 3, between Calles 78 and 80 (© 7/204-5370); in Vedado, check out **Habana Sí,** Calle 23 no. 301, at the corner of Calle L (© 7/838-3162), across from the Tryp Habana Libre.

SHOPPING A TO Z
Art Galleries

Galería Acacia This gallery is the place to go for high-end contemporary Cuban art, and a good place to see who the up-and-coming hot artists are. Calle San José 114 (btw. Calles Industria and Consulado), Centro Habana. © 7/863-9364. www.galeriascubanas.com.

Galería Víctor Manuel This place has a pretty good selection of modern decorative paintings, crafts, and a few pieces that could qualify as real artwork. Given its prime location and popularity, don't expect anything to come cheap. Calles San Ignacio and Callejón del Chorro, Plaza de la Catedral, La Habana Vieja. © 7/861-2955.

La Casona Located in a series of rooms over two floors of the Casa de los Condes de Jaruco on Plaza Vieja, this wonderful gallery has similar works to those found at Víctor Manuel, but the selection is better, and there's less of a cattle-car mass-market feel to the place. Calle Muralla 107 (corner of Calle San Ignacio), Plaza Vieja, La Habana Vieja. © 7/863-4703. www.galeriascubanas.com.

Ceramics

Terracota 4 This working studio-cum-gallery in La Habana Vieja features the works of Amelia Carballo, Angel Norniella, and José Ramón. The pieces show a wide range of

The Real Deal

Authentic boxes of Cuban cigars should be sealed and have HECHO EN CUBA (Made in Cuba) burned into the bottom of the box.

influences and utilize wide-ranging techniques. One or more of the artists is usually on hand, and sometimes you'll get a chance to see them working. Calle Mercaderes (btw. Calles Obrapía and Lamparilla), La Habana Vieja. ✆ 7/866-9417.

Cigars

Cigars are Cuba's most-prized product. The word *Cubans* is synonymous with the highest quality cigars on the planet. Locally, they are called *puros* or *habanos;* the latter is the name of the country's official cigar company. All of the various brands—Partagas, Cohiba, Romeo y Julieta, Punch, and so on—are marketed by Habanos S.A. Cigars not officially sold by Habanos fall into the various categories of black- and gray-market stogies. Habanos markets its product through a series of storefronts, usually called something like La Casa del Tabaco or La Casa del Habano. Official sales are also held at shops at most cigar factories, as well as at many higher-end hotels, restaurants, and attractions around town. *Beware:* Black- and gray-market cigars sold on the street or by *jineteros* (hustlers) are more often than not falsely marked, lower-quality cigars.

Cuban cigars range widely in size and shape. Prices range from around CUC$30 to CUC$50 (US$54/£27) per box for the smallest, lowest-quality *puros,* to over CUC$400 (US$432/£216) per box for the more coveted cigars. Most shops sell only complete boxes, although certain cigars are usually available individually, or in boxes of five.

The best **La Casa del Habano** shops are those in the Hostal Conde de Villanueva at Calle Mercaderes 222, La Habana Vieja (✆ 7/862-9293); the Partagas cigar factory at Calle Industria 524, behind El Capitolio (✆ 7/862-4604); and in the Quinta y 16 shopping minicomplex at Avenida 5 and the corner of Calle 16, Miramar (✆ 7/204-7973). Another nice one in La Habana Vieja is the **Casa del Ron y Tabaco Cubana,** Calle Obispo and Calle Bernaza (✆ 7/867-0817), where you can combine two of Cuba's greater pleasures—smoking cigars and drinking rum.

Fashions

In addition to the shop mentioned below, perhaps the most distinctive clothing items a traveler can buy include T-shirts with the image of Che Guevara on the front, and the revolutionary's signature green *boina* (beret) with a little red star in front.

Men might want to pick up a *guayabera* or two. This cool, pleated, and embroidered tropical shirt comes in a variety of (mostly) solid colors, and in both long- and short-sleeve versions. As a rational alternative to heavy suits and ties in a tropical clime, *guayaberas* are appropriate for everything from informal occasions to high-level government and business meetings (in Cuba, at least). You'll find *guayaberas* for sale all over; some of the typically touristy gift shops even carry them. One good place to shop for a guayabera is **El Quitirín,** Calle Obispo and San Ignacio (✆ 7/862-0810). For a more upscale selection, head over to Miramar and shop at **La Maison** (see below); **Le Select,** Avenida 5 and Calle 28 (✆ 7/207-9681); or **Joyería Quinta y 16** (see "Jewelry," below).

La Maison This minicomplex in an old Miramar mansion is the home of Cuban haute couture, but that's not saying much. Several stores spread around the rambling

converted home feature a limited range of men's and women's fashions, jewelry, and **123**
accessories. There's a nightly runway fashion show (CUC$10/US$11/£5.40), as well as a
modest cabaret show, combined with the fashion show on weekends. Calle 16 no. 701
(corner of Av. 7), Miramar, Playa. © **7/204-1543.**

Handicrafts

Cuba doesn't have a particularly strong tradition in producing handicrafts, but the rise in
tourism has seen local artisans quickly making up for lost time. Tourist gift shops as well
as the street markets discussed below are well stocked with locally produced handicrafts.
The best buys are woodcarvings and statues, papier-mâché masks and religious figures,
and simple jewelry made from shells and seeds. You'll also find a host of Afro-Cuban
percussion instruments for sale. Drums you'll find include the two-headed, hourglass-
shaped *bata* drums; paired bongos, carved African-style religious drums; and congas, the
modern salsa backbone. *Shékeres* (gourd shakers) and claves (two wooden sticks used to
play the fundamental rhythm in various Cuban genres) are also available. The Calle
Tacón street market (see below) is your best bet for any of the above.

Jewelry

There are few good jewelry shops in Cuba, which has no real history of producing fine
jewelry. You'll find a plethora of simple, artisan-produced necklaces, bracelets, rings, and
earrings at most tourist shops and street markets. If you look hard enough, you'll actually
find some well-made and attractive pieces. Unfortunately, the nicest jewelry being produced in Cuba is usually made with tortoiseshell or black coral, both natural resources
slow to replenish and easily endangered by overharvesting.

The most common jewelry worn by Cubans are bracelets and necklaces of colored
glass or plastic beads representing the various Afro-Cuban deities. You can pick these up
at the street markets mentioned below. Be sure to ask about the significance of the pieces
you are interested in and what deities they represent.

Joyería Quinta y 16   This is the trendiest jewelry shop in the trendiest little mini-
mall in Havana's trendiest neighborhood. Come here if you want to drop a wad of cash
for some strands of gold, silver, and diamonds, although the selection is far from inspiring. Av. 5 and Calle 16, Miramar. © **7/204-7963.**

Music

Music is one of Cuba's greatest exports. Many CDs available in Cuba are also widely
available abroad or via the Internet. Most CDs in Cuba sell for between CUC$8 and
CUC$15 (US$8.65–US$16/£4.30–£8). However, be careful: Unless you are shopping at
one of the official state-run stores, the CDs you buy may be low-quality bootlegs.

If you're looking for salsa, pick up a disc or two by Los Van Van or NG La Banda. Fans
of Cuban folk music should definitely stock up on recordings by Silvio Rodriguez and
Pablo Milanes. Jazz fans will want some Chucho Valdés with Irakere, and Gonzalo Rub-
alcaba, while those looking to groove to some Afro-Cuban sounds should check out
Síntesis, Los Muñequitos de Matanzas, Yoruba Andabo, and Clavé y Guaguanco. For *son*
and mambo, pick up discs by Adalberto Alvarez y su Son, or the classic rereleases of Beny
Moré and Peréz Prado. Finally, since you've probably already got a copy of *Buena Vista
Social Club,* you might stock up on solo albums by its various members: Compay
Segundo, Rubén Gonzales, Eliades Ochoa, and Omara Portuona. If you enjoy Reggae-
ton, Eddy-K is your group.

(Tips) **Don't Run to Buy** *Ron*

Your best bet for buying rum is the duty-free shop at the airport. The prices and selection are as good here as you'll find anywhere on the island, and you'll save yourself the hassle of hauling heavy bottles around with you while traveling.

Egrem (www.egrem.com.cu) is the national recording industry's signature label, the home of many prominent Cuban musicians. Egrem has a series of storefronts around the country called **Casa de la Música Egrem.** You can also buy discs at one of the many **ARTex** shops around Havana, or you can shop the ARTex catalog online at **www. discuba.com.**

Casa de la Música Habana   Housed in a classic old apartment building in Centro Habana, this is the nicest and best stocked of the Egrem storefronts. It also features daily concerts at 5 and 10pm. Calle Galiano (btw. Calles Concordia and Neptuno), Centro Habana. ℂ 7/860-8296.

Longina Música   This ARTex shop has an excellent selection of CDs and cassettes, as well as sheet music, magazines, and one of the better stocks of Afro-Cuban drums, shakers, and claves you'll find. Calle Obispo 360, La Habana Vieja. ℂ 7/862-8371.

Perfume

Habana 1791   This attractive shop in Old Havana sells traditional perfumes and aromatherapy distillations in faux-vintage glass jars and vials. The place is sometimes marketed as a "perfume museum." Calle Mercaderes 156 (corner of Calle Obrapía), La Habana Vieja. ℂ 7/861-3525.

Rum

After cigars, rum is one of Cuba's signature products. Cuba produces several fine rums. The most commonly sold brand, **Havana Club,** comes in white and dark varieties of various vintages and ages. The premier rum in Cuba is Havana Club's 15-year-old Gran Reserva. This sells for anywhere from CUC$75 to CUC$100 (US$81–US$108/£41–£54) per bottle. It's good, but I don't think it's worth the price tag. However, their 7-year-old Añejo Reserva is a damn fine rum at around CUC$12 (US$13/£6.50) per bottle. Other good rums include **Ron Varadero, Matusalém, Ron Caney, Ron Santiago,** and **Ron Mulata.**

Street Markets

The biggest and best street market in Havana comprises three narrow rows of stalls stretching over a full city block. It's open Wednesday to Sunday from 9am to 6pm in La Habana Vieja on **Calle Tacón** ★★, between Calles Empedrado and Chacón. In addition to the typical arts and crafts and souvenir T-shirts, you'll find scores of local painters selling their wares. Most are rather amateurish renderings of street scenes and famous landmarks. However, you'll find a few good painters and graphic artists here if you look hard enough.

A much **smaller street market** occurs daily in Vedado in a small open area on the south side of La Rampa, at Calle 23 between Calles M and N. The market, which is open daily from 9am to 5pm, has less artwork than the market on Calle Tacón, but it has plenty of woodcarvings and simple jewelry for sale.

the huge gap between the peso and hard currency economies, Cubans often have a hard time understanding the true value of the convertible peso. Prices are often grossly inflated for tourists, on the principle that they "must all be rich." Bargaining is possible at street markets, but it's not necessarily a fluid and enjoyable process. Still, if you think something is overpriced, definitely feel free to offer whatever you believe to be fair, or whatever you are prepared to pay.

8 HAVANA AFTER DARK

Some would say Havana only really gets going after dark, when the slow pace and heat-induced stupor of the day finally wears off. This is a vibrant and truly cosmopolitan city with scores of bars, dance clubs, and theaters to choose from.

THE PERFORMING ARTS

Cuba has a strong tradition in the performing arts. Cuban musicians, playing in a range of styles, are world renowned. The **Cuban National Ballet** ★ (© 7/866-0142; www. balletcuba.cult.cu) has been garnering international accolades for decades, under the seemingly eternal direction of Alicia Alonso. There's an active theater scene (and plenty of movie theaters), both of which are popular with locals, given the scant offerings of Cuban television. The major venues for the classical performing arts are the **Teatro Nacional de Cuba,** Paseo and Calle 39, Vedado (© 7/879-3558), which specializes in live theater performances by local and visiting companies; the **Gran Teatro de La Habana,** Paseo de Martí and Calle San Rafael, Centro Habana (© 7/861-3077, ext. 115), which is home to the Cuban National Ballet, as well as a prime venue for concerts and dance performances; and the **Teatro Amadeo Roldán,** Calle Calzada, between Calles D and E, Vedado (© 7/832-1168), which is home to the National Symphony Orchestra. Other important and working theaters include the **Teatro Mella** (© 7/833-5651), **Teatro Karl Marx** (© 7/203-0801), and the **Café Teatro Brecht** (© 7/832-9359).

Visit **www.cubaescena.cult.cu** and **www.paradiso.cu** for a rundown of annual festivals and events. **Paradiso** (© 7/832-9538), the tourism arm of the Ministry of Culture, publishes the elusive *Cartelera* magazine, a free periodic bilingual magazine with listings for movies, theaters, bars, and live music, which is sometimes available at the front desk

---

(Moments **Feel the Beat**

The **Conjunto Folklórico Nacional de Cuba (Cuban National Folklore Group)** hosts the weekly **Sábado de la Rumba,** a mesmerizing show of Afro-Cuban religious and secular dance and drumming. The 2-hour shows are presented every Saturday at 3pm, at **El Gran Palenque,** Calle 4, between Calzada and Avenida 5 in Vedado. Call © **7/830-3060** or 7/830-3939 for more information or to make a reservation.

Similar shows are offered Thursday through Sunday at 10pm by the group **Obbara** at the Palacio de la Artesanía, Calle Cuba 64, between Calles Peña Pobre and Cuarteles, La Habana Vieja.

of most hotels in Havana. The *H* **magazine** also provides updated information (**www. thehmagazine.com/agenda/havana_listings.php**) as does *Cuba Absolutely* (**www. cubaabsolutely.com/events/whats_on.htm**). Your best bet for any advance planning is to go online or call the venue when you are in Havana. You can call any of the theaters listed above directly for performance schedules and ticket information.

THE CABARET, CLUB & DANCE SCENE

I'll bet Havana has more floor shows per capita than Las Vegas. In addition to the clubs and cabarets listed below, there are nightly and entirely respectable cabaret shows at the Habana Riviera's **Copa Room,** Paseo and Malecón, Vedado (© 7/836-4051); ARTex's **Patio de la Casa 18,** Calle 18, between Avenidas 5 and 7, Miramar (© 7/204-1212); and the **Cabaret Nacional,** Calle San Rafael and Paseo de Martí, La Habana Vieja (© 7/863-2361).

Habaneros love to dance and party, and you'll find a wild dance and club scene here. In fact, dance aficionados come to Havana from all over to learn the basic steps, fine-tune their moves, and watch the locals strut their stuff. Most clubs don't get going until after 10pm, and most stay pretty vibrant until the wee hours of the morning. While salsa is king in Cuba, most of the popular dance clubs catering to travelers have been putting some house, techno, Reggaeton, and other modern dance tunes into the mix. Dress codes are somewhat casual, but locals still like to put on the ritz as much as possible before a night of dancing, so bring some finery if you plan to hit any of the more popular clubs.

Cabaret Parisien Located at the Hotel Nacional, this venerable cabaret show is a vibrant and extravagant spectacle. Still, it will always play second fiddle to the Tropicana, which trumps it in terms of size and setting. Nevertheless, the show here is less expensive, and certainly more convenient, if you're staying at the hotel or in Vedado. Calle O (corner of Calle 21). © 7/836-3663. Show CUC$35 (US$38/£19); dinner packages from CUC$55 (US$59/£30).

Café Cantante Mi Habana Top acts often perform at this popular club. They also have a much more informal dance scene happening every afternoon between 4 and 7pm. This is a place where locals come to mix it up with foreigners who are in town specifically to learn how to salsa. Teatro Nacional, Paseo and Calle 39, Plaza de la Revolución. © 7/878-4275. Cover CUC$5–CUC$10 (US$5.40–US$11/£2.70–£5.40).

Casa de la Música Centro Habana ★★ This place, with its massive dance floor and concert space in the heart of Centro Habana, is currently considered the best salsa-dancing venue in town. The crowd is predominantly Cuban, and most of the folks can really dance. About half of the cover is usually applied to your food and drink tab. Calle Galianao 225, btw. Neptuno and Concordia. © 7/860-8296. Cover CUC$5–CUC$20 (US$5.40–US$22/£2.70–£11).

Casa de la Música Miramar ★★ Housed in a beautiful, former Masonic Lodge Hall, this place is associated with the national recording label Egrem. It has nightly concerts that range from bolero to salsa to jazz in the in-house club, Diablo Tun Tun. Still, for me, the real treat here is the afternoon jam sessions, which take place daily from 4 to 7pm. Calle 20 (corner of Calle 35), Miramar. © 7/204-0447.

El Rincón del Bolero ★ If you're looking for a slightly mellower scene, this is your spot. One of several bars and restaurants at the Dos Gardenias complex, this place specializes in the sad and sultry songs of bolero, and usually features some fine performers. Dos Gardenias, Av. 7 and Calle 26, Miramar, Playa. © 7/204-2353.

(Tips) A Way In

Cuban women (and to a lesser extent Cuban men) tend to hang out at the entrance to popular clubs looking for an unattached foreigner to pay their admission. Their pleadings can be quite earnest. You are by no means obligated, but they really have no other means of being able to enter. Remember that you'll also be liable for paying for the drinks.

Habana Café This place is loosely modeled after the Hard Rock Cafe chain. There's an old propeller fighter dangling overhead and a vintage 1957 Chevy in the middle of the joint. There's a good-size dance floor, and the evening's entertainment is part cabaret, part revue show, and part dance party. The atmosphere is far less formal and far livelier than you'll find at most other cabarets. In the Meliá Cohiba, Paseo, btw. Avs. 1 and 3, Vedado. © 7/833-3636, ext. 2630. www.cohiba-habanacafe.com. Cover CUC$20 (US$22/£11) includes CUC$10 (US$11/£5.40) worth of food and drink).

Salón Turquino Located on the top floor of the Tryp Habana Libre, this dance club is one of the hotter and more popular dance spots in Havana. The views are great, there's a nightly cabaret show at 10:30pm, and the club periodically features top-billed live bands. Tryp Habana Libre, 25th floor, Calles L and 23, Vedado. © 7/834-6100. Cover CUC$10–CUC$20 (US$11–US$22/£5.40–£11).

Tropicana ★★★ Accept no substitutes. This is the real deal. It's expensive—in fact, overpriced—but if you're going to see a cabaret show in Havana, it should be at the Tropicana. First opened in 1939, this open-air dinner theater is still the defining cabaret show in Cuba, if not the world. You enter the lush garden theater after passing the club's signature sculpted *Fountain of the Muses*. Dinner service starts around 8pm and is an uninspired, but acceptable affair. The show itself begins around 10:30pm. Once the show begins, the stage and verdant surroundings become an orgy of light, color, spectacular costumes, and pulsating movement. Scores of scantily clad showgirls and dancers seamlessly weave together a series of different numbers. The 2-hour-long spectacle covers most of the bases of popular Cuban show and dance music, from *son* to bolero to *danzón* to salsa, with a bit of Afro-Cuban religious music thrown into the mix. After the show, you can continue the celebration by dancing the night away at the adjoining Salón Arcos de Cristal.

Virtually every hotel and tour agency in Havana can book you a night at the Tropicana; some include dinner and a bottle of rum at the nightclub, others are just for the show (including a complimentary *cuba libre,* a rum-and-Coke drink), or include dinner first at El Ajibe or another Miramar restaurant. Packages with transportation and dinner are only slightly more than for the show alone, and are therefore a decent deal. Since it's open air, rain cancels the function. You'll get your money back on a rainout, but they offer no guaranteed reservations for a makeup show. Calle 72 (btw. Calles 41 and 45), Marianao. © 7/267-1010. reserves@tropicana.gca.tur.cu. Show CUC$50–CUC$60 (US$54–US$65/£27–£32); packages with transportation and dinner from CUC$70 (US$76/£38).

In addition to the bars listed below, **La Bodeguita del Medio** (p. 102) and **El Floridita** (p. 101) are two famous watering holes. I also enjoy the rooftop bar at the **Hotel Ambos Mundos** (p. 90).

Bar Dos Hermanos　This is a slightly seedy port bar, but well within the safety net of restored La Habana Vieja. A few *jineteras* and a *conjunto* (small musical band) are usually in attendance. There are tables scattered across two rooms, and a long, wooden bar with a good selection of call liquors. This place is open 24 hours. Av. del Puerto 304 (corner of Calle Santa Clara), La Habana Vieja. ℂ 7/861-3514.

Café Monserrate　I like the relaxed vibe at this popular bar, which attracts a mix of travelers and Cubans. The club's signature drink, the *coctel Monserrate*, is a tasty blend of rum, grapefruit juice, mint, sugar, and grenadine that gives the *mojito* a run for its money. There's usually live music here, as well as *jineteros* and *jineteras*. Calles Monserrate and Obrapía, La Habana Vieja. ℂ 7/860-9751.

Café O'Reilly　While this bar and restaurant combo occupies two floors of this decaying building in Old Havana, all the action happens on the second floor. French doors open onto a small veranda, giving a good view of the folks strutting by on the street below. The food is mediocre, but the ambience is energetic, without feeling forced. Calle O'Reilly 203 (corner of Calle San Ignacio), La Habana Vieja. No phone.

Café París　This place is almost always crowded and rowdy. The *conjunto* plays loud, and the patrons try to top them. Known as a *jinetera* hangout, this is still a good place to go for a good time. Open noon to midnight. At the corner of Calle San Ignacio and Calle Obispo, La Habana Vieja. No phone.

Club Imágenes　This place is done up like an upscale piano bar. The lighting is dark and the mood more subdued than you'll find at other joints. Still, they put on a nightly show, and even get things pumped up with karaoke every now and again. The small menu here includes a selection of tapas, making it a good choice when you want a snack. Calzada 602 (corner of Calle C), Vedado. ℂ 7/833-3606. CUC$5 (US$5.40/£2.70) minimum.

El Gato Tuerto ★　This hyperhip little club attracts a good mix of travelers and Cuban intelligentsia. The mood is dark, with walls of mirrors behind the tiny stage, and a long bar running the length of the longest wall. The club is small, so either reserve a table in advance or get here early. The entertainment runs the gamut from old-style bolero to *nueva trova* and modern jazz. Performers range from mediocre to top-notch. On most evenings, Alden Night, a melodramatic storyteller and poet, serves as master of ceremonies. The admission is applied to your first drink, so ask for the call liquor first. Calle O (btw. Calles 17 and 19), Vedado. ℂ 7/838-2696. Cover CUC$5 (US$5.40/£2.70).

Jazz Café ★　This place feels a little too slick and modern to be a jazz club, with chrome-trimmed tables and chairs, a curving wall of windows, and fairly bright lighting. But a jazz club it is, and next to La Zorra y El Cuervo (see below), this is the top spot to search out Cuba's best and brightest jazz talents. Third level of the Galerías Paseo mall, Avs. Paseo and 3, Vedado. ℂ 7/838-3556. CUC$10 (US$11/£5.40) minimum.

La Zorra y El Cuervo ★★　This is the premier jazz club in Havana and the first place to check if you want to catch any of the A-list jazz performers while you're in town. Modeled after an English pub, the basement-level bar space is small and cozy and relatively plain. The standard cover might double if someone like Chucho Valdés is playing.

La Rampa, Calle 23 no. 155 (btw. Calles N and O), Vedado. © **7/833-2402.** Cover CUC$10
(US$11/£5.40).

Lluvia de Oro ★   Open noon to midnight, this is a raucous and rowdy bar in the
heart of Old Havana. There's often live music and a lively mix of tourists, locals, *jineteros,*
and *jineteras.* Calle Obispo no. 316 (corner of Habana), La Habana Vieja. © **7/862-9870.**

Piano Bar Delirio Habanero   This subdued and low-lighted club is a good place for
a quiet and romantic evening. It's on the fourth floor of the Teatro Nacional, and the
walls of glass windows offer great nighttime views of Havana. The *criolla* cuisine is decent
here. You can either come here to enjoy the joint's singular charms, or duck in for a break
after dancing your butt off next door at the Café Cantante Mi Habana. Teatro Nacional,
Paseo and Calle 39, Plaza de la Revolución. © **7/878-4275.**

Viñales & Western Cuba

Western Cuba is a pastoral and underdeveloped region, with some stunning scenery. When folks talk about western Cuba, they mean **Pinar del Río** province, the third-largest province in Cuba. The area has been inhabited continuously for over 4,000 years, beginning with the Guanahatabey, Ciboney, and Taíno indigenous tribes that settled this section of the island prior to the Spanish arrival. In addition to the province of Pinar del Río, the general geographic area of western Cuba also includes the Archipiélago de los Canarreos (the Canary Archipelago), considered a "special municipality." The two largest islands of the chain, **Isla de la Juventud** and **Cayo Largo,** are developed for tourism.

Pinar del Río province is Cuba's prime ecotourism destination. Rock climbing, spelunking, mountain biking, hiking, and bird-watching are all excellent in this area. **La Güira National Park,** the **Guanacahabibes Peninsula,** and the **Sierra del Rosario Biosphere Reserve** make this one of Cuba's richest and wildest areas. The small hamlet of **Viñales** is widely considered one of the most beautiful places in the country, and it is rapidly becoming the

region's center for nature and adventure tourism. At the far western tip of the island, **María la Gorda** is one of Cuba's signature scuba-diving destinations. And the diving at **Cayo Levisa, Isla de la Juventud,** and **Cayo Largo** isn't too shabby either. To top it all off, Cayo Largo has some of the nicest and least-crowded beaches in Cuba.

Pinar del Río province is also Cuba's most heralded tobacco-growing region. Cigars made from tobacco grown in the **Vuelta Abajo** area, just west of the city of Pinar del Río, are coveted the world over.

Note: Pinar del Rio sustained direct hits from Hurricanes Gustav and Ike in September 2008, resulting in considerable damage to much of the province, especially Viñales and Isla de la Juventud. Housing took a serious hit in Isla de la Juventud, with many homes completely destroyed. The fishing industry there was severely damaged, but tourist operations have rebounded. If you plan to stay in *casas particulares,* it's best to call ahead to confirm that they're open. Many homes suffered roof damage and building materials are scarce and very expensive for local residents, so rebuilding will take a long time.

1 PINAR DEL RÍO

174km (108 miles) SW of Havana

Pinar del Río, the provincial capital, is named for the pine trees that grow along the banks of the Río Guamá, where the city is set. Originally founded as Nueva Filipina (New Philippine), it was re-christened Pinar del Río in 1774 and is one of the last major cities founded by the Spanish in Cuba. Pinar del Río is an animated little city of around 150,000, with a university, several hospitals, and some industries. The city's architecture is a mix of colonial and neoclassical in varying states from finely restored to postrevolutionary decay. The city's major attractions can easily be visited in a day, and you'd be

Tips **Watch Out**

If you're driving a rental car, you will be swarmed by bicycle-riding *jineteros* (hustlers) offering you *casas particulares* and *paladares* (private-home rooms and restaurants) as soon as you enter town. They will latch on to your car at any traffic light, stop sign, or slow section and follow alongside if their pedaling can keep pace as you drive through town. For some reason, they are particularly aggressive in Pinar del Río. If you want to lessen the attention, you might have to roll up your windows and shake your head a lot. Ambulatory *jineteros* and *jineteras* will also try to attach themselves to you as you walk around town.

better off giving more time and attention to the province's less urban destinations, although the city provides a glimpse of a town unfettered by major tourism.

ESSENTIALS

Getting There

BY BUS   The **bus station** (© 48/75-5255) is located at Calle Adela Azcuy, between Avenidas Colón and Comandante Pinares. **Víazul** (© 7/881-1413 in Havana, or 48/75-2571 in Pinar del Río; www.viazul.com) has two daily buses at 9am and 2pm from Havana to Pinar del Río. The trip takes 2¹/₂ hours and costs CUC$12 (US$13/£6.50) each way. This bus continues on to Viñales. If you pick the bus up here, it costs CUC$6.50 (US$7/£3.50) to Viñales, although it's only CUC$13 (US$14/£7) direct, one-way from Havana to Viñales. Víazul buses to Havana leave Pinar del Río at 8:50am and 2:50pm daily.

BY CAR   Take the Autopista Nacional (A4) west to Pinar del Río. It's a straight shot, and the Autopista actually ends as it enters Pinar del Río. Two alternative routes are the old Carretera Central, which runs roughly parallel to the newer Autopista, and connects Havana with Pinar del Río, and the Circuito Norte or "northern circuit," a road that runs from Havana to Mariel to Bahía Honda. At La Palma, you'll want to head south on the Viñales highway and then on to Pinar del Río. Both of these routes are two-lane affairs that are slower and more picturesque than the Autopista. On either of these, slow-moving ox carts and heavy trucks combine with bicycle traffic, pedestrians, and potholes to slow you down—not necessarily a bad thing if you want to take in some of the scenery. I recommend integrating the Circuito Norte route into an itinerary that encompasses Pinar del Río, Viñales, and either Cayo Levisa or Cayo Jutías.

Getting Around

You can easily walk to most places in Pinar del Río. Taxis are also readily available all around town, and are either at hand, or can be called, at most hotels and *casas particulares*. Call **Cubataxi** (© 48/75-3616) or **Havanautos** (© 48/77-8015), which has an office at the Islazul Hotel Pinar del Río.

Orientation

The Autopista Nacional ends and turns into Calle Martí as it enters Pinar del Río from the east. As you enter town, you'll see the Hotel Pinar del Río on your right. The heart of downtown is straight ahead. At the western end of downtown, you'll find the small, triangular-shaped Plaza de la Independencia. The main north-south byway, Calle Isabel Rubio, is also the old Carretera Central, and bisects Calle Martí by the post office.

Havanatur and **Islazul** have offices downtown; they're your best sources of information. For currency exchange, there's a **CADECA** on Calle Gerardo Medina, next to the local Coppelia ice-cream outlet and at Martí 46, virtually opposite the post office. On the same street, 2 blocks east of Coppelia, there's an **Etecsa** phone office where you can make local, national, and international calls and connect to the Internet. The main **post office** is located at the corner of Calle Martí and Calle Isabel Rubio (© **48/5442**); it's open Monday through Sunday from 8am to 8pm. The **León Cuervo Rubio hospital** (© **48/2010**) is at the junction of the Carretera Central and the Viñales highway.

WHAT TO SEE & DO

The principal attraction in town is **Fábrica de Tabacos Francisco Donatién** (© **48/75-3424**), Calle Antonio Maceo, just off the Plaza de la Independencia. Several fine brands are rolled at this renowned cigar factory. You can walk through the timeless rolling station, where a caller reads news and short stories to keep the rollers interested. You'll also

---

Smoke 'Em If You Got 'Em

When Christopher Columbus first visited Cuba, he found the local population smoking a local herb, *cohiba,* through a pipe, or *tobago.* They called the act of smoking *sikar.* He brought back some samples, and it wasn't long before millions of Europeans were smoking tobacco rolled into cigars and cigarettes. Tobacco was grown commercially in Cuba as early as the 16th century, and by the late–17th century, it was the country's most important export crop. By all accounts, the finest cigars in the world come from Cuba. And of the Cuban cigars available, the crème de la crème are made with tobacco grown in the **Vuelta Abajo,** the low plains spreading west from the city of Pinar del Río.

Most of the tobacco grown in Cuba is grown on small farms. Seeds are planted each year beginning in late October and throughout November to stagger the harvest. In a little over a month, seedlings are transplanted to the fields or *vegas.* Plants are carefully tended and regularly topped to stimulate leaf growth lower down. The highest-quality wrapper leaves, *capa,* are grown in semishade under protective mesh. Harvesting takes place from January through April. Leaves are classified by plant type, growing region, growing condition (sun or shade), and where they grow on an individual plant. All go through an intensive and carefully monitored process of drying, sorting, preparing, fermenting, aging, and finally, rolling. Real care is taken in handling the prized *capas.* Lesser-quality leaves end up as *capote* (binders) and *tripa* (filler).

Throughout Vuelta Abajo, you'll pass field after field planted with tobacco and see the traditional high-peaked, thatched-roof drying sheds. Tobacco from the Vuelta Abajo region is shipped to various factories in the region and around Cuba. The finest brands—Cohibas, Partagas, Romeo y Julieta, Montecristo, Robaina, H. Upmann, Corona, and Hoyo de Monterey—are all made with tobacco from Vuelta Abajo.

visit rooms where the final selection and grading, labeling, and boxing take place. You can buy some of the wares here, or at the well-stocked **Casa del Habano** across the street. The factory is open Monday through Friday from 9am to noon and 1 to 4pm and Saturday from 9am to noon. Admission is CUC$5 (US$5.40/£2.70), and includes a guided tour that lasts about 15 to 20 minutes.

The other main attraction in Pinar del Río is the **Casa Garay Fábrica de Guayabitas del Pinar** (© 48/75-2966), Calle Isabel Rubio, 3¹/₂ blocks south of Calle Martí. This little factory produces the town's signature Guayabita del Pinar liquor. They produce two types, *dulce* (sweet) and *seco* (dry). Both are cane liquors distilled with the fruit berries of a local bush. I like the *seco* quite a bit. It's a good-quality sipping liquor that, if you stretch your imagination, is almost brandy-like. The factory is open during the same hours as Fábrica de Tabacos Francisco Donatién. Admission is CUC$1 (US$1.10/55p), and usually includes a quick guided tour and a stop at the tasting room. Bottles of Guayabita are on sale for around CUC$4 (US$4.30/£2.15).

Aside from the city's two main draws, you can easily spend a few hours walking around town, and perhaps stopping in at either the **Museo Provincial de Historia (Museum of Province History)** at Calle Martí 58 (© 48/75-4300), or the **Museo de Ciencias Naturales (Museum of Natural Sciences)** at Calle Martí and Avenida Pinares (© 48/75-3087). Neither contains exhibits or collections of great interest, although the latter is housed in a wonderful old building with ornate Moorish architecture. You could also check out the **Teatro Milanés** (© 48/75-3871), Calles Martí and Colón, a striking 19th-century theater that is open for visits during the day, and sometimes hosts evening concerts and performances. Admission to each of the above attractions is CUC$1 (US$1.10/55p).

WHERE TO STAY

I personally recommend staying in Viñales (see section 2, below) and visiting the attractions in Pinar del Río on a day trip.

There is a host of *casas particulares* in Pinar del Río. You'll find them both congregated around the busy downtown area, as well as in the more typically residential neighborhoods on the outskirts of the city. Most charge between CUC$15 (US$16/£8.10) and CUC$20 (US$22/£11) per person and usually offer reasonably priced meal options. One recommended option is the **Casa de Eloina,** run by a very friendly family of seven women, right in downtown with a terrace, at Isabel Rubio 14, Apto 4 between Martí and Adela Azcuy (© 48/75-3496).

Moderate

Hotel Vueltabajo ★   This is by far the best option in downtown Pinar del Río. The hotel occupies a large and meticulously restored old mansion in the heart of the city. The rooms are simply furnished and there is little in the way of decor. Still, the rooms are very spacious and all have immensely high ceilings. Fifteen of them underwent an upgrade in 2008. It's worth the very slight splurge for the rooms with views and small balconies. Only four rooms here have king-size beds; the rest have two twin beds. The suite is not worth the extra cost, as the seating area is uncomfortable.

Calle Martí 103, Pinar del Río. © **48/75-9381.** www.islazul.cu. 39 units. CUC$52–CUC$65 (US$56–US$70/£28–£35) double; CUC$72 (US$78/£39) suite. Rates include breakfast buffet. MC, V. **Amenities:** Restaurant; bar; tour and activities desk; car-rental desk; laundry service. *In room:* A/C, TV, fridge, safe.

Hotel Pinar del Río   Serving both Cuban and international guests in equal measure, this is by far the largest hotel in town. It's uninspired and largely unappealing. It is perennially run-down, and I'm not sure it's ever seen better days. Still, the rooms are adequate and the beds have new mattresses. The hotel has a broad range of facilities and services, and it's an acceptable option if you're staying in Pinar del Río for a night or two. The several bars and in-house dance club make it a lively joint. In fact, be sure you get a room as far from the club as possible, or you might not sleep much; the fifth-floor rooms are quieter. The pool is open to visitors for CUC$10 (US$11/£5.40) per person, CUC$8 (US$8.65/£4.30) of which can be spent on food and drink.

Calle Martí, Pinar del Río. ☎ 48/75-5070. www.islazul.cu. 149 units. CUC$34–CUC$38 (US$37–US$41/£18–£21) double. Rates include breakfast buffet. MC, V. **Amenities:** 2 restaurants; 3 bars; dance club; outdoor pool; tour and activities desk; car-rental desk; laundry service. *In room:* A/C, TV.

Hotel Aguas Claras   This countryside hotel with the rooms in casitas spread about the grounds is much more idyllic than anything in town. The focus is around the pool and pool bar, popular with locals on weekends (visitors can pay CUC$2/US$2.15/£1.10 to use the pool), so you may want to opt for more tranquil casitas up the hill. The casitas are a mix of one-level with two rooms or two-levels with four rooms. The rooms are small with two single beds and some could do with a touch of paint. A river runs through the property and there's a field you can frolic in; at the center of the field is a picturesque green-and-white *casa del campo* (country house) with two rooms for rent.

Km 7.5 Carretera a Viñales. ☎ 48/77-8427. www.cubamarviajes.cu. 50 units. CUC$36–CUC$40 (US$39–US$43/£19–£22) double. Rates include breakfast buffet. No credit cards. Free parking. **Amenities:** Restaurant; bar; outdoor pool; horseback riding. *In room:* A/C, TV, minibar.

WHERE TO DINE

Moderate

Rumayor ★ CRIOLLA   This is probably the best dining option in Pinar del Río. Run by the Islazul chain, it's both a restaurant and nightly cabaret. The specialty here is slow-smoked chicken, and it's excellent. There are also several fish and meat dishes. Of these, the *cherna frita,* a fried fish in a garlic sauce, is good. The main dining room is indoors in a dark room decorated with Afro-Cuban motifs. Service is quick and attentive, a relative rarity in Cuba.

On the Viñales hwy., 1km (½ mile) north of town. ☎ 48/75-3007. Reservations not required. Main courses CUC$6–CUC$26 (US$6.50–US$28/£3.25–£14). MC, V. Daily noon–9:40pm.

Inexpensive

La Casona (Value) CRIOLLA   This is certainly the most atmospheric place to eat in Pinar del Río proper. About 13 heavy wooden tables with bench seating fill up the main dining room in this old colonial building. High ceilings, modern sculpted wall hangings, and long French doors that open onto the street give this place its character. The food is mediocre and simple. Avoid the pastas and stick to the roasted chicken or sandwiches. In the evenings, they open up a little patio beer garden with live music and an informal atmosphere.

Calles Martí and Colón. ☎ 48/77-8263. Main courses CUC$1–CUC$5 (US$1.10–US$5.40/55p–£2.70). MC, V. Daily 11:30am–11:30pm.

Rumayor ★ (see review above) offers up a nightly cabaret-style show in its large outdoor amphitheater space. The show here leans more on Afro-Cuban dances and traditions than the shows in Havana, and is less ornate, but it's still a pretty good spectacle. The show starts at around 11pm and finishes at 1am on Thursday, Friday, and Sunday and at 2am on Saturday. Admission is CUC$20 (US$22/£11) per table of four, which includes one drink per person.

Alternately, you could see what's happening at **La Casona** (see review above), the dance club at Hotel Pinar del Río, or **Café Pinar,** Calle Vélez Caviedes 34 (© **48/77-8199**). You can also see what's playing at the old **Cine Praga,** Calle Gerardo Medina, next to the Coppelia ice-cream parlor. Admission is just a couple of pesos, and you should be able to pay with Cuban pesos.

2 VIÑALES ★★★

200km (124 miles) SW of Havana; 26km (16 miles) N of Pinar del Río

Viñales is an extremely picturesque town in the heart of Cuba's prime tobacco-growing region. The town itself sits in the center of a flat valley surrounded by stunning karst hill formations known locally as *mogotes.* The *mogotes* are irregularly shaped, steep-sided geological formations that rise as high as 300m (984 ft.) and have bases ranging from just a few hundred yards in diameter to as much as a couple of kilometers in length. The *mogotes* are part of the Sierra de los Organos mountain chain, and were formed by eons of erosion. Many consider this to be the most naturally beautiful spot in Cuba and the view of the Viñales Valley from any of the surrounding hillsides is stunning, particularly at sunrise or sunset. The Viñales Valley is a great spot to bicycle around, and there are good options for bird-watching, hiking, and in particular, rock climbing and spelunking.

ESSENTIALS

GETTING THERE **Víazul** (© **7/881-1413** in Havana; www.viazul.com) has two daily buses at 9am and 2pm from Havana to Viñales, via Pinar del Río. The trip takes 3 hours and 15 minutes and costs CUC$13 (US$14/£7) each way.

The **bus station** (© **48/79-3195**) is located at Salvador Cisnero 63, just across the street from the town's main plaza. Víazul buses for Havana depart Viñales daily at 8am and 2pm, passing through Pinar del Río about 40 minutes later, before continuing on to the capital. You can hire a taxi to Havana for CUC$56 (US$60/£30) for up to four people, as well as to Cienfuegos and Trinidad.

To get here **by car,** take the Autopista Nacional (A4) west to Pinar del Río. From Pinar del Río, it's another 26km (16 miles) north on the well-marked Carretera Viñales. Entering Pinar del Río from the Autopista, you'll want to turn right at the post office, on Calle Isabel Rubio, and follow the signs for Viñales.

GETTING AROUND Taxis can be hired in Viñales, or called from your hotel. They tend to congregate around the central plaza. A cab to any of the local attractions costs between CUC$2 and CUC$6 (US$2.15–US$6.50/£1.10–£3.25) You can hire a cab for a full-day trip to anywhere around the region for around CUC$30 (US$32/£16) or CUC$60 (US$65/£32). If you'd rather rent a car, **Transtur** (© **48/79-6060**) has an office downtown just off the central park, and **Havanautos** (© **48/79-6390**) has an office diagonally opposite the Viñales Cupet gas station. Mopeds *(motos)* can now be rented from a place next to the Casa Don Tomás (℃ **48/79-6300**) for CUC$23 (US$25/£12) a day. The new Viñales Bus Tour has 18 stops and is a hop-on/hop-off service for CUC$5 (US$5.40/£2.70) a day.

This is a good region to bicycle around. The valley itself is almost perfectly flat and most of the major attractions can be reached along well-paved roads. You can rent bikes in pretty good shape for CUC$5 to CUC$10 (US$5.40–US$11/£2.70–£5.40) per day from your *casa particular* or Cubanacán offers a 1-day guided biking tour in the valley for CUC$20 (US$22/£11).

WHAT TO SEE & DO
Outdoor Adventures

Caves abound in this area and are one of the major attractions in and around Viñales. **La Cueva del Indio (the Indian's Cave;** ℃ **48/79-6280)** is the most popular cave and it's become a real tourist trap. Located about 5km (3 miles) north of Viñales at Km 33 on the Carretera de Puerto Esperanza, this cave gets its name from the fact that indigenous remains were found here. Only 1km (¹/₂ mile) or so of the extensive cave system here is open to travelers. A well-lit path leads from the entrance through a few small and narrow galleries to a tiny dock on an underground river. Here, you board a small rowboat powered by an outboard engine for a quick trip of about 180m (591 ft.) up and down this river, before exiting the cave at a dock area crowded with souvenir stands and a little snack bar. The entrance fee is CUC$5 (US$5.40/£2.70), and I don't think it's justified. Moreover, when the buses arrive in force, the line to get in is long and slow-moving.

Those with an interest in more serious spelunking should head to **Las Cuevas de Santo Tomás** ★. With over 45km (28 miles) of connected tunnels, chambers, and galleries, it's the largest explored cave system in Cuba. Some of these chambers and galleries are quite massive, with impressive stalagmite and stalactite formations. Unlike La Cueva del Indio, this cave system has been left in its natural state and you must visit it with headlamps and flashlights. So far, a relatively simple 1km (¹/₂-mile) section has been opened for guided tours, although more adventurous spelunking tours are in the works. Visits here, including a guide and equipment, cost about CUC$10 (US$11/£5.40), and are best booked in advance with the new **Centro de Visitantes,** located on the highway into Viñales, just beyond the Hotel Los Jazmines (open 8am–5:30pm daily; no phone).

In addition to caving, the limestone mountains and karst formations of Viñales make for excellent **rock climbing.** Although climbing is still in its infancy as a sport in Cuba, the Viñales Valley is rapidly becoming a mecca for local and visiting climbers. So far, over 140 routes have been identified and climbed in the area. Some carry colorful names, such as "Razor's Edge" and "Friday 13th." A few attest to some of the hazards of the area, such as "Feeding Mosquitoes" and "Poison Oak, Guano, and Spines." For more information, check out **www.cubaclimbing.com**.

Unless you plan on scaling several *mogotes* (steep geological formations), most of the **hiking** here is on gentle, well-groomed trails. There are several popular trails and routes, although you must hire an official guide to hike most of these. One of the most popular hikes is a simple walk through the *fincas* (farms) of the valley just outside of town. This provides wonderful views of the surrounding *mogotes,* and allows for encounters with the local farmers and a firsthand view of the tobacco-growing process. More athletic forays into the nearby forests and hills include hikes to and around the isolated little communities of **Los Acuáticos** and **Ancón,** as well as climbs to the summits of several *mogotes.* Guided hikes should run you between CUC$6 and CUC$20 (US$6.50–US$22/£3.25–£11) per person, depending on the route and length of the hike. Do-it-yourself

ACCOMMODATIONS ■
Hotel La Ermita **4**
Hotel Los Jazmines **6**
Hotel Rancho San Vicente **1**

DINING ◆
Casa de Don Tomás **5**
El Palenque de los Cimarrones **3**
Las Terrazas **4**

NIGHTLIFE ●
Discoteca Las Cuevas **2**

To Puerto Esperanza

La Cueva
del Indio

SIERRA LA GUASASA

SIERRA DE VIÑALES

Río Palmarito

Mogote
de Robustiano

Mogote
La Esmeralda

Los Acuáticos

Mogote
Rústico

Mogote
del Valle

VALLE DE VIÑALES

Mural de
la Prehistoria

Casa de Caridad
■ Botanical Gardens
VIÑALES

Mogote
Dos Hermanos

To Las Cuevas
de Santo Tomás

Casa del
Verguero

Havana
Viñales ★

0   1 mi
0   1 km

■ Centro de
Visitantes

C U B A

To Pinar del Río

VIÑALES & WESTERN CUBA

6

VIÑALES

hikers can wander the dirt roads and byways of the Viñales Valley, but must stay off the marked trails of **Viñales National Park.** For more information on guides and organized hikes, ask at your hotel, or check with **Centro de Visitantes** (no phone; open 8am–5:30pm daily), on the highway into Viñales, just beyond the Hotel Los Jazmines. It offers three options: a sociocultural trail through the valley, a flora-and-fauna trail, and a trip to the Cueva de Santo Tomás with departures at 9:30am and 2:30pm daily, for CUC$6 to CUC$10 (US$6.50–US$11/£3.25–£5.40) per person.

There are few well-defined trails for serious **mountain biking,** although there are plenty of dirt roads you can explore all around. Horseback riding can be arranged through the Hotel La Ermita or in the town's agencies.

Attractions & Organized Tours

The Viñales Valley is part of the heart of Cuba's tobacco-growing region and a great place to take a tobacco tour. Typical tours start at the **Casa del Verguero,** a small farm that grows and dries the primary material, followed by a visit to the nearby de-veining station, or *despalilladora.* Here, you'll see workers handle and sort the prized leaves for *capas,* or outer layers. You might also be given a quick tour of a final curing station, where the

Tips **Avoid the Crowds**

Viñales is an extremely popular destination for day trips out of Havana. If you're staying here, try to visit the various attractions early, before the buses arrive, and then spend the afternoon walking around town, hiking a more remote trail, or lazing around your hotel.

leaves emit an ammonia gas that will make your eyes tear. Finally, you'll visit a local cigar shop, **El Estanco.** However, you'll have to go into Pinar del Río if you want to visit an actual cigar factory.

Feel free to pass up the **Mural de la Prehistoria (Prehistoric Mural; ℭ 48/79-6260).** Sure it's big, but this over-hyped attraction can't quite cut it as kitsch, is decidedly uninteresting as art, is woefully inadequate as narrative, and is just not impressive enough in execution to merit all the attention. Despite some fresh paint, which restored—and even improved on—the vibrant colors of artist Leovigildo González Morillo's original work, this massive mural lacks the style and weight of the works of his mentor, Diego Rivera. The mural is located 4km (2¹/₂ miles) west of Viñales and is open daily from 8am to 7pm. The CUC$1 (US$1.10/55p) admission is waived if you eat at the on-site restaurant.

One of the nicer attractions in Viñales is the little **Casa de Caridad Botanical Gardens** ★ at the northeastern end of town. The lush gardens feature a mix of ornamental and medicinal plants and flowers, as well as orchids, bromeliads, palms, and fruit trees. If you're really lucky, you'll be able to munch on some freshly harvested fruit. No admission is charged, but donations are warmly accepted.

Cubanacán and **Havanatur** have offices right off the town's main square and offer a variety of tour options (the latter is not recommended due to poor customer service). Organized tours of the Viñales Valley can be booked with either of these operators or at any of the hotels in town. These jam-packed full-day tours cost between CUC$25 and CUC$35 (US$27–US$38/£14–£19) per person and usually include a visit to the Casa del Verguero, El Estanco, the Mural de la Prehistoria, the Cueva del Indio, and El Palenque de los Cimarrones, with lunch at one of the last three places, as well as a sunset cocktail at Hotel Los Jazmines. Other tour options include day trips to Pinar del Río, Cayo Levisa, Cayo Jutías, and María la Gorda, and cost between CUC$20 and CUC$75 (US$22–US$81/£11–£41) per person.

WHERE TO STAY
Moderate

The hotels below do a brisk business with tour groups. It is essential that you have a reservation in advance. At the end of 2009, British company Esencia (www.esencia hotelsandresorts.com) is due to open an ecospa resort in the valley, north of the village.

Hotel La Ermita Similar in style and setting to Hotel Los Jazmines (see review below), this is a lovely and modest hotel set on the hillside just above the town of Viñales. There are excellent views from the grounds and restaurant here, although only 12 rooms have the area's signature view. Those that do, such as second-floor corner room no. 64, are real steals. The rooms themselves are a little more spacious than those at Hotel Los Jazmines, and regular and recent upgrades have greatly improved them in terms of decor and comfort. Those in the newer buildings have a private porch or balcony, with a couple of heavy Adirondack chairs. There's a popular kidney-shaped pool in the center of the grounds and a poolside barbecue restaurant that I prefer to the hotel's principal buffet option. Even if you don't stay here, I recommend coming for sunset and perhaps staying for dinner at their Las Terrazas restaurant (see "Where to Dine," below).

Carretera de La Ermita Km 1.5, Viñales, Pinar del Río. (©) **48/79-6071.** Fax 48/79-6069. www.hotelescubanacan. com. 62 units. CUC$67–CUC$74 (US$72–US$80/£36–£40) double. Rates include breakfast buffet. MC, V. **Amenities:** 2 restaurants; 2 bars; outdoor pool; tennis court; tour and activities desk; gift shop; massage; laundry service. *In room:* A/C, TV, safe.

Hotel Los Jazmines ★ I give this hotel the nod over its nearby sister Hotel La Ermita, if only because you have much better odds of landing a room with a view. Most of the rooms are housed in two, three-story buildings set on a hillside overlooking the Viñales Valley. All are clean and comfortable, if a tad on the small side, and feature French doors opening onto a little balcony from which you can soak in the sights. Touches of gingerbread wrought-iron work and stained glass give the place a sense of elegance. If possible, request one of the third-floor rooms in the newer block, nos. 301 to 316. Sixteen duplex *cabañitas* (cabins) are located in a row heading downhill from the pool. These are a little bit smaller than the standard rooms, but are charming nonetheless.

Carretera de Viñales Km 25, Viñales, Pinar del Río. (©) **48/79-6205.** Fax 48/79-6215. www.hotelescubanacan. com. 78 units. CUC$67–CUC$74 (US$72–US$80/£36–£40) double. Rates include breakfast buffet. Rates lower in off season. MC, V. **Amenities:** 2 restaurants; 2 bars; outdoor pool; tour and activities desk; gift shop; massage; laundry service. *In room:* A/C, TV, safe.

Hotel Rancho San Vicente ★ Located about 270m (886 ft.) north of the Cueva del Indio, this quiet nature hotel can almost be considered a spa. A half dozen or so semi-private soaking pools (CUC$5/US$5.40/£2.70) are fed by tepid mineral springs, and massage and mud treatments (CUC$15/US$16/£8) are available at very reasonable prices. Most of the clean and comfortable rooms are actually individual little bungalows, with two twin beds and a tiny front porch; those housed in little ranch-style triplexes are slightly bigger inside, although less atmospheric. By far, the best rooms are the 20 new units housed in a series of two-story wooden buildings spread around the grounds. The whole complex is set amid a shady grove of pine, palm, and fruit trees. There's good bird-watching here, although the hotel doesn't afford any of the classic views for which Viñales is so famous.

Carretera de Puerto Esperanza Km 33, Viñales, Pinar del Río. (©) **48/79-6201.** Fax 48/79-6265. www. hotelescubanacan.com. 53 units. CUC$55–CUC$58 (US$65–US$68/£30–£34) double. Rates include breakfast. Rates lower in off season. MC, V. **Amenities:** Restaurant; bar; outdoor pool; tour and activities desk; massage; laundry service; Internet access. *In room:* A/C, TV, safe.

Inexpensive

There is a host of *casas particulares* in Viñales, which for some reason are called *villas* here. Most are on either the main street through town or on the street 1 block southeast and parallel to it. All charge between CUC$15 and CUC$25 (US$16–US$27/£8–£14) per person and usually offer reasonably priced meal options. I recommend **Casa Oscar Jaime Rodríguez,** Adela Azcuy 43 (© **48/79-3381**), with its friendly family and communal areas; **Garden House,** Salvador Cisneros 44 (© **48/79-3297**), for its lovely garden and big porch; **Villa Ernesto,** Salvador Cisneros 20 (© **48/79-3261**), so that you can enjoy a *mojito* with freshly plucked mint made by Ernesto, who was the barman at Hotel Los Jazmines for 37 years; **El Relojero,** off Adela Azcuy on Orlando Nodarse 7 (© **48/69-5429;** eliorentroomvinales@correodecuba.cu), with its welcoming family; or **Casa Lumino and Heriberto,** Calle Orlando Nodarse 3 (© **48/69-6952**) for Lumino's great cooking.

In addition to the places listed below, there are official—and uninspired—restaurants at most of the major tourist attractions, including the Mural de la Prehistoria and the Cueva del Indio. If you're staying at either Hotel Los Jazmines or Hotel La Ermita, you'd probably do well to venture away from their buffets and try one of the a la carte options. All *paladares* in Viñales have been closed by the government, although *casas particulares* are permitted to serve meals to their guests, and most will accept other diners with a certain amount of discretion.

Casa de Don Tomás CRIOLLA/SPANISH   This is probably the most popular restaurant in Viñales, and it's touted in most guidebooks as well as by tour and hotel operators throughout the region. The atmosphere in this restored 1889 colonial mansion is wonderful, and the building itself has been declared a national monument. You'll want to choose a table on either the small front patio or the more spacious back patio. The restaurant's signature dish, *Las Delicias de Don Tomás,* is a paella-like dish of Spanish rice cooked and served in an earthenware bowl and featuring bits of chicken, pork, fish, ham, and even lobster. It's usually slightly overcooked and underseasoned. You'd definitely be better off opting for a simpler pork steak in *criolla* sauce, or the hefty portion of fried chicken. The house drink is called a *Trapiche,* and it's made of rum, pineapple juice, and honey, and served with a sliver of sugar cane as the swizzle stick.

Calle Salvador Cisnero 140 (the main street in Viñales). ✆ **48/79-6300.** Reservations not accepted. Main courses CUC$5–CUC$14 (US$5.40–US$15/£2.70–£8). No credit cards. Daily 10am–10pm.

El Palenque de los Cimarrones ★ CRIOLLA   This is definitely a tourist trap catering to tour groups. However, the food is surprisingly good, and the show and setting are interesting and informative, without being too kitschy or corny. You reach the restaurant after paying a CUC$1 (US$1.10/55p) entrance fee and walking about 270m (886 ft.) through a narrow cave that bisects one of the area's signature *mogotes*. At the end of the path, you come to a re-creation of one of the nomadic homes set up by runaway slaves who lived and hid in these caves. After a brief bit of Afro-Cuban music and dance, you reach the restaurant, which is a series of interconnected *ranchos* (thatched huts), each decorated and representing a different orishá, or Afro-Cuban deity. The main dish here is a slow-roasted chicken seasoned with oregano, cumin, garlic, and lime juice—it's excellent. And, the yellow rice with bits of ham, bacon, sausage, and peas puts Casa de Don Tomás's version to shame. The restaurant is only open for lunch, but the bar and snack bar located in the cave at the joint's entrance are open 24 hours. This spot also serves as a popular dance club on Saturday (see "Viñales After Dark," below).

Km 36 on the highway to Puerto Esperanza, north of Viñales. ✆ **48/79-6290.** Reservations not required. Main courses CUC$5–CUC$5.80 (US$5.40–US$6.25/£2.70–£3.15). No credit cards. Daily 11am–4pm.

Las Terrazas ⟨Value⟩ CRIOLLA   This hotel restaurant has a wonderful perch above and view over the Viñales Valley. The view itself is worth the price of admission, and the food is pretty good as well, but the price of a bottle of Cuban wine is a shock—a staggering CUC$13 (US$14/£7). Standard Cuban cuisine is featured here, but there are a few twists. You can get turkey fricassee, which is turkey meat stewed in a tomato and white-wine sauce. I like the chicken Viñales, which is a boneless breast served au gratin. It's a good idea to arrive in time for the sunset over the valley.

At the Hotel La Ermita, Carretera de La Ermita Km 1.5. ✆ **48/79-6071.** Reservations recommended. Main courses CUC$4.85–CUC$9.85 (US$5.25–US$11/£2.60–£5.30). MC, V. Daily 7am–10pm.

Viñales has a couple of low-key little bars on the main road through town and, if you're lucky, there might be a concert taking place at the local **Casa de la Cultura,** or the hugely popular **Patio de Polo Montañez** ★, both of which are right on the central plaza, just off the church, or at the nearby smaller ARTex venue, **Patio del Decimista.** Sol del Valle and its leader, who plays the recorder through his nose, is worth seeking out. The scene at either Hotel Los Jazmines or Hotel La Ermita is dependent upon the type of groups and guests in residence. The **Discoteca Las Cuevas** is located at the entrance to El Palenque de los Cimarrones (see review above). Flashing lights and loud music get an atmospheric boost from the hanging stalactites. There's a cabaret-style show here on Saturday beginning around 9pm; admission is CUC$3 (US$3.25/£1.60).

---

3 SIERRA DEL ROSARIO BIOSPHERE RESERVE & SAN DIEGO DE LOS BAÑOS ★

Soroa: 87km (54 miles) W of Havana; San Diego de los Baños: 120km (75 miles) W of Havana

The mountainous region between Havana and Pinar del Río is another prime destination in the country's budding ecotourism industry. With both the **Sierra del Rosario Biosphere Reserve** and **La Güira National Park,** as well as ecotourism projects in **Soroa** and at **Las Terrazas,** the area offers a wealth of opportunities to explore the flora and fauna of Cuba's inland mountain forests. Add the sulfurous mineral springs of **San Diego de los Baños** into the mix, and you've got the perfect recipe for some nature-based rest and relaxation.

SIERRA DEL ROSARIO BIOSPHERE RESERVE

Declared a UNESCO biosphere reserve in 1985, the 25,000-hectare (61,776-acre) **Sierra del Rosario** encompasses a mountainous area of rapidly recovering, secondary tropical deciduous forests, cut with numerous rivers and waterfalls. Nearly 100 species of birds can be spotted here, including over half of Cuba's 22 endemic species. Currently, there are few trails and facilities in the reserve, which is not open to individual exploration and trekking. Most activity is confined to two tourism developments, **Las Terrazas** and **Soroa,** which are connected by a loop of paved roads, which begins and ends on the Autopista Nacional.

Essentials

GETTING THERE & GETTING AROUND   The only public transportation to Las Terrazas is the once-a-day Víazul drop-off leaving Havana at 9am and arriving at Las Terrazas at 10:35am, returning at 4:30pm. If you want to spend more time, you will either have to rent a car, hire a taxi, or come with an organized tour (which can be booked at any major tour operator or hotel tour desk). Las Terrazas is about 75km (47 miles) west of Havana. Take the Autopista Nacional (A4) west to Km 51. Here you'll see the not-hugely-visible sign and turnoff for Las Terrazas on your right. The heart of the complex is about 8km (5 miles) from the turnoff. About halfway there, you'll hit the entrance, where you have to sign in and pay an entrance fee of CUC$4 (US$4.30/£2.15) per person, although this is waived for guests at the hotel here.

To get to Soroa, continue through Las Terrazas or on the Autopista until the town of Candelaria at Km 62. The turnoff here is marked and it's another 8km (5 miles) to Soroa.

ORIENTATION The main offices at Las Terrazas are at Rancho Curujey; the community and Hotel Moka are a couple of kilometers away. Everything is well marked and connected by paved roads. If you don't have a reservation at Hotel Moka, you'll have to check in at Rancho Curujey before undertaking any tours or explorations of the reserve. The reserve gets busy in the high season and on weekends; reservations are recommended, even for day visits.

What to See & Do

Las Terrazas ★ (© 7/204-3739 in Havana, or 48/57-8555 on-site; open 9am–6pm) is a neat and organized project designed around a working community. The community and Hotel Moka are set just above the shores of the diminutive **Lago San Juan.** There are a half dozen or so trails and swimming holes, along with a smattering of other attractions, including the **Cafetal Buenavista,** an abandoned coffee plantation, and a few artists' and artisans' studios. If you're lucky, you might spot one of the area's endemic lizards or amphibians, including the world's second-smallest frog.

Officially you must have a guide to hike any of the trails here. Guides can be provided either by Hotel Moka or by the administrative offices at Rancho Curujey (© 48/57-8555, ext 221 or 7/204-3739 in Havana; reserva@terraz.co.cu or reservas@commoka.get.tur.cu). The trails around the **Cafetal Buenavista** make for a good couple of hours of gentle hiking, and the restaurant here makes the whole thing rather convenient. Another popular hike is the slightly more rugged **La Cañada del Infierno (the Gorge of Hell),** which follows a mountain river down beyond the ruins of yet another coffee plantation, ending a couple of kilometers later at the Santa Catalina sulfur springs. A guide costs between CUC$12 and CUC$39 (US$13–US$42/£6.50–£21) per person, depending on the group size and length of your hike.

The newest attraction and adventure here is a zip-line and harness-style **Canopy Tour.** The tour features five platforms connected by long steel cables, which you traverse with a climbing-style harness and pulley setup. The cables crisscross the little lake here two times. The tour takes about 50 minutes and costs CUC$25 (US$27/£14) per person, or CUC$15 (US$16/£8) if you are staying at the hotel.

Fans of the brilliant Polo Montañez can stop off at the **Peña Polo Montañez** (closed Mon) where the singer used to live. The small house overlooking the lake contains dozens of newspaper cuttings, his guitar, and his hat. His brother, Luis Borrego, is usually hanging around talking to visitors.

Soroa is a small community with one basic mini-resort (see "Where to Stay," below). The area's claims to fame are a lovely 22m (72-ft.) waterfall and a wonderful botanical garden. You reach the base of **Salto de Soroa** after a gentle hike of around 250m (820 ft.). There's a small pool here fit for wading. If you're more adventurous, you can hike or hire a horse for CUC$5 (US$5.40/£2.70) to ride the steep 1.8km (1-mile) trail to the natural lookout, El Mirador. The rainbow that sometimes forms in the mist of this waterfall has earned the whole town the moniker *El Arcoiris de Cuba* (the Rainbow of Cuba). The entrance to the trails is just a few hundred yards from the hotel, on the road to Havana; admission costs CUC$3 (US$3.25/£1.60) per person for those not staying at the hotel. Another nearby road leads up to a hilltop lookout called **El Castillo de las Nubes,** where you'll find a derelict building built to resemble a small fortress.

With more than 6,000 species of tropical plants and flowers from around the world, including 700 species of orchids, the **Jardín Botánico Orquideario Soroa** ★ (© 48/52-3871) is a must-see for anyone passing through Soroa. The compact grounds are well tended and pleasant and there are usually at least 20 or so species of orchids in bloom (most flowering blooms are btw. Dec and Apr). There's also a good chance of hearing and spotting the national bird, the tocororo. Admission is CUC$3 (US$3.25/£1.60) and includes a 15- to 20-minute guided tour. Open 8:30am to 4:30pm daily.

A 1-day taxi trip to this area from Havana costs around CUC$80 (US$86/£43).

Where to Stay
Expensive
Hotel Moka ★   This is the principal hotel in Las Terrazas and the nicest ecolodge in Cuba. The first-floor rooms have vaulted redbrick ceilings, while those on the second floor have high-pitched ceilings. Each of the well-lit and spacious rooms has colorfully tiled floors and a small balcony; however, there are no queen- or king-size beds. The marble bathrooms come with a tub/shower combination and a bidet. The restaurant serves food that is neither spectacular nor imaginative, and I recommend that you take some meals at the nearby La Fonda de Mercedes and Buena Vista restaurants. You can also rent small villas, attached to the homes of local residents, on the little lake below the hotel. These are charming and all have bathtubs except one; one also has an additional outdoor shower.

Autopista Nacional Km 51, Las Terrazas. © **48/57-8600** at the hotel, or 7/204-3739 in Havana. Fax 7/204-5305. 26 units, 5 villas. CUC$64–CUC$110 (US$69–US$119/£35–£59) double; CUC$50–CUC$85 (US$54–US$92/£27–£46) villa. Rates include breakfast. MC, V. **Amenities:** Restaurant; bar; small outdoor pool; tennis court; horse rental; activity desk; Internet access; laundry service. *In room:* A/C, TV, minibar, safe.

Moderate
Hotel & Villas Soroa   The clean and compact rooms at this mini-resort are not nearly as nice as those at Hotel Moka; however, the best rooms are those set up the stairs around the pool (nos. 16–24). Most have either two or three full-size beds, although a few have queen-size beds. The furnishings are simple and spartan. This place has a fair amount of group traffic and is also popular with Cubans, especially on weekends, when they gather around the large pool and the sound system is at full throttle. This is a good base for exploring Soroa, but I wouldn't recommend more than a night or two here. One advantage is that the pool can be used by day-trippers for CUC$10 (US$11/£5.40), and CUC$7 (US$7.55/£3.80) of that can be spent on food and drink; there's also a very well-stocked (food) shop on the premises.

Carretera de Soroa Km 8, Pinar del Río. © **48/52-3534.** www.hotelescubanacan.com. 49 units. CUC$53–CUC$65 (US$57–US$70/£29–£35) double. Rates include breakfast buffet. **Amenities:** 2 restaurants; 3 bars; outdoor pool; activities desk; massage; laundry service. *In room:* A/C, TV, safe.

Where to Dine
La Fonda de Mercedes (Finds)   CRIOLLA   This is clearly the top dining option in Las Terrazas, even though there are only six items on the menu. The best dish is the Camagüey-style lamb, which is served shredded and cooked in wine, although the grilled chicken a la Pinareña, which is seasoned with orange juice, garlic, and cumin, is also good. There are only five large wooden tables on the open-air patio of Doña Mercedes Dache's apartment in this residential block of housing just below Hotel Moka, so reservations are a good idea. The wine list features the moderately priced and almost drinkable, Soroa-brand red and white wines.

Edificio 9, Apto. 2, Las Terrazas. (✆ **48/57-8647.** Reservations recommended. Main courses CUC$6.45–CUC$8 (US$6.95–US$8.65/£3.50–£4.30) No credit cards. Daily 9am–9pm.

SAN DIEGO DE LOS BAÑOS & LA GÜIRA NATIONAL PARK

Just west of the Sierra de los Rosario, in the foothills of the Sierra de los Organos, you'll find La Güira National Park and San Diego de los Baños. **La Güira** is a small park that is nonetheless a favorite stop for bird-watching tours and general sightseers. **San Diego de los Baños** is a tiny back-of-beyond town built on the edge of a lovely river and some natural mineral springs. The springs have been famed for their medicinal properties for centuries, and the local baths are a very popular destination for Cubans looking for a relaxing getaway, basic spa treatments, and physical therapy.

Getting There & Getting Around

There is no regular or reliable public transportation to San Diego de los Baños. You will either have to rent a car, hire a taxi, or come with an organized tour. San Diego de los Baños is located about 133km (83 miles) southwest of Havana. Take the Autopista Nacional (A4) west to Km 102. You should see the sign and turnoff to your right. From here, it's another 21km (13 miles) to town. A taxi from Havana to San Diego de los Baños costs between CUC$40 and CUC$50 (US$43–US$54/£22–£27) one-way. A few taxis are available in town. They charge from CUC$3 to CUC$5 (US$3.25–US$5.40/£1.60–£2.70) one-way to La Güira.

What to See & Do

San Diego de los Baños is a tiny town built on the edge of a lovely river and some natural mineral springs. The **San Diego de los Baños Spa** ((✆ **48/54-8880**) is a relatively desultory facility that shows the wear and tear it has borne over the years. This place does a heavy business in therapeutic and vacation care for Cubans. A host of physical and occupational therapists, and doctors, are on staff here. This is no Canyon Ranch; in fact, you'll feel as if you're heading down to a dungeon as you descend the two stories to the ground-level baths. Still, if you're staying at El Mirador next-door (see "Where to Stay & Dine," below), you'd do well to stop in for a massage (CUC$25/US$27/£14). The rest of the complex was closed in 2008 due to water contamination.

La Güira National Park is 5km (3 miles) west of San Diego de los Baños. You enter the park through the grand gates of the former Hacienda Cortina. There are some ruins and tended gardens near the entrance, as well as a restaurant. There are no marked trails and no signs, but a heavily potholed road leads through the park (keep going straight) and up to the **Cueva de Los Portales** (marked by a Campismo sign), a small cave complex from which Che Guevara coordinated the Cuban defense forces during the Cuban missile crisis. The latter is probably the most interesting site in the area, and a must-see for anyone on the Che trail. Inside, you can tour the compound and see where Che hung his hammock for afternoon siestas, where he and the men took target practice, where they cooked and ate, and where they played chess. You can even peek into the tiny room where the revolutionary icon slept during those troubled times. Admission is CUC$1 (US$1.10/55p); it's the same price for a guide and to take pictures.

Where to Stay & Dine

Hotel El Mirador   This little hotel is a surprisingly neat and well-run option in this neck of the woods. The rooms are all set in a two-story building above and behind the pool and reception. All of the rooms are clean and comfortable, with good light (but more so on the first floor) and well-kept rattan furnishings, though the bathrooms are a tad small and the beds a bit soft. There are well-tended gardens and grounds and a mid-size pool. The main restaurant is actually pretty good for a Cuban chain hotel in the middle of nowhere; it serves unimpressive, but acceptable, international fare. Hotel El Mirador does a mixed business of tourists and Cubans, and the pool and poolside bar are both usually lively.

San Diego de los Baños, Los Palacios, Pinar del Río. © **48/54-8866.** www.islazul.cu. 30 units. CUC$37–CUC$41 (US$40–US$44/£20–£22) double. CUC$55 (US$59/£30) suite. MC, V. **Amenities:** Restaurant; poolside grill; 2 bars; outdoor pool; activities desk; car rentals. *In room:* A/C, TV, safe.

4 CAYO LEVISA ★

113km (70 miles) W of Havana; 53km (33 miles) N of Viñales

Cayo Levisa is an isolated little island accessible only by boat. The island is around 3km (1³/₄ miles) long and just several hundred yards wide at most points. The entire northern shore of Cayo Levisa is one long stretch of white sand fronting a calm and startlingly turquoise blue sea. The beach is backed alternately by small stands of pine trees and stretches of thick mangrove. There's excellent bird-watching and scuba diving here. Cayo Levisa is part of the Archipiélago de los Colorados, which includes Cayo Paraíso, an even smaller little island reputed to have been a favorite fishing haunt of Ernest Hemingway.

Several Havana, Pinar del Río, and Viñales tour agencies run day tours to Cayo Levisa, so the island's resort and beaches can fill up with 50 to 100 extra visitors between 10:30am and 5pm in high season. Still, there's enough beach to go around, and if you spend the night, you'll really feel like you've got the island to yourself and a few good friends.

GETTING THERE

Hotel Cayo Levisa (see "Where to Stay & Dine," below) runs two **boats** daily to Cayo Levisa leaving from Palma Rubia at 10am and 6pm. The trip takes 30 minutes. It may be possible to hire a boat to take you out if you miss the morning trip, but don't count on it. Return boats from Cayo Levisa leave for Palma Rubia at 9am and 5pm. If you don't have a prearranged tour to the island, the boat ride will run you CUC$10 (US$11/£5.40) per person round-trip.

To get to Palma Rubia from Havana by **car,** drive the northern highway from Mariel to Bahía Honda and continue on for another 40km (25 miles) west to Palma Rubia. If you're coming from Viñales, drive north to La Palma and then another 21km (13 miles) northeast to the embarkation point.

There is no regular or reliable **bus service** to Palma Rubia or Cayo Levisa. You could hire a **taxi** from Havana (CUC$45–CUC$55/US$49–US$59/£24–£30 each way) or take a tour from Viñales or Pinar del Río (CUC$25/US$27/£14), but make sure you prearrange a pickup for your return trip if you come by taxi, or you could have trouble getting out of Palma Rubia.

FUN ON & OFF THE BEACH

The beach encompasses 450m (1,476 ft.) on either side of the main lodge and is excellent for **sunbathing** and **swimming,** with broad stretches of soft sand and a gentle entry into the sea that allows you to walk out literally hundreds of yards before it gets too deep. The water can get a little rough and the weather cool when cold fronts blow through in the winter months, but this is the exception rather than the rule.

Cayo Levisa is an excellent destination for **diving** and **snorkeling.** There's a good dive operation on-site (cayolevisa@cubanacan.co.cu) and some 23 identified dive sites within a 45-minute boat ride of the island. Most of the sites are less than 15 minutes away, and some are excellent for snorkeling. Rest stops often include a packed lunch at some deserted little island. Two tank dives per day will run you CUC$72 (US$78/£39), including equipment, and multiday packages are available. Rental of snorkeling equipment costs CUC$5 (US$5.40/£2.70) per day.

If you're looking to follow in Papa Hemingway's footsteps, take a day trip to **Cayo Paraíso.** This small island is about 10km (6 miles) east of Cayo Levisa. There's a small bust of Papa and a little shack that functions as a bar and grill, where you can buy lunch and drinks. The trip costs CUC$25 (US$27/£14), including transportation, snorkeling, and refreshments. Snorkeling gear will run you an extra CUC$5 (US$5.40/£2.70). There have been reports of the dive/excursion boat being broken on several occasions. Check with Cubanacán before setting off, if your heart is set on diving.

WHERE TO STAY & DINE

Hotel Cayo Levisa ★ (Finds) If you land one of the oceanfront bungalows here, you may never want to leave this idyllic little resort. I prefer the older rooms, which are individual bungalows, built in two rows parallel to the shore and staggered so they all get an ocean view. The rooms themselves are rather spartan, although they are relatively spacious with two twin beds. Perhaps their best feature is an ample front porch with a couple of sitting chairs. The newer rooms are slightly more plush, but you sacrifice a bit of privacy and isolation in these more modern, wooden units. Scuba diving and snorkeling are the prime activities here, although you can organize a game of beach volleyball, or get an open-air massage from the resident massage therapist under the shade of palm trees at the water's edge. Dining here is a la carte and the little restaurant serves good fresh seafood and *criolla* (Cuban creole) cuisine at reasonable prices.

Cayo Levisa, Pinar del Río. © **48/75-6506.** Fax 48/75-6506. www.hotelescubanacan.com. 33 units. CUC$67–CUC$74 (US$72–US$80/£36–£40) double. Rates include breakfast. Round-trip transportation from Palma Rubia $15. No credit cards. **Amenities:** Restaurant; bar; massage. *In room:* A/C, TV, minibar (in some), safe.

ANOTHER NEARBY ISLAND: CAYO JUTIAS

A little bit west of Cayo Levisa, you can find similar attractions and isolated wonder at **Cayo Jutías** ★. Unlike its nearby sister, Cayo Jutías is connected to the mainland by a 8km (5-mile) *pedraplén,* or low-lying causeway. The island is a popular destination for day trips out of Pinar del Río and Viñales. Aside from the 8km (5 miles) of deserted white-sand beach, there's an open-air beachside restaurant serving standard *criolla* fare at reasonable prices. There's a new *náutico* (nautical) center from which excursions are arranged to Starfish Beach—a real highlight with dozens of enormous starfish—and to Isla Mégano, among others, for CUC$5 to CUC$17 (US$5.40–US$18/£2.70–£9.20) per person. Fishing trips can also be arranged for CUC$40 to CUC$45 an hour (US$43–US$49/£22–£24). You can also rent pedal boats, kayaks, snorkeling equipment, and beach loungers. Diving activities were under consideration at press time.

To get to Cayo Jutías from Havana, drive the northern highway from Mariel to Bahía Honda and continue west to Santa Lucía. If you're coming from Viñales, drive north to

San Vincente, then continue to San Caetano and Santa Lucía. The *pedraplén* to Cayo Jutías begins about 5km (3 miles) northwest of Santa Lucía. The toll for the *pedraplén* is CUC$5 (US$5.40/£2.70) per person (open 10am–6pm daily). All of the major tour agencies offer day trips to Cayo Jutías from Viñales and Pinar del Río for between CUC$20 and CUC$25 (US$22–US$27/£11–£14) per person, including lunch.

5 MARIA LA GORDA ★

306km (190 miles) SW of Havana

María la Gorda is a tiny beach and dive resort on the eastern end of the Bahía de Corrientes (Current Bay), which is formed by the long, curving Peninsula de Guanacahabibes. If you want to get away from it all, this is a good choice. The one hotel here caters almost exclusively to divers and dive groups, although it's also a good base for naturalists looking to explore the flora and fauna of the Guanacahabibes Peninsula, which UNESCO has declared an International Biosphere Reserve. The beach and hotel are named for a legendary Venezuelan beauty who was marooned here by pirates. María allegedly gained quite a reputation for her fleshy charms. She's long gone, but if you're looking to admire raw physical beauty, the sunsets here are some of the best in Cuba.

ESSENTIALS

GETTING THERE   There is no regular **bus service** to María la Gorda. If you are coming, check with the Gaviota hotel chain, which runs the only hotel here (see "Where to Stay & Dine," below)—they can arrange transportation to and from Havana, leaving daily at 8am and returning at 2pm, for CUC$60 (US$65/£32) per person one way, or CUC$100 (US$108/£54) round-trip. (It becomes cheaper the larger the group.)

To get here by **car,** take the Autopista Nacional (A4) west to Pinar del Río. From Pinar del Río, it's another 94km (58 miles) to María la Gorda on the old Carretera Central passing through the prime tobacco-growing towns of San Juan y Martinez and Isabel Rubio, and then continuing on to Sandino and La Fe. There are two left turns on the route without signs, so you will need to seek directions. You'll hit the water at Bahía de Corrientes at La Bajada. The road to the left leads 14km (8¾ miles) to María la Gorda. The road to the right heads out the peninsula another 54km (34 miles) to Cabo de San Antonio.

The **Marina María la Gorda** (© 48/75-0123) is an official entry and exit port for yachts. When arriving by sea, contact the marina before entering Cuban waters (19km/12 miles offshore) on VHF channels 16 or 19, or HF channel 2760. Theoretically, there's a Customs and Immigration officer on 24-hour duty, and water, electricity, and fuel can be had while tying up to the small pier here.

GETTING AROUND   Rentacar Vía (©/fax **48/77-8131**) has a car- and scooter-rental desk here. A four-door compact car with air-conditioning will run you between CUC$55 and CUC$80 (US$59–US$86/£30–£43) daily, including insurance and unlimited mileage, while scooters go for CUC$24 (US$26/£13) per day; hourly rates are available.

FUN ON & OFF THE BEACH

The beach right in front of the hotel quickly hits coral and rock outcroppings as soon as it meets the water. In fact, sand is at a premium here. You'd definitely be wise to bring along a pair of waterproof aquatic shoes or sandals. The best beach for sunbathing and swimming is about 1km (¹/₂ mile) southwest of the hotel near an abandoned marina. There are also some excellent beaches out toward Cabo San Antonio on the Guanaca-habibes Peninsula.

Scuba diving ★★★ is the principal activity here, and this is one of the top dive destinations in Cuba. More than 50 dive sites are within a 1-hour boat ride of the resort, and many are much, much closer. Visibility is excellent and the waters of the bay here stay calm year-round, making entry and exiting a breeze. The place has a bit of a reputation for whale sharks that apparently congregate near here in October and November. However, my dive master had been working here for almost 2 years and had yet to see a whale shark. What you will see are fabulous coral and sponge formations, colorful tropical fish, turtles, eels, barracuda, and rays. It costs CUC$42 (US$45/£23) per dive, including a complete equipment package. The boat goes out at 8:30am, noon, and 3pm. There are also nightly scuba dives for CUC$40 (US$43/£22). Multiday dive packages are available for CUC$135 (US$146/£73). Snorkelers can reach some decent coral outcroppings in 3 to 7.5m (10–25 ft.) of water within 90 to 180m (295–591 ft.) of the coast. Mask, fins, and snorkeling will cost you CUC$12 (US$13/£6.50) per day.

Depending on boat availability, half-day **fishing** trips can also be arranged for between CUC$150 and CUC$250 (US$162–US$270/£81–£135) for up to four persons, with your own equipment only. Possible catches range from tarpon to bonefish to a variety of deepwater fish.

Aside from the watersports mentioned above, the other main attraction here is exploring the nearby **Guanacahabibes National Park** ★. There are three trails in the park, and you must have a guide to hike any of them. The land here is flat and you'll find a mix of lowland scrub, pine forests, and mangrove, dotted with numerous little lakes and lagoons. There are quite a few endemic bird, lizard, and mammal species. This was also the last refuge of Cuba's indigenous tribes as the Spaniards completed their conquest, and several small archaeological sites have been uncovered. There's a little lighthouse, Faro Roncali, at the point at Cabo San Antonio, and a park ranger station (Estación Ecológica; ⓒ **48/75-0366;** open 9am–5pm daily) at La Bajada. It costs CUC$6 to CUC$10 (US$6.50–US$11/£3.25–£5.40) per person to hike the trails (starting at 9am; insect repellent required), including a multilingual guide, depending upon which trail you hike. Specialist trips for the same price can be organized for snorkelers, bird-watchers, spelunkers, and photographers. If you just plan on driving your car or scooter out the road to Cabo San Antonio and visiting some of the beaches here, you may be able to get away without a guide; however, as a rule, they are averse to foreigners roaming around the park unaccompanied. You can book the excursions from Villa María La Gorda (see below), too. Tours from Pinar del Río and Viñales include a bag lunch and cost CUC$40 (US$43/£22) and CUC$45 (US$49/£24) respectively.

WHERE TO STAY & DINE

Villa María La Gorda   Also known as the International Diving Center, this place is run by the Cuban Gaviota chain, and exists somewhere in that gray area between a no-frills dive camp and a modern resort. The rooms are adequate and fairly spacious, if nothing fancy. You'll definitely want to land one of the older oceanfront units, if possible. A series of newer units are set back from the beach, and are pleasant, quiet, and spacious as individual and two-story wooden bungalows. The resort's restaurants are uninspired, although there are really no other options around. I actually spied quite a few guests buying cookies and crackers at the little gift shop here and calling it a meal. Still, the

Península de Guanacahabibes, Pinar del Río. ©/fax **48/77-8131** or 48/77-8077. www.gaviota-grupo.
com. 55 units. CUC$58–CUC$68 (US$63–US$73/£31–£37) double. Rates include breakfast buffet. $5 extra
for oceanview room. MC, V. **Amenities:** 2 restaurants; bar; car- and scooter-rental desk; gift shop; laundry
service; full-service dive shop; medical service. *In room:* A/C, TV, fridge, safe.

6 ISLA DE LA JUVENTUD

162km (101 miles) S of Havana

Isla de la Juventud hangs like an apostrophe off the southern coast of Cuba and is the
largest and westernmost island in the Archipiélago de los Canarreos. Sometimes referred
to as the Island of a Thousand Names, it was called variously Siguanea, Guanaja, and
Camarco by the early indigenous populations. The island was later christened El Evangelista by Columbus, Parrot Island by pirates, and Isla de Pinos (Isle of Pines) throughout
most of the 19th and 20th centuries. Some even call it Treasure Island, claiming Robert
Louis Stevenson used it as a model for his book of the same name. Following the Cuban
Revolution, it was renamed Isla de la Juventud, or Isle of Youth, after a slew of secondary
schools and colleges were built here to educate both Cuban and foreign students.

For travelers, Isla de la Juventud's primary attraction is its stellar scuba diving. The one
working hotel serving foreigners caters almost entirely to divers. Other attractions include
some of the most elaborate and best-preserved indigenous cave paintings in the entire
Caribbean basin and the eerie prison buildings where Fidel Castro was incarcerated.

ESSENTIALS
Getting There
BY PLANE   **Cubana** has three daily flights to **Rafael Cabrera Mustelier Airport**
(© **46/32-2300;** airport code GER) on Isla de la Juventud from José Martí International
Airport in Havana. Fares cost CUC$43 (US$46/£23) each way. Demand is often very
high, as the flights are quicker and cheaper than the ferry, so be sure to make your return
reservation as far in advance as possible.

Regular public buses connect the airport and Nueva Gerona, 6.5km (4 miles) away.
These are marked SERVICIO AEREO. The official fare is 1 peso, but foreigners are usually
charged CUC$1 (US$1.10/55p). A taxi between the airport and downtown costs around
CUC$5 to CUC$7 (US$5.40–US$7.55/£2.70–£3.80).

BY BUS & FERRY   Isla de la Juventud is connected to the mainland by regular ferry
service between Nueva Gerona, on the island, and the town of Batabanó, on the coast
71km (44 miles) south of Havana. Several types of ferries make the trip. You'll definitely
want to book one of the two high-speed modern catamaran ferries. Either of these will
make the trip in between 2 and 3 hours, and costs CUC$50 (US$54/£27) each way.
These ferries depart Batabanó daily at 8am, with return trips leaving Nueva Gerona at
11am. The ferries often have varying schedules, according to demand. The company,
Empresa Viamar, which books all of the vessels, has a desk in the main Astro bus termi-
nal in Havana (© **7/870-9401** or 47/588-240 in Batabanó, or 46/32-4415 in Nueva
Gerona). Here, you can buy a bus-ferry combination ticket, which I highly recommend.
Buses leave the terminal for Batabanó four times a day and cost MN$5 (US20¢/10p).
Sometimes the connections at the Batabanó end do not work like a fine Swiss watch. In

Nueva Gerona, the ferry terminal and dock are approximately 4 blocks east of Calle José Martí (© **46/32-4415**). It is highly recommended that you buy a return ticket at the time of purchase and that you buy tickets at least a day or two in advance, because schedules are subject to change.

Getting Around

Taxis are plentiful on Isla de la Juventud and around Nueva Gerona (**Cubataxi;** © **47/32-3121**). Rides around town, out to the airport, or to one of the nearby beaches costs between CUC$2 and CUC$7 (US$2.15–US$7.55/£1.10–£3.80). A trip down to the Hotel El Colony costs CUC$18 to CUC$22 (US$19–US$24/£9.70–£12). There are three or four daily buses between Nueva Gerona and the Hotel El Colony. A full day with a driver cost from CUC$60 to CUC$80 (US$65–US$86/£32–£43). If you want to rent a car, **Cubacar,** Calle 32 corner of 39 (© **46/32-6666**); **Havanautos,** Calle 32 and 39 (© **46/32-4432**); and **Transtur,** at the ferry terminal and Hotel El Colony (©/fax **46/32-6666**), have offices on the island. Havanautos also rents mopeds.

There are also numerous horse-drawn taxis, which generally charge from CUC$1 to CUC$2 (US$1.10–US$2.15/55p–£1.10) for short rides, or between CUC$4 and CUC$6 (US$4.30–US$6.50/£2.15–£3.25) per hour.

Orientation

The main city, **Nueva Gerona,** sits near the northern tip of the island on the banks of the Río Las Casas, while the better beaches and scuba-diving locations are on the southwest and southeastern shores. The **Hotel El Colony** (see "Where to Stay & Dine," below) is located on the shores of Siguanea Bay, on the central western coast of the island. The southern third of the island is an almost entirely uninhabited area of swamp and mangrove.

There are several banks and a **CADECA** office (Calle José Martí corner of Calle 20) in Nueva Gerona. There's a **post office** at Calle José Martí corner of Calle 18, a 24-hour **Farmacia José Martí** (© **46/32-2484**) on Calle José Martí and Calle 24, and an **Etecsa** Telepunto phone and center at Calles 41 and 28. All of the above are located either on or within a 1- or 2-block radius of the Calle José Martí pedestrian mall.

The downtown offices of **Cubanacán** (© **46/32-6369**) and **Ecotur** (© **46/32-7101**) are your best sources of local information, and where you should head to book a tour to the attractions listed below.

WHAT TO SEE & DO

The island's most publicized attraction is the **Presidio Modelo (Model Prison;** © **46/32-5112),** located about 5km (3 miles) east of Nueva Gerona. The massive, five-story, circular prison blocks are dire and imposing, the remaining metal brackets whining in the silence, and even brief visits give you an idea of how uncomfortable they must have been. This is the prison where Fidel Castro and other surviving conspirators were sent following the failed Moncada raid. There's a small museum in the block where Fidel and his compadres did time, and you can even visit the Comandante's former cell, no. 3859. The museum is open Monday through Saturday from 8am to 4pm, and Sunday from 8am to noon; admission is CUC$2 (US$2.15/£1.10). There's an extra CUC$3 (US$3.25/£1.60) charge for taking photos, and a CUC$15 (US$16/£8) fee for taking video.

If you're spending much time in downtown Nueva Gerona, you might want to stop in at the **Museo Provincial** (© **46/32-3791**) on the park. Housed in an old building dating from the 1830s, this museum features a wide range of exhibits illustrating the island's history from pre-Columbian times to the modern era. Admission is CUC$1 (US$1.10/55p).

Nueva Gerona's **downtown park,** the Parque Julio Antonio Mella, is a great place to hang out, with some strategically placed benches for sitting and watching the townsfolk stroll on by. There's a pretty little colonial, mission-style church, **Nuestra Señora de los Dolores,** on the northern edge of the park, and the snazzy-looking Art Deco **Cine Caribe** on the eastern edge. Beginning at the park's western edge and running north for 5 blocks, Calle 39, also known as **Calle José Martí,** is a pedestrian-only street. This is where most of the town's shops, restaurants, and bars are located, and it's the site of the town's nightlife.

About 27km (17 miles) south of Nueva Gerona is an interesting botanical garden dubbed **La Jungla de Jones,** or the Jungle of Jones (✆ 46/39-6246). A rather unkempt attraction, the gardens nonetheless have a broad and varied collection of tropical flora. Admission is CUC$3 (US$3.25/£1.60). Farther south, beyond the town of La Fe, you'll find the **Criadero de Cocodrilos,** a crocodile-breeding project. The facilities are basic, but there are hundreds of these impressive reptiles here, ranging in size from little tots to monstrous adults. The facility is open daily from 8am to 5pm, and the CUC$3 (US$3.25/£1.60) entrance fee will get you a brief guided tour.

On the southeastern coast of Isla de la Juventud, 59km (37 miles) from Nueva Gerona is the **Cueva de Punta del Este** ★, a small complex of caves with more than 200 ancient pictographs well preserved on its walls. This cave system has been called the Sistine Chapel of Caribbean indigenous art. The paintings are of abstract and geometric patterns and are thought to have both religious and celestial significance. There's a pretty white-sand beach here as well, so you can combine a visit to the caves with some beach time. There's no entrance fee to the caves, but you'll need a special permit and guide to enter this area; your best bet is to visit as part of an organized tour, which can be arranged at your hotel or with **Cubanacán** (✆ 46/32-6369) or **Ecotur** (✆ 46/32-7101) in town.

ON THE BEACH & UNDER THE SEA

Isla de la Juventud is one of Cuba's premier **dive destinations** ★★★, and the diving here is wonderful. The waters are crystal clear, and there are walls, corals, caves, and even a few wrecks. The **Centro Internacional de Buceo Colony** (✆ 46/39-8181) is the main dive operator on the island, with its dive center at the small marina a few kilometers beyond the Hotel El Colony (see "Where to Stay & Dine," below). Most trips head to **Punta Francés** ★★, a national maritime park, with a beautiful stretch of white-sand beach fronting a calm and protected sea on the southwestern tip of the island. From here, many of the island's best dive sites are easily accessible. There are a couple of long piers out into the calm waters here. One has a buffet restaurant and bar at the end of it. On shore, there's a small park station, with bathroom facilities and some picnic tables. The park station also has several hundred chaise longues, which are taken out and spread along the beach whenever a cruise ship pulls in for a day tour. When this happens—once or twice a week—this quiet, isolated beach becomes a swarming mass of up to 1,500 sun worshipers. When the cruise ships aren't around, you'll have the joint almost to yourself. Dive trips cost CUC$60 (US$65/£32) for a two-tank dive, including a full-equipment package. However, if you stay here for any length of time, you are best off buying a multiday, multidive package. Day-trippers can take the boat ride out for between CUC$8 and CUC$30 (US$8.65–US$32/£4.30–£16); the higher fees include lunch.

Fishing can also be arranged through **Avalon** (✆ 535/286-1818; www.avalonfishing center.com), which runs 7-day packages based out of the Hotel Rancho El Tesoro or on the live-aboard boat, the *Perola*. Prices start from CUC$3,009 (US$3,250/£1,625) with the hotel as your base and CUC$ 4,028 (US$4,350/£2,175) for the live aboard in the low season. Enormous and abundant bonefish, tarpon, and permit are among the dozens of fish species encountered here.

The most popular beaches close to Nueva Gerona are the white-sand **Playa Paraíso** and the dark-sand **Playa Bibijagua.** These beaches are 5km (3 miles) and 8km (5 miles) east of town, respectively, and both are served by regular bus service from town. Oddly, the dark-sand Playa Bibijagua is the more popular spot, although neither is a prime beach destination by any standard.

WHERE TO STAY & DINE

In addition to the hotel listed below, there are many *casas particulares* in Nueva Gerona. You'll definitely be offered a few as soon as you set foot on the island, whether you arrive by sea or by air. Check out the offerings of whomever gives you the best vibe, or head to either **Villa Niñita,** Calle 32 no. 4110 between Calles 41 and 43, Nueva Gerona (© **46/ 32-1255**), or **Villa Peña,** Calle 10 no. 3710, between Calles 37 and 39, Nueva Gerona (© **46/32-2345**). Both offer clean, air-conditioned rooms with meals for between CUC$20 and CUC$25 (US$22–US$27/£12–£15) per person, as well as reasonably priced rides around the island.

Hotel El Colony   This is primarily a dive resort, and I only recommend it for hard-core divers. The hotel itself was built in two stages. The original horseshoe-shaped, two-story main building feels perpetually run-down. The newer "bungalows" are in better shape. These rooms are in one- and two-story blocks, and are spacious and modern, with two firm double beds, wicker furniture, and a small private terrace or balcony. The buffet restaurant is mediocre and overpriced. The nicest feature is the long pier and the Mojito Bar & Grill that sits at the end of it. This is a great place for sunsets and, when the wind is right, a good place to escape the fierce swarms of mosquitoes and sand fleas that often plague the nights here.

Carretera Siguanea Km 42 (49km/30 miles southwest of Nueva Gerona), Isla de la Juventud. © **46/39-8181.** reservas@colony.turisla.co.cu. 77 units. CUC$64–CUC$84 (US$69–US$91/£35–£45) double. Rates include breakfast buffet. MC, V. Taxis to or from Nueva Gerona or the airport CUC$18–CUC$22 (US$19–US$24/£9.70–£12); public buses make the run 3 times daily for 2 Cuban pesos. **Amenities:** 2 restaurants; 2 bars; outdoor pool; watersports equipment/rentals; tour desk; car- and scooter-rental desk; laundry service. *In room:* A/C, TV, safe.

ISLA DE LA JUVENTUD AFTER DARK

Start your evening with a stroll and mingle on Calle José Martí. If you get tired of that, you can check out what's playing at the **Cine Caribe,** Calle 37 and Calle 28, or stop in at the **Caberet El Patio,** Calle 24 between Calles Martí and 37, which offers up this island's somewhat anemic version of a traditional cabaret show (admission CUC$3/ US$3.25/£1.60), and then becomes a dance club. Other spots right on Calle Martí include the neighboring **Casa de las Mieles** and **Nuevo Café Virginia,** which are good options for a few drinks. The latter sometimes has live music and dancing. Or you can see if there's any live music or performance at the **Casa de la Cultura,** on Calle 24 at the corner of 37.

7 CAYO LARGO DEL SUR ★★★

177km (110 miles) S of Havana; 120km (75 miles) E of Isla de la Juventud

Cayo Largo del Sur—or more simply, Cayo Largo—is the second-largest island in the Archipiélago de los Canarreos, and the only other island in the chain to support any population or tourism activity. The island's primary attraction is its uninterrupted kilometers of pristine white-sand beach, perhaps the best in Cuba. The island also provides fabulous scuba-diving and snorkeling opportunities, excellent wildlife viewing, and great bonefish, tarpon, and deep-sea fishing.

Cayo Largo has a long and rich history as a stomping and fishing ground for nomadic Caribe and Siboney indigenous populations. It was also visited by Christopher Columbus on his second voyage in 1494, and used as a base and stopover point by pirates and corsairs, including Sir Francis Drake, Henry Morgan, and Jean Lafitte.

Over three-quarters of all visitors to Cayo Largo come direct on charter packages to the island, never even setting foot on mainland Cuba.

ESSENTIALS

GETTING THERE The modern **Juan Vitalio Acuña Airport** (© 45/24-8141; airport code CYO) accepts international traffic. Charter flights arrive here from Canada and Europe regularly throughout the year, with greater frequency during the high season. There are also daily flights here from Havana by **AeroCaribbean** (© 45/24-8364 or © 7/879-7524 in Havana). These are best booked in Havana with any of the many tour agencies (for contact information, see "Getting Around," in chapter 3). Fares are CUC$108 (US$117/£58) and run around CUC$137 (US$148/£74) for the day tour. A taxi from the airport to any hotel on the island costs between CUC$3 and CUC$6 (US$3.25–US$6.50/£1.60–£3.25).

The **Marina Internacional Cayo Largo del Sur** (© 45/24-8213; www.nautica marlin.com) is an official port of entry to Cuba. If you're arriving by sea, contact the marina before entering Cuban waters (19km/12 miles offshore) on VHF channel 16 or 19.

GETTING AROUND There's a shuttle that periodically runs a route connecting the marina and all the major resort hotels here; fare is CUC$1 (US$1.10/55p). Taxis are also readily available on Cayo Largo. A ride anywhere on the island costs between CUC$2 and CUC$10 (US$2.15–US$11/£1.10–£5.40). You can also rent a car or scooter from **Transtur** (© 45/24-8245), which has desks at most of the hotels on the island, as well as at the airport. Rates run about CUC$8 (US$8.65/£4.30) per hour for the first hour on a scooter, and about CUC$3 (US$3.25/£1.60) per hour for each additional hour; it's CUC$60 (US$65/£32) per day for a small jeep, including your first tank of gas and insurance.

FUN ON & OFF THE BEACH

Most visitors to Cayo Largo spend most of their time sprawled out on the 25km (16 miles) of uninterrupted white-sand beach. While the beaches fronting most of the hotels here are some of the finest to be found in the Caribbean, both **Playa Paraíso** ★★★ and **Playa Sirena** ★★★ on the western end of the island deserve special mention. Protected from the prevailing southeasterly trade winds, these beaches are broad expanses of some of the finest white sand to be found, and they are fronted by calm, clear Caribbean waters of postcard-perfect blue hues. Most of the beaches here are clothing optional, and the large number of European and Canadian visitors to Cayo Largo make topless and nude sunbathing quite common. Shade can be at a premium here, so you'll want to park your towel or beach mat close to a coconut palm, or under a beach umbrella or one of the thatched-roof *palapas* that are spread around. Be forewarned, demand usually far exceeds supply. If you have a portable beach umbrella or shade device, I highly recommend you bring it to Cayo Largo. The marina runs a basic restaurant and grill on Playa Sirena, and you can also rent Hobie Cats and windsurfers there. Playa Paraíso is almost entirely undeveloped, with a few thatched-roof A-frame structures on the sand for shade.

Full- and half-day **boat trips,** either on large sailing catamarans or converted fishing boats, are a popular activity here. The trips usually include a stop at Cayo Iguana, a small island with a large population of endemic iguanas, as well as some snorkeling on the barrier reef. These trips often stop at a spot called the *piscina natural* (natural pool). This slightly submerged sandbar is a beautiful and protected spot for a refreshing swim. These trips cost from CUC$69 to CUC$73 (US$75–US$79/£37–£39) per person, including lunch. Most of the all-inclusive resorts on the island allow guests unlimited use of small sailboats, catamarans, and windsurfers. You can rent a larger cruising sailboat for the day, or even overnight, from the marina. Boats go for between CUC$250 and CUC$600 (US$270–US$649/£135–£324) per day, with a skipper and crew.

Right beside the marina is a small turtle breeding and protection project, **La Granja de las Tortugas.** You can visit the facility and usually see various young turtles in holding tanks or protected nests. The farm is open daily from 9am to 6pm; admission is CUC$1 (US$1.10/55p). Between April and September, the folks here occasionally offer night-time trips to see the nesting turtles lay eggs. Inquire at your hotel or at the farm for details.

There's great **bonefishing** on the shallow flats and mangroves all around Cayo Largo. Tarpon, permit, Jack Crevalle, snook, and barracuda are also plentiful. Serious fishermen should contact **Casa Batida** (www.fishingtime.it) or **Avalon** (© 535/286-1818; www.avalonfishingcenter.com), which offers 7-day packages starting from CUC$3,935 (US$4,250/£2,125) in the low season; or contact the **marina** (© 45/24-8212; nautica.marina@repgc.cls.tur.cu).

With rich coral reefs, steep walls, and numerous wrecks, Cayo Largo has excellent **scuba diving** and **snorkeling,** and unlike two of the island's nearby celebrated dive spots, María la Gorda and Isla de la Juventud, you can actually stay in a very comfortable hotel here. Scuba-diving and snorkeling trips are run by the International Dive Center at the marina here (© 45/24-8214; buceo.marina@repgc.cls.tur.cu), but can be booked by any hotel on the island. A two-tank dive trip costs CUC$60 (US$65/£32), with a full equipment package costing an additional CUC$15 (US$16/£8). Avalon is on the verge of opening a new dive center (www.divingincuba.com) with accommodations: Villa Marinera. A 7-day package costs from CUC$1,266 (US$1,367/£684) for six dives. Whale sharks can be seen around October and November and at a new dive site, Cayo Blanco, it's possible to dive with dolphins.

Nightlife on Cayo Largo is pretty much limited to the bars, dance clubs, and revue shows at its all-inclusive hotels.

WHERE TO STAY & DINE

I find the hotel listed below to be the best choice by far on Cayo Largo, but the Sol Meliá company has another property just next door, the **Sol Pelícano** (© 45/24-8333; www.sol-pelicano.com), which is another good option geared more toward families. In addition, the **Barceló Cayo Largo** (© 800/227-2356 in the U.S. and Canada, or 45/24-8080 on Cayo Largo; www.barcelo.com) is yet another luxury resort, while **Gran Caribe** (© 7/204-6366 in Havana, or 45/24-81111 on Cayo Largo; www.gran-caribe.com) runs several more rustic options here, including the **Villa Lindamar, Villa Coral,** and **Villa Soledad.** Of these, Villa Coral, with a lively small-village feel, and Villa Lindamar, with its spacious A-frame bungalows, are the best.

Sol Cayo Largo ★★ (Finds) This is an animated and, at the same time, romantic all-inclusive resort set amid rolling dunes and limestone outcroppings bordering a stretch of Cayo Largo's fabulous Lindamar beach. The two-story blocks of rooms are done in a Cape Cod style, with faux stressed paint that gives the place a worn and lived-in feel. The rooms are quite spacious and comfortable, with either one king- or two queen-size beds and a private balcony or terrace. I think it's worth the CUC$20 (US$22/£11) supplement for one of the 60 oceanview standard rooms. All of these are located on the second floor and come with some added amenities, including a little nightstand CD player, stocked minibar, and—my favorite feature—an inviting, siesta-inducing, Yucatán hammock strung on the balcony. The junior suites come with a connecting sitting room and an extra TV.

Cayo Largo del Sur, Archipiélago de los Canarreos (6km/3³/₄ miles from the airport). © **45/24-8260.** Fax 45/24-8265. www.sol-cayolargo.com. 296 units. CUC$353–CUC$413 (US$381–US$446/£191–£223) double. Rates are all-inclusive. Children 2 and under stay free in parent's room; children 3–12 stay for half-price in parents' room. MC, V. **Amenities:** 5 restaurants; 4 bars; dance club; large free-form outdoor pool; 2 lit outdoor tennis courts; well-equipped health club; nonmotorized watersports equipment; children's programs; game room; concierge; tour and activities desk; car- and scooter-rental desk; salon; massage; babysitting; laundry service. *In room:* A/C, TV, fridge, hair dryer, safe.

Varadero & Matanzas Province

An easy ride from Havana, Matanzas is Cuba's second-largest province, and the site of its principal beach destination: **Varadero.** In addition to Varadero, the province is home to the lovely colonial-era cities of **Matanzas** and **Cárdenas,** as well as the **Ciénaga de Zapata,** a vast wetlands area of mangrove and swamp taking up most of the southern half of the province. The southern section of Matanzas province also holds great historical and sentimental value to modern Cubans, as it was here, in the Bahía de Cochinos (Bay of Pigs), that the nascent Cuban revolutionary state defeated an invasion force trained, supplied, and abetted by the United States. Matanzas remains an important agricultural region with huge sugar plantations, as well as citrus groves and cattle ranches.

1 MATANZAS

98km (61 miles) E of Havana; 40km (25 miles) SW of Varadero

Matanzas is a city of many names: City of Bridges, City of Rivers, and the Venice of Cuba. They all refer to the fact that the city is divided by two major rivers, and connected back by a series of pedestrian, auto, and rail bridges. Due to its slow pace and laid-back nature, Matanzas is also sometimes called Cuba's Sleeping Beauty. However, the city is probably most proud of its moniker as the Athens of Cuba, a name reflecting Matanzas's important cultural tradition and history. The first *danzón,* a languid and lyrical original dance and musical form, was originally composed and played in Matanzas in 1879 by native son Miguel Faílde, and Matanzas has a rich legacy of prominent poets, writers, painters, and musicians. Still, today's reality is that aside from its beautiful old city center, Matanzas is a relatively unappealing industrial port city of only passing interest to travelers. While it is a popular destination for day trips out of Havana and Varadero, there are no notable hotels or restaurants in Mantanzas.

ESSENTIALS
Getting There
BY PLANE   The nearest airport is Varadero's **Juan Gualberto Gómez International Airport** (© **45/24-7015;** airport code VRA), located more or less midway between Varadero and Matanzas. See "Varadero," below, for more information.

BY BUS   The **bus station** is located at the corner of Calzada de Esteban and Calle Terry. **Víazul** (© **7/881-1413** in Havana, or 45/29-1473 in Matanzas; www.viazul.com) has three buses daily for Varadero, stopping in Matanzas to drop off and pick up passengers. The buses depart Havana daily at 8am, noon, and 6pm. The trip takes about 2 hours to Matanzas, and the one-way fare is CUC$7 (US$7.55/£3.80). The return bus for Havana leaves Matanzas at 9am, 12:15pm, and 7pm.

BY TRAIN The main **train station** (© 45/29-2409) is located on the southern outskirts of town on Calle 181. There are a half-dozen or so trains departing daily from Havana's Central Station to Matanzas. Matanzas is on the main train line to eastern Cuba, and most trains bound for Holguín, Santiago de Cuba, and other points east stop in Matanzas. The 90-minute ride costs CUC$3 to CUC$5 (US$3.25–US$5.40/£1.60–£2.70).

One interesting alternative means of reaching Matanzas is the **Hershey Train** ★, a legacy of the famous chocolate company's formerly vast network of sugar plantations in Cuba. This slow-moving electric train leaves from Havana's **Casablanca Station** (© 7/862-4888). The Hershey Train station in Matanzas is located at Calle 67, in Reparto Versalles, just north of the Río Yumurí (© 45/24-7254). This scenic trip takes between 3 and 4 hours, making numerous stops, and costs CUC$3 (US$3.25/£1.60). There are five departures daily in each direction, leaving more or less simultaneously from each terminal station at roughly 4:30am, 8:30am, 12:30pm, 4:10pm, and 9pm.

BY CAR Matanzas is connected to Havana by a modern coastal highway, the Vía Blanca, which begins as you exit the tunnel connecting Habana Vieja with Habana del Este. It's a straight shot and scenic drive that generally takes around 90 minutes.

Getting Around

You can easily visit all the principal sites in downtown Matanzas on foot. **Taxis** are readily available in Matanzas, and tend to gather around the Plaza de la Vigía and Plaza de la Libertad. A taxi out to the Castillo de San Severino from downtown should cost around CUC$2 (US$2.15/£1.10) each way.

Orientation

Matanzas is divided into three distinct sections by the Yumurí and San Juan rivers. All let out onto the broad bay, Bahía de Matanzas. The northern section and the first you'll reach coming in on the Vía Blanca from Havana is **Reparto Versalles.** The central section, **Reparto Matanzas,** is where you'll find the city center and most of the local attractions. Heading south and out of town toward Varadero is **Pueblo Nuevo.**

There are currently no tour agencies with offices in Matanzas, but that is expected to change soon. The main **post office** is located at the corner on Calle 85 between Calles 288 and 290. There's an **Etecsa** center at Calles 288 and 83 (© 45/24-3123). There's a **CADECA** branch on Jovellanes and Milanés (© 45/25-3558).

WHAT TO SEE & DO

Matanzas has a very compact city center, and a few hours of walking around are generally enough to get a good feel for the place. There are two small plazas that anchor the social and cultural life of Matanzas, the **Plaza de la Vigía** and the **Plaza de la Libertad.** Both are within 5 blocks of each other in Reparto Matanzas, the central section of the city.

Probably the most visited site in Matanzas is the stunning neoclassical **Teatro Sauto** ★★, on the Plaza de la Vigía (© 45/24-2721). The theater, which was finished in 1863, is the design of Italian architect and artist Daniel Dal'Aglio, who also painted the beautiful frescoes that adorn the ceiling. Dance, theater, and classical music performances are still regularly held here, and it's worth checking to see if there's anything playing while you're in town. Otherwise, you may be able to take a guided tour of the theater; a major renovation of the theater was underway in 2008, so check in advance.

The other main attraction in town is the **Museo Farmacéutico** ★, Calle 83 no. 4951, Plaza de la Libertad (© 45/24-3179). Seemingly little has changed here since its founding in 1882 by the French pharmacist Ernesto Troilet. Porcelain jars of potions and elixirs are stacked high in beautiful floor-to-ceiling wood cabinets. The museum is open daily from Monday to Saturday 10am to 5pm and on Sunday from 10am to 2pm; admission is CUC$3 (US$3.25/£1.60).

At the head of the harbor, close to the downtown center, you'll find a couple of small stretches of beach, where there will almost always be a few locals swimming, fishing, and sunbathing. However, the harbor is quite industrial and I'd highly recommend you head over to Varadero for some more inviting beaches.

Out on the northern edge of the bay is the **Castillo de San Severino,** Avenida del Muelle. Built in 1734, this small fort served as a line of defense, slave-trading post, and long-standing prison. It's been restored and is definitely worth a visit, if for nothing other than the great view of Matanzas Bay. The Castillo is open daily from 9am to 5pm; admission is CUC$2 (US$2.15/£1.10).

On the outskirts of the city, you'll find the **Cuevas de Bellamar** ★, Finca La Alcancia (© 45/25-3538), a cave complex of nearly 3km (1³/₄ miles) of galleries and passageways, with intricate stalactite and stalagmite formations, indigenous pictographs, and several underground streams and rivers. You can tour the first kilometer or so of caves for CUC$5 (US$5.40/£2.70) per person, including a guide. This section is lit, so no equipment or flashlights are needed. The caves are located 5km (3 miles) southeast of Matanzas, off a well-marked access road. They are open daily from 9:30am to 4:15pm.

WHERE TO STAY & DINE

There are currently no hotels catering to travelers in Matanzas, and no restaurants worthy of a hearty recommendation. Most folks—and I recommend this—come here on day trips from either Havana or Varadero. In a pinch, there's the rather run-down **Hotel Louvre,** right on the Parque de la Libertad (© 45/24-4074), which accepts foreigners, as well as a handful of *casas particulares* congregated around the downtown center. The most happening spot in town is the **Café Atenas,** Calle Magdalena and Calle Milanés, Plaza de la Vigía (© 45/25-3493), a simple 24-hour cafe and snack bar, with an easygoing ambience and comfortable seating both indoors and outdoors on a cool patio.

MATANZAS AFTER DARK

Matanzas is a quiet city without much nightlife, with one notable exception. The younger sister to the venerable Tropicana in Havana, **Tropicana Matanzas** ★★, Autopista del Sur Km 4.5 (© 45/26-5555), seeks to provide the classic Tropicana cabaret experience to the thousands of tourists who come to Cuba and never venture far from Varadero. I don't know why they didn't just build it in Varadero, but whatever the reason, it is located on the outskirts of Matanzas, about a 20-minute drive from Varadero. Like its famous sibling, this is a large open-air theater with extravagant nightly performances. The artistic direction is shared between the two venues, and the show here is quite up to snuff. Scores of scantily clad showgirls and dancers seamlessly weave together a series of different numbers. Costumes are tight-fitting, garish, and often feature gravity-defying headgear. The spectacle covers most of the bases of popular Cuban show and dance music, from *son* to bolero to *danzón* to salsa, with a bit of Afro-Cuban religious music thrown into the mix. The 90-minute show starts around 10:30pm each night. After the show, you can continue the celebration by dancing the night away at the adjoining dance club.

Virtually every tour agency in Varadero can book you a night at the Tropicana Matanzas; packages include a complimentary *cuba libre* (cocktail with rum and Coke). All include round-trip transportation. Tickets for the show are CUC$49 (US$53/£26). Since it's open-air, rain cancels the function. You'll get your money back on a rainout, but there are no guaranteed reservations for a makeup show.

2 VARADERO ★★

140km (87 miles) E of Havana; 40km (25 miles) NE of Matanzas

Varadero is Cuba's most renowned and popular beach destination. Varadero is the common name for the entire length of the Hicacos Peninsula. The peninsula, which takes its name from a local spiny cactus, is 21km (13 miles) long, with a nearly continuous broad band of fine white sand fronting a clear blue sea. Backed by mangroves and the calm waters of Cárdenas Bay, it is less than a mile at its widest point. Large resort hotels take up a large percentage of the entire length of this peninsula.

Home to indigenous populations and a base camp for itinerant Taíno and Carib fishermen, Varadero was largely ignored throughout the Spanish colonial period. While it was first developed as a summer retreat by some 10 families from Cárdenas in 1887, its real potential as a tourist destination was realized relatively late. The first hotel was built here in 1910, and U.S. industrial magnate Irénée Dupont built his Xanadú Mansion here in 1928. A small cadre of celebrities and gangsters followed, including Al Capone. Still, at the time of the Revolution, there were only three hotels in Varadero. Today, there are over 55, with more than 15,000 rooms . . . and construction continues.

ESSENTIALS
Getting There
BY PLANE The **Juan Gualberto Gómez International Airport** (☎ **45/24-7015; airport code VRA**) is located 18km (11 miles) west of Varadero, roughly midway between Matanzas and Varadero. Direct charter and scheduled commercial flights arrive in Varadero from Montreal, Toronto, Vancouver, Cancún, Nassau, Montego Bay, and most major European hubs. The major international carriers servicing Varadero include **Air Canada, Air Transat, British Airways, Condor, Martinair, Mexicana, KLM,** and **LTU.** A taxi between the airport and Varadero costs CUC$25 to CUC$30 (US$27–US$32/ £14–£16). If you coincide with a Víazul departure, it will cost you CUC$6 (US$6.50/ £3.25) to the bus station and an additional CUC$2 (US$2.15/£1.10) on another Víazul bus to your hotel.

BY BUS Víazul (☎ 7/881-1413 in Havana, or 45/61-4886 in Varadero; www.viazul. com) has three buses daily for Varadero, leaving Havana at 8am, noon, and 6pm. The trip takes 3 hours to Varadero. The return buses for Havana leave Varadero at 8am, 11:25am, and 6pm. The fare is CUC$10 (US$11/£5.40) each way. Víazul also has a daily bus from Varadero to Trinidad leaving at 7:30am (6 hr.; CUC$20/US$22/£11 each way). The return bus leaves Trinidad at 2:25pm. The bus to Santiago leaves at 9:25pm (15 hr.; CUC$49/US$53/£26 each way). The return bus leaves Santiago at 8:30pm. The **bus station** is located at Calle 36 and the Autopista del Sur.

In addition, most of the hotels and tour agencies in Havana can arrange transportation on periodic transfer buses to Varadero, including a pickup at your hotel. In a similar vein, all of the hotels and tour agencies in Varadero can book you on similar buses heading

ACCOMMODATIONS ■

Breezes Varadero **11**

Gran Caribe Club Kawama
   Resort **2**

Hotel Dos Mares **6**

Hotel Los Delfines **4**

Hotel Pullman **5**

Iberostar Playa Alameda **21**

Mansión Xanadú **13**

Meliá Las Americas **14**

Meliá Varadero **15**

Paradisus Princesa del Mar **22**

Paradisus Varadero **18**

Tryp Peninsula Varadero **20**

ATTRACTIONS ●

Delfinario **17**

Marina Chapelin **16**

Marina Dársena Varadero **1**

Marina Gaviota Varadero **23**

Museo Municipal Varadero **8**

Parque Ecológico Varahicacos **19**

Parque Josone **7**

Varadero Golf Club **12**

ⓢ Bank; CADECA

Ⓒ Etecsa

ⓘ Information

✚ International
   Clinic

DINING ◆

El Criollo **3**

Las Americas **14**

Las Antiguedades **9**

Mesón del Quijote **10**

back to the hotels and airport in Havana. The fare is CUC$25 to CUC$35 (US$27–US$38/£14–£19) each way.

BY CAR Varadero is connected to Havana by a modern, four-lane, coastal highway, the Vía Blanca, that begins as you exit the tunnel connecting Habana Vieja with Habana del Este. It's a straightforward, scenic drive to Matanzas. The highway then threads its way through Matanzas, generally hugging close to the coast, and continues on the final 40km (25 miles) to Varadero. About 13km (8 miles) outside of Varadero there's a tollbooth (CUC$2/US$2.15/£1.10 per vehicle each way). The trip generally takes around 2 hours. A taxi between Havana and Varadero costs around CUC$80 (US$86/£43).

Getting Around

Taxis are plentiful in Varadero. A trip from one end of the peninsula to the other costs from CUC$13 to CUC$15 (US$14–US$16/£7–£8.10), and most trips to other places in the area cost CUC$5 to CUC$10 (US$5.40–US$11/£2.70–£5.40). If by some chance you can't flag one down, or there's none hanging around your hotel, you can call **Cubataxi** (✆ 45/61-4444), **Transgaviota** (✆ 45/61-9761), or **Transtur** (✆ 45/61-4444). Víazul now offers a transfer from the station to any hotel in Varadero for CUC$2

(US$2.15/£1.10) after the long-distance buses pull in. As in Havana, open-air **Coco Taxis** are also available for CUC$25 (US$27/£14) per hour. In theory, they should charge CUC$.50 (US55¢/27p) a kilometer, but they often cost more than a metered taxi. A **horse-and-carriage ride** costs CUC$10 (US$11/£5.40) for a city tour.

Sol Melía operates a free **open-air tourist train** between various points of the peninsula. The **Varadero Beach Tour buses** (© **45/66-8992**) that ply a loop from one end of Varadero to the other operate a day pass, with unlimited use of the route; it costs CUC$5 (US$5.40/£2.70) per day.

One of the best ways to get around Varadero is on a **scooter.** Rental agencies abound. Most rent modern, easy-to-use Vespa-style scooters for CUC$12 to CUC$15 (US$13–US$16/£6.50–£8) per hour, and CUC$24 to CUC$30 (US$26–US$32/£13–£16) per day.

There are a host of **car-rental agencies** at the airport and around town. Virtually every hotel either has a car-rental desk, or can easily facilitate renting a car. The official contacts for the various agencies are **Cubacar** (© **45/66-7326**), **Havanautos** (© **45/61-4409**), **Transtur** (© **45/66-7715**), and **Vía Rent a Car** (© **45/61-9001**).

(Moments) **Take a Detour**

At 110m (361 ft.), the **Bacuanayagua Bridge** ★ is the highest in Cuba. It spans the beautiful Yumurí Valley. Most tourist buses will stop here for a quick break and photo opportunity, and if you are driving, you'll probably want to do so as well. A rugged side road leads off the highway if you want to explore this largely undeveloped valley. The bridge is located 7km (4¼ miles) west of Matanzas, right on the Vía Blanca en route from Havana to Matanzas and Varadero.

Orientation

Cubatur, Cubanacán, and **Havanatur** have offices all over Varadero and in the hotels. **CADECA** (© 45/66-7870) is at the airport and Avenida Paya between Calles 41 and 42, and **Banco Financiero Internacional** (© 45/66-7002) is at Avenida 1 and Calle 32. The **Banco de Crédito and Comercio** (© 45/61-2616), Avenida 1 (btw. Calles 35 and 36) has a Visa ATM. The **Clínica Internacional Varadero,** Avenida 1 and Calle 61 (© 45/66-8611), is open 24 hours for emergency and routine medical care. It also has a 24-hour pharmacy. **Etecsa** has an office with Internet access open daily at the corner of Avenida 1 and Calle 30. **Infotur,** a network of information offices, has its base at Calle 13 and Avenida 1 (© 45/66-5966; infovar@enet.cu).

WHAT TO SEE & DO

This is a beach destination and, aside from lying on the beach and swimming in the clear waters of the Straits of Florida, most of the attractions and activities here are either found or conducted on or under the water. The nicest spot to visit in "downtown" Varadero is the **Parque Josone,** Avenida 1 between Calles 55 and 58 (© 45/66-7228), a beautifully maintained little city park with cool, shady grounds and gardens. There are paths winding around and over little lakes with fountains, several restaurants, and food stands, and the park is dotted with gazebos and park benches. The park is open daily from 9am to 11pm.

If it's raining, or you just can't take any more sunbathing, active adventures, or shopping, you could make a quick visit to the **Museo Municipal Varadero,** Calle 57 and Avenida de la Playa (© 45/61-3189). Open daily from 10am to 7pm (CUC$1/US$1.10/55p), the exhibits inside are of less interest and appeal than the beautiful old building that houses the collection. The perfectly maintained blue-and-white, two-story wooden building, with its gingerbread trim and red-tile roof, is a tribute to colonial Caribbean architecture and design.

Near the Marina Chapelín, on the ocean side of the road, you'll find the **Delfinario,** Autopista Sur Km 12 (© 45/66-8031). Open daily from 9:30am to 5pm, this attraction offers a 40-minute show with trained dolphins at 11am and 3:30pm. Admission is CUC$15 (US$16/£8.10) per person; it's CUC$5 (US$5.40/£2.70) extra to take photos and CUC$93 (US$100/£50) for a 15-minute swimming session with the dolphins (CUC$80/US$86/£43 Sat–Sun). While this place is highly touted by agencies and hotel tour desks, I personally find this type of attraction—and this one in particular—to be depressing and on the cruel side.

If you want a bird's-eye view of things, the **Centro Internacional de Deportes Aéreos,** Vía Blanca Km 1.5, off a little side road across from the Marina Dársena (© 45/66-7256), offers parachute jumps and ultralight flights. Tandem parachuting costs

CUC$150 (US$162/£81) per person. Ultralight flights start at CUC$45 (US$49/£24) for 10 minutes. You can also usually find ultralight flights leaving from different spots up and down the beach.

The **Varadero Golf Club** ★ (© 45/66-8482; www.varaderogolfclub.com) features a lovely little resort course, with plenty of water, few trees, and almost no rough. There are beautiful views of Cárdenas Bay from most holes. Greens fees run CUC$70 (US$76/£38) for a round, plus an extra CUC$40 (US$43/£22) for a cart. Club rental will cost you CUC$50 (US$54/£27). You can play a twilight round of 9 holes for just CUC$48 (US$52/£26) after 4pm.

A large swath of the eastern end of the peninsula is protected as the **Parque Ecológico Varahicacos (Varadero Ecological Park).** There are some gentle paths through the scrub forests here, and you can visit a series of small caves, some of which contain ancient indigenous pictographs. The park is actually broken up into two sections, with a small area close to the major hotel district, and the larger section farther east. Both are open daily from 9am to 4:30pm; admission is CUC$3 (US$3.25/£1.60).

Fun on & Under the Water

If you want to take out a Hobie Cat, windsurfer, paddle boat, or sea kayak, chances are your hotel will have them, either as part of your all-inclusive package or for hire. If not, simply hit the beach and walk a bit until you find some for rent.

There are three main marinas on Varadero: **Marina Gaviota Varadero,** at the far eastern end of the Autopista del Sur (© 45/66-7755); **Marina Dársena Varadero,** at the western end of the Autopista del Sur (© 45/61-4448); and **Marina Chapelín,** Autopista del Sur Km 12.5 (© 45/66-7550). The latter two also operate under the umbrella name of **Marlin** (© 45/66-8000; www.nauticamarlin.com). At any of these, you can charter a sailboat, organize a fishing excursion, or arrange to go scuba diving. Moreover, the tour agencies and hotel activities desks can book any of these activities.

FISHING The waters off Varadero provide the opportunity to go deep-sea fishing for marlin, sailfish, tuna, snapper, dolphin, and more. Rates run between CUC$240 and CUC$290 (US$259–US$313/£129–£157) for a half-day.

Fishing trips can also be arranged to the **Ciénaga de Zapata** area in southern Matanzas province. See "The Zapata Peninsula & Playa Girón," later in this chapter, for more details.

SAILING There are many charter sailboat options available at each of the marinas mentioned above. The most popular outfit, **Seafari** ★, Marina Chapelín (© 45/66-7550), has a fleet of broad and comfortable catamarans. A range of cruise options is available, from half-day and full-day cruises to simple sunset sails. Many of the sailing adventures make stops at the small, uninhabited cays off the eastern coast of the peninsula; these trips can include lunch on one of the cays, as well as snorkeling adventures on close-in coral reefs. Rates are CUC$30 (US$32/£16) for a half-day and CUC$45 to CUC$75 (US$49–US$81/£24–£41) for a full day. Many of these boats are outfitted with a bar or two and carry either a live band or loud, recorded dance music. Some boats head out for a floating sunset party or a raging dance party under the moonlight.

The popular **Boat Adventure** ★, Marina Chapelín (© 45/66-8440), is a 2-hour tour on small, sit-on-top motorized watercraft, or Aqua-Rays, through the canals and mangroves backing the peninsula. A guide leads a caravan of the small craft, which can hold up to two adults. This tour leaves roughly every hour, with a total of eight departures daily; it's CUC$39 (US$42/£21) per person. You can book this trip at any hotel or tour agency in town.

The **Discover Tour (Jeep & Boat Safari; ©️ 45/66-8000)** involves speedboating up the Rio Canimar, swimming in the Saturno Cave, visiting Matanzas, and off-roading in jeeps for CUC$73 (US$79/£39).

SCUBA DIVING & SNORKELING   Most of the large hotels on Varadero either have their own dive operations or can arrange scuba-diving and snorkeling trips around the area. Scuba diving and snorkeling off Varadero is generally pretty good, although rarely spectacular. There's an assortment of sites, including a black coral bed, various coral reefs, and an old wreck. True aficionados prefer the diving found in southern Matanzas province off the coasts of Playa Larga and Playa Girón. It's about a 90-minute drive from Varadero, and all of the dive operations here offer trips to these dive spots, an especially good choice if a northern wind is blowing and the waters are rough off of Varadero. If your hotel can't arrange this for you, contact **Centro Internacional de Buceo Barracuda,** Calle 59 and Avenida 1 (©️ **45/61-3481;** www.nauticamarlin.com).

One popular scuba-diving and snorkeling site worth mentioning is the **Cueva de Saturno,** located outside of Matanzas, on the road to the airport. This large cave houses a large deep *cenote* (pool) that can be explored with a mask and snorkel, or with full tank gear. The cave is open daily from 9am to 6pm; admission is CUC$5 (US$5.40/£2.70). Most agencies and hotels can arrange a half-day trip for CUC$25 to CUC$30 (US$27–US$32/£14–£16) per person, or CUC$60 (US$65/£32) for a one-tank dive. There's even a 24-hour cafeteria on-site.

Organized Tours

All of the tour agencies in town offer a host of guided excursions to the principal cities and attractions within striking distance of Varadero. Options include half-day tours to Matanzas or Cárdenas, day tours to Havana or Trinidad, and overnight excursions to Cayo Largo, Cayo Coco, or Santiago de Cuba. Rates run around CUC$15 (US$16/£8.10) for half-day tours and from CUC$49 to CUC$99 (US$53–US$107/£26–£53) for full-day excursions. Overnight trips vary widely depending on the means of travel (air or bus) and the type of accommodations. Your best bet for booking any of these is to check at your hotel, or contact **Cubanacán,** Calle 24, between Avenida 1 and Avenida de la Playa (©️ **45/66-7836;** www.cubanacan.cu); **Gaviota Tours,** Calle 56 and Avenida de la Playa (©️ **45/61-1844**); or **Havanatur,** Avenida de la Playa, between Calles 33 and 34 (©️ **45/66-7589**).

Gran Car (©️ **45/61-0555**) offers various trips for CUC$166 to CUC$187 (US$179–US$202/£90–£101), including a day trip spent tooling around Havana in a classic car. The trip includes a tour of Habana Vieja, with stops at the four major plazas, as well as a visit to a cigar factory, the Plaza de la Revolución, and a stop at the Hotel Nacional. Classic car trips start at CUC$30 (US$32/£16) for 2 hours.

SHOPPING

There's no lack of souvenir stands, T-shirt outlets, and overpriced hotel gift shops here, but good shopping options are limited. There are several outdoor arts and crafts markets around Varadero; the best, **Artesanía,** is at Avenida 1 and Calle 12. The **Plaza de los Artesanos** at Avenida 1 between Calles 46 and 48 is also good. **ARTex** has stores at each of these sites, as well as at Avenida 1 and Calle 35. At each, you will find a broad (and standard) collection of trinkets, T-shirts, musical instruments, posters, and CDs.

Taller de Cerámica Artística, Avenida 1 between Calles 59 and 60 (©️ **45/66-7554**), is a working pottery studio and factory with a broad selection of finished goods for sale.

Some are quite good and quite expensive. The work ranges from abstract and artistic to purely functional. You can usually watch a potter at work while shopping.

For a dense collection and variety of shops, **Plaza las Américas,** Autopista Sur Km 11 (© **45/66-8181**) has a modern mini-mall and convention center with clothing boutiques and T-shirt shops, along with an art gallery and a music shop thrown in. There's even a small supermarket here, and several restaurants.

If you want cigars, the best-stocked shop in Varadero is **Casa de los Tabacos,** Avenida 1 and Calle 38 (© **45/61-4719**). They usually have one or two rollers making fresh stogies here, and there's a comfortable bar for enjoying their wares, while sipping a glass of rum or a strong espresso.

WHERE TO STAY
Hotels
Most of the hotels on Varadero operate as all-inclusive resorts. Still, there are a few options for those who just want a room and breakfast, and the ability to pick and choose where they eat the rest of their meals. You can also purchase a day pass at many of the local all-inclusive resorts for between CUC$30 and CUC$80 (US$32–US$86/£16–£43), which will allow you access to their facilities, including buffet meals and endless drinks.

Expensive
Mansión Xanadú ★ The former mansion of Irénée Dupont de Nemours is now a high-end boutique hotel. While this is certainly the most distinctive boutique hotel in Varadero, its 1930s grandeur feels a little dated, and almost dingy in some instances. Moreover, the fact that it is such a tourist attraction takes away any real sense of intimacy and isolation. Still, you will be staying at what was once, and in some respects still is, the most luxurious address in town. The rooms are all spacious and meticulously maintained, with sparkling marble floors, Persian rugs, and antique furnishings. Most have narrow, intricately carved wooden balconies overlooking the ocean. However, be careful, for a couple of the rooms only come with narrow full-size beds. All of the rooms are on the second floor, and on the third floor, there's a lively bar with good views all around. The hotel is right on the Varadero golf course and guests enjoy unlimited privileges at the course. The hotel sits on a rocky outcropping a hundred or so yards from the beach, and while there's no pool or beach right here, guests can use both at the neighboring Meliá Las Américas.

Carretera Las Américas Km 8.5, Varadero. © **45/66-8482.** Fax 45/66-8481. www.varaderogolfclub.com. 6 units. CUC$150–CUC$210 (US$162–US$227/£81–£113) double. Rates include full breakfast and unlimited greens fees. MC, V. **Amenities:** Restaurant; bar; 24-hr. room service; massage; laundry service; dry cleaning. *In room:* A/C, TV, minibar, safe.

Inexpensive
In 1998, the Cuban government outlawed *casas particulares* in Varadero, wanting to steer all business to the official state-owned hotels and resorts. The ban is still in effect, although there are folks who will rent out rooms in private houses. Still, since it's not legal, they don't like to advertise or call attention to themselves. If you really want to find a *casa particular,* ask a taxi driver or tour guide, or walk around the area between Calle 13 and Calle 64 in the heart of Varadero's downtown, and you should be able to find something.

Hotel Dos Mares This little hotel is housed in an old, three-story Spanish-style stucco building. The rooms here are a tad dark, but they are clean and comfortable. However, they come with big, wall-mounted air-conditioning units that can be a bit loud. The good news is that you're centrally located and the beach is less than 90m (300 ft.) away.

Calle 53, btw. Avs. 1 and Playa, Varadero. ✆/fax **45/61-2702**. www.islazul.cu. 34 units. CUC$45–CUC$60 (US$49–US$65/£24–£32) double. Rates include breakfast. No credit cards. **Amenities:** Restaurant; bar; tour desk; laundry service. *In room:* A/C, TV, safe.

Hotel Pullman (**Value**) This old hotel probably has the most personality of any budget hotel in Varadero. It's across the street from the beach, in a three-story stone building, with some pretty decorative masonry work crowning it. The compact rooms are all clean and well maintained, and the hotel is well located in the heart of Varadero's little town. There's a charming patio restaurant here, and a couple of the rooms even share a nice veranda.

Av. 1, btw. Calles 49 and 50, Varadero. ✆/fax **45/61-2702**. www.islazul.cu. 16 units. CUC$45–CUC$60 (US$49–US$65/£24–£32) double. Rates include breakfast. No credit cards. **Amenities:** Bar; laundry service. *In room:* A/C, TV, safe.

All-Inclusive Resorts

There are literally scores of large, all-inclusive resorts in Varadero. I've listed my top choices. In addition to the places listed below, good options include the **Barceló Marina Palace** (✆ 45/66-9966; www.barcelomarinapalace.com), **Brisas del Caribe** (✆ 45/66-8030; www.hotelesoasis.com), **Coralia Club Playa de Oro** (✆ 45/66-8566; www.accorhotels.com), **Iberostar Varadero** (✆ 45/66-9999; www.iberostar.com), **Sandals Royal Hicacos Resort & Spa** (✆ 800/545-8283 in the U.S. or Canada, or 45/66-8844; www.sandalshicacos.com), and **Sol Palmeras** (✆ 45/66-7009; www.solmeliacuba.com).

The rack rates listed below are actually the high end of what you might pay. In fact, you should expect to pay much less. Most of these hotels sell the bulk of their rooms to wholesalers and package tour operators, who in turn sell quite attractive all-inclusive packages. Competition is fierce, and it pays to shop around. However, as this is a segment of the industry that depends on volume, some resorts try to make up for the low prices by skimping on food and drink quality, and upkeep. So be careful: If you come across a resort not listed here at a deal that seems too good to be true . . . it just might be.

Note: Since so much of the market here is European, many of the large resort hotels operate either exclusively on 220-volt electricity or a combination of 110-volt and 220-volt electricity. Although most hotels will lend you an adapter and converter, it's best to check beforehand and come with the proper adapters, if necessary.

Very Expensive

Meliá Las Américas ★★ Located just off the clubhouse and first tee of Cuba's only 18-hole golf course, this upscale hotel should be a golfer's top choice, although guests at any hotel in town can play the course. The Meliá Las Américas is a large resort hotel, with the bulk of its rooms in the five-story main building, as well as one- and two-bedroom bungalows in a series of smaller buildings spread around some lush gardens amid a maze of swimming pools and ponds. Still, the rooms in the main building are all large, spacious, and well maintained, and I'd choose them over the bungalows, if only for their comfortable balconies with views over either the Straits of Florida or the golf course and bay. The hotel sits right on a small section of beautiful beach, smack-dab in front of the golf course and next to the Plaza las Américas mall, making it one of the more strategically located hotels in Varadero. This hotel was recently reserved for adults only, and converted to an all-inclusive. It recently inaugurated a new sushi restaurant.

com. 290 units. CUC$295–CUC$545 (US$319–US$589/£159–£294) double; CUC$435–CUC$685 (US$470–US$740/£235–£370) suite; CUC$475–CUC$725 (US$513–US$783/£257–£392) Grand or Presidential suite. Rates are all-inclusive. MC, V. Children under 18 not allowed. **Amenities:** 5 restaurants; snack bar; 4 bars; lounge; dance club; 4 outdoor pools; 18-hole golf course; small, well-equipped health club; nonmotorized watersports equipment; concierge; tour and activities desk; car-rental desk; salon; 24-hr. room service; massage; laundry service; dry cleaning; Internet access. *In room:* A/C, TV, minibar, hair dryer, safe.

Meliá Varadero ★★ This large hotel sits on a rocky outcrop with small sections of fine beach on either side. Seven pyramid-like spokes extend off a massive and lush central atrium lobby. Rooms are large, contemporary, and comfortable. All come with either a king-size bed or two twin beds and a private balcony with a couple of sitting chairs. While the bathrooms aren't exactly small, some are a bit narrow, with the toilet and bidet a bit close to the tub and shower. Almost all of the rooms have some view of the water; the farther out on each spoke you go, the better the view. The hotel is just off the Plaza las Américas complex, so between the in-house arcade and the neighboring mall, you'll have a few more shopping and dining options.

Autopista del Sur Km 7, Carretera Las Morlas, Varadero. ℂ **45/66-7013.** Fax 45/66-7012. www.melia-varadero.com. 490 units. CUC$260–CUC$510 (US$281–US$551/£140–£275) double; CUC$400–CUC$650 (US$432–US$702/£216–£351) suite. Rates are all-inclusive. Children under 2 stay free in parent's room; children 3–12 stay for halfprice in parent's room. MC, V. **Amenities:** 5 restaurants; snack bar; 3 bars; lounge; outdoor nightly show; large outdoor pool; 2 lit outdoor tennis courts; small gym; nonmotorized watersports equipment; bikes; children's center and programs; concierge; tour and activities desk; car-rental desk; shopping arcade; salon; 24-hr. room service; massage; babysitting; laundry service; dry cleaning. *In room:* A/C, TV, minibar, coffeemaker, hair dryer, iron/ironing board, safe.

Paradisus Princesa del Mar ★★ The rooms, facilities, and grounds here are all quite grand. There's a sort of modern plantation styling throughout and lovely white parasols and gazebos with wafting curtains surrounding the pool. The best rooms here are the royal and presidential suites, which almost qualify as a hotel within the hotel. All of these come with ocean or lagoon views, private Jacuzzis—some on the balcony—and a host of other perks, including full room service 24 hours a day. The rest of the rooms are extremely attractive with handsome linens, and can all be considered junior suites, at the very least. The decor is subdued and elegant. The resort has a wide range of dining options, activities, facilities, and entertainment programs.

Autopista del Sur, Carretera Las Morlas, Varadero. ℂ **45/66-7200.** Fax 45/66-7201. www.solmeliacuba. com. 434 units. CUC$395–CUC$635 (US$427–US$675/£213–£343) double; CUC$470–CUC$710 (US$508–US$767/£254–£383) royal suite; CUC$1,200–CUC$1,500 (US$1,296–US$1,620/£648–£810) presidential suite. Rates are all-inclusive. MC, V. Children under 18 not allowed. **Amenities:** 7 restaurants; snack bar; 5 bars; lounge; dance club; 2 large outdoor pools; 4 lit outdoor tennis courts; well-equipped health club and spa; watersports equipment; tour and activities desk; car-rental desk; salon; massage; laundry service; dry cleaning; Internet access. *In room:* A/C, TV, minibar, coffeemaker, hair dryer, safe.

Paradisus Varadero ★★★ Set at the eastern end of the peninsula on a gorgeous and remote section of beach, this is the Sol Meliá chain's fanciest hotel in Varadero and part of its top-end brand Paradisus. Most rooms here are large junior suites with sunken sitting rooms that let out onto either a private terrace or balcony. The walls are done in a light pastel faux-faded wash, with hand-painted murals. Only a small percentage of the rooms here have an ocean view. A few suites have separate sitting areas and extra half-bathrooms. About half the units come with king-size beds, and the rest come with two twins. The one Garden Villa, however, is almost a world unto itself, set on a point of land just above the ocean. It has separate dining and sitting rooms, a full kitchen, a private lap

Tips **Stake Your Claim**

At some resorts, finding a chaise longue under a shady *palapa* is a cutthroat endeavor. You will either have to stake out your turf early, or find a local worker who, for a small gratuity, will save you a prime spot.

pool and Jacuzzi, and a private three-story tower with a fabulous lookout. Service is attentive and friendly. The hotel has a new Japanese restaurant, a growing trend in hotel resorts in Cuba.

Autopista del Sur Km 15, Rincón Francés, Varadero. ✆ **45/66-8700.** Fax 45/66-8705. www.solmeliacuba. com. 421 units. CUC$600–CUC$773 (US$648–US$835/£324–£417) double; CUC$1,999 (US$2,159/£1,079) Garden Villa. Rates are all-inclusive. Children under 2 stay free in parent's room; children 3–12 stay for 75% of adult rate in parent's room. MC, V. **Amenities:** 7 restaurants; 3 bars; lounge; cabaret; large outdoor pools; 3 lit outdoor tennis courts; small, well-equipped health club and spa; extensive watersports equipment; children's center and programs; game room; bikes; concierge; tour and activities desk; car-rental desk; 24-hr. room service; massage; babysitting; laundry service; dry cleaning; nonsmoking rooms. *In room:* A/C, TV, fridge, coffeemaker, hair dryer, safe.

Expensive

Breezes Varadero ★ This adults-only resort is part of the SuperClubs chain, and sits on a beautiful section of beach near the western edge of the Varadero Golf Club. All rooms are either junior suites or suites; my favorites are the juniors housed in a separate three-story building on the eastern edge of the property. Some of the third-floor units here have excellent ocean views, but others are a bit too close to the popular dance club. I'd avoid the Tropical Suites, which have relatively uninviting separate sitting rooms. Overall, there's an exuberant party vibe here. The expansive grounds are filled with tropical trees and flowers, most of which are marked. All watersports are included.

Carretera Las Américas Km 3, Varadero. ✆ **45/66-7030.** Fax 45/66-7005. www.superclubscuba.com. 270 units. CUC$196–CUC$238 (US$212–US$257/£106–£129) double; CUC$206–CUC$248 (US$222–US$268/ £111–£134) suite. Rates are all-inclusive. MC, V. Children 13 and under not allowed. **Amenities:** 4 restaurants; snack bar; 8 bars; lounge; dance club; outdoor nightly show; large outdoor pool; 2 lit outdoor tennis courts; small gym; watersports equipment; bikes; tour and activities desk; massage; laundry service; dry cleaning; Internet access. *In room:* A/C, TV, coffeemaker, hair dryer, safe.

Iberostar Playa Alameda ★★★ Located on the eastern edge of the peninsula, this is one of the newer and more upscale resorts in Varadero. The rooms here are housed in a series of three-story units spread around the resort's expansive grounds. The rooms are all junior suites, with two twin beds or one king-size bed, separate sitting areas, separate tub and shower units, walk-in closets, and either a balcony or terrace. Thick iron headboards, marble-topped tables, and large Italian tiles lend the rooms a fair amount of class. A broad pedestrian-only avenue leads from the reception and restaurant area to the large complex of pools, which includes a well-designed children's pool and play area. The resort's dance club and nightly cabaret theater are well removed from the rooms, so noise isn't a problem at night. There's an inviting bar with a lookout tower down by the beach.

Las Morlas Km 15, Punta Hicacos, Varadero. ✆ **45/66-8822.** Fax 45/66-8833. www.iberostar.com. 391 units. CUC$260–CUC$440 (US$281–US$475/£140–£238) double. Rates are all-inclusive. MC, V. **Amenities:** 7 restaurants; 2 snack bars; 4 bars; lounge; dance club; 2 pools; 2 lit outdoor tennis courts; small, well-equipped health club; Jacuzzi; sauna; nonmotorized watersports equipment; bikes; children's

Tryp Península Varadero ★★★ (Kids) This is my first choice for a family resort in Varadero. The facilities are top-notch, and the children's area is a standout, with a large children's pool area that's a virtual amusement park, with several fountains, an island castle, a crocodile slide, and a spouting whale. There's a separate area for toddlers, a large game room, and a beached galleon that serves as the jungle gym playground area. The rooms, housed in a series of attractive three-story Key West–style buildings, are all junior suites, with rattan furniture and a host of amenities. Most have two twin beds, although a small percentage have king-size beds, and there are five suites. The whole complex is tied together by a series of wooden decks and bridges and concrete walkways passing over ponds and skirting a large lagoon. Located toward the far eastern end of the peninsula, the hotel is on a beautiful stretch of beach.

Autopista del Sur Km 17.5, Punta Hicacos, Varadero. ☎ **45/66-8800.** Fax 45/66-8805. www.solmeliacuba. com. 591 units. CUC$269–CUC$420 (US$291–US$454/£145–£227) double; CUC$600 (US$648/£324) suite. Rates are all-inclusive. Children 2 and under stay free in parent's room; children 3–12 stay for half price in parent's room. MC, V. **Amenities:** 4 restaurants; snack bar; 4 bars; lounge; cabaret; 2 outdoor pools; 2 lit outdoor tennis courts; small, well-equipped health club and spa; extensive watersports equipment; bikes; children's center and programs; game room; concierge; tour and activities desk; car-rental desk; small business center; salon; massage; babysitting; laundry service; dry cleaning. *In room:* A/C, TV, fridge, coffeemaker, hair dryer, safe.

Moderate

Gran Caribe Club Kawama Resort (Value) One of the oldest resort hotels in Varadero, the Gran Caribe has, over time, become one of the best midrange all-inclusive options in the area. Built between 1930 and 1947, the original resort still stands as a series of two-story stone buildings built around a central courtyard. Inside, the rooms are totally modern, with attractive furnishings and good-size balconies, but no ocean views. The massive limestone blocks used to construct the buildings are polished and buffed on the inside, giving the interiors a cool and comforting feel. A host of newer units have less character, but are equally comfortable, and most are either right on or just off the beach; some of these do have ocean views. Part of the price savings here is reflected in the tiny 13-inch television sets and the rather insipid buffet meals. The resort is set on a nice stretch of beach toward the western end of the peninsula.

Av. 1 and Calle 1, Reparto Kawama, Varadero. ☎ **45/61-4416.** Fax 45/66-7334. www.gran-caribe.com. 488 units. CUC$97–CUC$226 (US$105–US$244/£524–£122) double. Rates are all-inclusive. MC, V. **Amenities:** 7 restaurants; 2 snack bars; 10 bars; lounge; 2 dance clubs; nightly show; 6 pools; small exercise room; sauna; nonmotorized watersports equipment; tour and activities desk; car-rental desk; massage; laundry service. *In room:* A/C, TV, fridge, safe.

Hotel Los Delfines (Value) This is a pretty little hotel complex and a pretty decent value. The beachfront resort was built in several stages, with a midsize swimming pool at its center. Rooms are standard issue, but they're clean, spacious, and comfortable, and everything is well maintained. For some reason, this 100-plus-room resort almost feels intimate, especially when compared to all the monster all-inclusives that are the rule of the roost here. The restaurant and buffet meals are unspectacular, but the hotel is in the heart of Varadero's downtown, close to plenty of dining and entertainment options. Since the rates are so low, you might not mind splurging on a meal out.

Av. 1 btw. Calle 38 and Calle 39, Varadero. ☎ **45/66-7720.** Fax 45/66-7729. www.islazul.cu. 103 units. CUC$100–CUC$120(US$108–US$130/£54–£65)double,all-inclusive;CUC$48–CUC$60(US$52–US$65/£26–£32) double only. MC, V. **Amenities:** 2 restaurants; 2 bars; outdoor pool; children's pool; tour and activities desk; laundry service. *In room:* A/C, TV, safe.

WHERE TO DINE

Since most hotels in Varadero are all-inclusive, most folks take the majority of their meals at their hotels. However, it's natural to want some variety when faced with a week or more at one resort, even if it has several dining options.

I recommend **Mi Casita** (© **45/61-3787**) at Avenida Camino del Mar, between Calles 10 and 11. The restaurants inside **Parque Josone** are also dependable, if unspectacular options; of these, the little lakeside Italian restaurant **Dante** (© **45/66-7738**) is my top choice.

Expensive

Las Americas ★ INTERNATIONAL   Arguably the most elegant restaurant in town is found at the most exclusive address in town, occupying a couple of ground-floor rooms and the oceanfront veranda of the Mansión Xanadú. The best seats are those on this veranda, at heavy wooden tables set with heavy china. The food is old-school French and Continental fare, adequately done, but no more. Service is semiformal and surprisingly inattentive at times. There's a good, fairly priced wine list. Several hotels offer discount coupons here, so be sure to ask your concierge.

At the Mansión Xanadú, Carretera Las Américas Km 8.5. © **45/66-7388.** Reservations required. Main courses CUC$12–CUC$45 (US$13–US$49/£6.50–£24). MC, V. Daily noon–4pm and 7–10:30pm.

Moderate

Las Antiguedades ★ CRIOLLA   The heads of mythical beasts, religious statues, enormous vases, and glass chandeliers crowd out this popular restaurant. Sit on French chairs at tables laid with Italian cutlery and dine on grilled lobster or *criolla* cuisine. A consommé is served to all guests. If you don't opt for the seafood, I recommend the *mixto de lonjas de cerdo y ropa vieja* (a mix of pork and sautéed, shredded beef, onions, and peppers), accompanied by rice, beans, plantain, and salad. The *ropa vieja* (shredded beef) is particularly tasty. Along with Las Americas, this is by far the most atmospheric place to eat in Varadero.

Av. 1 and Calle 59. © **45/66-7329.** Main courses CUC$11–CUC$25 (US$12–US$27/£5.95–£14). MC, V. Daily noon–10:45pm.

Mesón del Quijote ⓥalue SPANISH/SEAFOOD   Located on a small hillside between the Autopista and the beach resorts, the dining room of this popular restaurant is in a small building set beside the turret of a three-story imitation medieval castle. There are plenty of windows to enjoy the limited views afforded from its modest perch. I found the paella a bit of a disappointment, but the seafood and lobster are fresh and well prepared. If you don't order one of the many lobster entrees, try the fresh fish filet with olive oil. There's pork in brandy sauce and chicken breast in pepper sauce for those not inclined toward fish dishes.

Carretera Las Américas, Reparto La Torre. © **45/66-7796.** Reservations recommended. Main courses CUC$6.75–CUC$25 (US$7.30–US$27/£3.65–£14). MC, V. Daily noon–11pm.

Inexpensive

In addition to the place listed below, **La Vicaria,** Avenida 1 and Calle 37 (© **45/61-4721**), is a good and very popular spot for light, inexpensive bites, in a pleasant open-air setting.

El Criollo ★ CRIOLLA This popular place is probably your best bet for straight-ahead Cuban cuisine in Varadero. The restaurant is housed in an atmospheric old building that re-creates the vibe of a typical Cuban country home. You'll definitely want a table on the large, open-air veranda under a gently sloping red-tile roof. Simple roast chicken and pork dishes are reasonably priced and well prepared. Even the lobster dishes are a good value here. This restaurant is not to be confused with El Bodegon Criolla, a weak imitation of Havana's signature La Bodeguita del Medio.

Av. 1 and Calle 18. (✆ **45/61-4794.** Reservations recommended. Main courses CUC$5–CUC$18 (US$5–US$19/£2.70–£9.70). No credit cards. Daily noon–midnight.

VARADERO AFTER DARK

Almost every hotel here has some form of nightly entertainment, usually a Broadway theater review or local cabaret-style show. These can vary from sadly comic to totally professional. Most give way to a dance party. By far, the biggest and best cabaret show, the **Tropicana Matanzas** ★★, is located about 20 minutes away on the outskirts of Matanzas; see "Matanzas After Dark," earlier in this chapter for details. Other cabaret options include the **Cabaret Continental** at Varadero Internacional (✆ **45/66-7038;** cover CUC$10/US$11/£5.40); the **Mambo Club** at Gran Hotel, Carretera Las Morlas Km 14 (✆ **45/66-8565;** cover CUC$15/US$16/£8.10); and the **Palacio de La Rumba** at the Hotel Bella Costa, Avenida Las Américas (✆ **45/66-8210;** cover CUC$15/US$16/£8.10).

The new Egrem-run **Casa de la Música,** Avenida Playa (✆ **45/66-7568**), kicks off at 10:30pm with different shows and turns into a disco afterward. Admission is CUC$10 (US$11/£5.40). It's open Tuesday to Sunday.

Perhaps my favorite place for a show is the new **La Comparsita** ★★, Calle 60 and Avenida 3 (✆ **45/66-7415**), which is a lovely open-air space built to re-create the feel of a colonial-era courtyard. There are good sightlines from all the tables here and an excellent nightly show with wide-ranging Cuban music and dance styles. Admission is CUC$3 (US$3.25/£1.60). The place also has a happening bar upstairs.

Cueva del Pirata, Autopista Sur Km 11 (✆ **45/66-7751**), is a midsize cave that has been converted into a popular cabaret and dance club. Lights create eerie shadows among the stalactites. The cabaret show begins around 10:30pm from Tuesday to Sunday and has a pronounced Afro-Cuban emphasis. It's followed by dancing to either a live band or a DJ. Admission is CUC$15 (US$16/£8.10).

The **Mirador,** atop the Mansión Xanadú (✆ **45/66-8482**), is a good spot for a quiet drink with a nice view.

A SIDE TRIP TO CARDENAS

Located 18km (11 miles) southeast of Varadero, Cárdenas is a small, quiet city with beautiful colonial-era architecture and a timeless quality. Horse-drawn carriages and bicycles far outnumber cars on the streets here. Cárdenas is known as Cuba's "Ciudad Bandera" (Flag City), as it was here, in 1850, that the national flag was first flown. Because it's so close to Varadero, Cárdenas is popular—we'd say almost overrun—with day tours.

The city center is quite compact, and you can easily see most of the sights in a couple of hours while strolling around. There are several small squares and parks in Cárdenas. The diminutive **Parque Colón,** Avenida Céspedes, between Calles 8 and 9, has an important statue of Christopher Columbus dating from 1862. Fronting it is the beautiful **Catedral de la Concepción Inmaculada** ★, which is famous for its stained glass. In another main park, **Parque Echeverría,** sits the **Museo Casa Natal José Antonio Echeverría,** Calle Jenes 560, between Calzada and Coronel Verdugo (℡ **45/52-4145;** Mon–Sat 9am–6pm, Sun 9am–1pm; admission CUC$1/US$1.10/55p). This beautiful old home features tributes to various independence fighters and revolutionary heroes, including the museum's namesake, a murdered revolutionary student hero who was born here in 1932. The town's main market, **Plaza Molokoff,** Calle 12 and Avenida 3, is housed in an interesting two-story, L-shaped iron building, topped with a large and high ornate dome. Out by the water's edge is the **Arrechabala Rum Factory,** where the brand Havana Club was born and where present-day Varadero and Buccanero rums are made. Tours of the factory are given daily between 9am and 4pm; admission is CUC$2 (US$2.15/£1.10).

Cárdenas is the birthplace and home of Elián Gonzalez, the little boy who became the center of an international custody dispute in late 1999 when he washed up on the shores of Miami after his mother died at sea. While you're unlikely to see Elián, almost anyone in town will gladly point out his humble home on one of the main avenues. There's always at least one guard out front. The **Museo Batalla de Ideas (Museum of the Ideological Battle),** Calle Vives 523 at the corner of Coronel Verdugo (℡ **45/52-3990),** is housed in a beautifully restored old building, and features exhibits honoring the child celebrity, alongside numerous other displays documenting Cuba's revolutionary battles. The centerpiece here is a statue of a young Cuban boy, dressed in the uniform of the Young Pioneers, tossing away a Superman doll. The museum is housed in a beautifully restored old firehouse. Admission is CUC$1 (US$1.10/55p), and a guided tour is CUC$2 (US$2.15/£1.10). It will cost you an additional CUC$5 (US$5.40/£2.70) to take photos and CUC$15 (US$16/£8.10) to take videos. Open Monday to Saturday, from 9am to 6pm and Sunday 9am to 1pm.

Very few travelers stay in Cárdenas, and there are currently no hotels or official *casas particulares* accepting foreign tourists in the city, although that may change. There's regular public bus service between Varadero and Cárdenas, but it's geared primarily to commuting Cuban workers. A taxi from Varadero to Cárdenas costs around CUC$15 (US$16/£8.10).

3 THE ZAPATA PENINSULA & PLAYA GIRON ★

202km (126 miles) SE of Havana; 194km (121 miles) S of Varadero

The Zapata Peninsula juts off the southern coast of Matanzas province. The peninsula itself is almost entirely uninhabited; most of it is protected as part of the **Parque Nacional Ciénaga de Zapata (Zapata Swamp National Park)** ★, a haven for bird-watchers and naturalists. The eastern edge of the peninsula is defined by the Bahía de Cochinos (Bay of Pigs), the site of the failed 1961 U.S.-backed invasion of Cuba. The Bay of Pigs, and Playa Girón in particular, is a sort of national shrine to this stunning David-over-Goliath victory. Just off the shore, all along the Bay of Pigs and toward the east, the coast drops off steeply for 305km (1,000 ft.) or more, making this a true haven for scuba divers.

Note: Bring plenty of mosquito repellent. Since this is an area of vast swampland, mosquitoes can be fierce, particularly if there's no wind. I personally also pack lightweight, long-sleeved shirts and pants.

(Moments) **Battle Marks**

As you walk along the beaches of Playa Girón and Playa Larga, and drive the coastal road connecting them, you will notice tall concrete monuments marking the spots where a Cuban soldier died in the fighting. You will also notice many low-lying concrete machine gun nests, with their open rears for easy entry and thin front slits for wide-angle aiming. Feel free to try one on for size and a unique photo opportunity.

ESSENTIALS

GETTING THERE The nearest **airport** is in Varadero; see "Varadero," earlier in this chapter, for complete details. There is no dependable **public transportation** to this area, although most tour agencies in Havana and Varadero offer trips here.

The Zapata Peninsula and the beaches of Playa Larga and Playa Girón are connected to the Autopista Nacional—and each other—by a well-maintained two-lane highway. If you're coming **by car**, get off the highway at the exit for Australia and Jagüey Grande, and head south for 17km (11 miles) to Boca de Guamá. From there, it's another 13km (8 miles) to Playa Larga, and 34km (21 miles) to Playa Girón.

GETTING AROUND Public transportation is very sporadic and unreliable in this area. Most visitors either have their own rental car or come on a guided tour. Both of the hotels listed below have car- and scooter-rental desks, so if you somehow end up here without wheels, you can easily rent some to get around. Local taxis also can be hired at either of the hotels listed below.

ORIENTATION Heading south from the highway, you come first to Boca de Guamá. Continuing on, the road hits the head of the bay at Playa Larga and then follows the coast, in a southeasterly direction to Playa Girón. There are small communities in both Playa Larga and Playa Girón, but aside from the resorts, restaurants, and few attractions, there's little of interest to travelers.

WHAT TO SEE & DO

Most organized tours and independent travelers make a stop at **Boca de Guamá** (© 45/91-3224), a contrived tourist attraction, built as a re-creation of a Native American village on a series of small islands at the center of the large **Laguna del Tesoro (Treasure Lake)**. Boat tours of the lake and canals (CUC$10/US$11/£5.40) are available. On one small island in the middle of the lake, you'll be able to walk among 32 life-size figures of Taíno Indians sculpted by the late Cuban artist Rita Longa. You can also lunch or dine on crocodile meat at **La Boca,** a decent little tourist restaurant here. You can even stay at the **Guamá Hotel** (© 45/91-5515; www.hotelescubanacan.com; CUC$49/US$53/£26 double) here. The hotel features a series of individual circular bungalows built on stilts over the lagoons. The rooms themselves are decidedly spartan, but the setting is pleasant and there's a pool.

At the entrance to Boca de Guamá, you'll find a roadside mini-mall of shops and restaurants (which also serve crocodile steaks), and the **Criadero de Cocodrilos (Crocodile Farm;** © 45/91-5562). If you've never seen a crocodile up close, you will be awed by the size, power, and prehistoric aspect of these impressive reptiles. Admission is CUC$5 (US$5.40/£2.70) and includes a brief guided tour, with explanations of the

The Bay of Pigs

On April 16, 1961, an invasion force of 1,400 Cuban exiles, trained and backed by the United States, landed at several beach points along the Bay of Pigs in an ill-fated attempt to overthrow the Castro regime. They were quickly met by Cuban forces, led by Fidel Castro himself, and soon defeated. Fighting lasted less than 72 hours. Though they were entirely trained and supported—and even escorted—by the U.S. military and CIA, the invaders were left to fight on their own. President Kennedy was reluctant to commit any direct U.S. forces to the fight. The lack of air support and several serious tactical blunders contributed to the rout. The battle took the lives of some 160 Cubans and around 120 mercenary fighters. Some 1,195 of the invading troops were captured, and most of them were released 20 months later in a bartered exchange with the U.S. government for food, medical supplies, and hospital equipment. Today, the Bay of Pigs continues to be a source of great pride to Cuba's communist government and supporters, and an equally bitter pill for anti-Castro exiles and opponents.

crocodile's natural history and habits. A series of walkways and wooden bridges will carry you past numerous pens and cages of crocs of all ages and sizes. You can't exactly pick out your dinner, but it doesn't take much imagination to figure out where all the crocodile meat is coming from—at least you know it's fresh.

If you go to Playa Girón, it's worth taking a quick tour of the little **Museo Playa Girón** (© **45/98-4122**). Two rooms inside this simple building contain a series of photos, relics, and a written history detailing the Bay of Pigs invasion and battles, as well as some local history. A 15-minute documentary video (in Spanish) is shown throughout the day, and outside you can see the wreckage of tanks, heavy artillery, and a downed U.S. plane. The museum is open daily from 8am to 5pm; admission is CUC$2 (US$2.15/£1.10) for adults. It is an additional CUC$3 (US$3.25/£1.60) for a guide, CUC$1 (US$1.10/55p) to see the documentary, and CUC$1 (US$1.10/55p) to take photos. Unfortunately, the written explanations are in Spanish only.

See also **Caleta Buena,** p. 175.

Outdoor Activities

You'll need a permit to enter Zapata Swamp National Park. The park station and entrance (© **45/98-7249**) is located 2km (1¼ miles) west of Playa Larga. The permit costs CUC$10 (US$11/£5.40) per person, and includes a local guide. The state-run tour center located near the entrance has naturalist and fishing guides familiar with this area. In addition, all of the hotels and tour agencies in the area can arrange bird-watching excursions and fishing trips with local guides.

BIRD-WATCHING ★★★ The Zapata Peninsula is probably Cuba's richest bird-watching destination. Some 18 of Cuba's 24 endemic bird species can be spotted here, as well as large flocks of resident waterfowl and seasonal migrants. The Zapata wren, Zapata sparrow, and Zapata rail are just some of the endemic species. Hurricane Michelle flattened much of the forest here, and it's currently much harder to spot some species, including the bee hummingbird, which in the past were quite common. Several trails through and around the national park are available to birders.

FISHING ★★★ Fishing for bass, trout, tilapia, tarpon, permit, bonefish, and the bizarre looking *manjauri* (alligator gar, a type of fish) is excellent in this area. Prime fishing sites include the saltwater flats and mangroves of **Las Salinas de Brito** on the eastern edge of the peninsula, the **Hatiguanico River** deep within the national park, and the lagoons of **Boca de Guamá**. Rates range from CUC$25 to CUC$50 (US$27–US$54/£14–£27) per person for a simple outing, and from CUC$200 to CUC$500 (US$216–US$540/£108–£270) per day for a boat, guide, tackle, and lunch for up to three people. Ask at your hotel or any tour agency for details.

SCUBA DIVING ★★ The waters off the coast between Playa Larga and Playa Girón offer some of Cuba's best scuba diving. A steep wall, rich in coral and sponges, plunges to depths of over 300m (984 ft.). There are numerous caves to explore and visibility is typically excellent. In many cases, the drop-off is within 90 to 180m (295–591 ft.) of shore. The dive shops at both of the hotels here typically load people and gear into small buses or trucks and drive to one of numerous put-in points all along the shoreline. Both of the resorts listed below have full-service dive facilities on-site and offer a full menu of multiday dive packages. If you just want to try a dive or two, it will cost you around CUC$30 to CUC$40 (US$32–US$43/£16–£22) for a one-tank dive, and around CUC$45 to CUC$60 (US$49–US$65/£24–£32) for a two-tank dive, including equipment.

WHERE TO STAY & DINE

Most visitors to this area take all their meals at their hotels. The few available alternatives include the restaurants at Boca de Guamá, and a couple of simple state-run roadside restaurants geared to tourists between Playa Larga and Playa Girón. The best of these is the **Cueva de los Peces,** Carretera Playa Larga a Girón Km 18 (© **45/98-4183**), with good seafood and *criolla* cuisine. There is a handful of *casas particulares* in both Playa Larga and Playa Girón.

Hotel Playa Girón Originally designed and built as a residential community, this place is now a midsize all-inclusive resort. The rooms are housed in a series of one-, two-, and three-bedroom ranch bungalows and duplexes. Most have a separate sitting area, although sometimes the unit's only television is in the sitting room. Most have a fridge and sink in a sort of kitchenette area. Recent remodeling has greatly improved the furnishings and decor here. Still, this place is really only for hard-core divers or bird-watchers, because if you're looking for a week of sun and fun at an all-inclusive, Cuba has many more appealing options.

The best feature is the resort's **Caleta Buena** ★, a recreation area based around a series of natural pools in the coral and rock, located about 8km (5 miles) from the hotel. There's a grill restaurant, some sailboats, paddleboats, and windsurfers.

Playa Girón, Montemar Natural Park, Matanzas province. © **45/98-7206.** Fax 45/98-7241. 282 units. www.hotelescubanacan.com. CUC$76–CUC$84 (US$82–US$91/£41–£45) double. Rates are all-inclusive. MC, V. **Amenities:** 2 restaurants; snack bar; 2 bars; dance club; 2 outdoor pools; nonmotorized watersports equipment; bikes; moped rental; game room; tour desk; car-rental desk; laundry service. *In room:* A/C, TV, safe.

Hotel Playa Larga The entire complex here feels rather depressing, despite ongoing efforts to spruce things up. The problem, as far as I'm concerned, is the inherently desultory

Soviet-era architecture. Some of the rooms are quite cramped, with worn, soft beds and noisy air-conditioning units. Other rooms are more spacious, although precious few have queen-size beds (most just have two full beds). The small patch of beach here is acceptable, but it doesn't compare to other premier beaches. This place is best for serious divers and bird-watchers, and even they would probably do better at the Hotel Playa Girón.

Playa Larga, Montemar Natural Park, Matanzas province. Ⓒ/fax **45/98-7294.** www.hotelescubanacan. com. 68 units. CUC$46–CUC$53 (US$50–US$57/£25–£29) double. Rates include breakfast. MC, V. **Amenities:** Restaurant; snack bar; 3 bars; outdoor pool; 2 outdoor tennis courts; limited watersports equipment rental; moped rental; game room; tour desk; car-rental desk; laundry service. *In room:* A/C, TV, safe.

Trinidad & Central Cuba

Central Cuba is an area rich in both historical and natural attractions. It is home to several wonderful colonial-era cities, as well as isolated and pristine beaches. Heading east from Matanzas into Cuba's central heartland, you first hit Villa Clara province, which is devoted largely to sugar cane, citrus, tobacco farming, and cattle ranching. The provincial capital, **Santa Clara,** a lively university town, is often called Che Guevara's City and features an impressive monument and plaza dedicated to the fallen revolutionary. To the north of Santa Clara lie the tiny and well-preserved colonial-era city of **Remedios** and the stunningly beautiful beach resort destination of **la Cayería del Norte.**

Abutting Villa Clara to the south is Cienfuegos province. The city of **Cienfuegos** is affectionately known as *La Perla del Sur* (The Southern Pearl). Cienfuegos is a busy port city with a pretty, colonial-era center and the country's second-longest seaside promenade, or Malecón. Cienfuegos is connected to Trinidad by a pretty coastal highway, and is definitely worth a visit on a loop trip around the region.

The province of Sancti Spíritus is the only one in Cuba to count two of the original seven *villas* (towns) in Cuba among its offerings. The preserved colonial city **Trinidad,** tucked in the southwest corner of the province, is the highlight of a visit to the central section of the country, or all of Cuba for that matter. The provincial capital, **Sancti Spíritus,** isn't a great deal larger than Trinidad, and though it is more ramshackle and rough around the edges, lacking Trinidad's remarkable collection of perfectly preserved architecture, it is still worth a visit to see a couple of its colonial highlights.

1 SANTA CLARA ★

270km (168 miles) E of Havana

Santa Clara was founded in 1689 by settlers from Remedios looking for a site inland that would be less vulnerable to pirate attack. Heading east from Havana, Santa Clara marks the start of Cuba's central region. The city is strategically located on the island's spine, right on the main highway and train lines, and is the capital of Villa Clara province. Santa Clara is home to one of Cuba's principal colleges, la Universidad Central de las Villas (Las Villas Central University), and it played an important role in both the independence and revolutionary wars. Thanks to the latter, Santa Clara is known as Che Guevara's City. Today, it is also home to several industrial factories, the legacy of Guevara's tenure as Minister of Industry and his special relationship with this city. In addition to being an interesting destination in its own right, Santa Clara serves as the gateway to the colonial treasure of **Remedios ★★★** and the up-and-coming beaches of **la Cayería del Norte (the Northern Cays) ★★★.**

Getting There

BY PLANE Santa Clara's **Abel Santamaría Airport** (© 42/20-9138; airport code SNU) accepts both national and international flights. The latter are predominantly international charter flights bringing tourists on package tours to la Cayería del Norte.

BY BUS **Víazul** (© 7/881-1413 in Havana, or 42/22-2523 in Santa Clara; www.viazul.com) travels daily to Santa Clara on the Havana–Santiago de Cuba and Varadero-Trinidad lines. From Havana, the bus departs at 9:30am and 3pm, arriving at 1:55pm and 7:30pm, respectively; the fare is CUC$18 (US$19/£9.70). From Santiago, departure times are 9am, 3:15pm, and 10pm, arriving at 10pm, 3:40am, and 9:35am; the fare is CUC$36 (US$39/£19). From Varadero, the bus leaves at 8:15am and 9:25pm and arrives at 11:30am and 12:40am; the fare is CUC$11 (US$12/£5.95). The main **bus station** is on the western edge of town, on the Carretera Central, between Independencia and Oquindo.

BY CAR Santa Clara sits right on the Carretera Central, and just off the Autopista Nacional, 270km (168 miles) east of Havana. It's a straight shot on the highway and generally takes about 3 hours.

BY TRAIN Santa Clara is on Cuba's main train line. It is serviced several times a day on commuter lines connecting Havana with Holguín and Santiago de Cuba. Schedules change, so your best bet is to check at the station (© 7/861-8540 in Havana). Rates run up to CUC$15 (US$16/£8.10), depending on the train and class you choose. The Santa Clara **train station** (© 42/28-1543) is located at the northern end of town, at the end of Calle Luis Estévez.

Getting Around

Taxis are plentiful and inexpensive in Santa Clara. If you can't find one on the street or if your hotel can't hook you up, call **Cubataxi** (© 42/22-2555) or hop on a horse and carriage or *tuk-tuk* (bicycle or motorbike with a carriage).

Car-rental agencies in Santa Clara include **Havanautos** (© 42/20-5895), **Cubacar** (© 42/20-2040), and **Micar** (© 42/20-4570).

Orientation

Parque Vidal, also called Plaza Mayor, is Santa Clara's center. In addition to having the greatest concentration of colonial-era buildings, most of the city's banks, businesses, and tourism operators are based within a 2-block radius of the park. The city is ringed by a beltway, or *Circunvalación.*

Cubanacán, Colón 101 corner of Maestra Nicolasa (© 42/20-5189), **Cubatur,** Marta Abreu 10, between Máximo Gómez y Villuendas (© 42/20-8980), and **Havantur,** Máximo Gómez, between Independencia and Alfredo Barreras (© 42/20-4001), can supply you with information and arrange a wide range of tour and onward-travel options (to Remedios, CUC$29/US$31/£16; to the cayes with a stop in Remedios, CUC$40/US$43/£22). There are a couple of banks and a **CADECA** branch near the Parque Vidal.

For medical emergencies, head to the **Policlínico Nazareno** (© 42/28-399-1) on Serafín García Oeste, between Alemán and the Carretera Central.

ACCOMMODATIONS ■
Casa Héctor Martînez **16**
Casa Olga Riviera Gómez **9**
Hostal Casa Mercy **18**
Hostal Florida Center **19**
Hotel Santa Clara Libre **17**
Villa La Granjita **12**
Villa Los Caneyes **1**

DINING ◆
Colonial 1878 **7**
La Concha **3**
La Casa del Gobernador **5**
Park View **6**
Pizzeria Toscana **6**
Sabor Latino **4**

ATTRACTIONS ●
Fábrica de Tabacos **10**
La Casa del Tabaco, Ron y
  Café La Veguita **11**
Monumento a la Toma del
  Tren Blindado **13**
Monumento Ernesto
  Che Guevara **2**
Museo de Artes Decorativas **14**
Parque Vidal **15**
Teatro La Caridad **8**

$ Bank; CADECA
Ⓒ Etecsa
✉ Post office

Havana
★
Santa Clara
•
C U B A

WHAT TO SEE & DO

Santa Clara is a great town to walk around. Thanks to the university here, the city has a bit of a typical college-town vibe. The heart of the city is the central **Parque Vidal.** The double-wide streets ringing the park are pedestrian-only and often crowded with locals and lovers strolling in leisurely circles. There's a separate 5-block-long pedestrian-only mall (the Boulevard), a block behind the **Teatro La Caridad** (ⓒ **42/20-5548**), where you'll find a series of shops and restaurants aimed at travelers and dollar-spending Cubans. The active and ornate 19th-century theater, modeled after the Paris Opera, often features concerts and shows, and is worth a quick tour (CUC$1/US$1.10/55p) during the day; at presstime, it was closed and undergoing restoration.

The biggest attraction in town is the **Monumento Ernesto Che Guevara** ★, Plaza de la Revolución Che Guevara (ⓒ **42/20-5878**), which features a huge sculpture of the revolutionary hero, overlooking a vast plaza where massive demonstrations and music concerts are often held. Underneath the statue is a museum with exhibits detailing the life and exploits of "El Che" and a separate mausoleum holding Guevara's remains, as well as tombstones (and some of the remains) of 37 other revolutionary fighters killed

Che Guevara

Perhaps no one person, not even Fidel Castro, is so clearly representative of the Latin American revolutionary movement in both image and deed as Ernesto "Che" Guevara. In broad terms, Cubans respect and fear Castro, but they love Che Guevara. Fidel gave the Revolution its brains and brawn, but Che gave it sex appeal.

Born June 14, 1928, in Rosario, Argentina, to a middle-class family, he set off on a motorcycle trip through the Americas in 1953, having just graduated with a medical degree. (For a good glimpse into this period of his life, see the 2004 film *The Motorcycle Diaries*.) In 1954, he got caught in the crossfire of the CIA-supported overthrow of Guatemala's democratically elected leftist president Jacobo Arbénz. Exiled to Mexico in the aftermath of the coup, he met fellow exile Fidel Alejandro Castro Ruz. The two hit it off immediately, and soon, Guevara was a principal figure in the Cuban revolutionary struggle.

Despite chronic asthma and an overall weak constitution, Guevara was famous for his gritty work ethic and dogged determination. Guevara led the decisive December 1958 battles to seize Santa Clara, and was later rewarded with several high posts in the new revolutionary government, including Minister of Industry and president of the National Bank. As the story goes, Fidel Castro, in need of someone to head up the National Bank said, "We need a good economist." Hearing him incorrectly, Guevara said, "I'm a good communist." Despite the misunderstanding, he was given the post. However, Guevara soon tired of the bureaucratic life of politics and government, and embarked on a crusade to spread the Revolution and liberate the rest of the world. A falling-out with Castro, never fully clarified, may have also been behind his renewed revolutionary wanderings.

In 1966, after a brief foray in the Congo, Guevara went to Bolivia—namesake of Simón Bolívar, an early Latin American freedom fighter and Pan-American nationalist—and began organizing a guerilla army. However, the United States military and CIA were already on his trail, and on October 8, 1967, Guevara was caught by a unit of the Bolivian army, aided by U.S. "advisors." After consultations with Washington, the injured Guevara was summarily executed in the remote highlands of Bolivia.

alongside Guevara in Bolivia. This place is deeply revered by most Cubans, so don't joke or take it lightly. The monument is located on the western outskirts of the city and is open Tuesday through Sunday from 9am to 5:30pm; no cameras or video cameras are allowed.

Another popular revolutionary landmark is the **Monumento a la Toma del Tren Blindado (Armored Train Monument)** at Carretera Camajuani and the train line. It's a small park built around the spot where Che Guevara and his soldiers derailed an armored train during the critical battles for control of Santa Clara in 1958. In addition to the five cars and some sculptures, there's a tiny museum in this pleasant open-air park. The museum is open Monday to Saturday from 9am to 5:30pm; admission is CUC$1(US$1.10/55p).

Santa Clara has an excellent **Fábrica de Tabacos** ★ at Calle Maceo 181 (© **42/20-2211**). The factory occupies a full city block and produces high-quality Montecristo, Partagas, Romeo y Julieta, Punch, and Robaina cigars. It's open Monday through Friday from 9 to 11am and 1 to 3pm. A 20-minute guided tour costs CUC$3 (US$3.25/£1.60) per person, but the ticket can only be bought at one of the three tour agencies in town (see "Orientation," above). Across the street, there's a well-stocked shop, **La Casa del Tabaco, Ron y Café La Veguita** ★, Maceo 176-A (© **42/20-8952**). The cigar sommelier here, Marilín Morales Bauta, is quite charming and one of the premier experts in the field.

The **Museo de Artes Decorativas,** Parque Vidal (© **42/20-5368**), is in an 18th-century house whose last owner was named Clara Cartas. The house is stuffed full of Baccarat crystal and chandeliers, including a "spaghetti" chandelier. Its other unusual items include a rocking chair with a carved protruding face at its tip to stop the nanny from falling asleep and a wall plate imprinted with the image of the Crystal Palace in London. It is open Monday to Thursday 9am to noon, Friday 1 to 6pm, Saturday 1 to 6pm and 7 to 10pm, and Sunday 6 to 10pm. Admission is CUC$2 (US$2.15/£1.10).

WHERE TO STAY

There are scores of *casas particulares* (private rooms for rent) in Santa Clara. Most are within a block or two of either the Parque Vidal or the Plaza del Carmen. Recommended *casas particulares* in Santa Clara include: **Hostal Florida Center** ★★ Calle Maestra Nicolasa (Candelaria) 56, between Colón and Maceo (© **42/20-8161**), a gorgeous 1876 colonial house full of interesting historic furniture and blessed with a flourishing garden and a welcoming host, Angel—as well as some of the best food served in Cuba; **Hostal Casa Mercy,** Calle E Machado 4 (San Cristóbal) between Cuba and Colón (© **42/21-6941;** iselmm@gmail.com), run by the friendly Mercedes and Omelio with two bright rooms, a terrace, a cocktail menu, and book exchange; **Casa Olga Rivera Gómez,** Calle Evangelista Yanes 20 between Máximo Gómez and Carolina Rodríguez (© **42/21-1711;** www.netssa.com/santaclarahouse.html; zaidabarreto2006@yahoo.es), a lovely house with a roof terrace and beautiful floor tiles, fronting Plaza del Carmen and its church; and **Casa Héctor Martínez,** Calle Rolando Pardo (Buen Viaje) 8 between Maceo and Parque (© **42/21-7463**), a smart house close to all the action, with a small patio garden, hammock, and interesting objects and books.

Moderate

Villa La Granjita　Octagonal one and two-story, thatched-roof buildings scattered around rural grounds make up this quiet hotel that is around 4km (2½ miles) from the city center. Rooms are on the small side, but are comfortable and most have balconies; some have views toward the inviting pool. The hotel also has green credentials: solar power heats the water. By the time you read this, the disco should have been soundproofed; if not, steer clear on Friday, Saturday, and Monday. A clutch of royal palms tower over the entrance and near the mini-farmyard the hotel keeps, which children will love.

Carretera de Maleza Km 2.5 © **42/21-8190.** Fax 42/21-8149. www.hotelescubanacan.com. 65 units. CUC$65–CUC$72 (US$70–US$78/£35–£39) double; CUC$75–CUC$82 (US$81–US$89/£41–£44) suite. Rates include buffet breakfast. MC, V. **Amenities:** Restaurant; snack bar; bar; outdoor pool; Jacuzzi; dance club; horseback riding; gift shop. *In room:* A/C, TV, fridge, safe.

Villa Los Caneyes ★   Built to resemble a Taíno Indian village, this mini-resort is the most comfortable option in Santa Clara. Most of the rooms are housed either in large, round, six-unit structures or in individual bungalows. All are clean and roomy enough, although some have pretty low ceilings. The nicest rooms by far are in the two-story "H" block; two of these are actually two-room suites. The grounds are planted with tall trees and flowering plants, and there's good bird-watching all around. The buffet meals are unspectacular, to say the least. This place does a brisk business in tours, so don't be surprised if you're sharing it with a large group or two. Like the Villa La Granjita (see above), it's located about 2km (3 miles) from downtown, so if you're staying here, you can't just wander around Santa Clara at will—you'll either be taking taxis or you'll need your own wheels.

Av. de los Eucaliptos and Circunvalación, Santa Clara. ⓒ/fax **42/21-8140.** www.hotelescubanacan.com. 96 units. CUC$65–CUC$72 (US$70–US$78/£35–£39) double; CUC$80–CUC$87 (US$86–US$94/£43–£47) suite. Rates include buffet breakfast. MC, V. **Amenities:** Restaurant; snack bar; bar; outdoor pool; game room; gift shop. In room: A/C, TV, fridge, safe.

Inexpensive

Hotel Santa Clara Libre   This 10-story hotel fronting Parque Vidal is currently the only true hotel option right in Santa Clara. It definitely has seen better days. The rooms are dingy and only just acceptable; anything above the fourth floor should give you a good view, but the place does suffer from regular water supply problems. If you really want to stay here, it would be worth forking out the extra CUC$10 (US$11/£5.40) for the suite (no. 414) where Fidel once stayed and whose walls are lined with photographs. There's a rooftop bar here and a disco.

Parque Vidal 6, Santa Clara. ⓒ **42/20-7548.** www.islazul.cu. 108 units. CUC$36 (US$39/£19) double; CUC$46 (US$50/£25) suite. Rates include buffet breakfast. MC, V. **Amenities:** 2 restaurants; bar; dance club. In room: A/C, TV.

WHERE TO DINE

Dining options are rather scant and uninteresting in Santa Clara apart from the dinner at Hostal Florida Center. Most folks end up eating at their hotel, particularly those staying at either Villa Los Caneyes or Villa La Granjita or in their *casa particular*. There's little to recommend right around Parque Vidal, although for a quick and inexpensive bite, the **Pizzería Toscana, Colonial 1878,** and the air-conditioned bliss of **Park View,** all on or just off the park, would do in a pinch. The Palmares-run **La Concha,** on Carretera Central at the corner of Calle Danielito (ⓒ **42/21-8124**), is a dependable though unexciting option near the Che Guevara Monument. By far the best place to eat is the **Hostal Florida Center** ★★ (ⓒ **42/20-8161**), a popular *casa particular* with enormous platters of delicious seafood and chicken, plus salads and fruit dishes. The garden is candlelit at night. Stop by to reserve in advance. **Sabor Latino,** Esquerra 157 between Julio Jover and Berenguer (ⓒ 42/20-6539), is a friendly *paladar* serving up large portions of all the favorite meat and fish staples. Tables are spread around a couple of rooms and an open-air interior courtyard of **La Casa del Gobernador,** an old colonial home on Calle Zayas corner of Independencia (ⓒ **42/20-2273**); it's closed Monday. The front room lets out onto the street. The food is standard *criolla* (Creole) fare.

SANTA CLARA AFTER DARK

The **Bar La Marquesina,** just off the Teatro La Caridad, is a good bar, and it's open 24 hours daily. It usually draws a mix of college students, locals, and tourists. There's often a small group playing. With an artsy bohemian vibe, **Club Mejunje** ★★, Calle Marta Abreu 12 (📞 **42/28-2572**), is probably my favorite spot, featuring regular concerts, poetry readings, gay night on Saturday, and theater pieces put on in their brick-walled, open-air courtyard. Cover CUC$2 (US$2.15/£1.10).

Bar Club Boulevard, Independencia 225, between Maceo and Unión (📞 **42/21-6236**), is the most upscale joint in Santa Clara (closed Mon). This Cubanacán property features live music, the occasional cabaret show, and a popular dance club.

A SIDE TRIP TO REMEDIOS

The tiny old city of **Remedios** ★★★ is considered one of Cuba's colonial highlights. It's 45km (28 miles) northeast of Santa Clara on a direct two-lane highway. There's not a whole lot to see in Remedios, but that's part of its charm. The small Plaza Martí sits at the colonial center of Remedios, watched over by the beautiful **Iglesia de San Juan Bautista** ★★, with its stunning baroque-style altar covered in 22-karat gold and celebrated pregnant Madonna statue (open Mon–Fri 9am–noon and 2–5pm and Sat 2–5pm).

For several weeks at the end of each year, the quiet town of Remedios becomes the site of one of Cuba's great street parties and religious carnivals, **Las Parrandas.** The infectious revelry keeps things lively throughout the holiday season. Everything culminates on Christmas Eve in an orgy of drums, floats, and fireworks. The whole thing allegedly began in 1820, when the local priest sent some altar boys out to bang on pots and pans and scare some parishioners into the midnight Advent Masses. It later evolved into a sort of battle of the bands and fireworks between two sections of the small town. Today, the festivities drag out over the weeks leading up to Christmas Eve, and have even spread into neighboring hamlets. Still, Plaza Martí in Remedios is the place to be, and the night to be there is December 24. Be prepared to stay up late, and bring some ear protection. If you're not here near year's end, pop in at the **Museo de las Parrandas,** Calle Máximo Gómez 71, where you can get an idea of the pageantry by examining the small display of photos, costumes, and floats. It's open Tuesday through Saturday from 9am to noon and 1 to 6pm and Sunday from 9am to 1pm; admission is CUC$1 (US$1.10/55p). No visit to Remedios would be complete without at stop at the atmospheric **Café El Louvre** ★ (📞 **42/39-5639**), which is set on a corner facing the town's central plaza and church.

For trips to the cay, contact **Cubacar,** Carretera Caibarien (📞 **42/39-5555**).

Currently, the only hotel option in Remedios is the quaint and modest **Hotel Mascotte,** Máximo Gómez 114, between Calle Margal and Avenida del Río (📞 **42/39-5144;** www.hotelescubanacan.com; CUC$43/US$46/£23 double), which faces the small central park here. It is currently closed while undergoing a complete renovation and is being transformed into a Hoteles E brand by Cubanacán. The same chain will be opening Hotel Barcelona just two blocks away in 2009. However, there are also various *casas particulares* within a few blocks of the central park. Of these, head first to **Hostal Villa Colonial,** Calle Antonio Maceo 43 between Avenida General Carrillo and Fe de Valle (📞 **42/39-6274;** www.villacolonial.de.ki), which has a gorgeous front room and friendly owners; or to the delightful **Hostal el Patio** ★, Calle José Antonio Peña 72, between Antonio Romero and Hermanos García (📞 **42/39-5220**); or to **La Paloma,** Balmaseda 4 between Máximo Gómez and Ramiro Capablanca (📞 **42/39-5490**), which boasts huge bathrooms, but no real outdoor space; or to **Casa Rivero Méndez (Hostal El Chalet),** Calle Brigadier González 29, between Independencia and José Antonio Peña (📞 **42/39-6310**), a 1950s house with Art Deco ironwork.

About 8km (5 miles) east of Remedios, you'll hit the small coastal town of Caibarién where Osmani from **Villa Virginia,** Ciudad Pesquera 73 (© 42/36-3303; www.virginia spension.com) will give you a grand welcome and help you with transport if necessary. Just outside of Caibarién, you'll come to the toll (CUC$2/US$2.15/£1.10 each way) for the 50km (31-mile) *pedraplén,* or causeway, that leads to **la Cayería del Norte ★★★**, a small string of tiny islands, mangrove swamps, and coral reefs with some of the nicest beaches in Cuba. There's the small Aeropuerto Las Brujas (© 42/35-0009) close to the toll. **AeroCaribbean** operates charter flights to here.

While the beaches on both Cayo Las Brujas and Cayo Santa María are spectacular, perhaps the premier beaches in this area are **Playa Ensenachos ★★★** and **Playa Mégano ★★★**, both on Cayo Ensenachos. The protected waters here are as crystal clear as you can imagine, and you can usually wade out a couple hundred yards without the water getting much above your waist. However, these once public beaches are now the exclusive domain of guests at the new **Royal Hideaway Ensenachos** (see "Where to Stay & Dine," below). The hotes charges half the price of their rack rate for a day pass that can be bought at their reception desk. Villa Las Brujas charges a bargain CUC$5 (US$5.40/£2.70). Public beaches include La Salina, Punta Madrugilla, which is good for snorkeling, and Perlas Blancas.

Aside from premier beaches, the hotels listed below offer a wide range of watersports activities, as well as nature tours and bird-watching outings into the mangroves here, and organized tours to Remedios, Santa Clara, and beyond.

The **Marina Cayo Las Brujas** (© 42/35-0013/0213; www.gaviota-grupo.com; gaviota tourscsm@enet.cu) is next to Villa Las Brujas and offers catamaran cruises, diving, and aquabike tours.

In addition to the resorts listed below, the **Barceló Cayo Santa Maria Beach Resort,** the newest and largest property on these cays, is under construction. This massive mega-resort, a member of the Spanish chain Barceló, will open in two phases starting at the end of 2008 and have 2,780 rooms across four hotels. All three of the Sol Meliá properties (Meliá Cayo Santa María, Meliá Las Dunas, and Sol Cayo Santa María) share the delightful new **Aguas Claras Spa.**

Where to Stay & Dine
Expensive

Meliá Cayo Santa María ★★ This resort is a slight step up from its sister Sol property next-door—the whole operation is slightly larger, slightly more luxurious, and slightly more elegant. The rooms, facilities, and setting are wonderful, although only 28 rooms have sea views. The rooms themselves are quite spacious, with large wrought-iron furnishings, large checkerboard-tile floors, and private balconies. There is a variety of dining options, of which we recommend the Mediterranean restaurant, and a stream of activities and entertainment options throughout the day and night. The beach in front of the hotel is a long, beautiful stretch of soft white sand fronting a turquoise sea. The guests at this hotel can use the facilities at the Sol Cayo Santa María resort, but not vice versa. This is now an adults-only hotel.

Cayo Santa María, Villa Clara province. ✆ **42/35-0500.** Fax 42/35-0505. www.melia-cayosantamaria.com. 358 units. CUC$220–CUC$370 (US$238–US$400/£119–£200) double; CUC$370–CUC$491 (US$400–US$530/£200–£265) suite. Rates are all-inclusive. No children allowed. MC, V. **Amenities:** 4 restaurants; 3 bars; cabaret; 2 outdoor pools; 2 outdoor tennis courts; well-equipped health club and spa; extensive free watersports equipment; bikes; games; tour desk; car-rental desk; salon; 24-hr. room service; massage; gift shop; laundry service; nonsmoking rooms. *In room:* A/C, TV, minibar, hair dryer, safe, CD player.

Meliá Las Dunas   This vast complex of more than 900 rooms is like a minicity that requires golf buggies to move around; the farthest room is some 200m (656 ft.) from the lobby. If you like the impersonal and don't want to see the same face twice, then this is the place for you. Those who have difficulty with a lot of walking and want something more intimate should consider the other two Meliás (Meliá Cayo Santa María or Sol Cayo Santa María). All the main services are close to the lobby, while the rooms are either ringed around the kids' pool for families or the adults' pool in two residential zones. The gardens are as lush as you would expect. Only a disappointing 53 rooms have sea views, but rooms are in the same style and layout as the Meliá Cayo Santa María, only they feature more attractive, light-wood furniture. Superior rooms are closer to the lobby; the standard rooms are only a little smaller.

Cayo Santa María, Villa Clara province. ✆ **42/35-0100.** Fax 42/35-0105. www.melia-lasdunas.com. 925 units. CUC$194–CUC$241 (US$210–US$260/£105–£130) double; CUC$234–CUC$281 (US$253–US$303/£126–£152) suite. Rates are all-inclusive. MC, V. **Amenities:** 7 restaurants; 3 snack bars; 5 bars; cabaret; 3 outdoor pools; 2 outdoor tennis courts; spa; extensive free watersports equipment; bikes; games; tour desk; car-rental desk; salon; 24-hr. room service; baby club and 3 childrens' and teenage programs; laundry service; gift shop. *In room:* A/C, TV, minibar, hair dryer, safe, CD player.

Occidental Royal Hideaway Ensenachos ★   This massive resort has top-notch facilities and virtually total dominion over two of the best beaches on the entire island, the namesake Playa Ensenachos and neighboring Playa Mégano. The resort is divided into three sections: the Royal Hideaway, Royal Spa, and Royal Suites. All the rooms are large, modern, and luxurious, with marble floors and a private balcony or porch. Every block of rooms at the resort has its own private concierge. Guests at the Hideaway and Spa areas get to share all the common facilities, restaurants, pools, shops, and spa, whereas those in the Royal Suites section have their own private grounds and some separate facilities. The suites are massive, with kitchen facilities, large living rooms, private outdoor Jacuzzis, and private butlers. The resort's spa facilities are lovely. The elegance and luxury here are over the top and the snootiness of some staff is beyond belief. Some guests have complained that the food is under par for a five-star hotel billing.

Cayo Ensenachos, Villa Clara province. ✆ **42/35-0300.** Fax 42/35-0301. www.occidental-hoteles.com. 506 units. Royal Hideaway: CUC$502 (US$542/£271) double; CUC$554 (US$598/£299) superior; CUC$617 (US$666/£333) suite. Royal Spa: CUC$502 (US$542/£271) double. Royal Suite: CUC$617 (US$666/£333) double. Rates are all-inclusive. Children 12 and under not allowed. MC, V. **Amenities:** 6 restaurants; 2 snack bars; 4 bars; cabaret; 4 outdoor pools; 2 outdoor tennis courts; well-equipped health club and spa; 4 Jacuzzis; extensive free nonmotorized watersports equipment; bikes; game room; concierge; tour desk; car-rental desk; salon; gift shop; 24-hr. room service; massage; laundry service; nonsmoking rooms. *In room:* A/C, TV, minibar, hair dryer, safe.

Sol Cayo Santa María ★★   Although neighboring resorts have upped the ante some, this is still one of my favorite all-inclusive options in Cuba. The facilities and service are excellent, the location is spectacular, and the place manages to provide a sense of isolation and escape, despite the fact that there are some 300 rooms here. The rooms themselves are quite comfortable, with plenty of space, large windows, modern furnishings, and private balconies. Only 82 rooms have ocean views, and these are the choice rooms here, obviously. The entire complex is relatively compact and easy to navigate. The beach in front of the hotel is long and almost immediately deserted, just 91m (299 ft.) or so away from the hotel, and of the three Meliá hotels here, it has the loveliest stretch of sand. The large percentage of European and Canadian tourists here has made it a comfortable place for topless and nude bathing. Close by is the private and beautiful house of Villa Zaida del Río bounded by verandas with two rooms, a private pool, Jacuzzi and solarium, dining and butler service.

Cayo Santa María, Villa Clara province. © **42/35-0200.** Fax 42/35-0505. www.solmeliacuba.com. 301 units. CUC$148–CUC$265 (US$160–US$286/£80–£143) double; CUC$320 (US$346/£173) suite; CUC$1,147–CUC$1,457 (US$1,239–US$1,574/£619–£787) villa. Rates are all-inclusive. Children 2 and under stay free in parent's room; children 3–12 stay for half price in parent's room. Rates lower in off season; higher during peak weeks. MC, V. **Amenities:** 5 restaurants; 3 bars; dance club; cabaret; large free-form outdoor pool; children's pool; small, well-equipped health club and spa; extensive free watersports equipment; bikes; children's program; games room; concierge; tour desk; car-rental desk; gift shop; salon; massage; babysitting; laundry service; nonsmoking rooms. *In room:* A/C, TV, fridge, hair dryer, safe.

Moderate

Villa Las Brujas ★ (Finds)   Perched on a rocky outcrop over the turquoise Caribbean, the individual and duplex villas here are connected by a raised, rugged wooden walkway through scrub and mangrove. At the end of the row of buildings, there's a long stretch of beautiful white-sand beach, which is seldom crowded, as there are so few rooms here. The rooms themselves are spacious and well-appointed, with marble bathrooms, and separate sitting areas—making them all like minisuites. All but five have ocean views. Of these, the second-floor units have the best views. The restaurant, El Farallón, serves respectable *criolla* fare and fresh seafood, and there's a fun second-floor lookout above the restaurant. This is one of the few beach resorts in Cuba that has the feel of a boutique hotel. Watersports equipment can be rented from the nearby marina. Staff members are very friendly.

Cayo Las Brujas, Villa Clara province. © **42/35-0199.** Fax 42/35-0599. www.gaviota-grupo.com. 24 units. CUC$75–CUC$85 (US$81–US$92/£41–£46) double. MC, V. **Amenities:** Restaurant; bar; 2 outdoor Jacuzzis. *In room:* A/C, TV, stocked minibar, coffeemaker, hair dryer, safe.

---

2 CIENFUEGOS ★

256km (159 miles) SE of Havana; 67km (42 miles) S of Santa Clara

Known as *La Perla del Sur* (the Southern Pearl), Cienfuegos is an uncharacteristically calm and inviting port city. Although Columbus visited the deep and protected harbor here on his second voyage, and the Spanish built the Castillo de Jagua in 1745, it wasn't until 1819, when a group of French colonists settled here, that Cienfuegos began to grow and develop. The French influence continued through most of the city's history, particularly throughout the 19th century, when Cienfuegos became a major shipping point for sugar, tobacco, and coffee. As trade with the United States increased, Cienfuegos lost some of its strategic importance to the northern ports of Havana and Matanzas.

ACCOMMODATIONS ■
Casa Amistad **18**
Casa Ana Maria **2**
Casa Piñeiro **9**
Casa Wilfredo **10**
Hostal Palacio Azul **8**
Hotel Jagua **4**
Hotel La Union **12**
Vista al Mar **5**
Villa Lagarto **1**

DINING ◆
Café Cienfuegos **7**
Palacio del Valle **3**
Pizza Dinos **11**

ATTRACTIONS ●
Catedral de la Purísma
  Concepción **13**
Cementerio de Reina **19**
Club Cienfuegos **7**
Marina Cienfuegos **6**
Museo Provincial **16**
Palacio del Valle **3**
Palacio Ferrer **17**
Parque José Marti **14**
Teatro Tomás Terry **15**

Nevertheless, today Cienfuegos is still a busy port, with an assortment of heavy industry and important sugar-producing plantations surrounding it. In fact, the industrial smokestacks, high-tension electrical towers, and an abandoned nuclear plant significantly mar the landscape. However, the historic center, now a UNESCO World Heritage Site, and the beautiful bay and harborfront buildings and Malecón make it a wonderful city to explore and enjoy.

ESSENTIALS

Getting There

BY PLANE   Only international flights now use the small **Jaime González International Airport** (© 43/55-1328; airport code CFG) located 5km (3 miles) northeast of downtown. A taxi from the airport to downtown costs CUC$6 (US$6.50/£3.25).

BY BUS   **Víazul** (© 7/881-1413 in Havana, or 43/51-8114 in Cienfuegos; www.viazul.com) has two daily buses to Cienfuegos (actually an intermediate stop on the Trinidad route) leaving Havana at 8:15am and 1pm, arriving at 12:05pm and 4:55pm, and returning at 9:25am and 4:55pm. The fare is CUC$20 (US$22/£11) each way. The trip takes 3¹/₂ hours. From Cienfuegos to Trinidad, the fare is just CUC$6 (US$6.50/£3.25), and the ride around 1¹/₂ hours. The **bus station** is at Calle 49, between Avenidas 56 and 58 (© 43/51-5720).

BY CAR   From Havana, take the Autopista Nacional east. There are several possible turnoffs for Cienfuegos. The first and most popular is at Aguada de Pasajeros. This is marked and will bring you through the towns of Rodas and Abreus, before leading you into Cienfuegos. If you continue farther on the Autopista Nacional, your next turnoff will be at Cartagena. If you are coming from Santa Clara, you can take the turnoff at Ranchuelo, which is a straight shot into Cienfuegos. The trip should take 3¹/₂ to 4 hours from Havana.

Getting Around

Taxis are readily available around Cienfuegos. Most rides will cost between CUC$1 and CUC$3 (US$1.10–US$3.25/55p–£1.60). If you can't find one, call **Taxi OK** (© 43/55-1172) or **Cubacar** (© 43/51-8454). Tourists are technically not supposed to use the common horse-drawn taxis, as they are not licensed to carry foreigners, though some drivers will let you ride but will only accept CUC$1 or CUC$2 (US$1.10–US$2.15/55p–£1.10). There are also plenty of bicycle-powered cabs around town.

Car-rental agencies in Cienfuegos include **Havanautos,** Calle 37 at the corner of Avenida 18, Punta Gorda (© 43/55-1211), and **Cubacar** at the Hotel Jagua (© 43/55-1030) and opposite the Hotel La Unión (© 42/55-1645).

Orientation

There are two main areas you should be concerned with in Cienfuegos: the **historic center** of town that contains the city's central park, Parque José Martí, and other historic buildings; and **Reparto Punta Gorda,** a slightly newer section that heads out on a narrow strip to the southern point of the city, where you'll find the Hotel Jagua and the Palacio del Valle. Calle 37, or Prado, is the main north-south street and runs all the way to the tip of Punta Gorda. For a long stretch, it runs along the seafront, earning it the moniker the "Malecón" (boardwalk). It is bisected by Avenida 54, an east-west street, also called the "Bulevar," which is pedestrian-only for several blocks between the Parque José Martí and Prado.

The principal tour agencies in town are **Cubanacán,** Av. 54 no. 2903, between Calles 29 and 31, which is extremely helpful (© **43/55-1680**); and **Havanatur,** Avenida 54 between Calles 29 and 31 (© **43/55-1639**). In addition to their main offices listed above, they are represented at or can be booked by most hotels in town.

There's a **Banco Financiero Internacional** at the corner of the Bulevar and Calle 29 (© **43/55-1625**), and the Banco Popular de Ahorro, Avenidas 54 and 33, which has two ATMs; there's a **CADECA** branch on Avenida 56 between Calles 33 and 35 (© **43/55-2164**). The **Clínica Internacional,** Calle 37 no. 202, between Avenidas 2 and 0, Punta Gorda (© **43/55-1622**), is a small, modern facility that can handle most emergencies and medical needs, and has a 24-hour pharmacy. The **post office** is located at Avenida 56 between Calles 37 and 35 (© **43/55-1686**). There's an **Etecsa** office at Calle 31 between the Bulevar and Avenida 56 (© **43/51-3046**), which has Internet access.

WHAT TO SEE & DO
In Town

The **Parque José Martí,** formerly the Plaza de Armas, is the city's hub. It's a broad city park with a gazebo/bandstand at its center and a little Arco de Triunfo (Arc of Triumph) dating from 1902 at its western end. Surrounding the park, you'll find Cienfuegos' most interesting historical buildings. The 1918 **Palacio Ferrer** (© **43/51-9722**), on one corner here, is the city's Casa de la Cultura. This is a good place to find out if there are any interesting art exhibits or concerts going on while you're in town. You should also check out the view from the rooftop cupola here; admission is CUC$.50(US55¢/27p). The building is closed and undergoing renovation until reopening in January 2009. On the eastern end of the park, you'll find the **Catedral de la Purísima Concepción,** a beautiful neoclassical church finished in 1870. The church features wonderful stained-glass work imported from France. On the north side of the park is the **Teatro Tomás Terry ★** (© 43/51-3361; www.azurina.cult.cu). Inaugurated in 1890, the theater has been wonderfully maintained. It has been declared a national monument, and stars such as Enrico Caruso, Sarah Bernhardt, and Anna Pavlova performed here. Check to see if there will be any performances while you're in town; if not, you can tour the facility during the day. Admission is CUC$1 (US$1.10/55p) and includes a quick, guided tour. Across the park, on its south side, is the small **Museo Provincial,** which is only of interest to die-hard museum and local-history buffs.

Out on the end of Punta Gorda is the historic old **Palacio del Valle ★★** (© 43/55-1226), an eclectic architectural masterpiece, which covers vast stylistic ground in its compact floor plan. The centerpiece here is the Salón Comedor (dining room), which dates to 1917 and tries to imitate the intricate Moorish stucco and tile work of Spain's Alhambra. Other rooms are done variously in baroque, neoclassical, and Gothic styling. The whole thing operates as a restaurant (see "Where to Dine," below), and there's also a wonderful third-floor rooftop balcony bar and lookout.

At the very tip of Punta Gorda, there's now **La Punta,** a small garden, snack bar, and bar open late.

Cienfuegos has two picturesque cemeteries, featuring elaborate marble headstones, mausoleums, and aboveground burial crypts. The **Cementerio de Reina ★** is the older of the two and located on the western extreme edge of the city beyond the downtown center. The **Cementerio Tomás Acea** is in an eastern suburb of the city and features an elaborate entrance modeled after the Parthenon in Greece.

Popular tours from Cienfuegos include visits to the **Castillo de Jagua** (© 43/9-6402; open Mon–Sat 9:30am–5pm, Sun 9:30am–1pm; admission CUC$1/US$1.10/55p), which is located on the western flank of the narrow entrance to the harbor. Built between 1738 and 1745, the little fort sits on a hill above the quaint fishing village of Perché. Although the moat is dry, you still enter the castle by crossing the wooden drawbridge. Inside, there are some basic museum-like exhibits and a mediocre state-run restaurant. You reach the castle by driving to the Hotel Pasacaballos, then parking and taking the constant little ferry across; the cost one-way is CUC$1(US$1.10/55p).

The **Jardín Botánico Soledad** ★, Calle Central 136, Pepito Tey, Cienfuegos (© 43/54-5334), was begun by U.S. sugar magnate Edwin Atkins in 1900, and taken over by Harvard University in 1919. With more than 2,000 species of plants covering some 90 hectares (222 acres), it is the largest and most extensive botanical garden in Cuba. The grounds are beautiful to walk around, and there's usually good bird-watching here, although everything tends to be overgrown and unkempt, and markings are sorely lacking. The gardens are 17km (11 miles) east of downtown, via the road to Trinidad. The garden is open daily from 8am to 4:30pm; admission costs CUC$3 (US$3.25/£1.60) for adults and CUC$1 (US$1.10/55p) for children.

Near Playa Rancho Luna is the new **Delfinario** ⓘ Overrated **(Dolphin Show;** © 43/54-8120). Captive trained dolphins and sea lions perform several times daily here. Although the amphitheater around a penned-in saltwater lagoon is spiffy, these types of shows and facilities are rather depressing. The main pool and side pens here are particularly small and shallow. This place is open Thursday through Tuesday from 8:30am to 4:30pm, and has a reasonably priced little restaurant. Shows are at 10am and 2pm. Admission is CUC$10 (US$11/£5.40) for adults and CUC$6 (US$6.50/£3.25) for children. It will cost you an extra CUC$1 (US$1.10/55p) to take photos, CUC$2 (US$2.15/£1.10) to shoot video, and CUC$3 (US$3.25/£1.60) to get a kiss from a dolphin. A 15- to 20-minute swimming session with a dolphin costs CUC$50 (US$5.40/£2.70); a show is included in this price. Cubanacán offers a package for CUC$45 (US$49/£24).

Farther away is **El Nicho,** in the Escambray mountains, a series of waterfalls from which you can plunge into a natural pool; there's a restaurant on-site. Agencies organize trips for CUC$30 (US$32/£16).

On & Below the Water

While Cienfuegos sits on a large and beautiful protected bay, the best (and really the only) beach is 17km (11 miles) away at **Playa Rancho Luna.** The beach here is a long expanse of white sand, although the sand isn't quite as fine and silky as that found at some of Cuba's more famous beaches.

Marina Cienfuegos, Calle 35 between Avenidas 6 and 8, Punta Gorda (© 43/55-1699 or 43/55-1241; www.nauticamarlin.com), is your one-stop shop for all nautical needs. Here you can charter a sailboat or sportfishing excursion, book a cruise around the harbor, rent a Hobie Cat or windsurfer, and go fishing and diving. The elegant 1920s-built **Club Cienfuegos** entertainment complex, Calle 35 between Avenidas 8 and 12 (© 43/55-1275), has a small patch of sand with a little swimming area in front of it; some locals and tourists use it as a place to sunbathe and cool off. Several international regattas, fishing tournaments, and speedboat races are held in Cienfuegos each year. Check with the marinas or your hotel for details. You can book scuba-diving trips out of

Beny Moré

Maximiliano Bartolomé Moré, better known as Beny Moré and perhaps most descriptively dubbed "El Bárbaro del Ritmo" (The Rhythm Barbarian), is Cienfuegos' pride and joy. Born in the nearby hamlet of Santa Isabel de las Lajas on August 24, 1919, Moré was probably the greatest Cuban singer and bandleader of his time. He sang and composed in a variety of genres, from mambo to *son* to cha-cha-chá. Tall and thin, with a velvet-smooth voice, Moré was the epitome of the debonair Cuban bandleader of the '40s and '50s. Although he never enjoyed the overseas success of Xavier Cugat or Pérez Prado, in Cuba, Beny Moré is considered the king.

the **Faro Luna Diving Center** (© 43/54-8040; buceocom@nautica.cfg.cyt.cu) out at Hotel Faro Luna (see "Where to Stay," below) or with the Whale Shark Diving Center at Hotel Rancho Luna (© 43/54-8020) or book through Cubanacán in town. Dives are CUC$30 (US$32/£16).

SHOPPING

The best shop in town is the **Galería Maroya,** Av. 54 no. 2506, between Calles 25 and 27, located on the southern flank of the Parque José Martí, next to the Palatino Bar. This place features a broad selection of Cuban arts and crafts, with a decent representation of local works. There's an excellent cigar shop, **Casa del Habano El Embajador,** at Avenida 54 between Calles 33 and 35. There's an **ARTex** shop on the Bulevar (Av. 54 btw. Calles 37 and 27) stocking a selection of typical souvenirs, and it usually has a good selection of CDs, including some by Beny Moré.

WHERE TO STAY
In Cienfuegos
Expensive
Hotel La Unión ★ (Finds)   This hotel, housed in a marvelously restored mint-green 1869 colonial mansion right on the Bulevar a block off of the Parque José Martí, is one of the nicest boutique hotels in the country. The standard rooms could use a little more elbow room, so you might consider an upgrade to one of the 10 junior suites, which are quite spacious. The neoclassical furnishings are elegant, and the service is attentive, but some repair work is needed in the rooms. The inviting pool here is located in an interior courtyard, with a fragment of an old arched brick wall and a couple of sculpted lions standing guard over it. The open-air central courtyard bar is another great space to hang out and relax, as is the rooftop bar. The main restaurant (ca. 1869) is merely acceptable, with uninspired buffets and a limited a la carte menu.

Calle 31 (corner of Av. 54), Cienfuegos. © **43/55-1020.** Fax 43/55-1685. www.hotelescubanacan.com. 49 units. CUC$100 (US$108/£54) double; CUC$130 (US$140/£70) junior suite; CUC$170 (US$184/£92) suite. No seasonal variations in rates. MC, V. **Amenities:** Restaurant; snack bar; 2 bars; outdoor pool; small exercise room; sauna; Jacuzzi; concierge; limited room service; in-room massage; laundry service. *In room:* A/C, TV, fridge, hair dryer, safe.

Hotel Jagua ★ (Value) Following a complete remodeling, this hotel has fully recovered from the effects of Hurricane Michelle and is quite comfortable. The seven-story hotel is situated out on the end of Punta Gorda, just across from the Palacio del Valle. The modern rooms are spacious, comfortable, cool, and bright, with a large sliding-glass door to let in light, white tile floors, and plenty of amenities. Those on the higher floors of the main building have wonderful views over the city and harbor from private balconies. Only 20 of the rooms come with king-size beds; the rest have two twin beds. There's a large rectangular pool at the center of this complex.

Calle 37 no. 1, Punta Gorda. (℡) **43/55-1003.** Fax 43/55-1245. www.gran-caribe.com. 149 units. CUC$85–CUC$105 (US$92–US$113/£46–£57) double. MC, V. **Amenities:** 2 restaurants; bar; snack bar; cabaret; outdoor pool and children's pool; watersports equipment rental; tour desk; car-rental desk; laundry service. *In room:* A/C, TV, fridge, hair dryer, safe.

Inexpensive

Cienfuegos has scores of good *casa particular* options. You'll find no shortage of *jineteros* (hustlers) offering to show you a room. You'll find the greatest concentration of *casas particulares* all along the Prado (Av. 37), as well as surrounding the Parque José Martí and on Punta Gorda. In addition to the Hostal Palacio Azul listed below, dependable and clean choices include: **Casa Amistad,** Av. 56 no. 2927, between Calles 29 and 31 ((℡) **43/51-6143;** casamistad@correodecuba.cu), run by the superfriendly and knowledgeable Armando and Leonor, a colonial house with a wonderful front living room, two rooms, and some hearty home-cooked food (it's a stone's throw from Parque José Martí); **Casa Piñeiro,** Calle 41 no. 1402, between Avenidas 14 and 16, Punta Gorda ((℡) **43/51-3808;** www.casapineiro.com), an enormous house with friendly owners and a great outdoor oven; **Casa Wilfredo,** Av. 14 no. 4308 between Calles 43 and 45 ((℡) **43/52-8918;** wmoralesmartines@yahoo.es) with a small, independent rooftop apartment; and **Vista al Mar,** Calle 37 no. 210, between Avenidas 2 and 4, Punta Gorda ((℡) **43/51-8378;** www.vistaalmarcuba.com; gertrudis_fernandez@yahoo.es), in a convenient location with a small, sea-front patio.

Villa Lagarto, Calle 35 no. 4B ((℡) **43/51-9966;** villalagarto_16@yahoo.com), is run by the very friendly Tony and Maylin and has two breezy, comfortable top-floor rooms, a seawater pool, and a garden overlooking the sea right at the tip of Punta Gorda. **Casa Ana María,** Calle 35 no. 20 ((℡) **43/51-3269**), is an old colonial home, also out on Punta Gorda. Hostess Ana María Font D'Escoubet prepares filling meals for reasonable rates, and can help arrange tours and activities around Cienfuegos.

Hostal Palacio Azul ★ (Value) This newly restored waterfront building is an excellent value, offering clean and comfortable rooms just off the Malecón, out near the tip of Punta Gorda. Rooms in the 1920s building have high, decorated ceilings and beautiful tiled floors (ca. 1921). A grand marble staircase leads up to the second floor, where you'll find my favorite room, Dalia, a corner unit with a view of the Club Cienfuegos, the harbor, and the nightly sunset. All but two rooms come with a private little balcony. There's a solarium on the roof.

Calle 37 no. 1201, btw. Avs. 12 and 14, Punta Gorda. (℡) **43/55-5828.** Fax 43/55-1020. www.hotelescubanacan.com. 7 units. CUC$60 (US$65/£32) double. No seasonal variations in rate. Rate includes breakfast. MC, V. **Amenities:** Restaurant; bar; 24-hr. room service; laundry service. *In room:* A/C, TV, fridge, hair dryer; safe.

In addition to the moderately priced Hotel Club Amigo Faro Luna listed below, **Hotel Pasacaballos,** Carretera de Rancho Luna, Km 22 (© **43/59-2100**), is a dour option catering to both Cubans and foreign budget travelers. The only true beach hotel close to Cienfuegos is **Club Amigo Rancho Luna** (© **43/54-8012;** www.hotelescubanacan. com); however, this is a rather mediocre place catering to package-tour groups of folks who must be unaware that they have scores of better options all over Cuba. Still, if you want to go swimming for a few hours or the day, the beach here will certainly do. **Finca Los Colorados,** Carretera Rancho de Luna, Pasacaballos Km 18 (© **43/54-8044**), a *casa particular*, is on the road close to the lighthouse.

Hotel Club Amigo Faro Luna ★   This small hotel appeals primarily to scuba divers on multiday dive packages. There's a well-equipped dive center here, and scores of great dive sites offshore. The rooms are fairly comfortable, albeit spartan, and most even have an ocean view. Room nos. 209 and 210 have spacious private terraces overlooking the sea. A nice stretch of white-sand beach is about 180m (591 ft.) away. It's a little bit removed from downtown to serve as a base for exploring Cienfuegos, although if you've got a rental car and you want to mix some beach time with your city fun, this is an option.

Carretera Pasacaballo Km 17.5, Cienfuegos. © **43/54-8034.** 46 units. CUC$55–CUC$70 (US$59–US$76/ £30–£38) double. MC, V. **Amenities:** Restaurant; snack bar; 2 bars; outdoor pool; watersports equipment rental; tour desk; car-rental desk; laundry service. *In room:* A/C, TV, fridge, safe.

WHERE TO DINE

In addition to the places listed below, you can get acceptable pizza and pastas at **Pizza Dinos,** Calle 29 between Avenidas 54 and 56 (© **43/51-2020**). La Cueva del Camarón has closed and apparently is being turned into a small hotel.

Café Cienfuegos Ⓕⁱⁿᵈˢ   CONTINENTAL/SEAFOOD   This is the most refined dining to be had in Cienfuegos. The elegant, second-floor dining room is part of the Club Cienfuegos complex. While not as ornate or elaborate as the Palacio del Valle, the ambience here is still very pleasant, and the food is a bit better to boot. While there is an assortment of steak, pork, and poultry dishes, we recommend you stick to the fresh fish and seafood. If you have an aversion to meat, the Paella Cienfueguera will come with more chicken than seafood. The large, first-floor open-air bar area is set underneath a modern tent structure, with soaring spires. This is a great place to catch the sunset before heading in for dinner.

Calle 37 (Prado) btw. Avs. 8 and 10, Punta Gorda. © **43/51-2891.** Reservations recommended in high season. Main courses CUC$6.25–CUC$38 (US$6.75–US$42/£3.40–£21). No credit cards. Daily noon–10pm.

Palacio del Valle ★   CONTINENTAL/SEAFOOD   The food is not nearly as spectacular as the setting, but the luxurious and ornate surroundings just about make up for it. Music and entertainment in the main dining room are provided by the charismatic María del Carmen Iznaga Guillén, the niece of the great Cuban poet Nicolás Guillén. She is a genuine character, and worth a visit just to see and hear her play. The cuisine here is uninspired, but certainly acceptable. This place, now belonging to the hotel, is the de rigueur stop in town and there's a cattle-car feel to the operation at times. My favorite draw here is the rooftop bar, with its fabulous views over the harbor. At the time of this writing, a tapas bar and wine cellar with live music was about to open in the basement.

Calle 37 (Prado) and Av. 0, Punta Gorda. 🕿 **43/55-1003.** Reservations recommended in high season. Main courses CUC$9–CUC$25 (US$9.70–US$27/£4.85–£14). No credit cards. Daily 10am–midnight.

CIENFUEGOS AFTER DARK

The biggest draw in town is the **Club El Benny,** Av. 54 no. 2907 (the Bulevar) between Calles 29 and 31 (🕿 **43/55-1105**). There's a nightly cabaret show here (admission CUC$5/US$5.40/£2.70) that features the classic sounds and songs of the club's namesake. The place also serves as one of the city's most lively dance clubs. The other popular spot to dance the night away is the **Guanaroca Disco** at the Hotel Jagua, Calle 37 no. 1, Punta Gorda (🕿 **43/55-1003**). There's also music nightly at the large, open-air bar at the **Club Cienfuegos** (🕿 **43/51-2891**). A local **Casa de la Trova** (Patio del ARTex, also known locally as El Cubanísimo), at Avenida 16 and Calle 35 (🕿 **43/55-1255**), has nightly concerts (admission CUC$3/US$3.25/£1.60).

For a quieter time, pick out a sidewalk table at the **Palatino Bar,** overlooking the Parque José Martí at Av. 54, corner of Calle 27; or saddle up to a seat at the little hole-in-the-wall local hangout **Don Luis** on Calle 31, across from the Hotel La Union.

A similar option is found at the **Marina Cienfuegos** (🕿 **43/55-1699**). Ask at your hotel, or check down at the docks to see what's happening.

3 TRINIDAD ★★★

334km (208 miles) SE of Havana; 261km (162 miles) S of Varadero; 649km (403 miles) W of Santiago de Cuba

Tiny Trinidad is, quite simply, one of the finest colonial towns in all the Americas. Wholly disproportionate to its diminutive size, Trinidad ranks as one of Cuba's greatest attractions. A few square blocks of cobblestone streets, pretty pastel-colored 18th- and 19th-century houses, palaces, and plazas, Trinidad's colonial-era core can be toured in just a few hours. However, its serenity is so soothing that many visitors are easily coaxed into much longer stays. Magically frozen in time and tastefully scruffy where it needs to be, the city has streets that are more populated by horse-drawn carts than automobile traffic, and old folks still crouch by windows, behind fancy wrought-iron grilles, to peer out at passersby.

Founded in 1514 on the site of a native Taíno settlement, Villa de la Santísima Trinidad was the fourth of Diego Velázquez's original seven *villas* (towns). Trinidad quickly grew and later prospered in princely fashion from the sugar-cane industry concentrated in the outlying Valle de los Ingenios. The sugar boom that took root by the mid-1700s created a coterie of wealthy local sugar barons, who built magnificent estates in the valley and manor houses in town and imported thousands of African slaves to work the fields. Trinidad's golden age, though, proved to be short-lived. Slave uprisings on plantations, intense European competition, and, finally, independence struggles throughout the Caribbean all took their toll on the Cuban sugar industry.

When the bottom dropped out of sugar by the 1860s, Trinidad's economy collapsed and the town drifted into obscurity. Its economic failure in the late–19th century is a true blessing in the 21st: Trinidad escaped further economic development and modernization that surely would have obscured the colonial nucleus that UNESCO honored as a World Heritage Site in 1988. Even in the 1950s, in prerevolutionary, capitalist Cuba, the beauty and historical value of Trinidad prompted the government to declare it off-limits to further development.

ACCOMMODATIONS ■

Casa Bastida **1**
Casa de José y Fátima **27**
Casa del Historiador
  (Casa Carlos Zerquera) **12**
Casa Elda **21**
Casa Font **6**
Casa Meyer **7**
Casa Sotolongo **15**
El Mesón del Regidor **18**
Grand Hotel Iberostar
  Trinidad **24**
Hostal Casa Muñoz **3**
Hostal La Rioja **26**
Hostal Sandra y Victor **28**
Hotel La Ronda **23**
Hotel Las Cuevas **25**

DINING ◆

Cafeteria La Begonias **5**
Casa de la Música **19**
Paladar Estela **11**
Paladar La Coruña **2**
Restaurante El Jigüe **9**
Restaurante Trinidad
  Colonial **22**
Sol y Son **4**

ATTRACTIONS ●

Casa de la Trova **20**
Convento de
  San Francisco **10**
La Parroquial Mayor **17**
Museo de
  Arqueología **13**
Museo de Arquitectura
  Colonial **16**
Museo de la Lucha Contra
  Bandidos **10**
Museo Historico
  Municipal **8**
Museo Romántico/Palacio
  Brunet **13**
Plaza Mayor **14**

ESSENTIALS

Getting There

BY PLANE Chartered **AeroCaribbean** light-aircraft flights from Havana, Cienfuegos, and Varadero arrive in Trinidad at the little **Aeropuerto Alberto Delgado,** Carretera Casilda Km 1.5 (📞 **41/99-6393;** airport code TND), a couple of kilometers beyond the historic center of Trinidad. A taxi from the airport to Trinidad costs around CUC$5 (US$5.40/£2.70).

BY BUS   The quickest and best bus service to Trinidad is **Víazul** (② **41/99-4448** in Trinidad; www.viazul.com), which operates from Havana (② **7/881-1143**), Varadero (② **45/61-4886**), and Santiago de Cuba (② **22/62-8484**). From Havana, buses depart twice daily, at 8:15am and 1pm, arriving at 1:40pm and 6:30pm, respectively; the fare is CUC$25 (US$27/£14) one-way. From Varadero, buses leave at 7:30am and arrive at 1:25pm; the fare is CUC$20 (US$22/£11) one-way. From Santiago de Cuba, buses leave at 7:30pm, arriving at 7am the following day; the fare is CUC$33 (US$36/£18) one-way. Return buses leave Trinidad for Havana at 7:30am and 3pm; for Varadero at 9am and 3:30pm; and for Santiago at 8am.

The bus terminal, or **Terminal de Omnibuses** (② **41/99-4448**), in Trinidad is on Gustavo Izquierdo between Piro Guinart and Simón Bolívar, close to the Plaza Mayor.

BY CAR   From Havana, the fastest route is to drive along the Autopista Nacional to Santa Clara (about 4 hr.), and then drop down through Jibacoa to Trinidad along the local road south. Another option is to continue on the Autopista Nacional to Sancti Spíritus (perhaps stopping for a look, if you're not planning an overnight visit there), and circle back southwest to Trinidad for a scenic drive through the Valley of the Sugar Mills (see "Side Trips from Trinidad," later in this chapter). If you're driving in from Cienfuegos, there are actually two routes. We prefer the coastal road, which gives you some good sea views as you get close to Trinidad. From Santiago de Cuba, start out northwest on the unfinished Autopista Nacional and then take the Carretera Central through Bayamo, Camagüey, Ciego de Avila, and Sancti Spíritus. The journey from Santiago to Trinidad takes about 8 hours.

Getting Around

Getting around Trinidad is a simple affair. Almost everything of interest in town is clustered around the Plaza Mayor in the historic center. The streets of old Trinidad were made for exploring on foot, and you can easily get around the whole of the old city, and most of the newer parts just beyond the colonial core, very easily on foot.

BY TAXI   State-owned, registered taxis are available for travel back and forth between Playa Ancón and Trinidad, up the hill to Hotel Las Cuevas, or private hire for excursions. Call **Cubataxi** (② **41/99-2214**), **Taxi OK** (② **41/99-6110**), or **Transtur** (② **41/99-3454**). Taxis charge CUC$8 (US$8.65/£4.30) to Playa Ancón. Little yellow Coco Taxis, slightly slower, non-air-conditioned three-wheel vehicles, charge CUC$4 (US$4.30/£2.15).

BY CAR   Though it is far easier to sign on for an organized tour to visit the surrounding area, including Topes de Collantes in the Sierra del Escambray, you might choose to rent a car to explore central Cuba or travel to more distant destinations. The drive northeast to Sancti Spíritus through the Valle de los Ingenios is particularly alluring. The major car-rental companies are **Cubacar** (② **41/99-6110**) and **Vía Rent a Car** (② **41/99-6388**). Rates range from CUC$45 to CUC$80 (US$49–US$86/£24–£43) per day for a standard four-door to CUC$80 (US$86/£43) and up per day for a 4WD vehicle.

BY BICYCLE   Locals sometimes rent out bikes (usually functional cruisers for CUC$2–CUC$4/US$2.15–US$4.30/£1.10–£2.15 per day) that you can use to get back and forth to the beach. However, be forewarned: It's downhill, then flat on your way to the beach, but the final few kilometers coming home will be uphill. The best place to ask is at your *casa particular*. **Ruinas del Teatro Brunet** (② **41/99-5547**) rents out bikes for CUC$3 (US$3.25/£1.60) a day.

Maceo and Francisco Cadahía. It departs at 9am, 11am, 2pm, 4pm, and 7pm and picks up at a few stops in town, including the Cubatur office, before heading to Playa La Boca and the hotels on Playa Ancón. It returns from the beach at 10:15am, 12:15pm, 3:15pm, 5:15pm, and 8:15pm. The fare is CUC$2 (US$2.15/£1.10) per person.

Orientation

The streets of Trinidad go by both original colonial and newer, post-Revolution names. Locals usually don't know both; what one person may call Boca another calls Piro Guinart. Streets are haphazardly labeled. Many longtime residents use the old names, but most businesses and institutions adopt the newer names, which are used in this section. Be prepared to encounter some confusion if asking for an address, though Trinidad is so small that it's nearly impossible to be lost for long.

Your best bets for information about Trinidad and nearby excursions are any of the major state-run travel agencies. **Cubatur** (✆ **41/99-6314;** www.cubatur.cu), is at Antonio Maceo at the corner of Francisco Javier Zerquera, as well as at Maceo at the corner of Bolívar and in the Hotel Ancón (p. 202). More helpful is **Cubanacán,** located on José Martí between Francisco Javier Zerquera and Colón (✆ **41/99-6142**), and at Cafe Las Begonias where the employees are extremely helpful. **Infotur** is inside the Restaurante Santa Ana, but keeps irregular hours and is too far out of the center to be of any use.

Banco de Crédito y Comercio is located at José Martí 264 between Colón and Francisco Javier Zerquera (✆ **41/99-2405**). It's open Monday through Friday from 8am to 3pm and Saturday from 8am to 11am. A **CADECA** is at José Martí 166 (✆ **41/99-6263**); its hours are Monday through Saturday from 8am to 6pm and Sunday from 8am to 1pm.

For medical attention, go to the 24-hour **Clínica Internacional** located at Lino Pérez 103, at the corner of Reforma (✆ **41/99-6492**). There's a pharmacy in-house too. **Etecsa Internet terminals** are at the Etecsa office on Lino Pérez (on the east side of Parque Céspedes, between José Martí and Miguel Calzada). There are also Internet terminals inside the Cafetería Las Begonias.

The main **post office** is situated at Antonio Maceo 418, between Colón and Francisco Javier Zerquera. It is open Monday through Saturday from 8am to 7pm.

WHAT TO SEE & DO

Unquestionably, the greatest attraction in Trinidad is the town itself, which constitutes one of the finest colonial centers in the Americas and, justifiably, has been designated a UNESCO World Heritage Site in its entirety. The town's cobblestone streets contain a treasure-trove of small and grand colonial homes, churches, and quiet squares. Walking aimlessly about the curving streets of the old town is unmatched in Cuba for tranquillity and charm. About the only feature not authentically colonial is the neon cross that crowns the church on Plaza Mayor. Remarkably, as quaint as it is, Trinidad feels like a real town where Cubans live and work, rather than the film set it first appears to be.

A good way to get your bearings in Trinidad is to trace a path from the **Plaza Mayor,** the heart of the old town, heading west on Echerri and then down Piro Guinart to **Plazuela El Jigüe,** a quiet and pretty little square. Then head down Peña to Simón Bolívar and east on Antonio Maceo, the closest thing there is to a main drag in Trinidad.

A couple blocks south of here, along Lino Pérez, is **Parque Céspedes,** the focal point of the "new" town (though newer than the colonial core of Trinidad, it remains anything but shiny and modern).

Northeast of the old town, following Fernando H. Echerri to José Mendoza for several blocks, you'll reach **Plaza Santa Ana** and the ruins of **Iglesia Santa Ana,** which looks ancient, but dates only to 1812. On the square is a former 19th-century prison, **Real Cárcel,** which today houses a touristy restaurant and souvenir shop.

Around the Plaza Mayor ★★

The neo-baroque, 19th-century Plaza Mayor, elaborately adorned with serene sitting areas, statuary, towering palm trees, and gardens enclosed by white wrought-iron fences, is one of Cuba's most beautiful plazas. It's ringed by magnificent palaces and pastel-colored houses with red-tile roofs and wood shutters. On the northwest corner is the cathedral, Iglesia de la Santísima Trinidad, which most locals refer to as **La Parroquial Mayor.** The cathedral, completed in 1892, replaced the original 17th-century church that was destroyed in 1812 by a hurricane. The new construction, completed at the end of the 19th century, is rather simple on the outside, but the restored interior reveals a Gothic vaulted ceiling and nearly a dozen attractive carved altars. The cathedral can be visited Monday through Saturday from 10:30am to 1pm. Mass is at 9am on Sunday.

The highlight of the Plaza Mayor, and the most evocative reminder of Trinidad's glory days, is the lovingly restored **Palacio Brunet,** Fernando H. Echerri 52 at the corner of Simón Bolívar. The colonial mansion dates to 1704 (the second floor was built in 1808) and houses the **Museo Romántico ★★** (✆ **41/99-4363**). Its splendid collection of period antiques culled from a number of old Trinitario families convincingly evokes the life of a colonial sugar baron in the 1800s. Don't miss the enormous kitchen, covered in *azulejo* (glazed ceramic tiles), with a wood-burning stove. The views from upstairs are marvelous. The museum is open Tuesday through Saturday from 9am to 5pm and Sunday from 9am to 1pm. Admission is CUC$2 (US$2.15/£1.10); allow about 45 minutes for your visit.

In a pale yellow colonial building on the west side of the main square, **Museo de Arqueología** (✆ **41/99-3420**) features a collection that encompasses natural sciences and pre-Columbian Cuba. It's mostly an uninspired hodgepodge of exhibits, though; you'll find bones of Indian natives and slaves, glass-enclosed stuffed animals, and a 19th-century kitchen, which, though interesting, is hard to classify as either archaeology or natural science. It is currently closed and has no scheduled reopening date.

On the east side of the Plaza Mayor, in a squat, sky-blue mansion once belonging to the Sánchez Iznaga family, the **Museo de Arquitectura Colonial** (✆ **41/99-3208**) features moderately interesting exhibits that trace the development of Trinidad, including examples of woodwork and ironwork, maps, models, and photographs. What is on display, though, can hardly compare to the real-life exhibits beyond the museum's doors. It's open Monday, Thursday, and Saturday from 9am to 5pm and Sunday from 9am to 1pm. Admission is CUC$1 (US$1.10/55p).

The former Palacio Cantero, an 1830 palatial residence built by a noted sugar baron, houses the **Museo Histórico Municipal ★**, Simón Bolívar 423 between Peña and Gustavo Izquierdo (✆ **41/99-4460**). In addition to antiques and 19th-century furnishings, there are bits and pieces of slave history, old bank notes, and exhibits of revolutionary Cuba. For many visitors, though, the highlight is the climb up the narrow and rickety wooden stairs to the tower, which has terrific bird's-eye views of Trinidad and the surrounding area. The museum is open Saturday through Thursday from 9am to 5pm; admission is CUC$2 (US$2.15/£1.10). Allow about an hour for your visit, a bit longer if you want to linger over the views.

Tips **Know Where You're Going**

Be careful. I've received reports of *jineteros* meeting incoming buses and taxis with the names of tourists they've gleaned from friends inside the bus or taxi company. They then proceed to tell the tourists either that their reservation at a specific *casa particular* has been canceled, or that they are taking them to that *casa,* when in fact they are bringing them to a different *casa* altogether. If you have and trust your confirmed reservation at a *casa particular,* make sure you know the exact address and location of the house, and distrust touts who take you elsewhere.

The second of Trinidad's two major towers is the picturesque, yellow-and-white domed bell tower belonging to the former 18th-century **Convento de San Francisco (Convent of Saint Francis of Assisi),** Fernando H. Echerri at Piro Guinart. Today the building hosts the dogmatic, but rather fascinating **Museo de la Lucha Contra Bandidos** (© **41/99-4121**), which focuses on revolutionary Cuba and the continuing "struggle against bandits." Exhibits document Fidel's battles against counterrevolutionaries—the *bandidos* in question—who sought to overturn the regime's ideals by winning support among *guajiros* (poor rural farmers) and fighting in the Sierra del Escambray in the 1960s. In addition to newspaper reports, you'll find machine guns, military maps, a CIA radio, and photos of the ragtag principals who finally, and quite extraordinarily, overthrew the Batista government in 1959. As is the case with the Museo Histórico, though, the biggest draw may be the panoramic views from atop the bell tower. The museum is open Tuesday through Sunday from 9am to 5pm; admission is CUC$1 (US$1.10/55p). Allow 45 minutes or so, including the visit to the tower.

WHERE TO STAY

Trinidad has an abundance of *casas particulares*—around 380 at last count, including several in fine colonial homes that rank as excellent bargains and are particularly appropriate accommodations in this beautifully preserved old town. Visitors who arrive on the Víazul bus are confronted by a rabble of dozens of card- and placard-waving folks hoping to get you to follow them to their homestays. They are perfectly innocuous and, for the most part, honest folks just trying to make a buck. Not all the *casas* are officially registered, however, and many are not as close to the colonial center as you might wish to be. Have a map ready so they can show you clearly where their houses are located. If you already have the name of a *casa,* don't mention that you are looking for "José" or "María" (for example); the homeowner you're talking to will morph into that person in no time. Houses in the old center of town generally charge CUC$25 to CUC$35 (US$27–US$38/£14–£19) double; those a bit farther out (usually no more than a 15-min. walk from the Plaza Mayor) charge CUC$20 to CUC$25 (US$22–US$27/£11–£14) double. Alternatively, you could stay at one of the large resorts on Playa Ancón, 12km (7¹⁄₂ miles) away.

In Trinidad

The venerable old **Hotel La Ronda,** José Martí no. 239 (© **41/99-2248;** www.hotelescubanacan.com), has been closed for some time for extensive remodeling. It is expected to open some time in 2009, as an elegant little downtown boutique hotel run by Cubanacán.

Grand Hotel Iberostar Trinidad ★★ Facing the quiet Parque Céspedes, this restored and remodeled old building is now a beautiful and refined hotel in the heart of colonial Trinidad. Opened in February 2006, this is by far the most luxurious and opulent hotel in the area. A stately air pervades this place, from the large lobby area, with its soaring atrium ceiling and central fountain and broad marble staircase, to the rooms, restaurant, and all the rest. All the rooms are very spacious and tastefully done, with a broad range of amenities, including a phone in the bathroom. The junior suites are somewhat bigger, with a separate tub and shower, and walk-in closet. My favorite rooms are the second-floor standard units, nos. 106 through 111, with balconies facing the park. Avoid no. 218, as it's next to the noisy laundry room. No children under 15 are allowed.

Calle José Martí and Calle Lino Perez, Trinidad. ℂ **41/99-6073.** Fax 41/99-6077. www.iberostar.com. 40 units. CUC$172–CUC$290 (US$186–US$313/£93–£157) double; CUC$220–CUC$250 (US$238–US$270/£119–£135) suite. Rates include breakfast. MC, V. Children under 15 not allowed. **Amenities:** Restaurant; bar; tour desk; gift shop; room service 10am–11pm; laundry service. *In room:* A/C, TV, minibar, hair dryer, iron/ironing board, safe.

Moderate

Hotel Las Cuevas ★ Perched on a hill 1.6km (1 mile) north of (and up above) the old colonial core of Trinidad, this hotel is named for the caves that dot the hillside. Built in the 1950s, the hotel is surprisingly large, featuring rows of concrete bungalow-style rooms, a round pool, and a fantastic underground cave dance club (a short distance from the property). The remodeled rooms are very comfortable, with exposed stone walls and good bathrooms. While it's a little inconveniently located up a steep hill (a quiet setting many will appreciate), you can easily walk (downhill) to the restaurants and nightlife of Trinidad, and then take a taxi home. The hotel is popular with tour groups.

Finca Santa Ana, Trinidad. ℂ **41/99-6133.** Fax 41/99-6161. www.hotelescubanacan.com. 109 units. CUC$84–CUC$91 (US$91–US$98/£45–£49) double; CUC$99 (US$107/£53) suite. Rates include breakfast. MC, V. **Amenities:** 2 restaurants; 2 bars; dance club; nightly show; outdoor pool; outdoor tennis court; laundry service. *In room:* A/C, TV, safe.

Inexpensive

In addition to the *casas* reviewed below, following are some other recommended options. **Hostal La Rioja,** Frank País 389 between Simón Bolívar and Francisco Javier Zerquera (ℂ 41/99-3879; tereleria@yahoo.com.mx), is run by the superfriendly and welcoming Teresa. There's a new rooftop bar with city views. **Hostal Sandra y Victor,** Maceo 613, between Piro Guinart and Pablo Pichs Girón (ℂ 41/99-6444; www.sandra.trinidad photo.com; hostalsandra@yahoo.com), has two modern rooms and a great terrace with a rustic bar. The welcoming **Casa Bastida** ★, Maceo 537, between Simón Bolívar and Piro Guinart (ℂ 41/99-6686; julio_cecilia@hotmail.com), boasts wonderful rooftop views. One room has a cute balcony overlooking the street and there's an attractive communal dining area under a bamboo roof. **Casa Elda,** Jesús Menéndez 166, between Fernando Hernández Echerri and Ernesto Valdés Muñoz (ℂ 41/99-3283; mdleon@pol1tdad.ssp.sld.cu), is run by a friendly couple; the rooms can be connected and the bathroom is not en suite. **Casa del Historiador** (Casa Carlos Zerquera), Fernando Hernández Echerri 54 (ℂ 41/99-3634), the lovely colonial home of Trinidad's official historian, has two rooms, one quite small with a tiny bathroom. There is also **Casa Sotolongo,** Real 33, between Francisco Javier Zerquera and Simón Bolívar (ℂ 41/99-4169), which is located right on the main plaza, and **Casa de José y Fátima,** Francisco

Tips Check in Before You Check In

In Trinidad, if you make a reservation with one of the more popular *casas particulares*, it's a very good idea—if not essential—to reconfirm your reservation a couple of days in advance. *Casas* often let out rooms that haven't been reconfirmed.

Javier Zerquera 159 between Frank País and Fco Peterson (© **41/99-6682**), which has comfortable rooms with a balcony, in a colonial house with a gorgeous blue porch.

Casa Font ★★   A gorgeous, late-18th-century colonial house with a green facade, just a few steps from the bus station and in the heart of the old center, this family home has a great collection of antiques and a light, airy feel. For a *casa particular,* this is about as grand as it gets: chandeliers of Baccarat crystal, thick wood doors, colonial- and republican-era oil paintings, and mediopunto (stained-glass, fan-shaped) windows above doors. Out back is a pretty courtyard with a well. One room has a bed dating from 1800, richly decorated with mother-of-pearl, and a lovely tiled bathroom; the other room has two beds. There are also stunning *modernista mámparas* doors (half doors in the Modernista design) in the house.

Gustavo Izquierdo 105 (btw. Piro Guinart and Simón Bolívar), Trinidad. © **41/99-3683.** 2 units. CUC$25 (US$27/£14) double. No credit cards. *In room:* A/C, no phone.

Casa Meyer ★   A few paces from Casa Font, this is another spectacular, 200-year-old colonial home, with a garden courtyard. The house has very high, wood-beamed ceilings and very nice antiques, though it is a bit darker than Casa Font. One bedroom is huge, with antique beds, one decorated with mother-of-pearl, while the new room set back in the garden is just as nice and perhaps even more tranquil, with a huge, bronze four-poster bed. An original pram and 1903 gramaphone grace the main front room.

Gustavo Izquierdo 111 (btw. Piro Guinart and Simón Bolívar), Trinidad. © **41/99-3444.** 2 units. CUC$20–CUC$25 (US$22–US$27/£11–£14) double. No credit cards. *In room:* A/C, no phone.

El Mesón del Regidor   This small, state-run inn is atmospheric. The four rooms here are simple, but recently renovated, with redbrick floors and exposed beam and tile ceilings. Each has a private staircase leading up to it from the central courtyard and restaurant area. A couple of these staircases are steep and narrow. This hotel is just a few steps away from the Plaza Mayor. It is currectly closed as it undergoes further renovation by Cubanacán and is due to reopen in 2009.

Simón Bolívar 242 (btw. Muñoz and Rubén Martínez Villena), Trinidad. © **41/99-6572.** 4 units. CUC$45–CUC$55 (US$49–US$59/£24–£30) double. Rates include breakfast. No credit cards. *In room:* A/C, TV.

Hostal Casa Muñoz ★   This charming place is run by English-speaking Julio and his wife Rosa. A breezy and centrally located colonial house built in 1800, it has two bedrooms with en-suite bathrooms and a shady patio, plus a rooftop terrace with fantastic views. Julio is a photographer and has considerable advice on Trinidad's cultural scene; check out his collection of slides and pictures adorning the house. This place is popular and advance reservations are a must.

José Martí 401 (corner of Santiago Escobar), Trinidad. ©/fax **41/993673.** www.casa.trinidadphoto.com. 2 units. CUC$30–CUC$35 (US$32–US$38/£16–£19) double. No credit cards. *In room:* A/C, no phone.

Brisas Trinidad del Mar ★ The fanciest beach hotel in the general area of Trinidad, this place is semi-luxurious and easygoing. For those looking to combine beach time, great sea and mountain views, and easy access to Cuba's finest colonial city, this is without doubt the best option. The all-inclusive hotel imitates the famed colonial architecture of nearby Trinidad, with pastel colors and pastel-colored imitations of the town's more famous landmarks, including the San Francisco tower and the Plaza Mayor. The hotel is on one of the best sections of Playa Ancón, and it has a great pool and all the services one could want, including language and dance classes and diving. Rooms are handsomely outfitted, nicely decorated with pale yellow walls and blue accents. If there's a drawback, it's that the food can be pretty average and bland.

Península Ancón, Trinidad. ℂ 41/99-6500. Fax 41/99-6565. www.hotelescubanacan.com. 241 units. CUC$135–CUC$165 (US$146–US$178/£73–£89) double. Rates are all-inclusive. Discounts available for longer stays. MC, V. **Amenities:** 3 restaurants; 2 bars; 24-hr. snack bar; outdoor pool; 2 outdoor tennis courts; gym; Jacuzzi; sauna; scooter and bike rental; children's center and programs; massage; laundry service. *In room:* A/C, TV, safe.

Hotel Ancón While this place definitely plays second fiddle to the neighboring Brisas Trinidad del Mar, the Hotel Ancón is nonetheless a good option for travelers looking for plenty of services and amenities on the beach at a reasonable price. The older-style hotel—a large Soviet block plunked down on the sand—is pretty uninspiring, and rooms are moderate in size and simply decorated (bare bones, even). About half of the rooms have oceanview balconies, and these are a definite plus. Still, we recommend you ask for a room in the newer wing, although these are in no way new, having been built in 1995. Rooms here have either mountain or sea views, balconies, and slightly more space and more modern decor. Activities include salsa and language classes, volleyball, aerobics, and more.

Carretera María Aguilar, Playa Ancón, Trinidad. ℂ 41/99-6120. Fax 41/99-6121. www.hotelescubanacan. com. 279 units. CUC$110–CUC$140 (US$119–US$151/£59–£76) double. Rates are all-inclusive. MC, V. **Amenities:** 4 restaurants; 5 bars; 24-hr. cafeteria; nightly show; outdoor pool; 2 outdoor tennis courts; massage; laundry service. *In room:* A/C, TV, safe.

WHERE TO DINE

The dining scene in Trinidad is one of the more enjoyable ones in the country—which, admittedly, is not saying much—not so much for the excellence of its restaurants, but for the low-key atmosphere and a mix of both pretty good state-run establishments and *paladares* (private restaurants). Plenty of self-appointed guides will make their presence known, trying to lead you to an unofficial *paladar;* these are safe and often quite good, even if illegal (though that status has no consequence for you—feel free to dine wherever you like).

In addition to the restaurants listed below, the state-run **Plaza Mayor** (ℂ 41/99-6470) is an acceptable option serving a decent buffet, in a beautifully restored old home and an even more beautiful courtyard.

Expensive

Grand Hotel Iberostar Trinidad INTERNATIONAL The Grand Hotel's restaurant is the only place with fine dining in Trinidad. The main course is a la carte, but the starters and dessert are a little odd for such an expensive menu; however, you get the variety and no doubt avoid the wastage that is the curse of many Cuban resort hotels. Try the delicious entree of beef carpaccio with spicy tomato and the rarely-to-be-found Danish blue and manchego cheeses. For main courses, the grilled filet of *pargo* (snapper) with Parmesan vegetables or the candied tenderloin steak tournedos in red wine with fresh marrow and creamy potatoes are recommended.

Calle José Martí and Calle Lino Perez. ℂ **41/99-6073.** Prix-fixe menu CUC$28 (US$30/£15) for hotel guests, CUC$35 (US$38/£19) for nonguests. MC, V. Daily 12:30–3pm and 7–10pm.

Moderate

Casa de la Música CRIOLLA   It's not an obvious place to eat, perhaps, but one of Trinidad's best spots for live music also has a restaurant attached, and if you're lucky enough to score one of the tables on the terrace, you'll be within earshot of the band playing on the platform on the steps below. The restaurant is, on the whole, no better or worse than other state-run places in town. It serves the standard main courses—grilled chicken, pork, and fish, as well as lobster and a couple of inexpensive sandwiches. We also like this spot for lunch.

Fernando H. Echerri 3. ℂ **41/99-6622.** Reservations not accepted. Main courses CUC$3.50–CUC$26 (US$3.80–US$28/£1.90–£14); sandwiches CUC$1.50–CUC$3 (US$1.60–US$3.25/80p–£1.60). Daily 10am–10pm.

Paladar Estela ★★ (Finds) CRIOLLA   Enter through an elaborately decorated colonial house, 2 blocks north of the cathedral, into this private restaurant. It has a handful of tables set in an exuberant backyard garden setting, with tons of flowering plants, including red *estrella de navidad,* and a wall festooned with vines. Portions are nearly as voluminous as the flora, and light eaters can share one dish between two people. Dishes include roast pork *a la cubana,* fried chicken, grilled fish, and ham omelet. However, my favorite is the perfectly spiced *ropa vieja* made with shredded lamb. All are served with *moros y cristianos* (black beans and rice), salad, fried banana, crackers, and fruit.

Simón Bolívar 557. ℂ **41/99-4329.** Reservations not accepted. Main courses CUC$8–CUC$10 (US$9–US$11/£4.30–£5.40). No credit cards. Mon–Fri 7–10pm.

Paladar La Coruña ★ CRIOLLA   A pleasant private home restaurant with just two tables on the patio just beyond the living room, under a welcome ceiling fan, this is another of Trinidad's excellent *paladares.* It has an oral menu only, but you can already guess what's served: chicken, pork, grilled fish. Meals begin with a salad and veggie plate, and the main course is served with a heaping mound of rice and beans, followed by a small plate of bananas and mango. Tables are very informal, with plasticized tablecloths and wood chairs upfront. One wall of the *paladar* is decorated with souvenir money from customers around the world.

José Martí 430. No phone. Reservations not accepted. Main courses CUC$8–CUC$15 (US$9–US$16/£4.30–£8.10). No credit cards. Daily 11am–11pm.

Restaurant El Jigüe CRIOLLA   El Jigüe (*Hee*-gweh) is a brightly lit, nearly formal dining room in a handsome, airy colonial house. It sits on one of the old town's prettiest and tiniest squares, next to a massive shade tree. Just a block from the Plaza Mayor, the restaurant has high-backed chairs, white and plum tablecloths, and prominent chandeliers, which lend it an elegance not often seen in official restaurants in Cuba. Its specialty is *pollo El Jigüe,* which comes in a clay pot with pasta and cheese and is served with salad and coffee. Other dishes worth checking out are grilled fish, standard chicken, and lobster.

Rubén Martínez Villena 69 (corner of Piro Guinart), Plazuela El Jigüe. 🕐 **41/99-6476.** Reservations not required. Main courses CUC$7.50–CUC$24 (US$8.10–US$26/£4.05–£13). Daily 11am–10:30pm.

Restaurante Trinidad Colonial CRIOLLA This state-owned restaurant is more notable for its setting than its menu. It's in a pretty, mauve-colored house set back from the street, with a couple of tables in a sunny courtyard and more inside surrounded by chandeliers, fading oil paintings, and enormous dressers. The standard dishes of grilled fish, pork filet, grilled shrimp, and lobster are decent-size portions, but are a bit unexciting. The *filete de pescado Trinidad Colonial,* grilled fish topped with grated carrot, potato, and melted cheese, is small in size, but surprisingly good.

Antonio Maceo 55. 🕐 **41/99-6473.** Reservations not required. Main courses CUC$6–CUC$15 (US$7–US$16/£3.25–£8). Daily 9.30am–midnight.

Sol y Son ★★ CRIOLLA One of Trinidad's long-standing *paladares,* this place is housed in an art- and furniture-bedecked, 19th-century house that could double as an antiques store. Out back, on the porch of a very attractive, verdant courtyard, the restaurant offers one of the more extensive menus among private restaurants. Choose from soups, spaghetti, a long list of fish (including a breaded filet stuffed with cheese), and grilled and roasted chicken and pork dishes. Check out the *cerdo borracho* (drunk pork), which is grilled and doused with rum and the house cocktail made from seven-year-old rum and honey. The patio has mounted ceiling fans and, during the day, you should do your level best to sit beneath one, as it can get bloody hot.

Simón Bolívar 283 (btw. José Martí and Frank País). No phone. Reservations not accepted. Main courses CUC$6–CUC$9 (US$6.50–US$9.70/£3.25–£4.85). No credit cards. Mon–Thurs noon–3pm; Sun–Fri noon–3pm and 6:30–11pm.

Inexpensive

Cafetería Las Begonias SANDWICHES/SNACKS Once one of Trinidad's better restaurants, Las Begonias is now not much more than a snackateria, with 10 glass-topped tables on a red-tile floor, open to the street. Still, it's good enough for breakfast or a cheap light lunch. It serves mostly *emparedados* (sandwiches), pizzas, and hamburgers, as well as the ubiquitous fried chicken. This place has an Internet cafe attached.

Corner of Simón Bolívar and Maceo. No phone. Reservations not accepted. Main courses CUC$1.50–CUC$3.50 (US$1.60–US$3.80/85p–£1.90). No credit cards. Daily 9am–10pm.

SHOPPING

Trinidad, given its starring role on the tourist circuit, is one of the better shopping towns in central and eastern Cuba (though far from a shopper's paradise). In addition to the requisite cigar and music shops, several of Trinidad's atmospheric, cobblestone streets are converted daily into **street markets** featuring handicrafts, lace, and clothing items. While lace and clothing are the main attractions, you can also find interesting woodcarvings, musical instruments, masks, and a host of ceramic works. The street with the most variety tends to be Peña, near the Museo Municipal de Historia tower, while most of the lace and textile merchants, who occasionally have good *guayabera* shirts (simple, short-sleeved cotton shirt, with pockets and pleats, worn by men), tend to cluster on the small streets just east of the Plaza Mayor.

The art gallery on the south side of the Plaza Mayor, **Galería de Arte ARTex,** has two floors of contemporary art, much of it very accessible, and the traditional souvenir renderings of Trinidad.

The place for cigars and tobacco paraphernalia in town, **La Casa del Tabaco,** has two branches and carries all the finest Cuban cigars, carefully stored. The shop at Lino Pérez 296 (at the corner of José Martí) is open daily from 10am to 6pm; the branch on Francisco Javier Zerquera (at the corner of Maceo), is open daily from 10am to 6pm.

Many of the ceramic wares you'll see for sale around Trinidad are produced by the Santander family, whose history in this artform goes back generations. You can visit their small factory, **El Alfarero Casa Chichi,** Andrés Berro 51, between Abel Santamaría and Pepito Tey (© **41/99-3146**), although it's best to call in advance and tell them you're coming.

The most complete Cuban CD store in town, **ARTex,** is annexed to the Casa de Música on Fernando H. Echerri, where you'll find nightly performances of live music. The clerks will usually play just about anything you want to hear.

TRINIDAD AFTER DARK

While most of Trinidad's old-town streets are coffin-quiet after dark, several joints bop with live Cuban music nightly. One of the best spots to sit outside, have a *mojito* or beer, and hear good traditional bands is the small plaza midway up the steps leading to the **Casa de la Música** ★. The dance floor is usually a good mix of polished, semiprofessional locals and foreigners whose hips are somewhat less smoothly oiled. The steps are often overflowing with people checking out some free music under the stars from 8:30pm until midnight. Inside the Casa de la Música, a more raucous environment prevails until the wee hours for a cover charge of CUC$1 (US$1.10/55p). Just around the corner on Fernando H. Echerri, **Palenque de los Congos Reales** ★★ has an open-air stage where you can sometimes catch Grupo Folclórico performing Afro-Cuban music and dance (performances aren't regularly scheduled). At other times, there may be a standard *trova* or *son* group playing. It's open Sunday to Friday from 1:30pm to midnight, and until 1am on Saturday. The **Casa de la Trova,** Fernando H. Echerri 29, a block east of the Plaza Mayor, is the traditional spot to listen to Cuban bands and try out a few dance steps; it's open daily from 10am to 1am, and there's a cover charge of CUC$1 (US$1.10/55p). A similar spot is **Casa Fisher** (ARTex), on Lino Pérez 306 between José Martí and Francisco Cadahía, but the scene here can be hit-or-miss.

The **Ruinas del Teatro Brunet** ★, Maceo, between Zerquera and Simón Bolívar, puts on a nightly Afro-Cuban cabaret-style show in the spacious courtyard of the ruins of the city's first theater. Another bar set in a delightful open-air courtyard in the ostensible ruins of a colonial home, the **Ruinas de Segarte** ★, Jesús Menéndez s/n between Callejón Gado and Juan Manuel Marquéz, is an intimate affair and open from 10:30am to 1:30am daily, and also has live music most nights.

La Canchánchara, Rubén Martínez Villena at Pablo P. Girón, sometimes has a few musicians assembled, but it's mostly just a little open-air courtyard bar in an atmospheric colonial house, a good place to kick back in old wooden chairs and have a *mojito* or the eponymous house drink, made with *aguardiente* (firewater), lime, and honey. It's open daily from 9am to 10pm (but no food is served).

One of the most unusual nightspots in Cuba has to be the dance club carved out of a deep two-level cave, **Discoteca Ayala,** also called La Cueva (© **41/99-6133**). Though it can be deadly hot, and the kitsch factor is undeniable, it's still pretty cool to dance to blasting disco-salsa tunes as colored lights bounce off stalactites. The crowd on weekends is largely Cuban. Now if they could only install air-conditioning to go with the lights and sound system, nocturnal spelunking would be even more appetizing. To get there, you can either walk up a path leading directly behind the cathedral, off Juan Manuel Márquez, or take the longer route from Hotel Las Cuevas (it's not actually on the premises of the hotel, though it's under the same management). It's open Tuesday to Sunday 10pm to 2am (later Fri–Sat); admission is CUC$3 (US$3.25/£1.60).

SIDE TRIPS FROM TRINIDAD

Though the colonial streets of Trinidad are the main draw, the town is perfectly situated for quick trips to the beach (one of the best on the southern coast) and gorgeous surrounding countryside, which includes the Sierra del Escambray mountains and a picturesque valley that was once home to the sugar plantations that made Trinidad wealthy in the 18th and 19th centuries.

PLAYA ANCON ★ Though it can't quite compare with Cayo Largo, Varadero, Cayos Coco and Guillermo, Cayo Santa Maria, or Guardalavaca—Cuba's prettiest and most prestigious beaches—Playa Ancón is still a very beautiful beach with one distinct advantage over those other, isolated stretches of sand: the proximity to Trinidad. At just 13km (8 miles) from town, Ancón, a 3km (2-mile) strip at the end of a peninsula, is a quick and easy ride to and from Trinidad, so beach lovers can stay here and visit the colonial wonder of Trinidad at their will. The beach is made up of wonderful white sand, and there's good snorkeling and diving at some 30 offshore dive sites. Both the Brisas del Mar Trinidad and Playa Ancón hotels, as well as the major travel agencies in town, offer diving and snorkeling excursions beginning at CUC$30 (US$3.25/£1.60) per person, as well as watersports. **Cayo Blanco** is a tiny offshore island reputed to be one of the best dive spots, with a huge variety of coral. Local operators also offer "seafari" expeditions to Cayo Blanco, with boat trips to the island, lunch, and snorkeling. Trips depart from the Marina Nautica Marlin (© **41/99-6205**).

Northwest of Playa Ancón, about 8km (5 miles) from Trinidad, is **La Boca,** a small fishing village that's the popular beach spot among locals. Few tourists make it to La Boca, though there are a couple of *casas particulares* that rent rooms.

To get to Playa Ancón, take a taxi or Coco Taxi. Alternatively, energetic folks can rent a bike; see "Getting Around," earlier in this section.

VALLE DE LOS INGENIOS ★★ Trinidad got rich off the sugar trade back in the 18th and 19th centuries, and the Valle de los Ingenios (Valley of the Sugar Mills) was one of the most productive sugar-cane growing areas in all of Cuba. The gorgeous, verdant valley is no longer king of the sugar trade, which once supported 60 mills, but for visitors, it makes a wonderful day trip. The zone has been declared a UNESCO Cultural Heritage Site. A 1907 American steam train, especially for tourists, departs daily for the valley, making the journey out to one of the old sugar estates, **Manaca-Iznaga,** in just over 30 minutes from Trinidad. However, the train has broken down several times in the last year; a replacement bus costs CUC$19 (US$21/£10), but it's not nearly as atmospheric. The old manor house (Casa Hacienda) remains and is now a pretty good tourist restaurant; however, the main attraction is the fantastic, 45m-high (148-ft.) pointed tower, built in 1845, which visitors can ascend (for a fee of CUC$1/US$1.10/55p) for spectacular views of the surrounding area. A huge bell once hung here and tolled for the toiling slaves in the fields, signaling the beginning and end of their working days. There's a surprisingly good little restaurant in a hacienda-style home here, that serves up a filling lunch for between CUC$4 and CUC$8 (US$4.30–US$8.65/£2.15–£4.30).

If it's working, the steam train departs Trinidad daily at 9am, leaves Manaca-Iznaga at 1:30pm, and returns back in Trinidad around 3pm. Tickets (CUC$10/US$11/£5.40

round-trip) can be purchased from any tour operator around town, or directly at the train station 1km (¹/₂ mile) from the center of Trinidad on Calle Antonio Guiteras Final (© **41/99-3348**).

PARQUE NACIONAL TOPES DE COLLANTES (SIERRA DEL ESCAMBRAY) ★★

Northwest of Trinidad, along dangerously curving roads, are the thickly pine-covered mountains of the Sierra del Escambray, a beautiful range that cuts across central Cuba. From Trinidad, the Topes de Collantes National Park, which covers 175sq. km (68 sq. miles), is the main draw, a cool refuge from the heat that usually bakes the stone streets of Trinidad. It's a splendid area for hiking, though a sad and lifeless resort village of Soviet-style hotels also provides therapeutic spa treatments.

Of the several well-established trails, the most popular route is **Salto del Caburní,** a hike that begins near a graffiti-covered house, the Casa de la Gallega (where simple lunches are served), and terminates in a great 75m (246-ft.) waterfall and swimming hole. The clearly marked trail, through dense forests of palm, pine, and eucalyptus trees, is fairly challenging, with several steep descents, often along a muddy, narrow path. The water in the deep green pool makes for a brisk swim. Another popular hike, which also has a waterfall as its reward at the end, is **Salto Vega Grande.** Each of these trails is a 4km (2.5-mile) hike each way.

The Topes de Collantes resort, about 20km (12 miles) from Trinidad, welcomes mostly Cubans; but several of its hotels accept foreign guests. Of these, the top choice is **Villa Caburní** (© **42/54-0189;** www.gaviota-grupo.com). The massive and rather unattractive **Kurhotel Escambray** (© **42/54-0180;** www.gaviota-grupo.com) is most notable as a sort of lakeside spa offering a variety of therapies, including hydrotherapy. Still, it's hard to recommend this place, when most visitors have access to such vastly better services at home.

Though it's possible to rent a car and explore the region on your own, paying a CUC$6.50 (US$7/£3.50) entrance fee at the Topes de Collantes resort (**Complejo Turístico Topes de Collantes;** © **42/54-0193/0219;** reserva@topes.com.co.cu; run by Gaviota), hikers are advised to sign on for organized bookings, since many trails are not well marked. The Trinidad travel agencies, such as Havanatur and Cubatur, offer Sierra del Escambray jeep excursions for CUC$29 to CUC$37 (US$31–US$40/£16–£20) per person.

4 SANCTI SPIRITUS

70km (43 miles) NE of Trinidad; 386km (240 miles) E of Havana

Sancti Spíritus lies smack-dab in the middle of the island and is the capital of the province of the same name. Perched on the banks of the Río Yayabo, the old town is a warren of corkscrew streets, many lined with fine, if weathered, colonial homes. Like Trinidad, the town was one of the original seven *villas* founded by Velázquez in the early 16th century. Today, Sancti Spíritus is a small and not greatly significant, mostly modern provincial capital with an unassuming, lived-in feel. Though much of the city is run-down, it is beginning to renovate some of its more important colonial buildings, including one of the finest house-museums and one of the best-preserved colonial churches in the country, with the hopes of attracting a greater percentage of the travelers that stop off in nearby Trinidad.

Getting There

BY BUS Víazul (① 7/881-1143 in Havana; www.viazul.com) has three daily buses to Sancti Spíritus on the Havana–Santiago de Cuba line leaving at 9:30am, 3pm, 6:15pm, and 10pm. From Havana, the trip takes just over 5 hours. The fare is CUC$23 (US$25/£12). Víazul also makes the 1-hour trip to Sancti Spíritus directly from Trinidad (① 41/99-4448; CUC$6/US$6.50/£3.25) daily at 8am on the Trinidad–Santiago de Cuba route. From Santiago, buses leave at 9am, 3:15pm, and 10pm, and the trip takes around 10 hours. The fare is CUC$28 (US$30/£15).

The bus terminal in Sancti Spíritus (① 41/32-4142) is located at Carretera Central Km 388, between Circunvalación and the Carretera de Jíbaro. Taxis charge CUC$2 or CUC$3 (US$2.15 or US$3.25/£1.10 or £1.60) for a ride to the center of town.

BY TRAIN The no. 17 train travels daily from Havana's Estación Central to Sancti Spíritus, departing at 9:45pm and arriving at 6am; the fare is CUC$14 (US$15/£7.30) for adults. For more information, call ① 7/862-1920 or 7/861-4259. The **Estación de Tren** (① 41/32-9218) in Sancti Spíritus is located at the end of Avenida Jesús Menéndez, southwest of the Puente Yayabo.

BY CAR Driving from Havana, the fastest route is along the Autopista Nacional (A1) to Santa Clara, and then continuing along the Carretera Central to Sancti Spíritus (about 5 hr.). The short drive from Trinidad, along the Circuito Sur, is one of the prettiest in Cuba, as the road rolls through fields of sugar cane with the Sierra del Escambray looming in the background. From Santiago de Cuba, start out northwest on the unfinished A1 and then take the Carretera Central through Bayamo, Camagüey, and Ciego de Avila (about 6 hr.).

Getting Around

Call **Cubataxi** (① 41/32-2133) for a taxi, or hop aboard one of the horse-drawn *coches* (carriages), which officially only accept pesos, but most will accept an offer for the fare of CUC$1 to CUC$2 (US$1.10–US$2.15/55p–£1.10). Unlicensed taxis also circulate on the streets of Sancti Spíritus. To rent a car, call **Cubacar** (① 41/32-8533). Rates are about CUC$55 to CUC$75 (US$59–US$81/£30–£41) per day for a standard four-door car.

Orientation

For a relatively small town, Sancti Spíritus is rather spread out. However, you're unlikely to spend much time beyond the old town, where you can easily walk everywhere. You'll only need a taxi (or horse-drawn *coche*) for getting to the bus terminal, train station, or your hotel, if you choose to stay at one of the inconveniently located, large hotels on the outskirts of town.

The closest Sancti Spíritus comes to having a tourist information office is the travel agency **Cubatur** (① 41/32-8518), Máximo Gómez 7 on the west side of Plaza Sánchez. Cubatur also offers hotel discounts and discounted set meals at various restaurants in the city, including Quinta Santa Elena and Restaurant Mesón de la Plaza; ask for details.

The **Banco Financiero Internacional,** Independencia 2 between Plaza Sánchez and Honorato (① 41/32-8479), is open Monday through Friday from 8am to 3pm. The **CADECA** branch at Independencia 31 (① 41/32-8535) is open Monday through Saturday from 8am to 6pm and Sunday from 8am to 1pm.

ACCOMMODATIONS ■
Casa de Estrella **2**
Hostal del Rijo **7**
Hostal Paraíso **14**
Hotel Plaza **5**
Los Richards **4**

DINING ◆
Mesón de la Plaza **8**
Restaurant Hostal del Rijo **7**
Restaurant Quinta
  Santa Elena **12**

ATTRACTIONS ●
Biblioteca Provincial
  Rubén Martínez **6**
Calle Llano **11**
Casa de los Refranes **1**
Iglesia Parroquial Mayor del
  Espíritu Santo **9**
Museo de Arte Colonial **10**
Plaza Serafin Sánchez **3**
Puente Yayabo **13**

Ⓢ CADECA
Ⓔ Etecsa
✉ Post office

If you need medical attention, **Hospital Provincial Camilo Cienfuegos** is located on Carretera Central at Bartolomé Masó (☎ **41/32-4017**).

You can make long-distance or international phone calls or log on for CUC$6 per hour (US$6.50/£3.25) with the Etecsa card at the **Etecsa** office on Independencia 14 Sur opposite the CADECA; it's open daily from 8:30am to 7:30pm. The main **post office** is at Independencia 8 Sur, between Plaza Sánchez and Honorato. It's open Monday through Saturday from 8am to 8pm.

It won't take much more than a morning or afternoon to check out Sancti Spíritus's principal attractions. The old town is very untouristy and unassuming, and perfect for an easygoing stroll.

Calle Llano ★ is the most atmospheric street in Sancti Spíritus, a bent-elbow cobblestone alleyway (one of the only remaining stone streets in town) of pastel-colored and tiled-roof houses. It's often very still, except for a few kids playing stickball. **Puente Yayabo,** the bridge over the river at the southern edge of the old town, is a 19th-century take on a European Romanesque stone bridge. Locals don't pause long enough to wonder whether a medieval-style bridge built in 1825, in a town not founded until well into the 16th century, looks odd or not; they bound over it at great speed, on bicycles, in horse-drawn wagons, and in 1950s Chevys on their way to and from the Colón residential district.

The main hub of life in Sancti Spíritus is **Plaza Serafín Sánchez,** a large public square with a handful of fine colonial buildings in various states of disrepair mixed in with bland modern constructions. It certainly doesn't qualify as one of Cuba's most attractive plazas, but it is perennially busy with cars buzzing around and people meeting up. One of the most notable edifices on the square, on the corner of Solano and Máximo Gómez, is the **Biblioteca Provincial Rubén Martínez,** an early-20th-century library that looks more like the local opera house. The main sights in town are a short walk south of here.

Perhaps Sancti Spíritus's most splendid colonial home, **Museo de Arte Colonial** ★★, Plácido 74 at Jesús Menéndez (© **41/32-5455**), is the city's standout attraction. The opulent former palatial mansion of one of Cuba's most elite families, the Valle-Iznaga clan, who fled Cuba after the Revolution, it became the property of the state in 1961. Ninety percent of what you see inside, from furniture to paintings, is original. Though the family obviously kept an impressive collection of Limoges porcelain, French gilded mirrors, Italian marble tables, and Baccarat crystal chandeliers here, this wasn't their primary residence; the house was used mostly to host family members in transit, so the furnishings were rather eclectic. The three bedrooms are decorated in grand style, though, with handmade lace, embroidered sheets, and hand-painted glass. Note the gorgeous and very Cuban leather *sillón fumador* (smoking chair) and, in the music room, the mid-18th-century American piano, one of only two of its type in Cuba. In the tearoom is the family seal, which says a lot about the arrogance of the rich and powerful: *"El que más vale no vale tanto como Valle vale"* ("He who has the greatest worth isn't worth as much as a Valle is worth"—playing off the Spanish word for "worth" with the family surname). The museum is open Tuesday through Saturday from 9:30am to 5pm and Sunday from 8am to noon. Admission is CUC$2 (US$1.10/55p) with a guided tour in English, Spanish, or French; there is a fee of CUC$1 (US$1.10/55p) to take photos and taking video costs CUC$5 (US$5.40/£2.70).

Iglesia Parroquial Mayor del Espíritu Santo ★, Jesús Menéndez between Honorato and Agramonte, is one of the best-preserved colonial churches in Cuba and the oldest building in Sancti Spíritus. A small, faded blue church with a tall bell tower, the austere construction dates to 1680. The church's massive ceiling beams are impressive, as is the blue-and-yellow painted nave. Though the church is unlikely to wow most visitors, it is a quietly evocative, authentic colonial sight that recalls a day when Sancti Spíritus may have looked more like Trinidad. It's open Tuesday through Saturday from 9 to 11am and from 2 to 5pm; admission is free.

If you have occasion to be north of downtown, take a peek at the curiosity that is the **211** so-called **Casa de los Refranes (House of Aphorisms).** The bricks that make up the exterior of Tomás Alvarez's modest roadside house are covered with hundreds of sayings and slogans, some banal and others philosophical (they look like graffiti, but they're actually baked in a ceramic-like process). The house is on Carretera Central, just past the bus stop, up the road from Villa Los Laureles hotel.

If you have occasion to be north of downtown, take a peek at the curiosity that is the

If you have occasion to be north of downtown, take a peek at the curiosity that is the **211** so-called **Casa de los Refranes (House of Aphorisms).** The bricks that make up the exterior of Tomás Alvarez's modest roadside house are covered with hundreds of sayings and slogans, some banal and others philosophical (they look like graffiti, but they're actually baked in a ceramic-like process). The house is on Carretera Central, just past the bus stop, up the road from Villa Los Laureles hotel.

WHERE TO STAY

Sancti Spíritus has one of the best new boutique hotels in Cuba, as well as a good collection of *casas particulares* clustered within easy walking distance of the old town's main attractions. Three recommended *casas* are **Casa de Estrella,** Máximo Gómez 26 Norte (✆ 41/32-7927), a comfortable and friendly bargain option with two rooms, one an apartment; **Los Richards,** Calle Independencia 28 (Altos; ✆ 41/32-3029), a great spot just off Plaza Sanchéz, with two good rooms with an independent entrance (the family also runs a place at Independencia 17 Sur); and **Hostal Paraíso,** Máximo Gómez 11 Sur between Honorato and Cervantes (✆ 52/71-1257 cellphone), with two comfortable rooms—one in an old doctor's consulting room where an original glass cabinet is embedded in the wall.

Hostal del Rijo ★★ (Value)   This handsomely restored, light-blue colonial mansion on Plaza Honorato del Castillo is part of a growing trend in elegant boutique hotels, and best of all, it's a steal. The house was in complete ruins just several years ago, but it has been completely redone and now exudes colonial character and charm. The rooms are huge, especially nos. 5, 6, 7, and 8, which look out onto the plaza and have balconies with views of the tower of La Parroquial church. If at all possible, reserve one of these second-floor rooms, as they have much more style than those on the ground floor. The accommodations have restrained decor, with sedate colors and old photos of Sancti Spíritus. Ceilings are so high that chirping birds often flutter in and fly around in the public rooms in the morning. The two-story structure is built around a lovely patio with a fountain, where you'll find the hotel's excellent little restaurant. There's also a nice cafe and bar that opens onto the plaza.

Honorato del Castillo 12, Sancti Spíritus. ✆ **41/32-8588.** Fax 41/32-8577. www.hotelescubanacan.com. 16 units. CUC$49 (US$53/£26) double; CUC$55 (US$59/£30) suite. **Amenities:** Restaurant; bar; limited room service. *In room:* A/C, TV, fridge, safe.

Hotel Plaza   This small hotel right off Plaza Sánchez was closed at presstime and is being completely remodeled into a Hoteles E boutique hotel by Cubanacán. It has a rooftop terrace and mirador with long views of Sancti Spíritus. Rooms have high ceilings and the largest rooms face the plaza and the street.

Independencia 1 (Plaza Sánchez), Sancti Spíritus. ✆ **41/32-7102.** Fax 41/32-8577. www.hotelescubanacan. com. 27 units. Rates include breakfast. MC, V. **Amenities:** Bar; car-rental desk; limited room service. *In room:* A/C, TV.

WHERE TO DINE

Mesón de la Plaza ★ CRIOLLA   Set on one of Sancti Spíritus's most attractive plazas, this handsome 1850s house is open to the street and has two rooms with high ceilings and picnic-style tables with benches. The restaurant is very clean, well managed, and popular, especially with a lunchtime tourist crowd. It breaks out of the Cuban restaurant doldrums with a couple of house specialties: garbanzo soup with bacon, pork, and sausage; and *ropa vieja* (shredded beef), served in an earthenware pot. Those two dishes, plus a glass of excellent and refreshing sangria, make for a very good meal, but you might also opt for grilled shrimp or fish filet. *Note:* The restaurant is apt to close early at night, around 9pm, if there are no customers.

Máximo Gómez 34, Plaza Honorato. *C* **41/32-8546.** Reservations recommended for lunch. Main courses CUC$4.80–CUC$9 (US$5.20–US$9.70/£2.60–£4.85). Daily 10am–10pm.

Restaurant Hostal del Rijo ★★ CRIOLLA Set in an airy central courtyard beside a stone fountain and surrounded by an abundance of potted plants, this restaurant features wrought-iron furniture and an overall elegant ambience. Aside from the wonderful environs, this place also has a creative and deft young chef, who takes chances with local ingredients and dishes—an uncommon occurrence at most state-run restaurants. We recommend the roast pork in a fruit glaze, or the *camarones casilda* (shrimp cooked in white wine). You'll even find a fairly decent and reasonably priced wine list here. The *serrano helado,* an expreso coffee with vanilla ice cream, grenadine and syrup, is a delicious way to end your meal.

Honorato del Castillo 12, Sancti Spíritus. *C* **41/32-8588.** Main courses CUC$3.50–CUC$18 (US$3.80–US$19/£1.90–£9.70). Daily 7am–11pm.

Restaurant Quinta Santa Elena ★ CRIOLLA This restaurant near the river and Puente Yayabo occupies a lovely colonial home with handsome rooms and a relaxing grand terrace that opens onto the garden backyard, with river views. Popular with groups, especially at lunch, it features traditional Cuban music and good meals and service. Standard dishes like fried fish filet and pork and beef steaks are enlivened by a twist, of *vaca frita,* a traditional dish of roast beef, accompanied by white rice and vegetables.

Padre Quintero (btw. Llano and Manolico Díaz). *C* **41/32-8167.** Reservations recommended for lunch. Main courses CUC$5.50–CUC$9 (US$5.95–US$9.70/£2.95–£4.85). Daily 10am–10pm.

Camagüey & the Northeastern Coast

The extraordinary, powdery beaches of **Cayo Coco** and **Cayo Guillermo,** the cays that lie off the mainland and jut into the deep blue of the Atlantic Ocean, are the primary attractions of Ciego de Avila province. It is a remote area, but one with the infrastructure and natural gifts that make it perfect for idyllic sun, sand, and sea holidays. The namesake provincial capital Ciego de Avila and other towns and cities in this province hold few attractions for visitors.

A little farther east, the predominantly flat, low-lying Camagüey province, southeast of Ciego de Avila, is the largest in the country, though it is also the least densely populated. It occupies the widest swath on the island, 120km (75 miles) from the Atlantic coast to the Caribbean coast. **Camagüey,** the provincial capital, is Cuba's third-largest city, after Havana and Santiago de Cuba, and is a relatively undiscovered, fine colonial city that is worth exploring.

1 CAYO COCO & CAYO GUILLERMO ★★

98km (61 miles) N of Ciego de Avila; 550km (342 miles) E of Havana; 270km (168 miles) NE of Trinidad; 202km (126 miles) NW of Camagüey

One of Cuba's premier beach destinations, distinguished by some of the most pristine sand and water on the island, Cayo Coco and Cayo Guillermo are cousin cays *(cayos)* reached by crossing a 27km (17-mile) *pedraplén,* or man-made causeway, that extends from the mainland over the shimmering, shallow waters of the Atlantic. The cays share some of the same attributes as Varadero, but with a more isolated and natural feel, and without the interminable string of hotels.

Though these cays were explored way back in 1514, when Diego Velázquez named the stretch of islands and cays along the north coast **Jardines del Rey (the King's Gardens),** Cayo Coco was only developed for tourism in the early 1990s. The development on its neighboring cay, Guillermo, is newer still. Until construction of the causeway in 1988, the Cayos remained completely isolated, exclusively known to local fishermen and adventurous sailors like Ernest Hemingway.

The cays are part of the Archipélago de Sabana-Camagüey, which extends 300km (186 miles) along the north coast and consists of some 400 large islands and small cays. Cayos Coco and Guillermo, the most developed of the entire stretch, are populated by just a handful of resort hotels—although more are planned. The unspoiled beaches have spectacular white and powdery sand and the waters are a classic Caribbean-style crystalline turquoise. The area's natural gifts are some of the best in Cuba: nearly 400km (250 miles) of coral reefs, plus an ecotourist's bundle of lagoons, marshes, and one of Cuba's most abundant populations of birds, with more than 150 species. The latter include the Americas' largest native colony of pink flamingos, estimated at upwards of 10,000 birds, which often appear as a gauzy pink haze shimmering on the horizon (except in May, when they venture close to the causeway), as well as herons, pelicans, black and white egrets, white ibis, and other tropical species. The waters off the cays are flush with grouper, snapper, and mackerel, while deeper off the coast, fishermen find marlin and swordfish.

A third cay—east of Cayo Coco, Cayo Romano, and the beaches out on Cayo Paredón Grande (tiny despite its name)—is the next bull's-eye targeted for Cuban hotel development in the archipelago, although no construction has yet begun. For now, the main resorts are Cayo Coco and Cayo Guillermo, and they're quite popular with Canadian and British travelers, as well as a good number of Germans and French. The focus for most guests is trained squarely on the beaches, swimming pools, watersports, dining and drinking, in-house activities, and nightly entertainment; rare is the traveler who comes seeking something else. If you have other activities in mind, your sense of isolation could be significant, although for those who get antsy, all the hotels offer local excursions as well as day trips and overnights to Trinidad, Camagüey, and Havana.

ESSENTIALS
Getting There
BY PLANE   The **Aeropuerto Internacional Jardines del Rey,** Carretera a Cayo Coco (© 33/30-9165; airport code CCC), accepts international flights from Canada, Mexico, Germany, the U.K., and Spain. There are twice-daily domestic flights on **AeroCaribbean** (© 33/30-9106) from Havana for CUC$108 (US$117/£58).

The hotels all have airport pickup services for clients. If you have not prearranged transportation to your hotel, there are usually a couple of state-owned taxis hanging about. The fare from Aeropuerto Internacional Jardines del Rey is about CUC$8 (US$8.65/£4.30) to Cayo Coco and CUC$14 (US$15/£7.55) to Cayo Guillermo.

BY BUS   If you're traveling independently to the cays from within Cuba, getting there on your own without a rental car or legal taxi is complicated. The only bus services that travel across the checkpoint are those belonging to official tour operators, such as **Cubanacán, Cubatur,** and **Havanatur.** All of these operators offer package deals and transportation options to the cays from all of their major operational points, including Havana, Santiago, Varadero, Trinidad, and Ciego de Avila.

A more complicated way to the cays is to take a **Víazul** (© 7/881-1413; www.viazul. com) bus to Ciego de Avila, and then hire a taxi all the way to the cays for CUC$40 to CUC$50 (US$43–US$54/£22–£27). All Víazul buses on the Havana-Santiago route stop in Ciego de Avila. The fare is CUC$30 (US$32/£16) from Havana, and CUC$26 (US$28/£14) from Santiago. Make sure you hire a state cab, as a driver with his own car is still not allowed to transport foreigners to the cays.

BY CAR/TAXI   To drive to the cays, head north out of Ciego de Avila toward the city of Morón, and follow the signs out to the cays. You can pick up a taxi in either Ciego de Avila or Morón, the two nearest cities of note. Call **Turistaxi** (© 335/22-9997 in Ciego de Avila) or **Cubataxi** (© 33/22-3129). A taxi from Trinidad costs CUC$100 (US$108/ £54). One has to pass a guarded checkpoint with a toll each way of CUC$2 (US$2.15/ £1.10) to access the *pedraplén* that bridges the distance between the mainland and the cays.

Getting Around
You won't get very far on foot. The cays are deceptively large, and there's no place to go on foot anyway, unless you want to visit an adjacent hotel. The best way to get around

ACCOMMODATIONS ■
Iberostar Daiquiri **3**
Meliá Cayo Coco **11**
Meliá Cayo Guillermo **2**
NH Krystal Laguna
  Villas & Resort **9**
Sol Cayo Coco **10**
Sol Cayo Guillermo **1**
Tryp Cayo Coco **8**
Villa Cojimar **4**

DINING ◆
Meliá Cayo Guillermo **2**
Las Caletas **11**

ATTRACTIONS ●
Acuavida Centro Spa-Talaso **7**
La Cueva de Jabalí **6**
Parque Natural El Bagá **5**

the cays is by **moped.** Most of the hotels have mountain bikes (free for guests) and mopeds that rent for CUC$20 (US$22/£11) a day.

There is a tourist bus, Jardines del Rey Bus Tour, which makes the entire circuit from one end of Playa Coco to the far end of Playa Guillermo. The bus runs around every 1¹/₂ hours, and costs CUC$5 (US$5.40/£2.70).

All of the hotels can call you a cab, or you can try **Taxi OK** (*©* **33/30-2222**). If you prefer to drive yourself, there are car-rental companies located on both Cayo Coco and Cayo Guillermo, and the majority of the hotels have agencies on the premises. **Havanautos** has an office at Calle Libertad between Honrato del Castillo and Maceo, Ciego de Avila (*©* **33/21-2570**); **Cubacar** has an office at the bus terminal in Ciego de Avila (*©* **33/22-5105**) and in the Hotel Morón in Morón (*©* **33/50-2028**); **Micar** has agencies in Ciego de Avila (*©* **33/26-6169**). All have operational centers on Jardines del Rey, with desks at most of the major hotels. Due to high demand and isolation, rates are relatively expensive on the cays, about CUC$80 to CUC$100 (US$86–US$108/£43–£54) per day for a standard four-door vehicle. You're sometimes better off renting a car in Ciego de Avila or another city before traveling to the cays.

Papa & the Cayos

Ernest Hemingway's love of sailing and deep-sea fishing is well documented, a great source of his love affair with Cuba. The novelist was one of the first to explore Cayo Guillermo; in the '30s and '40s, Hemingway used to set sail off the coasts of the northern cays in dogged pursuit of marlin and swordfish in the Atlantic. The celebrated beach on Cayo Guillermo, Playa Pilar, is even named for the author's beloved fishing boat, *Pilar*. In an episode befitting his he-man, roguish character, Hemingway enlisted his crew and boat to hunt for Nazi submarines off Cuba's northern cays at the height of World War II (according to some, the island was awash with Nazi sympathizers and agents). Papa's companion was, as ever, Gregorio Fuentes, the model for the aged fisherman in *The Old Man and the Sea*.

In Hemingway's novel *Islands in the Stream*, the main character looks longingly across the bay at Cayo Guillermo, asking rhetorically, "See how green she is and full of promise?" Evidently the Cuban authorities, intent on developing the cays a half century after Hemingway first explored them, feel the same way.

All the hotels offer a variety of **organized excursions,** either directly or through tour representatives, which transport guests by bus or minibus from one cay to the other, or to other destinations, such as Playa Pilar on Cayo Guillermo. You're probably just as well off using whatever operator is working out of your hotel, or you can call **Cubanacán** (© **33/30-1225**), **Cubatur** (© **33/30-1029**), or **Havanatur** (© **33/30-1371**) to set something up.

Orientation

Banco Financiero Internacional (© **33/30-1252**) has several branches on the cays. For medical attention, go to **Clínica Internacional Cayo Coco** (© **33/30-8150**), next to the Villa Gaviota on Cayo Coco.

Several of the hotels have Internet access for their guests. International and domestic mail can be handled at any of the hotels.

WHAT TO SEE & DO

Cayo Coco is the better known of the two cays, probably due to its earlier development. The best-known **Cayo Coco beaches** ★★ are **Playa Larga** and **Playa Colorada; Playa Los Flamencos,** a few kilometers west, is a slightly more isolated and quieter beach, and beyond this is **Playa Prohibida.** Together, they're among the most stellar beaches to be found in all of Cuba. In the interior of the cay are lagoons and marshlands, havens for the local bird and animal populations.

Cayo Guillermo is connected to Cayo Coco by a 15km (9-mile) *pedraplén*. **Cayo Guillermo beaches** ★★ (**Playa El Paso, Playa del Medio,** and **Playa Larga**) are every bit as spectacular as those on Cayo Coco; in fact, at low tide, the crystal-clear waters are so shallow that you can comfortably wade out several hundred meters, making them preferable to the beaches on Cayo Coco for many guests. The landscape is very similar to Cayo Coco, but Guillermo boasts the most spectacular beach of either cay, and per- **217** haps the entire northern coastline: **Playa Pilar ★★★**, long ago explored by Ernest Hemingway and today a popular day trip for hotel guests on both cays.

Diving & Other Watersports

With long, pristine stretches of coral reef, and warm, crystal-clear waters, the cays are one of the best diving spots on the planet. There are a couple of dozen dive sites, including five superior sites easily accessible from the cays, which range in depth from 5 to 40m (16–131 ft.). All the hotels on Cayo Coco and Cayo Guillermo can organize diving excursions, but you may wish to directly consult one of the main outfits, like **Blue Diving** (© 33/30-8180 or 33/30-8179), which has a dive center at the Meliá Cayo Coco, right on the beach. They offer certified programs, several dive packages to choose from, international licensing courses, and diving excursions to Playa Santa Lucía and Trinidad. A two-tank dive is CUC$80 (US$86/£43), including equipment.

Most of the hotels have their own catamarans, sailboards, and other vehicles and facilities for watersports; kite surfing and paragliding are also possible. **Cubanacán Náutica** on Cayo Coco (© 33/30-1221 or 33/30-1411) has a wide range of watersports programs, including "seafari" catamaran trips to Paredón Grande, east of Cayo Coco; glass-bottom boat trips out to the coral reef with opportunities for snorkeling; and a complement of kayaks and windsurfing boards. The **Marlin Marina** on Cayo Guillermo (© 33/30-1737/1323) has a six-vessel pier and similar capabilities and facilities, including diving and sportfishing trips. Full-day catamaran trips run about CUC$75 (US$81/£41) per person; half-day trips are CUC$40 (US$43/£22). An hour-long glass-bottom boat trip is just CUC$20 (US$22/£11).

Boat Adventure ★ (© 33/30-1516) offers small speedboat trips (self-driven, with a guide) through a maze of mangrove canals, marshes, and wetlands of Cayo Guillermo, a scenic trip with stops for snorkeling. There are four departures daily; the cost is CUC$41 (US$44/£22) per person.

Organized Tours

All the hotels offer day trips to remote beaches, including the finest in the cays, **Playa Pilar,** as well as **flamingo tours, jeep tours,** and **city tours** by minibus to Morón, Trinidad, and Camagüey, or to Havana and Santiago by plane. Other options include **sugar cane tours** and visits to **Sitio La Güira** (a purpose-built dude ranch). Horseback treks and jeep safaris through the interior of the cays and to Morón are also available. A popular trip is to **Laguna de la Leche ★**, a massive lake on the outskirts of Morón with plenty of pelicans, flamingos, and other native birds. The lake's name comes from the water's murky, milky appearance (caused by limestone deposits). Another, much smaller lake that's worth a visit is **Lago La Redonda,** where you'll find thick mangroves, swamps, and funky woodlands growing out of the still waters. It's best seen by *lancha* (motorboat) tour leaving from the entrance of the little restaurant. On a cruise, you'll see huge spider webs, massive mounds of termites in trees, and thick Spanish moss. Both lakes are most often visited in combination with a city tour of Morón. Consult a tour operator representative from **Havanatur, Cubatur,** or **Cubanacán** in the lobby of any of the hotels for information and current prices.

One of the only true attractions here, aside from the beaches and nature, is the **Parque Natural El Bagá** (© 33/30-1062, ext. 103), an interesting little complex that features a series of nature trails and lookouts through mangroves and litoral forest, and on raised

A Stopover in Morón

Located 37km (23 miles) north of Ciego de Avila, Morón (Moh-*rohn*) is the small gateway city to the cays, and home to most of the 3,500 Cubans who work at the resort hotels. With just a few dusty streets traveled by bicycles, horse-drawn carriages, and antique American autos, charmingly low-key Morón is most notable for its splendid, but dilapidated collection of colonial buildings that line the main street, **Calle Martí.** Most visitors arrive by bus or taxi from Ciego de Avila or Camagüey or on an organized tour from one of the hotels on the Cayos. Though Morón possesses a **Municipal Museum,** Calle Martí 374 (© **33/50-4501;** admission CUC$1/US$1.10/55p) with pre-Columbian artifacts and idols, and an evocative **1920s railway station,** most travelers are content to stroll up and down Martí, absorbing the relaxed local flavor. The town mascot is the cock of Morón, a bronze statue placed at the foot of a clock tower near the Hotel Morón (the cock crows twice daily).

Some visitors decamp to Morón as a less-expensive alternative to the all-inclusive luxury hotels on the cays. By far the best place to stay in town is **La Casona,** Cristóbal Colón 41-C (© **33/50-2236;** fax 33/5-2128), an elegant and beautiful, if simple, small hotel in a yellow colonial manor house. It has seven

platforms over lagoons. There is also a small reconstruction of an ancient indigenous village, with periodic live shows of local actors engaged in re-creations of Taíno dances. (*Parents, be forewarned:* The women in the shows are topless.) A wonderful stretch of beach is also right here. Admission to the whole complex is CUC$25 (US$27/£14).

Time for Some Pampering

Although nowhere near as opulent as many modern spas, the new **Acuavida Centro Spa-Talaso** (© **33/30-215;** www.servimedcuba.com) offers a wide range of massage and spa treatments. Options range from mud baths and seaweed scrubs to full-body massages and a host of water-based treatments. The large facility has five pools in a range of sizes and temperatures. Some are freshwater pools, while others take advantage of the neighboring seawater. There's a salon on the premises, as well as a small medical facility.

WHERE TO STAY & DINE ON CAYO COCO

Almost all visitors to Jardines del Rey come as part of an all-inclusive package and take all their meals at their hotels. If you want to take a break from your hotel fare, check out the simple shack, **Ranchón Playa Prohibida,** located out on Playa Prohibida, where a full lobster meal, with rice and beans and two good-size tails, will run you around CUC$15 (US$16/£8.10). If you're out at Playa Pilar, there's the similar **Ranchón El Pilar** serving similar fare at similar prices.

Very Expensive

Meliá Cayo Coco ★★★ This elegant flagship of the Meliá chain is the top hotel on Cayo Coco and one of the finest hotels in Cuba. Popular with wedding parties and honeymooners, it is now an adults-only resort. The property is hip and stylish enormous but sparsely furnished rooms with extremely high ceilings, marble floors, private bathrooms, and air-conditioning, and the hotel has a family-style restaurant, small pool, and an open-air bar out back. Though rooms could perhaps be a bit better cared for, the hotel is an atmospheric place to crash for CUC$36 (US$39/£19) double occupancy. The large, unattractive, and uninviting **Hotel Morón,** Avenida de Tarafa (© **33/50-2230;** www.islazul.cu), run by Islazul, is a distant second choice. It does have a pool, however. Double rooms cost just CUC$36 to CUC$42 (US$39–US$45/£19–£23).

Easily the best spot for a meal in Morón is **Restaurante-Bar La Fuente,** Calle Martí 169 between Libertad and Ignacio Agramonte (© **33/50-5758**). The upscale and very cute restaurant has original art on the walls and an open central patio and fountain. Focusing on the tourist trade, it serves lots of salads, omelets, and main courses like grilled fish and lobster for CUC$5 to CUC$20 (US$5.40–US$22/£2.70–£11). At night, the essential visit is to the **Casa de la Trova,** Calle Libertad between Narciso López and Martí, for a dose of traditional Cuban tunes.

throughout, chic for an all-inclusive beach hotel. The resort has 76 fantastic bungalow rooms built out over a natural lagoon, separate from the other facilities and very private. Suites and junior suites are huge, with dining tables, inviting screened balconies, and very nice bathrooms. Superior standard doubles on the lagoon have refined decor and unscreened balconies. In this case, we actually prefer the first-floor units, as they have fabulous private balconies close to the lapping water. The rest of the grounds away from the lagoon are nicely landscaped, and rooms in the main part of the hotel are arranged like a tropical village. The hotel's excellent stretch of beach, Playa Las Coloradas, fronts a pretty, protected bay. The hotel's Las Caletas restaurant is a beautiful open-air, tentlike affair built on a dock over the lagoon. An interesting feature on the premises is the Club Cubano, an information center that offers Spanish classes, seminars, dance lessons, and information on Cuban culture. Guests are free to patronize the dance club and other facilities at the Sol Meliá hotel next-door. There's also an open-air theater with nightly entertainment.

Cayo Coco, Jardines del Rey. © **33/30-1180.** Fax 33/30-1195. www.solmeliacuba.com. 250 units. CUC$343–CUC$417 (US$370–US$450/£185–£225) double. Rates are all-inclusive. MC, V. Children under 18 not allowed. **Amenities:** 4 restaurants; snack bar; 4 bars; outdoor pool; 2 lit outdoor tennis courts; fitness center; Jacuzzi; sauna; full-service dive shop; watersports equipment; free bikes; scooter rental; game room; concierge; tour desk; car-rental desk; salon; massage; laundry service. In room: A/C, TV, minibar, hair dryer, safe.

Expensive

NH Krystal Laguna Villas & Resort ★★   One of the newer hotels on the cays and one of the largest in Cuba, this resort is made up of two conjoined complexes, connected by a system of asphalt walkways. The grounds are extensive and chock-full of facilities, including three amphitheaters and a host of restaurants and bars. Half of the rooms are corporate-style blocks, while the others are very attractive, wooden cabinlike casitas built over a natural lagoon. The latter, considered the "villas" here, are the best feature of the hotel, and have living rooms with a sofa bed, two-room bathrooms, high ceilings, and open balconies overlooking the lagoon. The standard rooms are housed in large blocks with an apartment-complex feel, and all are junior suites with a connected sitting room. The beach, hidden behind the lagoon, isn't visible from the property; to get to the sands on Playa Larga, you've got to walk about 5 minutes. The impressive resort was recently taken over by the NH hotel group, and is currently receiving more than $8 million dollars in renovations and improvements.

Cayo Coco, Jardines del Rey. © **33/30-1470.** Fax 33/30-1498. www.nh-hotels.com. 690 units. CUC$130–CUC$190 (US$140–US$205/£70–£103) double; CUC$170–CUC$240 (US$184–US$259/£92–£130) suite; CUC$210–CUC$270 (US$227–US$292/£113–£146) villa. Rates are all-inclusive. Children 2 and under stay for free in parent's room; children 3–12 stay for CUC$35 (US$38/£19) per day in parent's room. MC, V. **Amenities:** 2 restaurants; 2 bars; dance club; 4 outdoor pools; 3 lit outdoor tennis courts; gym; Jacuzzi; dry sauna; free bikes; scooter rental; children's center and programs; game room; concierge; tour desk; car-rental desk; babysitting; laundry service. *In room:* A/C, TV, fridge, hair dryer, safe.

Sol Cayo Coco ★ (Kids)

Yet another of Sol Meliá's hotels on Cayo Coco, this is probably the best-suited hotel on the cay for families. (*Note:* It will be closed for a complete refurbishment May–Oct 2009.) Constructed in 1997, the large hotel has a very relaxed feel. Families make up a great percentage of clients, and the kids' club, minigolf, soccer field, and kid's corner restaurant are tailored to youngsters. It's the only hotel on the cays with two beaches—it sits on a nice expanse of Playa Las Coloradas and also offers guests access to a sensational, secluded section of Playa Larga reached by crossing a bridge over a river to spectacularly limpid, shallow waters. Rooms are a good size, with an airy, beachy feel, and light blue walls, and almost all of them have sea views. The hotel's Nautical Club is one of the largest in Cuba, with more than 10 catamarans and other watersports facilities. The hotel offers all kinds of special packages.

Cayo Coco, Jardines del Rey. © **33/30-1280.** Fax 33/30-1285. www.solmeliacuba.com. 270 units. CUC$283–CUC$319 (US$306–US$345/£153–£172) double. Rates are all-inclusive. Children under 2 stay free in parent's room; children 3–12 stay for half price in parent's room. MC, V. **Amenities:** 4 restaurants; 3 bars; dance club; 2 outdoor pools; 2 lit outdoor tennis courts; gym; Jacuzzi; sauna; watersports equipment; free bikes; scooter rental; children's center and programs; game room; concierge; tour desk; car-rental desk; salon; massage; babysitting; laundry service. *In room:* A/C, TV, minibar, hair dryer, safe.

Tryp Cayo Coco ★★

The granddaddy of all the Cayo hotels is the Tryp Cayo Coco, built in 1996 and restructured and remodeled in recent years. The resort has refurbished smart, cheery double rooms, with red-tile floors, headboards, and mirrors. The rooms are adorned with big, colorful pillows and vibrant tropical paintings above the beds, and all have open-air balconies. Many of the rooms have sea views. The buildings and restaurants are spread out across the extensive, villagelike property. The pool areas are ample, with lots of greenery. There is even a small pond area with some resident flamingos.

Cayo Coco, Jardines del Rey. © **33/30-1300.** Fax 33/30-1386. www.solmeliacuba.com. 508 units. CUC$283–CUC$319 (US$306–US$345/£153–£172) double. Rates are all-inclusive. Children under 2 stay free in parent's room; children 3–12 stay for half price in parent's room. MC, V. **Amenities:** 8 restaurants; 3 bars; dance club; 2 outdoor pools; 3 lit outdoor tennis courts; gym; Jacuzzi; sauna; watersports equipment; dive center; free bikes; scooter rental; children's center and programs; concierge; tour desk; car-rental desk; massage; babysitting; laundry service. *In room:* A/C, TV, fridge, hair dryer, safe.

Very Expensive

Meliá Cayo Guillermo ★★   The fanciest property on Cayo Guillermo, this imposing luxury hotel wraps around the extensive pool area, with several restaurants (including a brand-new buffet restaurant) and bars scattered about the property, including a breezy, open-air grill restaurant down by the beach. The section of beach the hotel fronts is one of the finest on the cays, with thick palm trees sprouting out of pristine white sand. The hotel has a beautiful, long wooden pier that extends out into the surf, where you can venture for total privacy, as well as a couple of shaded hammocks set out in the sea, grazing the shallow waters. Rooms are second only in elegance to the Meliá Cayo Coco, and a recent remodeling has really spruced them up substantially. Suites are very large bungalows with a sitting area, backyard, and Jacuzzi, while junior suites have two rooms and two bathrooms. Rooms sport a beachy decor that is surprisingly informal for a luxury hotel, though it doesn't take away from its abundant comforts. The grounds are lush and luxurious, and feature several lotus gardens.

Cayo Guillermo, Jardines del Rey. ✆ **33/30-1680.** Fax 33/30-1685. www.solmeliacuba.com. 301 units. CUC$343 (US$370/£185) double. Rates are all-inclusive. Children under 2 stay free in parent's room; children 3–12 stay for half-price in parent's room. MC, V. **Amenities:** 3 restaurants; 4 bars; dance club; outdoor pool; 2 lit outdoor tennis courts; fitness center; Jacuzzi; sauna; watersports equipment; dive center; free bikes; scooter rentals; children's center and programs; game room; concierge; tour desk; car-rental desk; salon; massage; babysitting; laundry service. *In room:* A/C, TV, stocked minibar, coffeemaker, hair dryer, safe.

Expensive

Iberostar Daiquirí ★★   This large resort hotel sits on a beautiful section of beach. Run by a Spanish chain, the hotel has several long, three-story blocks constructed around a large pool surrounded by gardens, as well as a host of smaller three-story buildings spread around their ample grounds. The rooms are a good size with modern and tasteful decor, tile floors, and multicolored bedspreads. Every room has either a balcony or terrace. The better rooms have views of the ocean. All the rooms have two full beds, though the suites have queen-size beds and a separate sitting room. The Iberostar has an excellent children's program, and a host of available activity and tour options.

Cayo Guillermo, Jardines del Rey. ✆ **33/30-1650.** Fax 33/30-1641. www.iberostar.com. 312 units. CUC$180 (US$194/£97) double. Rates are all-inclusive. MC, V. **Amenities:** 3 restaurants; 4 bars; dance club; outdoor pool; 2 outdoor tennis courts; gym; sauna; watersports equipment; bike and scooter rental; children's center and programs; game center; concierge; tour desk; car-rental desk; babysitting; laundry service. *In room:* A/C, TV, minibar, hair dryer, safe (for a fee).

Sol Cayo Guillermo ★★   Although its nearby sister, the Meliá Cayo Guillermo, may be a bit swankier, this is still my favorite place to stay on Cayo Guillermo. This well-designed hotel, completely refurbished in 2008, has plenty of personality and a relaxed vibe. All the accommodations are loosely described as bungalows, although there are a few two-story blocks and duplex units here. The rooms are bright and cheery, decorated in sunny yellow and blue beach tones. They have beamed, peaked wooden ceilings, and nice tile-and-marble bathrooms (all with showers only). We especially like the built-in luggage racks made from driftwood. The best rooms are the individual bungalows set close to the beach, although the second-floor superior rooms are also a good bet, with large private balconies equipped with hammocks. The grounds are very nicely designed and maintained, and the beach is a wonderful long stretch of white sand. The hotel is popular with a broad range of travelers, from honeymooners and families to singles and retirees.

Cayo Guillermo, Jardines del Rey. ⓒ **33/30-1760.** Fax 33/30-1748. www.solmeliacuba.com. 268 units. CUC$283 (US$306/£153) double. Rates are all-inclusive. Children under 2 stay free in parent's room; children 3–12 stay for half price in parent's room. MC, V. **Amenities:** 4 restaurants; 4 bars; dance club; outdoor pool; 2 lit outdoor tennis courts; fitness center; Jacuzzi; steam room; watersports equipment; free bikes; scooter rental; children's center and programs; game room; concierge; tour desk; car- and scooter-rental desk; salon; massage; babysitting; laundry service. *In room:* A/C, TV, minibar, coffeemaker, hair dryer, safe.

Moderate

Villa Cojímar The oldest of the four Cayo Guillermo hotels (built in 1992), this Gran Caribe hotel has received some long overdue upgrading in recent years. The rooms are now quite modern and attractive, although overall this hotel still lags far behind the competition in terms of style, facilities, and amenities. That said, it's one of the cheapest options on the cays, it's right on the beach, and the rooms are certainly acceptable. It has rather skimpily manicured grounds, a large central pool area, and a meager open-air theater where dance classes and the nightly show are staged.

Cayo Guillermo, Jardines del Rey. ⓒ **33/30-1712.** Fax 33/30-1725. www.gran-caribe.com. 212 units. CUC$115–CUC$145 (US$124–US$157/£62–£78) double. Rates are all-inclusive. MC, V. **Amenities:** 3 restaurants; snack bar; 3 bars; dance club; nightly show; outdoor pool; 2 outdoor tennis courts; fitness center; watersports equipment; bike and scooter rental; children's club; game room; concierge; tour desk; car-rental desk; massage; babysitting; laundry service. *In room:* A/C, TV, fridge, hair dryer, safe.

Jardines del Rey After Dark

Most folks simply take advantage of the bars and nightly shows at their all-inclusive resorts. The Sol Cayo Coco has one of the largest, most atmospheric, and liveliest dance clubs of the large resorts. Another alternative is the Wednesday night cabaret show at **La Cueva de Jabalí** ★ (ⓒ **33/30-1206**). The show is rather simple and pedestrian, but the setting is quite interesting in the belly of a small underground cave. Admission is CUC$5 (US$5.40/£2.70). The show starts at 10pm and dancing follows. Mosquitoes are sometimes a problem inside the cave, so wear some insect repellent or long-sleeved clothing.

Another alternative is **La Bolera,** a four-lane bowling alley/bar/cabaret near the Meliá Playa Guillermo.

Farther South: Jardines de la Reina

South of Ciego de Avila is the protected pristine chain of islands known as the **Archipiélago de los Jardines de la Reina** ★★. Here, there are hundreds of uninhabited virgin cays, but the real attraction lies under the water with some of the best diving and fishing in the Caribbean. There are some 80 dive sites that offer the possibility of seeing whale sharks, hammerhead sharks, bull sharks, and hawksbill turtles, among others. (Whale shark high season runs Aug–Jan, with the peak months being Oct–Dec.) Anglers can hope to catch an abundance of bonefish, thousands of tarpon, and huge numbers of permit. Other species that can be caught are horse eye jacks, mutton snapper, and silky sharks. There is only one authorized diving and fishing operation based out of Júcaro, south of Ciego de Avila: **Avalon** (www.divingincuba.com and www.avalonfishingcenter. com), which runs 7-day diving packages on three live-aboard boats or the floating hotel, La Tortuga, starting at CUC$1,731 (US$1,869/£935) in low season; and 7-day fishing packages on three live-aboard boats or the floating hotel, La Tortuga, with seven cabins, starting at CUC$3,407 (US$3,680/£1,840) in low season.

553km (344 miles) E of Havana; 110km (68 miles) E of Ciego de Avila; 328km (204 miles) W of Santiago de Cuba

One of Cuba's most historic and important cities, Camagüey is an excellent place to visit to get a feel for Cuba's colonial-era grandeur. Founded as the sixth of Cuba's original seven *villas* in 1514—as a port town originally named Santa María del Puerto del Príncipe—the city was later moved to a different spot by Diego Velázquez himself in 1516 and transplanted again to its present, inland location in 1528. The town didn't receive its final name, which means "Son of the Tree" in the Taíno language, until after the conclusion of the Spanish-American War in 1898.

Camagüey retains a strong colonial imprint, with a highly irregular layout and warren of narrow, bending streets and alleyways, handsome colonial houses, two of the most dignified colonial plazas in Cuba, and an unequaled collection of impressive, if evocatively dilapidated 16th-, 17th-, and 18th-century churches. In fact, Camagüey is often called *la ciudad del Barroco* (city of baroque) or *la ciudad de las iglesias* (city of churches). Another symbol of the city is the *tinajón*, a massive terra-cotta water jug used in the 18th and 19th centuries to collect rainwater. These now largely decorative items can still be seen in the serene gardens and courtyards of the city's colonial houses.

Travelers intent on experiencing the cultural offerings of urban, interior Cuba should not skip Camagüey. The birthplace of Cuba's national poet, Nicolás Guillén, Camagüey claims some of the strongest artistic and literary traditions in Cuba and one of the country's most vital cultural scenes, with an active community of plastics artists and the internationally renowned Camagüey Ballet. Camagüey is also recuperating its distinguished historical character, plowing ahead with invaluable restoration work of the city's classic colonial structures. The 1998 visit of Pope John Paul II gave the city added impetus to refurbish its crumbling set of colonial churches. Yet, it is not just a museum set piece—it's a lively city that explodes with a vibrant cultural life and fiestas. Travelers could conceivably blow through and see the principal attractions in a day, but Camagüey requires at least 2 or 3 days or more to unfurl its significant charms and visit the nearby beaches and ecological attractions.

ESSENTIALS
Getting There

BY PLANE   You can fly from Havana to Camagüey on **Cubana** daily except Tuesday and Saturday for CUC$94 (US$102/£51); there are also international charter flights from Canada. Flights arrive at **Aeropuerto Internacional Ignacio Agramonte,** Carretera Central Nuevitas Km 8 (© **32/26-1889** or 32/26-7276; airport code CMW), 9km (6 miles) west of the city. A local bus runs from the airport to Parque Finlay and back, but a taxi is probably your best bet.

BY BUS   **Víazul** (© **7/881-1413** in Havana, or **32/27-0396** in Camagüey; www.viazul.com) travels daily to Camagüey on the Trinidad–Santiago de Cuba and Havana–Santiago de Cuba lines. From Havana, the bus departs at 8:40am, 9:30am, 3pm, and 10pm, arriving at 5pm, 6:05pm, 11:55pm, and 6:05am, respectively; the fare is CUC$33 (US$36/£18). From Santiago, departure times are 9am, 3pm, and 10pm, arriving at 4:35pm, 10:45pm, and 3:20am; the fare is CUC$18 (US$19/£9.70). From Trinidad, the bus leaves at 8am and arrives at 1:15pm and the fare is CUC$15 (US$16/£8.10).

The main bus terminal for long-distance buses, the **Terminal de Omnibuses** (© 32/27-2601) is located 2km (1¼ miles) southeast of the city, at Carretera Central 180 at the corner of Calle Perú. For buses to locations within Camagüey province, there is a separate **Terminal Municipal** (© 32/28-1525), several blocks north of the old center, near the intersection of Padre Olalla and Avenida Carlos J. Finlay (just north of the railway station).

BY TRAIN Camagüey is on the main Havana–Santiago de Cuba railway line, with nearly a half-dozen daily trains originating in Havana and Santiago de Cuba. Train schedules change frequently, and depending on the season, many trains don't operate on a daily basis; verify the current schedule by calling © 7/861-8540, though it's often better to go in person to the train station and purchase tickets at least a day in advance. Trains arrive in Camagüey from Morón, Santa Clara, and Ciego de Avila as well. The large and busy, local train station (© 32/29-2633) is on Avenida Carlos J. Finlay, across from the Hotel Plaza.

Getting Around

The labyrinthine layout of Camagüey's old town is extremely complicated, though it is pretty compact. The best way to get to know the historic center is on foot. In fact, in and around Camagüey, you will mostly depend on leg power, though taxis may be necessary to get back and forth between a couple of the hotels.

BY TAXI There are a few taxis around town. Call **Cubataxi** (© 32/28-1247) for local and long-distance hire. Bicycle-powered rickshaws also function as taxis around the historic center and are ubiquitous.

BY CAR A car isn't necessary if you are planning to stay put in Camagüey, but if you're looking to go beyond the city, the major car-rental companies are **Havanautos** (© 32/27-2239) and **Cubacar** (© 32/272439); the latter is in the Hotel Plaza and in Parque Casino. There are also company offices in the airport. Rates are about CUC$55 to CUC$80 (US$59–US$86/£30–£43) per day for a standard four-door car.

Orientation

You'll find a **Banco Financiero Internacional** (© 32/29-4846) at Independencia 221, at Plaza de Maceo. It's open Monday through Friday from 8am to 3pm. There is a **CADECA** (© 32/29-5220) at República 353, open Monday to Saturday from 8am to 6pm and Sunday from 8am to 1pm. The above branches are two of the most centrally located ones, but you'll find several other banks and money exchange houses around the city.

If you need medical attention, **Servicios Médicos Internacionales** is located at Ignacio Agramonte 449, opposite the church of La Merced (© 32/33-6370).

An **Etecsa** Telepunto telephone and Internet center is on Calle República 453; it's open daily from 8:30am to 7:30pm. The main branch of **Correos** is at Ignacio Agramonte 461; it's open Monday through Saturday from 7:30am to 8pm.

Most of the major Cuban tour agencies operate several tour desks around Camagüey, and at all the major hotels. **Cubatur** operates at Ignacio Agramonte 421 (© 32/25-4785). **Havanatur** (© 32/28-1564) and **Islazul** (© 32/27-2018) were both moving their offices to unspecified locations at presstime. Cultural promoter **Paradiso** at Ignacio Agramonte 413 (© 32/28-6059; esme@sccm.artex.cu) can arrange trips to see ballet rehearsals and a ballet shoe factory for CUC$5 (US$5.40/£2.70), and a tour of local

Havana

Camagüey

C U B A

To Airport

Av. Carlos J. Finlay

Roosevelt

Lugareño

Santa Rita

O. Primelles

General Gómez

M. Ramos

Plaza de los Trabajadores

Av. de los Mártires

Padre Olalla

E. Varona

F. Céspedes

República

Ignacio Agramonte

Maceo

Marti

Independencia

Cisneros

Luaces

Cristo

Matías Varona

Carretera Central

La Caridad

Río Haibonico

Plaza de la Revolución

Estadio

Av. Ignacio Agramonte

Casino Campestre

Av. de la Libertad

F. Rodríguez

Cuba

0   0.25 mi
0   0.25 km

$ CADECA
C Etecsa
✉ Post office

ACCOMMODATIONS ■
Casa Los Vitrales **21**
Casa Manolo **5**
Casa Manolo Banegas **12**
Casa Xiomara & Rodolfo **6**
Gran Hotel **11**
Hotel Colón **4**
Hotel Plaza **3**

DINING ◆
Don Ronquillo Restaurant **10**
El Ovejito **17**
La Campana de Toledo **22**
Restaurante Isabella **14**
Salón Caribe **11**

ATTRACTIONS ●
Casa de la Trova **19**
Casa Natal del Mayor
 (Ignacio Agramonte) **8**
Casa Natal Nicolás Guillén **13**
Hospital de San Juan de Díos **23**
Iglesia de Nuestra Señora de la Merced **9**
Iglesia de Nuestra Señora del Carmen **16**
Iglesia San Juan de Díos **23**
La Catedral **20**
Museo Provincial General Ignacio Agramonte **2**
Parque Agramonte **18**
Plaza del Carmen **15**
Plaza San Juan de Díos **23**
Teatro Principal **7**
Tifereht Israel Synagogue **1**

artists' studios. It also offers city tours, and courses in dance, singing, design, and ceramics. Trips to the beach also seem to be cheaper with Paradiso at CUC$40 (US$43/£22), including transport and a day pass at one of the hotels.

WHAT TO SEE & DO

Camagüey's *casco histórico* (old quarter) is the primary draw, and most sights of interest are within easy walking distance of its epicenter, just north and west of the Hatibonico River. The historic zone represents one of the largest colonial sectors in Cuba, spread over 300 hectares (741 acres), and Camagüey boasts more than a dozen colonial churches. As in Havana, the office of the city historian is actively engaged in restoring as many of the city's historic buildings as it can manage, and by law, all businesses in the district contribute 2% of their revenues toward the restoration cause.

Parque Agramonte, which occupies the spot where the old Plaza de Armas existed in 1528, shortly after the transfer of the city to its present location, is the best place to get your bearings. In its center is a bronze and pink granite equestrian statue of the most famous citizen of Camagüey, Ignacio Agramonte. Each corner of the park is marked by a tall royal palm, planted to pay tribute to four local martyrs of the struggle for independence, who were executed in the square by Spanish forces for treason. The park is an agreeable spot, with elegant street lamps and marble benches popular with locals. It is flanked by attractive colonial houses, including the **Casa de la Trova** (where live traditional Cuban music can be heard daily), and the early-18th-century **Catedral** on the south side. The church is a good example of the city's ongoing efforts to resurrect neglected historic buildings. Dedicated to Nuestra Señora de la Candelaria, patron saint of Camagüey, the cathedral has been transformed, in the span of less than 3 years, from a dull and uninspiring church to an attractively austere house of worship, showing off beautiful *vigas* (wood ceiling beams).

Calle Maceo, just north of Parque Agramonte, is the city's principal shopping avenue, a busy pedestrian artery stuffed with shops and bars. The other principal reference point of downtown Camagüey is the much-trafficked, but disappointingly pedestrian **Plaza de los Trabajadores (Workers' Square).** On it are two of the city's more important sights: the birth house of Ignacio Agramonte, and the church of La Merced.

Southeast of the historic core, across the unspectacular Hatibonico River, lies **Casino Campestre,** the largest natural city park in Cuba. Inaugurated in 1860, it was transformed into a public park at the beginning of the 20th century. Its tall, shady royal palms, public monuments, and children's attractions make it a favorite with Camagüeyanos. Nearby, on the other side of the Cándido González baseball stadium, is the **Plaza de la Revolución,** a massive but cold square honoring Cuba's revolutionary legends past and present: Agramonte, Che, and Fidel. Pope John Paul II said Mass at this spot in 1998.

The Top Attractions

Casa Natal del Mayor (Ignacio Agramonte)   Ignacio Agramonte y Loynaz, Camagüey's favorite son and the national hero of the independence struggle—known to all as "El Mayor"—was born December 23, 1841, in this pale yellow 18th-century house. Agramonte's birthplace displays classical colonial elements, both baroque and Hispanic-*mudéjar* (Hispanic-Moorish). The house, now a national monument, may interest those with a thirst for Cuban history; others may simply be interested in viewing the lovely carved wooden ceilings upstairs and smattering of period furnishings (only some are original to the house) of an authentic colonial house. A number of artifacts aim to reveal

Agramonte's boyhood life here and his later achievements, with documents including love letters to Amalia Simoni (who would later become his bride), photographs, newspaper accounts of battles, and Agramonte's pistol.

Ignacio Agramonte 459, Plaza de los Trabajadores. (C) **32/29-7116.** Admission CUC$2 (US$1.10/55p). Tues–Sat 10am–5pm; Sun 8am–noon.

Casa Natal Nicolás Guillén   Camagüey's most important literary figure, considered Cuba's national poet, was born in this house, which stands as a simple tribute to his life and enduring work. Guillén, born here in 1902, only lived in the house for 2 years, though he returned to Camagüey after studying law in Havana and worked as a journalist for a local paper. The house now functions primarily as a research and cultural center, with occasional poetry readings and concerts. A smattering of photographs, personal memorabilia, and copies of a handful of poems connect the house to the life and work of Guillén.

Calle Hermanos Agüero 58 (btw. Cisneros and Príncipe). (C) **32/29-3706.** Free admission. Mon–Fri 8am–5pm.

Iglesia de Nuestra Señora de La Merced ★   The most significant structure on the rather plain Plaza de los Trabajadores is this massive, 18th-century brick church, Camagüey's most distinguished and, in its day, the largest in Cuba. A chapel existed on this spot in 1601; the present structure dates to 1748 (it was reconstructed in 1848 and again in 1909 after a fire). To one side of a lush cloister is the old convent, which still houses a rapidly decreasing number of nuns. The church is an eclectic architectural mix. Adorning the ceiling are surprising Art Nouveau murals, added in the 20th century. Also of note are the painted wood, neo-Gothic altar and the **Santo Sepulcro,** a 1762 casket elaborately fashioned from 25,000 silver coins and carried high by eight men during Easter processionals. Down narrow stairs behind the principal altar is a mysterious crypt, the remains of an extensive underground cemetery. Most of it was closed off after fire damage, but six macabre tombs with skeletons remain and are on creepy view alongside a small museum of 18th- and 19th-century objects uncovered at the church.

Av. Agramonte 4 (Plaza de los Trabajadores). (C) **32/29-2783.** You'll have to tip to see the catacombs, as they're padlocked. Free admission to the church. Mon–Sat 8am–1:30am and 3m–5pm; Sun 8am–1am and 4:30–6pm.

Museo Provincial General Ignacio Agramonte   Several blocks north of the historic center of the city, Camagüey's largest and most important museum houses the second-largest collection of paintings in Cuba, bettered only by the Museo de Bellas Artes in Havana. The museum concentrates on Cuban fine arts (from the early 19th c. to contemporary works), but also packs in moderately interesting collections of natural history and archaeology. There is also a selection of decorative arts, including furnishings and porcelain from the colonial and Republican periods. The natural history rooms display native Cuban species, such as sharks, fish, and exotic fauna. These exhibits may be interesting for kids bored with Cuban history and fine art, but you've surely seen better. The building itself is worth a look around, as it features a handsome patio with a wealth of indigenous trees and *tinajones* (large ceramic pots). The museum was closed for much of 2008, but was due to be open by the time this guide went to print.

Av. de los Mártires 2 (btw. Ignacio Sánchez and Rotario). (C) **32/28-2425.** Admission CUC$2 (US$2.15/£1.10) adults, free for children under 12. Mon 1–5pm; Tues–Thurs and Sat 10am–5pm; Fri noon–7pm; Sun 10am–2pm.

Tips   Camagüey's Synagogue

Camagüey has one of the more active, if still tiny, Jewish communities in Cuba, and many Jewish visitors from overseas pay a visit to the city's small synagogue, **Tifereht Israel,** Calle Andrés Sánchez 365, between Capdevila and J. de Agüero, La Vigía (© **32/28-4639**). Inaugurated in 1998, the synagogue serves just a handful of families, and the community is in the process of restoring the small Jewish cemetery in the city, which had suffered from neglect.

Plaza del Carmen ★★ (Finds)   A narrow, pedestrian-only street of pastel-colored colonial row houses opens onto an irregularly shaped square. Renovations have revamped the 18th-century square with street lamps, huge *tinajones* (clay pots used for storing water), and slightly larger-than-life sculptures of locals in various poses of daily work and pleasure by ceramacist Martha Jiménez. The restored spot has done much to uncover a classic Camagüey colonial plaza.

Not long ago, the church and convent at the end of the open square stood roofless, in utter ruins. The baroque-style **Iglesia de Nuestra Señora del Carmen,** which dates to 1825, is now immaculately restored. It is the only church in Camagüey, and indeed in the whole eastern half of Cuba, topped by two towers. The early-19th-century **Monasterio de las Ursalinas (Ursuline Convent)** next-door is now an architectural showpiece distinguished by handsome arches framing the expansive patio. Built in 1829, the convent later became a refuge for hurricane victims and a school for the poor after the sisters transferred their headquarters to Havana. In the years subsequent to the Revolution, it served several purposes; most recently, it was a nondescript warehouse. The building was taken over in 1999 by the city historian's office, and today the convent is an eye-pleasing beauty, well worth a peek inside from the entrance, but the main building is now closed to visitors.

Plaza del Carmen. Daily 24 hr.

Plaza San Juan de Dios ★★★   A national monument and one of the most remarkable colonial relics in Cuba, this elegant and serene square looks like a meticulously designed movie set. Its charms are subtle, but undeniable. The colonial arches, cobblestones, and houses with red-tile roofs and window grilles speak volumes about Camagüey's colonial past. The square, whose present design dates to 1732, holds great significance for Cubans: The body of the national independence war hero Ignacio Agramonte was brought here, after being burned by the Spaniards, for identification in 1873.

On one side of the square are the 17th-century church and hospital of the order of San Juan de Dios. **La Iglesia San Juan de Dios** features a baroque colonial interior with dark-toned woods and the original brick floor. The church adjoins the handsome **Hospital de San Juan de Dios,** established to serve the poor. Padre José Olallo Valdés (1815–89), who furthered that mission, has been beatified by the Catholic Church and is on his way to being made a saint. Off one side of the cloisters are the remains of Agramonte, making the buildings even more of a sacred place for Camagüeyanos. The city now puts on art exhibits, concerts, and historical displays, such as old pharmaceutical objects, in one corner of the hospital. The understated, but noble colonial structure contains a notable courtyard, thick doors, and an elegant wood staircase. Climb the stairs to the tower from which there is a splendid view of all the church belfries spread across the skyline of the *centro histórico*.

Plaza San Juan de Dios. (℃ **32/29-1318.** Admission CUC$1 (US$1.10/55p). Tues–Sat 9am–5pm; Sun 9am–noon.

SHOPPING

You'll find *artesanía* (handicrafts) stands set up on **Plaza San Juan de Dios** Friday through Sunday. Another spot for handicrafts is **Centro/Galería ACAA (Asociación Cubana de Artesanos Artistas),** just off the Plaza de los Trabajadores at Calle Padre Valencia 2 (℃ **32/28-6834**), which features exhibits and sales, including clay and ceramics, with artisans working out back.

If you want to visit an **artist's studio,** we highly recommend the work of the amiable husband-wife team Joel Jover and Ileana Sánchez. Their home studio is Calle Martí 154, on the north side of Parque Agramonte (℃ **32/29-2305;** jover@pprincipe.cult.cu). They also have a gallery on Plaza San Juan de Dios (**Finds**). Another well-known and very welcoming artist is Oscar Rodríguez Lasseria, a talented **ceramicist** whose studio is on Calle Luis A Varona (Vista) 420, between Alfredo Adán and 25 de Julio (℃ **32/28-1400** or 32/28-6909; lasseri@pprincipe.cult.cu), a bit removed from the *centro* in La Vigía district. Oscar conducts invitational seminars with ceramics artists from around the world. *Note:* If you purchase any artworks in Camagüey, you'll need to take them to the **Registro de Bienes Culturales** (℃ **32/29-1388**) to get official permission and documentation to export them from Cuba. The local office is situated on the second floor of the old hospital on Plaza San Juan de Dios; it's open Monday through Saturday from 8:30am to 1pm; fees vary.

Check out the **Casa del Tabaco** in the Galería Colonial, Ignacio Agramonte 406 (℃ **32/28-3944**), for a fine selection of Cuban cigars. The gentleman in the shop is very willing to educate customers about the fine art of Cuban tobacco. He'll tell you that Fidel used to smoke a Cohiba Lancero (which goes for about CUC$350/US$378/£189 a box).

Pick up CDs and tapes of Cuban music at any **ARTex** shop. Perhaps the best one is within the Casa de la Trova, on Calle Cisneros (℃ **32/29-1357**). Other branches are on República 38 and Ignacio Agramonte 109. Those interested in Cuban memorabilia, stamps, and coins should drop in at Ignacio Agramonte 433 between Lopez Recio and Independencia.

WHERE TO STAY

Camagüey has an appealing supply of attractive and affordable hotels—most owned and operated by the Cuban Islazul chain—and several have undergone extensive restorations that have brought back their old-world charm. For visitors interested in homestays, the city also provides a host of excellent private accommodations.

Moderate

Gran Hotel ★ Camagüey's most classic hotel dates from 1939. Its clubby, old-world feel is accentuated by an abundance of watering holes—this midsize hotel has four bars, including the Piano Bar, a great dark place that's one of the best cocktail lounges in Cuba. Another good bar is the spot on the rooftop. There's more to the Gran Hotel than places to wet your whistle, though. It has a medium-size terrace pool that features a nightly show that's part water ballet; a pretty triangular patio with a fountain; a top-floor restaurant with panoramic views; and a handsome, breezy lobby with an old elevator of beautiful wood, and displays of local art and handicrafts. The rooms are nicely appointed and have high ceilings and small TVs. A handful of corner "special" rooms (nos. 1 and 7 on each floor) are the prize, though; they are larger, with separate, but small, sitting rooms and handsome dressers. A few interior rooms on each floor have no windows to speak of.

Maceo 67 (btw. General Gómez and Ignacio Agramonte), Camagüey. © **32/29-2093.** Fax 32/29-3933. www.islazul.cu. 72 units. CUC$52–CUC$58 (US$56–US$63/£28–£31) double. Rates include buffet breakfast. MC, V. **Amenities:** Restaurant; cafeteria; 4 bars; nightly show; small outdoor pool. *In room:* A/C, TV, safe.

Inexpensive

Recommended *casas particulares* include **Casa Manolo Banegas** ⓕ**inds** , Calle Independencia 251, between Hermanos Agüero and General Gómez (© **32/29-4606**), a gorgeous first-floor flat stuffed with objets d'art, including an ancient Rigonda Bolshoi radio and quite possibly the largest hat stand in the world. The rooms are lovely; the first has a large bronze bed and the second has two large beds and white furniture. Both have private bathrooms, although, as it is a colonial house, they are not en suite. A wraparound balcony and its great central location complete the appeal. **Casa Manolo,** Santa Rita 18, between República and Santa Rosa (© **32/29-4403;** yohsbany@hotmail.com), is run by a friendly, welcoming household and has two bedrooms with en-suite bathrooms; one is larger with a bathtub, the other with shower. **Casa Xiomara & Rodolfo,** Oscar Primelles 615, between Lugareño and San Ramón (© **32/28-1948;** cubarentur@gmail.com), has an amazingly large and well-equipped apartment that's a very nice option for two couples or a family traveling together. **Casa Los Vitrales,** Calle Avellaneda 3, between General Gómez and Martí (© **32/29-5866;** requejobarreto@gmail.com), is a centrally located *casa* run by a very helpful family. The rooms are spacious and quiet and the breakfasts are very filling.

Hotel Colón ★ ⓥ**alue** Having undergone a massive face-lift, this midsize hotel is now one of the best options in Camagüey. Opened in 1927 by Catalan owners, the lobby—decorated with colorful glazed tiles, columns, and a marble staircase—features a handsomely restored, antique dark-wood bar. The rooms, many of which are set around a pretty open-air colonial patio, have also been redone. Though some of the rooms are smaller than those at the Hotel Plaza (see below), they are very clean and have high ceilings, colorful tile floors, fairly elegant appointments, and nice bathrooms. The five "matrimonial" rooms at the back off the patio on the second floor are the largest and have queen-size beds, though they are the same price as all other rooms. Other rooms off the long, airy hallway that leads to the street are less appealing and only have either two or three twin beds. The rooms at the end of the hallway—nos. 201 and 235—do have small balconies overlooking the street, though, and they're larger than others along the hall. However, with these two, street noise from Camagüey's main artery below could be an issue. The open-air grill restaurant in the patio is a good place for a bite to eat. The lobby bar, though, should be your last stop of the evening; it's a splendid spot for a *mojito*.

Calle República 472, Camagüey. © **32/28-3346.** www.islazul.cu. 48 units. CUC$38–CUC$44 (US$41–48/£21–£26) double. Rates include continental breakfast. MC, V. **Amenities:** Restaurant; bar. *In room:* A/C, TV, safe.

Hotel Plaza ⓥ**alue** This character-filled place is directly across from the train station. Built in 1907, it's a little funky, but oddly cool for the right kind of traveler—one who values uniqueness over strict adherence to hotel standards. The lobby has two welcoming bars; one is chilly with air-conditioning, while Bar Pergola has high ceilings, glowing green light from skylights, and slow-moving ceiling fans. The main restaurant, El Dorado, is, surprisingly enough, almost elegant. Each of the 67 large rooms is different, with sizes and shapes determined by the structure of the building. Most are newly refurbished, with new furniture, tile floors, and new, but tiny TVs. Try to get a room with a private balcony on the north- or west-facing side of the building; although rooms on the interior, with views of the patio, are quieter than those facing the street, but they do suffer from bar noise. The most unusual option is no. 221, from which the first radio transmission in Cuba was broadcast in 1924; the original microphone is in the room along with photographs on the walls.

Van Horne 1 (btw. República and Avellaneda), Camagüey. ℭ **32/28-2457.** www.islazul.cu. 67 units. CUC$32–CUC$38 (US$35–US$41/£17–£21) double. Rates include continental breakfast. MC, V. **Amenities:** Restaurant; 24-hr. cafeteria; 2 bars; car-rental desk. *In room:* A/C, TV, safe.

WHERE TO DINE

In addition to the places listed below, **Café Callejón de la Soledad** (ℭ **32/29-1961**) is an atmospheric outdoor cafe on a cobblestone alley, just beside the 18th-century Iglesia de Nuestra Señora de la Soledad.

Don Ronquillo Restaurant ★ CRIOLLA Tucked back in the Galería Colonial, this upscale colonial-style restaurant is one of the best in town. The restaurant has a breezy feel, lemon-yellow walls, and mural paintings at either end. The menu offers a nice assortment of well-prepared dishes, including breaded shrimp, chicken *cordon bleu*, and a juicy steak "Mayoral" in a red-wine sauce. Unusual for a Cuban restaurant outside of Havana or the beach resorts, it has a pretty decent wine selection.

In Galería Colonial, Calle Ignacio Agramonte 406 (btw. República and Lopez Recio). ℭ **32/28-5239.** Main courses CUC$6–CUC$12 (US$6.50–US$12/£3.25–£6.25). No credit cards. Daily noon–9:30pm.

El Ovejito ★ (Finds) CRIOLLA Set just off the quaint little Plaza del Carmen, this restaurant specializes in lamb dishes, hence the name "Little Lamb." Heavy wooden tables and wood and rough-cowhide chairs are spread through several rooms of this lovingly restored home dating to 1827. There are huge, soaring arched wooden doorways and several ceramic murals by Oscar Lasseria on the walls. When the weather permits, grab one of the several tables under large canvas umbrellas on the cobblestone plaza in front of the restaurant. The house special is a roasted leg of lamb, stuffed with bacon and carrots and served with a thick and tasty red sauce. There are several other meat dishes on the menu.

Plaza del Carmen, Calle Hermanos Agüero 152, btw. Onda and Carmen. ℭ **32/24-2498.** Reservations recommended. Main courses CUC$2.10–CUC$6.65 (US$2.25–US$7.20/£1.15–£3.60) No credit cards. Daily noon–9:40pm.

La Campana de Toledo ★ CRIOLLA Although it's a tad touristy, this elegantly rustic restaurant still ranks as the city's most enjoyable dining experience. The gorgeously restored, 18th-century house has a lovely patio with great shade trees and several tables out by the aged bell (which gives the restaurant its name). The well-prepared dishes go beyond the standard offerings: Try *picadillo a la Habanera* (beef hash), the house specialty; *boliche mechado*, beef stuffed with fatty bacon and served with French fries; a dish of rice and beans; or choose from among a number of salads and grilled fish. Service is excellent. The restaurant is most popular for lunch, but at night, the patio is illuminated and the square is wonderfully quiet.

San Juan de Dios 18 (btw. Ramón Pinto and Padre Olallo), Plaza San Juan de Dios. ☎ **32/28-6812.** Reservations recommended. Main courses CUC$4.20–CUC$18 (US$4.55–US$20/£2.25–£9.80). MC, V. Daily 11am–10pm.

Restaurant Isabella ★ (Value) ITALIAN   This new restaurant is the first state restaurant in Cuba to show any modern artistic flair. Named in honor of local actress Isabel Santos, the restaurant is a whirl of visual excitement. Royal blue director's chairs imprinted with famous names on the backs sit smartly around glass-topped tables. Film posters line the wall at one end, while old film reels hang on the other. There's low metallic lighting and set lights creating a suitably filmic ambience. If this isn't enough to entice you inside, the pizzas are huge and thin, don't scrimp on the ingredients, and are a good value. If pizza isn't your thing, choose from the director's clapboard menu, which lists spaghettis, pastas, and lasagna.

Calle Ignacio Agramonte btw. Independencia and Lopez Recio. ☎ **32/22-1540.** Main courses CUC$2–CUC$8 (US$2.15–US$8.65/£1.10–£4.30). Daily 11am–10pm.

Salón Caribe ★ (Value) INTERNATIONAL/CRIOLLA   This sophisticated, top-floor restaurant of Camagüey's coolest hotel has panoramic views of the city. Surprisingly elegant, it has large, faux-crystal chandeliers, large mirrors, cool breezes, and black-and-white tile floors. During the day, there's lunch a la carte with a variety of soups, fish, and Creole fried chicken; there's also a good-value buffet dinner for CUC$12 (US$13/£6.48).

In the Gran Hotel, Maceo 67 (btw. General Gómez and Ignacio Agramonte). ☎ **32/29-2314.** Main courses CUC$3.50–CUC$7.50 (US$3.80–US$8.10/£1.90–£4.05). MC, V. Daily noon–3pm and 7–10pm.

CAMAGÜEY AFTER DARK

There's a Cartelera Cultural board with weekly events listings posted in a building at 432 Ignacio Agramonte or consult the Cartelera Cultural page at www.pprincipe.cult.cu.

Built in 1850, the neoclassical **Teatro Principal,** Padre Valencia 64, between Tatán Mendéz and Lugareño (☎ **32/29-3048**), is an elegant showpiece with a grand marble staircase and chandeliers. The theater often showcases the distinguished **Ballet de Camagüey** ★★. Camagüey's **Casa de la Trova** ★★, Salvador Cisneros 171 (☎ **32/29-1357**), is one of the liveliest in Cuba, with good bands and great local crowds. It's open Tuesday through Thursday from noon to 6pm and 9pm to midnight; Friday and Saturday from noon to 6pm and 9pm to 1am; and Sunday from 11am to 4pm and 9pm to 1am. Admission is CUC$3 (US$3.25/£2.70) and includes CUC$2 (US$2.15/£1.10) worth of drinks.

El Oriente

Prior to the 1959 Revolution, the eastern half of Cuba was a single province, straightforwardly called El Oriente, or the East. Most Cubans still refer to everything east of Camagüey—a region much more scenically and historically interesting than most of central Cuba—as El Oriente, even though it is now composed of the distinct provinces of Holguín, Granma, Santiago de Cuba, and Guantánamo. The region is less known and visited than the western half of Cuba, but every bit as rewarding for travelers (and perhaps more so). The farther east you go, the more emphatically Caribbean it feels. The region's remarkable landscapes include the north coast's exuberant banana and coconut groves, densely wooded peaks of the Sierra Maestra, and tropical rainforest on the east coast.

The wars of independence began in El Oriente in the 1860s, and nearly a century later, Castro concentrated his power base in the inaccessible **Sierra Maestra.** Quiet but dignified **Bayamo,** which played a pivotal role in Cuba's revolutionary struggles, is the capital of Granma province. The gorgeous beaches of **Guardalavaca,** part of Holguín province, make it the fastest-growing resort area in Cuba, while tiny, remote **Baracoa,** where Columbus first dropped anchor at the extreme northeastern edge of Guantánamo, is one of the most beautiful, rugged spots on the island. The former capital city of the Spanish colony, **Santiago de Cuba,** is not only known as a vibrant musical center, but also as the cradle of the Revolution; see chapter 11 for full coverage of Cuba's "Second City."

Note: The eastern end of Cuba was especially hard hit from Hurricanes Gustav and Ike in September 2008. More than 100,000 people were evacuated from Guantánamo province, including the popular tourist spot of Baracoa, where communications were still down in late September. In Holguín, the main areas affected were Banes and Gibara. Call before arriving to confirm that your *casa particular* or hotel is open.

1 GUARDALAVACA ★★

56km (35 miles) N of Holguín; 190km (118 miles) NW of Santiago de Cuba; 258km (160 miles) NE of Camagüey

Guardalavaca's rural and somnolent past is reflected in the resort's poetic name, which literally means "watch the cow." Though today the moniker evokes a pastoral setting that hardly seems consistent with the coterie of full-fledged, all-inclusive resort hotels that gaze out over some of the finest beaches in Cuba. Guardalavaca remains charmingly low-key. However, it is one of the hottest destinations on the island.

Guardalavaca is both a bucket-term for a series of neighboring beaches north of Holguín and the namesake for one small town and specific beach. Guardalavaca is the finest, and really the only resort area in the eastern half of the island. Guardalavaca's appeal is its stunning, three-stripe canvas of intensely green tropical vegetation, stone-white sand, and pristine turquoise seas well protected by coral reefs.

Christopher Columbus first sailed around the coast at Guardalavaca, landing just to the west at the Bay of Bariay in late 1492. He declared it "the most beautiful land that

Tips **When Not to Come to Guardalavaca**

The month of May in Guardalavaca is heavy with tropical rains, as is the early part of June. August is sweltering and too humid for all but the most committed sun worshipers.

human eyes have ever seen." Columbus may have been given to hyperbole, repeatedly touting the unrivaled virtues of the places where he dropped anchor, but his assessment of Guardalavaca remains pretty accurate. The area was originally home to several indigenous groups, and today it is recognized as Cuba's archaeological capital, primarily for the discovery of the 15th-century Arawakan Indian village and burial site near Guardalavaca, one of the most important pre-Columbian sites in the Caribbean. The *bohíos* (thatched-roof huts) that dot the thickly wooded hills still evoke a sense of Caribbean discovery more than 500 years later.

The town of Guardalavaca remains a dusty country backdrop to the resort hotels that now dwarf it. The foundations of Guardalavaca's resort development were laid in the late 1970s: Fidel Castro himself inaugurated the first hotel here, swimming laps in its large square pool. "Guardalavaca" now denotes not only the eponymous town and beach, but is also used to refer to the entire resort, strung along several nearby beaches and continuing to expand. Playa Esmeralda and Playa Pesquero (also known as Costa Verde) are the two newest and most exclusive beaches to be developed.

The backdrop to the beaches is a bucolic region thick with sugar-cane fields, grazing cattle, and luxuriant, rolling hills sprinkled with royal palms. The zone is being touted as an ecotourist paradise; in addition to scuba diving at a dozen dive sites, hiking, biking, and horseback-riding trips are primed to take off in the near future. A dozen nature preserves, including one declared a UNESCO World Biosphere Reserve, dot the region. Side trips from Guardalavaca are easy to arrange.

ESSENTIALS
Getting There
BY PLANE The gleaming **Aeropuerto Internacional Frank País,** Carretera Central Vía Bayamo Km 11.5 (© **24/46-8148;** airport code HOG), is about 70km (43 miles) south of Guardalavaca, and 14km (8¼ miles) south of Holguín, the provincial capital. The airport is about an hour from hotels in and around Guardalavaca. Both national and direct international flights from Canada and Germany (via **Air Canada, Air Transat, LTU,** and various package charters) arrive at the airport here. The main domestic carriers are **Cubana** (© **24/42-5707** in Holguín, or 7/834-4446 in Havana; www.cubana.cu) and **AeroCaribbean** (© **24/46-8556** in Holguín, or 7/879-7524 in Havana; www.aerocaribbean.com), which offer three daily flights between them from Havana. Flights cost from CUC$104 to CUC$110 (US$112–US$119/£56–£59) each way.

The hotels all have airport pickup services (buses and minibuses) for clients. If you have not prearranged transportation to your hotel, there are usually a couple of state-owned taxis hanging about. Rates run between CUC$30 and CUC$35 (US$32–US$38/£16–£19).

BY BUS Víazul (© **24/46-1036** in Holguín, or 7/881-1413 in Havana; www.viazul.com) travels to Holguín on its Havana-Santiago and Trinidad-Santiago (3 times daily)

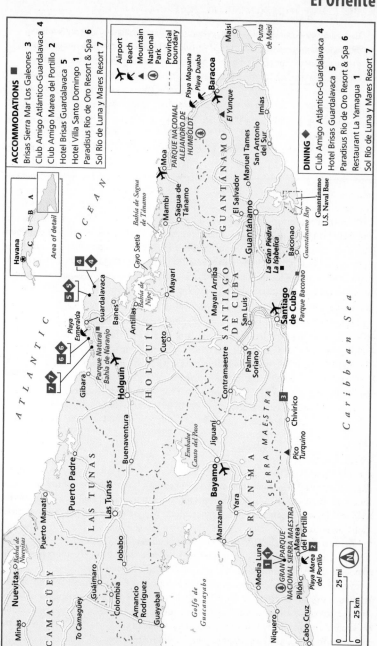

ACCOMMODATIONS ■

Brisas Sierra Mar Los Galeones **3**
Club Amigo Atlántico-Guardalavaca **4**
Club Amigo Marea del Portillo **2**
Hotel Brisas Guardalavaca **5**
Hotel Villa Santo Domingo **1**
Paradisus Rio de Oro Resort & Spa **6**
Sol Rio de Luna y Mares Resort **7**

✈ Airport
⏣ Beach
▲ Mountain
⚫ National Park
‒ ‒ ‒ Provincial boundary

DINING ◆

Club Amigo Atlántico-Guardalavaca **4**
Hotel Brisas Guardalavaca **5**
Paradisus Rio de Oro Resort & Spa **6**
Restaurant La Yamagua **1**
Sol Rio de Luna y Mares Resort **7**

(Tips) **Day Trips to Guardalavaca**

The relatively expensive all-inclusive hotels pretty much have a lock on the splendid beaches around Guardalavaca. If you would like to visit the beaches and spend the day there without paying for the privilege of sleeping at one of the hotels, you can design a day trip from Holguín if you have a rental car. (*Note:* If you don't have your own wheels and have to take a taxi, the cost could equal the cost of staying in one of the less-expensive all-inclusive hotels, and you'd have to travel 1¹/₂ hr. back to your hotel in Holguín, making it hardly worth the effort.) The major hotels sell day passes, generally from CUC$40 to CUC$70 (US$43–US$76/£22–£38), that allow you to use the facilities, including pool and beaches, and eat and drink all you wish.

lines. From Havana, the buses depart at 9:30am, 3pm, and 10pm, and arrive at 10:45pm, 3:20am, and 9:55am, respectively; the fare is CUC$48 (US$52/£26). From Trinidad (© 41/99-4448), the bus leaves at 8am and arrives in Holguín at 4:45pm; the fare is CUC$26 (US$28/£14). From Santiago, departures are at 9am and 3:15pm, arriving at 1:25pm and 6:40pm, respectively; the fare is CUC$12 (US$13/£6.50). The main bus station in Holguín is located on Carretera Central between 20 de Mayo and Independencia (© 24/42-2111), just west of downtown.

BY CAR/TAXI   The easiest way to get to Guardalavaca, if you don't have a prearranged bus service to take you from the airport, is by rental car or state-owned taxis, such as **Taxi OK** (© 24/43-0243). Getting from the airport, through the city of Holguín, and out onto the highway to Guardalavaca is quite confusing. One of the best ways to navigate it is to hire a local tout for a few dollars to ride with you until you're on your way.

Guardalavaca's beauty and proximity to areas of interest, including Baracoa, make it one of the better areas in Cuba to rent a car for some regional sightseeing. Car-rental agencies in Holguín include **Cubacar** (© 24/46-8217, ext. 116), and **Transgaviota** (© 24/43-4996). Almost all of these have desks at the airport, as well as at one or more beach resorts. Car rentals average from CUC$45 to CUC$80 (US$49–US$86/£24–£43) per day for a standard economy car.

Getting Around

Playa Guardalavaca is small enough that you can easily walk from any of the hotels here to the La Roca dance club and the restaurants in town. Playa Esmeralda is about 3km (1³/₄ miles) from Guardalavaca, a manageable walk. The rest of the beaches and attractions are quite far.

The best way to get around the beaches of Guardalavaca is by **bicycle** (if you're feeling fit) or **moped** *(moto)*. Most of the hotels have mountain bikes (free for guests) and mopeds that rent for around CUC$25 (US$27/£14) a day.

Any of the hotels can arrange a taxi for side trips in the area. You can also call directly **Cubataxi** (© 24/46-1895) or **Taxi OK** (© 24/46-1212) on Playa Guardalavaca. All the hotels also offer excursions either directly or through tour operator representatives.

Each of the major hotels has representatives of one or more car-rental agencies on the premises. You could also contact **Cubacar** (© 24/46-8217, ext. 116 in Holguín; or © 24/43-0389 on Playa Guardalavaca), or **Transgaviota** (© 24/43-4966 in Guardalavaca, or © 24/46-8421 at the Frank País airport).

a hop-on/hop-off service in the area. The fare is CUC$5 (US$5.40/£2.70) for the day.

Orientation

The best sources of visitor information are the hotels themselves and the representatives of the major tour operators (Havanatur, Cubatur, and Cubanacán) that operate out of the hotels.

Currency exchange and **postal services** are available at any of Guardalavaca's hotels. Most of the large resort hotels have **Internet access** for their guests.

For medical assistance, contact **Clínica Internacional,** Calle 2 no. 15, Playa Guardalavaca (𝒞 24/43-0291). It has a pharmacy on the premises; pharmacies are also located in the **Paradisus Río de Oro** hotel (p. 239), Hotel Costa Verde, Hotel Occidental Grand Playa Turquesa, and Hotel Playa Pesquero.

WHAT TO SEE & DO

Most folks come here on all-inclusive packages, and many are content to spend their entire time in a chaise longue on the beach or beside the pool. However, a wide range of tours and activities are available for the more active.

Beaches, Diving & Other Watersports

The spectacular beaches around Guardalavaca are this resort area's main attraction. Tracing the coast are more than 1,200km (746 miles) of pure white beaches lined by royal palm trees, framed by exuberant vegetation, and fronting some of the clearest, most inviting waters of Cuba. The best beaches are **Esmeralda, Pesquero, Yuraguanal,** and **Guardalavaca**—all of which have major hotels lining them—and small **Don Lino.** Many of the beaches are long and wide expanses of sand, but the jagged coastline is also peppered with tiny coves that are nearly private. Near the gentle arc of Esmeralda is a series of tiny cove beaches that in practice are almost exclusively for the guests of the Paradisus Río de Oro hotel (p. 239).

Guardalavaca has a dozen excellent dive sites, including Boca de las Esponjas (Mouth of Sponges), El Salto (the Waterfall), and El Cañón de los Aguajies (Grouper Canyon), and is well-known for its abundant and vibrant sponges. Near Guardalavaca is a group of submerged caves, Los Tanques Azules, which are popular with experienced divers. **Eagle Ray** (𝒞 24/43-0316; sales_nautica@guard.gvc.cyt.cu) and **Coral Reef Scuba Diving Center** (𝒞 24/43-0185) are on Playa Guardalavaca, and **Sea Lovers Scuba Diving Center** (𝒞 24/43-0060) is on Playa Esmeralda. They offer dive packages, underwater camera rental, and diving gear rental. Certification programs are also provided, with several dive packages; a single dive costs CUC$35 to CUC$45 (US$38–US$49/£19–£24).

The most popular watersports are sailing, kayaking, wind surfing, canoeing, and pedal boating. Most of the hotels have their own catamarans and other vehicles and facilities for watersports. **Marina Internacional Puerto de Vita** (𝒞 24/43-0491 or 24/43-0446) operates catamaran cruises around the coral reef beyond the cays for either a half- or full day. **Cubanacán Náutica** (𝒞 24/43-0491) has a wide range of watersports programs, including "seafaris" with snorkeling to Playa Pesquero, and yacht rentals for sportfishing.

Parque Natural Bahía de Naranjo

The **Bahía de Naranjo,** about 5km (3 miles) west of Guardalavaca, is a 1,000-hectare (2,471-acre) nature park of mangrove swamps and thickly wooded wilderness. Within the park, visitors can hike along trails and take boat rides. There are plenty of man-made attractions to round out the more ecologically oriented offerings. The **aquarium** at Cayo Naranjo, a sliver of an island reached by boat, isn't really a large-scale aquarium in the traditional sense; it's part of a *parque recreativo* (tourist complex), but it does feature tropical fish as well as a daily marine show at noon and, best of all, an opportunity to swim with dolphins for CUC$99 (US$107/£53). While we are normally fairly appalled by the conditions of most dolphin attractions, including others around Cuba, this place has some of the largest natural ocean pens you'll find anywhere. You'll also find rodeo, watersports, horseback riding, and a seafood restaurant with an Afro-Cuban show. The park is open daily from 7am to 4pm. The best way to visit is by organized excursion, offered by all the beach hotels; most packages are CUC$99 (US$107/£53) per person and include transportation, admission, and a dolphin swim.

On Dry Land

One of the most popular activities on dry land here is **horseback riding.** There's plenty of wide-open terrain and wonderful sea views to be enjoyed. However, be sure to bring plenty of sunscreen as protection from the often-brutal sun here. Most hotels can arrange a riding excursion for you. There are stables in front of Hotel Club Amigo Guardalavaca (© **24/43-0780**), or you can contact Gaviota's **Centro Hípico Playa Esmeralda** equestrian center (© **24/43-0433**) and sign up for an organized horseback excursion.

Banes

A slow-moving, dusty little town about 30km (19 miles) southeast of Guardalavaca, Banes is best known for its unlikely association with the towering figures of 20th-century Cuba. Fulgencio Batista, whose government the rebels deposed in 1959, was born here in 1901. Fidel Castro and his brother, Raúl, were born nearby in Birán. The hotels and tour operators in Guardalavaca arrange guided excursions to Banes, though if you wish to go independently, you could easily do so by rented moped or taxi.

Fidel married the daughter of the conservative mayor of Banes in 1948 at the small **Iglesia de Nuestra Señora de la Caridad,** on a plaza at the edge of the park. (They divorced 6 years later.) Of perhaps greater significance in town is the **Museo Indocubano** ★, Av. General Marreo 305 (© **24/48-2487**), specializing exclusively in Cuba's pre-Columbian history. Its collection is among the best in Cuba; among the 20,000 or so items, exhibits include fragments of ceramics, jewelry, tools, and a valuable 13th-century gold "idol of Banesa," just 4cm (1½ in.) high. The museum is open Tuesday through Saturday from 9am to 5pm, and Sunday from 8am to noon; admission is CUC$1 (US$1.10/55p).

Tucked into the hills of the Banes zone are 96 archaeological sites from the Native American groups that once populated the area. **Museo El Chorro de Maíta (Maíta's Stream Museum)** ★, Cerro de Yaguajay (© **24/43-0421**), represents the largest and most important discovery of a Native American cemetery in Cuba. The community dates from 1490 to 1540. The burial ground contains the remarkably well-preserved remains of 108 Taíno men, women, and children (62 are on display), including a single Spaniard, most likely a friar, whose body is marked by a cross. A *cacique* (tribal chief), lying in a fetal position, is distinguished by a copper medal placed on his shin. Several skulls are deformed, the result of a beautification practice that involved applying two pieces of wood to the head with ropes. Found among the remains were Spanish ceramics and jewelry and objects crafted from gold, copper, coral, and quartz; many are displayed in cases. The museum is open Monday through Friday from 9am to 5pm and Sunday 9am to 1pm. Admission is CUC$2 (US$2.15/£1.10); it's CUC$1 (US$1.10/55p) extra to take photographs and CUC$5 (US$5.40/£2.70) for video.

The entire area is developed around the all-inclusive resort concept, and visitors have no other options. Playa Guardalavaca was the original beach resort developed in the late 1970s, but today, resort hotels are distributed on several beaches along the coast. Principal among them are Playa Esmeralda, Playa Turquesa, and Playa Pesquero, where the hotels are more upscale than Guardalavaca, and the beaches even finer. Guardalavaca is dominated by Cubanacán properties, for the most part older and more affordable than newer hotels in other parts. The Spanish chain Sol Meliá has concentrated its hotels in a row along Playa Esmeralda.

Playa Guardalavaca

Club Amigo Atlántico-Guardalavaca

Over the years, several neighboring projects here have been fused into one massive all-inclusive resort. The oldest hotel at this resort, the Atlántico, was built in 1976 and its age shows in its basic structure. Three large, '70s Soviet-style blocks are situated around a square old-style pool. However, the newer section of villas is considerably nicer and closer to the beach, and really should be your first and only choice here. These large, tastefully decorated villas are much more modern, with marble bathrooms and small terraces; some have good sea views. The pool is much better as well. But the rooms and the grounds still can't compare with nicer properties in the area. The hotel has only a tiny cove beach; you have to walk along a boardwalk to get to the real beach, a considerable jaunt. On the whole, it's a decent if unexciting hotel that clings to its glory days as the first property on the beach, when Fidel himself swam in the pool.

Playa Guardalavaca, Banes, Holguín. (✆ **24/43-0180.** Fax 24/43-0200. www.hotelescubanacan.com. 144 villas. CUC$70–CUC$79 (US$76–US$85/£38–£43) double. Rates are all-inclusive. MC, V. **Amenities:** 4 restaurants; 2 snack bars; 4 bars; dance club; nightly show; 4 outdoor pools for adults; 4 outdoor pools for children; watersports equipment; gym; sauna; outdoor tennis court; children's programs; concierge; tour desk; car- and scooter-rental desk; bike rental; massage; babysitting; laundry service. *In room:* A/C, TV, safe.

Hotel Brisas Guardalavaca ★

Like a couple of other all-inclusive beach hotels in the area that have upgraded their facilities, this hotel is a hybrid: part standard resort hotel with a big and rather uninteresting block structure, and part more intimate villa-style accommodations. The two sections are connected and considered one property, but guests would be wise to draw a firm distinction; the one-star rating we have given applies only to the villas, which are much more striking. Mediterranean in style and set amid pleasant gardens, the pastel-colored, red-tile-roof villas are large and luxurious, with balconies. The atmosphere is one of tranquillity, with easy access to an attractive stretch of beach. The standard hotel next-door, built in 1994, doesn't fare well in comparison. Rooms aren't very inspiring for the price, but many of them have good sea views.

Playa Guardalavaca, Banes, Holguín. (✆ **24/43-0218.** Fax 24/43-0418. www.hotelescubanacan.com. 206 villas. CUC$100–CUC$106 (US$108–US$114/£54–£57) double. Rates are all-inclusive. MC, V. **Amenities:** 4 restaurants; snack bar; 4 bars; dance club; nightly show; 2 outdoor pools for adults; 2 outdoor pools for children; 2 lit outdoor tennis courts; watersports equipment; bikes; children's programs; Jacuzzi; concierge; tour desk; car- and scooter-rental desk; massage; babysitting; laundry service. *In room:* A/C, TV, minibar, hair dryer, safe.

Playa Esmeralda

Paradisus Río de Oro Resort & Spa ★★★

One of the finest and most luxurious all-inclusive resort hotels in Cuba, this Sol Meliá flagship hotel is perched above a low, rocky cliff overlooking Playa Esmeralda. Set amid lush, meticulously landscaped gardens are handsome two-story blocks of rooms and slightly more exclusive casitas, consisting of two apartments with separate terraces and outdoor showers. The rooms are very large and well-appointed, with separate sitting areas, balconies, and large bathrooms with heated floors. Of these, those on the second floor have higher ceilings than those below, and those on the corners have larger balconies. There are also two massive, private oceanview villas, with private swimming pools, that are easily the top accommodations in Guardalavaca. Walkways wend through lush vegetation and around ponds; scattered about the grounds are private sitting areas and hammocks strewn lazily between trees. All the specialized restaurants are in high demand, so it's a good idea to make reservations for the duration of your stay upon arrival. The restaurants' selections and the food in general is considerably better than most other all-inclusives. (The Japanese restaurant is excellent.)

The superb main beach is a short walk down some stairs built into the cliff, but the hotel also features three nearly private, tiny cove beaches accessed through the gardens (few guests seem to know about them). A serene, blue wood bridge over a large pond leads to the other two Meliá hotels on Esmeralda. At night, the bridge is illuminated and is a particularly good spot if you're in the mood for a romantic walk after dinner. This hotel was recently reserved for adults only and new spa facilities have opened, including some open-air massage gazebos built out over the ocean. By summer 2009, this hotel will have introduced Royal Service for new deluxe bungalows in the forest.

Carretera a Guardalavaca, Playa Esmeralda, Holguín. ℭ **24/43-0090.** Fax 24/43-0095. www.solmeliacuba. com. 300 units. CUC$367 (US$396/£198) double; CUC$511 (US$552/£276) superior suite; CUC$1,460 (US$1,577/£788) villa. Rates are all-inclusive. MC, V. Children are not allowed. **Amenities:** 7 restaurants; 2 bars; nightly show; outdoor pool; 3 lit outdoor tennis courts; gym; spa; Jacuzzi; sauna; watersports equipment; bikes; game room; concierge; tour desk; car- and scooter-rental desk; salon; massage; 24-hr. room service; laundry service. *In room:* A/C, TV, minibar, coffeemaker, hair dryer, iron/ironing board, safe.

Sol Río de Luna y Mares Resort ★★ (Kids)

This complex, which underwent a complete renovation in 2008, consists of two formerly separate Sol Meliá properties on Playa Esmeralda joined at the hip. Formerly the Río de Luna and Río de Mares, they've merged—and guests at either one are free to use the facilities at both—but the two hotels deserve to be thought of separately, since they're slightly different in character and design. We prefer the Río de Luna, which was built in 1992. It has a sedate, open-air lobby and medium-size pool, and the overall design of the hotel is more intimate. Suites have two rooms, with two bathrooms and a large balcony or small terrace. The Río de Mares, while somewhat newer, has a slightly more impersonal feel, with rooms built in large wings in a U-shape around the pools. However, the rooms on the third and fourth floors here have excellent views, and the junior suites are immense, with massive terraces. The rooms are all very cute and playfully rustic, with amenities that include a large TV and CD player. The long stretch of beach fronting the two hotels is superb. The wide range of activities, facilities, and a well-run children's program make this an excellent choice for families.

Carretera a Guardalavaca, Playa Esmeralda, Holguín. ℭ **24/43-0060.** Fax 24/43-0065. www.solmelia cuba.com. 464 units. CUC$183–CUC$280 (US$198–US$302/£99–151) double; CUC$203–CUC$306 (US$219– US$330/£110—165) suites. Rates are all-inclusive. Children under 2 stay free in parent's room; children 3–12 stay for half-price in parent's room. MC, V. **Amenities:** 6 restaurants; 4 bars; dance club; nightly show; 2 outdoor pools; 2 lit outdoor tennis courts; gym; Jacuzzi; sauna; watersports equipment; bikes; children's center and programs; concierge; tour desk; car- and scooter-rental desk; salon; massage; babysitting; laundry service. *In room:* A/C, TV, minibar, coffeemaker, hair dryer, iron/ironing board, safe.

Blau Costa Verde Beach Resort ★★ (Kids   This resort has a decidedly tropical feel, with light pastel colors. The huge concrete structure you drive up to, though, is not the most attractive. It consists of six big building blocks, with three open-air restaurants built around a large figure-eight pool. Rooms are cheery, done in light colors with an ocean theme, but not overly large, and TVs are rather small. The bathrooms, however, are surprisingly large and nicely designed in tile and marble. Some rooms have distant beach views. The sands are a 50m (164-ft.) walk away, but the beach is lovely, and the water has amazing crystal-clear turquoise tones. A kids' club, kiddie pool, playground, shallow "children's beach," and child care will appeal to families. The food here is actually pretty good for a large-scale all-inclusive.

Playa Pesquero, Rafael Freyre, Holguín. © **24/43-0510.** Fax 24/43-0515. www.blau-hotels.com. 309 units. CUC$108–CUC$212 (US$117–US$229/£58–£114) double; CUC$120–CUC$224 (US$130–US$242/£65–£121) suite. Rates are all-inclusive. Children under 2 stay free in parent's room; children 3–14 stay for half price in a separate room. MC, V. **Amenities:** 4 restaurants; snack bar; 3 bars; dance club; nightly show; outdoor pool for adults; outdoor pool for children; 2 lit outdoor tennis courts; gym; Jacuzzi; sauna; watersports equipment; children's center and programs; concierge; tour desk; bikes; car- and scooter-rental desk; salon; massage; babysitting; laundry service; nonsmoking rooms. *In room:* A/C, TV, minibar, hair dryer, safe (for a fee).

Occidental Grand Playa Turquesa ★★ (Kids   This large resort is set above a beautiful broad beach and next to some lovely natural forests. Perhaps the most distinctive features here are the seven swimming pools, several connected in cascading fashion by waterfalls. Rooms are large, modern, and well kept. They have large, cool, ceramic tile floors in a checkerboard pattern, and stylish wrought-iron headboards over the beds. All have private balconies, although many of these are quite compact. The grounds here are lush and shady. There are several good a la carte dining options, as well as the ubiquitous large buffets. The pizza and ice-cream stand on the beach is a big hit here. This hotel has an extensive array of watersports and activities, and an excellent children's program.

Playa Yuraguanal, Rafael Freyre, Holguín. © **800/858-2258** in the U.S. and Canada, or 24/43-0540. Fax 24/43-0545. www.occidental-hoteles.com. 500 units. CUC$251 (US$271/£136) double; CUC$314 (US$339/£170) suite. Rates are all-inclusive. Children under 2 stay free in parent's room; children 2–12 stay for CUC$51 (US$55/£28) in parent's room. MC, V. **Amenities:** 5 restaurants; 2 snack bars; 6 bars; dance club; nightly show; 7 outdoor pools; 8 lit outdoor tennis courts; gym; football court; Jacuzzi; sauna; watersports equipment; children's center and programs; concierge; tour desk; car- and scooter-rental desk; massage; babysitting; laundry service; nonsmoking rooms. *In room:* A/C, TV, minibar, hair dryer, safe.

Playa Costa Verde ★★ (Kids (Value   Originally built for and run by the Jamaican SuperClubs chain, this attractively designed property is now managed by the Cuban Gaviota company. The resort is an excellent value for families, with whom it is extremely popular. Although rooms do not have sea or beach views, they are quite large, with very nice decor in bright greens and deep blues, tile floors, and balconies or terraces. They represent some of the best-equipped and best-designed rooms I've seen among high-end beach hotels in Cuba. In addition to the beautiful rooms, this hotel has a wide range of activities and an excellent children's program. A spectacular section of Playa Pesquero is a 5-minute walk from the pool over a bridge and through wetlands. The Japanese restaurant here is especially worthy of mention.

Playa Pesquero, Rafael Freyre, Holguín. © **24/43-3520.** Fax 24/43-3525. www.gaviota-grupo.com. 480 units. CUC$80–CUC$125 (US$86–US$135/£43–£68) double; CUC$110–CUC$150 (US$119–US$162/£59–£81) suite. Rates are all-inclusive. Children under 2 stay free in parent's room; children 2–12 stay for half price in separate room. MC, V. **Amenities:** 4 restaurants; snack bar; 13 bars; dance club; nightly show; 2 outdoor pools; 4 lit outdoor tennis courts; fitness center; Jacuzzi; sauna; watersports equipment; children's center and programs; game room; concierge; tour desk; bikes; car- and scooter-rental desk; salon; massage; babysitting; laundry service. *In room:* A/C, TV, minibar, coffeemaker, hair dryer, safe.

Playa Pesquero ★★ (Kids)   This massive hotel is one of the largest in Cuba. Your experience here begins with a fabulous open-air lobby with lily pools, large sculptures, and several romantic sitting areas. The rooms are all in two-story blocks spread around the massive grounds ringing the large free-form pool, spa, and entertainment area. Rooms are all spacious and cheery, and all have a private balcony or porch. The superior rooms are really junior suites, and the extra space and sitting area is quite nice. This resort has a whole host of organized activities and entertainment options, as well as a broad selection of restaurants and bars. Of the a la carte restaurants here, La Trattoria is particularly appealing, with a series of private dining gazebos spread around a small re-creation of Venice's canal system, replete with a real gondola. Be sure to reserve one of these in advance if you're looking for a romantic dinner.

Playa Pesquero, Rafael Freyre, Holguín. © **24/43-3530.** Fax 24/43-0535. www.gaviota-grupo.com. 912 units. CUC$140–CUC$180 (US$151–US$194/£76–£97) double; CUC$170–CUC$230 (US$184–US$248/£92–£124) suite. Rates are all-inclusive. Children under 2 stay free in parent's room; children 3–12 stay for half price in separate room. MC, V. **Amenities:** 7 restaurants; 2 snack bars; 7 bars; dance club; nightly show; massive outdoor pool; 3 lit outdoor tennis courts; fitness center; 4 Jacuzzis; sauna; watersports equipment; children's center and programs; game room; concierge; tour desk; car- and scooter-rental desk; salon; shopping arcade; pharmacy; massage; babysitting; laundry service. *In room:* A/C, TV, dataport, coffeemaker, safe.

WHERE TO DINE

Few visitors eat anywhere besides their all-inclusive hotels, of course. However, if you're just day-tripping to Guardalavaca, or you can't take another hotel buffet, check out **El Cayuelo,** near the Las Brisas hotel on Playa de Guardalavaca (© **24/43-0736**), which serves decent *comida criolla* (Cuban creole food) and seafood; **El Ancla,** Playa de Guardalavaca (© **24/43-0381**), for seafood; and **Pizza Nova,** Playa de Guardalavaca (© **24/43-0137**), for excellent thin-crust pizzas and basic Italian fare. Other tourist restaurants in the zone include **El Conuco de Mongo Viña,** Playa Esmeralda (© **24/43-0915**), as well as **Restaurante Cayo Naranjo** (© **24/43-0132**) and **Yaguajay Restaurant** (© **24/43-0422**), both within the tourist complex of Parque Natural Bahía de Naranjo.

GUARDALAVACA AFTER DARK

All of the all-inclusive hotels provide free nightly entertainment of varying quality; as a general rule, the stages, dancers, and musicians increase in quality along with the price, so expect the nightly cabaret at the Río de Oro to far outclass what Club Amigo puts on. Some are well-produced, professional, lively affairs and give you a pretty good time. Others are, well, cheesy and embarrassing. Most hotels change the program every night over a 1- or 2-week schedule, so if you want to drop in every night, you'll at least see a new presentation (the musicians and dancers, though, may very well be the same).

When the tourist-targeted entertainment gets to be too much, head for the one place where you can be assured of spotting (and maybe even interacting with!) locals. For those who need a break from packaged entertainment, the **Disco La Roca** (© **24/43-0167;** CUC$5/US$5.40/£2.70 cover) in Guardalavaca is the place to be outside of the hotels. It is partly open air and has good beach views.

The following are the most common and easily accessible side trips from Guardalavaca. Though it may seem unfair to characterize the largest city and provincial capital, Holguín, as a day trip from the beach, the fact of the matter is that the overwhelming majority of visitors to this section of northeastern Cuba have sun and surf on their minds.

Holguín

56km (35 miles) SW of Guardalavaca; 734km (456 miles) E of Havana; 134km (83 miles) NW of Santiago de Cuba

The provincial capital, officially called San Isidoro de Holguín, may be known across Cuba as the "city of parks," but it doesn't get a whole lot of tourist traffic. Holguín is a pleasant but unremarkable city with only a modicum of attractions. Still, it makes a good day trip for resort visitors who would otherwise see nothing of Cuba save Guardalavaca's all-inclusive hotels and brilliant beaches.

Holguín, the fourth-largest city in Cuba, has a compact center that's easy enough to get around; visitors can manage the highlights in an unhurried day. The city's few elegant plazas, colonial buildings, and small dose of museums do not rival the highlights of Trinidad or Camagüey, and much of the city's historical character has been subsumed by industrial expansion. The great majority of the city's buildings date from the 19th and 20th centuries.

Pleasant **Parque Calixto García** (also called Parque Central), named for a 19th-century patriot, represents the heart of the city. The hero of the wars of independence is paid tribute with a large marble statue in the park's center. Benches are usually occupied by locals watching the town and time pass by. Two nearby churches of note are the handsome domed **Iglesia de San José** (on Plaza Carlos Manuel de Céspedes), which has an unusual baroque interior to go with its remade neoclassical facade, and the imposing 18th-century **La Catedral de San Isidro de Holguín** (Calle Mandulay, on Parque de las Flores), which features *mudéjar* (Moorish-style) carved wooden ceilings.

Of special note in Holguín is the unusual **Familia Cuayo Fábrica de Organos,** a studio that still produces handmade *órganos pneumáticos* (air-compression organs) with hand-cut music sheets, and restores musical instruments—perhaps the very last of a breed. Eighteen workers make only four organs per year. A large organ, for which there is today a very limited market, costs about CUC$23,148 (US$25,000/£12,500). You can drop in during business hours at Carretera a Gibara 301 (© **24/42-4162**), and someone is sure to give you a look around.

La Loma de Cruz (Hill of the Cross), 3km (1¾ miles) north of the city, can be climbed by ascending the nearly 500 steps to the top, where there's a wooden cross that was placed there in 1790. Though the often-windy hill has excellent views of Holguín in the flat valley and the surrounding countryside, the hilltop is a little forlorn. The **Mirador de Mayabe** is the other acclaimed viewpoint, about 10km (6 miles) from the city center. On the hill, **Cerro de Mayabe,** is a hotel and restaurant.

Holguín's **Cabaret Nuevo Nocturno** ★ (© **24/42-5185**) is an open-air cabaret show. Its Corazón Caribeño show (Wed–Mon, 10pm–2am) is very professional and entertaining, considerably better than the ones put on nightly by the all-inclusive hotels in Guardalavaca. Afterward, the stage becomes a hopping dance club. Admission is CUC$10 (US$11/£5.40), or you can buy a package at any of the hotel tour desks for around CUC$30 (US$32/£16), which includes transportation from your hotel and a cocktail.

For details on getting to Holguín, see "Getting There," earlier in this section.

35km (22 miles) N of Holguín

A sleepy, charming, early-19th-century provincial port, Gibara ★—sometimes referred to as *La Villa Blanca,* or the White Village, due to its one-time whitewashed appearance—is home to a number of fine colonial-style buildings. Today, Gibara, a modest fishing town, has great scenery and overlooks a wide natural bay, with a very tranquil atmosphere. Two pretty little beaches and a Malecón (promenade) line the picturesque bay, and inland is the **Silla de Gibara,** a flat-topped mountain that locals claim is the hill described by Columbus when he first happened upon Cuba (it is much more probable that he landed in Baracoa, much farther east of here, and that the mountain described in his journal is El Yunque).

On the top of Los Caneyes hill are the ruins of an old **fortress,** which protected merchants involved in trade with Europe and the U.S. (a 30-min. walk up the hill rewards hikers with excellent views of the town and bay). Trade soon diminished with the introduction of the railroad, and the fortunes of Gibara suffered, leading to an exodus of a significant portion of its population. Gibara's moment in the sun is still reflected in the handful of grand mansions and public buildings.

The main plaza is marked by an attractive yellow church with red-tiled cupolas and African oak trees. Of greatest interest is the **Museo de Ambiente Cubano,** Independencia 19 (© **24/43-4687**), housed in an impressive neoclassical house constructed in 1872. The sumptuous mansion, which once belonged to an elite merchant, features huge mediopunto stained-glass windows, yellow and blue tiles, and quality period furnishings. It's open from Tuesday to Saturday 8am to 5pm and Sunday 8am to noon.

For all intents and purposes, there's no public transportation available to tourists connecting either Holguín or Guardalavaca to Gibara. This is just as well, since it is quick and convenient to take a taxi there and back for around CUC$30 to CUC$40 (US$32–US$43/£16–£22). Gibara is also featured as a day trip by most of the tour operators in Guardalavaca.

Cayo Saetia

130km (81 miles) SE of Guardalavaca

This pristine cay, on the eastern side of the Bahía de Nipe, isn't terribly easy to get to, but if isolated and totally unpopulated, sugar-white cove beaches and wild game are of interest to you, it might be worth the effort. This erstwhile exclusive game resort was once the private stomping and hunting grounds of Cuba's military and political brass. The cay has an exceptional roster of flora and fauna, which includes not only deer and wild boar, but also a wild collection of exotics such as antelopes, ostrich, water buffalo, and zebras. Most excursions include snorkeling, boat rides, jeep safaris, horseback riding, and lunch on the beach. While this place is billed as an ecotourist getaway, this seems to include stalking semicaptive and imported game under the rubric of "ecotourism." There's only one hotel on the cay, **Villa Cayo Saetía** ★ (© **24/9-6900;** www.gaviota-grupo.com), with just a dozen simple, yet tasteful rooms and cabanas. Cayo Saetía is about 90 minutes from Guardalavaca by jeep and just 20 minutes by helicopter (the preferred method of transport). Contact **Gaviota Tours** (© **24/43-0907**), which runs the place, or any of the hotels or travel agencies in Guardalavaca.

757km (470 miles) E of Havana; 201km (125 miles) E of Camagüey; 127km (79 miles) W of Santiago de Cuba; 73km (45 miles) S of Holguín

Granma province is unusually easygoing and lethargic, even by the standards of stifling hot and dry eastern Cuba, but its retiring pace and unassuming nature belie a turbulent, indelible role in modern Cuban history. Bayamo, the capital of the province, and the densely forested, impenetrable mountains of the Sierra Maestra at the extreme southwest corner of the Oriente region have long been at the forefront of political turmoil and rebellion. The otherwise unassuming region may just be the place where Cuba's independent streak runs deepest.

Bayamo, one of Cuba's original seven *villas* and today a midsize city and the capital of Granma province, is considered the birthplace of Cuban independence. The *himno nacional,* or national anthem, was first sung here after the city was seized by the Liberating Army and became the capital of the Republic at Arms in 1869. South of Bayamo, the Sierra Maestra, a national park comprising a spectacularly verdant and rugged range that reaches right down to the Caribbean coast, is where Fidel Castro and his band of rebels sneaked back into Cuba in 1956 after a period of exile in Mexico. The rebels hid in the mountains, depending upon the assistance of sympathetic *guajiros* (peasants), and based their long-shot revolution there, covertly raising the antenna of Radio Rebelde and scoring decisive victories on the road to eventual triumph. How influential was the province as a turning point in 20th-century Cuban politics and society? Important enough that, after the Revolution, it received the name of the yacht in which Fidel and his brothers in arms sailed from Mexico, and the government-owned and operated national daily newspaper is now named for the province: Read all about it in *Granma.*

Today, Bayamo and the Sierra Maestra are considerably better known for their historical associations than they are as travel destinations. Bayamo is pleasant and peaceful, but its citizens and well-maintained colonial structures don't really try too hard to impress visitors, making it a tranquil stopover. Meanwhile, much of the Sierra Maestra remains difficult to penetrate due to controlled access. However, it is relatively simple and rewarding to trace the revolutionary steps of Fidel and Che Guevara, visiting the fascinating installations of the rebel group—preserved as they were in the tense days of the late 1950s—tucked high in the mountains. The dramatic coastline that bends around the southeastern base of the Oriente, where the mountains scrape the edge of the sparkling Caribbean, makes an excellent, if time-consuming, ground approach to Santiago de Cuba, and is worth the trip for the scenic value alone. A handful of package tourism hotels are perched on the rocky coast, where the sands aren't much to speak of, but the incomparable sea and mountain views, and diving and hiking opportunities—not to mention very favorable package prices—more than compensate for that.

ESSENTIALS

Getting There

BY PLANE   You can fly from Havana to Bayamo on **Cubana** (✆ **23/42-3916** in Bayamo, or 7/834-4446 in Havana; www.cubana.cu) on Tuesday and Friday. Flights arrive at **Aeropuerto Carlos Manuel de Céspedes,** Carretera a Holguín (✆ **23/42-7514;** airport code BYM), 10km (6 miles) north of the city. The fare is CUC$104 (US$112/£56) one-way. By registered taxi, the trip to town is about CUC$4 (US$4.30/£2.15).

BY BUS **Víazul** (© **23/42-4036** in Bayamo, or 7/881-1413 in Havana; www.viazul. com) is the most convenient mode of transportation for traveling to Bayamo from Havana and Santiago, and major cities in between. On the Trinidad–Santiago de Cuba line, the bus departs Trinidad at 8am and arrives in Bayamo at 5:50pm; the fare is CUC$26 (US$28/£14). Buses from Santiago bound for points west leave at 9am, 3:15pm, 6pm, and 10pm and stop in Bayamo 2 hours and 5 minutes later. The fare is CUC$7 (US$7.55/£3.80). On the Havana-Santiago line, there are four daily departures at 9:30am, 3pm, 6:15pm, and 10pm; the trip from Havana is roughly 14 hours and costs CUC$44 (US$48/£24).

The main bus terminal for long-distance buses, the **Terminal de Omnibuses,** is located on the outskirts of downtown, on Carretera Central near Avenida Jesús Rabi, on the road to Holguín. Horse-drawn carriages and unregistered taxis await passengers to ferry them downtown for a dollar or two.

BY TRAIN Though traveling by train is probably not the most comfortable or efficient way to get to Bayamo, train no. 13 departs Havana's Estación Central at 8:15pm and arrives the next morning at 10:30am. The fare is CUC$26 (US$28/£14). Not all Havana-Santiago trains stop in Bayamo, so check before boarding one. Train schedules change frequently, and depending on the season, many trains don't operate on a daily basis; verify the current schedule by calling © **7/862-1920** or 7/861-4259, though it's often better to go in person to the train station and purchase tickets at least a day in advance. The Bayamo train station is on Calle Línea between José Antonio Saco and Parada (© **23/42-2311**), 1km (¹/₂ mile) from the center.

Getting Around

The compact old town of Bayamo is very simple to get around on foot. You're only likely to need a taxi to get back and forth to your hotel, if you stay out at the large Hotel Sierra Maestra, or to get to the airport or bus or train station to move on. Contact **Cubataxi** (© **23/42-4313**) for local and long-distance taxis. Alternatively, you can take a horse-drawn or bicycle taxi anywhere in town for CUC$1 to CUC$2 (US$1.10–US$2.15/ 55p–£1.10).

Getting to the Sierra Maestra mountains is rather more complicated, necessitating a rental car, hired *carro particular,* or organized excursion. If you wish to explore the Sierra with any degree of independence, or make the coastal drive to Santiago de Cuba, your own wheels are virtually indispensable. There's a **Havanautos** office within the Servi-Cupet gas station on Carretera Central (© **23/42-7375**). Rates are about CUC$55 to CUC$80 (US$59–US$86/£30–£43) per day for a standard four-door compact car.

Cubanacán (see "Orientation," below) runs a bus to Playa Guardalavaca every Saturday and Sunday, leaving at 7am from Plaza Francisco Manuel Osorio and costing CUC$12 (US$13/£6.50) round-trip; it makes a stop in Holgúin too. It returns at 5pm.

Orientation

Bayamo's historic center sits on a high bluff overlooking the Bayamo River. For information about excursions in the province, visit one of the major tour operators. **Cubanacán** has an office inside the Hotel Royalton, and **Havanatur** (© **23/42-7672**) has an office on the western side of Parque Céspedes. The tour desk at the Hotel Sierra Maestra is also a good place to get information and arrange tours and car hire.

A **Banco de Crédito y Comercio** branch is on General García between Saco and Perucho Figueredo. It's open Monday through Friday from 8am to 3pm and on Saturday from 8 to 11am. There is a **CADECA** on Saco No. 5 between Donato Mármol and

For medical attention, go to **Hospital General Carlos Manuel de Céspedes,** Carretera Central on the way to Santiago de Cuba (© **23/42-2144**).

The main **post office** is on the west side of Parque Céspedes. It's open Monday through Saturday from 8am to 8pm. An **Etecsa** telepunto center with Internet access is at General García 109; it's open daily from 8:30am to 7:30pm.

BAYAMO

The second Spanish city founded in Cuba in 1513, as Villa de San Salvador de Bayamo, is small and quiet for a provincial capital. The laid-back town welcomes relatively few visitors, except for day-trippers, and locals refrain from hassling foreign visitors—unless it involves singing the Cuban national anthem for you, the city's pride and joy.

Bayamo grew wealthy in the 17th and 18th centuries from contraband and later sugar and cattle. Many of the local elite were privileged enough to send young men off to Spain and France to study, and a number of them returned with enlightened ideals about colonialism and a strong desire for Cuban independence. Carlos Manuel de Céspedes (1819–74) was a wealthy businessman who, in 1868, freed his slaves and formed a small army that set about achieving that goal. The movement was known as the *Grito de Yara,* a call for independence or death. His forces succeeded in capturing Bayamo and giving life to the War of Independence against Spain. The rebels held Bayamo for 3 months until it was evident that the superior numbers of Spanish troops would soon defeat them. Rather than surrender, the rebel army audaciously chose to burn the city, in the ultimate act of sedition. Most of the city was wiped out by this act of self-immolation in 1869.

What to See & Do

Parque Céspedes ★★ is the focal point of downtown Bayamo. It's an exquisite, peaceful square flanked by tall royal palm trees. The light-blue and pink building at one end of the square, which housed a pharmacy, is where the great blaze began. At one end of the plaza is a marble bust of the independence fighter Perucho Figueredo, which carries the words and music to "La Bayamesa" (later the national anthem), imploring followers not to fear "a glorious death" and encourages Cubans that to "die for the homeland is to live." At the other end of the plaza is a stately granite and bronze statue of Carlos Manuel de Céspedes. Ringing the square are handsome, pastel-colored, arcaded colonial-style (post-1869) buildings. Had the city not been consumed by fire, in all likelihood it would resemble the remarkable colonial core of Trinidad.

Next to the Hotel Royalton on the north side of the square, the **Casa Natal de Céspedes** ★, Calle Francisco Maceo Osorio 57 (© **23/42-3864**), the birthplace of the "father of the Cuban nation," is the only house on the square that escaped destruction from the fire. The significance of it alone being saved is not lost on Cubans. Today it is a museum, open Tuesday through Friday from 10am to 6pm, Saturday from 10am to 3pm and 8 to 10pm, and Sunday from 10am to 3pm and 8 to 10pm; admission is CUC$1 (US$1.10/55p). The house has been lovingly restored; the two-story building holds a chronological exhibit about the Céspedes family, elegant 19th-century colonial furnishings, objects belonging to Céspedes (such as his ceremonial saber), and a few odds and ends that help piece together the story of Bayamo's independent streak (including the original printing press that produced the first newspaper of free Cuba, *El Cubano Libre,* in 1868). The standout item, however, is the extraordinary, huge four-poster bronze bed complete with two oval shields depicting towns in mother-of-pearl decoration; the imagery changes as you glance at the depictions from left to right. Céspedes is remembered for refusing to trade his surrender for the life of his son, who was captured by the Spanish army; the Cuban patriot replied in writing that all Cubans were his sons and he could not be expected to trade their independence for the life of one man. The Spaniards promptly shot his son Oscar.

Just west of the museum and Parque Céspedes, dominating a small open square called **Plaza del Himno,** is **La Catedral de Bayamo** (or La Catedral del Santísimo Salvador), an immense, ocher-colored, 16th-century church that succumbed to the 1869 fire. Rebuilt several times over the course of its life, the church was recently magnificently restored. It features a high-peaked wood-beam ceiling and, above the altar, an attention-getting battle mural commemorating a pivotal local episode when the parish priest blessed the rebel army flag. This blurring of the lines between church and state was not the only overtly political statement to take place in the cathedral; the first singing of the revolutionary anthem was staged here in 1869. The cathedral is open to visitors daily from 9am to 1pm and from 3 to 5pm. To one side of the cathedral, the small chapel **Capilla de La Dolorosa (Chapel of the Lady of Sorrows),** which dates to 174, is distinguished by a lovely Moorish-style, carved wooden ceiling and fine baroque altarpiece; it was only one of three important buildings to survive the 1869 blaze (the others were the Casa de la Trova and Céspedes' home).

Heading south from Parque Céspedes, Calle General García has been turned into a pleasant pedestrian mall, with several shops, simple restaurants, and tour agency offices.

Where to Stay

Quite a few *casas particulares* can be found in the old center of Bayamo. **Casa Olga Celeiro Rizo,** Calle Parada 16 (Altos) between Martí and Mármol (© 23/42-3859; yaimara.grm@infomed.sld.cu), is a friendly house with two comfortable, air-conditioned rooms and a great terrace overlooking the pleasant Francisco Maceo Osorio plaza; Olga can help with excursions. **Villa Rose Mary,** Pío Rosado 22 between Ramírez and Avenida F.V. Aguilera (© 23/42-3984; www.cubahostal.com; varezsanchez@yahoo.es), is an attractive house with two comfortable, clean, air-conditioned rooms. **Casa Ana Martí Vázquez,** Céspedes 4 between Maceo and Canducha (© 23/42-5323; marti@enet.cu), has two rooms, each with a television, fridge, and air-conditioning; however, one is up an extremely steep flight of stairs in a converted attic section, so the other larger room is preferable.

Inexpensive

In addition to the hotels listed below, another good option and excellent value is the training school **Hotel Escuela Telégrafo,** Calle José Antonio Saco 108 (© 23/42-5510; www.ehtgr.co.cu), which is in the heart of downtown. It has 12 rooms and charges just CUC$20 (US$22/£11) for a double room with air-conditioning, a television, and a small refrigerator.

Hotel Royalton ★ Set facing Parque Céspedes, this charming hotel is to be refurbished as a boutique hotel under Cubanacán's Hoteles E brand and will be the top choice in town. Dating to the 1940s, four of the rooms have small balconies with great plaza views. Off to one side of the lobby is the dependable **Restaurant Plaza,** which has a nice sidewalk terrace and serves a generous plate of fried chicken with excellent french fries, as well as chicken fricassee and beef with garlic sauce.

Calle Maceo 53, Bayamo. © 23/42-2290. Fax 23/42-4792. www.hotelescubanacan.com. 33 units. CUC$29–CUC$35 (US$31–US$38/£16–£19) double. Rates include breakfast. These prices will rise once the refurbishment is complete. MC, V. **Amenities:** Restaurant; bar. *In room:* A/C, TV, fridge.

Hotel Sierra Maestra Located 2km (1¼ miles) from Parque Céspedes, this large and friendly hotel has an excellent outdoor swimming pool and a quiet, relaxed feel. Rooms are smallish, but well-appointed, with air-conditioning and TV, and most have a balcony of some sort. Most rooms are in a large, nondescript three-story block of a building backing the pool. My favorite rooms are in the separate cabana section of two-story units. At night, this place has a decent bar scene and probably the liveliest dance club in town.

Carretera Central Km 1.5 on the way to Santiago de Cuba. ☏ **23/42-7974.** Fax 23/42-7973. www.islazul. cu. 132 units. CUC$36–CUC$45 (US$39–US$49/£19–£24) double. MC, V. **Amenities:** Restaurant; bar; large outdoor pool; tour desk; car rental desk. *In room:* A/C, TV, safe.

Where to Dine

Only a few *paladares* remain in Bayamo. Aside from the place listed below, **Paladar El Polinesio,** Parada 125 between Pío Rosado and Capotico Bayamo (☏ **23/42-3860**) is the second-best restaurant in town. There's also a **Dino's Pizza** at General García 111.

For dessert, stand in line with locals at the ice-cream parlor **Tropicrema,** located just off the southwest corner of Parque Céspedes.

Dear Granma

In early December 1956, Fidel Castro, his brother Raúl, Ernesto (Che) Guevara, and a group of idealist revolutionaries, including some who had previously stormed the barracks in Santiago de Cuba and Bayamo, sailed back to Cuba from exile in Mexico with weapons and an audacious plan: to overthrow, once and for all, the Batista government. They set sail aboard a yacht christened the *Granma*, purchased from a couple of Americans in Veracruz. The stealth journey was beset by all manner of hitches, including bad weather and scarce provisions. Just 82 men disembarked at Las Coloradas beach 2 days later than planned, with few weapons and virtually no supplies.

Batista forces had been tipped off to the operation, and prompt aerial bombing killed about half the rebels; the others fled for the mountains in small groups. After suffering an ambush, only 16 men remained, and when the survivors eventually met up at Cinco Palmas in the Sierra Maestra, only a dozen men remained. They had but eight rifles to their names. Against monumental odds, they nonetheless began to plan their offensive. Batista, no doubt convinced that the attempted sedition had been effectively quashed, announced to the world that Castro and the other leaders had been killed and withdrew government forces from the area—a fatal mistake.

Crafty Castro slowly but surely began to gain adherents and advance the rebel cause of the 26th of July movement. Astonishingly, a band of just over a dozen fighters at the campaign's inception—propped up by a growing network of *guajiros* (poor rural farmers) and vast, inaccessible terrain—somehow ended up toppling the Batista regime just 2 years later.

Today, the spot where the rebels landed ashore, at the southwestern tip of Cuba near Cabo Cruz, is a national park, **Parque Nacional del Desembarco del Granma.** A monument features a replica of the *Granma;* the real vessel is in the Museo de la Revolución in Havana.

Restaurant Sagitario ★ CRIOLLA   This place serves large and well-prepared meals in a pleasant backyard patio. The house specialty is pork steak cooked with cheese; the *pargo* (red snapper) is also good. Service here is friendly and downright efficient.

Calle Mármol 107 btw. Maceo and Francisco Vicente Aguilera. ✆ **23/42-2449**. Main courses CUC$6–CUC$7 (US$6.50–US$7.55/£3.25–£3.80). No credit cards. Daily noon–11pm.

SIERRA MAESTRA ★ ★

Cuba's highest and longest mountain range stretches about 140km (87 miles) west to east, across three provinces: Granma, Santiago de Cuba, and Guantánamo. Its highest peaks are only several kilometers from the coastline, making for some exciting views, whether you're perched up in the mountains or cruising along the coast. The entire range forms part of the **Gran Parque Nacional Sierra Maestra,** and its thickly forested, rugged terrain, with steep, deep green mountains swathed in wispy clouds, is impenetrable for most traffic, though the area is splendid for hikers. While there are many trails just begging to be explored, until recently most remained closed to the public; hard-core hikers should perhaps anticipate encountering some closed trail heads. The heart of the Gran Parque is a park-within-a-park, the **Parque Nacional de Turquino** ★, which includes Turquino, the nation's highest summit at just under 2,000m (6,562 ft.).

Deep folds and craggy ravines make these mountains very inaccessible, and they are, not surprisingly, very sparsely populated, with only small numbers of *guajiros* (poor rural farmers)—many of whose families once gave shelter and support to the rebels in their midst—living very simply in *bohíos* (thatched-roof huts) with no electricity or running water. Also tucked away in the mountain range are dozens of endemic species of birds and plants.

Unless you're a physically prepared hiker with all your own equipment and several days or more for hikes, your best bet is to head to Turquino Park, where there is, at least, minimal infrastructure; there's also the lasting legacy of Fidel Castro and his committed band of rebels, which formed the **Comandancia de La Plata,** a base command for their guerrilla war in 1956 after returning from exile in Mexico (see "Dear *Granma,*" above). The two main trails into the mountains are the **Pico Turquino Trail** and the **La Plata Trail;** the latter visits the rebels' base camp.

The road south from Bayamo is a long, lush, tropical adventure; it cuts through beautiful sugar-cane fields where pigs, peacocks, and machete-wielding farmers roam, with the rounded, green peaks of the Sierra Maestra looming in the background. **Villa Santo Domingo,** 65km (40 miles) south of Bayamo by a good road, is where you'll find the entrance to the national park, as well as a rustic hotel and restaurant that serve as a perfect base camp for those who want to trace the trail of Fidel and Che, ascend Pico Turquino, or just explore the rugged beauty of the national park. The **Hotel Villa Santo Domingo** (ⓒ 23/56-5568; www.islazul.cu), where Fidel and his brother Raúl have been frequent guests in the past (Fidel favored cabin no. 6), sits down a bit on the left side of the road, on the banks of the Yara River. The 20 attractive little cabins have twin beds, private bathrooms, air-conditioning, TVs, solar-powered hot water, and fridges. They cost CUC$34 to CUC$37 (US$37–US$40/£18–£20) double, including breakfast. Also on the grounds are a good restaurant and outdoor grill, as well as a bar, and video/game room. Even for those not staying at the hotel, the rustic, open-air **Restaurant La Yamagua** is the best place to eat in the area if you didn't bring your own provisions. For groups, the restaurant does a good *parrillada* (barbecue) of *cerdo asado* (roast pork), salad, rice, dessert, and coffee for CUC$14 (US$15/£7.55) per person. The menu includes standards of *comida criolla* (Cuban creole food), several different preparations of chicken, and pork steak.

Hiking in the Sierra

Hiking deep into the Sierra Maestra is a superbly rewarding experience for any hiker, but—given the mountains' historic role in the success of the Revolution and the fact that much of the Sierra remains a military zone—the Cuban government zealously protects access to it. By law, you need permission and a guide to explore the national park. Remember, Fidel's cronies hid from Batista's forces and the CIA for more than 2 years in the dense forest of the Sierra, so finding your way around is a complicated task. Park authorities don't look kindly upon foreigners seeking to explore the park on their own.

Guides can be contracted at the official entrance to the national park, the **Centro de Visitantes,** about 200m (656 ft.) along the road beyond the Hotel Villa Santo Domingo. It is open daily from 7:30 to 10am. Visitors pay a minimum CUC$12 (US$13/£6.50) fee to enter the park, which includes a guide for hikes into the Sierra. An additional CUC$5 (US$5.40/£2.70) is payable to take pictures of La Comandancia. This also is the spot to arrange for treks and bird-watching. You will need to arrive with all necessary gear, as no one in the area rents equipment. The center offers a number of different hikes and prices. All prices are per person and include a guide:

- Comandancia La Plata del Ejército Rebelde (see below): CUC$12 (US$13/£6.50)
- Palma Mocha, a 1-day trek toward Pico Turquino: CUC$12 (US$13/£6.50)
- Aguada de Santo Domingo to Pico Turquino, includes 1 night in the Aguada refuge, which has beds and mattresses, but you'll need a sleeping bag: CUC$33 (US$36/£18)
- Santo Domingo–Aguada–Pico Turquino–La Majagua–Las Cuevas, includes 2 nights of camping: CUC$40 (US$43/£22)

To gain access to the Pico Turquino or La Plata trail, hikers must either climb or take a 4WD (CUC$5/US$5.40/£2.70) that takes 15 minutes one-way, or a tough-as-nails flatbed truck (CUC$5/US$5.40/£2.70) that takes 45 minutes one-way; the trip is up a treacherously steep paved road, with thrilling hairpin turns, to **Alto de Naranjo,** 5km (3 miles) from the visitor center. A minimum number of 10 to 12 hikers is usually required for the truck service.

Places to get more information about trekking in the Sierra Maestra are **Agencia de Reservaciones del Campismo (Cubamar),** General García 211, Bayamo (© 23/42-4200), and **Islazul,** General García 207, Bayamo (©/fax 23/42-3273), which runs the Villa Santo Domingo hotel at the entrance to the park. However, it is much cheaper to arrive independently at the national park or with a hired *carro particular* (private Cuban's car) to arrange a hike than it is to book through Cubamar whose prices are exorbitant.

Pico Turquino ★★

The hike to Pico Turquino, the highest summit in Cuba, requires a minimum of 2 nights in the area (1 night camping). The trek from Alto de Naranjo is about 15km (9 miles). Experienced, fast hikers can do the ascent and descent in a day, but most people choose to camp overnight at the *refugio* (refuge), several kilometers below the summit. The trek through an amazing array of tropical ferns, vines, and dense cloud forest, punctuated by the sharp calls of unseen birds, is terrific, with stunning panoramic views all around, and is only really difficult at the steep end. It gets quite cold at night, so make sure you're prepared with proper clothing and equipment.

Comandancia de la Plata ★★

Though not nearly as challenging a hike—you can do the 6km (4 miles) up and back in about 3 hours—the trail to La Plata perched on a mountain ridge reverberates with thrilling history, no matter on which side of the political fence you fall. Visiting the rudimentary installations of Fidel Castro's rebel base camp is a remarkable experience. When you learn the story of the rebellion and visit the crude installations from which Fidel directed his offensive, it's hard not to have at least some appreciation for why this man clung so tenaciously to power and the ideals of the Revolution: Look what he did to get there.

After about 20 minutes on the trail, about 800m (2,625 ft.) above sea level, hikers come to the **Alto de Medina,** a small wooden house. At the entrance to the base camp, it was the checkpoint building. Farther up along the trail, you come to a **small museum** about the revolutionary guerrilla warfare waged in these mountains. You'll see what, at one time, was a small hospital, and eventually, you'll arrive at the huts where Fidel lived with his *compañera* (partner) Celia Sánchez. Fidel never allowed anyone but Celia inside the shack; the bench outside the door where he conducted interviews is still there. Ingeniously constructed under the cover of thick forest, the installations make it quite apparent how the rebels eluded capture and assassination. The hilltop rising above the camp is

THE COASTAL ROAD TO SANTIAGO DE CUBA

The Sierra Maestra stretching down to the rocky beaches and black sands of the south coast, against the sparkling blue waters of the Caribbean, is one of the most dramatic sights in Cuba. To trace the coastline to Santiago de Cuba is to take the scenic route; it's a roundabout way to get to your destination, for sure, but well worth it if you're a fan of rugged, bravura landscapes. If you're pressed for time and headed to Santiago, the inland route from Bayamo is much more direct.

The coastline is remarkably absent of any sort of villages or installations for long stretches at a time: It's just you, the open road, and the sea to your right and Sierra Maestra to your left. The road is pretty good for most of the trajectory, although rockslides aren't uncommon. While you can usually make the trip in any normal sedan, a four-wheel-drive vehicle is recommended for the added clearance, if nothing else. The beaches, such as they are, range from passable soft gray stone to forbidding big black rock.

A smattering of large resort hotels are located at certain points along the coast, and while it's a stretch to describe them as beach resorts, they do offer splendid sea views, a host of watersports, and plenty of trekking opportunities. Most are package tourism confines, aimed largely at seniors. Canadian charter planes fly direct to Manzanillo, then the hotels bus in groups of 100 vacationers or more for an inexpensive, weeklong, coastal Cuban vacation. Whether those guests arrive expecting fine, white, powdery Caribbean sand we don't know (we certainly hope not). Although we were initially turned off by the notion of an all-inclusive hotel hovering illogically on "beaches" that suffer so in comparison with those along the north coast, we do admit that there are a couple of hotels that wouldn't be awful places to vacation, as long as your expectations are simple. They include the **Club Amigo Marea del Portillo,** Carretera Granma Km 12.5, Pilón (© **23/59-7081;** www.hotelescubanacan.com).

From Marea del Portillo, the road continues another 40km (25 miles) or so to Santiago de Cuba province. The views take in desertlike landscapes, the massive dry mountains of the Sierra Maestra, black rocky beaches, and large waves crashing ashore; it's a highly scenic drive. The only village of any real size is **Chivirico,** a small fishing settlement about 75km (47 miles) outside of Santiago de Cuba. The best hotel en route to Santiago de Cuba is the all-inclusive **Brisas Sierra Mar Los Galeones** ★ (© **22/32-9110;** www.hotelescubanacan.com), a massive, multitiered hotel overlooking a sandy brown beach. Though the overall facilities are fairly impressive—there are four restaurants, five bars, two tennis courts, a fitness room, and a large swimming pool—the rooms are standard and uninspiring, with ugly flowered curtains and tiny TVs. There are plenty of better all-inclusive hotels in other parts of Cuba, but this place does combine well with a visit to Santiago. Rates are CUC$118 to CUC$148 (US$127–US$160/£64–£80) double, all-inclusive. From here, it's another hour or so to Santiago; see chapter 11 for full coverage.

THE ROAD TO BARACOA

Guantánamo province, by virtue of a Cuban song seemingly known the world over ("Guantanamera") and an attention-getting, anachronistic U.S. military base, gets more ink and initial interest than it probably deserves. The easternmost province on the island only has one true draw, but it's one of the highlights of Cuba: the tiny tropical town of Baracoa. The only real reason to stop over in the sweltering and unappealing city of

Goin' (or Not) to Gitmo

On the radio in Guantánamo city and along the road to Baracoa, the unmistakable sounds of English-speaking DJs and American pop music can be heard, seemingly out of nowhere. The programming is courtesy of the U.S. government, emerging from behind barbed-wire fences at the base at Guantánamo Bay, known to American military personnel as "Gitmo." The base is an eyebrow-raising anomaly in revolutionary Cuba, as it's probably the least likely spot in the world for the U.S. to have a naval base. Washington continues to hold an indefinite lease on the base, which was established in 1903 as a reward for the U.S. role in the Spanish-American War—making it the oldest overseas American naval base.

Pursuant to the original agreement, signed by President Theodore Roosevelt, which called for an annual payment of 2,000 gold coins (worth US$4,085 in 1903), the U.S. government continues to send rent checks for that original amount, even though Fidel Castro has never cashed a single one since 1959. Castro understandably would rather forgo the paltry sum than lend legitimacy to the American presence in Cuba. A 1934 treaty that reaffirmed the lease of the base stipulated that both the U.S. and Cuba must mutually agree to terminate the lease—and when was the last time Washington, D.C., and Havana agreed on anything?

Though it has official missions (refueling and reconnaissance), in peace times the Guantánamo base has existed primarily to continue to poke thorns in Castro's side. That was, until 2001, when the U.S. military decided to send Al Qaeda prisoners captured in the conflicts in Afghanistan and Iraq to Guantánamo. Since then, the base has been a source of international news and controversy. Most of the detainees continue to be held and interrogated without access to lawyers or the filing of any formal charges.

Cubans have grudgingly learned to live with the base. They no longer expect a U.S. invasion at any moment, and the U.S. now returns those Cubans who, rather than attempting to cross the Atlantic, try to escape Cuba by crossing over to the American base. Only a small handful of Cuban workers still cross military checkpoints every day to get to their jobs on the base.

Gitmo has about 3,000 full-time residents who, though surrounded on three sides by Cuba, live as if they were in American "suburbotopia," with typical suburban homes, U.S. products, American cars, cable TV, a golf course, and, of course, a McDonald's. However, this gated community has a sign (on the Cuban side) that reads REPUBLICA DE CUBA, TERRITORIO LIBRE DE AMERICA (Republic of Cuba, Free Territory of America).

Guantánamo is to visit the distant lookout trained at the contentious **American naval base** isolated on Cuban soil. That's as close as you'll get—and honestly, outside of the novelty factor, there's nothing much to see.

The parched landscape of the southern coast begins to change gradually in color along the spectacular 40km (25-mile) road **La Farola** ★★★, which courses southeast of

Santiago and wends its way through the mountains along the route to Baracoa. Things get more and more lush, with thick tropical vegetation and beautiful views at every turn. *Be forewarned:* In addition to its beauty, this is a tight and winding road with a seemingly endless series of white-knuckle hairpin turns. Baracoa, isolated from the rest of Cuba before the building of the road, is a beguiling little town, known for its chocolate and coconut and connections to Columbus. It's been known to bewitch more than a few travelers into staying much longer than they'd planned.

3 BARACOA ★★★

236km (147 miles) NE of Santiago de Cuba; 150km (93 miles) NE of Guantánamo; 332km (206 miles) E of Holguín

Swathed in generous tropical vegetation and refreshed by 10 rivers, Baracoa is perhaps the most picturesque spot in all of Cuba. The historic town sits on a lovely oyster-shaped bay, **Bahía de Miel (Honey Bay)** ★★★, and the landmark flat-topped mountain known as **El Yunque (the Anvil)** looms in the background.

Not only is Baracoa, for my pesos, the most beautiful place on the island, it's also the oldest. That Baracoa was the first settlement established by Diego Velázquez in 1511—making it the oldest colonial city in the Americas—is not in doubt. Christopher Columbus is thought to have first landed at this spot in late November 1492, and locals claim that he planted a wooden cross here to mark his arrival (the cross, carbon-tested for age, is on display in the Asunción church in town).

After its founding, Nuestra Señora de la Asunción de Baracoa remained the capital of the new Spanish colony for just 4 years; when Velázquez moved the capital west to Santiago, on a bigger and deeper bay, Baracoa's isolation had already begun. The small fishing and farming village remained virtually cut off from the rest of Cuba, with no true road in until the 1960s, when a scenic roller coaster of a highway was cut through the mountains.

For such a small, isolated settlement, Baracoa is loaded with things to do and see. It swims with possibilities for hiking, white-water rafting, and boating. Baracoa really shines the first week of April, when heady street parties (part of a *semana de cultura,* or cultural week) commemorate the date General Antonio Maceo disembarked at nearby Playa Duaba in 1895, marking the beginning of Cuba's War of Independence. The greatest pleasure Baracoa offers, though, is just being here. Most people make the trek just to take in its extraordinary beauty, tranquillity, and abundant charms. A UNESCO Biosphere Reserve, the tropical seaside town is tucked into green hillsides covered with cocoa and coconut groves, and surrounded by beaches lined by royal palms. As the abundant greenery attests, Baracoa is huddled in the midst of the wettest region in Cuba. In 2011, Baracoa will celebrate the 500th anniversary of its founding.

ESSENTIALS
Getting There
BY PLANE There are flights on Thursday and Sunday on **AeroCaribbean/Cubana** from Havana to Baracoa; however, flights are often booked weeks ahead. Fares run between CUC$131 and CUC$140 (US$141—US$151/£71—£82) one-way. Flights arrive at the small **Aeropuerto Gustavo Rizo** (© **21/64-5376;** airport code BCA), west of the bay near the Hotel Porto Santo and about 4km (2¹⁄₂ miles) west of downtown. By

taxi, the trip to town costs CUC$3 to CUC$4 (US$3.25—US$4.30/£1.60—£2.15). Should the Baracoa flights be full, Moa, 38km (24 miles) down the road, has flights on Monday from Havana, for CUC$122 (US$132/£66), and flights operate daily, except Thursday, from Havana to Guantánamo, for CUC$122 (US$132/£66).

BY BUS Most visitors arrive overland; the ride from Santiago de Cuba is especially spectacular, if lengthy. A **Víazul** bus (© **22/62-8484** in Santiago, or 21/64-3880 in Baracoa; www.viazul.com) departs Santiago daily at 7:45am and arrives in Baracoa at 12:35pm; the fare is CUC$15 (US$16/£8.10). The bus stops in Guantánamo. The same bus departs Baracoa at 2:15pm and arrives in Santiago at 7:05pm. The route is very popular, especially in high season; make reservations for the trip at least a day in advance, as these buses sell out frequently and fast.

The Baracoa **Terminal de Omnibuses** (© **21/64-3880**) is located at the end of José Martí near Avenida de los Mártires.

BY CAR You can drive to Baracoa from either Santiago de Cuba, along the scenic La Farola highway (see "The Road to Baracoa," above), or from Guardalavaca/Holguín along the northern coastal road through Moa. Allow $3^1/_2$ to 4 hours for either route.

Getting Around

You can easily get around most of Baracoa on foot or *bicitaxi* (bicycle carriage). To reach the beaches, rivers, and mountains around Baracoa, you'll either need to contract a taxi, rent a car, or sign on for an organized excursion. **Cubataxi** (© **21/64-3737**) makes local and long-distance runs.

A car is a good idea if you really want to do some independent exploration of the surrounding area, or travel to, say, Santiago de Cuba or Guardalavaca. There's a **Havanautos** office at the Baracoa airport (© **21/64-5343**); **Cubacar** (© **21/64-5212**) and **Vía Rent a Car** (© **21/64-5137**) also have agencies in Baracoa. **Cubatur** on Calle Maceo (© **21/64-5306**) also rents cars. Rates are CUC$55 to CUC$65 (US$59–US$70/£30–£35) per day for a standard four-door compact car.

Transtur runs the BaracoaBusTour that travels a 56km (35-mile) circuit and stops at El Yunque and Playa Maguana. The hop-on/hop-off service costs CUC$5 (US$5.40/£2.70) a day.

Orientation

The **Havanatur** office at Antonio Maceo 120 (© **21/64-5358**) can provide travel information, as can the personnel of the tour desks at the Hotel El Castillo and Hotel Porto Santo. Other tour agencies include **Cubatur,** Maceo, corner of Pelayo Cuervo (© **21/64-5306**); and **EcoTur,** Coronel Cardoso 24 (© **21/64-3665**), which specializes in outdoor trips in the area.

A **Banco de Crédito y Comercio** branch is on Calle Antonio Maceo 99. Traveler's checks can be cashed at the Hotel El Castillo and Hotel Porto Santo.

For medical attention and a pharmacy, go to the Clinica Internacional Baracoa, Calle Martí, between Roberto Rey and Linvano Sánchez (© **21/64-1037-38;** www.servimed cuba.com).

The main **post office** is on Calle Antonio Maceo 136, near Plaza Independencia; it's open Monday through Saturday from 8am to 10pm and Sunday from 8am to 8pm. You can make local, long-distance, and international phone calls or use one of the computer terminals at the **Etecsa** office on Calle Antonio Maceo, opposite Plaza Independencia; it's open daily from 8:30am to 7:30pm.

ACCOMMODATIONS ■

Casa Brisas del Atlántico **1**
Casa Daniel Salomón Paján **10**
Casa de Nelsy Borges Téran **9**
Casa Isabel Garrido **13**
Casa la Colina **12**
Casa Tropical **4**
Casa Walter **11**
Hostal La Habanera **8**
Hotel El Castillo **14**
Hotel La Rusa **2**

ATTRACTIONS ●

El Castillo de
   Santa Bárbara **14**
El Yunque **15**
Fuerte Matachín/Museo
   Matachín **3**
Nuestra Señora de
   la Asunción **7**
Museo Arqueológico **17**
Parque de la
   Independencia **6**

DINING ◆

La Colonial **5**
La Punta **16**
Restaurante Duaba **14**

WHAT TO SEE & DO

Baracoa is its own greatest attraction. Its bustling streets are lined with gaily painted clapboard houses, and the rivers, beaches, and mountains beyond the city are perfect for outdoor exploration.

In the 18th and 19th centuries, Baracoan settlers built three fortresses to protect the town from pirate attacks. **El Castillo de Santa Bárbara,** the oldest of the bunch, sits high above town, with splendid views of the bay and surrounding countryside; it has now been converted into a hotel. **Fuerte de la Punta,** facing the seaside promenade, is now a restaurant. The third, **Fuerte Matachín,** near the entrance to town, houses the municipal museum, **Museo Matachín,** Calle Martí s/n at the Malecón (② **21/64-2122**). It holds a number of interesting historical exhibits related to the history of Baracoa and its legends and myths. The museum also has a collection of extraordinary, vividly colored and striped *polimitas* (snail shells), which locals used to make into necklaces sold to tourists before the supply dried up. (It is now illegal to sell them.) The museum is open daily from 8am to noon, and from 2 to 6pm; admission is CUC$1 (US$1.10/55p) with a guide, and photo and video privileges cost an extra CUC$1 (US$1.10/55p) and CUC$5 (US$5.40/£2.70), respectively. Ask here about a city tour for CUC$5 (US$5.40/£2.70).

Nuestra Señora de la Asunción, Maceo 152 (© **21/64-3352**), the rather austere cathedral, was constructed in 1512, though it was burned by the French in 1652. The current structure was rebuilt at the beginning of the 19th century. It is in a considerable state of disrepair, but is slated for massive improvement work. It is most notable for the **Cruz de la Parra,** a small wooden cross on display inside a glass case. Locals insist that Columbus himself planted the cross on the banks of the bay in 1492, shortly after disembarking on Cuban soil for the first time. Whether or not there's any truth to that claim, carbon dating has in fact established that the cross is more than 500 years old (making it one of the oldest Christian relics in the Americas, if not the oldest). The hardwood is native to Cuba, though, so if Columbus did leave it, the cross must have been fashioned in situ rather than having been brought with him, as was originally believed. The cross has greatly dwindled in size, due to the devout visitors over the years, who thought nothing of slicing off a memento for themselves. The church is open Tuesday through Saturday from 8am to noon and from 2 to 4pm.

Next to the church is **Parque de la Independencia** (also called Parque Central), a popular gathering spot for locals and tourists enjoying a few lazy days in Baracoa. A bust of the rebel Taíno Indian leader Hatuey (whose countenance today appears on beer bottles) adorns the square. Hatuey took up arms against the early conquistadores until he was caught by the Spanish and burned at the stake.

In the area around Baracoa are as many as 50 **pre-Columbian archaeological sites** related to the major Native American groups that inhabited the area (Siboney, Taíno, and Guanturabey). The only native group to survive is the Yateras, a small community that has succeeded in preserving its traditions, marrying only among each other and living along the Río Toa.

Above the town is the **Museo Arqueológico** in Reparto Paraíso, open Monday to Friday from 9am to 6pm and Saturday from 9am to noon; admission is CUC$3 (US$3.25/£1.60). It costs CUC$12 (US$13/£6.50) to take a video and CUC$1 (US$1.10/55p) for a guide. The remains of Taínos can be seen in a cave, as well as in a random collection of ceramics and artifacts supposedly belonging to this pre-Columbian tribe. The museum is only really worth the entrance fee to climb to the **mirador** ★★★, where you can admire and survey the entire bay; on a clear day, the vista is stunning.

OUTDOOR EXCURSIONS AROUND BARACOA

Baracoa's potential as an ecotourism destination has just begun to be exploited. The spectacular area around Baracoa affords excellent opportunities for treks and white-water rafting. The region features patches of secondary rainforest, and abounds in banana, yucca, mango, coconut, and tall royal palm trees, and at least 10 flowing rivers. The earth here is rich in iron, which gives it a red tone.

Distinctive **El Yunque** ★★, described in Spanish chronicles as an anvil-shaped, high (575m/1,886 ft.), and square mountain, dominates the landscape; Columbus wrote of seeing it on his approach to the bay. Frequently bathed in mist, the flat-topped limestone mountain is about 10km (6¼ miles) west of Baracoa, and its slopes can be climbed in 4 hours round-trip. The slopes have been declared a UNESCO Biosphere Reserve. El Yunque is part of the Parque Natural Duaba and is home to scores of bird species and unique plants. In fact, 16 of Cuba's 24 endemic bird species can be found in this area. You can also spot the endemic *coco thrinas* palms, which look like tall dandelions. The trek through tropical forest, with views of rare ferns and orchids, is beautiful, but it can be intensely humid. Those who aren't up for the hike can always drive, though it's rough going along the unpaved road. Adventurers in search of white-water rafting possibilities should check out **Río Toa,** the widest river in Cuba and part of a national park.

The UNESCO Natural World Heritage Site of **Parque Nacional Alejandro de Humboldt,** a mountainous rainforest area with karst scenery that extends for 32,560 hectares (80,458 acres) north of Baracoa, is rich in biodiversity. It is home to the ivory-billed woodpecker, Cuban parrot and parakeet, colorful *polimita* snails, Caribbean manatee, and rare Cuban *solenodon* (an insectivorous mammal).

Alexander Domínguez at **EcoTur,** Coronel Cardoso 24 (*©* **21/64-3665**), organizes a variety of nature outings with transportation and guides, including white-water rafting on the Río Toa, various treks, boating excursions along rivers (one of the best trips is along the gorgeous Río Yumurí, 30km/19 miles east of Baracoa, where there's a charming little fishing village), and an exclusive 10km (6.2-mile) hike to Juncal-Rencontra in the Toa area, not offered by other agencies. Currently, visitors must bring tents and sleeping bags for this latter trip, but EcoTur hopes to provide camping equipment in 2009. **Havanatur** (*©* **21/64-5358**) and **Cubatur** (*©* **21/64-5306**) also offer organized excursions. Prices run between CUC$16 and CUC$36 (US$17–US$39/£8.65–£19) per person, but there's often a six-person minimum. Baracoa is blessed with a few superb beaches, which, due to the town's isolation, haven't yet been built up with huge all-inclusive hotels (this will certainly change in the coming years). **Playa Maguana** ★ is about 22km (14 miles) from town on the road to Moa. It's a peaceful place with picture-perfect golden sands and is popular with local families and fishermen. There's a small hotel here (see "Where to Stay," below). Cubatur runs day excursions here from 10am to 4pm for CUC$5 (US$5.40/£2.70) per person that can be organized on the morning you wish to go. A smaller and more isolated beach, **Playa Nava,** is another 6km (3³/₄ miles) west. It's not as pretty as Maguana, but you're likely to have it to yourself.

WHERE TO STAY

There's nothing fancy or especially luxurious in easygoing Baracoa—except the spectacular views of the bay and surrounding mountains—but one of the main hotels, in the oldest fortress in town, is a charmer. The little town is populated by more than 150 *casas particulares,* most right within the old town; several are excellent and among the best deals of their kind in Cuba.

Moderate

Hotel El Castillo ★★ **Finds** Perched up on a hill with the best views of Baracoa and the bay, and a picture-perfect pool, this easygoing Gaviota hotel—the lower part of which inhabits an old fort—is the top place in town to stay. Its simple rooms don't quite measure up to the privileged location and general ambience, though they're of pretty good size, have colonial-style furnishings, and are set around the pool. If you can get room no. 201, do so, as it's a large corner room with a queen-size bed, and one of only two rooms with a bed big enough for a couple. All the rest have two or three twin beds. If we owned the place, we'd restyle it as a swank hotel. Advance reservations are essential in high season. Nonguests can use the pool for CUC$10 (US$11/£5.40), including CUC$8 (US$8.65/£4.30) worth of food and drink.

Calle Calixto García, Loma el Paraíso, Baracoa. *©* **21/64-5194.** www.gaviota-grupo.com. 34 units. CUC$54–CUC$58 (US$58–US$63/£29–£31) double. Rates include breakfast. MC, V. **Amenities:** Restaurant; snack bar; 2 bars; outdoor pool; laundry service. *In room:* A/C, TV, safe.

Hotel Porto Santo Gaviota runs this hotel right on the bay near the spot where Columbus supposedly deposited the cross marking his arrival in the Americas. Slightly larger than Hotel El Castillo, this one gets more tour groups. Its best feature is a large pool with a deck and thatched-roof bar overlooking the bay and cute private-cove beach. In fact, the view here may be even better than that from El Castillo, because from here you are looking at Baracoa. In truth, rooms aren't very large or nicely decorated, and all have rather small bathrooms, but those in the last wing have the best bay views (something I'd request). All come with a small balcony or private patio. The location is somewhat isolated, though, and can be a pain if you're looking to make frequent trips into town.

Carretera del Aeropuerto, Baracoa. ℂ **21/64-5106.** Fax 21/64-5339. www.gaviota-grupo.com. 83 units. CUC$54–CUC$58 (US$58–US$63/£29–£31) double. Rates include breakfast. MC, V. **Amenities:** Restaurant; grill; 2 bars; nightly show; outdoor pool; car- and scooter-rental desk; laundry service. In room: A/C, TV, minibar, safe.

Villa Maguana ★★ This little place, 21km (13 miles) from Baracoa, doesn't look like much from the outside. But the secluded and peaceful inn fronts a totally private, pretty cove next to a 2km (1¼-mile) white-sand beach. The four villas with 16 rooms are large and charmingly rustic, like private cabins, with dark-wood furniture and red-and-yellow decor; two have great terraces with rocking chairs overlooking the transparent water. Note that villas nos. 1 and 2 face the beach. The villas would be a great place for a large family or a band of couples to rent and just hang out here on the beautiful outskirts of Baracoa.

Carretera de Moa a Baracoa, Km 20, Baracoa. ℂ **21/64-5106.** Fax 21/64-5339. www.gaviota-grupo.com. 16 units. CUC$60–CUC$75 (US$65–US$81/£32–£41) double. Rates include breakfast. MC, V. **Amenities:** Restaurant; bar. In room: A/C, TV, minibar, safe.

Inexpensive

There are more than 150 *casas particulares* in Baracoa. Recommended *casas* include **Casa Daniel Salomón Pajón** ★, Calle Céspedes 28, between Rubert López and Maceo (ℂ **21/64-2122** or 529-17403; fifi@toa.gtm.sld.cu), which is one of the friendliest *casas* in Cuba. Daniel works at the museum and knows a lot about Baracoa's history. He has one comfortable room with a large bathroom and a central covered patio. Mountain bikes are also available for rent. **Casa Tropical** ★, Calle Martí 175 (ℂ **21/64-3437**), has very comfortable rooms in a lovely colonial house with an enormous blue porch and courtyard, and is run by a friendly and welcoming family; the very tasty swordfish in coconut sauce is a good enough reason to stay. **Casa Isabel Garrido** ★, Calle Calixto García 164A (ℂ **21/64-3515**; ysabel@toa.gtm.sld.cu), has a large terrace and a small balcony overlooking the street; there's also a separate entrance to the two upstairs bedrooms that share a sitting room and small kitchen. **Casa Walter,** Calle Rubert López 47, between Céspedes and Coroneles Galanos (ℂ **21/64-2346**; maribara@enet.cu), is a central option whose third-floor terrace has a high-pitched red-tile roof with dining tables and a bar. **Casa Brisas del Atlántico** ★, Calle Frank País 3, between Avenida Malecón and Máximo Gómez (ℂ **21/64-3457** or 21/64-3872), has two rooms with a separate entrance and a huge rooftop terrace with sea views. **Casa La Colina** ★, Calle Calixto García 158 altos, between Céspedes and Coroneles Gulano (ℂ **21/64-2729**), has a superb terrace. **Casa de Nelsy Borges Terán,** Calle Maceo 171 between Ciro Frías and Céspedes (ℂ **21/64-3569**; oteran@toa.gtm.sld.cu), has a great rooftop terrace and one of the rooms has a lovely street-front balcony. Filling dinners are served.

Hostal La Habanera ★ (**Value**)   Fronting the Plaza de la Independencia, this recently renovated, downtown colonial structure is an atmospheric, affordable, and perfectly located option. The rooms are all spacious, with high ceilings, bright-patterned bed linens, rattan headboards, sparkling tile floors, and tubs in the bathrooms. All come with two twin beds and, unfortunately, they aren't planning on adding larger beds anytime soon. However, for a budget option, you'll be surprised to find a large television, with four international cable channels. My favorite rooms are the four that share a long, broad veranda overlooking Calle Maceo. Gaviota was due to take over the management of this hotel under the Hoteles E brand at press time.

Calle Maceo 68, at the corner of Calle Frank País. (**C**) **21/64-5273.** www.gaviota-grupo.com. 10 units. CUC$40–CUC$55 (US$43–US$59/£22–£30) double. Rates include breakfast. MC, V. **Amenities:** Restaurant; snack bar/bar; laundry service. In room: A/C, TV, fridge.

Hotel La Rusa   This legendary little hotel was established by a Russian émigré (and princess) and former dancer ("La Rusa de Baracoa"), who, over the years, became active in Cuban revolutionary politics and later played host to Fidel, Che, and the poet Nicolás Guillén. Today, this big yellow house right by the sea hasn't really lived up to its storied past. As a very run-down hotel, its biggest plus is that it fronts the sea, across the street from Baracoa's Malecón. However, at press time, Gaviota was due to take over the management and spruce up the hotel.

Calle Máximo Gómez 161, Baracoa. (**C**) **21/64-3011.** Fax 21/64-2337. www.gaviota-grupo.com. 12 units. CUC$36–CUC$40 (US$39–US$43/£19–£22) double. Rates include breakfast. MC, V. In room: A/C, TV, minibar.

WHERE TO DINE

Diners resigned to the plain, unimaginative food in the rest of Cuba are in for a treat in Baracoa. The town and region revel in a unique cuisine found nowhere else in Cuba, one that makes ample use of local coconut and chocolate. The region produces about three-quarters of Cuba's coconuts, so logically it plays a strong part in the local diet. Try *cucurucho,* a coconut pudding with fruit (orange and papaya) and honey wrapped in palm leaves; fresh fish embellished with coconut sauce; and the drinks *sacoco,* rum and coconut milk drunk from green coconuts, and *chorote,* chocolate with cornstarch. **Casa de Chocolate,** Maceo 121, is the place to get thick hot chocolate and locally made candies.

La Colonial ★ BARACOAN/CRIOLLA   The only officially sanctioned *paladar* (private home restaurant) left in Baracoa, this well-run place in a lovely colonial home is quite good, and deserves to be supported by travelers. There's no fixed menu; ask about fresh dishes and catches from the daily roster of seven to eight main courses, including fish and shrimp cooked in *leche de coco* (coconut milk). Once you get beyond the floral tablecloths, the decor and ambience here are actually somewhat romantic.

Martí 123. (**C**) **21/64-5391.** Reservations recommended for large groups. Main courses CUC$7–CUC$9 (US$7.55–US$9.70/£3.80–£4.85). No credit cards. Daily 11am–11pm.

La Punta BARACOAN/CRIOLLA   On a covered terrace within the walls of one of the original three forts in Baracoa, this state-run restaurant is an elegant, tranquil spot, perfect for lunch. It has good service and well-prepared dishes such as dorado and *pargo* (grilled fish). Typical Cuban dishes such as beefsteak, pork, and fried chicken are also available. Spaghetti and beef fajitas are also served for those who want a bit of variety. Although the walls of the fort block most of the views, especially from the tables, if you walk around the grounds, you can peek through the cannon slots at the Atlantic Ocean, Baracoa bay, and some stunning scenery. The bar here is open from 10am to 10:30pm.

Fuerte de la Punta. ⓒ **21/64-5224.** Reservations not accepted. Main courses CUC$.80–CUC$4.50 (US85¢–US$4.85/45p–£2.45). No credit cards. Daily 7am–10:30pm.

Restaurante Duaba BARACOAN/CRIOLLA   The restaurant within the Hotel El Castillo does big business serving Baracoa specialties to its guests but it's a good option for anyone in Baracoa. Try any of the locally flavored dishes, such as Santa Bárbara fish filet, *jaiba* (sea crab), or *cobo enchilado,* a huge shellfish. There are also some good options for vegetarians, including stuffed eggplant and a vegetable plate. The daily set menu is pricey at CUC$12 (US$13/£6.50); try ordering a la carte instead.

In Hotel El Castillo, Calle Calixto García, Loma el Paraíso. ⓒ **21/64-5106.** Reservations recommended. Main courses CUC$5.10–CUC$12 (US$5.50–US$13/£2.75–£6.50). MC, V. Daily 7–10pm.

BARACOA AFTER DARK

Baracoa has an amazingly lively, after-dark scene for a town so small. In fact, its nightlife ranks among the best in Cuba. Virtually all the clubs and live-music venues are conveniently located on a single street, **Calle Antonio Maceo,** making Baracoa throb most nights like a tiny, tropical New Orleans, with traditional Cuban and contemporary dance music and revelers spilling out into the street until the wee hours. The scene is especially buoyant on Saturday nights *(El Sabado Baracoese),* when Baracoans host a massive street party along Maceo. Unique to Baracoa are the enthusiastic *animadores,* or emcees, who introduce songs and bands and entertain audiences with florid language, poetry, and humor. Club cover charges are generally CUC$1 to CUC$3 (US$1.10–US$3.25/55p–£1.60). Ask around for the possibility of listening to indigenous Baracoan music called *kiriba* and *el nengon.*

The first spot to stop is the local **Casa de la Trova** ★★, Maceo 149, a comfortable, well-lighted place loaded with locals and featuring good bands and a gregarious emcee. If you're lucky, you'll get to hear **Maravilla Yuqueña,** a wonderful group with a venerable old lead singer who should be far more famous than he is. Down the street is **485,** Maceo 485, with a Trova-like covered patio and the livelier **485 Disco** next-door. Across the street, **La Terraza** is a huge, open-air terrace on top of a building. It has a nightly show (10pm–midnight) and full-throttle, decibel-busting music under the stars, with dancers and occasional dance contests. A more sedate spot, within shouting distance of the sound system of La Terraza, is **El Patio ARTex,** a cute, brightly colored cafe with red lamps and a corrugated tin roof. The live music is pure Cuban *son.*

Santiago de Cuba

Set on the seaside, near the island's eastern tip, **Santiago de Cuba** ★★★ is the country's second-largest city. Vibrant, tropical, and often sweltering, Santiago is the country's liveliest cultural showpiece, outside of Havana. With a population just under a half-million people, Santiago is a world apart, with a unique history and rhythms all its own. The city has produced some of Cuba's greatest contemporary musicians as well as several of its most stalwart revolutionaries, and it has served as the stage for some of the most storied events in Cuba's modern history. As the capital of the old Oriente province, it has the largest Afro-Cuban population in Cuba and a resolutely Afro-Caribbean feel that distinguishes it from the rest of Cuba.

Founded in 1515, Santiago was one of the first of seven towns in Cuba and the Spanish colony's capital until 1553. Diego Velázquez, the founder of the original seven *villas,* built his mansion here, and the house still stands in the heart of the historic quarter. The Spanish character of the city would soon be supplemented by other influences. After the 1791 revolution in Haiti, a large number of French coffee plantation owners fled with their African slaves and made their way to Santiago. Black Haitian workers followed, as did large contingencies of West African slaves, sold to work on the plantations.

While downtown Santiago has the requisite noise, traffic, and urban chaos of a large city, it retains the intimate, friendly feel of a provincial capital, with peaceful neighborhoods where men play dominoes outdoors on hilly streets.

Santiago continues to earn its reputation as one of the liveliest and most individualistic cities in Cuba. The city's annual Carnival celebrations in July are famous throughout Cuba. Afro-Cuban religious traditions, including Santeria and other forms of worship, have their strongest hold here. And Santiagueros are also recognized for their take on Cuban Spanish, with a unique vocabulary and singsong rhythm.

Santiago fans out from a large, deep natural bay—guarded by the 16th-century El Morro fortress—and sits at the base of low mountains. Fine excursions await visitors with time to explore outside the city: **El Cobre** ★★ is a sacred shrine set in the beautiful foothills of the Sierra Maestra, while **Gran Piedra** is a great rocky area just outside the city that invites hiking and relaxation in its cool environs.

1 ORIENTATION

ARRIVING & DEPARTING

BY PLANE   Direct international scheduled and charter flights arrive at the **Aeropuerto Internacional Antonio Maceo** (© 22/69-1053; airport code SCU). Airlines regularly servicing Santiago include **Aerocaribbean** from Santo Domingo and **Cubana.** Charter flights run between Miami and Santiago several times each week.

Daily flights connect Santiago with Havana via **Cubana** (© 22/65-1578 in Santiago, or 7/83-4446 in Havana; www.cubana.cu) for CUC$113 (US$122/£61). **AeroCaribbean**

Plaza de la Revolución

Estadio Guillermón Moncado ■

$ CADECA
C Etecsa
⌧ Post office

0   0.5 mi
0   0.5 km

REPARTO PASTORITA

Av. General Cebreco

Matanzas
Las Villas
8
7
6
5
D
C
B
A

Av. de las Américas

REPARTO SUEÑO

G
24
F
E
J
23
K
L
M
25
N
2
3

Av. de Céspedes

Teresa
L
M
4

Autopista Nacional

4
6

Casa del Caribe ■

13 10
11
12
17
15
13

26 26
27

Av. Manduley 29
9
7
5
3

REPARTO VISTA ALEGRE

Victoriano Garzón

Escarlo (Juan C. Zenea)

Enramada (José A. Saco)

Aguilera

REPARTO SANTA BÁRBARA

Luis F. Marcané 28

■ Havanatur

Av. de Raúl Pujol

Bitirí

Anacaona
13

PARQUE ZOOLÓGICO

Pedrera (Prudencio Martínez)

Aguilera

Celda (Gal. Carlos Roloff)

Pizarro (Gal. F. Peraza)

D. Velázquez

REPARTO LAS FLORES

Gal. Julio Sanguily
Gal. S. Sánchez
Camino de la Laguna

REPARTO ASUNCIÓN

ACCOMMODATIONS ■
Casa Alejandro Thomás **18**
Casa Asensio **24**
Casa Florinda Chaviano
   Martínez **25**
Casa Gloria Boué Alonso **23**
Casa Hugo & Adela **16**
Casa Leonardo y Rosa **17**
Gran Hotel Escuela **13**
Hostal Basilio **20**
Hotel Casa Granda **11**
Hotel Las Américas **27**
Hotel Libertad **19**
Meliá Santiago de Cuba **26**

DINING ◆
El Cayo **2**
La Isabelica **26**
Paladar Las Gallegas **12**
Paladar Salón Tropical **28**
Restaurant El Morro **2**
Santiago 1900 **21**
ZunZún **29**

ATTRACTIONS ●
Ayuntamiento **9**
Balcón de Velásquez **6**
Barrio El Tivolí **5**
Casa Velázquez
   (Museo de Ambiente
   Colonial Cubano) **8**
Castillo El Morro **2**
Catedral de Nuestra Señora
   de la Asunción **7**
Cementerio Santa Ifigenia **1**
Cuartel de Moncada
   (Museo Histórico
   26 de Julio) **22**
Museo del Carnaval **15**
Museo de la Lucha
   Clandestina **3**
Museo Emilio Bacardí
   Moreau **14**
Padre Pico steps **4**
Parque Céspedes **10**

(© **22/68-7255** in Santiago, or 7/870-4965 in Havana) flies on Monday, Thursday, Friday, and Sunday for CUC$120 (US$130/£65). Flight duration is roughly 2 hours.

The airport is 8km (5 miles) south of the city. There are several car-rental agencies at the airport. The quickest and safest way to the city is by registered taxi; the trip into town is CUC$5 to CUC$6 (US$5.40–US$6.50/£2.70–£3.25).

BY BUS   Víazul's (© **22/62-8484** in Santiago, or 7/881-1413 in Havana; www.viazul. com) Havana–Santiago de Cuba line, with stops in Santa Clara, Sancti Spíritus, Ciego de Avila, Camagüey, Bayamo, and Holguín, is the best way to get to Santiago by bus, especially if you're planning to see any points of interest between Cuba's two main cities. For the trip from Havana, buses depart at 9:30am, 3pm, 6:15pm, and 10pm, arriving at 1:30am, 6:40am, 6:35am, and noon, respectively; the fare is CUC$51 (US$55/£28) one-way. From Trinidad (© **41/99-4448**), a bus leaves daily at 8am and arrives at 8pm; the fare is CUC$33 (US$36/£18) one-way. From Camagüey (© **32/27-2601**), the trip is about 7 hours; buses leave at 12:10am, 6:30am, 1:30pm, and 4:20pm and the fare is CUC$20 (US$22/£11) one-way. Buses depart Santiago for Havana at 9am, 3:15pm, 6pm, and 10pm.

Víazul also has once-daily service between Santiago and Baracoa, leaving Santiago at 7:45am and returning from Baracoa at 2:15pm. Duration is 4 hours and 50 minutes; the fare is CUC$15 (US$16/£8.10) one-way.

The **Terminal de Omnibuses** (© **22/62-8484**) for Víazul is located on Avenida de los Libertadores at the corner of Avenida Yarayó, about 2km (1¼ miles) from Parque Céspedes. A taxi to downtown costs about CUC$3 (US$3.25/£1.60).

BY TRAIN   The Cuban *ferrocarril* (railway) is relatively dependable, but delays, midrun breakdowns, and other problems are still quite common. Taking the train is a potentially adventurous experience for those who wish to see the "real Cuba," but can be frustrating for those who need to adhere to a schedule.

A special fast train, also known as the "French Train" or "Tren Francés," travels from Havana to Santiago on alternate days (12 hr. with stops in Santa Clara and Camagüey). It offers *primera especial* (first-class) service for CUC$62 (US$67/£33) and *segunda clase* (second-class) service for CUC$50 (US$54/£27), featuring reclining seats, air-conditioning, and cafeteria services. Prices are discounted by 50% for children under 7 years old, and **Ferrotur** claims it will refund the fare if arrival is more than 1 hour late. Daily departure from Havana in the high season is at 6:05pm, arriving at 6:30am in Santiago.

Other services include the following regular trains (also with air-conditioning and food services on board): no. 11, departing Central Station in Havana at 3:15pm and arriving at 5:15am; and no. 43, leaving La Coubre Station in Havana at 6:20am and arriving at 11pm (fare for both CUC$32/US$35/£17). Train schedules change frequently, and depending on the season, many trains don't operate on a daily basis; verify the current schedule by calling © **7/862-1920** or 7/861-4259, though it's often better to go in person to the train station and purchase tickets at least a day in advance.

In Santiago, the large, modern **Terminal Central de Ferrocarriles** is located on Avenida Jesús Menéndez at Paseo de Martí (© **22/62-2836**), across from the Caney rum factory.

BY CAR   Driving to Santiago is a good way to see the breadth of the country. The six-lane, toll-free Autopista Nacional (A1) and the Carretera Central run the length of Cuba, straight down the spine of the country from Pinar del Río to Santiago. However, east from Sancti Spíritus, it is just two lanes almost the entire way to Santiago, and the going can be slow at times, since there are equal numbers of cars, trucks, horse-drawn carriages, bicycles, and pedestrians making use of the Carretera Central. Santiago is 860km (534

Santiago, City of Struggle & Rebellion

Santiago has long demonstrated a fiercely independent streak. Among Cubans, the city is known affectionately as the *cuna de la Revolución,* or the cradle of the Revolution. The first slave uprisings in Cuba occurred in Santiago, and the city had prominent roles in the wars of independence against the Spanish in 1868 and 1895. Antonio Maceo rejected a pact with the colonial power, laying the foundation for continued resistance, and became one of the leaders of the rebel army. Each of the 29 generals during the 30-year war against the Spanish came from the city, and the Bay of Santiago was the site of the 1898 naval battles between the U.S. and Spain. Teddy Roosevelt and his Rough Riders stormed the Loma de San Juan, a low hill just east of the city, in battles against the Spanish, which led to Spain's imminent defeat and withdrawal from Cuba (though Cuba's independence was effectively usurped by the Americans in the years after the Spanish-American War).

In 1953, the young firebrand Fidel Castro and a band of insurgents attacked the Moncada military barracks in Santiago (the failed, but famous 26th of July episode). After many of his rebels were tortured and killed by the army, Castro was captured and he issued his famous declaration, "History will absolve me," in defense of his seditious actions. A local Santiago schoolteacher, Frank País, sparked an uprising of university students in 1957, attacking police headquarters. Assassinated by the Batista army in the streets of Santiago, he became a martyr of the Revolution. Castro returned from exile in Mexico in 1956 to wage war from the cover of the Sierra Maestra, west of Santiago, and 2 years later the rebel leader ultimately announced victory, on January 1, 1959, from the balcony of the governor's mansion (today Town Hall) in Parque Céspedes. Castro rewarded the city that supported him with the title "Heroic City of the Revolution."

miles) east of Havana, 127km (79 miles) east of Bayamo, and 134km (83 miles) southeast of Holguín.

VISITOR INFORMATION

Most of the major tour agencies, including **Cubanacán,** Calle M, corner of Avenida Las Americas (② **22/64-3445**), **Cubatur,** Calle Lacret 701, corner of Heredia (② **22/68-6033**), and **Havanatur** (② **22/64-3603**), have offices in the airport and at several hotels in town. They all offer guided city and area tours for CUC$36 to CUC$70 (US$39–US$)76/£19–£38; excursions to El Cobre for CUC$15 (US$16/£8.10), La Gran Piedra for CUC$42 (US$45/£23), Baconao for CUC$66 (US$71/£36), and Tropicana for CUC$28 to CUC$44 (US$30–US$48/£15–£24); and group trips to Baracoa for CUC$74 (US$80/£40) and more far-flung destinations.

CITY LAYOUT

The historic center of the city rolls across low hills to the east of the **Bahía de Santiago.** The focal point of colonial Santiago is **Parque Céspedes.** This historic square boasts perhaps the oldest house in the Americas. **Calle Heredia,** which leads east from the square, is a popular street with plenty of foot traffic, and it is lined with live music venues, colonial houses and museums, and artisans selling their crafts. South of Parque Céspedes is the charming, hilly **El Tivolí** district and its emblematic Padre Pico steps. Heading east of Parque Céspedes is **Plaza de Dolores,** an attractive and shady little square that's a popular and easygoing hangout ringed by a handful of restaurants, bars, and cafes. **Plaza de Marte** marks the divide between old Santiago and the newer section, leading along the long and wide avenue Victoriano Garzón out toward the nicest suburbs in Santiago and districts of several hotels and *casas particulares,* **Reparto Sueño, Reparto Vista Alegre,** and **Reparto Santa Bárbara.**

Old and new street names (pre- and post-Revolution) are still sometimes used interchangeably in Santiago. The most common pre-Revolution street names used in the old colonial center are: Enramada (for José Antonio Saco); San Basilio (Bartolomé Masó); San Pedro (General Lacret); Santo Tomás (Félix Peña); Marina (Aguilera); and Carnicería (Pío Rosado).

2 GETTING AROUND

BY TAXI Among the many taxi companies available for local and long-distance hire are **Taxis OK** (© 22/65-3333), **Transtur** (© 22/65-2329), and the least expensive, **Cubataxi** (© 22/64-1965/65-1038). Taxis of many different stripes and comfort levels, all varying by small degrees in price, congregate near the cathedral on Parque Céspedes and at the major tourist hotels. Be sure to ask prices before hiring one, as tourist gouging is a favorite local pastime (from the Meliá Santiago to Parque Céspedes, the fare is CUC$3/US$3.25/£1.60; from downtown to El Morro the fare is CUC$8–CUC$12/US$8.65–US$13/£4.30–£6.50). Cheaper taxis, both registered and unregistered, can be found parked around Plaza Marte. With the latter, negotiate a price, but understand that the driver may be uncomfortable taking you directly to the door of your hotel if he's not officially licensed to carry foreigners.

Coco Taxis are few and far between around Santiago. Coco Taxis should be a bit less expensive than regular taxis, although the drivers will usually first quote you the going cab rate, so try to negotiate. There are also *bici* (bicycle) and *moto* (motorcycle) taxis, both of which are convenient and inexpensive (usually CUC$1/US$1.10/55p), but occasionally hair-raising for many passengers, given the volume and often-chaotic nature of car traffic in Santiago.

BY CAR **Cubacar** (© 22/68-6107) has offices at the airport, opposite the Cupet gas station on Carretera Central; Hotel Casa Granda; Hotel Las Américas; Meliá Santiago; and Hotel Villa San Juan. **Vía Rent a Car** (© 22/62-4646) is inside the Cubatur office, Lacret 701, corner of Heredia. Rates are CUC$45 to CUC$80 (US$49–US$86/£24–£43) per day for a standard four-door compact car.

BY FOOT The area of greatest activity and cultural interest to many visitors in the historic center—the few streets around Parque Céspedes—is easy to get around on foot, though some areas, such as the Tivolí district, are extremely hilly. However, many hotels are at least a couple of kilometers from the city center, and a good number of the city's foremost attractions, such as El Morro, are beyond the city and require transportation.

(Fast Facts) **Santiago de Cuba**

Airport See "Arriving & Departing," above.

Car Rentals See "Getting Around," above.

Currency Exchange A **CADECA** ((C) **22/65-1383**) branch is on Calle Aguilera 508. The local branch of **Banco de Crédito y Comercio** ((C) **22/62-3316**), where you can exchange traveler's checks and get cash advances, is on Félix Peña 614. **Bandec** ((C) **22/62-7581**), with similar services, is on Félix Peña between Aguilera and Heredia with an ATM. Both are open Monday through Friday from 8am to 3pm and Saturday 8 to 11am. An ATM is at the **Banco Popular de Ahoro** ((C) **22/64-2454**) on Plaza Dolores. You can also change money at the Meliá Santiago and most other hotels in the city.

Emergency Dial (C) **116** for any emergency.

Hospitals & Medical Assistance **Clínica Internacional,** Avenida Raúl Pujol at Calle 10 in Reparto Vista Alegre ((C) **22/64-2589**), has 24-hour emergency services, a dentist, and English-speaking doctors. There are **pharmacies** at the clinic and along Calle José Antonio Saco.

Internet Access The **Etecsa** Multiservicios Céspedes on Heredia, corner of Sto Tomás ((C) **22/62-4784**) provides telephone and Internet service daily from 8:30am to 7:30pm. You can also find cybercafes at the Meliá Santiago.

Police The police station is located at Corona and San Gerónimo ((C) **116**). However, the probability of finding an English speaker is remote. In case of an emergency, one of the better hotels (such as the Casa Granda or Meliá Santiago) should be able to help or at least interpret for the police.

Post Office The main post office is on Calle Aguilera 517 at Padre Quiroga ((C) **22/65-2397**); it's open Monday through Saturday from 8am to 10pm. There are basic postal facilities in all the major hotels. A **DHL** office can be found at Calle Aguilera 310 at the corner of San Félix ((C) **22/68-6323**).

Safety Santiago is one of Cuba's less safe cities, if only because the local *jineteros* are relentless in accosting foreigners. They are, for the most part, innocuous. Still, if you're attending a street festival, concert, or Carnival, put your money in a money belt and leave your watch, jewelry, and knapsack behind (these items will be safer in your hotel or *casa particular*). Also, be careful and keep an eye on your bags at the Santiago bus and train stations. That said, Santiago, as with the rest of Cuba, is still relatively safe for a large city.

Taxis See "Getting Around," earlier in this chapter.

Telephone Santiago's area or city code is **22,** but many numbers are still published under the old system and area code 226. The "6" is now placed before the number.

You can make local, long-distance, and international phone calls with a phone card from **Etecsa** (see "Internet Access," above).

Many visitors in search of what makes Cuba unique actually prefer the country's second city to the capital, even though Santiago is unpolished and has few grand examples of colonial architecture.

THE TOP ATTRACTIONS

A major gathering spot day and night for Santiagueros, aggressive *jineteros*, and travelers alike, **Parque Céspedes** ★ is a menagerie of eclectic architecture, to put it mildly. Its benches, tall shade trees, and gas lamps are ringed by colonial, 19th-century, and modern structures, including the ancient mansion of Diego Velázquez (see "Casa Velázquez," below), as well as the handsome colonial governor's mansion (Town Hall), the baroque cathedral, and the city's oldest hotel, Casa Granda.

The **Ayuntamiento,** or Town Hall (also called the Palacio Municipal), a huge white building on the north side of the square with blue wooden grilles, was originally built in 1515. It was greatly renovated in the 1950s after an earthquake, but has retained its elegant colonial lines, balcony, and patio. Fidel Castro addressed the adoring masses here on January 1, 1959, after the rebel army had taken the city and announced the triumph of *La Revolución.*

Across the park, the early-19th-century **Catedral de Nuestra Señora de la Asunción** is a massive, ornate, pale-yellow-and-white basilica with twin towers—one of several churches to occupy the site since 1522 after its antecedents were destroyed by pirates, earthquakes, and other natural disasters. The frescoes on the arches and dome of the interior have been magnificently restored. Inside is a massive pipe organ, as well as the remains of the Spanish conquistador Diego Velázquez, although, since a 1678 earthquake, the whereabouts of those remains in the building are unknown. The graves of the first (Spanish) archbishop of Cuba and the first Cuban archbishop are clearly visible. The cathedral is open Tuesday through Saturday 8am to 12:30pm and 5 to 7:30pm, and Sunday 8 to 11am and 5 to 6:30pm.

Casa Velázquez (Museo de Ambiente Colonial Cubano) ★★   The mansion (ca. 1516) that once belonged to Diego Velázquez, founder of the original seven *villas* in Cuba, still stands despite the unrepentant fumes of tour buses and recent fires that have threatened it. The house has a notable Moorish influence, with a wonderful carved cedar ceiling (most of which had to be reconstructed after a fire). The top floor was the living quarters; the ground floor was the commercial part of the house, where Velázquez maintained offices and horse carriages were kept. The majority of the house's elaborate frescoes have been supplemented by very amateurish reproductions, a real sin against the authenticity that is so apparent elsewhere. The museum aims to depict the varied styles and epochs of colonial life, seen through period furnishings from the 16th to the 19th century. You'll find some splendid pieces of French, British, Spanish, and Cuban furniture; Spanish ceramics; carved chests; and French porcelain. Several dressers have extraordinary inlaid designs, proof of the wealth of the bourgeoisie in colonial Cuba. A second 19th-century house in back, blue, and white, with an attractive courtyard, is not part of the original Velázquez house. Allow an hour for your visit.

Félix Peña 612 (corner of Aguilera), Parque Céspedes. ℂ **22/65-2652.** Admission CUC$2 (US$2.15/£1.10); CUC$1 (US$1.10/55p) to take photos, CUC$5 (US$5.40/£2.70) to take video. Guided tours in Spanish or English available. Sat–Thurs 9am–1pm and 2–5pm; Fri 2–5pm.

Castillo El Morro ★★   Guarding the entrance to the Bahía de Santiago, this seemingly impregnable fortress is built atop a rocky promontory and entered across a formidable drawbridge. The medieval and Renaissance-style structure, a UNESCO World
Heritage Site, is a warren of platforms, passageways, and cells spread across five levels and
protected by 1.5m-thick (5-ft.) walls. It was engineered in 1638 by the Italian architect
who built similar fortresses in Havana, as well as Cartagena, Colombia and San Juan,
Puerto Rico, to protect against pirate attacks (which it didn't do so well, as pirates including Henry Morgan succeeded in ransacking the place).

The site, where the sun beats down unrelentingly, has magnificent views of the bay
and the Caribbean coastline stretching all the way to the Sierra Maestra. Inside the fortress, built above a dry moat, is a sparse museum (with display explanations in Spanish
only) detailing the history of piracy, El Morro, and Santiago de Cuba. One room contains artifacts related to the 1898 Spanish-American War—its principal naval battles were
fought right in the Bay of Santiago. The 19 modern American ships sank all seven Spanish ships; ironically, the Spanish ship *Cristóbal Colón* was the last to sink, thus closing the
door on the history of Spanish colonialism in the Americas.

A daily ceremony, called the Puesta del Sol, takes place at sunset, recalling the importance of the fortress in the 19th century. Youngsters dressed as *mambises,* or members of
the Cuban rebel army, lower the flag and shoot off the ancient (ca. 1805) Spanish cannon
to cries of "¡Viva Cuba Libre!" Visiting El Morro for the day-ending ceremony, when it
has cooled off some, is an excellent idea. You'll need about an hour to tour the complex.
Avoid the hours of 11am to 4pm at all costs; if you do come in the middle of the day,
two great spots for lunch—and cooling off—are the nearby Restaurant El Morro and El
Cayo (see "Where to Dine," later in this chapter for both).

To get there, an organized excursion or a car or taxi is required. The fortress is about
15km (9 miles) south of the center of Santiago along the Carretera del Morro.

Bahía de Santiago. ☏ **22/69-1569.** Admission CUC$4 (US$4.30/£2.15); CUC$1 (US$1.10/55p) to take
photos; CUC$5 (US$5.40/2.70) to take video. Free guided tours are available in English, French, and Italian. Daily 9am–8pm.

Cuartel de Moncada (Museo Histórico 26 de Julio) ★   The yellow barracks of
the Spanish army, east of downtown, represent a pivotal episode in modern Cuban history. The ocher-colored exterior is still pockmarked with bullet holes, a reminder of the
day in July 1953 when Fidel Castro and a band of ragtag, but idealistic rebels launched
an assault on the barracks, with the intention of stealing arms and jump-starting a revolution. First built by the Spanish in 1859, the barracks were burned down and then
rebuilt in the late 1930s. Today, the Art Deco–style barracks house a museum focused on
that day and the revolutionary struggle. For anyone interested in Cuban history, regardless of ideology, a visit to the museum is a must.

Fidel and his poorly funded troops, including his brother Raúl and Abel Santamaría,
arrived in the early hours of July 26 dressed like army soldiers (though the street shoes
they wore, rather than military boots, would give them away). Some 120 men attacked
the barracks, but the plan failed miserably and 61 were killed. The others escaped, but
were soon captured; many were tortured to death by Batista's army. Batista announced to
the press that 500 well-funded militiamen had attacked the barracks and been killed in
a gun battle. A young journalist succeeded in getting photographs of the tortured and
murdered young revolutionaries out of Santiago and to Havana, where the pictures were
published, galvanizing many Cubans against the Batista regime.

The museum exhibits the rebels' small rifles and pistols, bloodstained uniforms, photographs, letters, and other documents that tell the amazing story of the subsequent exile of the surviving rebels and guerrilla warfare in the Sierra Maestra. Exhibits are labeled in Spanish only, so a guide might be a good idea.

Calle Trinidad (corner of Moncada). (© 22/62-0157. Admission CUC$2 (US$2.15/£1.10); CUC$1 (US$1.10/ 55p) to take photos; CUC$5 (US$5.40/£2.70) to take video. Free guided tours are available in English, French, and Italian. Tues–Sat 9:30am–5:15pm; Sun 9:15am–12:30pm.

Museo Emilio Bacardí Moreau ★ Begun by Emilio Bacardí, the founder of the political and rum dynasty in 1899, this highly personal collection constituted one of the first museums in Cuba. Now a provincial museum, it remains an eclectic art and historical assembly. The grand, gleaming white neoclassical building was erected in 1928 to house the idiosyncratic collection. On the first floor is a wide variety of artifacts documenting indigenous peoples, slavery, and the wars of independence, including an extensive array of armaments and a peculiar coffin-shaped torpedo used by the Mambíses. Bacardí also collected personal items belonging to Cuban national heroes, including those of Antonio Maceo and Carlos Manuel Céspedes. Don't miss the tiny stage set of a colonial Santiago street (through a door on the south side of the first floor). In an annex, which must be entered from a side door on Calle Aguilera, is an archaeology room holding an Egyptian mummy (smuggled out of Egypt in 1913), a pair of Peruvian mummies belonging to the Paracas (pre-Inca) culture, various ceremonial objects, pre-Columbian ceramics, and an extraordinary decorated shrunken head from the Amazon. The second floor is an art museum exhibiting national and international paintings. There are several contemporary pieces, including a larger-than-life sculpture of Che Guevara in heroic pose. Allow an hour to see it all. All of the display information here is in Spanish, but English-speaking guides are available.

Calle Pío Rosado (at Aguilera). (© 22/62-8402. Admission CUC$2 (US$2.15/£1.10). Free guided tours are available in English. Mon noon–4:15pm; Tues–Sat 9–11:45am and 1–4:15pm; Sun 9am–noon.

OTHER ATTRACTIONS

Barrio El Tivolí (Finds) A charming, hilly neighborhood just south of Parque Céspedes (loosely bordered by Av. Trocha and Calle Padre Pico), El Tivolí was once the most fashionable place to live in Santiago. Today, it's a relaxed place of steep streets, weathered and decrepit wooden houses, and a couple of attractions, but mostly it's a good place to wander.

The famous **Padre Pico steps** are named for a Santiaguero priest who aided the city's poor. Castro once roared fire and brimstone down on the Batista government here, but today you'll find more pacifistic chess and dominoes players who've set up all-hours tables on the steps. Take the steps up to the **Museo de la Lucha Clandestina (Museum of the Underground Struggle),** General Rabí 1 between Santa Rita and San Carlos (© 22/62-4689), which is housed in a handsome 18th-century mansion on a hill, Loma del Intendente. Inside are disorganized exhibits related to the November 1956 attack on this former police headquarters, led by rebel leader and schoolteacher Frank País and his brother Josué, both executed by the army. Frank País's funeral was massively attended by Santiagueros, a signal that the Revolution would have significant local support. Other photos and documents attest to the phenomenal years of tension, rumors, and conflict that led to the rebels' triumph (labels are in Spanish only). The museum is open Tuesday through Sunday from 9am to 5pm; admission is CUC$1 (US$1.10/55p).

Barrio El Tivolí, just south and west of Parque Céspedes.

(Tips) **Terrace with a View**

The **Balcón de Velázquez,** at the corner of Heredia and Corona at the edge of El Tivolí district, is a marvelous lookout over red-tile rooftops of the city as it slopes down to the Bay of Santiago. Named for the Spanish conquistador who founded the city, the terrace was reconstructed in the 1950s and now is a site of cultural goings-on on Fridays; it has been said that the original terrace in this very spot was used by Velázquez himself to observe incoming ships in the bay. An escape tunnel once ran from the spot, protected by cannons, all the way to the bay. Admission is free, but you'll have to pay CUC$1 (US$1.10/55p) or CUC$5 (US$5.40/£2.70), respectively, if you want to take photographs or videos.

Cementerio Santa Ifigenia ★★   Northwest of the city center, this sprawling cemetery, dating to 1868, is a small city of the dead, populated by elaborate marble tombs and sarcophagi, including several spectacular mausoleums (many of which are pre-1868, having been moved here from other cemeteries). By far the most famous is that of José Martí, a massive stone and marble circular structure built in 1951 (Martí died in 1895). Don't miss the solemn changing of the guard ceremony. The Lincolnesque mausoleum is near the entrance to the cemetery, at the end of a private path. Martí once wrote that he wished to die, "without a homeland, but without a master" and to be buried with "a bouquet of flowers and a flag." In addition to Martí, the remains of Emilio Bacardí, Carlos Manuel de Céspedes, Pedro (Perucho) Figueredo (author of the Cuban national anthem), and heroes of the Moncada 26th of July rebel attack are interred here. The newest addition to the celebrated figures buried here is the great musician and native son, Compay Segundo. In addition, the cemetery's palm-lined paths abound with a wealth of other fascinating tombs for families both famous and unknown.

Calzada Crombet. (©) **22/63-2723.** Admission CUC$1 (US$1.10/55p), CUC$1 (US$1.10/55p) to take photos. Daily 7am–6pm.

Loma de San Juan   This low-rise hill in the center of Reparto Vista Alegre, a leafy, upscale neighborhood, is where the decisive last battle of the Spanish-Cuban-American War was fought. Teddy Roosevelt and his army of an estimated 6,000 Rough Riders stormed the hill and defeated the Spanish troops. At the entrance to the park is the Arbol de la Rendención (Tree of Surrender), where the Spanish forces capitulated to the Americans. Something that still irks Cubans today, besides the commonly used name of the war that leaves them out, is that the Cubans were not even signatories to the surrender. While there are several plaques and monuments in the neatly manicured park, which pay tribute to the North Americans who participated and died in the war, there are few dedicated to the Cuban fighters (though the Tomb of the Unknown Mambi, or independence fighter, can be found there).

Reparto Santa Bárbara, at the intersection of Av. de Raúl Pujol and Carretera de Siboney Km 1.5 (next to the Hotel San Juan).

Museo del Carnaval (Kids)   Santiago's Carnival is the most famous in Cuba, and this small museum, in one of the oldest houses on Calle Heredia, aims to give visitors some historical perspective. Carnival counts centuries of tradition; the first published reference to the celebration was in 1669. It displays old costumes, black-and-white photographs,

Tips **Bay of Santiago**

> Santiago's deep natural bay is one of the city's defining characteristics. The narrow entrance to the Bahía de Santiago, past the Castillo El Morro, stretches 8km (5 miles). During the Spanish-American War, the contingency of Spanish ships was huddled within the bay, and the Americans were perched on the coast waiting to ambush them.
>
> Today, Santiago's marina is popular with European and (believe it or not) U.S. yachts. Visitors can book a 1-hour trip around the entire bay for CUC$12 (US$13/ £6.50) per person. If you just want to cross over to the fishing village on the tiny island of Cayo Granma for lunch, the ferry is CUC$3 (US$3.25/£1.60) round-trip. For more information, contact the **Santiago Marina,** Calle 1 no. 4, Punta Gorda (*© **22/69-1446;** marlin@nautica.scu.cyt.cu).

huge papier-mâché masks, and hand-painted and embroidered *mamarrachos* (capes). Percussion instruments show how popular the celebration is: They include old car parts and simple wood instruments. The final room displays a couple of the most recent winners of the costume contests—elaborate and huge affairs. **Folklore and music and dance events** ★ are held at the museum if there is no rain Tuesday through Saturday at 4pm, with *rumba* performances in high season only on Sunday at 3pm. Plan to spend about a half-hour viewing the displays. All the printed display information here is in Spanish.

Calle Heredia 303 (corner of Pío Rosado). *© **22/62-6955.** Admission CUC$1 (US$1.10/55p); CUC$1 (US$1.10/55p) for a guide; CUC$1 (US$1.10/55p) to take photos. Tues–Sun 9am–5pm.

Plaza de la Revolución This massive, raised platform monument to Antonio Maceo features a startling equestrian statue of the great patriot surrounded by 23 enormous iron machetes slicing toward the sky, like daggers in the sides of the colonial power. Maceo, a Cuban of mixed blood, was called the "Bronze Titan" of the Cuban independence wars. Beneath the work is an eternal flame. The monument is an emphatic statement, to be sure. An underground room houses a small and rather uninspiring museum dedicated to the man.

Av. de las Américas (at Los Desfiles and Carretera Central). *© **22/64-3712.** Admission to museum CUC$1 (US$1.10/55p). Mon–Sat 9am–5pm; Sun 9am–1pm.

4 WHERE TO STAY

Santiago may not be blessed with the range of hotels that Havana has—in fact, it has less than a half-dozen hotels within easy reach of downtown—but it has enough variety among its few hotels that most guests shouldn't have trouble finding a decent place to stay at any price level. Only one of Santiago's major hotels is within the historic district, which is lively and fun, but too noisy and chaotic for many visitors. Most of the tourist hotels are on the outskirts of the city, an easy and inexpensive cab ride away.

Especially popular in Santiago are *casas particulares;* the city has hundreds of state-sanctioned private homestays, including some of the coolest *casas* in Cuba, several in historic homes in the heart of the old district and others in tranquil, leafy suburbs. Reparto Sueño alone has dozens of *casas.*

For those who might prefer to stay outside the city as an overnight excursion or even with plans to make a day trip out of Santiago, there are a couple of hotels along the coast and near some of the outlying attractions. Those hotels are listed in "Side Trips from Santiago de Cuba," later in this chapter.

CENTRO HISTORICO
Moderate

Hostal Basilio ★ (Value)   This little hotel is in a beautifully restored old home in the heart of downtown and now operates under the boutique Hoteles E brand. The good-size rooms have very high ceilings with ornate crown molding. Throughout the hotel, you'll find attractive tile work on the floors and wainscoting, nicely decorated and well-equipped bathrooms, and attractive blue bedspreads and curtains. Only two rooms here have anything besides two twin beds, and of these, no. 5 is the better bet, with a king-size bed. Still, my favorite room may just be no. 1, which has a lovely window overlooking the street—so this is not the room to choose for those easily bothered by street noise. The hotel has a small in-house restaurant serving reasonable local and international fare.

Calle Basilio 403 (btw. Calvario and Carnicería). ℂ **22/65-1702.** Fax 22/68-7069. www.hotelescubanacan. com. 8 units. CUC$60 (US$65/£32) double. Rate includes breakfast. MC, V. **Amenities:** Restaurant; bar. *In room:* A/C, TV, minibar, hair dryer, safe.

Hotel Casa Granda ★★   A large, elegant building right on Parque Céspedes, this classic Santiago hotel is a landmark in the city. Graham Greene's character Wormold, from *Our Man in Havana,* stayed in the 1914 hotel, which underwent a full-scale renovation in 1995. Best known perhaps for its terrace bar with live music and its roof garden with great views over the cathedral and Santiago, the Casa Granda is one of the best places to stay in the city. Its location is superb, as long as you don't mind the hustle and bustle of travelers and *jineteros* in the square. The hotel features large rooms with high ceilings and restrained decor. As with most state-run hotels in Cuba, double beds are at a premium here; in fact, just 15 rooms come with a queen-size bed, and the rest have two twins. Rooms either have views of the park, Calle Heredia, or the interior—noise-sensitive guests should opt for the latter. If you want a view of the park, room nos. 403 through 407 are your best bets. The tile-and-marble bathrooms are quite nice, with good tubs, but these rooms need an upgrade for the price. The elegant a la carte restaurant on the first floor is handsome, with good food and service, but it's not cheap.

Heredia 201 (btw. San Félix and General Lacret). ℂ **22/65-3021.** Fax 22/68-6035. www.gran-caribe.com. 58 units. CUC$96–CUC$110 (US$104–US$119/£52–£59) double; CUC$115–CUC$135 (US$124–US$146/ £62–£73) junior suite. Rates include breakfast. MC, V. **Amenities:** 2 restaurants; 2 bars; car-rental desk; tour desk; limited room service; laundry service. *In room:* A/C, TV, hair dryer, safe.

Inexpensive

There are scores of *casas particulares* in downtown Santiago; I've listed my favorites below. If these are full, you can also try **Casa Bertha Peña,** Calle Heredia 308 between Pío Rosado and Porfirio Valiente (ℂ **22/62-4097;** co8kz@yahoo.es), a very centrally located house with two rooms. The second bedroom, dominated by a handsome, wood-and-marble dresser, is buried farther into the house and may be quieter. **Casa Pedro Guillermo Martí Vazquez,** Calle Corona 805 between Santa Rita and San Carlos (ℂ **22/62-0101;** juan@film.cineclubes.com), a large house with an enormous front living room with original tiles and scarlet furniture, has two rooms. The one at the back of the house is larger. The house has large, unusual dado tiling of egrets catching fish. **Casa**

María de la Cruz Figueroa, Calle Rey Palayo 83 between Reloj and Calvario (✆ 22/62-2152; hospedajemaria@yahoo.com), is run by a very friendly family and has two rooms: one fairly spacious room upstairs at the back of the house with a decent-size bathroom that opens onto a shaded roof terrace, and the other room on the ground floor.

Casa Alejandro Thomás ★ A nicely furnished and airy, colonial-style home, this conveniently located place is just a 5-minute walk from Parque Céspedes. It has two small, but well-equipped rooms upstairs off a terrace. Each has its own bathroom, and one has its own independent terrace. The rooms share a small kitchen facility upstairs. Guests are welcome to lounge in the handsome family sitting room with leather club chairs, a sofa, and a TV.

Calle Aguilera 602 (corner of Barnada) btw. Barnada and Paraíso. ✆ **22/62-0844.** 2 units. CUC$15–CUC$25 (US$16–US$27/£8.10–£14) double. No credit cards. *In room:* A/C, no phone.

Casa Hugo & Adela ★ (Finds) High above the hubbub below, featuring an expansive, private corner terrace with incredible views of Santiago all the way to the bay, this place rents one large third-floor room with an independent entrance. The owners are very friendly and speak English. If this room is not available, there are about four other options on the same corner.

San Basilio (Bartolomé Masó) 501 (corner of Reloj). ✆ **22/62-6359.** 1 unit. CUC$25–CUC$30 (US$27–US$32/£14–£16) double. No credit cards. *In room:* A/C, fridge, no phone.

Casa Leonardo y Rosa ★ Very centrally located, just a couple of blocks from Parque Céspedes on a relatively quiet, short street, this large and gorgeous colonial house has an ornate green-and-cream facade. The house has extraordinarily high ceilings, chandeliers, and wainscoting on the walls. One room is in the main house; the other room, which we prefer, is on the second-floor of a cheerfully colored addition out back. The private bathroom is downstairs, off the spacious open-air courtyard filled with flourishing plants.

Calle Clarín 9 (btw. Aguilera and Heredia). ✆ **22/62-3574.** 2 units. CUC$20–CUC$30 (US$22–US$32/£11–£16) double. No credit cards. *In room:* A/C, no phone.

Casa Maruchi ★ (Finds) This is a lovely colonial house with a wonderful patio stuffed with orchids and other plants. A new, striking fountain now graces the tranquil patio. Two chic, comfortable rooms with exposed brickwork, Spanish colonial furniture, lace bedspreads, and candlesticks are off the patio. Maruchi is a friendly *casa* owner.

Calle Hartmann (San Félix) 357, corner of Trinidad and San Germán. ✆ **22/62-0767.** maruchi@infomeil. com. 2 units. CUC$20–CUC$25 (US$22–US$27/£11–£14). No credit cards. *In room:* A/C, no phone.

Gran Hotel Escuela (Value) This hotel-school offers good value and an excellent location in the heart of Santiago's historic center. The rooms themselves are rather uninspired and spartan, but they are clean and spacious (the triples are enormous and represent great value), with firm beds—although only two rooms here come with a double bed. A few rooms have tiny balconies overlooking bustling Calle Enramada. This hotel has historically been favored by local and visiting artists and musicians. *Be forewarned:* There's no elevator here, and all the rooms are on the second and third floors.

Calle Enramada 312 (corner of Calle San Félix), Santiago de Cuba. ✆ **22/65-3020.** www.granhotelstgo. cu. 15 units. CUC$32 (US$35/£17) double. **Amenities:** Restaurant; bar; cafeteria. *In room:* A/C, TV, fridge, safe.

Hotel Libertad Fronting the busy Plaza de Marte, this hotel is another good budget option, run by the Islazul chain. Only half of the rooms here have windows, and you will definitely want a room with a window. No. 214 is the hotel's largest and best room. All have simple furnishings, and small, but functional bathrooms. About half the rooms here have double beds, a high percentage for a state-run hotel chain. Aside from its central location, the best feature here is the third-floor rooftop bar that underwent a remodeling in 2008.

Calle Aguilera 658 (across from Plaza de Marte), Santiago de Cuba. ✆ **22/62-8360**. www.islazul.cu. 17 units. CUC$32–CUC$38 (US$35–US$41/£17–£21) double; CUC$43–CUC$51 (US$46–US$55/£23–£28) suite (no. 214). Rates include breakfast. MC, V. **Amenities:** Restaurant; 2 bars; laundry service. *In room:* A/C, TV.

THE OUTSKIRTS
Expensive
Meliá Santiago de Cuba ★★ (Kids) This unique, postmodern high-rise, a mass of blue, red, and gray steel girders and glass, is the largest hotel in Santiago and easily its most luxurious. It's in a peaceful area about 2km (1¼ miles) from the historic core, which is perfect for guests who need a little bit more tranquillity and space. It has facilities and services in spades, including the best outdoor pool in the city. Rooms are attractive and large, with huge windows and excellent views, particularly from the higher floors. The hotel has a show on Saturday in its atmospheric **Santiago Café**, which is an indoor reconstruction of a miniature colonial city. Nonguests can use the pool facilities for a fee of CUC$10 (US$11/£5.40), which includes CUC$5 (US$5.40/£2.70) worth of food and drink.

Av. de las Américas (at Calle M), Reparto Sueño, Santiago de Cuba. ✆ **22/68-7070**. Fax 22/68-7170. www.solmeliacuba.com. 302 units. CUC$115 (US$124/£62) double; CUC$145 (US$157/£78) junior suite; CUC$165 (US$178/£89) suite. MC, V. **Amenities:** 4 restaurants; 3 bars; Saturday show; 3 outdoor pools; volleyball court; gym; sauna; massage; tour desks; car-rental desk; business center; small shopping arcade; 24-hr. room service; laundry service. *In room:* A/C, TV, minibar, hair dryer, safe.

Moderate
Hotel Las Américas (Value) A comfortable and friendly, older-style hotel just down the street from the Meliá Santiago, Las Américas isn't fancy, but it's a good place to stay, with plenty of services, attractive gardens, and a midsize pool. The rooms have been upgraded with new curtains, blackout shades, and bedspreads; they are a good size and have nice gray-marble bathrooms and cable television. A new pirate-themed restaurant, Bucaneros del Caribe, opened in summer 2008. The hotel dance club is quite popular with young Santiagueros. Nonguests here can use the pool facilities for a fee of CUC$10 (US$11/£5.40), which includes CUC$8 (US$8.65/£4.30) worth of food and drink.

Av. de las Américas (at General Cebreco), Reparto Sueño, Santiago de Cuba. ✆ **22/64-2011**. Fax 22/68-7075. www.islazul.cu. 70 units. CUC$58–CUC$69 (US$63–US$75/£31–£37) double; CUC$84–CUC$100 (US$91–US$108/£45–£54) minisuite. Rates include breakfast. MC, V. **Amenities:** 2 restaurants; 2 bars; dance club; outdoor pool; tour desk; car-rental desk. *In room:* A/C, TV, fridge, safe.

Inexpensive
Casa Asensio ★ (Value) This fine house with an upstairs apartment is run by a friendly woman, Isabel. The huge apartment has an even larger, private rooftop terrace. There's an independent entrance and a separate kitchen, a large, comfortable bed, and good-size bathroom. Abstract art is painted on the walls, and you have access to the home's little garden.

Calle J no. 306 (btw. Calle 6 and Av. de las Américas), Reparto Sueño, Santiago de Cuba. ✆ **22/62-4600**. manuel@medired.scu.sld.cu. 1 unit. CUC$25 (US$27/£14) double. No credit cards. *In room:* A/C, kitchenette, fridge, no phone.

Casa Florinda Chaviano Martínez   This large and well-furnished house is impeccable. The lone bedroom for rent is big and meticulously maintained. It features a great rooftop terrace and breezy patio covered with vines.

Calle I no. 58 (btw. Calles 2 and 3), Reparto Sueño, Santiago de Cuba. ℰ **22/65-3660.** 1 unit. CUC$25 (US$27/£14) double. No credit cards. *In room:* A/C, TV, fridge, no phone.

Casa Gloria Boué Alonso   There is no shortage of nicely furnished 1950s-style houses in the Sueño district; this one has funky, overstuffed furniture and two rooms, one of which is upstairs with its own massive terrace. The other room is downstairs and is very spacious, with the largest private bathroom you're likely to find in Cuba. There's a common sitting room with a television showing only local channels.

Calle J no. 212 (btw. Calles 4 and 5), Reparto Sueño, Santiago de Cuba. ℰ **22/64-4969.** 2 units. CUC$20–CUC$25 (US$22–US$27/£11–£14) double. No credit cards. *In room:* A/C, fridge, no phone.

5 WHERE TO DINE

Santiago has a unique take on Cuban and Caribbean cuisine, but it isn't an especially great place for dining; there are few really good restaurants, and even fewer *paladares* (private home restaurants). A couple of the better restaurants are outside of downtown, and it's best if you plan ahead to combine them with sightseeing. The couple of officially sanctioned *paladares* and the state-run restaurants (many of which are concentrated around Plaza Dolores) are nothing to look forward to. Understandably, many visitors tend to eat at their hotel restaurants—as good an option as any. The Meliá Santiago de Cuba and Hotel Casa Granda have elegant restaurants that are worth a splurge even for nonguests; Hotel Las Américas has a new pirate-themed restaurant. Although you can only get sandwiches and simple dishes there, one of my favorite lunch spots is the open-air terrace bar at the Hotel Casa Granda. On a hot afternoon, this is the coolest place in town—in both senses of the word. A couple of appealing options are on the outskirts of the city—good ideas when organizing day trips to El Cobre or La Gran Piedra.

CENTRO HISTORICO
Moderate
Paladar Las Gallegas CRIOLLA   Four sisters run this friendly, down-home place just a couple of blocks from Parque Céspedes. Portions are reasonable, the food is okay, and the spacious dining room—a cross between a living room and a salon—has a peaked beam ceiling, seven tables (including two on narrow balconies overlooking the street), an ornate chandelier, and red satin curtains. There's the predictable fried chicken, but also chicken fricasse, pork steaks, and ham. All dishes come with rice and salad. Go early or late; on many nights, the tiny place is full, though the wait usually isn't long.

San Basilio 305 altos (btw. General Lacret and San Félix). ℰ **22/62-4700.** Reservations not accepted. Main courses CUC$8 (US$8.65/£4.30). No credit cards. Daily 1–10:30pm.

Santiago 1900 ★ Ⓥⓐⓛⓤⓔ CRIOLLA   Beyond the doorman controlling access with antique red-leather ropes on brass stanchions lies an elegant and reasonably priced restaurant. There are several interior dining rooms, as well as a wonderful open-air ground-floor patio with a stone fountain in its center, and two open-air spaces on the second-floor balcony. Some of the tables up here have a good view of the city's church steeples. The menu is pretty standard Cuban fare, but it is very well prepared, and the ambience is intriguing. This place attracts a mixed Cuban and foreign clientele.

Calle Basilio 354 (btw. Carnicería and San Félix). $\mathcal{C}$ **22/62-3507.** Reservations not required. Main courses CUC$3.50–CUC$6 (US$3.80–US$6.50/£1.90–£3.25). No credit cards. Daily noon–midnight.

THE OUTSKIRTS
Expensive

La Isabelica ★★ INTERNATIONAL   This small, romantic restaurant serves up French-influenced cuisine in a tranquil and elegant setting. We recommend the fresh grouper in a saffron sauce, served over a bed of spinach. You also can't go wrong with the curried chicken breasts with plum and pineapple. There's a decent and reasonably priced wine list, and the service is attentive and efficient. Dinner here gets you a free entrance into the hotel's nightly cabaret show.

In the Meliá Santiago, Av. de las Américas (at Calle M), Reparto Sueño. $\mathcal{C}$ **22/68-7070.** Reservations recommended. Main courses CUC$11–CUC$36 (US$12–US$39/£5.95–£19). MC, V. Daily 7–11pm.

ZunZún ★★ CRIOLLA   This elegant and upscale restaurant occupies a handsome 1940s house in the Vista Alegre neighborhood. It has four private salons for intimate dining, and a couple of tables on a broad front veranda, which are my favorites. With relatively soft lighting, marble floors, and period furnishings—some original to the house—ZunZún (formerly Tocororo) is the place in town to splurge. Everything is very well prepared and nicely presented. It's especially good for seafood, such as a delicious mixed grill of fish and shellfish; medallions of lobster, shellfish, and shrimp; and garlic shrimp. Carnivores can opt for a beef filet in red-wine sauce or *ropa vieja* (shredded beef). The tables here have white tablecloths and candles—rarities in Cuba.

Av. Manduley 159, Reparto Vista Alegre. $\mathcal{C}$ **22/64-1528.** Reservations recommended. Main courses CUC$6–CUC$21 (US$6.50–US$23/£3.25–£11). Daily noon–10pm.

Moderate

Paladar Salón Tropical ★ CRIOLLA   One of the most elegant *paladares* in Cuba—in fact, it's swankier than most state-owned and hotel restaurants—this attractively decorated place, with stained-glass windows, lovely tablecloths, and high-backed chairs, also has a terrific, breezy, plant-covered terrace. The views are excellent; it's a marvelous environment for having a couple of beers . . . and waiting interminably for your dinner. It's own popularity has overwhelmed this place, and service can be glacially slow at times. Depending upon what is available, the menu might offer a smorgasbord of choices, including chicken soup, shish kabobs, grilled fish, mixed grill, and barbecued chicken. The *paladar* is quite popular with smooching Cubans as well as bored *jineteras* with their romantic "dates." Reservations are highly recommended, and the operating hours listed below are not strictly enforced—this place often closes early or unexpectedly.

Luis Fernández Marcané 310 Altos (btw. Calles 9 and 10), Reparto Santa Bárbara. $\mathcal{C}$ **22/64-1161.** Reservations recommended. Main courses CUC$4–CUC$7.50 (US$4.30–US$8.10/£2.15–£4.05). No credit cards. Daily noon–11pm.

BAHIA DE SANTIAGO
Moderate

El Cayo Finds CRIOLLA   This relaxing spot for lunch is a boating excursion and dining outing rolled into one. In a pretty blue-and-white clapboard waterfront house on a tiny island in the middle of the Bay of Santiago—you have to take a CUC$3

(US$3.25/£1.60) round-trip ferryboat from the **Santiago Marina** (© **22/69-1446**) to get there—is this breezy, tranquil restaurant that's popular with organized groups, but is perfect for independent travelers, too. Sit on the covered wraparound balcony overlooking the water and try any of the specialties, which quite logically are seafood dishes: Spanish mackerel, lobster, red snapper, marlin, or fish soup.

Cayo Granma, Bahía de Santiago. © **22/69-0109.** Reservations recommended for lunch. Main courses CUC$6–CUC$25 (US$6.50–US$27/£3.25–£14). MC, V. Daily 11am–6pm.

Restaurant El Morro ★ CRIOLLA   A hugely popular and pleasant, open-air place, perched on the coast near the fortress of the same name and boasting spectacular views of the sparkling blue Caribbean Sea, this restaurant, happily, isn't a tourist trap. It also serves a good-value lunch (with choices) for groups. Try the lobster if you're in a mood to splurge; otherwise, there's a fish filet stuffed with cheese, spicy shrimp, and chicken with pineapple. The long black tables are under a wood-beamed canopy thick with vines and hanging plants and white *tumbergia* flowers, a most welcome refuge from the scorching sun that makes midday at El Morro fortress a daunting proposition.

Carretera del Morro Km 8.5, Bahía de Santiago. © **22/69-1576.** Reservations recommended for lunch. Main courses CUC$12 (US$13/£6.50). V. Daily noon–4pm.

6 SHOPPING

Opportunities for shopping in Santiago, despite the city's cultural traditions, aren't that much better than in many smaller cities in Cuba. Your best bets, as elsewhere in Cuba, are handicrafts, music and musical instruments, and the always-dependable rum and cigars.

ART & HANDICRAFTS

Sellers and craftspeople line both sides of **Calle Heredia** from Parque Céspedes on up to Calle Porfirio Valiente. The informal daily market features a range of handicrafts and souvenirs, including sculptures of shapely (as well as rail-thin) women carved from ebony and other precious woods, paintings, masks, papier-mâché dolls, musical instruments, and jewelry. A number of state-owned crafts and souvenir shops with similar merchandise, but inflexible pricing, occupy the storefronts at the base of the cathedral on **Parque Céspedes.** New crafts and souvenir shops line the road leading to the **El Morro** fortress (across from the El Morro restaurant).

Locally produced abstract and figurative art is available at a handful of galleries, including the one within the lobby of the **Hotel Casa Granda** and **Galería de Arte Oriente** on Calle General Lacret 653, between Aguilera and Heredia.

CIGARS & RUM

The **Barra de Ron Caney,** at the rum factory that used to be the original Bacardí plant before the Revolution (when the owners fled to the Bahamas and the U.S.), is a gift shop selling an array of types and vintages of Cuban-produced rum, as well as cigars, nice silver jewelry, and other souvenirs. You can taste before you buy. The factory and shop are on Av. Jesús Menéndez 703 between San Antonio and San Ricardo (© **22/62-5576**), across from the train station. The shop is open daily from 9am to 5:30pm. Alternately, you can check out the **Museo de Ron** (© **22/62-3884**), at San Basilio 358, which offers

> **Tips** **Bring on the *Béisbol***
>
> Santiago is yet another baseball-mad Cuban city, and the local professional team is usually among the best in the national league. The *pelota* (as it's popularly known) season begins in late winter and continues through the spring. Games are held at the **Estadio Guillermo Moncada** on Avenida de las Américas (✆ **22/ 64-5640**). Ask at your hotel about getting tickets (it's usually possible to purchase them right before game time at the stadium ticket booth).

a brief illustrated guide to the history and process of rum production, with a pleasant bar next-door. Museum admission is CUC$2 (US$2.15/£1.10).

Cigars can be purchased at hotel shops or **Casa del Habano,** next-door to the Caney rum factory (✆ **22/62-2366**), which even has a smokers' lounge and bar. *Note:* I'd be especially wary of the quality of cigars you are offered by *jineteros* on the street.

MUSIC

Santiago is the capital of *son* and other indigenous forms of Cuban music, and there are a few good spots to pick up CDs and tapes of Santiaguero musicians (though overall, Havana has a much better selection of music stores). The **EGREM** music label has shops at the Antonio Maceo airport. The **Casa de la Trova** (p. 284) has an **ARTex** store, and there's a small record shop attached to the **Casa de la Música,** Corona (Mariano) 564, between Aguilera and José Antonio Saco. Of the artists you may have an opportunity to see perform live, most sell CDs at their performances.

7 SANTIAGO DE CUBA AFTER DARK

THE PERFORMING ARTS

Besides the locally grown Cuban music scene, another nighttime draw is the **Cabaret Tropicana Santiago** ★★, Autopista Nacional Km 1.5, north of Santiago (✆ **22/64-2579**). It's second in size and fame only to Havana's internationally regarded Tropicana, but Santiago's show is no second banana. It's a slickly produced cabaret show—different from the one in Havana—with excellent singers and dancers and extraordinarily elaborate costumes. Dinner is available, and drinks aren't cheap, but the Tropicana is a must-see, only if you don't have an opportunity to catch the program in the capital. The show begins at 10pm daily; there's also a dance club on the premises, open until 3am. The show without dinner and including one drink is CUC$35 (US$38/£19). There's an additional CUC$5 (US$5.40/£2.70) charge for taking pictures during the show, and CUC$15(US$16/£8.10) if you want to shoot video. Packaged excursions with dinner and transportation can be purchased at the larger hotels and all tour operators.

You'll find a much more scaled-down and less-expensive Saturday night show at the **Santiago Café** ★ (✆ **22/68-7070**), in the Meliá Santiago. The cover here is just CUC$5 (US$5.40/£2.70), which includes two drinks.

The top spots for cultural events such as dance and theater (which inevitably take a back seat to live music) are the sleek **Teatro Heredia,** Avenida de los Desfiles, across from the Plaza de la Revolución (✆ **22/64-3178**); **Teatro Oriente,** Calle José Antonio Saco

Carnival & Other Santiago Festivals

Santiago is well known among Cuban cities for its sparkling music festivals, which thrust Afro-Caribbean culture and the local musical genius to the forefront of urban life. If you can stand the stultifying heat in late July, Carnival is the most exciting time to visit the city.

In Santiago, *Carnaval* is not a pre-Lenten celebration as it is in other Latin American countries. In the 17th century, slaves reshaped the traditional (and much more solemn) Catholic veneration of the city's patron saint, Santiago Apóstolo, and the attendant religious processions, into a festive celebration. The slaves' revelry was much more raucous than that of the white Christians, who began to refer to the slaves' participation as the *Fiesta de Los Mamarrachos* (party of the Crazies). Gradually, the rest of Santiaguero society began to appreciate and even participate in Carnival. French and Haitian elements were incorporated after the 18th-century influx of those populations. By the 20th century, Santiago's Carnival had gone the way of samba and *Carnaval* in Brazil, which was appropriated from marginal black communities and transformed into a mainstream cultural affair.

Today, unsurprisingly, even Carnival is linked to politics. The 3-day celebration also serves to commemorate the 26th of July movement that was the foundation for the Revolution. In the small wee hours of the 26th of July, a reconstruction of the Moncada attack is made, complete with a cavalcade of old cars and gun shots. It's a surreal event. Yet politics seems light-years away

115 (© **22/62-2441**); **El Quitrín,** San Gerónimo 463 (© **22/62-2528**); and **Ateneo Cultural** (© **22/62-3635**), in an old law school building on Félix Peña. Keep an eye out for performances by **Ballet Folklórico Cutumba** ★★★, an extraordinary Afro-Cuban outfit that has toured in North America and Europe. Cutumba has returned to Santiago and has its base at the old Cine Galaxia, Calle Trocha corner of Santa Ursula (Av V. Hierrezuelo; © **22/65-5173;** www.cubanfolkloricdance.com/cutumba.php). It hopes to be performing by the time this book goes to press. Also keep an eye out for **Conjunto Folklórico de Oriente,** which often performs at Hotel Casa Granda. You may not catch all the spiritual and cultural elements embedded in their show, but the music and dance are infectious nonetheless. Teatro Heredia is headquarters for the **Festival del Caribe** ★★ in July. The **Museo del Carnaval,** Heredia 303 (© **22/62-6955**), has folklore programs most days of the week, and a Sunday rumba show at 6pm. For other dance programs, see the **Casa del Caribe,** below.

LIVE MUSIC

Santiago is all about the music. Some of the biggest personalities on the Cuban music scene, such as **Compay Segundo, Eliades Ochoa,** and **La Vieja Trova Santiaguera,** hail from Santiago. Although Compay died at 95 in 2003, Ochoa is still active, touring both in Cuba and internationally. Calle Heredia, just off Parque Céspedes, is Cuba's version of Bourbon Street, but much less commercialized. Four or five places burst with addictive live, traditional Cuban music on any given night, and several have bands during the day, from the popular explosion that erupts on Santiago's sweltering streets. Garish floats, with parade queens atop, glide through the streets, frenetic drum-beating conga parades rock the neighborhoods (the biggest are the barrio congas of day 1), and masked *diablitos* (devils) dart daringly through the throngs. African elements, including representations of orishás (Yoruba gods), are omnipresent. *Comparsas,* the Carnival band processions, have marchers who don papier-mâché masks and brightly colored costumes.

Today, Carnival manages still to be exuberant, even though funds for fancy costumes are tough to come by and homemade instruments predominate (during the years of the so-called Special Period in the mid-1990s, economic conditions were so tough that Carnival had to be canceled for a couple of years). Some conga ensembles, such as Los Hoyos, trace their origins back to the 19th century. Dance troupes to be on the lookout for include Cabildos, La Placita, and Izuama y Olugo. The focal points of Carnival activities are along Avenida Jesús Menéndez and Victoriano Garzón, where the parade and float judging takes place.

Preceding Carnival is the **Fiesta del Fuego,** or **Festival del Caribe,** in the first week of July, which brings a cornucopia of cultural workshops, theater, and artistic performances to Santiago. Also worth catching, although not nearly as frenzied as Carnival, is the **Festival de Rumba** in mid-January, which is also celebrated with street dancing and music.

too. Personal local favorites include **Los Jubilados,** a band of gregarious septuagenarians who often play at the Casa de la Trova; **Kokoyé,** a folkloric band playing traditional Afro-Cuban and Afro-Haitian music; and the **Vocal Divas,** a talented women's a cappella group.

Several of the spots below are not only great for hearing live music, but also for watching local patrons who make dancing to Cuban music a sultry art form all their own. Give it a try yourself and don't worry about looking foolish; unless you've had professional training, you simply can't compete with Cubans on the dance floor, so don't even try. If you're without a partner, there's usually no shortage of Cuban men and women (most of whom will invariably be *jineteros* and *jineteras*) willing to give you a whirl. At places like the Casa de la Trova and other spots around town, you're likely to find music throughout the day, beginning around noon, and well into the night. At most clubs, the music starts around 9pm and really heats up from around 10pm until 2am.

Casa de las Tradiciones ★★★   More cramped and heaps more intimate than the more touristy Casa de la Trova, this old house (called "La Casona" by locals) in the Tívoli section of town is loaded with character and decorated with dozens of paintings and photos on the walls. It gets perfectly steamy when there's a tight band playing and more than two couples working the dance floor. Calle Rabí154. ✆ 22/65-3892. Cover CUC$1 (US$1.10/55p).

Casa de la Trova ★★★ Decades of raw and infectious Cuban music seep from the walls of this legendary live music venue, the greatest of the country's Casas de la Trova. Old-timers may complain that it doesn't have the character it once did, due to makeovers, but its long front room and back patio and the grand upstairs salon still outclass almost any other Cuban music joint. All the greats have played here; you may catch an up-and-coming star, or a band of octogenarians who rightly should be every bit as famous as the guys in Buena Vista. They aren't, but you'll enjoy their music all the more for their relative obscurity and chance to see them in such a welcoming environment. Heredia 206 (btw. San Félix and San Pedro). ✆ 22/65-2689. Cover CUC$1 (US$1.10/55p) daytime, CUC$3–CUC$10 (US$3.25–US$11/£1.60–£5.40) at night.

Casa del Caribe ★ This cultural center has a full schedule of music events and other goings-on starting between 4 and 7pm Thursday to Sunday. The program is eclectic, ranging from poetry to folkloric dancing to rumba and steel bands. It would be best to call beforehand before hiking out here. Concerts are held on two leafy outdoor patios. There are also cultural conferences and workshops. Contact the *casa* for the Fiesta del Caribe program. Calle 13 no. 154 (corner of Calle 8), Vista Alegre. ✆ 22/64-3609. Cover CUC$1–CUC$2 (US$1.10–US$2.15/55p–£1.10).

Patio de ARTex If there's not much happening at the Casa de la Trova, peek in here for live Cuban music every afternoon and night of the week; there's a gorgeous courtyard out back. Heredia 304 (btw. Pío Rosado and Porfirio Valiente). ✆ 22/65-4814. Cover CUC$2 (US$2.15/£1.10) at night only.

Patio de los Dos Abuelos This place on the Plaza de Marte is a good spot to listen to *boleros* and *filin* (feelin', a musical genre), daily from 10am to 2am. The scene is a little older and more sedate than most of the places listed above, but folks still get up and dance. Moreover, the patrons and players show real love for the romantic ballads and tragic love songs that are the staples here. Calle Pérez Carbó 5 (across from the Plaza de Marte). ✆ 22/62-3302. Cover CUC$2 (US$2.15/£1.10) at night.

BARS & CLUBS

In general, bars open around noon and stay open as long as there are patrons, usually between midnight and 2am. Dance clubs and music joints tend to get going around 10pm and stay open until at least 2am.

Bello Bar This bar occupies the entire 15th floor of the Meliá Santiago hotel and has stunning 360-degree views of Santiago. Live jazz and Cuban tunes can be heard daily. In Meliá Santiago hotel. (Av. de las Américas at Calle M, Reparto Sueño). ✆ 22/68-7070.

Club 300 This is a dark, enveloping nightclub with occasional live music and a fair share of *jineteras* "jes dying to meetchu," as Mick Jagger used to sing. Calle Aguilera (btw. General Lacret and San Félix). ✆ 22/65-3532. Cover CUC$2 (US$2.15/£1.10).

Discoteca La Iris This sweaty dance club, extremely popular with young locals, seems to be pumping at all hours of the day, with ear-shattering disco, salsa, merengue, and Latin rock. It underwent redecoration in mid-2008. Calle Aguilera 617 (btw. Bamada and Plácido). ✆ 22/65-4910. Cover CUC$2 (US$2.15/£1.10).

Hotel Casa Granda Terrace Bar A great spot for people-watching over the Parque Céspedes, this convivial terrace/balcony bar is always hopping, with a good mix of foreigners and Cubans hoping to meet foreigners. The hotel also has a **Rooftop Garden** bar on the top floor with excellent views of the cathedral and Santiago Bay, although this

La Taberna de Dolores (Finds)   This local hangout, and my favorite low-rent watering hole in Santiago, is in the pretty, leafy patio of an old colonial house. This joint always has cheap draft beer in plastic mugs. The crowd is mostly Cuban, with a few backpacker sorts. With a minimal bit of Spanish (like *cerveza,* meaning beer), you should be able to pay in Cuban pesos—be sure to ask about paying in *moneda nacional,* although be sure you have some *moneda nacional* in your pocket when they give you the bill. Calle Aguilera (at Reloj), Plaza Dolores. ⓒ **22/62-3913.**

---

8 SIDE TRIPS FROM SANTIAGO DE CUBA

Excursions to all the places listed below, as well as to Guantánamo and Baracoa (see chapter 10), can be arranged at the tour desks found in most hotels, or with **Cubanacán** (ⓒ **22/64-3445**), **Cubatur** (ⓒ **22/65-2560**), or **Havanatur** (ⓒ **22/64-3603**) in Santiago. Prices range from CUC$15 (US$16/£8.10) for a day trip to El Cobre, to CUC$42 (US$45/£23) for a trip to Gran Piedra and La Isabelica, to CUC$66 (US$71/£36) for a tour to Baconao.

BASILICA DEL COBRE
18km (11 miles) W of Santiago de Cuba

The most important shrine for Cubans and the most famous church in the country is lodged in the foothills of the Sierra Maestra near the old copper mines that give it its name. The triple-domed church with the name of **El Sanctuario de Nuestra Señora de la Caridad del Cobre,** built in 1927, rises on Maboa hill and is photogenically framed by green forest. The faithful come from across Cuba on pilgrimages to pay their respects to (and ask for protection from) a black Madonna, the *Virgen de la Caridad* (Virgin of Charity). She is nothing less than the protectress of Cuba, and her image, cloaked in a glittering gold robe, can be seen throughout the country. Her parallel figure in Afro-Cuban worship is Ochún, goddess of love and femininity, who is also dark-skinned and dressed in bright yellow garments. In 1998, the pope visited and blessed the shrine, calling the Virgin "La Reina de los Cubanos" (Queen of Cubans), and donated a rosary and crown.

According to legend, the statue of Cuba's patron saint was discovered bobbing in the Bay of Nipe in 1611 by three young fishermen (or miners, depending on who's telling the story) about to capsize in a storm. The Madonna wore a sign that read YO SOY LA VIRGEN DE LA CARIDAD (I am the Virgin of Charity). With the wooden statue in their grasp, the fishermen miraculously made it to shore. Pilgrims, who often make the last section of the trek on their knees, pray to her image and place *votos* (mementos) and offerings of thanks for her miracles; among them are small boats and prayers for those who have tried to make it to Florida on rafts. Ernest Hemingway—whose fisherman in *The Old Man and the Sea* made a promise to visit the shrine if he could only land his marlin—donated his Nobel Prize in Literature to the shrine, but it was stolen (and later recovered, but never again to be exhibited here). The Virgin sits on the second floor, up the back stairs, encased in glass. When Mass is being said, the push of a button turns the Virgin around to face the congregation. The annual pilgrimage is September 12, and the patron saint's feast day is July 25. The Basilica is open daily from 6am to 6:30pm; admission is free.

You can take a taxi to El Cobre for CUC$25 (US$27/£14) round-trip, but an agency tour is cheaper. The no. 2 bus runs between Santiago and El Cobre four times daily, leaving from the main bus station in Santiago. To enhance the spiritual experience, or to merely have a serene and incredibly cheap overnight stay, there's an inn behind the church, **Hospedería de la Caridad,** which welcomes foreigners who abide by the strict rules (10pm curfew and repeated requests for quiet); a stay costs a mere 15 pesos a night. If you can pay in *moneda nacional* this only comes out to about 58¢, although they generally charge foreigners a few CUCs. There are only 15 austere, but well-kept rooms; it's necessary to reserve by phone ((✆ **22/34-6246**) at least 15 days in advance.

LA GRAN PIEDRA & LA ISABELICA
27km (17 miles) E of Santiago de Cuba

A tortuous coastal road east of Santiago ascends the mountains to **La Gran Piedra (The Big Rock),** an enormous 25m-high (82-ft.) rock perched 1,200m (3,937 ft.) above sea level. You can climb a half-hour or so on foot to the top of the rock for a panoramic bird's-eye view of thickly wooded eastern Cuba and the majestic Sierra Maestra that extends to the Caribbean and as far as the eye can see. The air is much sweeter and cooler than in Santiago. Admission is CUC$2 (US$2.15/£1.10). Near the foot of the trail is the modest **Gran Piedra** ((✆ **22/68-6147;** www.islazul.cu), a rustic little hotel with a restaurant, as well as the **Jardín Ave de Paraíso,** a small botanical garden with birds of paradise and other flowers. The garden is open daily 8am to 5pm, and admission is CUC$1 (US$1.10/55p).

About 2km (1¼ miles) beyond Gran Piedra, a passable dirt track leads to **Museo La Isabelica,** Carretera de la Gran Piedra Km 14, an early-19th-century coffee plantation *finca* (country house) that once was the property of newly arrived French immigrants who fled Haiti after the slave revolt there in 1791. The owner named La Isabelica for his mistress (and later wife), a beautiful slave. The house was a stone mansion built in the style of rural French manor houses in Haiti. It was one of about 60 coffee plantations in the area, which proved very hospitable for planting coffee beans. The 200 Arabica coffee plantations in the region helped Cuba become the number-one coffee producer in the world until 1850, when it was surpassed by Brazil. These Franco-Haitian plantations were recently declared UNESCO World Heritage Sites. On the premises of La Isabelica is a workshop, along with the original furniture and slave instruments. The house has recently been renovated and provides a glimpse into the life of the period. It's open daily 9am to 5pm; admission is CUC$2 (US$2.15/£1.10).

GRAN PARQUE NATURAL BACONAO
25km (16 miles) SE of Santiago de Cuba

A UNESCO biosphere reserve, **Parque Baconao** is spread over some 40km (25 miles). The local dark-sand beaches are scruffy and the hotels are isolated, but the park hides a number of attractions, several of them man-made, for visitors with a couple of extra days in Santiago.

The road leading southeast out of Santiago is lined with 26 monuments to revolutionary heroes who died in the attack on the Moncada barracks. About 10km (6 miles) east is the **Valle de la Prehistoria,** Carretera Baconao Km 6.5 ((✆ **22/63-9239**), Cuba's very own Jurassic Park—a lifeless and cheesy attraction. Lodged on farmlands are 250 massive life-size statues of dinosaurs and a giant, club-wielding Stone Age man. The park is open daily from 8am to 5pm; admission is CUC$1 (US$1.10/55p). Nearby, in a nod to more recent history, the **Museo Nacional del Transporte (Automobile Museum),** Carretera Baconao Km 8.5 (© **22/63-9197**), has a decent number of old cars, some more valuable and in better shape than others. One vehicle, a 1951 Chevrolet, was driven by Fidel's brother Raúl to the Moncada attack (he got lost); a Cadillac on view belonged to the legendary singer Beny Moré. The museum's collection of vintage American cars has been built by the novel practice of offering Cubans new Russian-built Ladas for their old Cadillacs and Chevys. Next door is a collection of several thousand model and Matchbox cars. The museum is open daily from 8am to 5pm; admission is CUC$1 (US1.10/55p); an extra CUC$1 (US$1.10/55p) is charged to take photos.

On the coast, at Km 27.5, is the **Acuario Baconao** (© **22/35-0004**), a rather sad little aquarium that runs daily dolphin and sea lion shows. Admission is CUC$5 (US$5.40/£2.70). You can also swim with the dolphins for around 15 minutes for CUC$40 (US$43/£22).

Appendix A: Fast Facts, Toll-Free Numbers & Websites

1 FAST FACTS: CUBA

AREA CODES Area codes around the country range from one to two digits. See "Staying Connected," p. 56, for dialing instructions within area codes, from one area code to another, and from Havana to another area code.

ATM NETWORKS/CASHPOINTS See "Money & Costs," p. 41.

BUSINESS HOURS There are no hard-and-fast rules, but most businesses and banks are open Monday through Friday from 9am to 5pm. Some businesses and banks close for an hour for lunch. Shops and department stores, especially those that cater to tourists, tend to have slightly more extended hours, and are usually open on Saturday and Sunday.

CAR RENTALS See "Getting There & Getting Around," p. 37.

DRINKING LAWS Cuba has no firm or clear liquor laws. Beer, wine, and liquor are served at most restaurants and are available at most gift shops and hard-currency stores. Drinking and driving is against the law.

DRIVING RULES See "Getting There & Getting Around," p. 37.

ELECTRICITY You will find a mix of electrical currents and plug types used in Cuba. Around 90% of the hotels and *casas particulares* use a 110-volt current with standard U.S.-style two- or three-prong outlets. However, some outlets are rated 220 volts, particularly in hotels that cater to European clientele. These are usually marked and sometimes accept only two-prong round plugs. For all intents and purposes, you should have personal appliances rated for 110-volt current, with U.S.-style prongs, or the appropriate converters. It is also a good idea to carry a three-to-two-prong adapter for any appliance you have that has a three-prong plug.

Wherever you go, bring a **connection kit** of the right power and phone adapters, a spare phone cord, and a spare Ethernet network cable—or find out whether your hotel supplies them to guests.

EMBASSIES & CONSULATES All major consulates and embassies are in Havana. Canada also has other locations.

The embassy of **Canada** is at Calle 30 no. 518, at the corner of Avenida 7, Miramar (© 7/204-2516; fax 7/204-2044; http://havana.gc.ca). The Consulate of Canada is at Hotel Atlantico, Suite 1, Guardalavaca (© 24/430-320; fax 24/430-321; honcongvaca@canada.com); and at Calle 13, corner of Avenida 1 and Camino del Mar, Varadero (© 45/61-2078; fax 45/66-7395; honconvdero@canada.com).

The embassy of the **United Kingdom** is at Calle 34 no. 704, between Avenida 7 and 17, Miramar (☏ 7/214-2200; fax 7/214-2218; www.britishembassy.gov.uk/cuba).

Though neither an embassy nor a consulate, the **United States Interests Section,** Calle Calzada between Calles L and M, Vedado (☏ 7/833-3551; http://havana.usinterestsection.gov), is the official U.S. government representation on the island. There is no Australian embassy in Cuba. The Canadian embassy will assist.

EMERGENCIES In most cases, you will want to dial ☏ **106** for any emergency. This is the number for the police. Alternately, you can dial ☏ **104** for an ambulance in six of the country's provinces (for Havana, dial ☏ 838-1185; Pinar del Rio ☏ 76-2317; Isla de la Juventud ☏ 32-4170; Matanzas ☏ 2-8500; Ciego de Avila ☏ 185; Las Tunas ☏ 4-9192; Granma ☏ 185; Santiago ☏ 62-3300); and, although in Guantanamo, you can dial ☏ 104, in Baracoa, you must dial ☏ 4-3472, and ☏ **105** for the fire department. The three-digit emergency numbers are part of an ongoing effort to institute a national program for emergency response. However, in some areas of the country, it is still not fully functional. At none of these numbers can you assume you will find an English-speaking person. For legal emergencies, contact your diplomatic representation. All U.S. citizens can find assistance at the **U.S. Interests Section,** see above, with no questions asked about licenses.

ETIQUETTE & CUSTOMS Cubans are friendly, open, and physically expressive people. They strike up conversations easily and seldom use the formal terms of address in Spanish. However, be aware that as a foreigner, many Cubans who start a conversation with you are hoping in some way to get some economic gain out of the relationship. *Jineterismo,* or jockeying, is a way of life in Cuba. This may involve anything from offers to take you to a specific restaurant or hotel (for a commission) to direct appeals for money or goods.

Dress is generally very informal, in large part due to the tough economic times faced by the broad population. Suits are sometimes worn in business and governmental meetings, although a simple, light, short-sleeved cotton shirt with a tie, or a *guayabera,* are more common. The *guayabera* is a loose-fitting shirt with two or four outer pockets on the front and usually a few vertical bands of pleats or embroidery. The *guayabera* is worn untucked, and is quite acceptable at even the most formal of occasions.

Perhaps the greatest etiquette concern is about what you say. Open criticism of the government or of Fidel or Raúl Castro is a major taboo. Don't do it—especially in open public places. The police, community revolutionary brigades, and reprisals for vocal dissent are an ongoing legacy of Cuba's political reality. One effect of this is that while Cubans you meet will often be very open and expressive with you, they tend to immediately clam up the minute another Cuban unknown to them enters the equation.

GASOLINE (PETROL) See "Getting Around/By Car," p. 39.

HOLIDAYS See "Holidays" and "Calendar of Events," p. 34.

HOT LINES Asistur (☏ 7/866-4499; www.asistur.cu) can help with all types of travelers' emergencies—for a fee.

INSURANCE Medical Insurance For travel overseas, most U.S. health plans (including Medicare and Medicaid) do not provide coverage, and the ones that do often require you to pay for services upfront and reimburse you only after you return home. Even if your plan does cover overseas treatment, most out-of-country hospitals make you pay your bills upfront, and send you a refund only after you've returned home and filed the necessary paperwork with your insurance company. As a safety net, you may want to buy travel medical insurance, particularly if you're traveling to a remote or high-risk area where emergency evacuation might be necessary. If you require additional medical insurance, try **MEDEX Assistance** (✆ 410/453-6300; www.medexassist. com) or **Travel Assistance International** (✆ 800/821-2828; www.travelassistance. com); for general information on services, call **Worldwide Assistance Services, Inc.,** at ✆ 800/777-8710).

Canadians should check with their provincial health plan offices or call **Health Canada** (✆ 866/225-0709; www.hc-sc. gc.ca) to find out the extent of their coverage and what documentation and receipts they must take home in case they are treated overseas.

Travelers from the U.K. should carry their **European Health Insurance Card** (EHIC; ✆ 0845-606-2030; www.ehic. org.uk), which replaced the E111 form as proof of entitlement to free/reduced cost medical treatment abroad. Note, however, that the EHIC only covers "necessary medical treatment," and for repatriation costs, lost money, baggage, or cancellation, travel insurance from a reputable company should always be sought.

TRAVEL INSURANCE Check your existing insurance policies and credit card coverage before you buy travel insurance. You may already be covered for lost luggage, canceled tickets, or medical expenses. The cost of travel insurance varies widely, depending on the cost and length of your trip, your age and health, and the type of trip you're taking, but expect to pay between 5% and 8% of the vacation itself. You can get estimates from various providers through **InsureMyTrip.com.** Enter your trip cost and dates, your age, and other information, for prices from more than a dozen companies. Residents of the U.K. can purchase annual and single-trip travel insurance at a low cost through **www. travelinsuranceweb.com.**

Most tour operators and agencies that work in Cuba or book travel to Cuba offer a basic insurance package for around CUC$5 (US$5.40/£2.70) per day, which includes in-country medical coverage with a zero deductible of up to CUC$25,000 (US$27,000/£13,500); emergency evacuation and repatriation coverage of up to CUC$7,000 (US$7,560/£3,780); coverage for civil damages caused to third parties of up to CUC$25,000 (US$27,000/ £13,500); and lost luggage coverage of up to CUC$400 (US$432/£216). Other coverage options also exist. These policies are invariably bought through **Asistur** (✆ 7/ 866-4499; www.asistur.cu).

TRIP-CANCELLATION INSURANCE Trip-cancellation insurance will help retrieve your money if you have to back out of a trip or depart early, or if your travel supplier goes bankrupt. Trip cancellation traditionally covers such events as sickness, natural disasters, and State Department advisories. The latest news in trip-cancellation insurance is the availability of **expanded hurricane coverage** and the **"any-reason"** cancellation coverage—which costs more, but covers cancellations made for any reason. You won't get back 100% of your prepaid trip cost, but you'll be refunded a substantial portion. **Travel-Safe** (✆ 888/885-7233; www.travelsafe. com) offers both types of coverage.

INTERNET ACCESS In all cities outside of Havana, head to the main Etecsa office where you will find a bank of computers. Some hotels in the provinces and most in beach resorts also offer Internet access. In Havana, outside of the Etecsa office in Habana Vieja, all the top-end hotels offer Internet access at a minimum price of CUC$6 (US$6.50/£3.25) an hour. You'll get an Internet card with a scratch-off log-in number and password on the back, which will allow you to use any Etecsa computer around the country. Also, see "Staying Connected," p. 56.

LANGUAGE Spanish is the official language of Cuba. English is spoken at most tourist hotels and some restaurants and attractions. Outside of the tourist orbit, English is not widely spoken, and some rudimentary Spanish will go a long way.

Indigenous and African languages have had a profound and lasting influence, and you will find many words—like *cigar, barbacoa,* and *conga*—tracing their origin to indigenous and African sources used widely across the island. Various African dialects are still widely used in the songs and ceremonies of Santeria and other syncretic religions, although almost no one speaks them conversationally. In a legacy from the Soviet days, some Cubans speak Russian. Also, see the glossary in Appendix B, p. 297.

LAUNDROMATS Dry cleaners and laundromats—be they full service or self-serve—are few and far between in Cuba. Hotel laundry services, which can sometimes be expensive, are far more common. Your best bet is to ask at your *casa particular* when you stay in one. You'll be charged around CUC\$3 (US\$3.25/£1.60) for an enormous bag of laundry. It will cost extra to have your clothes ironed.

LEGAL AID If you get into legal trouble, immediately request to be put in touch with your embassy. All embassies have round-the-clock emergency numbers. Asistur (www.asistur.cu) may also be able to help. Its emergency numbers are © 7/866-8521, © 7/866-8339, and © 7/866-4920.

LOST & FOUND Be sure to tell all of your credit card companies the minute you discover your wallet has been lost or stolen and file a report at the nearest police precinct. Your credit card company or insurer may require a police report number or record of the loss. Most credit card companies have an emergency toll-free number to call if your card is lost or stolen; they may be able to wire you a cash advance immediately or deliver an emergency credit card in a day or two.

Visa does not have a toll-free emergency number for Cuba. You must dial © 119, then 01/410-581-994. For MasterCard, you must also dial © 119, then 01/636-722-7111. For American Express cards issued in Canada, you must dial © 119, then 01/905-474-0870.

If you need emergency cash over the weekend when all banks are closed, you can have money wired to you via **Western Union** (© **800/325-6000;** www.western union.com).

MAIL A post office is called a *correo* in Spanish. You can get stamps at post offices, gift shops, and the front desk in most hotels. The Cuban postal system is extremely slow and untrustworthy. You can count on every parcel and piece of mail being opened and inspected. The cost of a postcard or letter to the U.S. or Canada is CUC\$.75 (US81¢/41p), and it takes about 3 weeks for delivery. A postcard to Europe costs CUC\$.65 (US70¢/35p) and a letter to Europe is CUC\$.75 (US81¢/41p). A package of up to 1 kilogram (2.2 lb.) will cost CUC\$10 to CUC\$20 (US\$11–US\$22/£5.40–£11) to ship, depending upon your destination country, but can only be dealt with at principal post offices.

However, it is best to send anything of any value via an established international courier service. **DHL,** Calle 26 and Avenida 1, Miramar, Havana (© **7/204-1876;** www.dhl.com), provides broad coverage to most of Cuba. *Beware:* Despite what you may be told, packages sent overnight to U.S. addresses tend to take 3 to 4 days to reach their destination.

MAPS Most car-rental agencies and many hotels will give you a copy of basic nationwide and Havana road maps. The Cuban Geographic and Cartographic Institute publishes a couple of much more detailed maps; most tourist gift shops and Infotur kiosks carry these maps. If you're buying a map before your trip, try to get the **International Travel Map: Cuba** (ITMB Publishing; www.itmb.com). You'll also find good maps online at www.cubaroutes.com and **www.cubamapa.com**. Anyone doing any serious driving should purchase the Guia de Carreteras available in Havana (p. 86).

MEASUREMENTS See the chart on the inside front cover of this book for details on converting metric measurements to nonmetric equivalents.

NEWSPAPERS & MAGAZINES The nationwide Spanish-language daily, *Granma*, is a thin paper with sparse coverage of local and international news, and a strong party-line editorial bias. The paper is not nearly as widely available as daily papers in most other countries, but some street vendors and many hotels do have copies each morning. English-digest versions of *Granma* come out every few days and are available at many hotels. A handful of other daily and weekly newspapers are published, and are usually even harder to find than *Granma*. These include *Trabajadores, Juventud Rebelede,* and a host of regional rags.

Probably the most useful magazine for travelers is the elusive bilingual cultural publication **Cartelera,** which is sometimes available at the front desks of most hotels in Havana.

PASSPORTS The websites listed in this section provide downloadable passport applications, as well as the current fees for processing applications. For an up-to-date, country-by-country listing of passport requirements around the world, go to the "International Travel" tab of the U.S. State Department website at **http://travel.state.gov**.

FOR RESIDENTS OF AUSTRALIA You can pick up an application from your local post office or any branch of Passports Australia, but you must schedule an interview at the passport office to present your application materials. Call the **Australian Passport Information Service** at ℭ **131-232,** or visit the government website at www.passports.gov.au.

FOR RESIDENTS OF CANADA Passport applications are available at Passport Canada offices, Canada Post outlets throughout Canada or downloadable from the central **Passport Canada,** Department of Foreign Affairs and International Trade, Gastineau QC K1A 0G3 (ℭ **800/567-6868;** www.ppt.gc.ca). *Note:* Canadian children under 16 years who travel must have their own passport. However, if you hold a valid Canadian passport issued before December 11, 2001, which bears the name of your child, the passport remains valid for you and your child until it expires.

FOR RESIDENTS OF IRELAND You can apply for a 10-year passport at the **Passport Office,** Setanta Centre, Molesworth Street, Dublin 2 (ℭ **01/671-1633;** www.irlgov.ie/iveagh). A 3-year passport can be acquired for those under age 3; a 5-year passport may be acquired for those ages 4 to 17. Those over 65 may acquire a 10-year passport. You can also apply at 1A South Mall, Cork (ℭ **21/494-4700**) or at most main post offices.

FOR RESIDENTS OF NEW ZEALAND You can pick up a passport application at any New Zealand Passports Office or download it from their website. Contact the **Passports Office** at ℭ **0800/225-050** in New Zealand or 04/474-8100, or log on to www.passports.govt.nz.

FOR RESIDENTS OF THE UNITED KINGDOM To pick up an application for a standard 10-year passport (5-yr. passport for children under 16), visit your nearest passport office or major post office, or contact the **United Kingdom Passport Service** at ℭ **0870/521-0410** or visit its website at www.ips.gov.uk/passport.

FOR RESIDENTS OF THE UNITED STATES Whether you're applying in person or by mail, you can download passport applications from the U.S. State Department website at **http://travel.state.gov**. To find your regional passport office, either check the U.S. State Department website or call the **National Passport Information Center** toll-free number (© **877/487-2778**) for automated information.

POLICE Nationwide, you can dial © **116** for police, although you shouldn't expect to find an English-speaking person on the other end of the line. In general, the police are quite helpful and not to be feared. Bribery and graft are not an issue. In the event of robbery, the police are your best bet, but for physical emergencies or other threats of serious danger, you are probably best off contacting your embassy.

SMOKING Although Fidel gave up smoking years ago, Cuba remains a major producer of tobacco and tobacco products. Many Cubans smoke. Cuba introduced a nonsmoking ban in enclosed public places in February 2005, but it is not really enforced. Most restaurants have nonsmoking areas.

TAXES There are no direct or specific taxes on goods or services in Cuba. However, some tourist restaurants have begun adding a 10% service charge onto their bills. However, this charge goes directly to the restaurant and not the waiter, so you will need to leave a cash tip too. There is a CUC$25 (US$27/£14) departure tax that must be paid in cash upon leaving the country.

FAX Most hotels have **fax machines** available for guest use (be sure to ask about the charge to use it).

TELEPHONES See "Staying Connected," p. 56.

TIME Havana is 5 hours behind Greenwich Mean Time, or on a par with Eastern Standard Time in the United States and Canada. Daylight saving time is observed by setting clocks ahead 1 hour from the last Sunday in March to the last Sunday in October.

TIPPING Most Cuban workers earn incredibly low salaries in dollar terms—around CUC$8 to CUC$12 a month (US$8.65–US$13/£4.30–£6.50)—so tips are an extremely important and coveted source of supplemental income. With the rise in tourism, all sorts of workers now expect and work for tips, including taxi drivers, porters, waiters, guides, and restaurant musicians. Taxi drivers in particular are loath to give any small change on a fare. So if the meter reads CUC$2.30 (US$2.50/£1.25), you are expected to pay CUC$2.50 (US$2.70/£1.35), although you are certainly within your rights to ask for CUC$.20 (US21¢/10p) or so change. Porters should be tipped between CUC$.50 (US55¢/25p) and CUC$1 (US$1.10/55p) per bag. Some restaurants include a 10% service charge, although you should tip the waiter an additional 5% to 10% depending upon the quality of service, or even more (as this is how they actually survive, since they will not see any of that 10% service charge). If you stay in a resort, you should definitely tip the maid around CUC$1 (US$1.10/55p) a day, and also tip the waiters who serve you every day in the all-inclusive resorts, as they are on miserable salaries.

TOILETS Public restrooms are hard to come by. You must usually count on the generosity of some hotel or restaurant, or duck into a museum or other attraction. Although it's rare that a tourist would be denied the use of the facilities, you should always ask first. In broad terms, the sanitary conditions of public restrooms in Cuba is much higher than those found throughout the developing world, although at many establishments, toilet seats are sometimes missing. Always bring toilet paper with you wherever you go.

Many restrooms have an attendant, who is sometimes responsible for dispensing toilet paper. Upon exiting, you are expected to either leave a tip, or pay a specified fee. If the restrooms are not clean and you do not take the toilet paper, do not feel obliged to tip. Otherwise, leave up to CUC$.25 (US30¢/15p).

USEFUL PHONE NUMBERS
Overseas Citizens Services: ℂ 01/202-501-4444.

U.S. Passport Agency: ℂ 1-877-487-2778.

U.S. Centers for Disease Control and Prevention's international traveler's hot line: ℂ 404/332-4559.

WATER   Water is generally safe to drink throughout the country. However, since many travelers have tender digestive tracts, I recommend playing it safe and sticking to bottled water, sold as *agua mineral sin* or *con gas* and made by Ciego Montero.

---

2 TOLL-FREE NUMBERS & WEBSITES

MAJOR U.S. AIRLINES
(*flies internationally as well)

American Airlines*
ℂ 800/433-7300 (in U.S. or Canada)
ℂ 0207/365-0777 (in U.K.)
www.aa.com

Continental Airlines*
ℂ 800/523-3273 (in U.S. or Canada)
ℂ 0845/607-6760 (in U.K.)
www.continental.com

Delta Air Lines*
ℂ 800/221-1212 (in U.S. or Canada)
ℂ 0845/600-0950 (in U.K.)
www.delta.com

JetBlue Airways*
ℂ 800/538-2583 (in U.S.)
ℂ 801/365-2525 (in Canada)
www.jetblue.com

United Airlines*
ℂ 800/864-8331 (in U.S. and Canada)
ℂ 0845/844-4777 (in U.K.)
www.united.com

US Airways*
ℂ 800/428-4322 (in U.S. and Canada)
ℂ 0845/600-3300 (in U.K.)
www.usairways.com

INTERNATIONAL AIRLINES

Aerocaribbean
ℂ 7/879-7524 (in Cuba)
www.aero-caribbean.com

Aeroméxico
ℂ 800/237-6639 (in U.S.)
ℂ 0207/801-6234 (in U.K., information only)
www.aeromexico.com

Air Canada
ℂ 888/247-2262 (in U.S. and Canada)
ℂ 0871/220-1111 (in U.K.)

Air France
ℂ 800/237-2747 (in U.S.)
ℂ 800/375-8723 (U.S. and Canada)
ℂ 0870/142-4343 (in U.K.)
www.airfrance.com

Air Jamaica
ℂ 800/523-5585 (in U.S. or Canada)
ℂ 0208/570-9171 (in U.K.)
ℂ 876/922-3460 (in Kingston, Jamaica)
www.airjamaica.com

Air New Zealand
ℂ 800/262-1234 (in U.S.)
ℂ 800/663-5494 (in Canada)
ℂ 0800/028-4149 (in U.K.)
www.airnewzealand.com

Air Transat
ℂ 866/847-1112 (in U.S. and Canada)
www.airtransat.com

Alitalia
© 800/223-5730 (in U.S.)
© 800/361-8336 (in Canada)
© 0871/424-1424 (in U.K.)
www.alitalia.com

Aviacsa (Mexico and Las Vegas only)
© 800-967-5263 (in U.S.)
www.aviacsa.com.mx

Bahamasair
© 800/222-4262 (in U.S.)
© 242/377-5505 (in Nassau, Bahamas)
www.bahamasair.com

Cayman Airways
© 800/422-9626 (in U.S.)
© 345/743-8200 (in Grand Cayman)
www.caymanairways.com

Cubana
© 7/834-4446 (in Cuba)
© 888/667-1222 (in Canada)
© 0207/538-5933 (in U.K.)
© 52/50-6355 (in Mexico City)
© 52/998-887-7210 (in Cancún, Mexico)
© 876/978-3410 (in Kingston, Jamaica)
© 809/227-2040 (in Santo Domingo, Dominican Republic)

© 876/952-0527 (in Montego Bay, Jamaica)
© 242/377-3460 (in Nassau, Bahamas)
www.cubana.cu

Grupo Taca
© 800/400-TACA (in U.S. or Canada)
© 800/722-TACA (in Canada)
© 0870/241-0340 (in U.K.)
© 506/299-8222 (in San Jose, Costa Rica)
© 7/833-3114 (in Cuba)
www.taca.com

Iberia Airlines
© 800/722-4642 (in U.S. and Canada)
© 0870/609-0500 (in U.K.)
www.iberia.com

Martinair
© 7/833-3729 (in Cuba)
© 416/364-3672 (in Canada)
© 31/20-601-1767 (in Holland)
www.martinair.com

Mexicana
© 800/380-8781 (in U.S. and Canada)
www.mexicana.com

Virgin Atlantic Airways
© 800/821-5438 (in U.S. and Canada)
© 0870/380-2007 (in U.K.)
www.virgin-atlantic.com

BUDGET AIRLINES

Air Comet
© 900/9954-99 (in Spain)
© 0808/234-5186 (in U.K.)
© 7/207-9522 (in Cuba)
www.aircomet.com

Air Europa
© 902/401-501 (in Spain)
© 7/204-6904 (in Cuba)
© 0871/222-9122 (in U.K.)
www.aireuropa.com

Blue Panorama
© 39/06-6021-4737 (in Italy)
www.blue-panorama.com

Condor Airways
© 800/364-1667 (in U.S. and Canada)
www3.condor.com

CAR RENTAL AGENCIES

Cubacar
© 7/273-2277 (in Cuba)
cubacar@transtur.cu

Havanautos
© 7/835-3142 (in Cuba)
havanautos@transtur.cu

Micar
✆ 7/204-7777 (in Cuba)

Rex
✆ 7/835-6830 or 7/683-0303 (in Cuba)

MAJOR HOTEL CHAINS

Escencia Hotels & Resorts
www.esenciahotelsandresorts.com

Gaviota
✆ 7/866-9780
www.gaviota-grupo.com

Gran Caribe
✆ 0808/238-0042 (in U.K.)
www.gran-caribe.com

Habaguanex
✆ 7/867-1038
www.habaguanex.com

Iberostar
✆ 34 902/995-555 (in Spain)
www.iberostar.com

Transtur
✆ 7/862-2686 or 7/861-5885 (in Cuba)
www.transtur.cu

Vía Rent a Car
✆ 7/861-4465 (in Cuba)
www.gaviota-grupo.com

Islazul
✆ 7/832-0570
www.islazul.cu

NH Hoteles
✆ 0800/0115-0116 (in U.K. and Eire)
✆ 800/232-9860 (in U.S. and Canada)
www.nh-hotels.com

Occidental Hotels & Resorts
✆ 800/6460-6460 (in Europe)
✆ 800/858-2258 (in North America)
www.occidental-hoteles.com

Sol Meliá
✆ 0808/234-1953 (in U.K.)
www.solmeliacuba.com

Appendix B: Cuban Spanish Terms & Phrases

Cubans speak fast and furiously. There's a very nasal and almost garbled quality to Cuban Spanish. Cubans tend to drop their final consonants, particularly the *s*, and they don't roll their *rr's* particularly strongly, converting the *rr* into an almost *l* sound in words like *carro* or *perro*. Cubans seldom use the formal *usted* form, instead preferring to address almost everyone (except those much older or of particular social or political stature) as *tú*. Likewise, you'll almost never hear the terms *señor* or *señora* as forms of address—Cubans prefer *compañero* and *compañera*. Cubans are also direct. They will almost always answer the phone with a curt *"Diga,"* which translates roughly as a mix of "Tell me," "Say what?" and "Speak."

1 BASIC WORDS & PHRASES

English	Spanish	Pronunciation
Good day	**Buenos días**	*Bweh*-nohss *dee*-ahss
How are you?	**¿Cómo está?**	*Koh*-moh ehss-*tah*?
Very well	**Muy bien**	Mwee byehn
Thank you	**Gracias**	*Grah*-syahss
You're welcome	**De nada**	Day *nah*-dah
Goodbye	**Adiós**	Ah-*dyohss*
Please	**Por favor**	Pohr fah-*vor*
Yes	**Sí**	See
No	**No**	Noh
Excuse me (to get by someone)	**Perdóneme**	Pehr-*doh*-neh-meh
Excuse me (to begin a question)	**Disculpe**	Dees-*kool*-peh
Give me	**Déme**	*Deh*-meh
Where is . . . ?	**¿Dónde está . . . ?**	*Dohn*-deh ehss-*tah*?
the station	**la estación**	lah ehss-tah-*seown*
a hotel	**un hotel**	oon oh-*tel*
a gas station	**una estación de servicio**	*oo*-nah ehss-tah-*seown* deh sehr-*bee*-syoh
a restaurant	**un restaurante**	oon res-toh-*rahn*-teh

English	Spanish	Pronunciation
the toilet	**el baño**	el *bah*-nyoh
a good doctor	**un buen médico**	oon bwehn *meh*-thee-coh
the road to . . .	**el camino a/hacia . . .**	el cah-*mee*-noh ah/*ah*-syah
To the right	**A la derecha**	Ah lah deh-*reh*-chah
To the left	**A la izquierda**	Ah lah ees-*kyehr*-dah
Straight ahead	**Derecho**	Deh-*reh*-choh
I would like . . .	**Quisiera . . .**	Key-*syehr*-ah
to eat	**comer**	koh-*mehr*
a room	**una habitación**	*oon*-nah ah-bee-tah-*seown*
Do you have . . . ?	**¿Tiene usted . . . ?**	*Tyeh*-neh oos-*ted*?
How much is it?	**¿Cuánto cuesta?**	*Kwahn*-toh *kwehss*-tah?
When?	**¿Cuándo?**	*Kwahn*-doh?
What?	**¿Qué?**	Kay?
There is (Is there . . . ?)	**(¿)Hay (. . . ?)**	Eye?
What is there?	**¿Qué hay?**	Keh *eye*?
Yesterday	**Ayer**	Ah-*yer*
Today	**Hoy**	Oy
Tomorrow	**Mañana**	Mah-*nyah*-nah
Good	**Bueno**	*Bweh*-noh
Bad	**Malo**	*Mah*-loh
Better (best)	**(Lo) Mejor**	(Loh) Meh-*hor*
More	**Más**	Mahs
Less	**Menos**	*Meh*-nohss
No smoking	**Se prohibe fumar**	Seh pro-*hee*-beh foo-*mahr*

NUMBERS

1	**uno**	*ooh*-noh	17	**diecisiete**	dyess-ee-*syeh*-teh
2	**dos**	*dohss*	18	**dieciocho**	dyess-ee-*oh*-choh
3	**tres**	*trehss*	19	**diecinueve**	dyess-ee-*nweh*-beh
4	**cuatro**	*kwah*-troh	20	**veinte**	*bayn*-teh
5	**cinco**	*seen*-koh	30	**treinta**	*trayn*-tah
6	**seis**	*sayss*	40	**cuarenta**	kwah-*ren*-tah
7	**siete**	*syeh*-teh	50	**cincuenta**	seen-*kwen*-tah
8	**ocho**	*oh*-choh	60	**sesenta**	seh-*sehn*-tah
9	**nueve**	*nweh*-beh	70	**setenta**	seh-*ten*-tah
10	**diez**	*dyess*	80	**ochenta**	oh-*chen*-tah
11	**once**	*ohn*-seh	90	**noventa**	noh-*behn*-tah
12	**doce**	*doh*-seh	100	**cien**	*syehn*
13	**trece**	*treh*-seh	200	**doscientos**	doh-*syehn*-tohs
14	**catorce**	kah-*tor*-seh	500	**quinientos**	kee-*nyehn*-tohs
15	**quince**	*keen*-seh	1,000	**mil**	meel
16	**dieciseis**	dyess-ee-*sayss*			

DAYS OF THE WEEK

Monday	**lunes**	(*loo*-nehss)
Tuesday	**martes**	(*mahr*-tehss)
Wednesday	**miércoles**	(*myehr*-koh-lehs)
Thursday	**jueves**	(*wheh*-behss)
Friday	**viernes**	(*byehr*-nehss)
Saturday	**sábado**	(*sah*-bah-doh)
Sunday	**domingo**	(doh-*meen*-goh)

---

2 MORE USEFUL PHRASES

English	Spanish	Pronunciation
Do you speak English?	**¿Habla usted inglés?**	*Ah*-blah oo-*sted* een-*glehss*?
Is there anyone here who speaks English?	**¿Hay alguien aquí que hable inglés?**	Eye *ahl*-gyehn ah-*key* keh *ah*-bleh een-*glehss*?
I speak a little Spanish.	**Hablo un poco de español.**	Ah-*bloh* oon poh-koh deh ehss-pah-*nyol*
I don't understand Spanish very well.	**No (lo) entiendo muy bien el español.**	Noh (loh) ehn-*tyehn*-do mwee byehn el ehss-pah-*nyol*
The meal is good.	**Me gusta la comida.**	Meh *goo*-stah lah koh-*mee*-dah
What time is it?	**¿Qué hora es?**	Keh *oh*-rah ehss?
May I see your menu?	**¿Puedo ver el menú (la carta)?**	*Pweh*-doh vehr el meh-*noo* (lah *car*-tah)?
The check, please.	**La cuenta, por favor.**	Lah *kwehn*-tah, pohr fah-*vor*
What do I owe you?	**¿Cuánto le debo?**	*Kwahn*-toh leh *deh*-boh?
What did you say?	**¿Cómo? (colloquial expression for American "Eh?")**	*Koh*-moh?
I want (to see) . . .	**Quiero (ver) . . .**	*Kyehr*-oh (vehr)
a room	**un cuarto** or **una habitación**	oon *kwar*-toh, *oon*-nah ah-bee-tah-*seown*
for two persons	**para dos personas**	*pah*-rah dohss pehr-*soh*-nahs
with (without) bathroom	**con (sin) baño**	kohn (seen) *bah*-nyoh
We are staying here only . . .	**Nos quedamos aquí solamente . . .**	Nohs keh-*dahm*-ohss ah-*key* sohl-ah-*mehn*-teh
one night	**una noche**	*oon*-ah *noh*-cheh
one week	**una semana**	*oon*-ah seh-*mahn*-ah

English	Spanish	Pronunciation
We are leaving . . . tomorrow	**Partimos (Salimos)** . . . **mañana**	Pahr-*tee*-mohss (sah-*lee*-mohss) mah-*nya*-nah
Do you accept . . . ? traveler's checks? credit cards?	**¿Acepta usted . . . ?** **cheques de viajero?** **tarjeta de crédito?**	Ah-*sehp*-tah oo-*sted?* *cheh*-kehs deh byah-*heh*-ro? tar-*hay*-ta de *kray*-dee-toe?

3 TYPICAL CUBAN WORDS & PHRASES

Ahí Namá There it is, that's it!
Babalao Afro-Cuban religious priest
Bachata Party, hanging out
Bárbaro Great, fabulous
Bicitaxi Bicycle carriage
Bodega Store
Bohío Traditional, palm-thatched rural or indigenous dwelling
CADECA Acronym for *casa de cambio* (currency exchange office)
Camello Flatbed truck-bus hybrid
Carro particular Privately owned car
Casa de la trova Music club
Casa del campo A simple country house
Casa particular A private home with rooms for rent
Cerveza Beer
Chama Child
Chavito Cuban Convertible Peso
Chévere Cool, excellent
Cirilo Yes or yeah
Coche Horse-drawn carriage
Cola Line or queue
Comida criolla Cuban creole cuisine
Compañero/compañera Literally, "partner," most common form of an address, as opposed to *señor* or *señora,* which are almost never used
Compay Friend
Consumo Price inclusive of food and drinks
Coppelia National ice-cream chain, almost synonymous with ice cream
Cuba libre Cocktail with rum and Coke
Diga Literally, "speak"; this is a very common phone greeting
Divisa U.S. dollar/Cuban Convertible Peso
Fanoso Cheapskate
Fruta bomba Papaya
Fula U.S. dollar (slang)
Guagua Bus
Guajiro/Guajira Peasant or farmer
Guarachar To hang out or party
Guayabera Loose-fitting, embroidered and pleated men's shirt
Hacer botella To hitchhike

Jinetero/jinetera Literally, "jockey"; used to refer to anyone hustling a foreigner for money

Mojito A rum cocktail

Orishá Santeria deity

Paladar Private home restaurant

Paradero Train station

Por nada You're welcome

Puro Cuban cigar

¿Qué bolá? "What's going on?" (slang)

Santero Afro-Cuban Santeria religious priests

Villas Towns or settlements

Yuma Street slang for the United States of America

Zafra Sugar-cane harvest

INDEX

ABC Charters, 30, 51
Academic trips and language
classes, 55
Accommodations
Baracoa, 259–261
Bayamo, 248–249
best, 9–12
Camagüey, 229–231
Cayería del Norte, 184–186
Cayo Coco, 218–220
Cayo Guillermo, 221–222
Cayo Largo, 154–155
Cienfuegos, 191–193
Guardalavaca, 239–242
Havana, 87–101
Isla de la Juventud, 152
Las Terrazas, 143
María la Gorda, 148–149
Matanzas, 158
Pinar del Río, 133, 146
Sancti Spíritus, 211
San Diego de los Baños,
144–145
Santa Clara, 181–182
Santiago de Cuba, 274–278
tips on, 58–60
Trinidad, 199–202
Varadero, 165–170
Viñales, 138–139
Zapata Peninsula, 175–176
Acuario Baconao, 287
Acuario Nacional (Havana),
117
Acuavida Centro Spa-Talaso
(Cayo Coco), 218
Adventure and wellness
trips, 55
AeroCaribbean, 40
Afro-Cuban culture, 25–26
Air Transat Holidays, 51
Air travel, 37–38, 40–41
Ancón, 136
Arrechabala Rum Factory
(Cárdenas), 172
Artesanía (Varadero), 164
ARTex shops
Cienfuegos, 191
Havana, 121, 124

Trinidad, 204, 205
Varadero, 164
Art galleries
Cienfuegos, 191
Havana, 121
Asociación Cubana de Limi-
tados Físicos-Motores, 47
ATMs (automated-teller
machines), 44
Ayuntamiento (Santiago de
Cuba), 270

Bacuanayagua Bridge, 162
Balcón de Velázquez (Santi-
ago de Cuba), 273
Ballet de Camagüey, 232
Ballet Folklórico Cutumba
(Santiago de Cuba), 282
Banes, 238
Banks, 41
Baracoa, 255–262
road to, 253–255
Baradero, what's new in, 2
Bar Club Boulevard (Santa
Clara), 183
Bar Dos Hermanos (Havana),
128
Bar La Marquesina (Santa
Clara), 182
Barrio El Tivolí (Santiago de
Cuba), 272
Baseball, 53
Havana, 119
Santiago de Cuba, 281
Baseball Adventures, 53
Basilica del Cobre, 285–286
Batista, Fulgencio, 238
Bayamo, 245–250
Bay of Pigs invasion (1961),
174
Bay of Santiago, 274
Bazar Volveré (Havana), 121
Beaches. See also specific
beaches
Baracoa, 259
best, 8
Cayería del Norte, 184

Cayo Coco and Cayo
Guillermo, 216–217
Cayo Jutías, 146
Cayo Largo, 153–154
Cayo Levisa, 145–146
Guardalavaca, 237
Isla de la Juventud, 151, 152
María la Gorda, 147
Varadero, 159
Beers, 27
Bello Bar (Santiago de Cuba),
284
Beny Moré International Fes-
tival of Popular Music
(Cienfuegos), 36
Biblioteca Provincial Rubén
Martínez (Sancti Spíritus),
210
Biking and mountain
biking, 53
Havana, 119
Trinidad, 196
Viñales, 137
Bird-watching, 53–54
Zapata Peninsula, 174–175
Boat Adventure (Varadero),
163–164
Boating (boat rentals), Vara-
dero, 163
Boat travel and tours, 38
Cayo Largo, 154
Varadero, 163–164
Boca de Guamá, 173, 175
Boca de las Esponjas, 237
Books on Cuba, 23–24
Business hours, 288
Bus travel, 38–39

Cabaret Continental (Vara-
dero), 171
Cabaret Nacional (Havana),
126
Cabaret Nuevo Nocturno
(Holguín), 243
Cabaret Parisien (Havana),
126
Cabaret Tropicana Santiago
(Santiago de Cuba), 281

Caberet El Patio (Isla de la Juventud), 152
Cabo San Antonio, 148
CADECA, 41
Café Cantante Mi Habana (Havana), 126
Café El Louvre (Remedios), 183
Café Monserrate (Havana), 128
Café O'Reilly (Havana), 128
Café París (Havana), 128
Café Pinar (Pinar del Río), 135
Cafetal Buenavista (Sierra del Rosario), 142
Café Teatro Brecht (Havana), 125
Caibarién, 184
Caledonia, 55
Calendar of events, 34–37
Callejón de Hammel (Havana), 114
Calle Llano (Sancti Spíritus), 210
Calle Maceo (Camagüey), 226
Calle Obispo (Havana), 112
Camagüey, 64, 223–232
    accommodations, 229–231
    getting around, 224
    nightlife, 232
    orientation, 224
    restaurants, 231–232
    shopping, 229
    sights and activities, 226–229
    traveling to, 223–224
Cañonazo (Havana), 118
Canopy Tour (Sierra del Rosario), 142
Capilla de La Dolorosa (Bayamo), 248
Caracol (chainbn), 121
Cárdenas, 171–172
Caribbean Bound, 52
Caribbean Destinations, 52
Carnaval, Santiago de Cuba, 282–283
Carnival
    Havana, 36
    Matanzas, 36
    Santiago de Cuba, 36
Car rentals, 39–40
Cartelera magazine, 125
Car travel, 39
Casa Compay Segundo (Havana), 117
Casa de Africa Museum (Havana), 25
Casa de Caridad Botanical Gardens (Viñales), 138

Casa de la Cultura
    Isla de la Juventud, 152
    Viñales, 141
Casa de la Música
    Trinidad, 205
    Varadero, 171
Casa de la Música Centro Habana (Havana), 126
Casa de la Música Egrem, Havana, 124
Casa de la Música Habana (Havana), 124
Casa de la Música Miramar (Havana), 126
Casa de las Mieles (Isla de la Juventud), 152
Casa de las Tradiciones (Santiago de Cuba), 283
Casa de la Trova
    Baracoa, 262
    Camagüey, 232
    Cienfuegos, 194
    Santiago de Cuba, 284
    Trinidad, 205
Casa del Caribe (Santiago de Cuba), 284
Casa del Habano (Pinar del Río), 133
Casa del Habano El Embajador (Cienfuegos), 191
Casa de los Refranes (Sancti Spíritus), 211
Casa de los Tabacos (Varadero), 165
Casa del Ron y Tabaco Cubana (Havana), 122
Casa del Verguero (Viñales), 137–138
Casa Fisher (Trinidad), 205
Casa Garay Fábrica de Guayabitas del Pinar (Pinar del Río), 133
Casa Natal de Céspedes (Bayamo), 247
Casa Natal del Mayor (Ignacio Agramonte; Camagüey), 226–227
Casa Natal Nicolás Guillén (Camagüey), 227
Casas particulares, 59–60, 199, 201. See also Accommodations
    Havana, 87
Casa Velázquez (Santiago de Cuba), 270
Casino Campestre (Camagüey), 226
Castillo de Jagua (near Cienfuegos), 190
Castillo de la Real Fuerza (Havana), 109–110

Castillo de San Severino (Matanzas), 158
Castillo El Morro (Santiago de Cuba), 271
Castro, Fidel, 15, 238, 270, 271
    Comandancia de la Plata, 252
    Granma (boat), 250
    Guantánamo and, 254
    history of Cuba under, 17–22
    Sierra Maestra, 245
Castro, Raúl, 19, 238
    Cuba under, 22–23
Catedral de Bayamo, 248
Catedral de la Concepción Inmaculada (Cárdenas), 171
Catedral de la Purísima Concepción (Cienfuegos), 189
Catedral de San Cristóbal (Havana), 110
Cayería del Norte, 177, 178, 184–186
Cayo Blanco, 206
Cayo Coco, 213–220
Cayo Guillermo, 213–218
    accommodations, 221–222
Cayo Jutías, 146
Cayo Largo del Sur, 153–155
Cayo Levisa, 145–147
Cayo Paraíso, 146
Cayo Saetía, 244
Celebration of Classic Cars (Havana), 35
Cellphones, 57
Cementerio de Colón (Havana), 116
Cementerio de Reina (Cienfuegos), 189
Cementerio Santa Ifigenia (Santiago de Cuba), 273
Cementerio Tomás Acea (Cienfuegos), 189
Center for Constitutional Rights, 31
Centers for Disease Control and Prevention, 45
Central Cuba, 63–64
Centro Habana, 82
    accommodations, 92
    restaurants, 105
    sights and attractions, 114–115
Centro Internacional de Buceo Colony (Isla de la Juventud), 151
Centro Internacional de Deportes Aéreos (Varadero), 162

Centro Wifredo Lam
(Havana), 111
Ceramics, Havana, 121–122
Céspedes, Carlos Manuel de,
247
Chinatown (Havana), 114
Chivirico, 253
Cienfuegos, 186–194
Cigars, 53–54, 122, 132
Santiago de Cuba, 281
Cine Caribe (Isla de la Juven-
tud), 151, 152
Cine Praga (Pinar del Río),
135
Climate, 34
Club Cienfuegos, 190, 194
Club de Golf Habana
(Havana), 54
Club El Benny (Cienfuegos),
194
Club Habana (Havana), 119
Club Imágenes (Havana), 128
Club Mejunje (Santa Clara),
183
Club 300 (Santiago de Cuba),
284
Coco Taxis, 83, 161
Coffee, 27
Columbus, Christopher, 112,
132, 149, 153, 233–234,
244, 255, 258
statue of (Varadero), 171
Comandancia de Che Gue-
vara (Havana), 118–119
Comandancia de la Plata,
252–253
Complejo Turístico Topes de
Collantes, 207
Conjunto Folklórico de Ori-
ente (Santiago de Cuba),
282
Conjunto Folklórico Nacional
de Cuba (Havana), 125
Consulates, 288–289
Convento de San Francisco
(Trinidad), 199
Copa Room (Havana), 126
Coppelia (Havana), 116
Credit cards, 43–44
Criadero de Cocodrilos
Boca de Guamá, 173–174
Isla de la Juventud, 151
Crocodile Farm (Boca de
Guamá), 173–174
Cuartel de Moncada (Santi-
ago de Cuba), 271–272
Cubacel, 57
Cuba Climbing, 54
Cuba Direct, 52, 55
Cubalinda, 52
Cubana, 37, 40

Cubanacán, 78
Cienfuegos, 189
Isla de la Juventud, 150
Santa Clara, 178
Trinidad, 197
Varadero, 164
Viñales, 138
Cuban Embassy
London, 31
Ontario, 31
Cuban Embassy in London, 29
Cuban films, 24–25
Cuban Interests Section
(Washington, DC), 28, 30, 31
Cuban music, 23
Cuban National Balle
(Havana), 125
Cuban Revolution, 19–20
Cuban Solidarity
Campaign, 55
Cubataxi, 38, 83, 131, 150,
160, 178, 196, 208, 214,
224, 236, 246, 256, 268
Cuba Tourist Board Canada, 28
Cuba Tourist Board Great
Britain, 28
Cubatur, 78
Camagüey, 224
Sancti Spíritus, 208
Trinidad, 197
Cuba Welcome, 52–55
Cueva de Los Portales (La
Güira), 144
Cueva del Pirata (Varadero),
171
Cueva de Punta del Este (Isla
de la Juventud), 151
Cueva de Saturno (near
Matanzas), 164
Cuevas de Bellamar (Matan-
zas), 158
Currency and currency
exchange, 42–43
Customs regulations, 31–33

Days of Cuban Culture, 36
Delfinario
near Cienfuegos, 190
Varadero, 162
Disabilities, travelers with,
47–48
Disco La Roca (Guardala-
vaca), 242
Discoteca Ayala (Trinidad),
205–206
Discoteca La Iris (Santiago de
Cuba), 284
Discoteca Las Cuevas
(Viñales), 141

Discover Tour (Varadero),
164
Dolphin Show (near Cienfue-
gos), 190
Don Luis (Cienfuegos), 194
Dragon's Gate (Havana), 114
Drinking laws, 288
Drugstores, 46

Ecotur, Isla de la Juventud,
150
Egrem, 124
El Alfarero Casa Chichi (Trini-
dad), 205
El Cañón de los Aguajies, 237
El Capitolio (Havana), 114
El Castillo de las Nubes
(Sierra del Rosario), 142
El Castillo de Santa Bárbara
(Baracoa), 257
El Cobre, 285–286
ElderTreks, 48
Electricity, 288
El Estanco (Viñales), 138
El Floridita (Havana), 128
El Gato Tuerto (Havana), 128
El Gran Palenque (Havana),
125
El Malecón (Havana), 114–115
El Morro (Santiago de Cuba),
271
El Nicho, 190
El Oriente, 64, 233–262
what's new in, 2
El Patio ARTex (Baracoa), 262
El Quitirín (Havana), 122
El Rincón del Bolero
(Havana), 126
El Salto, 237
El Templete (Havana), 111
El Yunque, 258–259
Embassies, 288–289
Emergencies, 289
Entry requirements, 29–31
Escorted tours, 51–52
Estación Central (Havana), 41
Estadio Latinoamericano
(Havana), 119
Etiquette and customs, 289
Extreme weather, 45–46

Fábrica de Tabaco H.
Upmann (Havana), 115
Fábrica de Tabaco La Corona
(Havana), 115
Fábrica de Tabaco Partagas
(Havana), 115
Fábrica de Tabacos (Santa
Clara), 181

Fábrica de Tabacos Francisco Donatién (Pinar del Río), 132–133
Familia Cuayo Fábrica de Organos (Holguín), 243
Families with children, 48–49
  suggested itinerary, 69–70
Faro Luna Diving Center, 191
Faro Roncali, 148
Fashions (clothing), Havana, 122–123
Ferrocuba, 41
Festivals and special events, 34–37
Fiesta de la Virgen del Cobre (Santiago de Cuba), 36
Fiesta del Fuego (Santiago de Cuba), 35
Fiesta de Los Mamarrachos (Santiago de Cuba), 282
Films, Cuban, 24–25
Fishing, 54
  Cayo Largo, 154
  Havana, 120
  Isla de la Juventud, 151–152
  Jardines de la Reina, 222
  María la Gorda, 148
  Varadero, 163
  Zapata Peninsula, 175
Food and cuisine, 26–27
Frommers.com, 51
Fuerte de la Punta (Baracoa), 257
Fuerte Matachín (Baracoa), 257

Galería Acacia (Havana), 121
Galería de Arte ARTex (Trinidad), 204
Galería Víctor Manuel (Havana), 121
GAP Adventures, 52
Gasoline, 40
Gaviota Tours (Varadero), 164
Gays and lesbians, 48
Gibara, 244
Gifts and other assistance, 32
Global Exchange, 52, 55
Golf, 54
  Havana, 119
  Varadero, 163
Gran Car (Varadero), 164
Granma (boat), 250
Granma Memorial, 112
Granma province, 245
Gran Parque Nacional Sierra Maestra, 250–251
Gran Parque Natural Baconao, 286–287

Gran Teatro de La Habana (Havana), 125
Guanacahabibes National Park, 148
Guanaroca Disco (Cienfuegos), 194
Guantánamo, 254
Guardalavaca, 233–244
  accommodations, 239–242
  getting around, 236–237
  nightlife, 242
  orientation, 237
  restaurants, 242
  side trips from, 243–244
  sights and activities, 237–238
  traveling to, 234, 236
Guayabera shirts, 204
  Havana, 122
Guevara, Ernesto "Che"
  Monumento Ernesto Che Guevara (Santa Clara), 179–180
  The Motorcycle Diaries (film), 180
Guillén, Nicolás, Casa Natal (Camagüey), 227
Gyms, Havana, 119

HabanaBusTour coaches, 84
Habana Café (Havana), 127
Habana del Este (Havana), 82–83
  accommodations, 99–100
  restaurants, 108–109
Habana 1791 (Havana), 124
Habana Sí (Havana), 121
Habanos Festival (Havana), 35
Handicrafts
  Havana, 123
  Santiago de Cuba, 280
Hatiguanico River, 175
Hatuey, 258
Havana, 61–62, 75–129
  accommodations, 87–101
  arriving in, 75–76, 78
  currency exchange, 85
  dentists and doctors, 85
  drugstores, 85
  emergencies, 85
  express mail services, 85
  eyeglasses, 85
  Frommer's favorite experiences, 115
  getting around, 83–84
  hospitals, 85–86
  Internet access, 86
  layout of, 78
  maps, 86
  neighborhoods in brief, 82–83

nightlife, 125–129
outdoor activities, 119–120
photographic needs, 86
police, 86
post office, 86
restaurants, 101–109
safety, 86
shopping, 121–125
sights and attractions, 109–119
taxis, 83
tours, 109
visitor information, 78
what's new in, 1
Havana Biennale, 36
Havana International Ballet Festival, 36
Havanatur
  Camagüey, 224
  Cienfuegos, 189
  Havana, 78
  Pinar del Río, 132
  Santa Clara, 178
  Varadero, 164
  Viñales, 138
Health concerns, 44–46
Health insurance, 289–290
Hemingway, Ernest, 285
  Cayo Guillermo and, 216, 217
  Museo (Havana), 118
Hiking
  Salto del Caburní, 207
  Sierra Maestra, 251
  Viñales, 136–137
Historical sights, best, 5–6
History of Cuba, 15–23
Hitchhiking, 40
Holguín, 243
Holidays, 34
Horseback riding
  Cayo Coco and Cayo Guillermo, 217
  Guardalavaca, 238
Hotel Ambos Mundos (Havana), rooftop bar at, 128
Hotel Casa Granda Terrace Bar (Santiago de Cuba), 284–285
Hotels
  Baracoa, 259–261
  Bayamo, 248–249
  best, 9–12
  Camagüey, 229–231
  Cayería del Norte, 184–186
  Cayo Coco, 218–220
  Cayo Guillermo, 221–222
  Cayo Largo, 154–155
  Cienfuegos, 191–193
  Guardalavaca, 239–242
  Havana, 87–101

Isla de la Juventud, 152
Las Terrazas, 143
María la Gorda, 148–149
Matanzas, 158
Pinar del Río, 133, 146
Sancti Spíritus, 211
San Diego de los Baños, 144–145
Santa Clara, 181–182
Santiago de Cuba, 274–278
tips on, 58–60
Trinidad, 199–202
Varadero, 165–170
Viñales, 138–139
Zapata Peninsula, 175–176
Hurricanes Gustav and Ike, 3

Iglesia de Nuestra Señora de La Merced (Camagüey), 227
Iglesia de San Juan Bautista (Remedios), 183
Iglesia Parroquial Mayor del Espíritu Santo (Sancti Spíritus), 210
Iglesia Santa Ana (Trinidad), 198
Immigration and customs clearance, 37
The Indian's Cave (Viñales), 136
Industriales (Havana), 119
Infotur, 28
Trinidad, 197
Varadero, 162
Insurance, 289–290
International Association for Medical Assistance to Travelers (IAMAT), 45
International Blue Marlin Tournament (Havana), 36
International Book Fair (Havana), 34–35
International Festival "Boleros de Oro" (Havana), 35
International Festival "Matamoros Son" (Santiago de Cuba), 36
International Festival of "La Trova" Pepe Sánchez (Santiago de Cuba), 35
International Festival of New Latin American Film (Havana), 36
International Gay and Lesbian Travel Association (IGLTA), 48
International Jazz Festival (Havana), 35
International "Old Man and the Sea" Billfish Tournament (Havana), 35–36

International Percussion Festival PER-CUBA (Havana), 35
International Student Identity Card (ISIC), 50
International Student Travel Confederation (ISTC), 50
International Youth Travel Card (IYTC), 50
Internet access, 57–58, 290
Isla de la Juventud, 149–152
Isla Mégano, 146
Islazul, Pinar del Río, 132
Itineraries, suggested, 64–74

Jardín Botánico Orquideario Soroa (Sierra del Rosario), 143
Jardín Botánico Soledad (Cienfuegos), 190
Jardines de la Reina, 222
Jazz Café (Havana), 128
Jewelry, Havana, 123
Jinetera, 50
Jineteras and *jineteros,* 49, 199
Pinar del Río, 131
Jogging, Havana, 119–120
Journey Latin America, 52
Journeywoman, 50
Joyería Quinta y 16 (Havana), 122, 123
Juncal-Rencontra, 259

Kite surfing, 54

La Boca, 206
La Bodeguita del Medio (Havana), 128
La Cañada del Infierno (Sierra del Rosario), 142
La Canchánchara (Trinidad), 205
La Casa del Habano (Havana), 122
La Casa del Tabaco (Trinidad), 205
La Casa del Tabaco, Ron y Café La Veguita (Santa Clara), 181
La Casona (Havana), 121
La Casona (Pinar del Río), 135
La Cayería del Norte, 177, 178, 184–186
La Comparsita (Varadero), 171
La Cueva del Indio (Viñales), 136
La Farola, 254–255
Lago La Redonda, 217

Lago San Juan (Sierra del Rosario), 142
La Granja de las Tortugas (Cayo Largo), 154
La Gran Piedra, 286
La Güira National Park, 144–145
Laguna del Tesoro, 173
La Habana Vieja (Old Havana), 82, 109
accommodations, 87–92
restaurants, 101–105
La Jungla de Jones (Isla de la Juventud), 151
La Loma de Cruz (near Holguín), 243
La Maison (Havana), 122–123
Language, 290–291
La Parroquial Mayor (Trinidad), 198
La Plata Trail, 251
La Punta (Cienfuegos), 189
Las Cuevas de Santo Tomás (Viñales), 136
Las Parrandas (Remedios), 37, 183
Las Salinas de Brito, 175
Las Terrazas (Sierra del Rosario), 141
La Taberna de Dolores (Santiago de Cuba), 285
La Terraza (Baracoa), 262
Latin America Network Information Center, 28
Laundromats, 291
La Zorra y El Cuervo (Havana), 128–129
Legal aid, 291
Lennon Park (Havana), 116
Le Select (Havana), 122
Lluvia de Oro (Havana), 129
Loma de San Juan (Santiago de Cuba), 273
Longina Música (Havana), 124
Los Acuáticos, 136
Lost and found, 291
Los Tanques Azules, 237

Mail, 291
Mambo Club (Varadero), 171
Manaca-Iznaga, 206
Maps, 291–292
Maqueta de la Habana (Havana), 117
María la Gorda, 147–149
Marina Cayo Las Brujas, 184
Marina Chapelín (Varadero), 163
Marina Cienfuegos, 190, 194
Marina Dársena Varadero, 163

Marina Gaviota Varadero, 163
Marina Internacional Puerto de Vita, 237
Marlin (Varadero), 163
Matanzas (city), 156–159
Matanzas province, 63, 156
  what's new in, 2
May Day parades, 35
MedicAlert identification tag, 46
Medical insurance, 289–290
Medical requirements for entry, 31
Memorial *Granma,* 112
Memorial José Martí (Havana), 116–117
Mirador (Varadero), 171
Miramar (Havana), 82
Model Prison (Isla de la Juventud), 150
Money and costs, 41–44
Monumento a la Toma del Tren Blindado (Santa Clara), 180
Monumento Ernesto Che Guevara (Santa Clara), 179
Moré, Beny, 191
Morón, 218–219
The Motorcycle Diaries (film), 24, 180
Mountain and rock climbing, 54
Municipal Museum (Morón), 218
Mural de la Prehistoria (Viñales), 138
Museo Arqueológico in Reparto Paraíso (Baracoa), 258
Museo Batalla de Ideas (Cárdenas), 172, 173
Museo Casa Natal José Antonio Echeverría (Cárdenas), 172
Museo de Ambiente Colonial Cubano (Santiago de Cuba), 270
Museo de Ambiente Cubano (Gibara), 244
Museo de Arqueología (Trinidad), 198
Museo de Arquitectura Colonial (Trinidad), 198
Museo de Arte Colonial (Sancti Spíritus), 210
Museo de Artes Decorativas (Santa Clara), 181
Museo de Ciencias Naturales (Pinar del Río), 133
Museo de la Ciudad (Havana), 112

Museo de la Lucha Clandestina (Santiago de Cuba), 272
Museo de la Lucha Contra Bandidos (Trinidad), 199
Museo de la Revolución (Havana), 112
Museo de las Parrandas (Remedios), 183
Museo del Carnaval (Santiago de Cuba), 273–274, 282
Museo El Chorro de Maíta (Banes), 238
Museo Emilio Bacardí Moreau (Santiago de Cuba), 272
Museo Ernest Hemingway (Havana), 118
Museo Farmacéutico (Matanzas), 158
Museo Histórico 26 de Julio (Santiago de Cuba), 271–272
Museo Histórico Municipal (Trinidad), 198
Museo Indocubano (Banes), 238
Museo La Isabelica (near Gran Piedra), 286
Museo Matachín (Baracoa), 257
Museo Municipal Varadero, 162
Museo Nacional de Bellas Artes (Havana), 112–113
Museo Playa Girón, 174
Museo Provincial (Cienfuegos), 189
Museo Provincial (Isla de la Juventud), 150–151
Museo Provincial de Historia (Pinar del Río), 133
Museo Provincial General Ignacio Agramonte (Camagüey), 227
Museo Romántico (Trinidad), 198
Music, Cuban, 23
Music and dance trips, 55
Music stores
  Havana, 123–124
  Santiago de Cuba, 281

National Lawyers Guild, 31
Natural attractions, best, 6–7
Newspapers and magazines, 292
Nightlife
  Baracoa, 262
  best, 13–14
  Camagüey, 232
  Cayo Largo, 154
  Cienfuegos, 194

Guardalavaca, 242
Jardines del Rey, 222
Matanzas, 158–159
Pinar del Río, 135
Santa Clara, 182–183
Santiago de Cuba, 281–285
Trinidad, 205–206
Varadero, 171
Viñales, 141
Northeastern Cuba, 64
Nuestra Señora de la Asunción (Baracoa), 258
Nuestra Señora de los Dolores (Isla de la Juventud), 151
Nueva Gerona, 150, 151
Nuevo Café Virginia (Isla de la Juventud), 152

Obbara (Havana), 125
Office of Foreign Assets Control, 30
Outdoor activities, best, 7–8

Palacio Brunet (Trinidad), 198
Palacio de La Rumba (Varadero), 171
Palacio del Valle (Cienfuegos), 189
Palacio Ferrer (Cienfuegos), 189
Paladares, 26
Palatino Bar (Cienfuegos), 194
Palenque de los Congos Reales (Trinidad), 205
Parachuting, Varadero, 162–163
Paradiso, 52
Paradiso (Havana), 125
Parking, 39
Parque Agramonte (Camagüey), 226
Parque Calixto García (Parque Central; Holguín), 243
Parque Central (Havana), 111
Parque Céspedes
  Bayamo, 247
  Trinidad, 197
Parque Colón (Cárdenas), 171
Parque de la Independencia (Parque Central; Baracoa), 258
Parque Echeverría (Cárdenas), 172
Parque Ecológico Varahicacos (Varadero), 163
Parque Histórico Morro y Cabaña (Havana), 118–119

Parque José Martí (Cienfuegos), 189
Parque Josone (Varadero), 162
Parque La Maestranza (Havana), 113
Parque Lennon (Havana), 116
Parque Nacional Alejandro de Humboldt, 259
Parque Nacional Ciénaga de Zapata, 172
Parque Nacional de Turquino (Sierra Maestra), 251
Parque Nacional Topes de Collantes, 207
Parque Natural Bahía de Naranjo, 237–238
Parque Natural Duaba, 258–259
Parque Natural El Bagá, 217–218
Parque Vidal (Santa Clara), 178, 179
Passports, 29, 292–293
Patio de ARTex (Santiago de Cuba), 284
Patio de la Casa 18 (Havana), 126
Patio del Decimista (Viñales), 141
Patio de los Dos Abuelos (Santiago de Cuba), 284
Patio de Polo Montañez (Viñales), 141
Peña Polo Montañez (Sierra del Rosario), 142
Photography and writing trips, 55
Piano Bar Delirio Habanero (Havana), 129
Pico Turquino, 251, 252
Pico Turquino Trail, 251
Pinar del Río, 130–135
Playa (Havana), 82
  accommodations, 97–99
  restaurants, 106–108
  sights and attractions, 117
Playa Ancón, 206
  accommodations, 202
Playa Bibijagua, 152
Playa Ensenachos, 184
Playa Esmeralda, 237
  accommodations, 239–240
Playa Girón, 172–176
Playa Larga (Cayo Guillermo), 216, 220
Playa Larga (Zapata Peninsula), 173–176
Playa Maguana, 259
Playa Mégano, 184
Playa Nava, 259
Playa Paraíso, 152, 153
Playa Pilar, 217
Playa Rancho Luna, 190

Playas del Este (Havana), 82–83
  accommodations, 99–100
  restaurants, 108–109
Playa Sirena, 153
Plaza de Armas (Havana), 110
Plaza de la Catedral (Havana), 110
Plaza de la Libertad (Matanzas), 157
Plaza de la Revolución
  Camagüey, 226
  Havana, 82
    accommodations near, 94–97
    restaurants, 106
  Santiago de Cuba, 274
Plaza de la Vigía (Matanzas), 157
Plaza del Carmen (Camagüey), 228
Plaza de los Artesanos (Varadero), 164
Plaza de San Francisco (Havana), 111
Plaza las Américas (Varadero), 165
Plaza Mayor (Trinidad), 197, 198–199
Plaza Molokoff (Cárdenas), 172
Plaza San Juan de Dios (Camagüey), 228–229
Plaza Serafín Sánchez (Sancti Spíritus), 210
Plaza Vieja (Havana), 110
Plazuela El Jigüe (Trinidad), 197
Police, 293
Polo Montañez, Peña (Sierra del Rosario), 142
Posada Carriles, Luis, 113
Prehistoric Mural (Viñales), 138
Presidio Modelo (Isla de la Juventud), 150
Puente Yayabo (Sancti Spíritus), 210
Puesta del Sol (Santiago de Cuba), 271
Punta Francés (Isla de la Juventud), 151

Race relations, 49
Real Cárcel (Trinidad), 198
Regent Holidays, 52
Regions in brief, 61–64
Registro Nacional de Bienes Culturales, 32
Remedios, 177, 183
Restaurants
  Baracoa, 261–262
  best, 12–13
  Camagüey, 231–232
  Cienfuegos, 193–194

Guardalavaca, 242
Havana, 101–109
Las Terrazas, 143–144
Pinar del Río, 134
Sancti Spíritus, 211–212
Santa Clara, 182
Santiago de Cuba, 278–280
Trinidad, 202–204
Varadero, 170–171
Viñales, 140
Rock climbing, Viñales, 136
Ruinas del Teatro Brunet (Trinidad), 205
Ruinas de Segarte (Trinidad), 205
Rum, 124
Santiago de Cuba, 280–281
Rumayor (Pinar del Río), 135

Sábado de la Rumba (Havana), 125
Safety concerns, 47
Saga, 48
Sailing, 54
Salón Turquino (Havana), 127
Salto del Caburní, 207
Salto de Soroa (Sierra del Rosario), 142
Salto Vega Grande, 207
San Cristóbal agency, 78
Sancti Spíritus, 207–212
San Diego de los Baños, 144–145
San Diego de los Baños Spa, 144
San Isidoro de Holguín, 243
Santa Clara, 177–186
  accommodations, 181–182
  getting around, 178
  nightlife, 182–183
  orientation, 178
  restaurants, 182
  sights and activities, 179–181
  traveling to, 178
Santeria, 25
Santiago de Cuba, 64, 263–287
  accommodations, 274–278
  coastal road to, 253
  currency exchange, 269
  getting around, 268
  history of, 267
  hospitals and medical assistance, 269
  Internet access, 269
  layout of, 267–268
  nightlife, 281–285
  police, 269
  post office, 269
  restaurants, 278–280
  safety, 269

shopping, 280–281
side trips from, 285–287
sights and attractions, 270–274
telephone, 269
traveling to, 263–264, 267
visitor information, 267
what's new in, 3
Scuba diving, 54
Cayo Coco and Cayo Guillermo, 217
Cayo Largo, 154
Cayo Levisa, 146
Guardalavaca, 237
Havana, 120
Isla de la Juventud, 151
Jardines de la Reina, 222
María la Gorda, 148
Varadero, 164
Zapata Peninsula, 175
Seafari (Varadero), 163
Seasons, 33–34
Sea turtles, 154
Senior travelers, 48
Sierra del Escambray, 207
Sierra del Rosario Biosphere Reserve, 141–144
Sierra Maestra, 64, 245, 246–247, 250–253
Signature Travel, 52
Single travelers, 50
Smoking, 293
Snorkeling, 54
Cayo Largo, 154
Cayo Levisa, 146
Varadero, 164
Society for Accessible Travel & Hospitality, 47
Sol Cayo Coco, 222
Sol Meliá Cuba, 52
Soroa (Sierra del Rosario), 141–143
"Special Period," 21–22
Sportfishing. See Fishing
Starfish Beach, 146
STA Travel, 50
Street markets
Havana, 124–125
Trinidad, 204
Student travelers, 50
Sun exposure, 45, 46
Surfing, 54–55
Swimming, Havana, 120

Taíno Indians, 173, 194, 218, 238, 258
Taller de Cerámica Artística (Varadero), 164–165
Taxes, 293
Teatro Amadeo Roldán (Havana), 125

Teatro Heredia (Santiago de Cuba), 281, 282
Teatro Karl Marx (Havana), 125
Teatro La Caridad (Santa Clara), 179
Teatro Mella (Havana), 125
Teatro Milanés (Pinar del Río), 133
Teatro Nacional de Cuba (Havana), 125
Teatro Oriente (Santiago de Cuba), 281–282
Teatro Principal (Camagüey), 232
Teatro Sauto (Matanzas), 157
Teatro Tomás Terry (Cienfuegos), 189
Telephones, 56–57
Tennis, 55
Havana, 120
Terracota 4 (Havana), 121–122
Thomas Cook, 52
traveler's checks, 44
Tico Travel, 30, 51
Tiendas Panamericanas (Havana), 121
Tifereht Israel (Camagüey), 228
Time zone, 293
Tipping, 293
Tobacco, 132
Toilets, 293–294
Train travel, 41
Transportation, 38–41
Travel CUTS, 50
Traveler's checks, 44
Traveling to Cuba, 37
Travel insurance, 290
Travellers' Tales, 55
Trinidad, 63–64, 194–206
accommodations, 199–202
getting around, 196–197
nightlife, 205–206
orientation, 197
restaurants, 202–204
shopping, 204–205
side trips from, 206–207
sights and activities, 197–199
traveling to, 195–196
what's new in, 2
Trip-cancellation insurance, 290
Tropical illnesses, 45
Tropicana (Havana), 127
Tropicana Matanzas, 158–159, 171

Ultralight flights, Varadero, 162–163
Universidad de la Habana (Havana), 117

University of Havana, language classes, 55
University of the Oriente, Spanish classes, 55

Valle de los Ingenios, 206–207
Varadero, 63, 159–172
accommodations, 165–170
getting around, 160–161
nightlife, 171
organized tours, 164
orientation, 162
restaurants, 170–171
shopping, 164–165
side trip to Cárdenas, 171–172
traveling to, 159–160
Varadero Ecological Park, 163
Varadero Golf Club, 54, 163
Vedado (Havana), 82
accommodations, 94–97
restaurants, 106
sights and attractions, 116–117
Vegetarian travelers, 50–51
Víazul, 38
Villa Virginia, 184
Viñales, 62, 135–141
what's new in, 1
Viñales National Park, 137
Visas, 29–30
Visa traveler's checks, 44
Visitor information, 28–30
Volunteer and working trips, 55
Vuelta Abajo, 132

Water, 294
Watersports. See also specific sports
Cayería del Norte, 184
Cayo Coco and Cayo Guillermo, 217
Guardalavaca, 237
Websites
best, 14
traveler's toolbox, 57
visitor information, 28–29
Western Cuba, 62
Wheelchair accessibility, 47
White-water rafting, 259
Wi-Fi access, 57
Women travelers, 49–50

Yateras, 258

Zapata Peninsula, 172–176
Zapata Swamp National Park, 172–176

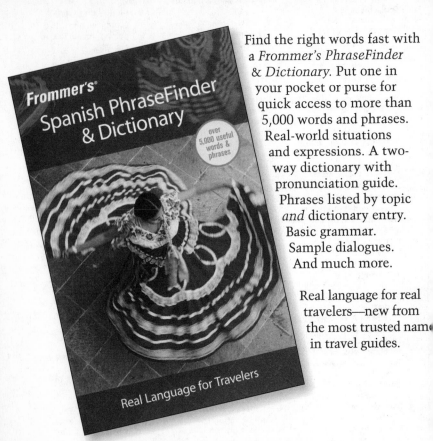

FROMMER'S® COMPLETE TRAVEL GUIDES

Alaska
Amalfi Coast
American Southwest
Amsterdam
Argentina
Arizona
Atlanta
Australia
Austria
Bahamas
Barcelona
Beijing
Belgium, Holland & Luxembourg
Belize
Bermuda
Boston
Brazil
British Columbia & the Canadian
  Rockies
Brussels & Bruges
Budapest & the Best of Hungary
Buenos Aires
Calgary
California
Canada
Cancún, Cozumel & the Yucatán
Cape Cod, Nantucket & Martha's
  Vineyard
Caribbean
Caribbean Ports of Call
Carolinas & Georgia
Chicago
Chile & Easter Island
China
Colorado
Costa Rica
Croatia
Cuba
Denmark
Denver, Boulder & Colorado Springs
Eastern Europe
Ecuador & the Galapagos Islands
Edinburgh & Glasgow
England
Europe
Europe by Rail

Florence, Tuscany & Umbria
Florida
France
Germany
Greece
Greek Islands
Guatemala
Hawaii
Hong Kong
Honolulu, Waikiki & Oahu
India
Ireland
Israel
Italy
Jamaica
Japan
Kauai
Las Vegas
London
Los Angeles
Los Cabos & Baja
Madrid
Maine Coast
Maryland & Delaware
Maui
Mexico
Montana & Wyoming
Montréal & Québec City
Morocco
Moscow & St. Petersburg
Munich & the Bavarian Alps
Nashville & Memphis
New England
Newfoundland & Labrador
New Mexico
New Orleans
New York City
New York State
New Zealand
Northern Italy
Norway
Nova Scotia, New Brunswick &
  Prince Edward Island
Oregon
Paris
Peru

Philadelphia & the Amish Country
Portugal
Prague & the Best of the Czech
  Republic
Provence & the Riviera
Puerto Rico
Rome
San Antonio & Austin
San Diego
San Francisco
Santa Fe, Taos & Albuquerque
Scandinavia
Scotland
Seattle
Seville, Granada & the Best of
  Andalusia
Shanghai
Sicily
Singapore & Malaysia
South Africa
South America
South Florida
South Korea
South Pacific
Southeast Asia
Spain
Sweden
Switzerland
Tahiti & French Polynesia
Texas
Thailand
Tokyo
Toronto
Turkey
USA
Utah
Vancouver & Victoria
Vermont, New Hampshire & Maine
Vienna & the Danube Valley
Vietnam
Virgin Islands
Virginia
Walt Disney World® & Orlando
Washington, D.C.
Washington State

FROMMER'S® DAY BY DAY GUIDES

Amsterdam
Barcelona
Beijing
Boston
Cancun & the Yucatan
Chicago
Florence & Tuscany

Hong Kong
Honolulu & Oahu
London
Maui
Montréal
Napa & Sonoma
New York City

Paris
Provence & the Riviera
Rome
San Francisco
Venice
Washington D.C.

PAULINE FROMMER'S GUIDES: SEE MORE. SPEND LESS.

Alaska
Hawaii
Italy

Las Vegas
London
New York City

Paris
Walt Disney World®
Washington D.C.

Frommer's® Portable Guides

Acapulco, Ixtapa & Zihuatanejo
Amsterdam
Aruba, Bonaire & Curacao
Australia's Great Barrier Reef
Bahamas
Big Island of Hawaii
Boston
California Wine Country
Cancún
Cayman Islands
Charleston
Chicago
Dominican Republic

Florence
Las Vegas
Las Vegas for Non-Gamblers
London
Maui
Nantucket & Martha's Vineyard
New Orleans
New York City
Paris
Portland
Puerto Rico
Puerto Vallarta, Manzanillo & Guadalajara

Rio de Janeiro
San Diego
San Francisco
Savannah
St. Martin, Sint Maarten, Anguila & St. Bart's
Turks & Caicos
Vancouver
Venice
Virgin Islands
Washington, D.C.
Whistler

Frommer's® Cruise Guides

Alaska Cruises & Ports of Call

Cruises & Ports of Call

European Cruises & Ports of Call

Frommer's® National Park Guides

Algonquin Provincial Park
Banff & Jasper
Grand Canyon

National Parks of the American West
Rocky Mountain
Yellowstone & Grand Teton

Yosemite and Sequoia & Kings Canyon
Zion & Bryce Canyon

Frommer's® With Kids Guides

Chicago
Hawaii
Las Vegas
London

National Parks
New York City
San Francisco

Toronto
Walt Disney World® & Orlando
Washington, D.C.

Frommer's® PhraseFinder Dictionary Guides

Chinese
French

German
Italian

Japanese
Spanish

Suzy Gershman's Born to Shop Guides

France
Hong Kong, Shanghai & Beijing
Italy

London
New York
Paris

San Francisco
Where to Buy the Best of Everything

Frommer's® Best-Loved Driving Tours

Britain
California
France
Germany

Ireland
Italy
New England
Northern Italy

Scotland
Spain
Tuscany & Umbria

The Unofficial Guides®

Adventure Travel in Alaska
Beyond Disney
California with Kids
Central Italy
Chicago
Cruises
Disneyland®
England
Hawaii

Ireland
Las Vegas
London
Maui
Mexico's Best Beach Resorts
Mini Mickey
New Orleans
New York City
Paris

San Francisco
South Florida including Miami & the Keys
Walt Disney World®
Walt Disney World® for Grown-ups
Walt Disney World® with Kids
Washington, D.C.

Special-Interest Titles

Athens Past & Present
Best Places to Raise Your Family
Cities Ranked & Rated
500 Places to Take Your Kids Before They Grow Up
Frommer's Best Day Trips from London
Frommer's Best RV & Tent Campgrounds in the U.S.A.

Frommer's Exploring America by RV
Frommer's NYC Free & Dirt Cheap
Frommer's Road Atlas Europe
Frommer's Road Atlas Ireland
Retirement Places Rated